T0226287

Lecture Notes in Computer Science

Lecture Notes in Computer Science

Edited by G. Goos and J. Hartmanis

237

CONPAR 86

Conference on Algorithms and Hardware
for Parallel Processing
Aachen, September 17–19, 1986
Proceedings

Edited by Wolfgang Händler, Dieter Haupt, Rolf Jeltsch,
Wilfried Juling and Otto Lange

Springer-Verlag
Berlin Heidelberg New York London Paris Tokyo

Editors

Wolfgang Händler
Universität Erlangen-Nürnberg
Institut für Mathematische Maschinen und Datenverarbeitung
Martensstr. 3, D-8520 Erlangen

Dieter Haupt
RWTH Aachen
Lehrstuhl für Betriebssysteme
Templergraben 55, D-5100 Aachen

Rolf Jeltsch
RWTH Aachen
Institut für Geometrie und Praktische Mathematik
Templergraben 55, D-5100 Aachen

Wilfried Juling
RWTH Aachen
Rechenzentrum
Templergraben 55, D-5100 Aachen

Otto Lange
RWTH Aachen
Allgemeine Elektrotechnik und Datenverarbeitungssysteme
Templergraben 55, D-5100 Aachen

CR Subject Classifications (1985): C.1.1, C.1.2, C.1.3, F.2.1, F.2.2

ISBN 3-540-16811-7 Springer-Verlag Berlin Heidelberg New York
ISBN 0-387-16811-7 Springer-Verlag New York Berlin Heidelberg

CONPAR 86

PREFACE

The second Conference on Algorithms and Hardware for Parallel Processing, CONPAR 86, has long been overdue. During the past five years since the first CONPAR was held in 1981 there has been a dramatic increase in awareness for the necessity of parallel processing. This resulted in many significant publications and an increasing number of related conferences in this field. The 1980s are proving to be the decade of parallel processing .

It is the goal of CONPAR to bring together researchers involved in parallel processing. It is intended to create a forum to allow for the interaction of people designing algorithms and architectures of different kinds of parallelism utilizing todays exploding hardware possibilities.

In contrast to CONPAR 81 where 29 papers were selected for presentations this year we received 106 papers. Reviewing these papers proved a tremendous task requiring the assistance of 43 referees. 42 papers from 13 countries are included in these proceedings. Academia, industry and research laboratories are all represented. Because of the large number of excellent papers submitted, the task of arriving at a program was an extremely difficult one. CONPAR 86 will have parallel sessions in order to accommodate more papers. But still there were many interesting papers which could not be included. Therefore, all of the papers finally accepted and included in these proceedings should be of the highest quality. We sincerely thank all of the authors who submitted papers for their interest in this conference.

CONPAR 86 will be complemented by presentations, demonstrations and exhibits of various manufacturers. The significant aspect of this joint event is that all of the parallel systems presented are commercially available today or will be in the immediate future and many more significant developments are expected soon.

Professor Arthur Burks from The University of Michigan, Ann Arbor, will act as the Honorary Chairman and will address the conference with his keynote " A Radically Non-von-Neumann-Architecture for Learning and Discovery".
Together with J. von Neumann and H.H. Goldstine, Professor Burks created what is now the "Classical General Purpose Computer". In spite of all criticism regarding what is called the "von-Neumann-Bottle-Neck" or the " von-Neumann-Programming-Style " the Burks/ Goldstine/ von-Neumann-Approach has proved to be viable and outstanding.

At CONPAR 86 several renowned experts have been invited to give presentations in their respective fields:
I.S. Duff, AERE Harwell, Oxfordshire, and A.H. Sameh, University of Illinois at Urbana Champaign,will concentrate on numerical algorithms for parallel processing, whereas Ph. Treleaven, University College London, S. Uchida, ICOT Tokyo, and U. Trottenberg, SUPRENUM Gesellschaft für numerische Superrechner m.b.H, Bonn, will introduce novel computer architectures and will report on the progress of current projects.
Finally, W. Händler, University of Erlangen-Nürnberg, will discuss trends in the general development of multiprocessors.

Our special thanks go to the referees who read and evaluated the manuscripts. We wish to acknowledge the efforts of the Organizing Committee and the staff of the RWTH - Computer Center for the local arrangements. We are also grateful to the Springer-Verlag for the kind assistance in preparing the proceedings.

Aachen, July 1986

W. Händler
D. Haupt
R. Jeltsch
W. Juling
O. Lange

ACKNOWLEDGEMENTS

For substantial help we are obliged to the members of the Program Committee

P. C. P. Bhatt	R. W. Hockney	K. Miura
G. Blaauw	R. Jeltsch	D. Parkinson
R. Dierstein	H. F. Jordan	G. Paul
A. Endres	G. Joubert	K. D. Reinartz
W. Händler	O. Lange	A.H. Sameh
D. Haupt	J. Mikloško	P. Spies

to the following referees

W. Ameling	J. Jersák	W. Schönauer
J. P. Banatre	J. S. Kowalik	D. Siewiorek
M. Broy	T. Legendi	G. Spruth
D. J. Evans	R. Mannshardt	M. Vajteršic
M. Feilmeier	K. Mehlhorn	R. Vollmar
G. Fritsch	P. Müller-Stoy	H. Wössner
F. Hossfeld	D. Müller-Wichards	Z. Xie
H. Hultzsch	J. Nievergelt	
K. Hwang	G. Regenspurg	

and to the Kernforschungsanlage Jülich GmbH for the layout and printing of the posters, the call for papers and the conference program.

TABLE OF CONTENTS

NONNUMERICAL ALGORITHMS (Session 2.2)

ARCHITECTURAL ASPECTS (Session 3.1)

NUMERICAL ALGORITHMS (Session 3.2)

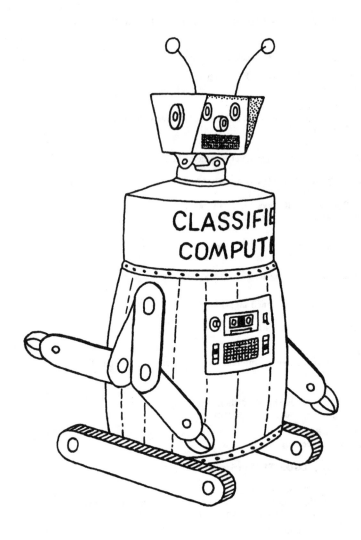

Classifier Robot

Figure 1

(Paper by Burks)

A RADICALLY NON-VON-NEUMANN-ARCHITECTURE FOR LEARNING AND DISCOVERY*

Arthur W. Burks
Electrical Engineering and Computer Science
The University of Michigan, Ann Arbor, Michigan 48109

1. What is a von Neumann Architecture?

It is a pleasure to keynote a second Conference on Algorithms and Hardware for Parallel Processing, and I wish to thank your chairman and my good friend Professor Wolfgang Händler for this double honor. My theme for CONPAR 81 was the logical interrelations between parallelism in hardware and parallelism in software, and the present paper will continue this theme (Burks 1981).

Since 1981 I have been working with my colleague and former student John Holland on architectures for a new type of programming system he has developed, called *classifier systems*. Classifier systems are capable of improving their performance, they are capable of discovering new ways of performing, they can compute in highly parallel mode, and they can recover from local damage. These properties all stem from the novel parallelism of the system. (Holland 1984, 1985, 1986; Burks and Holland 1985; Riolo 1986a, 1986b; Holland and Burks 1986; Holland, Holyoak et al. 1986; Burks 1987.)

This new architecture will serve as a good example for a discussion of parallelism. We will approach this subject by comparing different kinds of computer architectures.

It is common today to decry von Neumann's original single-bus architecture and to propose parallel "non-von" alternatives to it. A classifier machine is "non-von," even "radically non-von." But uttering these slogans does not really convey much information, for they have never been carefully defined. So let me distinguish three general types of computer organization: von Neumann's single-bus architecture, evolutionary von Neumann architectures, and radically non-von architectures.

(1) The von Neumann single-bus architecture. This was a centralized architecture comprised of (a) a memory [for instructions as well as data] and a single buffer register, (b) an arithmetic-logic unit with one accumulator and one register [both capable of shifting], (c) a control unit to interpret instructions and direct their execution, (d) magnetic tape units for input-output and auxiliary storage, and (e) a single bus interconnecting these blocks, transmitting both instructions and data, one word at a time, bit-parallel (Burks, Goldstine, von Neumann 1946).

Computer architectures should always be evaluated in terms of the intended problem domain and the available technology. Von Neumann wanted a computer for solving

---

*This research was supported by National Science Foundation grants SES82-18834 and DCR83-05830. Some of the material in the present paper is taken from Burks 1987, which gives a fuller exposition.

scientific and engineering problems. Given the cost and size of vacuum tube circuits
(for switching, communication, and short-term storage) and cathode ray-tube memories,
this architecture was admirably balanced between memory, arithmetic-control (processor), and communication bus.

(2) Evolutionary von Neumann architectures. Technology evolved rapidly, and in
the ensuing forty years there has been a rapid but gradual evolution from this original design to the designs of most contemporary computers. The main advances can
be categorized as follows.

Memories: extended hierarchies of various kinds and speeds of memory, stack
memories, and associative memories. *Arithmetic-logic unit*: overflow sensing; more
logical and arithmetic operations, including floating point and vector operations;
cellular structures for arithmetic. *Control*: index registers, from the specific to
the general; interrupts and break-points; microprogramming. *Input-output*: more
intelligent, more independent, more sophisticated terminals and peripherals. *Parallelism "in time"*: memory interleaving and cycle stealing, pipelining, interrupts,
time sharing (the appearance of parallelism) and paging. *Parallelism "in space"*:
vector and array processors, several arithmetic units, multiprocessors, multimemories.
Instruction parallelism: independent IO, multiprocessors. *Communication networks*:
many paths, buffers, hierarchies, etc.

The arrangement of computing units in cellular arrays is a form of spatial parallelism that deserves special comment because as integrated circuits become smaller it
becomes more important. The "cells" in a regular iterative array can be processors,
processors with memories, or whole computers. Von Neumann was the first to consider
these, in connection with his work on self-reproduction (von Neumann 1966, Burks 1970,
von Neumann 1986). ILLIAC IV was the first computer to be organized this way. It
combined a cellular architecture with a von Neumann centralized architecture, as have
most of its successors (Bell and Newell 1971; Hockney and Jesshope 1981).

ILLIAC IV had only 64 processor-memory units, but as integrated circuits have
become smaller, cheaper, and faster, larger arrays have been developed. Thus the
Connection Machine has a central computer operating an array of 2^{16} cells, each cell
containing a bit processor, small control tables, and 4096 bits of memory (Hillis
1986). These cells are interconnected by two neighborhood relations: each cell has
4 immediate neighbors, and is also connected to 16 neighbors via a Boolean 16-cube.

* * *

Though most computers today are a very long way architecturally from von Neumann's original design, they are all the product of a gradual evolution from this
starting point. Moreover, *there is a common and characteristic theme starting with
the original von Neumann single-bus organization and running through all evolutionary
von Neumann architectures: the syntax and semantics of von Neumann's program language*. Syntactically, each instruction has an address linking it to one or more (in
the case of branching) instructions to be executed next. Semantically, each instruc-

tion has an address or addresses linking it to the data variables it is to operate on.

This brief characterization needs to be elaborated a bit. The addresses may be implicit, as when instructions are executed in the order in which they are stored, or when an instruction operates on the top of a stack, or when the data are in designated registers. The datum may also be an instruction, as when one instruction causes the address of another instruction to be changed.

When one instruction points to a second, that pointer is used to transfer control from the first to the second. This transfer is like lowering a "go" flag or passing a baton in a race. If two or more processors are working on the same problem and using a common memory, then an instruction may need signals from two or more prior instructions before it is executed. Hence an instruction may have two or more addresses pointing to other instructions, and it may have two or more addresses pointing to it.

Thus there are two kinds of addresses in a von Neumann-type program. There are *instruction-to-instruction addresses* which sequence program execution by transferring control. And there are *instruction-to-data addresses* that link an instruction's operation code to the memory positions the instruction operates on.

(3) Radically non-von architectures. Almost all contemporary computers use this basic syntax and semantics of von Neumann's original program language. It is therefore appropriate to call any computer organization which has a different type of program language a *radically non-von architecture*.

Data flow and demand-driven machines are radically non-von. For they package instructions and their data together, thus collapsing the two kinds of addresses (instruction-to-instruction and instruction-to-data) into one kind. Classifier machines are also radically non-von, and are even more so, since at the bottom level they do not use any addresses.

A classifier system has three levels:

Bottom level: Basic classifier performance system
Middle level: Bucket-brigade learning algorithm
Top level: Genetic discovery algorithm.

A basic classifier system has classifiers (rules or instructions) and messages (data). At each major cycle all classifiers are applied to all messages to generate a new message set, and no addresses are used for this.

The bucket-brigade algorithm adds a market economy, in which each classifier has a strength (capital). A classifier must compete with other classifiers to get its messages carried over to the next major cycle and must pay for the messages it uses. If a classifier's messages are used by other classifiers it will receive payments in turn, so the strength of a classifier varies over a program run and depends on its success in the market. Tags are used for these payment transfers. Tags perform some functions usually performed by means of addresses, but tags are not used for transferring control or for picking out data locations.

The genetic algorithm periodically eliminates weak (poor) classifiers and replaces them by genetic combinations (offspring) of strong classifiers. Since the genetic algorithm selects the classifiers it operates on according to their strengths, it does not use addresses.

We will explore the three levels of a classifier system in the succeeding three sections. Then we will compare classifier machines to computers that use the syntax and semantics of von Neumann's program language.

2. Basic Classifier Systems

A classifier system has two kinds of basic entities, *classifiers* and *messages*. These correspond to the instructions and data of standard computer languages, but function quite differently. A classifier is a hypothetical statement, typically with two *conditions* as antecedents and a computing or action term as *consequent*. Messages are binary words (based on the alphabet 0,1). They express inputs to the system, results of calculations that are to be preserved, and outputs from the system. Classifiers are ternary words, based on the alphabet (0,1,#). The sign "#" functions somewhat differently in conditions and in consequents. It means "don't care" in a condition. But it means "pass through," or "place the corresponding bit of the message satisfying the first condition into the generated message," in the consequent.

The robot of Figure 1 has a sensory part on top, a classifier computer in the middle, and an effector part below. The classifier computer contains a set of classifiers and a set of messages. Each set is small compared to the totality of possibilities — a typical small classifier system has about 32 messages of 16 bits each, and 1024 classifiers of two conditions. The set of classifiers remains invariant in a basic classifier system; it will change during the computation when the genetic algorithm is added (sec. 4).

Classifier computation proceeds as a succession of *major cycles*. At each major cycle the computer receives input messages and adds them to the internal messages carried over from the proceeding major cycle. It then applies every classifier to every message to produce a new set of messages. The computer sends the output messages to the sensor and effector parts of the robot, and replaces the old message set by the remaining new messages. Input, internal, and output messages are distinguished by tags.

The following table shows how messages and conditions can be coded so that conditions can recognize sets of messages.

| Messages | Colors | | Conditions |
	Specific	Generic	
10	Dark red	Red	1#
11	Light red		
00	Dark green	Green	0#
01	Light green		

When the number sign "#" occurs in a condition it means "don't care," so that the messages "10" (dark red) and "11" (light red) both satisfy the condition "1#" (red). Note that the fraction of "don't cares" in a condition measures its generality; such a measure is used in the bucket-brigade algorithm (sec. 3). Classifiers are so-called because they classify messages.

To see how new messages are generated from old consider the very simple case of two classifiers

(α) If 1# and ## then 0#   (If the light is red then stop)
(β) If 0# and ## then 1#   (If the light is green then go)

and a single message 10 (dark red). If some message satisfies the second condition of a classifier (in this example all messages do), then each message satisfying the first condition is transformed into a new message. The method of constructing the new message from the old is as follows:

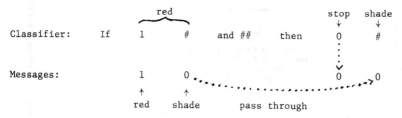

Note that the new message contains both new information ("stop") and old information (the shade of the stimulus).

While it is logically possible to process all classifiers against all messages simultaneously, it is not practical to build such a large logical switch with present technology. Figure 2 shows one practical organization, in which the classifiers are processed sequentially, but each classifier condition is compared with all messages in parallel. The Auctioneer and Genetic Processor of Figure 2 go beyond basic classifiers, and will be explained in the next two sections.

In this architecture the classifiers are cycled through the Classifier Processor. In each *minor cycle* the second condition of a classifier is compared in parallel with all old messages, and if it is satisfied the first condition is also compared, and (possibly) new messages are generated and sent to the new message store. At the end of the major cycle the old messages are erased and replaced by the new messages. Input messages are brought in at the beginning of a major cycle and output messages sent out at the end.

To get a feel for how a classifier computation goes, consider the following *object-location problem*. The classifier robot is placed somewhere in one end of the room, and it is to move around and find an object of a specified kind placed somewhere in the other end of the room. When the robot locates this object it should position itself next to the object, face it, and stop. Built into the robot is the capacity to recognize when it reaches its goal.

Suppose now that a programmer has written a set of classifiers such that the

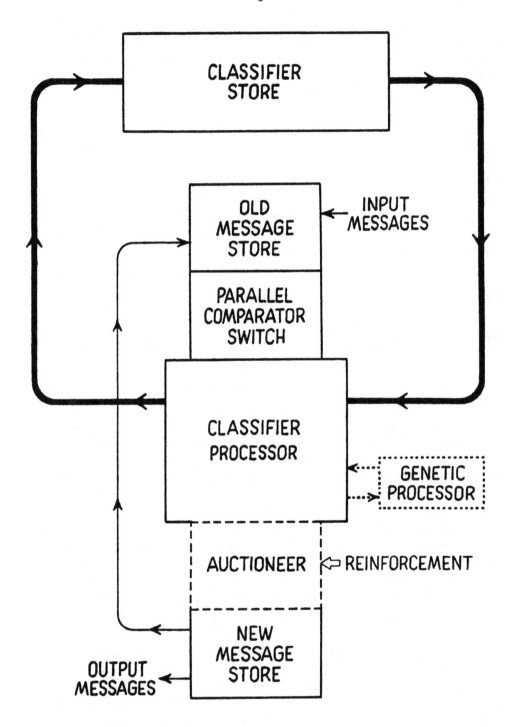

Classifier Computer

Figure 2

basic classifier computer, using this set, can solve the object-location problem, perhaps inefficiently. Figure 3 shows the series-parallel structure of such a computation. The classifiers are labeled C_1, C_2, etc. and the messages M_a, M_b, etc. Input and output messages are circled. Output message M_n caused the robot to reach its goal and stop the computation run.

This is the basic performance level of classifiers. A learning algorithm is added in the next section, and a discovery algorithm in the following one.

3. Learning by Repeated Competition

Consider the object location problem in the form of a set of similar but varying environments and a classifier program which usually solves this problem, perhaps inefficiently. Our next step is to add an algorithm which will enable this classifier program to improve its performance over a succession of runs.

For the moment, look at the simpler problem of selecting between alternative stimulus-response rules, each of which can be expressed by a single classifier. Associate a strength (an amount of capital) with each classifier and let the classifiers use their strengths to compete in an auction for the right to control the response of the robot to a stimulus. See the Auctioneer in Figure 2. For each stimulus message, those classifiers which produce potential response messages make bids for the right to control the robot's response. The winning classifier pays out its bid amount. Then the reinforcement mechanism is used to reward (pay) or penalize (charge) the classifier according to whether its response was correct or incorrect. Hence the strength or capital of a classifier increases {decreases} when it wins the auction with correct {incorrect} responses. It is obvious that in such a system the rule "If the light is red then stop" would quickly come to dominate the rule "If the light is red then go."

The procedure just described is easily implemented. But stimulus-response reinforcement does not take computer science very far down the road to learning, though perhaps it is as far as behavioral psychology can go. As Figure 3 illustrates, the solution to a typical problem involves a sequence of parallel interacting steps. Success cannot be judged and rewarded until the end of this sequence. The problem is then to allocate credit and blame to the constituent parts.

Human management systems normally make these credit allocations. Can this be done automatically? Yes, the bucket-brigade algorithm accomplishes this task. It gradually distributes pay-offs made at the ends of runs to classifiers which contribute earlier in those runs.

A classifier is a kind of producer, using messages supplied by other classifiers and transforming them into new messages (products). The *bucket-brigade algorithm* puts these producers into iterated market competition. The message list is restricted in size, so that classifiers must compete with one another in an auction to get their messages carried over to the next major cycle. Each classifier has a strength (capi-

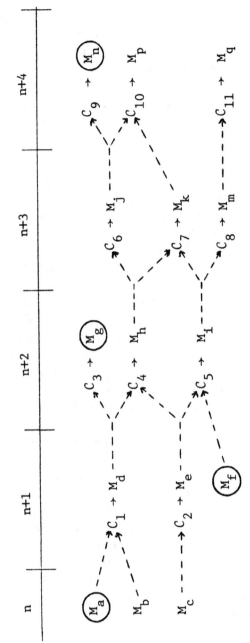

Major cycles

Series–Parallel Classifier Computation

Figure 3

tal), and it can use part of this to make a bid for the preservation of its message. If it wins the bid, it pays the bid amount to its suppliers. If its message is used successfully by one or more classifiers in the next major cycle, it will receive payments in return.

The amount bid by a classifier C is a function of the strength of C, the specificity of C's conditions, and other factors such as the degree of association of C with the classifiers that supplied it with messages (e.g., the sum of the bids made to get those messages carried into the present major cycle). The bucket-brigade algorithm modifies the bids probabilistically and then selects those messages with the highest modified bids to constitute the message set for the next major cycle. Such probabilistic variations contribute to adaptability.

A basic classifier calculation is a forward recursion of message generation. The bucket-brigade algorithm adds to this a virtual backward recursion of payments. For its success in the *present* major cycle a classifier pays another classifier for its success during the *previous* major cycle, the payments being made during the *next* major cycle. See Figure 4. In cycle $n+2$ classifier C_4 uses messages M_d and M_e to produce message M_h, and its bid $B(M_h)$ gets M_h carried into cycle $n+3$. Because of this success classifier C_4 pays .5 $B(M_h)$ to C_1 and to C_2 in cycle $n+3$. In turn, since M_h is used successfully by C_6 and C_7 in cycle $n+3$, C_4 receives $B(M_j)$ from C_6 and .5 $B(M_k)$ from C_7 in cycle $n+4$.

Return now to the object location problem mentioned earlier and suppose the robot contains a classifier program that solves the problem inefficiently, after much trial and error. Over successive runs the bucket-brigade algorithm will develop it into a program that performs well. The improvement is not in the classifiers (they do not change) but in the strengths associated with them. Initially all classifiers are assigned the same strength. At the end of each successful run those classifiers which posted messages in the last major cycle are rewarded, and over succeeding runs these rewards gradually work back and increase the strengths of those classifiers which contribute messages earlier in the runs. Thus classifiers that produce messages that are used by other classifiers gradually increase in strength while classifiers that fail in this gradually lose strength. In this way the classifier robot gradually develops a strength assignment to classifiers that produces good performance.

Strength is both a measure of past success in this learning process and the main determinant of future success. When the program succeeds it gains strength (the reinforcement reward) which is gradually distributed to the contributing classifiers by the auction market. There may also be negative reinforcement. The robot can be given an upper limit of time (number of major cycles) to solve the object location problem, and if it fails in that time given a negative payoff (punishment).

An economic analogy may help the reader picture how the bucket-brigade algorithm transforms the operation of basic classifiers. Consider the manufacture of automobiles, beginning with mining and proceeding through the stages of smelting, steelmaking, parts manufacture, assembly, and distribution. An organization of these

10

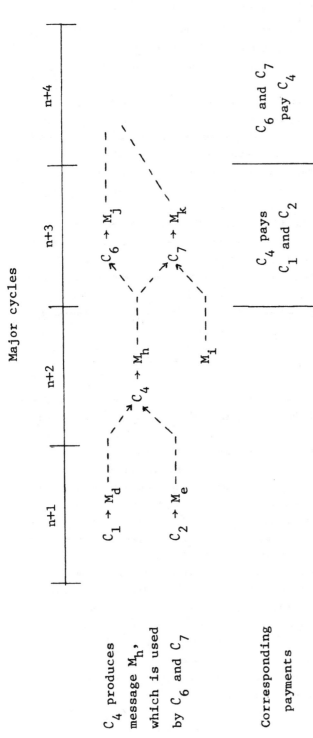

Timing of Bucket-Brigade Payments

Figure 4

producers into a planned economy in which products are produced by quotas is analogous to a basic classifier system. For the bucket-brigade analogy imagine that there are competing processors at each stage and that the output of each stage goes into an auction market that feeds it selectively into the next stage. Assume further that all the producers of this economic system begin with the same capital.

It is easy to see how rewards flow backwards in successive time steps through this economic system. The consumers who buy the cars make payments to the distributors, who use the money to buy more cars from assemblers, who then buy more parts, etc., on back through the stages of the system. The market will gradually route these payments so as to improve the efficiency of the system. The more efficient producers will prosper and this bucket-brigade economy will gradually learn to produce autos more cheaply.

In Figure 2 the payoff reinforcement is supplied from the outside. It can also be accomplished internally, for the payoff mechanism can be incorporated in the robot along with a definition of the goal.

Bucket-brigade accounting is done as follows. Each classifier is accompanied by an identification tag and the amount of its strength. When a classifier produces a new message the classifier's ID, those of the suppliers, and the bid amount are attached to the new message. If the bid is sufficient to get the new message carried over to the next major cycle, the Auctioneer posts the message on the new list with the producer's ID attached to it. The Auctioneer also stores the following string for accounting purposes: the IDs of the suppliers, the ID of the producer, and the producer's bid amount. During the next major cycle the Auctioneer debits the producer and credits the suppliers as these pass through the Classifier Processor (see figs. 2 and 4).

The tags used in the bucket-brigade algorithm are attached to both messages (data) and classifiers (instructions). It should be noted that they are for the purpose of accounting and are not addresses in the ordinary sense, for they are not used for transferring control or picking out data locations.

Finally, let us compare the performance roles of classifiers before and after the bucket-brigade algorithm is added. Suppose the robot is performing repeated runs of the object location problem. In the basic classifier system the contribution of a classifier to performance depends only on the environmental inputs. When the bucket-brigade algorithm is present the contribution of a classifier to performance depends also on the classifier's strength relative to the strengths of competing classifiers, and these relative strengths depend on the past performances of the classifiers in problem runs.

When the strength of a classifier has become so small that the classifier does not contribute significantly to performance, the classifier is not worth storing and processing, and should be eliminated. This is done by the genetic algorithm, which removes poor classifiers and replaces them with the offspring of strong classifiers.

4. Discovery by Genetic Mixing

The *genetic algorithm* is best introduced by means of a simple example. Suppose that at one major cycle of a bucket-brigade run the system has

Set of classifiers	C_0	C_1	C_2	C_3	C_4	C_5	C_6	C_7
Strengths	.11	.03	.26	.04	.20	.17	.05	.14

The Genetic Processor of Figure 2 operates with stochastic variation; it will probably delete the three weakest classifiers, C_1, C_3, and C_6. It will then replace them by three new classifiers, derived by genetic operators from the best of the remaining classifiers, probably C_2, C_4, and C_5.

The genetic algorithm can use various genetic-like operators. We employ two, mutation and crossover. For example, C_2 might be mutated to make a new classifier C_2', and C_4 crossed with C_5 to make new classifiers C_4' and C_5'. These new classifiers are assigned average strengths. The Genetic Processor receives a few classifiers each major cycle from the classifier processor, applies the genetic algorithm to them, and returns the results to the classifier processor.

Crossover operates at a higher grammatical level than mutation. Mutation alters single letters, while crossover rearranges blocks of letters. If these blocks express meaningful concepts then crossover rearranges concepts. For example, Figure 5 begins with two bad rules about responding to stop lights when driving, and the random crossover point falls so as to interchange the consequents of the two rules.

Thus the genetic algorithm creates new rules, substitutes them for poor rules, and tests them in competition with the remaining rules. This is a logic of discovery.

The learning power of the bucket-brigade algorithm is limited by the potentialities inherent in the starting set of classifiers. The genetic algorithm removes this limitation by creating new classifiers from old ones. It can also generate a new classifier condition that is relevant to the environment by replacing some of the bits of an input message by don't care symbols.

The environmental niche a robot can exploit is defined on the input side by its set of possible input messages and on the output side by its set of possible actions. Using this base the Genetic Processor can create classifiers ab initio, by generalizing received messages to make classifier conditions and generalizing possible output messages to make action terms. When a classifier robot embodies this mechanism, it can be taught a sequential task in successive training steps. The teacher first reinforces correct responses to simple stimuli, and then gradually trains the robot to sequence these.

5. Simulations

This completes our outline of classifier machines. It is also an outline of a logic of learning, economic competition, discovery, and evolutionary adaptation. This is only a small part of what is to be said, of course, for these processes are so complicated that they can only be expressed as computer programs and machine designs, and studied by simulation.

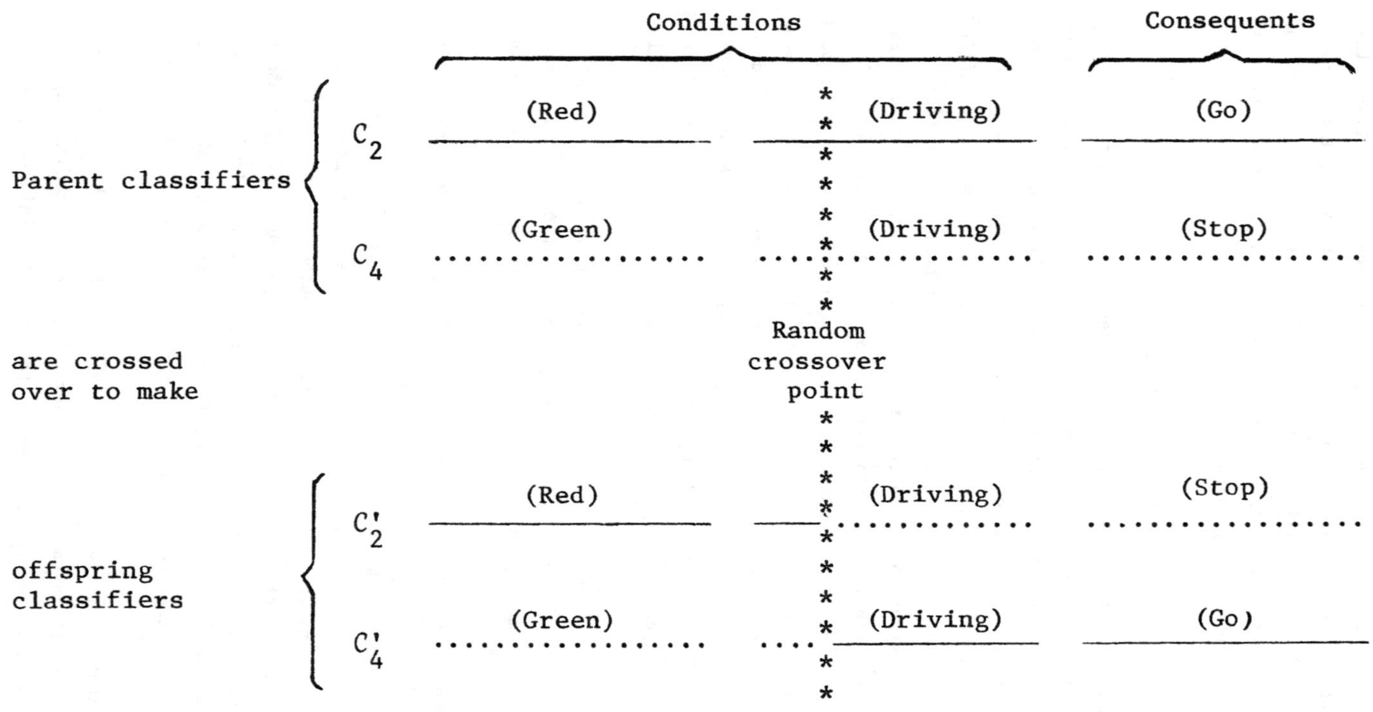

Conditions   Consequents

⎧   ⎫ ⎧
│ (Red) _____ * * (Driving) _____   │ │ (Go) _____
│   │ │
C₂ │   │ │
│ (Green) ·········· * * (Driving) ······· │ │ (Stop) ··········
C₄ ⎩   ⎭ ⎩

                    Random
                  crossover
                    point

⎧   ⎫ ⎧
│ (Red) _____ * * (Driving) ·········   │ │ (Stop) _____
C′₂ │   │ │
│ (Green) ·········· * * (Driving) _____ │ │ (Go) ··········
C′₄ ⎩   ⎭ ⎩

⎫
C₂ ⎬ Parent classifiers
C₄ ⎭

are crossed
over to make

⎫
C′₂ ⎬ offspring
C′₄ ⎭ classifiers

Crossover in the Genetic Algorithm

Figure 5

Several simulations have been done. Examples include control of an oil pipeline distribution system (Goldberg 1983), learning to play poker (Smith 1980), and learning to distinguish between alphabets (Gillies 1985). More work is in process (Grefenstette 1985). A general simulator has been written in the C language and simulations are being programmed in it (Riolo 1986a, 1986b).

6. Two Sources of Computer Architecture

We began with a general classification of architectures: the von Neumann single-bus architecture, evolutionarily von Neumann architectures, and radically non-von architectures. We saw that the syntactic and semantic structure of the original von Neumann program language was common to all architectures of the first two kinds, and we defined a radically non-von architecture as one whose program language has a basically different kind of syntax and semantics. Data flow and demand driven machines are radically non-von because they merge instruction-to-instruction and instruction-to-data addresses into a single kind of address linking one data-instruction package to another. Classifier machines are radically non-von because they use no addresses at all on the basic level, and only use tags to connect classifiers to each other for accounting purposes.

These non-von addressing structures permit highly parallel computing. In a data flow machine all the instruction-data packages that have fresh data can be computed simultaneously. The classifier machine of Figure 2 processes an instruction against all data simultaneously, and greater parallelism in classifier execution is logically possible.

Classifier computers are rooted in natural systems: market economies and genetic evolution. In contrast, the modern electronic computer arose from artificial or man-made systems. I will conclude my comparison of computer architectures by elaborating on this difference.

The so-called von Neumann architecture had both a hardware and a software side. Its vacuum tube circuits derived from Atanasoff's electronic computer and the fast ENIAC. The first stored program computers had either a mercury delay-line or a cathode ray tube store. Their one-memory and one-bus organization arose naturally from the nature of these memories and the desire to restrict the number of vacuum tubes in the machine. Many individuals contributed to the hardware side, but J. V. Atanasoff, J. P. Eckert, and von Neumann played the major roles (Burks 1980, Burks and Burks 1981 and 1987). Conrad Zuse and Helmut Schreyer started down the same path, but their work was interrupted by the war and they never had the resources available to us in the United States.

Von Neumann's contributions to software were more important than his contributions to hardware. Prior to the invention of mercury delay-line and cathode ray tube memories, *all* erasable computer memories were small, the largest holding only about eighty words. Hence these memories could store only the data for the problem, not the program. Programs were stored in read-only memories, punched tape or plugboard, and program languages used only fixed or constant addresses such as "register 1," "register 2," etc. Constant addresses were satisfactory for these machines, since they did not have very many registers or accumulators to refer to.

Von Neumann designed the first program language that incorporated variable addresses. In this language the same instruction could be used successively with different addresses, each address being substituted by means of a substitution instruction. (This result is accomplished today by means of index registers, but in the first stored program computers indexing was done in the arithmetic unit.) Variable addresses and the substitution instruction made it possible to write short programs that could operate on data items located in many different memory positions, and to write programs to transform other programs. This is the modern way. Thus von Neumann's invention led to the modern software world of assemblers, compilers, and automatic program languages.

Mathematical logic was the main source of von Neumann's programming contributions. He was influenced by the concept of a formal language, developed by Gottlob Frege, Bertrand Russell, David Hilbert, and Kurt Gödel. For his famous incompleteness proof Gödel designed a formal language in which recursive or computable functions could be expressed. Gödel's language was fine for his proof, but it was not a practical language for computation. For example, an integer n was expressed in it by a string of $n+1$ marks, and the basic arithmetic operation was the successor function "add one mark."

Von Neumann designed his program language so that it would be a practical tool for computing recursive functions. He used the positional notation and the standard arithmetic operations of the ENIAC, and added instructions for address substitution and branching. Computer instructions are the imperative versions of well-formed formulas, and a von Neumann substitution instruction referring to the instruction it is to modify is analogous to a metalanguage formula referring to an object-language formula. Also, a cyclic subroutine is analogous to a logical formula which has a bounded quantifier. The recursion of the formula is limited by the stated bound, while the subroutine cycles until it reaches its bound. And the free variables of a bounded quantifier expression correspond to the parameters of a subroutine which are set from outside (von Neumann 1986, pp. 381-384).

Thus artificial or man-made systems were the historical sources of modern computer architectures: prior computers and computing technology on the hardware side, read-only programs with constant addresses and formal logical languages on the software side.

Natural systems process information and hence are possible sources of computer architectures, though little use has been made of this source so far. Von Neumann was the first to propose a cellular automaton structure, and he did so to have a framework for the logical analysis of self-reproduction (von Neumann 1966 and Burks 1970). And the novel features of classifier computers are derived from natural systems.

The bucket-brigade algorithm applies the competitive system of economics to products (messages) by having producers (classifiers) compete in a free market to get their products carried over to the next major cycle. The genetic algorithm applies the competitive system of biological evolution to classifiers by deleting poor performers and replacing them by new classifiers created by genetic recombination techniques from good performers. This competition can be sharpened by assessing taxes of classifiers for the space and processing capacity they consume.

The parallelism of classifiers occurs on both an abstract level and in execution. Genetic variation is a kind of parallel sampling of the logical space of possible classifiers (instructions). When classifiers are computed every classifier can be applied to all messages in parallel. This kind of computational parallelism occurs in nature; antibodies searching out antigens is one example, the operation of control chemicals another. Moreover, this natural parallelism contributes to the robustness of classifier systems. In an ordinary computer program if an instruction is damaged or instructions get out of order the program generally fails. In a classifier program the order does not matter, and if a classifier is damaged it is usually replaced by competing classifiers.

References

Bell, C. Gordon and Allen Newell: 1971. *Computer Structures: Reading and Examples.* McGraw-Hill, New York.

Burks, Alice R. and Arthur Burks: 1987. *The First Electronic Computer — The Atanasoff Story.* To be published.

Burks, Arthur: 1970 (ed.). *Essays on Cellular Automata.* University of Illinois Press, Urbana.

_____: 1980. "From ENIAC to the Stored Program Computer: Two Revolutions in Computers." *A History of Computing in the Twentieth Century*, pp. 311-344. Nicholas Metropolis, Jack Howlett, and Gian-Carlo Rota (eds.). Academic Press, New York.

_____: 1981. "Programming and Structural Changes in Parallel Computers." *CONPAR 81: Conference on Analyzing Problem Classes and Programming for Parallel Computing, Nürnberg, June 10-12, 1981, Proceedings*, pp. 1-24. Wolfgang Händler (ed.). Springer-Verlag, Berlin.

_____: 1987. "The Logic of Evolution and the Reduction of Coherent-Holistic Systems to Hierarchical-Feedback Systems." To be published in *Probability and Causation*. Bryan Skyrms and William Harper (eds.). Columbia University Press, New York.

Burks, Arthur and Alice R. Burks: 1981. "The ENIAC: First General-Purpose Electronic Computer." *Annals of the History of Computing* 3, 310-389. Comments by John V. Atanasoff, J. G. Brainerd, J. Presper Eckert and Kay Mauchly, Brian Randell, and Conrad Zuse, together with the authors' responses to these comments, pp. 389-399.

Burks, Arthur and John Holland: 1985. "A Radically non-von Architecture for Learning and Discovery." Logic of Computers Group, Electrical Engineering and Computer Science, University of Michigan, Ann Arbor.

Burks, Arthur, John von Neumann, and H. H. Goldstine: 1946. *Preliminary Discussion of the Logical Design of an Electronic Computing Instrument.* Institute for Advanced Study, Princeton. Second edition, 1947, pp. vi + 42.

Dennis, Jack, J. B. Fosseen and J. P. Linderman: 1974. "Data Flow Schemas." *Inter-*

national Symposium on Theoretical Programming, pp. 187-216. A. Ershov and V. A. Nepomniaschy (eds.). Springer-Verlag, New York.

Dennis, Jack and David Misunas: 1974. "A Preliminary Architecture for a Basic Data-Flow Processor." *ACM-SIGARCH*, vol. 3, no. 4, pp. 126-132.

Gillies, Andrew: 1985. "Machine Learning Procedures for Generating Image Domain Features." Doctoral thesis, University of Michigan.

Goldberg, David: 1983. "Computer-Aided Gas Pipeline Operation Using Genetic Algorithms and Rule Learning." Doctoral thesis, University of Michigan.

Grefenstette, John J. (ed.): 1985. *Proceedings of an International Conference on Genetic Algorithms and Their Applications, July 24-26.* Carnegie-Mellon University, Pittsburgh.

Hillis, W. Daniel: 1985. *The Connection Machine.* M.I.T. Press, Cambridge, MA.

Hockney, R. W. and C. R. Jesshope: 1981. *Parallel Computers.* Adam Hilger, Bristol.

Holland, John: 1975. *Adaptation in Natural and Artificial Systems — An Introductory Analysis with Applications to Biology, Control, and Artificial Intelligence.* University of Michigan Press, Ann Arbor.

_____: 1984. "Genetic Algorithms and Adaptation." *Adaptive Control in Ill-Defined Systems*, pp. 317-333. O. G. Selfridge, E. S. Rissland, and M. A. Arbib (eds.). Plenum Press, New York.

_____: 1985. "Properties of the Bucket-Brigade Algorithm." *Proceedings of an International Conference on Genetic Algorithms and Their Applications, July 24-26*, pp. 1-7. John J. Grefenstette (ed.). Carnegie-Mellon University, Pittsburgh.

_____: 1986. "Escaping Brittleness: The Possibilities of General-Purpose Learning Algorithms Applied to Parallel Rule-Based Systems." *Machine Learning II*, forthcoming. R. S. Michalski, G. J. Carbonell, and T. M. Mitchell (eds.).

Holland, John and Arthur Burks: 1986. "Adaptive Computing System Capable of Learning and Discovery." United States Patent Application.

Holland, John, Keith Holyoak, Richard Nisbett, and Paul Thagard: 1986. *Induction: Processes of Inference, Learning and Discovery.* M.I.T. Press, Cambridge, MA.

Riolo, Rick: 1986a. "CFS-C: A Package of Domain Independent Subroutines for Implementing Classifier Systems in Arbitrary, User-Defined Environments." Logic of Computers Group, Electrical Engineering and Computer Science, University of Michigan, Ann Arbor.

_____: 1986b. "LETSEQ: An Implementation of the CFS-C Classifier System in a Task-Domain that Involves Learning to Predict Letter Sequences." Logic of Computers Group, Electrical Engineering and Computer Science, University of Michigan, Ann Arbor.

Smith, Stephen: 1980. "A Learning System Based on Genetic Algorithms." Doctoral thesis, University of Pittsburgh.

Treleaven, Philip, David Brownbridge, and Richard Hopkins: 1982. "Data-Driven and Demand-Driven Computer Architecture." *Computing Surveys* 14, 93-143.

Von Neumann, John: 1966. Arthur W. Burks (ed.). *Theory of Self-Reproducing Automata.* University of Illinois Press, Urbana.

_____: 1986. *Papers of John von Neumann on Computers and Computer Theory.* William Aspray and Arthur Burks (eds.). M.I.T. Press, Cambridge, MA.

The parallel solution of sparse linear equations

Iain S. Duff

Computer Science and Systems Division

AERE Harwell

Didcot, Oxon

England, OX11 0RA

Abstract

We discuss the solution of large sparse systems using Gaussian elimination on both local and shared memory parallel computers.

There is a natural parallelism to Gaussian elimination that has been frequently exploited. We can take advantage of this parallelism in addition to that provided by the sparsity itself. We discuss this latter parallelism in some detail.

We discuss an approach that exploits the parallelism due to the sparsity and that can automatically benefit also from the parallelism of Gaussian elimination. This approach, which is applicable to quite general systems, is based on a multifrontal technique.

We look at the implementation of the multifrontal approach on shared memory machines and discuss its implementation on a hypercube.

1 Introduction

A system of linear equations is called **sparse** if most of the entries of its coefficient matrix are zero. The solution of large sparse systems of linear equations is one of the major calculations in large-scale computing in science and engineering. It is thus of great importance to study the performance of existing and new solution techniques on the range of parallel processors which are currently or soon to be marketed.

In this paper, we consider direct methods for the solution of sparse systems. We see that these techniques, based on Gaussian elimination, exhibit a very natural small granularity parallelism even when used in the solution of **full** systems (that is systems where all entries of the coefficient matrix are treated as nonzero). Further parallelism can be obtained from the sparsity, and it is primarily the exploitation of this that we will discuss. We examine Gaussian elimination parallelism in Section 2 and illustrate the phenomenon of parallelism due to sparsity in Section 3. We discuss a general technique for automatically using both forms of parallelism in Section 4 and consider its implementation on both shared and local memory machines in Sections 5 and 6 respectively. We draw some conclusions in Section 7.

In this presentation, we have assumed that our readership has a background in computer science but not necessarily in numerical analysis. We have therefore defined the principal numerical analysis terms when they are first used.

2 Parallelism in Gaussian elimination

Gaussian elimination involves factorizing a matrix A into the product $A=LU$ of a lower triangular matrix L and an upper triangular matrix U so that the solution to the set of linear equations $Ax=b$ can be easily effected by solving the triangular system $Ly=b$ followed by the triangular system $Ux=y$. In the case of full matrices A, the work for the factorization is $O(n^3)$ for a matrix of order n, while the solution of the triangular factors only involves $O(n^2)$ work. Although the factorization of a sparse matrix has a much lower operation count and is dependent on the number and distribution of nonzeros (the **sparsity pattern**), it is still true that the factorization step is much more costly than the solution phase. We therefore concentrate on the factorization step in this paper.

Assume that the coefficient matrix A has entries a_{ij}, $1 \leq i,j \leq n$. Gaussian elimination on a system of order n consists of $n-1$ major steps. Major step k, $1 \leq k \leq n-1$, involves the selection of a **pivot** a_{kk}. This process of selection, called **pivoting**, is made to ensure good numerical performance and is followed by the elimination of the entries $a_{k+1,k},...,a_{nk}$ by adding appropriate multiples of row k to rows $k+1,...n$ producing the updating operations

$$a_{ij} = a_{ij} - a_{ik}[a_{kk}]^{-1}a_{kj} \quad k<i,j \leq n \tag{2.1}$$

on rows and columns $k+1$ to n of the matrix (the **reduced matrix**). The important feature is that each update to an entry a_{ij} is independent so that they can all be performed in parallel.

If each single update operation is considered separately then the amount of parallelism is large $((n-1)^2$ processes at the first stage) but the communication costs are high since the each process must have the entries necessary for forming its triple product (2.1). Indeed, the biggest problem in Gaussian elimination on a local memory machine is that the pivot row $(a_{k\bullet})$ and the pivot column $(a_{\bullet k})$ or the multipliers $(a_{\bullet k}[a_{kk}]^{-1})$ must be communicated to all other rows or columns of the matrix. The most common way to overcome this is to treat all the operations updating a submatrix or a column or row as a single unit, thus increasing the granularity although decreasing the number of parallel processes. Many authors have suggested doing this for the Cholesky factorization (Gaussian elimination on a symmetric A to produce the factorization $A=LL^T$) on a hypercube both by subdiving A into submatrices and assigning a submatrix to each processor (Saad 1986) or by splitting the matrix into columns and assigning columns to processors either in a wrap around fashion or by contiguous blocks (Geist and Heath 1985). It is fairly easy to incorporate pivoting with this approach, advantage being taken of its lower order of complexity relative to the (2.1) update (Geist 1985). It is also possible to design a sparse version of the Cholesky factorization although present experience with it is disappointing (George et al. 1986a, 1986b). In Section 4 we consider a more general technique for sparse systems.

For surveys of parallel algorithms for full systems we refer the reader to Heller (1978) or Sameh (1983).

3 Parallelism due to sparsity

In Gaussian elimination on full systems, the major steps must be done sequentially. Although it is not necessary to wait until the completion of the first step before commencing the second, the second pivot must be updated before it can be used. Similarly, the third pivot must have been updated by both first and second steps before it can be used. The wavefront approach to Cholesky decomposition (Kung et al. 1981, O'Leary and Stewart 1985) uses pivots as soon as they are updated but must still process the pivots in order. However, if sparsity is present, this constraint of sequential pivoting does not necessarily hold.

The easiest way to see the influence of sparsity in removing the sequential pivot restriction is to consider the simple example of a tridiagonal matrix, arguably the most common sparse matrix.

$$\begin{bmatrix} a_1 & b_1 & & & & & \\ c_2 & a_2 & b_2 & & & & \\ & c_3 & a_3 & \bullet & & & \\ & & \bullet & \bullet & \bullet & & \\ & & & \bullet & \bullet & \bullet & \\ & & & & \bullet & \bullet & b_{n-1} \\ & & & & & \bullet & a_n \end{bmatrix}$$

Figure 3.1. A tridiagonal matrix.

From the example of a tridiagonal matrix shown in Figure 3.1, it is clear that selecting pivots in order down the diagonal imposes a sequential restriction. However, without increasing the number of arithmetic operations, we can simultaneously choose the first and last diagonal entries as pivot. Continuing in this way on the reduced matrix, we get the burn at both ends (BABE) algorithm with a parallelism of two throughout most of the calculation. If we allow an increase in the number of arithmetic operations then far greater parallelism can be obtained. Indeed, we can choose as pivots diagonal entries a_1, a_3, a_5, ... and obtain a parallelism of $[n/2]$ at the first stage. Although this ordering causes some zero entries in **A** to become nonzero in the factors (that is it causes **fill-in**) and more work than the sequential or BABE algorithms, if it is applied successively to subsequent reduced matrices, the number of major steps is $[log_2 n]$ rather than the $n-1$ of the sequential algorithm. Indeed, this is just the pivotal ordering that the nested dissection ordering of George (1973) would give us. Duff and Johnsson (1986) have looked at the effect of ordering on general systems but we defer further comments until we describe our approach for general systems in the following section.

4 Multifrontal techniques

Multifrontal methods are described in some detail by Duff *et al.* (1986) and their potential for parallelism by Duff (1985). We do not intend to describe this class of methods in detail here but we will work through a small example shown in Figure 4.1 to give the reader a flavour for the important points and to introduce the notion of an elimination tree (discussed in detail by Duff 1985 and Liu 1985). In Figure 4.1, x denotes a nonzero entry and zeros are left blank.

$$\begin{matrix} x & & x & x \\ & x & x & x \\ x & x & x & \\ x & x & & x \end{matrix}$$

Figure 4.1. Matrix used to illustrate multifrontal scheme.

We assume the matrix in Figure 4.1 is ordered so that pivots will be chosen down the diagonal in order. At the first step we can perform the elimination step corresponding to row and column 1 by first **assembling** row and column 1 to get the submatrix

$$\begin{matrix} x & x & x \\ x & & \\ x & & \end{matrix} \quad ,$$

Figure 4.2. Assembly of first pivot row and column.

which is termed a **frontal matrix**. By 'assembling', we mean placing (or summing) the nonzeros of row and column 1 into an array of dimension the number of nonzeros in row and column 1. Thus the zero entries a_{12} and a_{21} have been omitted in Figure 4.2 and an index vector is required to identify the rows and columns in the frontal matrix. Column 1 is then eliminated using pivot $(1,1)$ to give a reduced matrix of order two with associated row (and column) indices 3 and 4. Note that at this stage no reference has been made to any of the other entries of the original matrix. The updating operations corresponding to the entries of the reduced matrix are not performed immediately and the reduced matrix can be stored until these updates are necessary. Row (and column) 2 is now assembled, the (2,2) entry is used as pivot to eliminate column 2, and the reduced matrix of order two, with associated row (and column) indices of 3 and 4, is stored. Before we perform the pivot operations using entry (3,3), the updating operations from the first two eliminations (the two stored submatrices of order two) must be performed on the original row and column 3. This is effected by summing or 'assembling' the reduced matrices with the original row and column, using the index list to control the summation. Note that this gives rise to a fill-in in positions a_{34} and a_{43}. The pivot operation which eliminates column 3 using pivot (3,3) leaves a reduced matrix of order one with row (and column) index 4. The final step sums this matrix with the (4,4) entry of the original matrix. The sequence of major steps in the elimination can be represented by the tree shown in Figure 4.3.

Figure 4.3. Elimination tree for the matrix of Figure 4.1.

Figure 4.4. Elimination tree for the matrix of Figure 4.3 after node amalgamation.

The same storage and arithmetic is needed if the (4,4) entry is assembled at the same time as the (3,3) entry, and in this case the two pivotal steps can be performed on the same submatrix. This corresponds to collapsing or amalgamating nodes 3 and 4 in the tree of Figure 4.3 to yield the tree of Figure 4.4. On typical problems, node amalgamation produces a tree with about half as many nodes as the order of the matrix. Duff and Reid (1983) employ node amalgamation to enhance the vectorization of a multifrontal approach. In the present context, node amalgamation creates a larger granularity at each node which can assist in realizing the parallelism of this technique.

The computation at a node of the tree is simply the assembly of information concerning the node together with the assembly of the reduced matrices from its sons followed by some steps of Gaussian elimination. We can represent this by the system

$$\begin{pmatrix} A_1 & A_2 \\ A_3 & A_4 \end{pmatrix} \tag{4.1}$$

where eliminations are performed corresponding to pivots from A_1 and the Schur complement $A_4 - A_3 A_1^{-1} A_2$ is passed on for assembly at the father node.

The main feature of general elimination trees is that computation at any leaf node can proceed immediately and simultaneously and computations at nodes not on the same path from the root are independent. All that is required for computations to proceed at a node is that the calculations at its sons have been completed. A full discussion of this is given by Duff (1985).

5 Implementation on shared memory machines

When implementing multifrontal techniques on shared memory machines we are concerned to reduce contention for shared data. In particular, we wish to design our data structures to avoid updating information used by more than one processor. Duff (1985) studies these issues in some detail. Here we will sketch the data structures employed and report on some work that has been done since that paper.

Clearly, information on tree nodes available for computation must be kept so that, when a processor is free, it can easily find work to do. We do this by keeping a list of available nodes in a queue. Free processors take the next item on the queue, and when calculations on the last son node are complete, its father node is added to the back of the queue. Thus we need only protect two sets of pointers to prevent simultaneous updating or simultaneous accessing of the queue by different processors. Additionally, for each non-leaf node a count must be kept of the number of its sons whose calculations have not completed. Again this information must be protected against simultaneous access and a node is added to the queue when its count reaches zero.

Reading the data from the sons presents no problems since only one processor at a time can be accessing a particular item and we do not update the information anyway. Furthermore, since it is possible to tell in advance how much storage is required for the assembled frontal matrix, this space can be reserved before starting the actual assembly and so only a pointer to the first location of free space need be protected.

At some point when we advance up the tree towards the root there cannot be sufficient available nodes to saturate the parallelism of our machine. However, as was observed by Duff and Johnsson (1986), the frontal matrices grow in size as we near the root, so it is natural to take advantage of parallelism within each node. That is, we utilize the inherent parallelism of Gaussian elimination that we discussed in Section 2. In our current implementation, we do this by identifying two types of work package, the selection of pivots and the elimination operations on a row. We hold both types of work in the same pool using flags to identify what type of work each entry in the pool represents. When a processor accesses the pool for more work, it interprets the flag and does the appropriate work. We have found this a good method for increasing the parallelism although at the cost of decreasing the granularity. We can, however, control things by making each unit correspond to elimination operations on a block of rows and are currently experimenting to find the best compromise between granularity and parallelism. Clearly the optimal parameters will depend on the architecture but our approach allows them to be set as input parameters to the code and so it should not be hard to adjust them for any shared memory machine. The issues involved when using local memory machines are, however, quite different and we discuss them in the following section.

6 Implementation on local memory machines

The elimination tree view of multifrontal Gaussian elimination lends itself fairly naturally to local memory machines. After the computations corresponding to a node of the graph have been completed on a processor, the resulting frontal matrix is passed to the processor at which the computations for the father node will be performed. Since that target processor may at that time be doing work on some other node, there may be much overlap between communication and computation. If we wish to achieve good processor utilization and keep communications between processors to a minimum, two major issues are the balanced assignment of tree nodes to processors and the change of parallelism as we advance to the root of the elimination tree.

The first constraint that we wish to impose on the elimination tree is that it is a binary tree and indeed most nodes, except the leaves, have exactly two sons. Furthermore, we wish the tree to be reasonably balanced, that is we wish the lengths of the paths between leaf nodes and the root node to be about the same. The reasons for these restrictions is that it is really not possible to determine a balanced assignment of the nodes of a general tree onto the processors of a multiprocessor system, but much work has been done on mapping binary trees (for example, see Bhatt and Ipsen 1985). Duff and Johnsson (1986) examined the structure of the trees produced by various ordering strategies and found that although the most popular ordering for sparse systems, the minimum degree ordering (Tinney and Walker 1967), gave a very irregular tree, the nested dissection ordering could be organized to give exactly the sort of tree we desire.

With a tree that is binary and nearly-balanced, we then look at the number of nodes at each level of the tree. At the first level going away from the root at which the number of nodes exceeds the number of processors, level k say, we allocate the subtrees routed at that level to different processors, allowing some processors to have two subtrees with the same father so that all of the tree below level k is allocated to processors. Each processor can then perform elimination and updating operations independently on its subtree without interprocessor communication. When two subtrees on different processors but with the same father complete, then several processors must co-operate in one elimination or updating operation and we must subdivide further computations using the parallelism of Gaussian elimination. We assume that each computation is of the form shown (4.1) and that submatrices of the kind A_4 from (4.1) will be assembled at the common father node. However, the calculations at this father node will be spread over the two processors originally holding the two subtrees. Following the earlier work on full systems (for example, see Geist and Heath 1985), we assemble columns 1, 3, 5, ... in one processor and columns 2, 4, ... in the other. At the next level in the tree, the frontal matrix will be distributed among four processors and so on. As the sparse parallelism reduces, we must subdivide the frontal matrices further to maintain a sufficient level of parallelism. On a hypercube, the natural way to distribute these increasing number of subdivisions is to use hypercubes of increasing dimension. The submatrix corresponding to the root is factorized on the whole cube.

7 Concluding remarks

The important feature about the work discussed in this paper is that we have developed a general approach for the direct solution of sparse systems of linear equations which can automatically take advantage of both parallelism in Gaussian elimination and parallelism due to sparsity. Furthermore, the approach can be implemented on both shared and local memory machines. Additionally, there are many parameters which can be varied both in the original generation of the tree and in the implementation of the factorization given the tree structure. It is still too early to pass judgement on the best method to adopt but we can say with some certainty that it will be strongly dependent on the computer architecture involved.

Acknowledgement

I would like to thank Ilse Ipsen for her most helpful comments.

References

Bhatt, S.N. and Ipsen, I.C.F. (1985). How to embed trees in hypercubes. Report YALEU/DCS/RR–443, Department of Computer Science, Yale University, Connecticut.

Duff, I.S. (1985). Parallel implementation of multifrontal schemes. Report CSS 174, Computer Science and Systems Division, AERE Harwell. *Parallel Computing* (To appear).

Duff, I.S. and Johnsson, S.L. (1986). Node orderings and concurrency in sparse problems: an experimental investigation. Proceedings International Conference on Vector and Parallel Computing, Loen, Norway, June 2–6, 1986. (To appear).

Duff, I. S. and Reid, J. K. (1983). The multifrontal solution of indefinite sparse symmetric linear systems. *ACM Trans. Math. Softw.* **9**, 302–325.

Duff, I.S., Erisman, A.M., and Reid, J.K. (1986). Direct methods for sparse matrices. Oxford University Press, London.

Geist, G.A. (1985). Efficient parallel LU factorization with pivoting on a hypercube processor. Report ORNL–6211, Engineering Physics and Mathematics Division, Oak Ridge National Laboratory, Tennessee.

Geist, G.A. and Heath, M.T. (1985). Parallel Cholesky factorization on a hypercube multiprocessor. Report ORNL–6190, Engineering Physics and Mathematics Division, Oak Ridge National Laboratory, Tennessee.

George, A. (1973). Nested dissection of a regular finite-element mesh. *SIAM J. Numer. Anal.* **10**, 345–363.

George, A., Heath, M., Liu, J., and Ng, E. (1986a). Sparse Cholesky factorization on a local-memory multiprocessor. Report CS–86–01. Department of Computer Science, York University, Ontario, Canada.

George, A., Heath, M., Ng, E., and Liu, J. (1986b). Symbolic Cholesky factorization on a local-memory multiprocessor. Proceedings International Conference on Vector and Parallel Computing, Loen, Norway, June 2–6, 1986. *Parallel Computing* (To appear).

Heller, D. (1978). A survey of parallel algorithms in numerical linear algebra. *SIAM Review* **20**, 740–777.

Kung, H., Sproull, R., and Steele, G. (Eds.) (1981). *VLSI systems and computations.* Computer Science Press, Rockville, Maryland.

Kung, S.-Y., Arun, K., Bhuskerio, D., and Ho, Y. (1981). A matrix data flow language/architecture for parallel matrix operations based on computational wave concept. In Kung, Sproull, and Steele (1981).

Liu, J.W.H. (1985). Computational models and task scheduling for parallel sparse Cholesky factorization. Report CS–85–01. Department of Computer Science, York University, Ontario, Canada.

O'Leary, D.P. and Stewart, G.W. (1985). Data-flow algorithms for parallel matrix computations. *Communications ACM* **28**, 620–632.

Saad, Y. (1986). Gaussian elimination on hypercubes. Report YALEU/DCS/RR–462, Department of Computer Science, Yale University, Connecticut.

Sameh, A.H. (1983). An overview of parallel algorithms in numerical linear algebra. Bulletin de la Direction des Etudes et Recherches, EDF, France. Serie C., 129–134.

Tinney, W.F. and Walker, J.W. (1967). Direct solutions of sparse network equations by optimally ordered triangular factorization. *Proc. IEEE* **55**, 1801–1809.

PARALLEL ALGORITHMS ON THE CEDAR SYSTEM[1]

M. Berry   K. Gallivan
W. Harrod   W. Jalby
S. Lo   U. Meier
B. Philippe   A. H. Sameh

Center for Supercomputing Research and Development
University of Illinois at Urbana-Champaign
Urbana, Illinois 61801

1. INTRODUCTION

One of the key factors in the success of a supercomputer is the use of parallelism in forms which can be effectively exploited in the design of algorithms for a large class of problems. The introduction of pipelined architectures, such as the CRAY and CYBER 205, was an initial step in the design of supercomputers general enough to perform a large number of application algorithms efficiently. These architectures make use of segmented functional units and interleaved memories and provide considerable speedup for applications which require a large number of homogeneous computations on regular data. This approach does, however, have limits. First, the approach is not scalable. For example, if one attempts to increase the performance of the machine by increasing the number of segments or the number of functional units, the length of the vector which achieves a fixed fraction of the peak performance increases thereby reducing the number of applications which can efficiently use the machine. Second, even for the present configurations of vector architectures there are a large number of applications which cannot be vectorized efficiently (the resulting vectors are too short or a second dimension of vectorization is required) or do not lend themselves to vectorization at all due to complex data dependencies or the presence of large grain parallelism.

These limitations have led supercomputer designers to explore architectures which provide concurrency in addition to vectorization. Since these concurrent/vector architectures are capable of higher calculation rates, more complex memory systems are needed to satisfy the increased need for rapid data transfer. The CRAY X-MP, CRAY 2, ETA 10 and CEDAR are all concurrent/vector architectures which make use of a hierarchical memory system to provide the required data rates.

While significant progress has been made in developing efficient algorithms for vector machines, the same cannot be said of parallel processors which provide concurrency and vectorization along with a complex memory system. The three aspects of these architectures must be addressed simultaneously and are often contradictory; increasing vector length may destroy data locality and thereby lead to inefficient use of the hierarchical memory system. In this paper, we consider the tradeoffs involved in designing algorithms for such architectures and present some results for a single cluster of the CEDAR machine.

The next section contains a brief description of the target machine. An analysis of a third level of the BLAS (matrix-matrix operations) is then presented along with a description of the implementation on a single cluster, of some classical linear algebra algorithms such as LU, Gram-Schmidt and Householder factorizations, as well as two algorithms for the algebraic eigenvalue problem on a single cluster.

[1]This work was supported in part by the National Science Foundation under Grant Nos. US NSF DCR84-10110, US NSF DCR84-06916, and US NSF DCR85-09970, the U. S. Department of Energy under Grant No. US DOE DE-FG02-85ER25001, and the IBM Donation.

26

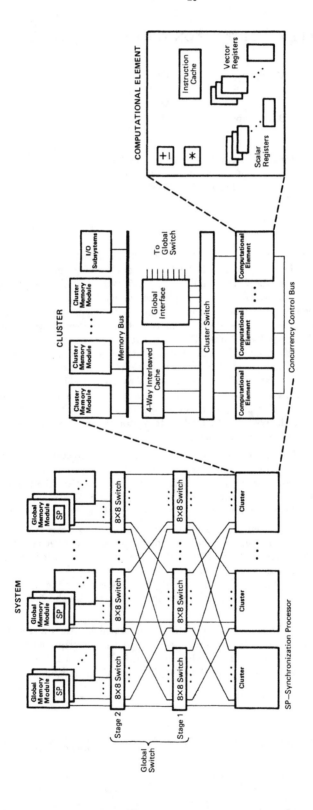

2. CEDAR ARCHITECTURE

Figure 1 illustrates the overall structure of the CEDAR architecture. In the Alliant FX/8 cluster, the eight floating point processors (CE's = computational elements) each have vector registers and an instruction cache, share a concurrency control bus for fast synchronization, and share a single four-module cache with ports that are twice as fast as a processor port. This cache is backed with a shared cluster memory. The cluster memory is backed by an I/O subsystem that contains several caches, processors, disks, and other I/O devices. A hardware coherence scheme is used to insure cache coherence. Each floating point processor is also connected through CEDAR logic to a private port of the global network that provides access to the shared global memory. A crossbar switch within each cluster connects each of these processors to its global switch port and to the shared cache ports.

Each of two unidirectional intercluster global switches is fully pipelined and employs two stages, each with 8×8 unidirectional crossbars and input buffering, for a system configuration of up to eight clusters. The global memory contains one module per floating point processor in the system. Each module contains two interleaved banks and a synchronization processor. The synchronization processor can perform an elaborate synchronization operation in response to a single input packet, thereby saving several round trips through the network while a memory port is locked up for each synchronization. The global memory may thus be used effectively for intercluster shared data and synchronization, for streaming long-vector access at high rate to the processors and as a fast backup memory for cluster memory. Each cluster has both a computational and an I/O complex of processors so that, as more clusters are added, the peak rates for processing and I/O grow.

3. ANALYSIS OF THE BLAS3

For a CEDAR cluster, the use of BLAS (vector / vector operations)[DBMS79] or even extended BLAS (matrix / vector operations)[DCHH84] may not be efficient since they mainly contain primitives involving an amount of data of the same order as the number of floating point operations; for example DAXPY (one of the BLAS) operating on vectors of length N will manipulate $3N+1$ data elements for executing only $2N$ operations. This may often result in an inefficient use of the hierarchical memory system, since less than one floating point operation per data accessed has to be performed. However, multiplying two square matrices of order N, involves $3N^2$ data elements for $(2N-1)N^2$ operations, so data elements fetched from the memory can be used several times before they are stored back again.

3.1. Description of the matrix multiplication algorithm

For the sake of simplicity, we consider here only the BLAS3 primitive: $C = C + A * B$. The similar cases $C = A * B$ and $D = C + A * B$ can be easily derived.

Let the $n_1 \times n_2$-matrix A be partitioned into $m_1 \times m_2$-blocks A_{ij}, the $n_2 \times n_3$-matrix B into $m_2 \times m_3$-blocks B_{ij} and the $n_1 \times n_3$-matrix C into $m_1 \times m_3$-blocks C_{ij}. The algorithm for obtaining the matrix C is as follows:

```
do i=1,k₁
   do j=1,k₃
      do k=1,k₂
         Cᵢⱼ=Cᵢⱼ+Aᵢₖ*Bₖⱼ
end do
```

where $n_1 = k_1 m_1$, $n_2 = k_2 m_2$ and $n_3 = k_3 m_3$ with k_1, k_2 and k_3 being integers greater than 1.

The block operations $C_{i,j} = C_{i,j} + A_{i,k} * B_{k,j}$ contain a reasonable amount of potential parallelism, so our algorithm proceeds by first partitioning the matrices and then dedicating the full resources of the cluster to each of the block operations in turn.

The total time required to perform the matrix multiplication can be expressed as:

$$T = lT_l + n_S T_S \qquad (3.1)$$

where l denotes the total number of loads executed from the memory (as opposed to cache), T_l the time of one load, n_S the number of submatrix multiplications that have to be performed, and T_S (kernel time) the time for one submatrix multiplication where the three relevant submatrices are kept in the cache. The first term represents the total time spent fetching data from the memory (pure transfer time) while the second represents mainly the time spent in computations. Each of them is a complex function of the three parameters m_1, m_2 and m_3, and trying to minimize their sum is difficult. In order to overcome this difficulty, we decouple the problem into independent subproblems: minimization of the transfer time and minimization of the computation time. The first subproblem involves the efficient use of the memory hierarchy in the cluster by properly exploiting data locality. The second requires the investigation of the tradeoffs encountered when implementing the matrix multiplication kernel using the two forms of parallelism available: concurrency and vectorization. The subproblems yield two regions in the parameter space where the values of the respective cost functions are close to minimal. By choosing a set of parameters within the intersection of these regions, near-optimal performance can be achieved in most cases.

3.2. Minimization of the computation time

The kernel to be considered is:

do $r=1,m_3$
  do $s=1,m_1$
    do $t=1,m_2$
      $c_{s,r}=c_{s,r}+a_{s,t}\,b_{t,r}$
end do

where c_{sr}, a_{st} and b_{tr} denote the elements of C_{ij}, A_{ik} respectively B_{kj}.

We introduce parallelism by performing the r-loop concurrently on all 8 processors using vectorization for the s-loop in each of them. Each processor computes an m_2-adic operation, the product of the submatrix A_{ik} with a column of B_{kj}.

Values of m_1, m_2, and m_3 which yield near-optimal values of the computation time for the kernel are highly dependent on the particular machine under consideration. A detailed discussion of this topic for the ALLIANT FX/8 is contained in [JaMe86] but the following reasoning can give some insight into the choice of the parameters.

The value of m_1 is the length of the vector operations used in the kernel algorithm. The vector registers of the ALLIANT FX/8 are of length 32 and therefore if m_1 is small it should be taken to be a multiple of 32. For larger values of m_1, greater than 160 on the ALLIANT FX/8, performance is not as sensitive to nonmultiples of 32 and any convenient value may be used. The algorithm performs m_2-adic operations and hence m_2 must be chosen large enough so as to achieve near-optimal performance. On the ALLIANT FX/8, $m_2 \geq 32$ delivers such performance. Since concurrency is used on the columns of the submatrices of B, the value of m_3, if small, should be a multiple of the number of processors available or large enough so that the processors are all kept busy for a significant fraction of the time. On the ALLIANT FX/8, this implies that $m_3=8k$ or is large.

3.3. Minimization of the transfer time

In this section, the values for submatrix sizes which minimize the number of data loads from main memory are presented. The following assumptions are made: each block C_{ij} is loaded into the cache only once and kept there for the duration of the k-loop; the blocks A_{ik} and B_{kj} are loaded each time they are involved in a submatrix multiplication.

In [JaMe86] it is shown that the optimal values of m_1, m_2 and m_3 are obtained by minimizing the total number of "loads" $(m_1n_2+m_3n_2+m_1m_3)(n_1m_1^{-1})(n_3m_3^{-1})$, or by minimizing:

$$\rho = (m_1+m_3)(m_1m_3)^{-1} = m_1^{-1}+m_3^{-1} \tag{3.2}$$

under the constraint

$$m_1 m_2 + m_1 m_3 < CS \qquad (3.3)$$

where CS denotes the cache size.

Assuming equality in (3.3), we obtain the following estimate of the optimal parameters as a function of m_2 and the cache size CS:

$$m_1 \approx \frac{CS}{m_2 + \sqrt{CS}} \quad ; \quad m_3 \approx \sqrt{CS}. \qquad (3.4)$$

The optimal ρ is then given by

$$\rho_{opt} \approx \frac{m_2}{CS} + \frac{2}{\sqrt{CS}}. \qquad (3.5)$$

Note that (3.4) requires m_1 and m_3 to be large which fits well the constraints for the computation time, while (3.5) indicates that the effect of m_2 is not dominant, allowing us to choose m_2 large enough to get an efficient m_2-adic operation. Finally, we would like to point out that enlarging the cache size by a factor of 4 leads to reducing ρ_{opt} only by a factor of 2.

For large n_1, n_2, and n_3, we now determine the optimal partitioning for the Alliant FX/8.

A good choice seems to be $m_1 = 96$, $m_2 = 32$ and $m_3 = 128$. Note that m_1 is a multiple of the length of a vector register, m_2 the optimal value for the m_2-adic operation and m_3 a multiple of the number of CE's. Fig.2 shows the experimental results for our optimal partitioning and for two other partitionings achieving the same kernel performance as the optimal one but involving a larger number of loads. We observe, as predicted above, a good correspondence between the decrease of the value of ρ ($\rho = 0.15625$, for $m_1 = 32$ and $m_3 = 8$; $\rho = 0.03125$, for $m_1 = m_3 = 32$; and $\rho = 0.01823$, for $m_1 = 96$ and $m_3 = 128$) and the improvement in performance. Also note that our optimal partitioning achieves a constant high performance for a large range of matrix sizes. Here, and throughout this paper all experiments on the Alliant FX/8 are performed in 64-bit, double precision arithmetic.

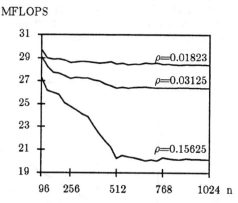

Fig. 2. Performance of the multiplication of two square matrices of order n

4. MATRIX FACTORIZATIONS

To demonstrate the superiority of BLAS3 over BLAS2 on the CEDAR architecture we consider some classical linear algebra algorithms which can be formulated in terms of matrix/vector as well as matrix/matrix operations. These are the LU decomposition, the modified Gram-Schmidt algorithm, and the Householder reduction.

4.1. Block LU Decomposition

The goal of the LU decomposition is to factor a $n \times n$-matrix A into the product of a lower triangular matrix L and an upper triangular matrix U. The classical LU factorization (see e.g. [DBMS79] consists essentially of dotproducts, i.e. the classical BLAS or BLAS1, it can however also be expressed in terms of rank one updates, i.e. BLAS2.

In order to use the efficient BLAS3, a block LU factorization must be performed. This algorithm decomposes A into the products of block lower triangular matrix L_k and a block upper triangular matrix U_k with blocks of size $k \times k$ (We assume for simplicity that n is divisible by k.). Let A be a diagonally dominant matrix partitioned in the following way:

$$A = \begin{pmatrix} A_{11} & A_{12} \\ A_{21} & A_{22} \end{pmatrix} = \begin{pmatrix} I & 0 \\ L_{21} & I \end{pmatrix} \begin{pmatrix} U_{11} & U_{12} \\ 0 & B \end{pmatrix} \tag{4.1}$$

where A_{11} is of order k. The first step of the algorithm is:

$$A_{11} \leftarrow A_{11}^{-1}, \quad L_{21} = A_{21} A_{11}, \quad B = A_{22} - L_{21} A_{12} \tag{4.2}$$

The above computations are then performed recursively on the smaller matrix B. Note that the BLAS2 version of the classical LU decomposition is a special case of this algorithm for $k = 1$.

This block LU algorithm consists mainly of matrix-matrix operations. The only difficulty lies in inverting $k \times k$ blocks. This can be done by using the Gauss-Jordan algorithm which can be implemented efficiently on a CEDAR cluster. Such an algorithm is numerically stable for our case, e.g. see [PeWi75]. A more general algorithm has been coded on the Alliant by [DoSo86].

The block-LU-algorithm is more expensive by a factor of approximately $(1 + 2/k^2)$ than the classical LU factorization which requires about $2n^3/3$ flops.

Both algorithms are implemented on the ALLIANT FX/8 using BLAS2 for the classical case and BLAS3 for the block variant. The performance of both methods as well as the speedup of the block LU-factorization applied to a 960×960-matrix for a varying number of processors are given in Fig. 3 . The block sizes chosen here, are 16 for $n \leq 320$, 24 for $320 < n < 832$ and 32 for $n \geq 832$. The block algorithm is about 3.5 times as fast as the classical LU factorization if $n > 500$.

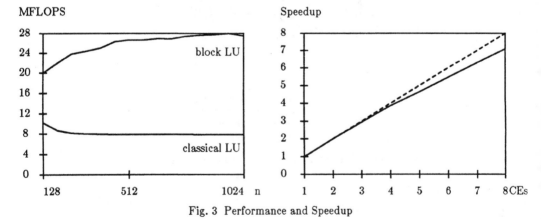

Fig. 3 Performance and Speedup

4.2. A Block Householder Scheme

We propose a block generalization of Householder's reduction for the orthogonal factorization of an $m \times n$ matrix A of rank n. Such formulations of the Householder transformations have been reported by Brenlund and Johnsen [BrJo74], Dietrich [Diet76] and Bischof and Van Loan [BiVa85].

A Householder transformation is an orthogonal matrix P of the form $P = I - uu^T$ where $u \in \mathbf{R}^m$ and $u^T u = 2$. If $x \in \mathbf{R}^m$, then Px is a vector in the orthogonal compliment of the set $\{u\}$. In particular P can be constructed so that Px is a multiple of e_1, the first column of the identity matrix. The Bischof and Van Loan method is based on the observation that the product of k Householder transformations $Q_k = P_k \cdots P_2 P_1$, can be written in the form,

$$Q_k = I - V_k U_k^T, \quad U_k, V_k \in \mathbf{R}^{m \times k}$$

where $U_k = (u_1, u_2, ..., u_k)$, and $V_k = (P_k V_{k-1}, u_k)$. In [BiVa85], it is stated that the floating point operation count is approximately $(1 + 2/p)n^2(m - n/3)$, where $p = n/k$. Also, it is shown that such a block scheme has the same numerical stability properties as the classical Householder factorization method. We will assume that k divides n, $m > n$, and a_j denotes the j th column of A.

Algorithm 4.2.1: Block Orthogonal Factorization Algorithm

$p = n/k \quad k_2 = 0$
do $j = 1, p$
$\quad k_1 = k_2 + 1, \quad k_2 = k_2 + k$
$\quad$ do $i = k_1, k_2$
$\quad\quad$ compute u_i such that for $P_i = I - u_i u_i^T$,
$\quad\quad$ $P_i a_i$ has zeros in the entries $i+1, ..., m$
$\quad\quad V_{i+1-k_1}^j = (P_i V_{i-k_1}^j, u_i)$
$\quad\quad U_{i+1-k_1}^j = (U_{i-k_1}^j, u_i)$
$\quad\quad$ if $(i \neq k_2)$ then
$\quad\quad\quad a_{i+1} \leftarrow (I - V_{i+1-k_1}^j U_{i+1-k_1}^{j\ T}) a_{i+1}$
$\quad\quad$ endif
$\quad$ enddo
$\quad$ if $(j \neq p)$ then
$\quad\quad (a_{k_2+1}, ..., a_n) \leftarrow (I - V_k^j U_k^{j\ T})(a_{k_2+1}, ..., a_n)$
$\quad$ endif
enddo

This orthogonal factorization algorithm is written in high level modules; vector-matrix, matrix-vector, and matrix-matrix, while the classical algorithm is based on the vector-vector modules, e.g. BLAS [see DBMS79]. Both have been programmed on the Alliant FX/8 in FORTRAN-8X, [see Harr86]. The classical Householder factorization method [DBMS79], has been programmed using vector optimization (no concurrency). In the following figures this program is referred to as VECTOR. We also compare our block scheme, for k > 1, with the case in which k = 1, we refer to this case as COLBLK. The optimal size of the blocks in the generalized Householder method is determined depending on the number of columns of the matrix A.

Figure 5 shows the performance obtained by the block orthogonal factorization when applied to a matrix with 1000 rows and n columns. The performance ranges from 19.53 MFLOPS to 27.30 MFLOPS for a matrix of order 1000 ×1000. The orthogonal factorization of a matrix of order 1000 × 1000 is realized in 52 seconds. Figure 6 shows the speedup over the program VECTOR for a matrix with 1000 rows and n columns; speedups range from 8.83 for a matrix of order 1000 ×100 to 16.30 for a matrix of order 1000 × 1000. This reflects the speedup realized by the block scheme and the eight CE's. Also, Figure 6 shows the speedup over the program COLBLK, this demonstrates the superiority of the block scheme in managing the CE vector registers and the cache. The speedups range from 1.83 for a matrix of order 1000 ×100 to 3.11 for a matrix of order 1000 ×1000.

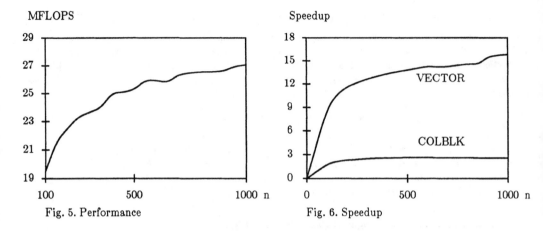

MFLOPS   Speedup

Fig. 5. Performance   Fig. 6. Speedup

4.3. A Block Gram-Schmidt Algorithm

The goal of this algorithm is to factor an $m \times n$-matrix A into the product of an orthonormal $m \times n$-matrix Q and an upper triangular $n \times n$-matrix R where $m > n$ and A is of maximal rank. A is partitioned into two blocks A_1 and B where A_1 consists of s columns of order m, with Q and R partitioned accordingly.

$$\left(A_1, B \right) = \left(Q_1, P \right) \begin{pmatrix} R_{11} & R_{12} \\ 0 & R_{22} \end{pmatrix} \tag{4.3}$$

The first step of the algorithm comprises the computations:

$$A_1 = Q_1 R_{11}, \quad R_{12} = Q_1^T B, \quad B_1 = B - Q_1 R_{12}. \tag{4.4}$$

The above computations are then performed recursively on the smaller problem $B_1 = PR_{22}$, etc. It is easily seen that this algorithm consists mainly of matrix operations. The decomposition of A_1 into the orthonormal matrix Q_1 and the upper triangular matrix R_{11}, which is performed by using the modified Gram-Schmidt algorithm, requires only $2ms^2$, while the rest of the matrix operations require $2m(n-ks)^2$ flops.

The BLAS2 version of the modified Gram-Schmidt algorithm is obtained by setting s to 1. This version, as well as a BLAS3 version of the algorithm with $s = 32$, are implemented on the ALLIANT FX/8. Fig. 4 shows the computational rates for both cases as well as the speedup of the BLAS3 version applied to a 960×960-matrix using a varying number of processors. Increasing the order of A obviously improves the performance for the BLAS3 version as the matrix-matrix operations dominate the whole computation.

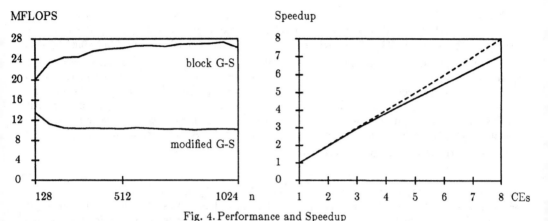

MFLOPS

Speedup

Fig. 4. Performance and Speedup

5. THE ALGEBRAIC EIGENVALUE PROBLEM

In this section, we discuss parallel algorithms for the determination of eigenvalues and eigenvectors for symmetric dense and tridiagonal matrices on one CEDAR cluster. A multiprocessor algorithm for the singular value decomposition of rectangular matrices is also presented.

5.1. Jacobi's Method

We have developed two parallel algorithms based on Jacobi's method for the determination of complete eigensystems of dense real symmetric matrices and of the singular value decomposition of rectangular matrices on the Alliant FX/8. Our intent has been to compare the performance of Jacobi and Jacobi-like schemes vs. existing EISPACK and LINPACK routines on the Alliant FX/8 computer system. For dense symmetric eigenvalue problems, we have obtained promising results for small-order matrices and matrices having multiple eigenvalues. A "one-sided" Jacobi algorithm which produces the singular value decomposition of a rectangular matrix has demonstrated superior performance on rectangular matrices in which the number of rows is much larger than the number of columns.

(a) For the standard eigenvalue problem

$$\mathbf{A}\mathbf{x} = \lambda\mathbf{x} \tag{5.1}$$

where $\mathbf{A}$ is a real $n \times n$ dense symmetric matrix, Jacobi's method reduces the matrix $\mathbf{A}$ to diagonal form by an infinite sequence of plane rotations

$$\mathbf{A}_{k+1} = \mathbf{U}_k \mathbf{A}_k \mathbf{U}_k^{\mathrm{T}}, \quad k = 1, 2, \cdots,$$

where $\mathbf{A}_1 \equiv \mathbf{A}$ and $\mathbf{U}_k = \mathbf{U}_k(i, j, \theta_{ij}^k)$ is an orthogonal plane rotation. Each $\mathbf{A}_{k+1}$ remains symmetric and differs from $\mathbf{A}_k$ only in rows and columns i and j. By annihilating an element a_{ij}^k at each step k which is at least of average magnitude, $\mathbf{A}_k$ approaches the diagonal matrix $\mathbf{\Lambda} = diag(\lambda_1, \lambda_2, \cdots, \lambda_n)$. Similarly, $(\mathbf{U}_k \cdots \mathbf{U}_2 \mathbf{U}_1)^{\mathrm{T}}$ approaches a matrix whose j-th column is the eigenvector corresponding to λ_j.

A parallel version of the classical cyclic Jacobi algorithm as discussed in [Same71] and [BeSa86] is obtained by the simultaneous annihilation of several off-diagonal elements by a given $\tilde{\mathbf{U}}_k$ rather than only one as is done in the serial version. For example, let $\mathbf{A}$ be of order 8 and consider the orthogonal matrix $\tilde{\mathbf{U}}_k$ as the direct sum of 4 independent plane rotations, ie.,

$$\tilde{\mathbf{U}}_k = \mathbf{R}_k(1,3) \oplus \mathbf{R}_k(2,4) \oplus \mathbf{R}_k(5,7) \oplus \mathbf{R}_k(6,8),$$

where $\mathbf{R}_k(i,j)$ is that rotation which annihilates the (i,j) off-diagonal element. If we consider one sweep to be a collection of orthogonal similarity transformations that annihilate the element in each of the $n(n-1)/2$ off-diagonal positions (above the main diagonal) only once, then for a matrix of order 8 each sweep will consist of 8 successive $\tilde{U}_k$'s with each one annihilating 4 elements simultaneously. Although several annihilation patterns are possible, the Multiprocessor Jacobi Algorithm implememented on the Alliant FX/8 utilizes a scheme which requires a minimal amount of indexing [BeSa86].

To effectively use vectorization supported by the Alliant FX/8 computer system, we disregard the symmetry of A_k and operate with full vectors on the entirety of rows and columns i and j. To avoid the necessity of synchronization, all row changes specified by the $\lfloor n/2 \rfloor$ or $\lfloor (n-1)/2 \rfloor$ plane rotations for a given $\tilde{U}_k$ are performed concurrently with one processor updating a unique pair of rows. After all row changes are completed, we perform the analogous column changes in the same manner. The product of the $\tilde{U}_k$'s, which eventually yields the eigenvectors for A, is accumulated separately.

(b) For determining the singular value decomposition

$$A = U\Sigma V^T \tag{5.2}$$

where A is a real $m \times n$ matrix $(m \gg n)$, $U^T U = V^T V = I_n$, and $\Sigma = diag(\sigma_1, \cdots, \sigma_n)$, we have adapted a "one-sided" Jacobi algorithm [Luk80] for the Alliant FX/8. Recall that the orthogonal matrices U and V define the orthonormalized eigenvectors associated with the n eigenvalues of AA^T and $A^T A$, respectively. The singular values of A are defined as the diagonal elements of Σ which are the nonnegative square roots of the n eigenvalues of AA^T. The main goal of this algorithm is to determine an orthogonal matrix $\tilde{V}$ as a product of plane rotations so that

$$A\tilde{V} = Q = (q_1, q_2, q_3, \cdots, q_n) , \tag{5.3}$$

and

$$q_i^T q_j = \sigma_i^2 \delta_{ij} ,$$

where the columns of Q, q_i, are orthogonal, and δ_{ij} is the Kronecker delta. We then may write Q as

$$Q = \tilde{U}\Sigma \text{ with } \tilde{U}^T \tilde{U} = I_n ,$$

and hence

$$A = \tilde{U}\Sigma \tilde{V}^T .$$

The annihilation scheme of the Multiprocessor Jacobi Algorithm described in [BeSa86] can be easily adapted as the orthogonalization scheme for obtaining the matrix Q. This orthogonalization of the columns of matrix A is determined iteratively given the fact that the orthogonality established between any two columns by a particular rotation may be destroyed by subsequent rotations. In general, each $\tilde{V}_k$ will have the same form of $\tilde{U}_k$ of the "two-sided" Multiprocessor Jacobi Algorithm.

Whereas the two-sided Jacobi algorithm discussed earlier requires row and column updates following each similarity transformation, this one-sided scheme performs only postmultiplication of A , and hence the plane rotation (i,j) changes only the elements in columns i and j of matrix A. On the Alliant FX/8, each processor is assigned one rotation and hence orthogonalizes one pair of the n columns of matrix A. Upon termination, the matrix A has been overwritten by the matrix Q from (5.3), and hence the singular values σ_i can be obtained via the n square roots of the diagonal entries of $A^T A$. The matrix U in (5.2), which contains the left singular values of the original matrix A, is readily obtained by scaling the resulting matrix A (now overwritten by $Q = \tilde{U}\Sigma$) by the singular values σ_i, and the matrix V, which contains the right singular vectors of the original matrix A, is obtained as the product of the orthogonal $\tilde{V}_k$'s. We note that this One-Sided Multiprocessor Jacobi Algorithm is applicable for solving the eigenvalue problem (5.1) for real nonsingular symmetric matrices. If $m = n$, A is a positive definite matrix, and Q is given by (5.3), it is not difficult to show that

$$\sigma_i = \lambda_i \text{ and } x_i = \frac{q_i}{\lambda_i}, \quad i = 1, 2, ..., n , \tag{5.4}$$

where λ_i denotes the i-th eigenvalue of A, x_i the corresponding normalized eigenvector, and q_i the

i-th column of matrix $\mathbf{Q}$. Two advantages of this one-sided Jacobi scheme over the "two-sided" Jacobi method are that no row accesses are needed and that the matrix $\tilde{\mathbf{V}}$ need not be accumulated.

For comparison purposes in the evaluation of our two Jacobi schemes, we refer to the Two-Sided Multiprocessor Jacobi Algorithm as MUJAC, and the One-Sided Multiprocessor Jacobi Algorithm as OMJAC. In Fig. 7, we plot the number of MFLOPS and the speedup (over 1 CE) achieved by the Alliant FX/8 when MUJAC and OMJAC are used for the matrix $\mathbf{A} = [\, a_{ij} \,]$ with $a_{ij} = dfloat\, [\, max(i,j)\,]$, $i,j = 1,2, \cdots ,n$, for different values of n. The decrease in performance for MUJAC for matrix orders greater than 100 can be greatly attributed to the memory limitations of the computational processor cache, Although peak performance of 17 MFLOPS for MUJAC for $n = 50$ was much larger than the 14 MFLOPS for OMJAC, the variation from the peak performance for all n was certainly much smaller for the latter.

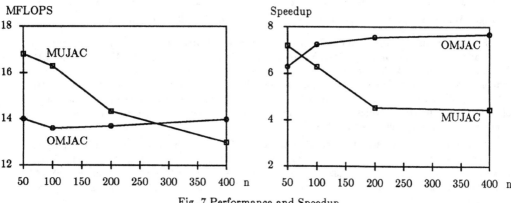

Fig. 7 Performance and Speedup

In Figs. 8, 9, and 10 we compare the performance in speed of MUJAC and OMJAC with that of new and existing EISPACK and LINPACK routines on the Alliant FX/8. For the dense symmetric eigenvalue problem we first compare MUJAC, OMJAC, and TRED2+TQL2 from EISPACK [SBDG76]. In order to compare a set of highly efficient subroutines that are optimized for vector as well as parallel processing, we compare MUJAC and OMJAC which use ASSEMBLER routines for applying rotations and computing dotproducts, with TQL2 and the new matrix-vector implementation of TRED2, TRED2V [DKH85]. In Fig. 8, we compare the timing of these three algorithms on 8 CEs with full optimization (global and vector) for $n \times n$ symmetric matrices in which $\lambda_i = i$. In Fig. 9, we compare the speeds when the $n \times n$ matrix has 1 as an eigenvalue with multiplicity $n-2$.

In Fig. 9, the largest n for which MUJAC executed faster than TRED2V+TQL2 is 90, while OMJAC consistently outperformed the other two algorithms and required only one-half the execution time of the EISPACK routines for each n. However, as shown in Fig. 8 for a matrix with uniformly distributed eigenvalues, the performance of both Jacobi schemes is approximately the same and TRED2V+TQL2 is superior for $n \geq 60$. Five to nine sweeps were required for both MUJAC and OMJAC for the experiments in Fig. 8, while only 3 to 4 sweeps were needed for those in Fig. 9. We note that for all our experiments, the accuracy in determining the eigenvalues and eigenvectors by these Jacobi algorithms is identical to that obtained by TRED2V+TQL2.

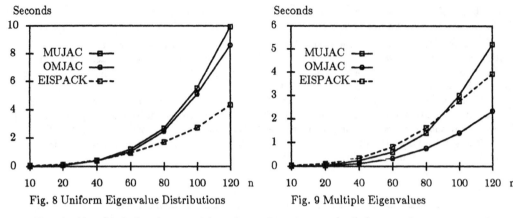

Fig. 8 Uniform Eigenvalue Distributions   Fig. 9 Multiple Eigenvalues

For the singular value decomposition of a real $m \times n$ matrix $\mathbf{A}$ ($m \gg n$) we compare the speed and accuracy of OMJAC with that of the appropriate routines from EISPACK and LIN-PACK: SVD and DSVDC. Recall that both routines SVD and DSVDC reduce the matrix $\mathbf{A}$ to bi-diagonal form via Householder transformations and then diagonalize this reduced form using plane rotations. We also compare our results from OMJAC with the new matrix-vector implementation of SVD: SVDV [DKH85], which has been demonstrated to achieve 50% speedup in execution time over SVD on machines such as the CRAY-1.

In Figure 10, we present the speedups for OMJAC over each routine used to compute the singular values and singular vectors of the matrix $\mathbf{A} = [a_{ij}]$, $a_{ij} = (i+j-1)/n$, $i = 1,2, \cdots ,m$, and $j = 1,2, \cdots ,32$, on the Alliant FX/8. With regard to accuracy, OMJAC was somewhat less accurate than SVDV and DSVDC for the smaller values of m, but very competitive for $m > 512$.

m	$\dfrac{t_s}{t_o}$	$\dfrac{t_d}{t_o}$	$\dfrac{t_{sv}}{t_o}$	
64	3.57	8.33	1.78	$t_d \equiv$ time for DSVDC
128	3.33	5.88	1.69	$t_o \equiv$ time for OMJAC, [3 sweeps]
512	3.45	3.03	1.13	$t_s \equiv$ time for SVD
2048	3.23	2.38	1.32	$t_{sv} \equiv$ time for SVDV
8192	3.13	2.70	1.26	

Fig. 10. Speed-ups for OMJAC

5.2. A Multiprocessor Method for Tridiagonal Matrices

A multiprocessor algorithm, TREPS, has been designed for finding few or all eigenvalues and the corresponding eigenvectors of a symmetric tridiagonal matrix [LoPS86]. This is a pipelined variation of EISPACK routines - BISECT and TINVIT which consists of the three steps: isolation, extraction - inverse iteration, and partial orthogonalization. Experiments on the Alliant FX/8 (one cluster of the CEDAR machine) and CRAY X-MP/48 multiprocessors show that this algorithm achieves high speedup over BISECT and TINVIT. In fact we show that this scheme, the origins of which date back to the Illiac IV [KuSa71] and [Huan74], is equally, or more effective than other multiprocessor schemes for obtaining either all the eigenvalues, or all the eigenvalues and eigenvectors of a symmetric tridiagonal matrix.

Let $\mathbf{T} = \left[e_{i,}\, d_{i,}\, e_{i+1} \right]$ be a symmetric tridiagonal matrix of order n with d_i and e_i as the diagonal and subdiagonal elements, respectively. Where $e_i \neq 0$. Let $p_n(\lambda) = \det(\mathbf{T} - \lambda\mathbf{I})$ be the characteristic polynomial of $\mathbf{T}$. The sequence of the principal minors of the matrix, Sturm sequence of $\mathbf{T}$ in λ, can be built using the following recursion :

$$p_0(\lambda) = 1, \quad p_1(\lambda) = d_1 - \lambda, \quad p_i(\lambda) = (d_i - \lambda)p_{i-1}(\lambda) - e_i^2 p_{i-2}(\lambda)\ , i = 2,...,n\ . \tag{5.5}$$

It is well known, [Wilk65], that the number of eigenvalues lying in a given interval [a,b] can be found by computing the difference of sign variations of the Sturm sequences at a and b. Therefore, given an initial interval, we can find the eigenvalues lying in it by repeated bisection or multisection of the interval until we have isolated each eigenvalue. Then, a method such as bisection, Newton's method or Zeroin scheme [FoMM77] can be used to extract the eigenvalues.

There are two possible means of parallelism that can be considered in the isolation process. One is in the computation of Sturm sequence, and the other is by performing simultaneously the computation of several Sturm sequences. The algorithm in [ChKS78] may be used to vectorize the linear recurrence of the Sturm sequence (5.5). However, the arithmetic redundancy, which varies between 2.5 and 4, makes this algorithm only efficient when vector operations are at least 4 times faster than sequential operations. Among the various ways of computing simultaneously several Sturm sequences, two options are : (1) performing bisection on several intervals (parallel bisection), (2) performing a partition of one interval into several subintervals (multisection). A multisection of order k splits an interval into $k+1$ subintervals. If there exists only one eigenvalue in the interval, to compute this eigenvalue with an absolute error ϵ requires $\log_2 \left\lceil \dfrac{(b-a)}{(2\,\epsilon)} \right\rceil / \log_2\left(k+1\right)$ multisections of order k.

Thus, the efficiency of the multisection of order k compared to bisection (multisection of order 1) is $E_f = \left\lceil \log_2(k+1) \right\rceil / k$. Thus, multisectioning is preferred in the partitioning process because: (i) a multisection creates more tasks than bisection, and (ii) there are several eigenvalues in one interval. Whereas, for extraction of eigenvalues, we prefer to perform parallel bisections rather than one multisection of high order.

After an isolated eigenvalue has been computed, the corresponding eigenvector can be found by inverse iteration [GoVa83]. This is a very fast process where one iteration is often sufficient to achieve convergence. The computation of an eigenvector is performed in the same task which extracts the corresponding eigenvalue. Thus, the order of potential parallelism depends on the number of desired eigenvalues. Observing that, there can be loss of orthogonality only for those eigenvectors corresponding to close eigenvalues, we orthonormalize the corresponding eigenvectors by the Modified Gram-Schmidt method.

The reader may refer to [LoPS86] for the specific implementation of TREPS on the Alliant FX/8 and the Cray X-MP/48. Two versions of TREPS have been developed, TREPS1 adopts the parallel bisection method in the extraction step, while TREPS2 uses Zeroin. This method is based on the secant and bisection method, is faster than the pure bisection method, but due to the adoption of the linear recurrence scheme (5.5), there is the potential of over- or underflow. The bisection method uses a modified nonlinear recurrence scheme to evaluate the Sturm sequences, it is more robust than the Zeroin method, especially for those eigenvectors corresponding to clustered eigenvalues.

Typical test matrices [-1,2,-1] of different orders have been used in the experiments. TREPS, in vector-concurrent mode, realizes high speed-up when the number of desired eigenvalues exceeds the number of processors, using some synchronization directives on the FX/8.

We have compared the performance of our algorithm with BISECT+TINVIT, TQL2, and SESUPD (a multiprocessor version of TQL2 using a divide and conquer technique [DoSo86]), when **all** the eigenvalues and eigenvectors are required. We have also compared our algorithm with BISECT and TQL1 when only the eigenvalues are needed. To evaluate the numerical performance, we compare the norm of the residuals, $\max\|Tz_i - \lambda_i z_i\|_2$, for the computed eigenvalues and eigenvectors for TREPS, BISECT+TINVIT, TQL2, and SESUPD. Orthogonality of the eigenvectors is also checked by computing the $\max|Z^T Z - I|_{i,j}$, where Z is the eigenvector matrix. For the test matrix of order 500, both the residuals and the quality of the eigenvectors of TREPS1 and TREPS2 are close to that of BISECT+TINVIT but not as good as those of TQL2 and SESUPD. $O(10^{-12})$ vs. $O(10^{-14})$, (Machine precision on the FX/8 is around 10^{-16}).

In Fig. 11 we compare the performance of the above algorithms on both the FX/8 and the CRAY X-MP. Note that the time for TQL2 on one CE is 131 times slower than the time required by TREPS2 on 8 CE's, and the time for TQL2 on 8 CE's is 28 times slower than that of TREPS2. Furthermore, TREPS2 is 4.8 times faster than SESUPD. TREPS2 also proved to be superior to TREPS1, TQL1 and BISECT for obtaining all the eigenvalues only for the above test matrix.

i	Algorithm		Alliant				CRAY X-MP	
			1 CE	8 CE	SP1*	SP8*	1 CPU	4 CPU
1	TREPS1	time (sec)	116	15			11	3
		speed-up	1	7.8	32.9	7.	1	3.6
2	TREPS2	time (sec)	26	3.7			1.7	.64
		speed-up	1	6.9	131.5	28.	1	2.7
3	TQL2	time (sec)	486	103			6.7	---
		speed-up	1	4.7	4.7	1.	1	---
4	BISECT+TINVIT	time (sec)	141	136			13**	---
		speed-up	1	1.0	3.6	.8	1	---
5	SESUPD	time (sec)	---	18			---	---
		speed-up	---	---	27.1	5.8	---	---

Test matrix is of order 500.

$$* \quad SP1 = \frac{Time(TQL2\ on\ 1\ CE)}{Time(algorithm\ i\ on\ 8\ CEs)}, \quad SP8 = \frac{Time(TQL2\ on\ 8\ CEs)}{Time(algorithm\ i\ on\ 8\ CEs)}$$

Fig. 11. Time and speed-up for computing all the eigenvalues and eigenvectors.

REFERENCES

[BeSa86]   M. Berry and A. Sameh, Multiprocessor Jacobi schemes for dense symmetric eigenvalue and singular value decompositions, CSRD Report No. 546, CSRD, University of Illinois at Urbana-Champaign, 1986.

[BiVa85]   C. Bischoff and C Van Loan, The WY representation for products of Householder Matrices, TR 85-681, Department of Computer Science, Cornell University, 1985.

[BrJo74]   O. Bronlund and T. Johnsen, QR-factorization of partitioned matrices, Computer Methods in Applied Mechanics and Engineering 3, pp. 153-172, 1974.

[ChKS78]   S. Chen, D. Kuck and A. Sameh, Practical parallel band triangular system solvers, *ACM Trans. Math. Software*, Vol. 4, pp. 270-277, 1978.

[DBMS79]   J. Dongarra, J. Bunch, C. Moler, and G. W. Stewart, **LINPACK User's Guide,** SIAM, 1979.

[DCHH84]   J. Dongarra, J. Du Croz, S. Hammarling, R. Hanson, A proposal for an extended set of fortran basic linear algebra subprograms, ACM SIGNUM, March 1985.

[Diet76]   G. Dietrich, A new formulation of the hypermatrix Householder-QR decomposition, Computer Methods in Applied Mechanics and Engineering 9, pp. 273-280, 1976.

[DoKH85]   J. Dongarra, L. Kaufman, and S. Hammarling, Squeezing the most out of eigenvalue solvers on high-perfomance computers, Technical Memorandum No. 46, MCSD, Argonne National Laboratory, 1985.

[DoSo86]   J. Dongarra and D. Sorensen, A fully parallel algorithm for the symmetric eigenvalue problem, Argonne National Laboratory Report MCS-JM-62, Jan 1986. [Submitted to SISSC]

[DoSo86]   J. Dongarra, D. Sorensen, Linear algebra on high performance computers, Technical Report ANL-82-2, Argonne National Laboratory, 1986.

[GoVa83]   G. Golub and C. Van Loan, **Matrix Computations,** The John Hopkins University Press, 1983.

[FoMM77]   G. Forsythe, M. Malcom and C. Moler, **Computer Methods for Mathematical Computations,** Prentice Hall, 1977.

[Harr86]   W. Harrod, Solving linear least squares problems on an Alliant FX/8, CSRD Report, CSRD, University of Illinois at Urbana-Champaign, 1986.

[Huan74]   H. Huang, A parallel algorithm for symmetric tridiagonal eigenvalue problems. CAC Document No. 109, Center for Advanced Computation, University of Illinois at Urbana-Champaign, Feburary 1974.

[JaMe86]   W. Jalby, U. Meier, Optimizing matrix operations on a parallel multiprocessor with a two-level memory hierarchy, Proc. ICPP, Aug. 1986.

[KuSa71]   D. Kuck and A. Sameh, Parallel computation of eigenvalues of real matrices. **IFIP Congress 1971,** North-Holland, Vol 2, pp. 1266-1272, 1972.

[LoPS86]   S. Lo, B. Philippe and A. Sameh, A multiprocessor algorithm for the symmetrics tridiagonal eigenvalue problem. CSRD Report no. 513, CSRD, University of Illinois at Urbana-Champaign, 1986. [to be published in SISSC].

[LukF80]   F. Luk, Computing the singular-value decomposition on the Illiac IV, ACM Trans. Math. Software, vol. 6, no. 4, pp. 524-539, 1980.

[PeWi75]   G. Peters, J. Wilkinson, On the stability of Gauss-Jordan elimination with pivoting, CACM 18, pp. 20-24, Jan. 1975.

[Same71]   A. Sameh, On Jacobi and Jacobi-like algorithms for a parallel computer, Math. Comp., vol. 25, pp. 579-590, 1971.

[SBDG76]   B. Smith, J. Boyce, J. Dongarra, B. Garbow, Y. Ikebe, V. Klema, and C. B. Moler, **Matrix Eigensystem Routines - EISPACK Guide,** Second Edition, Springer-Verlag, Berlin, 1976.

[Wilk65]   J. Wilkinson, **The Algebraic Eigenvalue Problem,** Oxford, 1965.

FUTURE PARALLEL COMPUTERS

Philip C. Treleaven

University College London
London WC1E 6BT

ABSTRACT

There is currently a veritable explosion of research into novel
computer architectures, especially parallel computers. In addition, an
increasing number of interesting parallel computer products are appearing. The design motivations cover a broad spectrum: (i) parallel UNIX
systems (e.g. SEQUENT Balance), (ii) Artificial Intelligence applications (e.g. Connection Machine), (iii) high performance numerical
Supercomputers (e.g. Cosmic Cube), (iv) exploitation of Very Large
Scale Integration (e.g. INMOS Transputer), and (v) new technologies
(e.g. Optical computers). This short paper gives an overview of these
novel parallel computers and discusses their likely commercial impact.

PARALLEL COMPUTERS

In October 1981 Japan launched its 10 year national Fifth Generation project
[9,14] to develop knowledge information processing systems and processors. Since
then other major industrial countries have started comparable national research programmes. In the United States the Strategic Computing Initiative, a $600 million
programme funded by the Department of Defence, is investigating "machine intelligence
technology that will greatly increase national security and economic power". In the
European Community the ESPRIT programme has a significant part of its $1.3 billion
funding devoted to future computers. In addition, the individual European countries
are funding major fifth generation programmes.

This competition between the national research programmes, to develop a new generation of computers, has been a catalyst for parallel computer research [1]. A
major question for the design of future parallel computers is the choice of the
parallel programming style. There are seven basic categories of computers (shown in
Figure 1). They range from "low level" computers, such as control flow, that specify
exactly how a computation is to be executed, to "high level" computers, such as Connectionist, that merely specify what is required. Associated with each category of
computer is a corresponding category of programming language.

Firstly, there are control flow computers and procedural languages [13]. In a
control flow computer (e.g. SEQUENT Balance, INMOS Transputer) explicit flow(s) of
control cause the execution of instructions. In a procedural language (e.g. ADA,
OCCAM) the basic concepts are: a global memory of cells, assignment as the basic
action, and (sequential) control structures for the execution of statements.

Secondly, there are actor computers and object-oriented languages [16]. In an
actor computer (e.g. APIARY) the arrival of a message for an instruction causes the
instruction to execute. In an object-oriented language (e.g. SMALLTALK) the basic
concepts are: objects are viewed as active, they may contain state, and objects communicate by sending messages.

Thirdly, there are data flow computers and single-assignment languages [13]. In
a data flow computer (e.g. Manchester) the availability of input operands triggers
the execution of the instruction which consumes the inputs. In a single-assignment
language (e.g. ID, LUCID, VAL, VALID) the basic concepts are: data "flows" from one

statement to another, execution of statements is data driven, and identifiers obey the single-assignment rule.

APPLICATION AREAS						
Numeric Computation		Symbolic Computation			. . .	
PROGRAMMING LANGUAGES						
Procedural Languages ADA, OCCAM	Object-Oriented Languages SMALLTALK	Single-Assignment Languages ID, VAL	Applicative Languages Pure LISP	Predicate Logic Languages PROLOG	Production Systems Languages OPS5	Semantic Nets Languages NETL
COMPUTER ARCHITECTURES						
Control Flow Machines TRANSPUTER	Actor Machines APIARY	Data Flow Machines MANCHESTER	Reduction Machines ALICE	Logic Machines ICOT PIM	Rule-Based Machines NON-VON	Connect-ionist Machines CONNECTION

Figure 1: Parallel Computers and Programming Styles

Fourthly, there are reduction computers and applicative languages [13,16]. In a reduction computer (e.g. ALICE, GRIP) the requirement for a result triggers the execution of the instruction that will generate the value. In an applicative language (e.g. Pure LISP, SASL, FP) the basic concepts are: application of functions to structures, and all structures are expressions in the mathematical sense.

Fifthly, there are logic computers and predicate logic languages [16,17]. In a logic computer (e.g. ICOT PIM) an instruction is executed when it matches a target pattern and parallelism or backtracking is used to execute alternatives to the instruction. In a predicate logic language (e.g. PROLOG) the basic concepts are: statements are relations of a restricted form, and execution is a suitably controlled logical deduction from the statements.

Sixthly, there are rule-based computers and production system languages [16]. In a rule-based computer (e.g. NON-VON, DADO) an instruction is executed when its conditions match the contents of the working memory. In a production system language (e.g. OPS5) the basic concepts are: statements are IF...THEN... rules and they are repeatedly executed until none of the IF conditions are true.

Lastly, there are connectionist computers and semantic net languages [16]. A connectionist computer (e.g. Connection Machine) is based on the modelling of inter-neural connections in the brain. In a semantic net language (e.g. NETL) networks are used to define the connections between concepts, represented as structured objects.

However, since most parallel computers are still based on control flow, we believe that the best way to survey future parallel computers is by their application area. Thus below we briefly examine each of the major application areas, namely: (i) fifth generation computers, (ii) numerical supercomputers, (iii) transaction processing systems, (iv) VLSI architectures, and (v) new technologies.

FIFTH GENERATION COMPUTERS

Fifth Generation computers are intended to be "knowledge-based" processing systems supporting AI applications. The design of Fifth Generation computers centres on the choice of the parallel programming style on which the computers are based. The three major approaches are: functional programming (e.g. Pure LISP), logic programming (e.g. PROLOG) and, what might be generally termed, knowledge-based programming including production system languages (e.g. OPS5) and semantic net languages (e.g. NETL). It is interesting to note that the main approach in Europe is reduction and data flow machines to support functional programming, whereas the main approach in Japan is logic computers and in the USA is rule-based and connectionist machines.

As an illustration of Fifth Generation computers we will briefly examine the MIT Connection Machine, based on the connectionist approach. Connectionists picture the brain as a densely-linked network of neurons (each neuron connected to as many as 10,000 others) capable of producing certain outputs when given certain inputs.

The Connection Machine [16] is designed to rapidly perform a few operations specific to AI, such as: (i) deducing facts from semantic inheritance networks; (ii) matching patterns against sets of assertions, demons or productions; (iii) sorting a set according to some parameter; and (iv) searching graphs for sub-graphs with a specific structure.

The Connection Machine is simply a collection of "intelligent" memory cells that are capable of connecting themselves to other such cells and hence representing some concept in the form of a semantic network. The initial design of the Connection Machine comprises 128K "intelligent" memory cells arranged as a uniform switching network. Each "intelligent" memory cell comprises a Communicator, Rule-Table, a State Register, a few words of storage, primitive ALU, and a message-register, as shown in Figure 2 below:

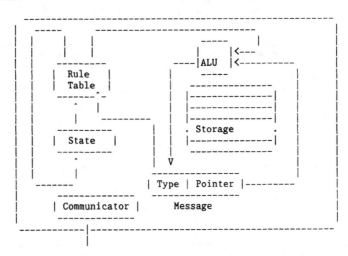

Figure 2: Connection Machine's Intelligent Memory Cell

The Communicators form a packet switched communications network being physically connected to only a few neighbouring communicators. When a communicator receives a message it decides (on the basis of the message address and local information) which direction the message should be routed, modifies the address and sends the message to the selected neighbour. The Rule Table is a simple table (shared with other cells) of rules that determine the behaviour of the "intelligent" memory cell under a received message. This behaviour may involve performing some elementary ALU operation, generating new messages or changing the state of the cell. The State Register is a vector of 10-50 bits storing so-called markers, arithmetic condition flags and the type of the cell. The Storage area comprises registers of a total 384 bits of memory holding relative addresses of other "intelligent" memory cells.

A prototype Connection Machine is currently operational at Thinking Machines Inc. The prototype, uses a conservative VLSI technology and comprises 64,000 nodes. In this prototype the processor has evolved from the initial design and looks less like a finite state machine and more like a general computer. It has been claimed by the designers that the 64,000-node processor has approximately 1000 times the logical-inference performance capabilities of current LISP workstations. Future Connection Machines will be based on a custom VLSI circuit suitable for use in a one million processor node machine.

SUPERCOMPUTERS

In the Supercomputer area, the 1970s was described as the decade of the single-instruction-multi-data stream (SIMD) computer [5], which includes both vector computers (e.g. CRAY-1) and array processors (e.g. ICL DAP). However, the 1980s is becoming the MIMD decade with computers ranging from a few CPUs (e.g. CRAY X-MP, ETA GF10) to parallel systems such as the Denelcor HEP and INTEL iPSC [5]. A number of the parallel numeric processors use the hypercube interconnection topology, which was pioneered in the CALTECH Cosmic Cube.

The Cosmic Cube [12] is a 2^6 hypercube of 64 nodes, with each node comprising an INTEL 8086 and 8087 floating-point coprocessor, together with 128K bytes of local memory. The interconnection topology of the Cosmic Cube, with each node being connected to 6 neighbours, is shown below. Communication between the nodes is by queued message passing along the edges of the hypercube at a rate of 2M bits/s.

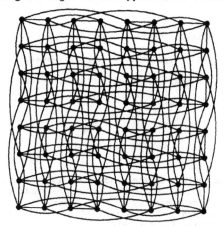

Figure 3: Cosmic Cube - Hypercube (binary n-cube) Topology

The programming model of the Cosmic Cube is based on concurrent processes that communicate by message passing, with a single node supporting a number of processes. Each process has a unique (global) ID that serves as an address for messages. All messages have headers containing the destination and the sender ID, and a message type and length. Messages are queued in transit, but message order is preserved between any pair of processes. Programs for the Cosmic Cube are written in conventional sequential languages (e.g. PASCAL, C) extended with statements and external procedures to control the sending and receiving of messages.

Even with current microelectronic technology, the 64-node Cosmic Cube is quite powerful for its cost and size. It can handle a variety of demanding scientific and engineering calculations 5-10 times faster than a VAX 11/780. A number of companies market versions of the Cosmic Cube [12]. The INTEL product is called the INTEL iPSC.

TRANSACTION PROCESSING SYSTEMS

An important new class of parallel computers has recently emerged in the market-place, namely parallel UNIX machines. Examples include the ELXSI 6400, ENCORE Multimax, FLEXIBLE Flex-32 and SEQUENT Balance 8000 etc. [6]. These machines start in price at $60,000, ranging up to $200,000, and are aimed at the high performance end of the DEC VAX computers. These parallel UNIX machines are multi-processor systems, with between 2-20 processors, each with a local cache, and a global memory of up to 30M bytes, all connected by a common bus. In addition, the processors are typically the 32-bit NS32032. As an illustration we will examine the SEQUENT Balance 8000.

The SEQUENT Balance 8000 system consists of 2 to 12 NS32032 processors, a high speed 26.7M bytes/s bus, and up to 28M bytes of global memory, as illustrated by Figure 4. There are three additional buses, namely the System Link and Interrupt Controller (SLIC) bus, the Small Computer System Interface (SCSI) bus and the 8-slot IEEE-796 Multibus. Each processor comprises five parts: the 32-bit CPU, a hardware floating point accelerator, a paged virtual memory management unit, a SLIC and an 8K byte cache. The system is managed by a version of the UNIX 4.2 BSD operating system, enhanced to make the multi-processor invisible to any application.

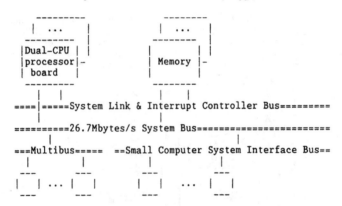

Figure 4: Parallel UNIX SEQUENT Balance 8000

This parallel UNIX system centres on the concept of a "processor pool" with all code and data residing in the global memory. When a processor becomes idle it is allocated, from the pool, to the next process on the process list. As the processor executes the process, the code and data are fetched over the System Bus into its local cache, thus reducing communication overheads.

Parallel UNIX systems, such as the SEQUENT Balance, combine the benefits of UNIX's existing applications with the scalable power of a multi-processor, and they are likely to have a significant impact on the market for parallel computers.

VLSI ARCHITECTURES

The term very large scale integration (VLSI) is generally applied to a chip containing over 100,000 devices. VLSI has very different properties from the earlier microelectronic technologies: (i) design complexity is critical, (ii) wires occupy most space on a circuit, and (iii) non-local communication degrades performance. In the design of VLSI architectures to exploit parallelism two approaches are notable [11,15]. The first to design specialised parallel grids of processors such as Systolic Arrays [7]. The second to design general-purpose, reduced instruction set (RISC) [10] parallel microcomputers like the INMOS Transputers [2]. Below we examine the Transputer.

INMOS' Transputer comprise a family of 16- and 32-bit microcomputers, capable of operating alone as a 10-MIPS (million instructions per second) processor or as a component of a parallel network of Transputers. Each microcomputer, as shown below, consists of four main parts: a reduced instruction set processor, 2K bytes of static RAM, a 32-bit multiplexed memory interface, and four INMOS standard serial links providing concurrent message passing to other Transputers. The processor has built-in support for multi-processing and parallelism. The execution state of each process is defined by six registers. These registers are arranged as a three-register evaluation stack, together with an instruction pointer, a workspace pointer, and an operand register. Instructions are eight bits, comprising a 4-bit function code and a 4-bit data value. Operands longer than four bits are built up four bits at a time in the operand register. Basic arithmetic instructions execute in 50 nsecs and a process switch takes only 600 nsecs.

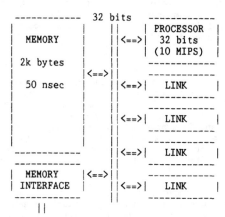

Figure 5: INMOS Transputer

Communication between Transputers is handled by the links. Each link implements two channels, an output and an input, over which messages are transmitted as a series of bytes.

Parallel programming in Transputers, and its OCCAM programming language [2], is based on communicating processes and message passing using explicitly defined channels. A network of Transputers corresponds directly to a network of processes, with each Transputer supporting one or more processes in a timeshared fashion.

NEW TECHNOLOGIES

Advances in technology have perhaps always constituted the driving force for developments in computer architecture. Three technologies that could have a big impact on future parallel computer design are: in the short term, Gallium Arsenide (GaAs) processors [8]; in the medium term, Optical computers [3]; and in the long term, Biological/Molecular computers [4].

GaAs technology [8] has made rapid progress in recent years particularly in the area of digital chip complexity. When comparing GaAs with silicon, its two main advantages are higher switching speed and greater resistance to adverse environmental conditions. But GaAs is inferior to silicon in terms of cost (of material and lower yield) and transistor count (related to yield and power considerations). However, for certain applications the advantages of GaAs are critical, leading to increasing interest in GaAs processors. A good discussion of processor architectures suitable for GaAs is given by Milutinovic et al [8].

Optical techniques for information processing have also made rapid advances in recent years. Within this area, the term Optical computing is defined [3] as: the use of optical systems to perform numerical computations on one-dimensional or multi-dimensional data that are generally not images. The goal of this work is to build an Optical binary digital computer which used photons as the primary information carrying medium rather than electrons. The potential advantages of optical computers include: (i) high space-bandwidth and time-bandwidth products, (ii) they are inherently two dimensional and parallel, (iii) optical signals can propagate through each other in separate channels with essentially no interaction, and (iv) optical signals can interact on a subpico-second time scale. Thus the potential for Optical parallel computers is clear. Discussions of the possible organisation of Optical computers is given in [3].

Finally, in the longer term Biological or Molecular computers promise an exciting research area. Although no molecular computing device seems so far to have been constructed [4], the possibility of organic switching devices and conducting polymers may come about from current developments in polymer chemistry, biotechnology, the physics of computation, and computer science. So far, however, there is no clear consensus as to the viability of biological/molecular computing or the best strategy for such computation. A good introduction to the topic is given in [4].

FUTURE TRENDS

Many factors support the adoption of a radically new generation of parallel computers. Firstly, the handling of non-numerical data such as sentences, symbols, speech, graphics and images is becoming increasingly important. Secondly, the processing tasks performed by computers are becoming more "intelligent", moving from scientific calculations and data processing, to artificial intelligence applications. Thirdly, computing is moving from a sequential, centralised world to a parallel, decentralised world in which large numbers of computers are to be programmed to work together in computing systems. Lastly, today's computers are still based on the thirty-year-old von Neumann architecture.

A number of trends in computer architecture are already discernible. Firstly, there is the growing agreement that future parallel computers will be constructed from large numbers of identical units (each with processing, memory and communications) suitable for implementation in VLSI and waferscale technology. The best current example is the INMOS Transputer [2] microcomputer.

Secondly, there is the need to integrate symbolic and numeric computing. Thus it is to be expected that the architectures of Fifth Generation computers and numeric Supercomputers will converge.

Thirdly, there are the increasing numbers of interesting parallel computer products, such as the parallel UNIX machines, that are appearing in the market. I believe these parallel "operating system" machines will become an industry standard over the next three years for mainframes, minicomputers and workstations, leading to parallel computers becoming the accepted commercial norm.

Lastly, in the longer term, say 10-20 years we have the stimulating prospect that Optical and Biological parallel might become available.

REFERENCES

[1] Almasi G.S. and Paul G., (eds.) "Special Issue on Parallel Processing", Parallel Computing, vol. 2, no. 3 (November 1985).

[2] Barron I., et al: "Transputer does 5 or more MIPS even when not used in parallel", Electronics, vol. 56, no. 23 (November 1983) pp. 109-115.

[3] Caulfield H.J., et al, "The Special Issue on Optical Computing", Proc. IEEE, vol. 72, no. 7 (July 1984).

[4] Conrad M., "On Design Principles for Molecular Computer", Comm. ACM, vol. 28, no. 5 (may 1985) pp.464-479.

[5] Hockney R.W., "MIMD computing in the USA - 1984", Parallel Computing, vol. 2 (1985) pp.119-136.

[6] Lineback J.R., "Parallel Processing: why a shakeout nears", ELECTRONICS, vol. 58, no. 43 (October 1985) pp. 32-34.

[7] Kung H.T., "Why Systolic Arrays," IEEE COMPUTER, vol. 15, no. 1, (January 1982), pp. 37-46.

[8] Milutinovic V., et al, "An Introduction to GaAs Microprocessor Architecture for VLSI", IEEE Computer, vol. 19, no. 3 (March 1986) pp. 30-42.

[9] Moto-oka T., "Overview to the fifth generation computer system project", Proc. Tenth Int. Symp. on Computer Architecture (June 1983). pp. 417-422.

[10] Patterson D.A., "Reduced Instruction Set Computers," Comm. ACM, vol. 28, no. 1, (January 1985), pp. 8-21.

[11] Seitz C.L., "Concurrent VLSI Architectures", IEEE Trans. on Computers, vol. C-33, no. 12 (December 1984) pp. 1247-1265.

[12] Seitz C.L., "The Cosmic Cube", Comm. ACM, vol. 28, no. 1 (Jan. 1985) pp. 22-33.

[13] Treleaven P.C. et al, "Data Driven and Demand Driven Computer Architecture", ACM Computing Surveys, vol. 14, no. 1 (March 1982) pp. 93-143.

[14] Treleaven P.C. and Gouveia Lima I., "Japan's Fifth Generation Computer Systems", IEEE COMPUTER, vol. 15, no. 8 (August 1982) pp. 79-88.

[15] Treleaven P.C., "VLSI processor architectures", IEEE COMPUTER, vol. 15, no. 6 (June 1982), pp. 33-45.

[16] Treleaven P.C., et al, "Computer Architectures for Artificial Intelligence", University College London, Computer Science Department, Tech. Report UCL-CS TR 119 (March 1986).

[17] Uchida S., "Inference Machine: From Sequential to Parallel", Proc. of the 10th Annual International Symposium on Computer Architecture, Sweden, (June 1983),

SUPRENUM - an MIMD multiprocessor system
for multi-level scientific computing

Ulrich Trottenberg

- SUPRENUM-Gesellschaft fuer numerische Superrechner mbH, Bonn
- Institut fuer Methodische Grundlagen, Gesellschaft fuer
  Mathematik und Datenverarbeitung mbH (GMD), St. Augustin
- Mathematisches Institut, Universitaet zu Koeln

1. The SUPRENUM idea

Multiprocessor computer and multi-level computing are the keywords
which characterize the SUPRENUM project. SUPRENUM stands for "supercomputer for numerical applications". More than a dozen institutions
from research, academia and industry work together in order to develop
an innovative computer system consisting of hardware, operating
system, programming environment, and - last not least - application
software for large scale scientific computing.

It was from three roots, represented by users, computer scientists and
mathematicians that the project grew:

- supercomputing - for which there is an immense demand in numerous
  disciplines in the natural sciences and engineering

- parallel computing - a major challenge for computer science (hard-
  and software sectors) aiming at the multiplication of computing
  power by using multiple processors strongly cooperating in a single
  system

- multi-level computing - the utilization of new algorithmic principles of numerical analysis which are capable of yielding sensational
  improvements in efficiency compared with classical algorithms.

The SUPRENUM idea is to combine these three developments and to translate them into **one** computer architecture. Accordingly, the concept
underlying the SUPRENUM computer is to ensure that performance gains
deriving from multi-processing on the one hand and from multi-level
computing on the other hand are multiplied wherever possible.

The start of the project in May 1985 was preceded by a project definition phase lasting over a year in which ideas were collected, a concept elaborated and the project partners selected. The decision on
architecture went in favour of the MIMD principle. By this, multi-processor architectures are meant in which the distributed computer units
are not subordinated to a central control (SIMD principle) but operate
autonomously. The current supercomputer scene is dominated almost exclusively by SIMD computers, especially vector computers featuring
highly sophisticated pipelining capabilities, pushing against the very
limits of attainable performance.

In the framework of a development scheme such as SUPRENUM, it is not
possible to make good the lead currently enjoyed by the major manufacturers (CDC, CRAY, Fujitsu etc.). In the field of MIMD, however, the
lead which other research institutions and manufacturers may hold is
not so great that it cannot be caught up. For numerous major problems

in the design, operation and application of MIMD computers, no solutions have so far been found which are acknowledged as being the final say. Commercial systems are only now appearing on the market.

Whereas in SIMD improvements in performance would be difficult to achieve on the basis of processor technology available now or in the near future, MIMD machines, in which each processor has its own memory fully available, would offer the advantage that the degree of parallelism, and hence attainable performance, is in principle unlimited provided that a sufficient number of processors is used. While limits are set by the demands made on interprocessor communication, these largely depend on the specific application.

The high-performance vector computers on the market are by definition (numerical) general purpose computers which hardly permit the specific properties of certain application classes to be fully exploited. (If they do so at all, then indirectly via the typical vector length and the like.) With MIMD architectures, in contrast, it is both possible and technically necessary to incorporate in the processor topology the communication structure characteristic of the class of algorithms under consideration.

It is therefore the aim of this project to realize a processor topology whose design is geared to the envisioned class of applications and algorithms and which supports as efficiently as possible the communication structure dictated by this field of application.

2. The kernel class of applications

There is a whole wealth of tasks whose solution by numerical analysis would require a computing power which is one or several orders of magnitude greater than the one available today. Their solution, however, would lead to new developments in technology and basic research. Such tasks are encountered in fluid mechanics, meteorology, multi-body problems in physics, plasma physics, nuclear physics, geology, microelectronics, etc.

Although the problems arise in a variety of technical and scientific disciplines and appear to be widely separated, a very large category of them is characterized by a remarkably uniform structure in terms of mathematics and computational requirements. They are characterized by local relationships on grid structures on which large systems of equations typically have to be solved. System magnitude can be very considerable: It is not uncommon to encounter a million unknowns to be determined; in some cases there are even problems with a thousand million unknowns waiting to be determined. Such "grid problems" always occur in the discretization of partial differential equations but also in connection with other models, e.g. in multi-body and elementary particle problems in physics.

3. The mapping: the multi-level principle and the SUPRENUM architecture

The local character of the grid problems described above, whose solution is the main aim of the SUPRENUM scheme, would initially suggest the application of "local" techniques in which the operations to be carried out predominantly link up quantities which are spatial neighbours (within the given grid structure). Most of the classic "single grid" techniques (relaxation techniques, explicit time-step methods etc.) have such a local character.

In recent years, however, remarkable performance increases have been achieved in the algorithmic area by the application of new numerical principles. For the grid problems of interest here, the **"multigrid"** (or - more generally - the **multi-level**) **principle** plays an outstanding role and can be put to a variety of general applications, see the introductory contributions in [1].

From the beginning of the project (preliminary considerations on project definition) and during the entire planning phase the declared aim was for the SUPRENUM architecture to support the multigrid principle: the partners were and are in agreement that development of a computer for grid problems is pointless if the computer does not allow the advances made through the multigrid principle to be utilized. Theoretical work in the project definition phase therefore concerned primarily the relationship of the multigrid principle and computer architecture (compatibility, support, optimization), see corresponding contributions in [2], [3], [4].

4. The SUPRENUM-1 system

All partners and specialists involved in the project are unanimous that a SUPRENUM supercomputer should not be realized in a single step. In a SUPRENUM-1 phase it is therefore planned initially to realize a high-performance MIMD computer which features the architecture required in the given class of applications and algorithms and which can be built up in a relatively short time on the basis of available components.

Based on the theoretical studies into the relationship between multigrid principle and computer architecture, a decision was taken in favour of a concept elaborated by Wolfgang K. Giloi, Head of the GMD Research Centre for Innovative Computer Systems and Technology:

- an MIMD computer consisting of p single-board processors ("nodes") connected by a two-stage bus system,

- node processor: 32/64-bit processor MC 68020, fast floating point accelerator with vector unit (Weitek 2264/65), private local memory,

- bus link of (up to) 16 nodes forming a cluster (a 19" pullout unit),

- at cluster level a 2D array of SUPRENUM-buses (horizontal and vertical bus link, based on the UPPER ringbus),

- overall computer system comprising the computer clusters, a programming computer, an operating system computer and a maintenance computer (each an MPR 2300).

The operating system will be based on UNIX. Languages supported will be concurrent MODULA 2 and FORTRAN expanded by MIMD features. Interprocessor communication will be by message passing.

A prototype with p = 256 = 4 x 4 x 16 nodes as well as some smaller development systems are scheduled to be operational by the end of 1988.

It is the object of the SUPRENUM-1 phase to develop these computers and provide them with system **and** numerical application software. For the typical major numerical users these computers are intended to represent an attractive package both in terms of the hardware performance offered and application software. They are also to offer the possibility of gaining experience with the programming and handling of

MIMD structures by reference to realistic numerical problems (not just elementary algorithms or model tasks).

5. Long-range SUPRENUM-2 goals

Of course, the fundamental question on how to use am MIMD-supercomputer for numerical applications properly, can not fully be answered within a project which only runs for a few years. There are so many problems involved here (fundamental questions concerning hardware and - still more difficult - software questions) that the SUPRENUM-1 part can be regarded only as the starting point for a more ambitious long-range research and development activity.

Such long-range investigations will be persued in the SUPRENUM-2 part of the project. Typical SUPRENUM-2 activities will be:

- **applications and algorithms**: extension of the kernel class of static grid structures (which are fixed or known a priori) to dynamic ones, data-dependent adaptive algorithms on irregular grid structures, high-dimensional grids, non-grid applications, etc.;

- **languages and programming environment**: consideration of more innovative language concepts which support an automatic distribution of processes and data (in particular in connection with dynamic grid structures), automatic vectorizing and parallelization, automatic MIMD compilation of standard programs, etc.;

- **system**: operating systems which support automatic distribution strategies; investigation of other interconnection structures, in particular with respect to dynamic grid structures; consideration of new technologies (for communication and computing), VLSI, GaAs etc.

6. The partners and their contributions

The idea of SUPRENUM was brought up by major research institutions whose cooperative brought to light the acute need for fast numerical methods and innovative computer structures. As a consequence, several major research institutions are now taking a substantive part in the project. The work is divided up into the three categories **application software**, **language level** and **system** (operating system and hardware). The institutes involved are:

- **application software**: Deutsche Forschungs- und Versuchsanstalt fuer Luft- und Raumfahrt (DFVLR) (German Aerospace Research Institute), Dornier GmbH, GMD, Kernforschungsanlage Juelich GmbH (KFA) (Juelich Nuclear Research Institute), Kernforschungsanlage Karlsruhe GmbH (KfK) (Karlsruhe Nuclear Research Institute), Duesseldorf University,

- **language level**: GMD, Darmstadt Technical University, Bonn University,

- **system**: GMD, Krupp Atlas Elektronik GmbH, Stollmann GmbH, Braunschweig Technical University, Erlangen-Nuernberg University.

For the actual handling of the project the main partners GMD, Krupp Atlas Elektronik GmbH and Stollmann GmbH have established the SUPRENUM GmbH, which will initially be vested with project management. It will also be involved in research and development and is later to undertake marketing of the SUPRENUM computers.

References

[1] W. Hackbusch, U. Trottenberg (eds.):
Multigrid Methods, Proceedings of the Conference Held at Köln-Porz 1981. Lecture Notes in Mathematics 960, Springer-Verlag 1982.

[2] W. Hackbusch, U. Trottenberg (eds.):
Multigrid Methods II, Proceedings of the Second European Conference on Multigrid Methods Held at Köln 1985. Lecture Notes in Mathematics, Springer Verlag, to appear.

[3] O. McBryan, S. McCormick, U. Trottenberg (eds.):
Proceedings of the Second Copper Mountain Conference on Multigrid Methods (1985). Applied Mathematics and Computation, North-Holland, to appear.

[4] U. Trottenberg, P. Wypior (eds.):
Rechnerarchitekturen für die numerische Simulation auf der Basis superschneller Lösungsverfahren.
Teil 1: GMD-Studie Nr. 88, St. Augustin 1984., Teil II: GMD-Studie Nr. 102, St. Augustin 1985.

An adaptable cluster structure of $(SM)^2$ -II

Chizuko Saito†, Hideharu Amano††, Tomohiro Kudoh†† and Hideo Aiso††

†IBM Japan,Ltd. ††Keio University

ABSTRACT

In analyzing electronic circuits, it is usually necessary to solve a sparse coefficient matrix comprised of simultaneous linear equations. In order to treat these problems effectively, we have developed a dedicated parallel machine called $(SM)^2$-II ('the Sparse Matrix Solving Machine' version II).

$(SM)^2$-II is composed of multiple clusters, each consisting of multiple PUs (Processing Units) connected by a special communication mechanism called RSM (Receiver Selectable Multicast).

Here, we propose an adaptive cluster structure and evaluate its performance. The characteristics of typical problems are analyzed at the beginning of computation. Then the size of each cluster and the connections between clusters are adapted to the problem automatically. Using this mechanism, effective computation is possible in various types of problems.

1. Introduction

In recent years, variable types of parallel machines have been proposed and developed. Shared bus and shared memory structures are popular types. In these parallel machines, a large number of processing units (PUs) are connected to obtain high performance. However, in a simple shared bus or memory structure, the number of PUs is limited because of congestion on the shared bus or memory.

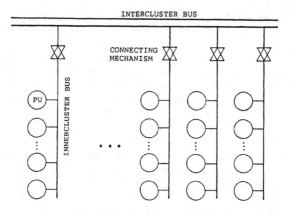

Figure 1 Typical cluster structure

To overcome this limitation, clustered structures have been introduced in many systems [1][2][3]. In these systems a cluster is constructed of a certain number of processers connected with a simple shared bus or memory (Figure 1). These clusters are connected with an upper hierarchy bus, shared memory, or other connection methods.

In general, the cost of intercluster communication is higher than that of innercluster communication. From this point of view, the larger the number of PUs in a cluster, the better the performance of the system. However, if a large number of PUs are connected in one cluster, congestion on a shared bus or memory cause performance degradation. For that reason, the number of PUs in a cluster must be chosen carefully. The optimum number of PUs is influenced not only by the features of the system (eg. the performance of PUs or the capacity of the connection mechanisms) but also by the target problems. Therefore, it is impossible to fix this number. A mechanism for changing this number depending on the characteristics of the target problems is advantageous.

In general purpose machines, it is difficult to decide the optimum number. Nevertheless, it is possible in a special field of target problems on a specific machine. Since 1983, we have been developing a specific parallel machine called $(SM)^2$-II (Sparse Matrix Solving Machine version II). $(SM)^2$-II is a dedicated parallel machine for solving problems with sparse matrices effectively. In this paper, a mechanism for changing the number of PUs in a cluster and a method for deciding the optimum number is proposed for this machine.

In section 2, the relationships between target problems and the number of PUs in a cluster is analyzed. The structure of $(SM)^2$-II and the mechanism for changing the size of a cluster are described in section 3. In section 4, an adjustment method for deciding the optimum number of PUs is introduced and some examples are shown. Finally, future work is discussed in section 5.

2. Clustered structures and target problems

Generally the capacity of innercluster communication is larger than that of intercluster communication. Therefore, if a target problem has no locality of communication, a clustered structure is not suitable. If locality of communication exists in target problems, the communication load is balanced over the whole system.

In this paper we focus on sparse matrix calculations. These problems are important in scientific calculation and they provide locality of communication. Usually, processes which correspond to several rows are mapped into a PU. If iterative methods are used, the relationships among communicating processes is determined by the coefficient matrix.

As an example, we can take multiplication between a matrix (A) and vector (x). This example is essential in the iterative method. In this method a PU receives the values of the vector from other PUs and multiplies elements of the matrix in local memory. Since calculations are only executed for non-zero elements of the matrix, the smaller the number of non-zero element number in a row, the shorter the interval of data transfer.

There are many types of sparse matrices in various fields of application. Matrices in electronic circuit analysis provide strong locality but its non-zero element number per row is small (from 3 to 5 on the average). In problems with these matrices innercluster communication is congested by frequent data transfer. However locality in intercluster communication may be strong. On the other hand, matrices in the problems using finite element methods provide less locality, but their non-zero element number per row is larger (6 on the average). In these problems intercluster communication is probably congested while communication within a cluster is not very frequent.

For the former type of problems clusters with a small number of PUs are advantageous in order to avoid congestion of the innercluster communication. However, a cluster with a larger number of PUs is advantageous for the latter type of problem in order to obtain high performance and avoid congestion of the intercluster communication. In order to balance the communication load over the whole system, the number of PUs in a cluster need to be adapted to each problem.

By analyzing matrices and the operation of the target system it is possible to set the optimum number of PUs. Before discussion about algorithms for setting the optimum number, the target system structure is described in the next section.

3. The structure of $(SM)^2$-II

3.1. RSM and the cluster structure.

$(SM)^2$-II is a MIMD-type parallel machine for treating scientific problems with sparse matrices. In order to use a large number of microprocessors effectively, $(SM)^2$-II provides the following characteristics:

a) Problems are described using a dedicated calculation model called the NC-model [4].

b) A special communication mechanism called RSM (Receiver Selectable Multicast) is utilized for effective data interchange [5].

c) A clustered structure is adopted to utilize the locality of communication.

d) A powerful process switching mechanism called DLOPS (Data driven Local OPerating System) is provided in every processing unit (PU).

In this paper, RSM and clustered structures are briefly described, while further information is available in [4] and [5]. Using RSM, data can be multicast quickly among PUs. the concept of RSM. All PUs share a global logical address, but there is no actual memory. In our target problems, relationships for communication among PUs are statically decided before calculation and communication channels are mapped into the global address. Therefore, a PU can determine whether or not data written into a certain address is necessary according to that address.

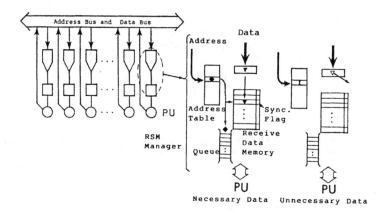

Figure 2 Diagram of RSM

RSM functions are shared memory in a sense, because they have the global shared address. On the other hand, RSM also has the message passing function because data is transferred only to necessary places. RSM has several other advantages and its effectiveness is confirmed in [4].

Figure 2 shows the diagram of RSM. The simplest method for realizing the RSM is to connect PUs with a bus. In this method the selection mechanism named RSM Manager attached to each PU selects the necessary data. RSM Manager refers to a table which is associated with the global address, and if the data is necessary for the PU, it stores the data in its own receive data memory. At that time the PU is informed of the arrival of the data.

In order to connect thousands of PUs, $(SM)^2$-II provides a clustered structure based on RSM. A certain number of PUs are connected using RSM with simple global address and data buses. This is called a 'cluster'. Clusters are connected with a selection mechanism which is called RSM Manager. It receives only required data, converts the address, and sends the data to another cluster.

Figure 3 shows the structure of $(SM)^2$-II. Because of the locality of communication in problems, dedicated AGENTs are provided for the neighboring clusters. Data is transferred to the other clusters by the third AGENT through the upper hierarchy bus. Each AGENT has two mechanisms corresponding to RSM Manager and communicates bidirectionally. When the data written by a PU is sent to another cluster, the AGENT obtains the address of the upper hierarchy (if the AGENT is for a neighboring cluster, it is the address of that cluster) by table reference. If the bus is not free, the data is held in data buffer and the obtained address is put into the queue. As soon as the bus is free, the stored data is sent.

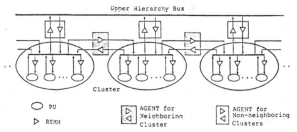

Figure 3 Structure of $(SM)^2$-II

3.2. Mechanisms for realizing variable size of cluster.

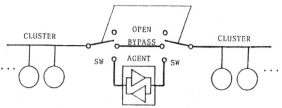

Figure 4 Connection Mechanism

It is ideal if the number of PUs in a cluster can be selected arbitrarily. However, large and complicated hardware is necessary to realize this. Therefore, we have determined a unit size for a cluster, called an 'atomic cluster'. A mechanism which can bypass data is introduced into AGENTs (Figure 4), and two atomic clusters connected with an AGENT in the bypass-mode work as a large cluster connected with simple buses. The size of a cluster can be changed only by changing the number of atomic clusters per cluster. Because of certain technical reasons, the number of PU in an atomic cluster is set at 8.

4. An algorithm for deciding the optimum cluster size

4.1. Adjustment method

In $(SM)^2$-II, if the innercluster bus is fully occupied with communication, the working ratio of PUs is rapidly degraded [5]. On the other hand, if the upper hierarchy bus is congested, the performance is degraded because of waiting for routed data. Therefore, the size of the cluster is chosen so as to avoid congestion at both innercluster buses and the upper hierarchy bus. However, congestion of buses is hard to analyze because buses are influenced by problems and mapping strategies. Therefore, we have adopted the following 'adjustment' method:

Step 1: Set the size of each cluster arbitrarily.

Step 2: Map the problem to the PUs.

Step 3: Evaluate the congestion both at the innercluster and upper hierarchy buses.

Step 4: If the upper hierarchy bus is fully occupied, increase the size of a cluster. If on the contrary the innercluster buses are fully occupied, decrease the size of a cluster. Repeat from Step 2 until neither bus is fully occupied.

If both kinds of buses are fully occupied, it is better to avoid congestion on innercluster. This is because the system performance is more influenced by innercluster bus congestion. PUs can execute computation during communication on the upper hierarchy bus because AGENTs control these communications. For the same reason, if the size decided by the above sequence has a certain range, it is advantageous to choose the size of cluster to be as large as possible.

To realize the above mentioned strategy, a high speed mapping strategy and a simple method for analyzing congestion on buses are needed. In the following sections we will describe them.

4.2. Mapping strategy

First, we introduce the process mapping strategy. It is difficult to obtain the optimum value as the process mapping is an NP-complete problem. Therefore, we should consider the relation between the cost of the mapping and the advantage gained by the mapping. Intricate mapping strategies are very expensive. However, the performance of the system does not improve significantly. Accordingly, we employ a simple strategy.

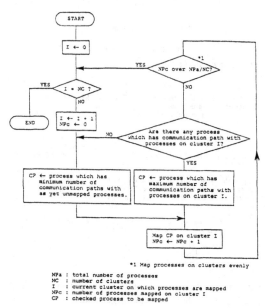

*1 Map processes on clusters evenly

NPa : total number of processes
NC : number of clusters
I   : current cluster on which processes are mapped
NPc : number of processes mapped on cluster I
CP : checked process to be mapped

Figure 5 Mapping strategy

Our mapping strategy is based on following principles:

(1) Minimize intercluster communications.

(2) Equalize the load of each PU.

(3) Employ simple strategy.

Figure 5 shows our mapping strategy.

4.3. Analysis of bus congestion.

For analysis, we use a kind of probability process model which is based on the model described in [5]. In the model, PUs and AGENTs are assumed to stay in one of the following three states:

(1) WRITING STATE: writing or in the queue for writing request (w:the number of PUs in this state / cluster W:the number of AGENTs on the upper hierarchy bus in this state),

(2) READING STATE: reading or being blocked by a writing request, (r:the number of PUs in this state / cluster R:the number of AGENTs on the upper hierarchy bus in this state),

(3) NON-ACCESS STATE: executing the operation without global address access. (a:the number of PUs in this state / cluster A:the number of AGENTs on the upper hierarchy bus in this state),

The system state is analyzed by the number of PUs and AGENTs in each state. Since $w+r+a$ is equal to the number of PUs (n) and $W+R+A$ is equal to the number of clusters (ncls), the system can be analyzed based on w,a,W and A. PUs and AGENTs change between these states at each step, and their expected number in the $(k+1)$th step is represented by the following expressions:

$$a^{k+1} = a^k \cdot Ra + f(w^k) + (1 - f(w^k)) \cdot (n' - a^k - w^k)$$
$$+ f(w^k) \cdot (n' - a^k - w^k) \cdot (1 - \frac{\lambda}{n})$$
$$n' = n + f(w^k) \cdot \frac{Ron}{\mu \cdot Rw} + f(W^k) \cdot \frac{Roo}{\mu \cdot Rw}$$
$$w^{k+1} = a^k \cdot Rw + w^k - f(w^k)$$
$$A^{k+1} = (1 - Roo - \frac{Roo}{\mu}) \cdot f(w^k) \cdot A^k + f(W^k) + (1 - f(W^k)) \cdot (ncls - A^k - W^k)$$
$$+ f(W^k) \cdot (ncls - W^k) \cdot (1 - \frac{\mu}{ncls})$$
$$W^{k+1} = \frac{Roo}{\mu} \cdot f(w^k) \cdot A^k + W^k - f(W^k)$$
$$(f(x) = x \text{ if } x < 1, \ f(x) = 1 \text{ if } x > 1)$$

Parameters are defined as shown in Table 1.

Table 1 Parameters

a: the number of PUs in a cluster in the NON-ACCESS state
w: the number of PUs in a cluster in the WRITE state
r: the number of PUs in a cluster in the READ state
   a+w+r=n

A: the number of AGENTs on the upper cluster bus in the NON-ACCESS state
W: the number of AGENTs on the upper cluster bus in the WRITE state
R: the number of AGENTs on the upper cluster bus in the READ state
   A+W+R=ncls

Ra: the probability of transition from NON-ACCESS state to WRITE state
Rw: the probability of transition from NON-ACCESS state to NON-ACCESS state
Ron: the ratios communication for neighboring clusters to whole communication
Roo: the ratios communication for other clusters to whole communication
Rblk: the blocking ratio in a cluster
μ: the average number of AGENTs to multicast data in the upper hierarchy bus
λ: the average number of PUs to multicast data in a cluster

N: the whole numbers of PUs in the system
ncls: the number of clusters
n: the number of PUs in a cluster
   ncls·n=N

When the problems contain matrix vector multiplication, these parameters can be obtained by the calculation speed of the PU, the speed of bus, and the target matrix. By iteration of the above expressions we obtain 'a_a', These numbers represent the system in an average state. When innercluster buses are fully occupied, 'w_a' becomes larger than 1, and when intercluster buses are fully occupied 'W_a' becomes larger than 1.

4.4. Examples of adjustment method

Table 2 Optimal size of clusters

Timer	NIU	FEM
16	8	32

Some examples using the adjustment method are shown in Table 2. The relationship between the size of the cluster and the congestion of the buses is shown in Figure 6. Congestion on an innercluster bus and the upper hierarchy bus is represented by 'w_a' and 'W_a', respectively. If these parameters become larger than 1, the bus is occupied by communication. The performance of the PUs is assumed to be 1MFLOPS and the communication time of the bus is assumed to be 400nsec.

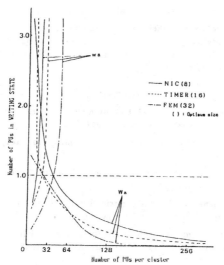

Figure 6 Bus Congestion vs. Size of Cluster

In this table, 'Timer' and 'NIU' are matrices for circuit simulation. These problems provide strong locality of communication, and the interval of data interchange is short. Thus a small sized cluster (8,16 PUs) is chosen by the adjustment method. These problems are innercluster bound. On the other hand, 'FEM' is the matrix for the finite element method. For these problems, a large sized cluster (32 PUs) is selected because this problem is bounded by intercluster communication. Using sizes decided by the adjustment method, 'w_a' and 'W_a' are within or close to 1, and congestion of the buses is minimized.

5. Conclusion

Using the proposed adjustment method, the size of the clusters is decided so as to avoid congestion on any bus in the system. However, if the locality of problems is very small, the upper hierarchy buses will still be congested using this method.

In this case, the division of the upper hierarchy bus and a three level hierarchy structure would be advantageous.

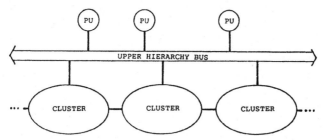

Figure 7 Structure which provides PUs on the upper hierarchy bus

In some application problems, congestion on the upper hierarchy bus is principally caused by a certain number of processes which need a large amount of intercluster communication. Such congestion can be avoided by using the structure shown in Figure 7. The particular processes are mapped into PUs directly connected to the upper hierarchy bus. This structure is realized with the bypass facility of the AGENTs for the upper cluster bus. Continued research is required in order to utilize these new structures and realize more effective structures.

ACKNOWLEDGEMENT

The authors would like to express their sincere gratitude to Professor Mario Tokoro of Keio University for his valuable advice. This research has advanced through valuable discussions with Mr. Taisuke Boku, Mr. Norio Takahashi and Mr. Tetsuro Wakatsuki. The authors are truly grateful to them for their encouragement and cooperation.

REFERENCES

[1] R.Kober, "The Multiprocessor System SMS201 Combining 128 Microprocessors to a Powerful Computer," pp.225-229 Digest of Papers Compcon Fall 1977.

[2] R.J.Swan, et al., "The implementation of the Cm* multi-microprocessor," Proc. of NCC, Vol 46, pp.645-655, 1977.

[3] D. Gajski, et al., "Cedar-a large scale multiprocessor," Proc. of the International Conference on Parallel Processing, pp.524-529 Aug. 1983.

[4] T.Kudoh, et.al., "NDL:A language for solving scientific problems on MIMD machines," Proc. of 1st Int. Conf. on Super Computing Systems Dec.1985 pp.55-64

[5] H.Amano, et.al., "$(SM)^2$-II: The new version of the Sparse Matrix Solving Machine," Proc. of 12TH annual International Symposium on Computer Architecture, June 1985

Memory conflicts in MIMD-Computers

– a performance analysis

Georg Ch. Pflug
Mathematisches Institut
Arndtstraße 2
D-6300 Gießen,BRD

1. Introduction and the models

Consider a computer architecture which consists of p parallel processors and a memory which is divided into m memory banks. To ensure data integrity, at most one processor gets the right to access a specific memory bank within one memory cycle. Whenever two or more processors request the same memory within the same cycle, a memory conflict occurs and has to be resolved by a certain strategy.

Of course, the possible waiting for conflict resolution lowers the efficiency of the system. It is the purpose of this paper to give a quantitative statement about this fact. As is well known, performances can be evaluated on the basis of a best-case, a worst-case and an average-case comparison. The latter - which will be considered here - requires the definition of a probabilistic model for the memory requests and their dependencies.

Every model is an abstraction of reality. This, is true in particular for probabilistic models of the instruction stream of parallel computer architectures. There are such many possible sequences of interleaved instructions and/or memory requests, that any particular model can depict only one particular aspect of the problem. When dealing with efficiency considerations for parallel memories, we consider the following simplified situation: The instruction stream is divided into smaller units, called steps, each of which contains exactly one memory request and (possibly) other instructions. For simplicity it is assumed that the execution of each step needs exactly one unit of time.
Graphically, each step may be represented by a box, containing the number of the memory bank:

$$\boxed{\quad j \quad} \qquad \text{memory bank no. } j$$

The so called execution graph contains all steps as nodes and is constructed according to the following rules

    (i)   All steps which are to be executed on the i-th processor appear in the i-th row of the graph

    (ii)   An arc connecting step i_1 to step i_2 symbolizes the dependency between both steps: i_2 can only be started, if i_1 has been completely finished.

In Figure 1, a typical execution graph for a system with p = 3 processors and m = 8 memories is shown. Given a specific execution graph containing n nodes it is a natural question to ask for the schedule which minimizes the "makespan" T_n , i.e. the total execution time. Unfortunately this is a problem of combinatorial optimization, which is of such high complexity, that it has to be replaced by good heuristics for practical purposes. Such heuristic algorithms are e.g.

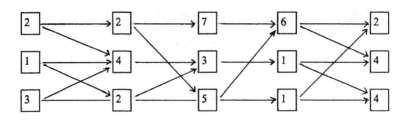

Fig. 1

(i)   the LEFT-strategy: For every memory conflict, it is always the processor with the lowest number (the leftmost processor) which gets the priority.

(ii)   the RANDOM-strategy: Among all processors waiting for service one request is chosen at random

(iii)   the LASF-strategy: The processor with the least attained service so far gets the priority.

The performance of a particular strategy will be measured by the <u>average bandwidth</u> B_a and the <u>steady-state bandwidth</u> B_s. These two quantities are defined as follows:

(1) $B_a = \lim\limits_{n} \dfrac{n}{E(T_n)}$, where $E(T_n)$ is the expected execution time for

                a program with n steps,

(2) B_s = mean number of active (= non waiting) processors in a steady state situation.

Evidently the inequalities

$$1 \leqslant B_a \leqslant p \quad , \quad 1 \leqslant B_s \leqslant p$$

and

$$B_a \leqslant B_s$$

hold true.

Since the variety of possible execution graphs is extremely large, we shall restrict our analysis to two interesting cases which reflect "extremal" situations. For the model I, we assume that all steps of cycle n have to be finished before the begin of cycle n+1 (i.e. the graph of dependencies is complete).

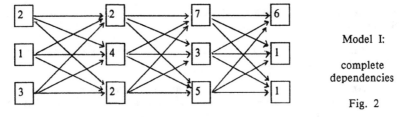

Model I:

complete dependencies

Fig. 2

Model I (Fig. 3) is the other extreme. Only the steps belonging to the same processor are dependent one from the other

For both models it is assumed that there are p processors and m = k . p memories. For the n-th step, the requested memories are $X_1^{(n)}, \ldots , X_p^{(n)}$. The best performance would be achieved if every processor would have its private memory; e.g. if the i-th processor accesses only the k memories, numbered as $(i-1) \cdot k+1, \ldots, ik$. In

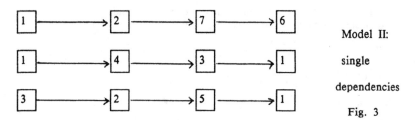

Model II:

single

dependencies

Fig. 3

that case, no memory conflict could occur. A worse case is encountered, if every processor can request all m memories with the same probability. In order to allow statements about the dependence of the performance on the degree of "privacy" for the m memories, we introduce the following distribution for the requests

$$(3) \quad P[X_i^{(n)} = j] = \begin{cases} (1 - \gamma) \frac{1}{m} & \text{if} \quad \lceil \frac{j}{k} \rceil \neq i \\ (1 - \gamma) \frac{1}{m} + \gamma \frac{1}{k} & \text{if} \quad \lceil \frac{j}{k} \rceil = i \end{cases}$$

$\lceil x \rceil$ denotes the ceiling of x. Equivalently $X_j^{(n)}$ could be described as

$$(4) \qquad X_j^{(n)} = \begin{cases} \overline{\overline{X}}_j^{(n)} & \text{with probability } \gamma \\ \overline{X}_j^{(n)} & \text{with probability } 1-\gamma \end{cases}$$

where $\overline{\overline{X}}^{(n)}$ is a "local" request (to one of the memories (i-1)k+1,...,ik with equal probability) and $\overline{X}^{(n)}$ is the "global" request (to one of all memories with equal probability). The parameter γ determines the degree of privacy: If $\gamma = 1$, then all requests are local and if $\gamma = 0$, all requests are global.

2. Model I: complete dependencies

In this model, the memory requests appear in groups of p (each processor issues exactly one) and the service of the next group cannot begin until all requests of the previous group are completely satisfied.

Let $X_1^{(n)}$, $X_2^{(n)}$, ... , $X_p^{(n)}$ be the numbers of the requested memories in the n-th group and let

$$(5) \quad Z_j^{(n)} = \# [X_i^{(n)} \mid X_i^{(n)} = j]$$

the number of requests for memory j in cycle n. Since each access takes one unit of time, the "service" of the group needs $M^{(n)}$ units of time, where

$$M^{(n)} = \max (Z_1^{(n)}, Z_2^{(n)}, ... , Z_m^{(n)})$$

The bandwith quantities B_a and B_s coincide here and may be expressed in terms of $M^{(n)}$ as

$$B_s = B_a = \frac{p}{E(M^{(n)})} .$$

Thus, for the evaluation of the bandwith, the calculation of $E(M^{(n)})$ is necessary. We consider first the case $\gamma = 0$. The superscript (n) may be omitted since everything is stationary and hence independent of n. The random variables $Z_1,...,Z_m$ are distributed according to a multinomial distribution with moments

$$E(Z_j) \quad = \quad \frac{p}{m}$$

(6) $\qquad$ $$Var\,(Z_j) \quad = \quad \frac{p(m-1)}{m^2}$$

$$Cov(Z_i,Z_j) \quad = \quad - \frac{p}{m^2} \qquad\qquad i \neq j$$

The exact distribution of M may be expressed by a recursion (cf. [CHA77]), but this leads to a complicated formula. However there is a very good approximation by a multivariate normal distribution with the same moments. Let

$$Z_j' = \frac{p}{m} + \frac{p}{m}\,V_j - \frac{1}{m}\sqrt{\frac{p}{m}}\,\sum_{j=1}^{m} V_j$$

where $V_1,...,V_m$ are independent $N(0,1)$ random variables. It is easily seen, that the Z_j' have exactly the same expectations and covariances as in (4). Let

$$M' = \max\,(Z_1',\,...\,,\,Z_m') = \frac{p}{m} + \frac{p}{m}\,\max V_j - \frac{1}{m}\sqrt{\frac{p}{m}}\sum_{j=1}^{m} V_j$$

The expectation of M' is

$$E(M') = \frac{p}{m} + \frac{p}{m}\,c_m$$

where

$$c_m = E(\max\,[V_1,\,...\,,\,V_m]) = \int_{-\infty}^{\infty} x\,d\,\Phi^m(x)$$

with Φ = standard normal distribution function, i.e. the constants c_m are the expectations of the maximal value of m independent $N(0,1)$ variables.

The exact values of c_m may be found by numerical integration

$c_1 = 0.0$	$c_{100} = 2.508$
$c_2 = 0.564 = \frac{1}{\sqrt{\pi}}$	$c_{200} = 2.746$
$c_5 = 1.163$	$c_{500} = 3.037$
$c_{10} = 1.539$	$c_{1000} = 3.241$

(cf. Tippet [TIP25]). Furthermore, it is known that $\dfrac{c_m}{s_m + \dfrac{\gamma'}{s_m}} \rightarrow 1$, as $n \rightarrow \infty$

where γ' is Euler's Konstant ($\gamma' = 0.57722$) and

$$s_m = 2\sqrt{\log m} - \frac{\log\log m + \log 4\pi}{2\sqrt{2\log m}}$$

(cf. David [DAV81], p. 264).

Because of

(7) $\qquad$ $$B_s = \frac{p}{E(M)} \approx \frac{p}{E(M')} = p\left(\frac{p}{m} + \sqrt{\frac{p}{m}}\,c_m\right)^{-1} = m\left(\frac{1}{1 + \sqrt{\frac{m}{p}}\,c_m}\right)$$

a good approximation for B_s is the function

$$g(m,p) = m \left(1 + \frac{m}{p} c_m \right)^{-1}$$

In Fig. 4 these functions are displayed for fixed m. Note that $g(m,p) < \min (p,m)$ and $\lim_{p\to\infty} g(m,p) = m$.

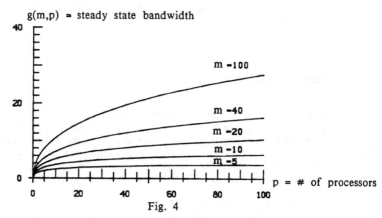

Fig. 4

We consider now the more general case $y > 0$. Since the exact calculation of B_s is even more complicated in this situation, we shall give a good approximation again. Let G be the number of "global" requests (cf.(4)) and let

$$Z_j^{(G)} = \text{number of all "global } X_i\text{'s such that } X_i = j.$$

We remark that for Z_j defined by (5) $Z_j = Z_j^{(G)}$ exactly for G indices and $Z_j = Z_j^{(G)} + 1$ for the remaining p - G indices.

We shall use the following fact:
If $Z_1,...Z_m$ are exchangeable integer valued random variables, then

$$(8) \quad \frac{t}{m} \leq E(\max(Z_1+1,Z_2+1,...Z_t+1,Z_{t+1},...Z_m)) - E(\max(Z_1,...Z_m)) \leq \frac{t}{m} \cdot E(A)$$

where A is the number of maximal elements in $Z_1,...,Z_m$. Since for multinomially distributed Z_j, E(A) is approximately equal to 1, the upper and the lower bound do nearly coincide in (8).

The previous result (7) implies that conditionally on G

$$E(\max(Z_1^{(G)},...Z_m^{(G)}) \mid G) \approx \frac{G}{m} + \sqrt{\frac{G}{m}} \cdot c_m$$

Since G is distributed according to a Binomial(p,1-y) distribution, we have

$$E(G) = p (1-y)$$

$$E(\sqrt{G}) = [\sqrt{p(1-y)} - \frac{1}{8} \frac{y}{\sqrt{p(1-y)}}]^+ + O(p^{-3/2})$$

where $[x]^+ = \max(x,0)$. This leads by (8) to the final formula

$$(9) \quad E(M') \approx \frac{py}{m} + \frac{p(1-y)}{m} + [\sqrt{p(1-y)} - \frac{y}{\sqrt{p(1-y)}}]^+ \frac{c_m}{m}$$

Of course, (9) will be replaced by p, whenever it is larger. Based on (9) B_s can be calculated as

$$B_s = \frac{p}{E(M')} \cdot$$

To illustrate the derived result, let us give a numerical example: If p=8 and m=10, then the approximative values for B_s are

γ	0.0	0.3	0.5	1.0
B_s	3.8	4.1	4.6	8

3. Model II : single dependencies.

As in the previous model, a memory conflict occurs if not all $X_i^{(n)}$ are distinct. However, all processors which are not affected by a conflict may continue their execution here. We consider first the steady state situation and assume that there is a non-terminating stream of requests. B_s, the mean number of active (=non waiting) processors is independent of the chosen strategy. Let $k_i^{(n)}$ be the length of the queue waiting for the memory i at time n. The $k_i^{(n)}$ form a markovian process :

$$(8) \qquad k_i^{(n+1)} = \max (k_i^{(n)} - 1 + \sum_{j=1}^{a} 1_{[X_j^{(n)} = i]}, 0) \qquad i = 1,...,m$$

where

$$a = p - \sum_{i=1}^{m} k_i^{(n)}$$

is the number of active processors. The state space of this process is $(k_1,...,k_m)$, where

$$0 \leqslant k_i \quad \text{and} \quad \Sigma k_i = p.$$

It is a nontrivial problem to find its stationary distribution . However it is a striking fact, that the interesting quantity $B_s = E(a)$,i.e. the mean number of active processors may be computed without the knowledge of the stationary distribution of (8). The reason is simply, that in every step the set of all unsatisfied requests (the old, waiting and the new ones) is a realisation of p independent r.v.'s $X_j^{(n)}$ and a is the number of distinct elements among these. Let G be the number of global requests (cf. (4)). W.l.o.g. we may assume that these requests are $X_{p-G+1}^{(n)},...,X_p^{(n)}$. The local requests $X_1^{(n)},...,X_{p-G}^{(n)}$ are all distinct. Let a_i be the number of distinct elements within $X_1^{(n)}...X_{p-G+i}^{(n)}$. Then

$$a_{i+1} = \begin{cases} a_i & \text{with probability } \frac{a_i}{m} \\ a_i+1 & \text{with probability } 1 - \frac{a_i}{m} \end{cases}$$

and

$$a_0 = p - G.$$

This implies that conditionally on G

$$E(a_i|G) = (p-G)(1- \frac{1}{m})^i + m(1 - (1 - \frac{1}{m})^i)$$

and hence

$$(9) \qquad E(a|G) = E(a_G|G) = (p-G)(1 - \frac{1}{m})^G + m (1 - (1 - \frac{1}{m})^G)$$

Since G is distributed according to a Binomial(p,1-y) distribution, we get after some easy calculations

(10) $B_s = B_s(m,p) = E(a) = (py - m + 1 - y)(1 - \dfrac{1-y}{m})^{p-1} + m$

as the final result.

Special cases are

(i) $y = 0$: $B_s = m(1 - (1 - \frac{1}{m})^p)$

(These functions are shown in Fig. 5. Notice that $B_s \to p$ for $m \to \infty$)

B_s = steady state bandwidth

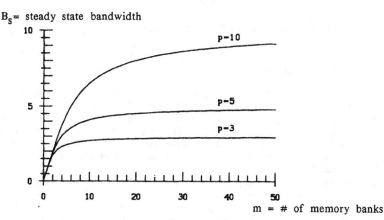

m = # of memory banks

Fig. 5

and (ii) $y = 1$: $B_s = p$.

As we shall see, the average bandwidth B_a depends here on the particular strategy. Let us first calculate the probability P(i) that the i-th processor is active in the steady state situation. For the LASF and the RANDOM strategies, all processors are indistinguishable and by symmetry

$$P(i) = \dfrac{B_s}{p} \qquad i=1,...,p$$

For the LEFT strategy however, this probability is independent of the number of processors with lower priority and hence (in the notation of (10))

(11) $P(i) = B_s(m,i) - B_s(m,i-1)$

with $B_s(m,0) = 0$. Of course, these probabilities decrease with increasing i. Let us give a numerical example. If p=8, m=10, then formula (10) gives

y	0.0	0.5	1.0
B_s	5.69	6.16	8

The probabilities P(i) are (for y= 0.5))

          $P(i) = 0.77$ $i=1,..8$ (LASF and RANDOM)
    $P(1) = 1$, $P(2) = 0.93$, $P(3) = 0.85$, $P(4) = 0.79$
    $P(5) = 0.73$, $P(6) = 0.67$, $P(7) = 0.62$, $P(8) = 0.57$.   (LEFT)

This last result (11) enables us to calculate the average bandwidth B_a. Since a program consisting of n steps is finished only if the last step is completed at the last processor, we get for large n

$$(12) \quad B_a = n \left[\frac{n}{p} \frac{1}{P(p)} \right]^{-1} = \begin{cases} B_s & \text{for LASF and RANDOM} \\ p(B_s(m,p)-B_s(m,p-1)) & \text{for LEFT} \end{cases}$$

For instance, the above numerical example yields

$$B_a = 6.16 \quad \text{for LASF or RANDOM}$$

$$B_a = 4.56 \quad \text{for LEFT}$$

The loss of efficiency of the LEFT strategy is evident.

4. Implications of the results

It has been conjectured in the seventies by M. Minsky, that the the performance of a parallel system increases only with the logarithm of the number of processors. Later, Lee stated a similar conjecture with a somewhat more optimistic rate of $p/\ln p$. The evident reason for not achieving the best factor p is the fact, that not all steps of a program can be executed in parallel. We have considered here only the subproblem of conflicting memory requests, which lower the system performance. It was shown, that the limited number of memory banks leads to a performance function which lies between Minsky's log p and Lee's $p/\ln p$. For existing computer architectures, such as Burroughs BSP (with $p=16$ and $m=17$) and CDC's ETA^{10} (with $m=8$ and $m=64$), the effective bandwidth of the memory system can be calculated analytically, if the stochastic characteristics of the memory requests are known. Usually the hardware descriptions contain only statements about the maximal bandwidth under ideal conditions with no reference to the steady state behavior under more realistic circumstances. Moreover, it was shown that the LASF strategy outperforms significantly the other strategies. This should be considered when designing the conflict resolution strategy.

5. References

[CHA77] Chang D.Y.; Kuck D.J.; Lawrie D.H.: On the effective bandwidth of parallel memories. IEEE Trans. Comp. C-26, No 5., 480-489 (1977)

[DAV81] David H.A.: Order Statistics.
J. Wiley & Sons, New York (1981)

[HOC83] Hockney R.W.; Jesshope C.R. Parallel Computers.
Adam Hilger, Bristol (1983)

[KNU75] Knuth D.E.; Rao G.S. Activity in an interleaved memory.
IEE Trans. Comp. Vol. C-24, 943-944 (1975)

[PFL86] Pflug G.Ch; Stochastische Modelle in der Informatik.
to appear 1986 with Teubner Verlag

[TIP25] Tipett L.H.C.: On extreme individuals and the range of a sample from a normal population. Biometrika 17 (1925)

THE DIGITAL OPTICAL COMPUTING PROGRAM
AT ERLANGEN

K.-H. Brenner, A. W. Lohmann

Physikalisches Institut der Universität
Erlangen-Nürnberg

Abstract

Optics is already penetrating the field of digital computing for example as read-only storage, as bus and as I/O devices. Protection against E.M.I. and E.M.P. is an incentive for replacing electronics by optics. Another incentive is the speed potential based on a carrier frequency of a million GHz.

Yet another incentive is the superior communications topology of optics: many light rays can criss-cross each other without disturbances. For comparison: only one wire can occupy any particular part of the three-dimensional space.

The specific projects at Erlangen deal with optics in conventional computers as well as with all optical computers.

1. Introduction

Progress in computer technology today is largely a progress in terms of miniaturization - not so much in terms of speed. While the density on a chip has increased by a factor of more than 100, computer speed has increased only by a factor on the order of 10. Interestingly, it is not the gates, that are responsible for this situation. Physical effects as a base for much faster gates do exist, but, as Josephson technology has demonstrated, faster gates are not sufficient to build faster computers. Equally important are the properties of the interconnections. Some of the main problems today are lack of connectivity, cross talk, clock skew and band limitation of the interconnections. Communication technology is starting to use the potential of optics, offering high bandwidth, low crosstalk interconnections and we believe that computer technology will follow. At Erlangen we pursue two main directions: Optics in conventional computers and all optical computers.

2. Optics in Conventional Computers

Optical hardware to a certain degree is already part of present day computers. Optical isolators are used in high performance computers in order to avoid ground loop problems. Fiber optical links enable high bit rate transmission in Local Area Networks. Work on an optical backplane for the next generation of computers is currently performed in Japan /1/. In Germany, an optical microprocessor bus has been demonstrated at the University of Duisburg /2/ and a dynamical, holographic interconnection network called HOLOLINK is currently under development /3/. In our group, the following projects are investigted.

2.1 Optical Perfect Shuffle Network

Processor performance can be increased considerably if the interconnection network is fast and reconfigurable. Possible structures of this kind are the Benes Network /4/, the Batcher Network /5/ and the Perfect Shuffle - Exchange Network /6/. An

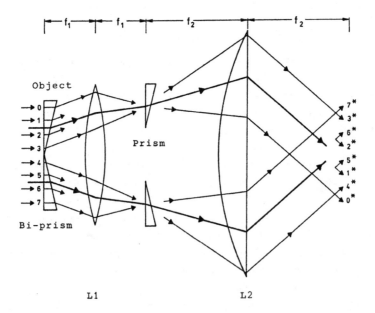

Fig. 1 Principle of the optical Perfect Shuffle.

important considerations here is the number of stages, required for non blocking interconnection. Another aspect concerns the control of these networks. Preferable to an external control is the property of being "self-routing". In IBM's new parallel computer GF11 an electronic Perfect Shuffle - Exchange Network is included to switch the interconnections with every clock cycle. At Erlangen /7/ as well as at AT&T Bell Laboratories /8/ an optical Perfect Shuffle unit for up to 100 000 inputs has been designed. Fig. 1 shows the optical principle. The large number of inputs is possible because the input data are arranged in a two-dimensional array. With suitable coding, N one-dimensional shuffles can be made equivalent to a large N^2 shuffle.

2.2   The Opto-Net

The Opto-Net /9/ was designed as the optical equivalent to a crossbar network. In contrast to an electronic crossbar with N inputs and N outputs, the optical version allows each of these N input lines to contain approx. 1000 parallel channels. Switching is achieved by using the polarization property of light in combination with electro-optic switchable halfwave plates.

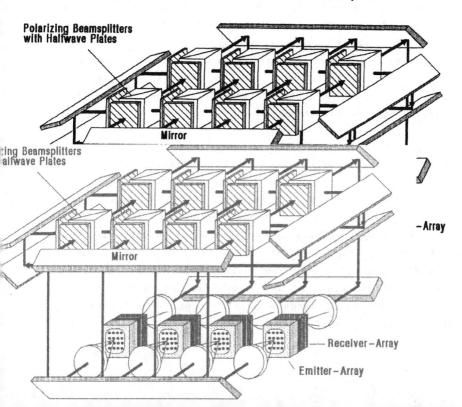

Polarizing Beamsplitters with Halfwave Plates

Mirror

...ng Beamsplitters ...alfwave Plates

Mirror

– Array

— Receiver – Array

Emitter – Array

Because the electro-optic effect is fast, the switching rate can be up to GHz. The geometry of this kind of network is shown in fig. 2. Here, the control signals have to be provided by an external unit.

2.3 Optical Chip to Chip Interconnections

Volume holograms are able to deflect light to arbitrary directions at almost 100% diffraction efficiency. In addition, focussing can be build into these holograms in order to collimate light. Using Dichromated Gelatine volume holograms a space variant interconnection of 823 channels has been demonstrated /10/. Further plans in this direction are oriented towards interconnecting an array of chips mounted on a common surface optically, hoping to substitute multilayer boards by optical wiring.

3. All Optical Computers

Faster and more reliable interconnections will increase computer speed to a certain degree. Then however, other speed-limiting factors will become prevailing. Problems of clock skew will enforce a regualar architecture and removal of the Von-Neumann bottleneck will require more connectivity. Optics offers both, equidistant path interconnections and a high degree of parallelism. This provides the base for new, parallel architectures. At Erlangen, we are pursueing two approaches: Parallel Optical Logic and Symbolic Substitution Logic.

3.1 Parallel Optical Logic using Spatial Filtering

Using Theta Modulation /11/, a technique which encodes information as the orientation of a grating structure, parallel logic can be performd by filtering operations in the Fourier plane of a coherent 8f-setup (fig. 3). With this technique, a large quantity of idential logic operations can be achieved in parallel, therefore favouring SIMD-types of architectures. The work at Erlangen is currently oriented towards a parallel optical adder /12/ for two-dimensional arrays of binary numbers.

73

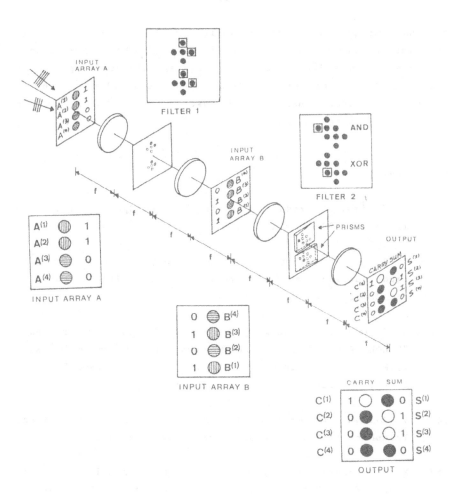

Fig. 3 A parallel optical adder with Theta Modulation

3.2 Symbolic Substitution Logic

Symbolic Substitution Logic /13,14/ can be considered as an extension of Cellular Logic. The elementary operations: recognizing
and substituting spatial binary pattern according to a given sub-
stitutuion rule, can be done optically in one step. In addition
to that, several such substitution rules can be performed simul-

taneously in parallel systems. Therefore, this kind of logic is well matched to the capabilities of optics. Although the optical hardware is space invariant, (i.e. regular) different operations can be performed on various areas of the input plane. In other words, the system appears to the user as a MIMD processor in spite of the homogeneous hardware.

References

/1/   H. Tajima, Y. Okada, K. Tamura: "A High Speed Optical Common Bus", TGCS 81, IECE, 1981.

/2/   K.-R. Hase: "Computer Internal Optical Bus System with Light Guiding Plate", in Proc. European Conference on Optical Communication, ECOC 85

/3/   D. Heger, P.-J. Becker, H. Bolle, W. Heil, P. Peschke: "HOLOLINK: A Conflictfree Holographic Interonnection Network of High Bandwidth for Highly Parallel Computing Systems", NTG Fachberichte 92, 1986, p. 280

/4/   V. Benes: "Mathematical Theory of Connecting Networks and Telephone Traffic", Acadmic Press New York, 1965

/5/   K.E. Batcher: "Sorting Networks and their Applications", in Proc. AFIPS 1968, SJCC 32, 2 Montvale N.J.: AFIPS Press, p. 307

/6/   C.L. Wu, T.Y. Feng: "The Universality of the Shuffle-Exchange Network", IEEE Trans. on Computers, C-30, 5 (1981) p. 324

/7/   A. Lohmann, W. Stork, G. Stucke: "Optical Perfect Shuffle", Appl. Opt. March 15, 1986

/8/   K.-H. Brenner, A. Huang: "Optical Implementations of the Perfect Shuffle Interconnection", Appl. Opt. 1986

/9/   A. Lohmann: "What Classical Optics can do for the Digital Optical Computer", Appl. Opt. March 15, 1986

/10/ H. Bartelt, S.K. Case: "Coordinate Transformations via Multifacet Holographic Optical Elements", Optical Engineering 22 (1983) p. 497

/11/ H. Bartelt, A. Lohmann, E.E. Sicre: "Optical Logic Processing in Paralel with Theta Modulation", J.Opt.Soc.Am. 1 (1984) p. 944

/12/ A. Lohmann, J. Weigelt: "A Digital Optical Adder Based on Spatial Filtering", Appl. Opt. Nov. 1, 1986

/13/ A. Huang: "Parallel Algorithms for Optical Digital Computers", Proc. 10th International Optial Computing Conference IEEE 1983, p. 13-17

/14/ K.-H. Brenner, A. Huang: "Digital Optical Computing with Symbolic Substitution", Appl. Opt. Nov. 1, 1986

HMESH: A VLSI ARCHITECTURE FOR PARALLEL PROCESSING

C. S. Raghavendra

Electrical Engineering-Systems Department
University of Southern California
Los Angeles, CA 90089-0781

ABSTRACT

Enhancements to array processors in the form of broadcast buses have been proposed for improving the speeds of algorithms in linear algebra, image processing and computational geometry. In this paper, we consider certain practical issues in such arrays which include fewer processors connected to the broadcast buses and finite time, namely $\log N$ time for broadcasting data to N processors. We propose a modified broadcast bus VLSI architecture which consists of a $\sqrt{N} \times \sqrt{N}$ mesh connected structure and a hierarchy of broadcast buses in each row and in each column such that every bus has k PE's. That is, in any row or column, in the first level there are $\frac{\sqrt{N}}{k}$ buses with groups of k PE's connected to each bus. One PE from each of this group is connected to second level of buses in a similar manner. This is recursively done until there are only k PE's left which are connected by a broadcast bus. With this architecture, maximum, minimum, or sum of N values can be found in $O(\log N)$, median row of a binary picture in $O(\log N)$, shortest distance between two points in $O(\log N)$. This architecture is well suited for parallel processing of applications in Linear Algebra, Image Processing, Computational Geometry and Numerical Computations. These restricted connections to buses reduces the I/O ports significantly, and therefore, is more suitable for VLSI implementation.

1. INTRODUCTION

Mapping algorithms to architectures has been an active area of research for quite some time. Designing parallel algorithms for many problems on specific architectures have been widely investigated. In particular, the mesh connected computers and its related structures have received considerable attention as they are well suited for VLSI implementation [HAMA 71, KUNG 77, STOU 82, GOPA

This research is supported by the NSF Presidential Young Investigator Award No. ECS-8452003 and a Grant from AT&T Information Systems.

85]. Two dimensional VLSI structures of processing elements (PE's) are naturally suited for image processing and computational geometry applications.

In such highly regular architectures the solution time complexities are dominated by the interprocessor communication times. For a given architecture, parallel algorithms need to be designed to minimize the routing of data between PE's. In a 2-dimensional MCC with N PE's data may have to be routed by a distance of $\sqrt{N}$ in the worst case. Therefore, many problems on the MCC will have $O(\sqrt{N})$ complexity (We use O for order no greater, and Ω for order at least). Since the MCC is a well suited structure for various problems, an extension to overcome long data movements can be accomplished by adding broadcast buses [BOKH 81, STOU 82, STOU 83].

With such a global broadcasting, in [BOKH 81] it is shown that solution to many problems can be speeded up; for example, finding maximum of N values will take $O(N^{1/3})$ instead of $O(N^{1/2})$. Several problems have been considered in [BOKH 81, STOU 83] with substantial improvements in computation time compared to MCC without broadcasting. Parallel algorithms to many problems including finding Closest pair, Geometric problems, and Graph problems have been designed for MCC in [STOU 83, GOPA 85]. A modified hierarchical mesh connected computer was proposed in [CARL 85].

A further extension to broadcasting is considered in [PRAS 85a] where a bus is employed in each row and column of PE's in a 2-dimensional MCC. It was shown that for many problems substantial speedups can be obtained. Problems such as finding max, closest pair, and several tasks in image processing can all be accomplished with $O(N^{1/6})$ time. It was also shown that broadcasting cannot improve solution times of certain problems such as sorting and matrix multiplication. That array architecture is well suited for many geometric and linear algebra problems, and the design of parallel algorithms involve in intelligently assigning the use of multiple buses.

In this paper we further generalize the idea of multiple buses and also consider certain practical aspects, such as the number of PE's that can be connected to a bus. The main idea is to provide multiple buses in each row and column of a 2-MCC such that there are some finite number of PE's connected to each bus. Our modified broadcast bus VLSI architecture consists of a $\sqrt{N}$ x $\sqrt{N}$ mesh connected structure and a hierarchy of broadcast buses in each row and in each column such that every bus has k PE's, where k is a small constant. That is, in any row or column, every group of k PE's share a bus and there will be $\frac{\sqrt{N}}{k}$ such groups. One PE from each of these groups is in turn connected by second level of buses in a similar manner and there will be $\frac{\sqrt{N}}{k^2}$ groups of PE's. This construction is repeated until there are only k PE's left which are connected by a broadcast bus. In all there will be $\log_k N^{1/2}$ levels of buses for each row and each column.

We consider several problems in Numerical linear algebra, semi group computations, Geometric problems, and problems in Image Processing and derive parallel algorithms on our architecture. We show that maximum of N values can be found in O($log\ N$), median row of a binary image in O($log\ N$) time, and closest pair problem in O($\log N$) time. All our algorithms are substantially faster than those running on MCC with a single broadcast feature and MCC with a broadcast bus in each row and column.

2. THE HIERARCHICAL MESH ARCHITECTURE

Before describing our hierarchical mesh architecture we briefly explain the use of broadcast buses in array processors. Figure 1 shows an array processor

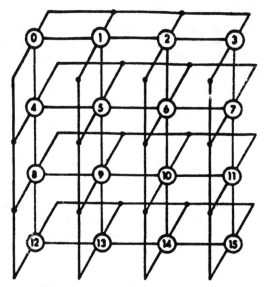

Figure 1. Array Processor with
Multiple Broadcasting

with broadcasting capability in each row and each column [PRAS 85a]. This is an SIMD architecture consisting of N PE's and each PE has a constant number of registers and is capable of executing simple arithmetic and logic instructions. There are two types of data transfer instructions that can be executed by the PE's: route data to one of the four nearest neighbors; and broadcast data to a row of PE's or a column of PE's. At any time only one type of data routing instruction can be executed by the PE's. Further, if broadcast instruction is executed only one PE per row (column) can send a value to all PE's in its row (column). Access to broadcast buses is controlled by the algorithm executed by the PE's and there will be no contention.

This architecture with row and column broadcast buses has shown to be powerful for solving many problems in parallel [PRAS 85a, PRAS 85b]. To illustrate how parallel algorithms are implemented on this architecture, we briefly explain computing the maximum of N elements distributed one per PE. Initially the PE's are grouped into blocks of size $O(N^{1/6} \times N^{1/6})$. In each block of PE's a maximum value is found using local communication and that value is moved to upper left corner PE of that block. Next, blocks of such corner PE's are formed and a maximum among them is found using broadcast buses. After this second step distance between PE's with a possible candidate will be $N^{1/3}$ along row as well as column. Also, in every active row (i.e., a row having at least one active PE) there are exactly $N^{1/6}$ PE's. The maximum of all these possible candidates can be found in $O(N^{1/6})$ time using row and column broadcast buses. This final maximum value can then be broadcast to all PE's in two steps.

The hierarchical mesh architecture (HMESH) proposed in this paper is an enhanced array structure. It is an SIMD architecture and consists of $\sqrt{N} \times \sqrt{N}$ processing elements with four nearest neighbor connections. Each PE consists of a few registers and is capable of performing arithmetic and logic computations. For routing data to long distances, the array of PE's are interconnected by a system of hierarchical broadcast buses. The PE's in each row and column are connected to the buses in such a way that there are exactly k PE's to each bus. The PE's are numbered as (i,j) where $0 \leq i,j \leq \sqrt{N} - 1$. In each row and column PE's are grouped and each group of size k share a common bus. The least index numbered PE's are again grouped in the next level, and again groups of k PE's share a bus. This construction is repeated until the top level is reached with k PE's which would require only one bus. There will be $\log_k N^{1/2}$ levels of buses in each row and column. The architecture for 16×16 PE's is shown in Figure 2.

The hierarchy of multiple buses allow fast data transfer between a pair of PE's. It takes at most $O(\log N)$ bus transfers for data to be routed from a source PE to a destination PE. Of course multiple PE's can be transferring data to other PE's simultaneously as long as different buses are used. However, there is potentially high parallelism in transfer of data between PE's. Also, a single PE can broadcast its data to all other PE's in $O(\log N)$ time. This can be accomplished by first broadcasting to local PE's, then to subsequent level of PE's, and after $\log N$ steps to the entire row of PE's. Then the same procedure can be repeated in all the column of PE's.

The HMESH architecture is highly modular and very powerful for mapping parallel algorithms. Each basic module will consist of k PE's and a common bus with the associated registers and control, and could be implemented in a single VLSI chip. All other bus connections are between chips. With the current state of technology about 4 to 10 16-bit PE's can be realized on a single chip. With $k = 10$ the number of levels in the hierarchy of buses is only three in a machine consisting of 10^6 PE's. Many parallel algorithms use divide and conquer technique which maps naturally to this architecture. Therefore, we can expect algorithms for this architecture to be much simpler and yet very efficient.

In this architecture the constant k is an important parameter and will appear in the complexity results of all our algorithms. When $k = 2$ the performance of this architecture would be comparable to that of mesh of trees, although there are no intermediate PE's in our architecture. If $k = N^{1/2}$ then there will be only one bus in each row and column and would reduce to the array processor with multiple broadcasting presented in [PRAS 85a]. When k is set to be $N^{1/6}$ there will be only three levels of buses in each row and column, and many of the results reported in [PRAS 85a] can be obtained with different algorithms within a factor of 3. However, with $k = N^{1/6}$, in the HMESH architecture max or min of elements in each row can be simultaneously found in $O(N^{1/6})$ time where as this requires $O(N^{1/4})$ time when there is only one broadcast bus in each row and column [PRAS 85a]. This property will be very useful in solving certain graph problems and in handling multiple figures in image processing.

3. PARALLEL ALGORITHMS

In this section we present parallel algorithms to several problems and our approach is similar to the ones presented in [PRAS 85a]. In all our algorithms we are interested in minimizing the number of data routing steps needed to solve the given problem. Our algorithms are faster than those known for MCC with single broadcasting and MCC with multiple broadcasting and are comparable to those for mesh of trees. We first consider finding Max, Min, or Sum of N data items.

Max, Min, or Sum

Let us consider the problem of finding maximum, minimum, or sum of N data items distributed one each among the PE's. This problem takes $O(N^{1/2})$ time on 2-MCC, $O(N^{1/3})$ time on 2-MCC with a global broadcast bus [BOKH 84], and takes $O(N^{1/6})$ time on 2-MCC with multiple broadcast [PRAS 85a].

Theorem 1: In a HMESH with constant k, the semi-group operation can be performed in $O(\log N)$ time.

Proof: Let us consider that we want to find the Max of N values. Basically, we find a Max value for each row and then find the global Max. First a local candidate for Max is found in each group of each row. This takes constant time k. Next, maximum of these candidates are found in the next level using broadcasting again taking k units of time. This procedure is repeated using the hierarchy of buses in each row, and in $k \log N$ time a candidate for Max is determined in each row. These values will all be stored in the first column of PE's. By repeating the same steps on the first column of PE's the Max of the N values can be found in $k \log N$ time. Therefore, the semi-group operation can be performed in $O(\log N)$ time.

Corollary: Maximum of $\sqrt{N}$ values in each row (column) can be found simultaneously in $O(\log N)$ time. Proof follows from Theorem 1.

Median Row of a Binary Picture:

Now we address the problem of finding median row of a given binary picture with pixels distributed one per PE. The median row divides the number of 1's in the binary picture into two halves such that about half the 1's are above this row and about half are below it. This can be accomplished in $O(\log N)$ time. We first count the number of 1's in each row simultaneously in $O(\log N)$ time and store this sum in left most PE in the respective row. Now the PE's in the first column compute the number of 1's above them as well as the total number of 1's in $O(\log N)$ time. With this the median row can be identified.

Closest Neighbor

We are given a binary picture with each PE containing a 0 or 1. We want to identify for each PE(i,j) with a 1 its closest neighbor $PE_c(i,j)$ containing a 1. The distance we use is the Manhattan distance. A simple algorithm to solve this on a 2-MCC with no additional buses is as follows: Each PE finds its left and right neighbors with 1 in its row. This can be done simply by propagating data left and then right updating the closest neighbor information along the way. These two pieces of data are then propagated up and down along columns with updates in a similar manner. At the end of this every PE with a 1 would identify its closest neighbor. On the MCC this algorithm takes $O(\sqrt{N})$ time. We use the same algorithm with propagating data through buses for better execution time.

Theorem 2: The Closest Neighbor problem can be solved on the HMESH architecture in $O(\log N)$ time.

Proof: We give a proof sketch by discussing the implementation strategy. The algorithm is exactly same as the simple scheme described above. First part of the algorithms involves in propagating information from left to right and then right to left such that every PE finds its closest left and right neighbor in the same row.

1) Find closest neighbors within the local group of k PE's. Move the address of rightmost PE in each group to the left most PE which is connected to the next level of broadcast bus. Now broadcast this information which contains possible candidates for left closest neighbors. This procedure is repeated on the hierarchy of buses. After $\log N$ steps each PE would have identified their left closest neighbor in its row. Similar steps are used to identify the right closest neighbor. Now these two pieces of data are propagated along columns in a similar fashion.

2) Move the data downwards in local groups and update closest neighbor data as data is propagated. Move the identified neighbors of bottom PE in each group to the PE which is connected to the next level of column bus. Repeat this procedure $\log N$ times and at the end every PE will know its left and right closest neighbors that are above them. Similarly move the data from bottom to top to identify two more neighbors coming from below. The minimum of all these four is the closest neighbor.

The total time needed is $O(\log N)$.

Marking Problem

In this problem, again, we are given a binary picture. Given two PE's, say A and B, we want to mark all the PE's that lie on a digitized straight line drawn between these two points.

Theorem 3: The PE's along the digitized straight line between two given ponts can be marked in $O(\log N)$ time.

Proof: We give the sketch of an implementation strategy. Essentially, if every

PE knows the address of the given points then the marking can be done by the PE's. We first move the address of given points, if any, to the left most PE in each row. This takes $O(\log N)$ time using the hierarchy of buses. Next the address of two points can be moved to the upper left corner PE in an additional $O(\log N)$ time. Finally, these two pieces of data can be broadcast to all PE's in an additional $O(\log N)$ time. Therefore, the marking problem can be solved in $O(\log N)$ time.

4. CONCLUSIONS

In this paper a generalized bus structure is proposed as an enhancement to array processors. The hierarchy of buses in each row and column provide a mechanism for fast data transfers between PE's allowing efficient algorithms for many problems in computational geometry and image processing. We are currently studying mapping of various problems in artificial intelligence applications on to the HMESH architecture.

REFERENCES

[BOKH 81]   S. H. Bokhari, "MAX: An Algorithm for Finding Maximum in an Array Processor with a Global Bus", in Proc. 1981 International Parallel Processing Conference, pp 302-303.

[BOKH 84]   S. H. Bokhari, "Finding Maximum on an Array Processor with a Global Bus", IEEE Transactions on Computers, Vol. C-33, No. 2, February 1984, pp 133-139.

[CARL 85]   D. A. Carlson, "Performing Tree and Prefix Computations on Modified Mesh-Connected Parallel Computers," Proc. 1985 Int. Conf. on Parallel Processing, August 1985, pp 715-718.

[FLYN 72]   M. J. Flynn, "Some Computer Organizations and their Effectiveness" *IEEE Trans. on Comput.,* Sept. 1972, pp. 948-960.

[GENT 78]   W. M. Gentleman, "Some Complexity Results for Matrix Computations on Parallel Processors", JACM, vol. 25, pp. 112-115, 1978.

[GOPA 85]   P. S. Gopalakrishnan, I. V. Ramakrishnan, L. N. Kanal, "An Efficient Connected Components Algorithm on a Mesh-Connected Computer," Proc. 1985 Int. Conf. Parallel Processing, August 1985, pp 711-714.

[HAMA 71]   V. C. Hamacher, "Machine Complexity Versus Interconnection Complexity in Iterative Arrays", IEEE Trans. on Comput., Vol. C-20, 1971, pp 321-323.

[HOCK 81]   R. W. Hockney and C. R. Jesshope, "Parallel Computers", Adam Hilger Ltd., 1981.

[HUNT 81]   Hunt, "The ICL DAP and its Application to Image Processing", in Languages and Architectures for Image Processing, M. J. B. Duff and S. Levialdi, eds., Academic Press, 1981.

[KUNG 77]   H. T. Kung, C. D. Thompson, "Sorting on a Mesh Connected Computer," Communications of the ACM, 1977.

[PRAS 85a]   V. K. Prasanna Kumar, C. S. Raghavendra, "Array Processor with Multiple Broadcasting," Proc. 12th Annual Symposium on Computer Architecture, June 1985, pp 2-10.

[PRAS 85b]   V. K. Prasanna Kumar, C. S. Raghavendra, "Image Processing on an Enhanced Mesh Connected Computer", Proc. IEEE Workshop on Computer Architecture for Pattern Analysis and Image Database Management, November 1985, pp 243-247.

[STOU 82]   Q. F. Stout, "Broadcasting on Mesh Connected Computers", 1982 Conference on Information Sciences and Systems, pp. 85-90.

[STOU 83]   Q. F. Stout, "Mesh Connected Computers with Broadcasting", IEEE Trans. on Computers, pp. 826-830, 1983.

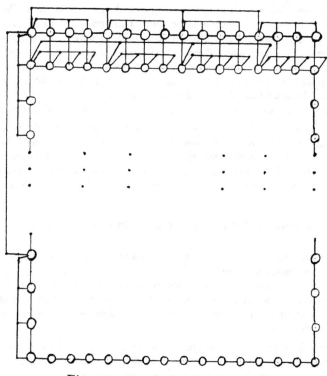

Figure 2. The HMESH Architecture

FFT on a New Parallel Vector Processor

K.K. Lau,
Dept. of Computer Science,
University of Manchester,
Oxford Road,
Manchester M13 9PL,
England.

X.Z. Qiao,
Dept. of Computer Architecture,
Institute of Computing Technology,
Academia Sinica,
Beijing,
China.

Abstract

A new parallel processing system has been proposed, and a prototype model of the system has been constructed. It is designed to perform parallel vector operations at maximum efficiency. In addition, it can also handle communicating vector operations, and hence exploit irregular parallelism present in many apparently sequential algorithms. The system is therefore suitable for a wide range of algorithms with varying degrees of parallelism. In this paper, we give a brief description of the system, and discuss the implementation of the Cooley-Tukey FFT on this system. We show that the system's versatility allows it to achieve a near maximum degree of parallelism for this algorithm in the asymptotic case.

1   Introduction

A new parallel processing system, called MU6V, was described in [5]. The novel features of this architecture offer a new kind of multi-processor facility which can function as a SIMD machine, or as a MIMD machine, or even as something in between. This versatility means that the system is suitable for a wide range of parallel algorithms. Principally, though, MU6V is designed to performed parallel vector operations at maximum efficiency, and hence the name "parallel vector processor". Nevertheless, it can also handle communicating or cooperating vector operations. As a result, the system can exploit irregular parallelism present in many algorithms which are apparently, and which therefore have been traditionally regarded as, sequential. Thus we can expect to implement a wide range of algorithms of varying degrees of parallelism efficiently on this system.

In this paper, we give a brief description of the architecture of MU6V. Its ability to cope with communicating vector operations is illustrated with the implementation of the Gauss-Seidel method for the iterative solution of linear equations. Then we discuss the implementation of the Fast Fourier Transform (FFT) due to Cooley-Tukey. We demonstrate how the system's versatility allows it to achieve a near maximum degree of parallelism for this algorithm in the asymptotic case.

2   MU6V : A Parallel Vector Processing System

The parallel vector processing system MU6V consists of a linear set of vector units, interconnected by a common communication highway, as shown in Figure 1. (In the prototype model, there are 3 vector units, but this number should eventually go up to 16) Each vector unit has a processor capable of both vector and scalar instructions. It also has its own memory, together with logic for input from and output to the common communication highway. Figure 2 shows the internal organisation of a vector unit.

Each vector unit is independently programmable, and thus potentially autonomous. So the units may run completely independent processes in parallel. However, they can also cooperate, and when they do, one of the participating processors acts as a master processor which initiates the other (slave) processors to perform particular tasks, and determines when the tasks are complete. The master processor can of course also take part in the computation if necessary.

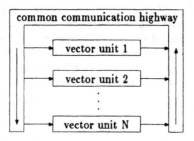

Figure 1: MU6V system organisation.

(The arrows in the diagram represent data flow)

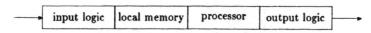

Figure 2: Internal organisation of a vector unit.

Since there is no common memory in MU6V, any global or shared variable exists in the form of multiple copies. When a vector unit updates its copy of a shared variable, it broadcasts the new value to all the other units by placing the value together with an identifier for the variable on the common communication highway. All vector units holding a copy of this variable must update their copies by accepting the broadcast value. A hardware synchronisation mechanism ensures that only the up-to-date values of all shared variables (and their copies) are used in all the vector units at all times.

Such a system is obviously designed to perform parallel vector operations at maximum efficiency. However, the built-in hardware communication and synchronisation mechanisms also allow the system to handle communicating or co-operating vector operations, i.e. vector elements updated in one unit can be passed to another unit which is operating in parallel, but which requires these updated values. As a result, it can extract maximum parallelism from what might appear to be an essentially sequential algorithm.

As an illustration, we will consider the Gauss-Seidel method for the iterative solution of the general system of n linear equations

$$A \underline{x} = \underline{b}$$

where A is $(n \times n)$, and $\underline{x}$, $\underline{b}$ are $(n \times 1)$. The method can be defined in pseudo-PASCAL as follows:

```
repeat
for i := 1 to n do
    begin
    s := 0 ;
    for j := 1 to i−1, i+1 to n do
    s := s + a[i,j] * x[j] ;
    x[i] := (b[i] − s) / a[i,i]
    end
until converged ;
```

where initially, x[i], i = 1, ... , n, are set to some approximate values, and "converged" is a boolean function which tests for convergence, i.e. the difference between the new and old values of x[i]'s.

Although its general form (the Successive Overrelaxation method) has the fastest rate of convergence in general, this method cannot be implemented efficiently on current parallel computers. On an array processor such as the ICL DAP, an inherently more parallel, though slower, method such as the Jacobi method is the preferred choice. On a vector computer such as the CRAY-1 and the CDC CYBER 205, the inner loop is vectorisable, though the outer loop is not. So, the algorithm can be efficiently implemented as a repeated sequence of vector operations. On closer examination, however, the Gauss-Seidel algorithm contains some "staggered" parallelism which these vector computers cannot exploit. This is illustrated by Figure 3, which shows for each element x[i] all the x[j]'s whose updated values are required for updating x[i] itself in the current iteration.

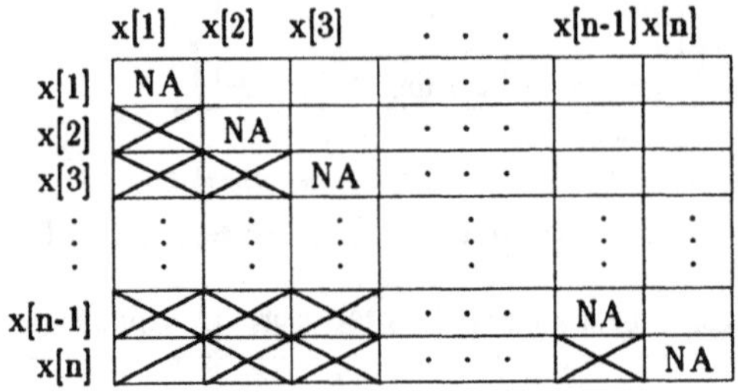

	x[1]	x[2]	x[3]	. . .	x[n-1]	x[n]
x[1]	NA			· · ·		
x[2]	⊠	NA		· · ·		
x[3]	⊠	⊠	NA	· · ·		
⋮	⋮	⋮	⋮	· · ·	⋮	⋮
x[n-1]	⊠	⊠	⊠	· · ·	NA	
x[n]	⊠	⊠	⊠	· · ·	⊠	NA

Figure 3: The "staggered" parallelism in Gauss-Seidel.

(NA stands for "not applicable".)

In each row, every crossed box represents an updated value which is required for updating x[i]. The empty boxes thus show all the scalar operations that could be carried out in parallel, i.e. the "staggered" parallelism at the beginning of each iteration. As the iteration proceeds, more and more crossed boxes become empty as more and more x[i]'s get updated, thus increasing the parallelism. On MU6V, this irregular pattern of parallelism can be exploited to the full. The algorithm can be expressed by the following code, which makes use of a notation loosely based on Actus [6] and CSP [4] :

```
procedure gauss-seidel (a : array ; x, b : vector ; n : integer);
    integer i ;
    repeat
    parallel i := 1 to n do
    row (i) ;
    until converged
```

where "converged" is a boolean function as before, and "row" is defined by

```
process row (i : integer ; a : array ; x , b : vector ; n : integer) ;
    real s ; integer j ;
    begin
    s := 0 ;
    parallel j := 1 to i−1, i+1 to n do
    s := s + a[i,j] * x[j]? ;
    ↑ x[i] := (b[i] − s) / a[i,i]
    end
```

where for an arbitrary variable v,
    v? means "consume the current value of v and immediately request for a new value";
    ↑ v means "broadcast the value of v".
(In addition, we shall use ?v to mean "accept a new value of v".)

Note that either parallel statement is not fully parallel, but each contains a certain amount of synchronisation. The parallel statement in process row has the same degree of parallelism as the number of already updated x[j]'s. The n processes row(i), i = 1, ... , n, in the <u>parallel</u> state-ment in <u>procedure</u> gauss-seidel are therefore synchronised, and exhibit the "staggered" parallelism illustrated in Figure 3. (For a detailed, more "tailor-made" implementation, see [5].)

The order in which the x[j]'s are updated in each iteration depends on the order in which the initial values of the x[j]'s are made available. Thus, it is possible not only to implement the traditional "sequential" Gauss-Seidel method by making the initial values of x[1], x[2], ... , x[n] available in that order, but also to implement other "asynchronous" parallel formulations such as those described in [1].

3   The Cooley-Tukey FFT on MU6V

The Cooley-Tukey algorithm [3] for computing the discrete Fourier transform is well-known. For a given sequence of n complex values x_k, $k = 0, \ldots , (n-1)$, the discrete Fourier transform is another sequence of n complex values X_j, $j = 0, \ldots , (n-1)$, defined by

$$X_j = \sum_{k=0}^{n-1} x_k \, \omega^{jk}, \quad j = 0, \ldots ,(n-1)$$

where $\omega = e^{-(2\pi/n)i}$, and $i = \sqrt{-1}$. (For the sake of simplicity, we shall assume that n is an even integer, i.e. $n = 2^m$ for some positive integer m.) For $n = 2^m$, the Cooley-Tukey algorithm computes $\underline{X}$ in m stages as follows. Express any j and any k as binary numbers, say

$$j = (j_{m-1}\, j_{m-2}\, \cdots\, j_0)_2 \ \text{and} \ k = (k_{m-1}\, k_{m-2}\, \cdots\, k_0)_2$$

and write

$$X_j \ \text{as} \ X[j_{m-1}\, j_{m-2}\, \cdots\, j_0]\,, \quad x_k \ \text{as} \ x[k_{m-1}\, k_{m-2}\, \cdots\, k_0].$$

Define $\underline{X}^{(0)}$ such that

$$\underline{X}^{(0)}[k_0\, k_1\, \ldots\, k_{m-1}] = x[k_{m-1}\, k_{m-2}\, \cdots\, k_0]\,,$$

i.e. the indices of the input elements are bit-reversed. Then the m stages of FFT are defined by

$$X^{(1)}[k_0\, \ldots\, k_{m-2}\, j_0] = \sum_{k_{m-1}=0}^{1} X^{(0)}[k_0\, \ldots\, k_{m-2}\, k_{m-1}]\omega^{2^{m-1}j_0 k_{m-1}}$$

$$X^{(2)}[k_0\, \ldots\, k_{m-3}\, j_1\, j_0] = \sum_{k_{m-2}=0}^{1} X^{(1)}[k_0\, \ldots\, k_{m-3}k_{m-2}\, j_0]\, \omega^{(2j_1+j_0)2^{m-2}k_{m-2}}$$

$$\vdots$$

$$X^{(m)}[j_{m-1}\, \ldots\, j_0] = \sum_{k_0=0}^{1} X^{(m-1)}[k_0\, j_{m-2}\, \ldots\, j_0]\, \omega^{(2^{m-1}j_{m-1}+2^{m-2}j_{m-2}+\ldots+j_0)k_0}\,.$$

And finally,

$$\underline{X} = \underline{X}^{(m)}\,.$$

For example, for $n = 8$, we have the signal flow graph [2] shown in Figure 4.

It is worth noting that the dual node space is constant at every stage, but increases logarith-mically (with respect to 2) from stage to stage. On a conventional vector computer, such as the CRAY-1 and the CDC CYBER 205, the dual node space determines the maximum possible vector

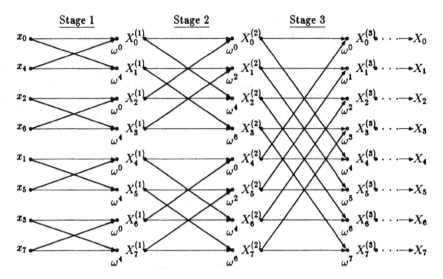

Figure 4: FFT signal flow graph for n = 8, with final result in natural order.

length at each stage. Therefore, the Cooley-Tukey FFT is only "pseudo-vectorisable" on these computers. (See [8], which contains a detailed study of implementing this and other FFT algorithms on vector computers.)

The ideal parallel processing system for implementing the Cooley-Tukey FFT for a fixed input vector length is the "perfect shuffle" interconnection pattern [7]. Unfortunately, in practice, there is no "perfect shuffle" system which can deal with general FFT. However, the idea of the perfect shuffle is a useful one nonetheless, and indeed forms the basis of our proposed implementation of FFT on MU6V.

We will show that using 2^p (slave) vector units (for some positive integer p) for the first $(m - p)$ stages of FFT for $n = 2^m$, the maximum parallelism possible on MU6V can be achieved by the 2^p vector units performing vector operations completely in parallel. For the last p stages, however, it is not profitable to use more than one vector unit, because the speed-up does not increase with the number of vector units employed.

To illustrate the basic idea of our implementation of the Cooley-Tukey FFT on MU6V, we shall first consider stage by stage the example shown in Figure 4. For this example, $p = 1$ is appropriate, and the signal flow graph in Figure 5 shows the 3 stages of parallel FFT on MU6V.

Initially, $X^{(0)}$ is split in half, the first and second half sent to vector units 1 and 2 respectively. In each vector unit, every dual node pair occupies adjacent positions. This enables vector operations to be carried out in Stage 1 involving vectors of length 2, in parallel with similar vector operations in the other unit. Two of these vectors are sub-vectors of $X^{(0)}$, formed respectively from the first and second elements of the dual node pairs, while the other two contain powers of ω. For example, in vector unit 1, the necessary computation can be described by the following vector operations :

$$\begin{pmatrix} x_0 \\ x_2 \end{pmatrix} + \begin{pmatrix} u_1 \\ u_2 \end{pmatrix} , \begin{pmatrix} x_0 \\ x_2 \end{pmatrix} - \begin{pmatrix} u_1 \\ u_2 \end{pmatrix} ,$$

where

$$\begin{pmatrix} u_1 \\ u_2 \end{pmatrix} = \begin{pmatrix} \omega^0 \\ \omega^0 \end{pmatrix} * \begin{pmatrix} x_4 \\ x_6 \end{pmatrix} ,$$

(since $\omega^4 = -\omega^0$) and for arbitrary vectors $\underline{u}$ and $\underline{v}$ of length n, "$*$" defines element-wise vector

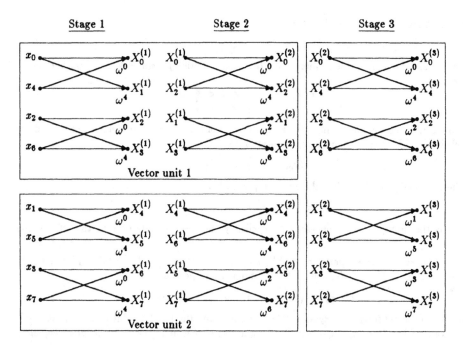

Figure 5: Parallel FFT with m = 3, p = 1.

multiplication. These parallel vector operations in the two vector units represent the maximum parallelism possible for Stage 1.

After Stage 1, there is no need for communication between the two vector units. However, in order to maintain the maximum possible degree of parallelism in Stage 2, it is necessary to permute the elements of the vector $\underline{X}^{(1)}$ in such a way that every dual node pair again occupies adjacent positions. This is done by performing the perfect shuffle on each half of $\underline{X}^{(1)}$ separately. Then, in Stage 2, parallel vector operations similar to those in Stage 1 are carried out in the vector units .

Stage 3 can be carried out in two different ways. One way is to continue using two vector units and proceed as before. However, this would necessitate a disproportionately large amount of inter-processor communication after Stage 2. We will show in the next section that the speed-up that could be achieved by this approach does not increase with the number of vector units used. We therefore prefer the other approach, i.e. to use just one vector unit for Stage 3. Again, we will show in the next section that the speed-up in this case is far more acceptable.

Before the computation in Stage 3, however, $\underline{X}^{(2)}$ is permuted by performing the perfect shuffle on the whole vector, in order to maintain the maximum parallelism possible as before. Then vector operations involving vectors of length 4 are carried out. Finally, after Stage 3, the vector $\underline{X}^{(3)}$ has now to be unscrambled (cf. Figure 4) in order to yield the result in natural order.

In general, for $n = 2^m$, using 2^p (slave) processors for the first $(m - p)$ stages, there will be no communication between the vector units in these stages. The maximum possible degree of parallelism is achieved by parallel vector operations involving vectors of length 2^{m-p-1} . In each of the last p stages, one vector unit is used to perform similar vector operations involving vectors of length 2^{m-1}.

Before giving the details of the implementation, we describe formally the permutation carried out after each stage. For a general vector

$$\underline{V} = (v_0, \ldots, v_{n-1})$$

where $n = 2m$, for some positive integer m, the perfect shuffle permutes $\underline{V}$ into another vector $\underline{V}'$, such that

$$v_i' = \begin{cases} v_{2i} & , \ 0 \le i \le \frac{n}{2} - 1 \\ v_{2i+1-n} & , \ \frac{n}{2} \le i \le n - 1 \end{cases}$$

This permutation can be conveniently described in terms of the binary representation of the indices of the elements of $\underline{V}$. Let the binary representation for k be

$$(k_{m-1} \ k_{m-2} \ \ldots \ k_0)_2$$

Then the kth element is shuffled to the position $p(k)$, where

$$p(k) = (k_{m-2} \ k_{m-3} \ \ldots \ k_0 \ k_{m-1})_2 \ ,$$

i.e. $p(k)$ is the binary number obtained by cyclically rotating the bits of k to the left by one position.

The permutation that we perform on $X^{(i)}$ after Stage i of our parallel FFT can be similarly described as follows. The kth element of $X^{(i)}$ is shuffled into position $q(i,k)$ where

$$q(i,k) = (k_{m-1} \ \ldots \ k_{i+1} \ k_{i-1} \ \ldots \ k_0 \ k_i)_2$$

i.e. $q(i,k)$ is obtained from k by cyclically left-rotating only the bits from bit 0 (k_0) to bit i (k_i). For the example in Figure 5, these permutations are as shown in Figure 6. In practice, these

Stage 1	Stage 2	Stage 3
0 0 0	0 0 0	0 0 0
0 0 1	0 1 0	1 0 0
0 1 0	0 0 1	0 1 0
0 1 1	0 1 1	1 1 0
1 0 0	1 0 0	0 0 1
1 0 1	1 1 0	1 0 1
1 1 0	1 0 1	0 1 1
1 1 1	1 1 1	1 1 1

Figure 6: Binary indices of elements of $X^{(i)}$ in Figure 5.

permutations may be computed beforehand and stored in an array, which can then be used for re-ordering the elements of $X^{(i)}$ at each stage.

Now we can give a general description of our parallel FFT for $n = 2^m$ using 2^p (slave) vector units on MU6V. Suppose $X^{(0)}$ is defined as before. Let us redefine $X^{(i)}$, $i = 1, \ldots, (m-1)$, such that their elements are in the permuted order at the beginning of each stage. That is, at the end of Stage i, $i = 1, \ldots, (m-1)$, we do

$$Y[k] := X^{(i)}[q(i,k)], \quad \text{for } k = 1, \ldots, n \ ;$$
$$X^{(i)} := Y \ ;$$

where Y is a temporary vector, and q is the permutation function defined earlier on. Then the m stages of computation are defined by

$$X^{(1)}[k_0 \ \ldots \ k_{m-2} \ j_0] = \sum_{k_{m-1}=0}^{1} X^0[k_0 \ \ldots \ k_{m-2} \ k_{m-1}] \ \omega^{2^{m-1} j_0 k_{m-1}}$$

$$X^{(2)}[k_0 \ \ldots \ k_{m-3} \ \dot{j}_0 \ \dot{j}_1] = \sum_{k_{m-2}=0}^{1} X^{(1)}[k_0 \ \ldots \ k_{m-3}\dot{j}_0 \ k_{m-2}] \ \omega^{(2\dot{j}_1+\dot{j}_0)2^{m-2}k_{m-2}}$$

$$\vdots$$

$$X^{(m)}[\dot{j}_0 \ \dot{j}_1 \ \ldots \ \dot{j}_{m-1}] = \sum_{k_0=0}^{1} X^{(m-1)}[\dot{j}_0 \ \dot{j}_1 \ \ldots \ \dot{j}_{m-1}k_0] \ \omega^{(2^{m-1}\dot{j}_{m-1}+2^{m-2}\dot{j}_{m-2}+\ldots+\dot{j}_0)k_0} \ .$$

The final result is obtained by unscrambling $\underline{X}^{(m)}$, i.e.

$$X[\dot{j}_{m-1} \ \dot{j}_{m-2} \ \ldots \ \dot{j}_0] = X^{(m)}[\dot{j}_0 \ \dot{j}_1 \ \ldots \ \dot{j}_{m-1}] \ .$$

Note that since the elements of $\underline{X}^{(i)}$ are now always "in order", these equations provide a means of determining the order of the powers of ω at each stage. Therefore, these terms also can be computed beforehand and stored in the correct order in an array.

The computation described by these equations can be implemented on MU6V as follows:

1. Use a global vector $\underline{X}$ to hold $\underline{X}^{(i)}$, $i = 0, \ldots, m$. Notionally split $\underline{X}$ into 2^p equal parts, and refer to them as $\underline{X}_j$, $j = 1, \ldots, 2^p$. Each $\underline{X}_j$ is thus of length 2^{m-p}.

2. In vector unit j, $j = 1, \ldots, 2^p$, use a local vector $\underline{S}_j$ to hold $\underline{X}_j$, and two local vectors $\underline{u}_j$ and $\underline{v}_j$, each of length 2^{m-p-1}, to hold the "odd" and the "even" elements of $\underline{S}_j$ respectively.

3. For each of the first $(m-p)$ stages, all 2^p vector units operate completely in parallel. In each vector unit, vector operations are carried out to :

   (a) update $\underline{u}_j$ and $\underline{v}_j$ using the above equations;

   (b) update and re-order $\underline{S}_j$, and form new $\underline{u}_j$ and $\underline{v}_j$.

4. Each vector unit communicates its $\underline{S}_j$ to $\underline{X}$ to update it.

5. A vector unit is then chosen to be used for the last p stages. In this vector unit, a local vector $\underline{S}$ is used to hold $\underline{X}$, and two other local vectors $\underline{u}$ and $\underline{v}$, each of length 2^{m-1}, to hold the "odd" and "even" elements of $\underline{S}$ respectively. Then, in each of the last p stages, this vector unit :

   (a) updates $\underline{u}$ and $\underline{v}$ using the above equations;

   (b) updates and re-orders $\underline{S}$, and writes $\underline{S}$ back into $\underline{X}$.

6. Unscramble $\underline{X}$.

To simplify the description, we have assumed that all the powers of ω, as well as the permutations defined by q, have been computed beforehand and passed to the vector units in the correct order. The appendix shows this implementation in detail, using the same notation that was used in section 2.

4 Performance Analysis

The hardware of MU6V supports parallelism at two levels. Firstly, the vector units can operate in parallel, producing a speed-up of up to the number of vector units employed. Secondly, within each vector unit, vector operations produce a speed-up which is a function of the length of the vectors involved. If we denote this function by $\alpha(l)$, where l is the vector length of the operations concerned, then $\alpha(l)$ increases with l up to a point. The maximum value of $\alpha(l)$, which we will denote by α'

is usually called the *asymptotic speed-up* of the vector operations. The overall maximum speed-up possible using 2^p vector units is therefore $\alpha' 2^p$.

In the first $(m - p)$ stages of our parallel FFT, since there is no inter-processor communication, the total computing time required, assuming asymptotic vector speed-up, is

$$T_{P_1} = (4T_X + (m - p - 1)(T_O + 2T_M) + T_O) * l/\alpha'$$

where

T_X	is the time required to communicate one element between X and $\underline{S}$;
T_O	is the total time taken to perform a scalar multiplication, a scalar addition and a scalar subtraction;
T_M	is the time "map" takes to map one element (see Appendix);
$l = 2^{m-p-1}$	is the vector length of the operations;
α'	is the asymptotic vector speed-up.

The dominant term in T_{P_1} is obviously

$$(m - p) * l * T_O/\alpha' \, ,$$

the total time required for the first $(m - p)$ stages of the transformation. This is especially so for a large value of $(m - p)$.

On a serial computer, these computations will need a total time of

$$T_{S_1} = (m - p) * T_O * 2^{m-1} \, .$$

Therefore, the speed-up for phase one is

$$T_{S_1}/T_{P_1} \approx \alpha' 2^p \, ,$$

ignoring the terms in T_O and T_M, i.e. for a large value of $(m - p)$, the speed-up in phase one tends to the maximum possible.

In phase two, if 2^p vector units are used, then the total computing time is dominated by inter-processor communication after every stage. In order to minimise the waiting time for elements to become available, it is possible to process a dual node pair as soon as its components arrive at the vector unit concerned. In other words, synchronised scalar operations instead of parallel vector operations should be carried out. In this case, communication and scalar operations can proceed in parallel, and the total communication time is almost equal to the total computing time.

If T_C is the time taken to communicate one element between two vector units, then the total computing time is at least

$$T_{P_2} = 2^m * p * T_C + T_O,$$

where the first term is the total communication time, and is the dominant term. Now the total time required for phase two on a sequential computer is

$$T_{S_2} = 2^{m-1} * p * T_O \, ,$$

and so the speed-up using synchronised scalar operations on 2^p vector units is at most

$$T_{S_2}/T_{P_2} \approx \frac{T_O}{2T_C} \, ;$$

ignoring the T_O term in T_{P_2}. This is not a function of p, and so the speed-up is far from acceptable.

On the other hand, if phase two is carried out using just one vector unit which performs vector operations on vectors of length 2^{m-1}, then the total computation time will be

$$T'_{P_2} = 2^{m-1}(p * T_O/\alpha' + 2p * T_M/\alpha' + 2T_C) .$$

The speed-up in this case is

$$T_{S_2}/T'_{P_2} \approx \frac{\alpha'}{1 + \frac{2\alpha'T_C}{pT_O}}$$

ignoring the term in T_M. If $T_C << T_O$, then this speed-up again approaches the maximum possible using just one vector unit, that is α'.

References

[1] R.H. Barlow and D.J. Evans, Parallel Algorithms for the Iterative Solution to Linear Systems, *Computer J.* **25** (1982) 56-60.

[2] E.O. Brigham, *The Fast Fourier Transform* (Prentice-Hall 1974).

[3] J.W. Cooley and J.W. Tukey, An Algorithm for the Machine Calculation of Complex Fourier Series, *Math. Comput.* **19** (1965) 297-301.

[4] C.A.R. Hoare, Communicating Sequential Processes, *Comm. ACM* **21** (1978) 666-677.

[5] R.N. Ibbett, P.C. Capon and N.P. Topham, MU6V : A Parallel Vector Processing System, *ACM Computer Architecture News* **13** (1985) 136-144.

[6] R.H. Perrot, A Language for Array and Vector Processors, *ACM TOPLAS* **1** (1979) 177-195.

[7] H.S. Stone, Parallel Processing with the Perfect Shuffle, *IEEE Trans. Comput.* **20** (1971) 153-161.

[8] P.N. Swarztrauber, FFT algorithms for Vector Computers, *Parallel Computing* **1** (1984) 45-63.

Appendix

```
procedure fft ( x : vector ; m, p : integer ; q, w : array );
integer i, j, tm, tp, tmp, tmp2, mp, mp1, mp2, jt1, jt2, jt3, jt4 ;
vector y[1 .. (2↑m)] ;
    begin
    tm := 2↑m ; tp := 2↑p ; tmp := 2↑(m−p) ; tmp2 := tmp/2 ;
    mp := m−p ; mp1 := mp−1 ; mp2 := mp+1 ;
    parallel j := 1 to tp do
        sequential
        begin
        jt1 := (j−1)*tmp + 1 ; jt2 := j*tmp ;
        jt3 := (j−1)*tmp2 + 1 ; jt4 := j*tmp2 ;
        phase1( j, tmp, mp, mp1, x, q[1 : mp1, jt1 : jt2], w[1 : mp, jt3 : jt4] )
        end ;
    parallel j := 1 to tm do
    y[j] := ?x[q[mp, j]] ;
    x := y ;
    phase2( tm, p, x, q[mp2 : m, #], w[mp2 : m, #] )
    parallel j := 1 to tm do
    y[j] := ?x[q[m+1, j]] ;
    x := y
```

<u>end</u>

where "phase1" and "phase2" are defined by

```
process phase1 ( j, tmp, mp, mp1 : integer ; x : vector ; q, w : array );
integer k, tm1 ; vector s, v2[1 .. tmp], v1[1 .. (tmp/2)] ;
    begin
    tm1 := tmp−1 ;
    parallel k := 1 to tmp do
    s[k] := x[(j−1)*tmp + k]?;
    for k := 1 to mp1 do
        begin
        v1 := s[2 : tmp ; 2] * w[k, #] ;
        v2[1 : tm1 ; 2] := s[1 : tm1 ; 2] + v1 ;
        v2[2 : tmp ; 2] := s[1 : tm1 ; 2] − v1 ;
        s := map( v2, q[k, #] ) ;
        end ;
    v1 := s[2 : tmp ; 2] * w[mp, #] ;
    s[2 : tmp ; 2] := s[1 : tm1 ; 2] − v1 ;
    s[1 : tm1 ; 2] := s[1 : tm1 ; 2] + v1 ;
    parallel k := 1 to tmp do
    ↑x[(j−1)*tmp + k] := s[k]
end
```

```
process phase2 ( tm, p : integer ; x : vector ; q, w : array ) ;
integer i, tm1, tm2 ; vector v1[1 .. (tm/2)], v2[1 .. tm] ;
    begin
    tm1 := tm − 1 ; tm2 := tm/2 ;
    for i = 1 to p do
        begin
        v1 := x[2 : tm ; 2] * w[mp+i, #] ;
        v2[1 : tm1 ; 2] := x[1 : tm1 ; 2] + v1 ;
        v2[2 : tm ; 2] := x[2 : tm ; 2] − v1 ;
        x := map( v2, q[mp+i, #]) end
    end
```

In <u>procedure</u> fft,

- the array q[1 .. m+1, 1 .. 2↑m] holds the permutations for all the m stages of computation, as well as that for the final unscrambling of the result;

- the array w[1 .. m, 1 .. 2↑(m−1)] holds the powers of ω in the correct order for the m stages of computation.

In <u>process</u> phase1, "map" is a vector operation which maps the elements of a vector onto those of another vector according to an ordering vector.

ANALYSIS OF MULTIGRID METHODS FOR NON-SHARED MEMORY SYSTEMS
BY A SIMPLE PERFORMANCE MODEL

O. KOLP, H. MIERENDORFF

Gesellschaft fuer Mathematik und Datenverarbeitung mbH

Schloss Birlinghoven, D-5205 Sankt Augustin 1, F. R. Germany

W. SEIDL

Institut für Mathematische Maschinen und Datenverarbeitung

Universität Erlangen-Nürnberg, Martensstr. 3, D-8520 Erlangen, F. R. Germany

ABSTRACT

The system behaviour of parallel processors normally depends in a complex way on many parameters. We investigate the quality of a linear model for the transport in non-shared memory systems by the example of a multigrid method. To this purpose, this method was implemented on the processor kit DIRMU-25 for measuring the required computing time. On the other hand, we have developed a simple abstract process model describing the computational work by one parameter and the transport work by two parameters. The simulation of the abstract model is compared with the implementation at the measuring points. In this way, we obtain information about the quality of the model and the interpretation of the parameters used. The results of this comparison enable us to forecast system performance for large systems by simulation. Though not being optimal for the DIRMU-25 system, the used algorithm is sufficiently complex to illustrate, in particular, the transport characteristics of the system.

1. INTRODUCTION

The considerations of the present paper are based on nearest-neighbour-systems (NN-system). The processors of this architecture are arranged at the crosspoints of a 2-dimensional orthogonal grid and each processor is directly connected with its 4 nearest neighbours. Every processor has a local memory. A common main memory does not exist.

A prerequisite for constructing large systems is a performance forecasting that considers the most important algorithms designated for a system. Since such a forecasting is desired long before constructing the first subsystem, it must in general be based on theoretical investigations and simulations. Such investigations will require the more work, the more parameters of the systems in question have to be considered. These parameters are the constants in the models which reflect the behaviour of system components during subproblem processing. For considering large systems and problems, we must try to obtain an optimum description of system behaviour by a minimum number of model parameters. For comparing different algorithms and processors, it is useful to cover many different situations by the same set of parameters.

Multigrid methods are among the fastest methods suitable for solving large problems described by differential equations. Their parallelization on different parallel processors of the type considered has repeatedly been investigated by means of the above methods (cf., [CS83], [CS85], [KM84], [KM85a] and [KM85b]).

These investigations have shown that asymptotic methods are of excellent suitability for large systems, in particular because of the simple form of the results they produce. In general, however, reality is described sufficiently well only for systems of some thousand processors (cf., [KM85a] and [KM85b]).

For systems of medium to small size, simulation should be preferred because of the great number of influential factors to be considered. Even in this field, simulation will also require much cost unless the reality is reduced to a simple model by suitable abstraction. For static multigrid methods of simplest type, we needed only one parameter for the computing cost of an operator. In this context, let an operation be the evaluation of a difference star, an interpolation or a defect computing for one grid point. If N is the number of inner grid points of the finest grid, the computing cost for a V-cycle will be of the order N. Apart from N, there is still a number of other functions to be connected with cost parameters (e.g. in two-dimensional problems $N^{1/2}$ with the cost required for organizing the inner loops of the program). All these influences were neglected. Only for very small systems of less than 8 processors, this has led to somewhat too optimistic efficiency values in simulation. Transport was considered by a linear model for the transport cost. It estimates the cost required for a data packet by means of the packet size and an additional constant. Such a model enabled us to compare a great number of different systems.

This paper presents an investigation on the quality of this simulation type. In chapter 2, we select a special multigrid algorithm and describe our cost model. Chapter 3 describes the system configuration DIRMU-25 we used, the implementation and the measuring results. Chapter 4 compares the results of simulation with those of measuring. Even for small systems, they show such a good coincidence that the precision of drawing hardly suffices to demonstrate the differences. This chapter also discusses the factors primarily influencing this result. We always consider only the main part of the multigrid method without I/O and loading processes.

2. DESCRIPTION OF THE ALGORITHM

Multigrid methods, described, for example, in [ST82], are assumed to be known here. We consider V-cycle iteration with regular grid generation. Let a problem be the Poisson equation defined by suitable boundarys condition on a two-dimensional quadratic domain R. We assume that this is discretized on a set $\{G_1, \ldots, G_n\}$ of point grids on R. G_1 has only one grid point that is the midpoint of R. G_1 is obtained from G_{i-1} by halvening the edges of the meshes, $i=2,...,n$. Let 'rel' be the cost required for the relaxation operator applied to an inner grid point. We here confine ourselves to odd-even point relaxation. Accordingly, let 'int' and 'res' be the cost for inter-polation and restriction operators. Let ν_1 and ν_2 be the number of relaxations per grid in transition from finer to coarser grids and vice versa. In odd-even relaxation it is sufficient to do the defect computing for the restriction only on the coarse points of a grid.

We estimate the average operation cost for a V-cycle required per grid point at

$$(\nu_1+\nu_2)\cdot\text{rel}'+(3/4)\cdot\text{int}'+(1/4)\cdot\text{res}'=a_0(\nu_1+\nu_2+1) \qquad \text{with } a_0=\text{'rel'}=\text{'int'}=\text{'res'}.$$

If the number of inner grid points for the grid G_i is $(2^i-1)^2$, the computational work for a V-cycle will be for a single processor

$$A(1)=a_0(\nu_1+\nu_2+1)\sum_{i=1}^{n}(2^i-1)^2$$

The mapping of the multigrid problem onto the multi-processor architecture 'nearest-neighbour system' (NN-system) is done as in [KM84]. First, the problem is mapped onto a binary tree, then the tree is mapped onto the nearest-neighbour struc-ture.

The m coarsest grids, $m\geq1$, are assigned to the top of the tree. If a domain of the i-th ($i\geq m$) grid is assigned to a node of the tree in the j-th tree level ($j\geq1$), sub-domains of this domain are assigned in the i+1-th grid to its two sons in the j+1-th tree level. The partition of a domain is done from tree level to tree level, alternating in parallel to the x- or y-axis (cf., fig. 1). If the grid G_{m+k} ($m+k\leq n$) is distributed over the leaves, the corresponding domains of the remaining n-(m+k) grids shall be assigned to the leaves, too; k denotes the depth of the tree.

Let us now define the different domains explicitly. Let the grids be $G_i=(0,2^i)\times(0,2^i)$ $i=1,...,n$. If $R=(x_1,x_2)\times(y_1,y_2)$ is assumed to be a rectangular in G_i, let $R^{(r)}=(x_1',x_2')\times(y_1',y_2')$ be defined as follows for $r=0,1,2...$: $x_1'=\max\{x_1-r,0\}$, $x_2'=\min\{x_2+r,2^i\}$, $y_1'=\max\{y_1-r,0\}$, $y_2'=\min\{y_2+r,2^i\}$, i.e., $R^{(r)}$ is the rectangular in G_i which results from R, by adding from all sides r rows of points as far as feasible. First, the so-called S-sets are defined recursively. Let an S-set S of G_i be given which is assigned to a process in the j-th tree level, $i=m+j$, $j=0,...,k-1$, $S=(x_1,x_2)\times(y_1,y_2)$. Let $S=G_m$ for $j=0$. Let S_1 and S_2 be the S-sets of G_{i+1} that are assigned to the two sons and that are defined as follows, $S_l=(x_{1l},x_{2l})\times(y_{1l},y_{2l})$, $l=1,2$:

a) partition of the y-component for j even:

$x_{11}=2x_1$, $x_{12}=2x_2$, $y_{11}=2y_1$, $y_{12}=y_1+y_2$, $x_{21}=2x_1$, $x_{22}=2x_2$, $y_{21}=y_1+y_2$, $y_{22}=2y_1$.

b) partition of the x-component for j odd:

$x_{11}=2x_1$, $x_{12}=x_1+x_2$, $y_{11}=2y_1$, $y_{12}=2y_2$, $x_{21}=x_1+x_2$, $x_{22}=2x_2$, $y_{21}=2y_1$, $y_{22}=2y_1$.

If $i=m+k+q$, $q=0,1,...,n-(m+k)$ no further partition is done. If S is a part of G_i, then the S-set $S'=(x_1',x_2')\times(y_1',y_2')$ of G_{i+1} that is assigned to the same processor can be determined as follows: $x_1'=2x_1$, $x_2'=2x_2$, $y_1'=2y_1$ und $y_2'=2y_2$.

For a domain S, the domains Q,Q',R,T,U and V are then defined. All of them can be represented in the form $S^{(t)}$ with: $t=4v_1+1$ for Q, $t=4v_1$ for Q', $t=\max\{4v_1+1,4v_2\}$ for R, $t=2v_1$ for T, $t=2v_2$ for U and $t=4v_2$ for V. By the definitions the relations $S \subset T \subset Q \subset Q' \subset Q \subset R$, $S \subset U \subset V \subset R$ and Q=R or V=R are obtained between the domains. Furthermore, in the grid i and with $S=S^{(0)}$, the following holds:

$$|S^{(t)}|=2^{2m+j}+(2t+1)2^m(2^{\lceil j/2 \rceil}+2^{\lfloor j/2 \rfloor})+(2t+1)^2 \quad \text{for } m \leq i \leq m+k, \; i=m+j \text{ and}$$

$$|S^{(t)}|=2^{2m+k+2q}+(2t+1)2^{m+q}(2^{\lceil k/2 \rceil}+2^{\lfloor k/2 \rfloor})+(2t+1)^2 \quad \text{for } m+k \leq i \leq n, \; i=m+k+q.$$

If we imagine the algorithm of a V-cycle in the binary tree, a process P in the j-th tree level will be as follows with $i=m+j$, $0<j<k$:

1) P receives data concerning T from the sons.

2) Relaxation (v_1-times) on T leads to the domain S.

3) Exchange of data concerning the j-th tree level for filling the domain R.

4) P executes the restriction on Q.

5) P sends coarse data from Q' to the father.

6) P receives coarse data concerning V from the father.

7) P executes the interpolation in the domain V.

8) Relaxation (v_2-times) on V leads to the domain U.

9) P sends data from U to its sons.

The process in the top (j=0) can treat the first m grids as in the sequential algorithm after having received from the sons data concerning G_m as in 1). This process will terminate with item 9), i.e., it sends data from G_m to the sons. The leaf processes (j=k) operate on domains of the grids G_i, $i \geq m+k$. That means, in this process the items 1) and 9) of the above algorithm are omitted for each i and items 5) and 6) for $i>m+k$.

The mapping of the tree structure onto a nearest-neighbour system (NN-system) of the size 2^k is done as in [KM84] like an 'H-tree' and is represented in fig. 2 by an example of 16 processors (i.e., k=4).

The algorithm represented here pursues the approach of restricting transport cost by minimising the number of transports. The disadvantage of this strategy is the fact that the domains to be actually processed by a processor, are quite extensive.

For the transport of data between two processors, we use the same model as in [KM84]. The transport cost is assumed to be $(a_1x+a_2)w$ for a data packet of x elements going from a source processor via w-1 intermediate processors to a target processor. We call a_1 the data parameter and a_2 the packet parameter. A system having dual port memories between two connected processors as communication facility can be considered as a prototype of this transport model.

The following specifies the cost in the NN-system ([KM84]). We distinguish between operation cost and transport cost. First, the operation cost of a V-cycle can be represented by the sum of the costs for the various grids G_i i=1,...,n.

$$A_c=a_0 \left(\sum_{i=1}^{n} \left(\sum_{l=0}^{2v_1-1} |S_i^{(2v_1-l)}| + \sum_{l=0}^{2v_2-1} |S_i^{(4v_2-l)}| \right)/2 + |Q_i|/4 + 3|V_i|/4 \right) \tag{1}$$

When calculating the operation cost we considered like in [GK84] that the application of the relaxation operator reduces the domain to which the relaxation operator is applied by one row of points with each half step of relaxation. We can reduce the cost in equation (1) for i=n in the last V-cycle, since no further step of the algorithm must be prepared.

With respect to the transport cost, we can distinguish between the data exchange (A_d) for neighbouring grids (G_i, G_{i+1}) according to items 1),5),6) and 9) of the algorithm and the exchange of boundary data (A_b) in a grid (item 3)).

$$A_d = \sum_{j=1}^{K} ((|R_i|/2)a_1 + 2a_2)w_j \text{ with } i=m+j. \tag{2}$$

$$A_b = \sum_{j=1}^{n-m} ((r|S_{xi}|a_1+a_2)w_j' + (r|R_{yi}|a_1+a_2)w_{j-1}') \text{ with } i=m+j \tag{3}$$

$|S_{xi}|$ and $|R_{yi}|$, respectively, denote the edge lengths of S_i or R_i in the direction of the x- or y-axis and $r=max\{4v_1+1, 4v_2\}$. Furthermore, the following holds for the path lengths w_j and w_j' (the term 1/2 is added to w_j for the overlay of transports in the source processor during the domain data exchange):

$w_j' = 2^{l(j)}$ with $l(j) = \lceil (k-j+1)/2 \rceil - 1$, $j=1,\dots,k$ and $w_j' = 1$ for $k \leq j \leq n-m$;

$w_j = 2^{l(j)-1} + 1/2$, $j=1,\dots,k$.

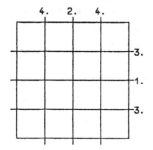

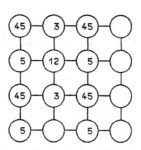

Fig. 1: j-th partition of the grid G_{m+4}, $j=1,\dots,4$.

Fig. 2: Mapping of the grid G_i to the NN-System. $k=4$, $i=1,\dots,n$, all processors work on the grid $i \geq 6$. The processor ⑫ is working on grids 1,2 and $i \geq 6$.

3. IMPLEMENTATION AND MEASUREMENTS

The parallel program for the above multigrid method has been implemented on the kit system DIRMU-25 of the University of Erlangen. The DIstributed Reconfigurable MUltiprocessor Kit allows the construction of a wide range of memory-coupled multiprocessor configurations with constrained neighbourhoods. Various problems of strong locality have already been solved on NN-fields, n-cubes, rings, trees and pyramids (cf., [HM85a], [HM85b]). At that time DIRMU was the only parallel computer available to test the algorithm, but the results of further implementations of multigrid methods have also shown its suitability for such problems by efficiency values > 0.9 (cf., [GH84]). The DIRMU basis is a general purpose microcomputer building block consisting of a processor module with private memory and a multiport-memory module (cf., fig. 3). For generating common memory domains, the P-module can access to the M-ports of a maximum of seven other modules via the P-ports and by means of plug-in cables, i.e. each multiport is part of the address space of all processors accessing it. A hardware priority control efficiently solves access conflicts. For more detailed information about the DIRMU-system we refer to [HM85b].

On account of the memory coupling, a parallel program, that makes full use of the DIRMU facilities, requires only very few transports when storing the data in the multiport (cf., [GH84]). Therefore, our model would not be applicable to such a program. For model testing, it was therefore necessary to simulate a system on DIRMU that was in accordance with the prototype described in chapter 2. On a 4x4 NN-system, the multiport of each processor was divided into four separate domains each of them being able to work as dual-port RAM in the communication with a neighbour. All required data are now located in the private memory. As example of the horizontal data exchange at grid level 4 (cf., fig. 2), fig. 4 illustrates the relationship of real structure and simulated structure for a part of the configuration.

The transport of grid boundaries is done by block transfer by means of high-speed assembler routines. Thus, we obtained a transport model similar to that described in chapter 2, except the difference of adding another parameter a_3 for each new grid row upon restoring the grid boundaries. For a data transport between multiport and private memory by the sender or the receiver, this will then yield the cost

$A_{sr}=(a_2+z(a_3+sa_1))/2$

where z is the number of rows and s is the number of columns, i.e., zs = x. The transfer of data by an intermediate processor is somewhat faster, since the packet is already structured suitably:

$A_t=a_2+a_3+xa_1$.

Hence, the cost for a data exchange via (w-1) intermediate processors is:

$A_d=2A_{sr}+(w-1)A_t$.

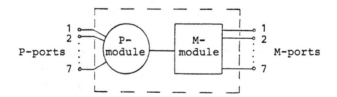

Fig. 3: DIRMU building block

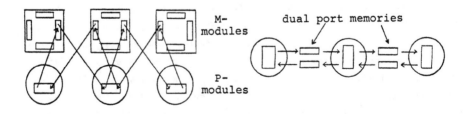

Fig. 4: Real and simulated system structures in data exchange

The quality of a simulation model can be estimated by the extent to which it tolerates program optimizations. In this respect, extensive efforts have been made, a.o. to determine the real speedup achievable by the method for relatively small grids. For example, it must be considered that the boundaries to be relaxed might be narrower at the finest level. Furthermore, the restriction of boundaries was dropped if these had been omitted for the father etc.

The program can execute V-cycles, W-cycles and full multigrid. Among the measurements performed, we want to demonstrate here only the measurements concerning two different V-cycles.

n	3	4	5	6	7
t_s	76	328	1377	5653	23000
t_p	68	190	446	932	2406

V-cycle with m=2, $\nu_1=\nu_2=1$

n	4	5	6	7	
t_s	581	2414	9885	40500	[msec]
t_p	443	1184	2758	5812	[msec]

V-cycle with m=3, $\nu_1=\nu_2=2$

Tab. 1: Comparison of runtimes for the serial program t_s and the parallel program t_p for different numbers of grid levels n and for 16 processors.

All measured times were allocated to computing cost, transport cost and overhead. The latter consists of synchronization cost and the passing through the control structure. In contrast to the computing cost, the overhead increases only linearly with increasing n and amounting to 110 µsec it is even inconsiderable for seven levels. By means of further measurements, the exact costs per grid for relaxation, restriction and interpolation were obtained as well as the parameters for the real transport model (cf., section 4). In our case, the influence of the transport cost is of minor importance according to the good transport design of the DIRMU system.

4. SIMULATION RESULTS AND COMPARISON WITH THE MEASUREMENTS

The simulation model is based on a group-sequential flow organization. It is assumed that not only the individual steps of the flow model of chapter 2 are processed sequentially, but also their partial steps. These are, for example, the relaxation half steps in the always assumed odd-even relaxation or the transport of boundary data to each of the four neighbours of a processor. In reality, this synchronization is not required. On account of the data dependencies of the algorithm, however, processing can hardly be done otherwise.

The cost of the various partial steps is considered in accordance with the formulas (1), (2) and (3). This requires a precise determination of the subsets of the grids involved in computation and transport. For example, the reduction of that set of correctly calculated points of a subdomain must be considered which is reduced by a boundary line after each relaxation step. Furthermore, at the boundary of the global domain, the absence of the 'inner' boundaries of the subdomains must be considered if only a few partitions are made in small systems.

As parameters we measured for the DIRMU-25 system 'rel'=401 μsec, 'res'=557 μsec and 'int'=335 μsec. For all cycle types and in two-dimensional problems we thus obtain a_0=401 with good approximation. Transport was carried out with a transport organization requiring 126 μsec per packet, 40.2 μsec per matrix row and 18.6 μsec per data element for the transport between the private memory of a processor and one of its communication memories. We consider only one row beginning per packet. By that, we obtain the cost function

$$(a_1 x + a_2) w = (37.2x + 332.4) w$$

for the transport of a packet of x elements via w-1 intermediate processors.

The results for simulation and measuring are represented in fig. 5 for different v_1, v_2 values in case of V-cycles. We consider the efficiency in each case. With a cost A(P) for an algorithm on P processors we understand as usual by speedup the function S(P)=A(1)/A(P) and by efficiency E(P)=S(P)/P. The quality of simulation is satisfactory even for the smallest systems. With decreasing system size, simulation tends to deliver somewhat too favourable efficiency values. This is due to the neglection of the cost for organizing the inner loops and the simplified transport model. Both costs are of the order $A(P)^{1/2}$.

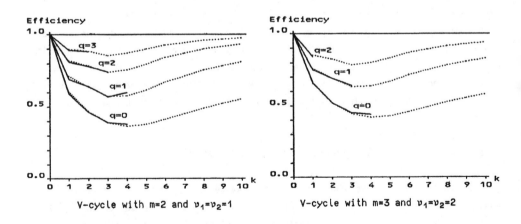

V-cycle with m=2 and $v_1 = v_2 = 1$

V-cycle with m=3 and $v_1 = v_2 = 2$

Fig. 5: Comparison of simulation and measurements.
—— measurements, ... simulation results, system size 2^k processors, problem size $(2^n-1)^2$ grid points in the finest grid (n=m+k+q).

5. FINAL REMARKS

With a single cost parameter for the average time requirements of a complex operator of the algorithm, with a maximum-precision count of the occurrences of these operators and by means of a linear transport cost function, we could obtain simulation results showing the quality of measuring results for a class of simple parallel multigrid algorithms for nearest-neighbour systems. The simple simulation model allowed an easy extension of the investigations to problems and systems of any size.

As far as small systems shall be considered by simulation, the size of the subproblems assigned to the processors must be estimated as exactly as possible. For larger systems, estimation can be less exact.

For systems with vector processors or in case of greater influence of the transport work, it may be necessary to use a larger number of parameters.

6. REFERENCES

[CS85] T. F. Chan and Y. Saad: Multigrid Algorithms on the Hypercube Multiprocessor; Yale University, report no. YALEU/DCS/RR-368, 1985.

[CS83] T. F. Chan and R. Schreiber: Parallel Networks for Multi-Grid Algorithms: Architecture and Complexity; Yale University, report no. YALEU/DCS/RR-262, 1983.

[GK84] B. Görg and O. Kolp: Parallele Rechnerarchitekturen für Mehrgitteralgorithmen; in Trottenberg and Wypior (eds.): Rechnerarchitekturen für die numerische Simulation auf der Basis superschneller Lösungsverfahren II, GMD-Studien no. 102, GMD, D-5205 St. Augustin, 1985.

[GH84] L. Geus, W. Henning, W. Seidl and J. Volkert: MG00-Implementierungen auf EGPA-Mehrprozessorsystemen; GMD-Studien no. 102, GMD, D-5205 St. Augustin, 1985.

[HM85a] W. Handler, E. Maehle and K. Wirl: DIRMU Multiprocessor Configurations; Proc. Int. Conf. on Parallel Processing, University Park, Pennsylvania, aug. 1985

[HM85b] W. Handler, E. Maehle and K. Wirl: The DIRMU-Testbed for High-performance Multiprocessor Configurations; Proc. 1st Int. Conf. on Supercomputing Systems, St. Petersburg, Florida, dec. 1985

[KM84] O. Kolp and H. Mierendorff: Systemunabhängige Organisation von Mehrgitterverfahren auf Parallelrechnern; in Ehrich (ed.): GI-14. Jahrestagung, Braunschweig, Okt. 1984, Proc.; Informatik-Fachberichte 88, Springer-Verlag.

[KM85a] O. Kolp and H. Mierendorff: Efficient Multigrid Algorithms for locally Constrained Parallel Systems; Proc. 2nd Copper Mountain Conf. on Multigrid Methods, march 31 - april 3, 1985, Copper Mountain, Colorado; subm. to AMC.

[KM85b] O. Kolp and H. Mierendorff: Bus Coupled Systems for Multigrid Algorithms; Proc. 2nd European Conf. on Multigrid Methods, Köln, oct. 1985; to appear.

[ST82] K. Stüben and U. Trottenberg: Multigrid Methods: Fundamental Algorithms, Model Problem Analysis and Applications; in Hackbusch and Trottenberg (eds.): Multigrid Methods, Proc. of the Conf. in Köln-Porz, nov. 1981; Lecture Notes in Mathematics, Springer, Berlin 1982.

Multitasking algorithms on CRAY computers for interval arithmetic Newton-like methods for a class of systems of nonlinear equations

Hartmut Schwandt

Technische Universität Berlin, Fachbereich Mathematik, MA 6 - 1

Straße des 17.Juni 135, D-1000 Berlin 12, FRG

Abstract: For several classes of systems of nonlinear equations interval arithmetic methods can be defined which converge to a solution essentially under the condition that an initial inclusion is known, i.e. the convergence can be said to be global. We consider vector algorithms for an interval arithmetic Newton-like method which is combined with an interval arithmetic "fast solver" for nonlinear systems with block tridiagonal Jacobian. As an example we consider a nine point discretization of a twodimensional nonlinear Dirichlet problem. More specifically we discuss efficient algorithms for multiprocessor computers with two and four vector processors. The algorithms are intended to use all processors in parallel as far as possible under the condition that the vector efficiency in the parallel tasks does not substantially decrease. We report numerical results for programs using the multitasking routines on 1 and 2-processor CRAY-X/MP.

1. Introduction: Systems of nonlinear equations

(1) $\qquad f(x) = 0, f(x) = Mx + \Phi(x), \qquad \Phi(x) = (\phi_i(x_i))_{i=1}^{N}, \Phi'(x) \geq O$,

with an $N \times N$ real block tridiagonal matrix

(2) $\qquad M = (-T, A, -T), \ A, T \ p \times p$ matrices, $N = pq, \ p = 2^{m+1} - 1, q = 2^{n+1} - 1$,

and a continuously differentiable componentwise nonnegative diagonal function Φ have to be frequently solved in difference methods for some types of partial BVP. We combine an interval arithmetic Newton-like method with an interval arithmetic block cyclic reduction method IBU used as a "fast solver" [6]

(3) $\qquad \forall \, k \in N_0: \quad x^{k+1} := \{m(x^k) - IBU(m(F^{\#}(x^k)), (m(F^{\#}(x^k)) - F'(x^k))(m(x^k) - x^k) + f(m(x^k)))\} \cap x^k$

where m(.) denotes the (vector, matrix of) midpoint(s) of an interval (vector, matrix) and where $F'(x^k)$ is the interval extension of the Jacobian of f in an interval vector x^k. With

$$F^{\#}(x^k) := M + D_k \, I, \ D_k := [\min_{1 \leq i,j \leq N} \{i(\Phi(X_{i,j}^{(k)}))\}, \max_{1 \leq i,j \leq N} \{s(\Phi(X_{i,j}^{(k)}))\}]$$

we include the diagonal of $F'(x^k)$ by an interval multiple of the identity matrix (i(.), s(.) denote lower and upper bounds of intervals) such that $F'(x^k) \subseteq F^{\#}(x^k)$ and that $m(F^{\#}(x^k))$ has the block tridiagonal form required for IBU. Similar methods have been introduced in [6,8,9], for example. Starting with an interval vector x^0 including the unique (see [5, 13.5.6]) solution y, $x^0 := [-M^{-1}|\Phi(o)|, M^{-1}|\Phi(o)|]$ with [5, 13.4.6c], for example, they yield a sequence of interval vectors x^k which all include y and which converge to y [4,6]. In contrast to most monotone methods we do not need any convexity condition.

The properties of interval arithmetic require a particular attention in order to obtain intervals of a reasonable width and to guarantee the applicability of all interval operations. We mention, for example, the subdistributivity for intervals: $A(B + C) \subseteq AB + AC$ and the treatment of systems (A, b) of equations with interval coefficients and linear form instead of linear systems $Ax = b$. Instead of a solution x we compute an inclusion interval vector **x** of the set of solutions $\{x \in \mathbb{R}^n | \ Ax = b, A \in \mathbf{A}, b \in \mathbf{b}\}$ which usually is not an interval vector. Interval methods are in most cases not simple modifications of floating point methods in which all real numbers are replaced by intervals. The necessary control of the interval width often leads to conflicts with respect to efficiency aspects.

The problems to which these methods can be applied suggest the use of a supercomputer. In [5] we have discussed aspects of their vectorization. In the present paper we are interested in efficient algorithms for the currently available 2- and 4-processor CRAY computers by using the CRAY multitasking routines. Multitasking on CRAY X-MP has been discussed by several authors, see [2,4] e.g.. In the present paper we discuss the applicability of multitasking to interval algorithms by taking account of interval arithmetic properties. The convergence to y of (3) or similar methods is based on inclusion properties of *IBU* which cannot be obtained for possible interval modifications of other common "fast solvers", in particular not for those using *FFT*. Therefore, an efficient vectorization (and an efficient multitasking) of *IBU* are crucial for the application of (3) on vector and multiprocessor computers.

2. Interval arithmetic block cyclic reduction method IBU: We repeat the definition of *IBU*, which can be considered as an extension and generalization of the Buneman algorithm [1], in a form which is suitable for (3): We are given a system (M',b), where **b** is an interval vector with N components and where $M' = M + m(D_k)$ I $= (-T, A', -T)$ preserves the block tridiagonal form of M in (2). We assume A' to be tridiagonal and T to be tridiagonal or diagonal. According to the block structure of M' we partition all vectors in q subvectors with p components, e.g. $\mathbf{x} = (\mathbf{x}_1,...,\mathbf{x}_q)$, $\mathbf{x}_i = (\mathbf{x}_{1,i},...,\mathbf{x}_{p,i})$, $1 \le i \le q$. For convenience we introduce for all vectors subvectors with index 0 and $q+1$ set to o. We define *IBU* as follows with

$$r := 0(1)k: \quad j := 1(1)2^r : G_j^{(r)} := A' + \{2\cos((2j-1)\pi/2^{r+1})\} T; \quad \mathbf{p}^0 := o; \quad \mathbf{q}^0 := \mathbf{b} :$$

reduction phase

$r := 0(1)n-1:$

    If $r+1 \le l$ then $LES := IGA$ else $LES := ICR$;

    $j := 2^{r+1}(2^{r+1})q + 1 - 2^{r+1}:$

$$\mathbf{p}_j^{r+1} := \mathbf{p}_j^r + LES(G_{2^r}^{(r)}, T\, LES(G_{2^r-1}^{(r)},...T\, LES(G_1^{(r)}, T(\mathbf{p}_{j-2^r}^r + \mathbf{p}_{j+2^r}^r) + \mathbf{q}_j^r)...);$$

$$\mathbf{q}_j^{r+1} := \mathbf{q}_{j-2^r}^r + \mathbf{q}_{j+2^r}^r + 2T\, \mathbf{p}_j^{r+1} ;$$

solution phase

$r := n(-1)0:$

    If $r \le l$ then $LES := IGA$ else $LES := ICR$;

    $j := 2^r(2^{r+1})q + 1 - 2^r:$

$$\mathbf{x}_j := \mathbf{p}_j^r + LES(G_{2^r}^{(r)}, T\, LES(G_{2^r-1}^{(r)} ... T\, LES(G_1^{(r)}, \mathbf{q}_j^r + T(\mathbf{x}_{j-2^r} + \mathbf{x}_{j+2^r})...) .$$

Depending on the number of simultaneous right-hand sides in each step we switch between the interval Gauß algorithm (*IGA*) and interval cyclic reduction (*ICR*) for tridiagonal interval systems. For small r many right-hand sides have to be treated and the usually totally recursive Gauß algorithm is sufficiently vectorizable. For larger r, where only one or a few right-hand side(s) have to be treated, we use cyclic reduction. The optimal level l cannot be determined analytically. But experience has shown that for $p > q$ $l = 1$ is always the optimal level, while for $p \le q$ there are several almost optimal levels l. An intervalarithmetic analogon of the Thomas algorithm cannot be used instead of *IGA* because this would be equivalent to the application of subdistributivity.

3. Simulation of an interval arithmetic: On none of the existing vector computers an interval arithmetic is available. Therefore we define a fully vectorizable simulation in FORTRAN. Interval operations can be defined by operations on their bounds. We represent intervals by two reals and interval vectors and matrices by two arrays for the upper and lower bounds, resp.. An interval vector subtraction $\mathbf{c} := \mathbf{a} - \mathbf{b}$, for example, is defined for $\mathbf{a} = (A_1,...,A_N)$, $\mathbf{b} = (B_1,...,B_N)$, $\mathbf{c} = (C_1,...,C_N)$, $A_i = [i(A_i), s(A_i)]$, $B_i = [i(B_i), s(B_i)]$ by

$$C_i = A_i - B_i = [i(C_i), s(C_i)] = [i(A_i) - s(B_i), s(A_i) - i(B_i)], \ 1 \le i \le N,$$

a general vector multiplication $\mathbf{c} := \mathbf{a} * \mathbf{b}$ by

$$C_i = A_i * B_i = [\min\{a_i\}, \max\{a_i\}], \ a_i := \{i(A_i)*i(B_i), i(A_i)*s(B_i), s(A_i)*i(B_i), s(A_i)*s(B_i)\}, \ 1 \le i \le N.$$

In order to get correctly rounded bounds we require that all rounding errors committed in the computation of the bounds by the floating-point arithmetic be included in the result interval. We achieve this by multiplying the bounds with $1 \pm FC$, $FC =$ relative machine precision, and by adding $\pm PM$, the smallest positive floating-point number x with $x + x \ne 0$. An interval vector subtraction, for example, is executed on a CRAY computer as

$$CL(I) = CVMGP(AL(I) - BU(I), (AL(I) - BU(I))*FC - PM, AL(I) - BU(I))$$

$$CU(I) = CVMGP((AU(I) - BL(I))*FC + PM, AU(I) - BL(I), AU(I) - BL(I))$$

for $1 \le I \le N$ with $FC = 2^{-48}$, $PM = 2^{-8190}$. For reasons of efficiency we do not carry out interval operations neither as a subroutine call nor by an individual loop for each operation. As far as possible we form loops with as many operations as possible. Because of the chaining and overlapping of operations this simulation is by far more efficient than comparable simulations on serial computers.

4. Multitasking on CRAY X-MP: We use the CRAY multitasking routines suitable for the creation of tasks on the subroutine level. In addition to the main program we start one (three) additional tasks before the iteration loop for (3) and we stop them after that loop. We synchronize the two (four) tasks by events [3]. The corresponding CRAY library routines EVPOST, EVCLEAR und EVWAIT require together up to about 3200 clock periods, i.e. about 30 μsec on a CRAY X-MP. While the tasks are running calls to other routines causing interrupts like I/O are avoided. We only measure the real time elapsed between the start of the first and the termination of the last task and the accumulated CPU-times. See also [4] for a detailed discussion of performance measurements on CRAY X-MP in multitasking mode.

5. Multitasking algorithms: The definition of interval operations by floating point operations on their bounds suggests the definition of 2-processor algorithms with two tasks treating lower and upper bounds independently as far as possible. The application of *IBU* reduces in the present case to

$$IBU(M, \mathbf{b}) = [IBU(M, i(\mathbf{b})), IBU(M, s(\mathbf{b}))],$$

i.e. to two independent applications of *IBU* to point (noninterval) systems, because *IGA* and *ICR* are applied to (point) M-Matrices $G_j^{(r)}$, because $T \ge O$ and because we have defined *IBU* without interval vector subtractions (In addition $IBU(M,\mathbf{b})$ is an optimal inclusion). Therefore, we can create two independent tasks in each of which we have to apply the simulation of the appropriate one-sided rounding. Most of the remaining parts of (3) are also reducible. Only the computation of $m(\mathbf{x}^k)$, $m(\mathbf{F}^{\#}(\mathbf{x}^k))$ and - depending on ϕ - of $\phi(m(\mathbf{x}^k))$ and $\Phi'(\mathbf{x}^k)$ has to be carried out by a splitting according to the indices of the unknowns. At these points and after the convergence test, the two tasks must be synchronized. In total we need 4-5 synchronization points in each iteration step. The synchronization overhead (abbreviated by SO in the sequel) is completely negligible. The arithmetic work for those operations in *IGA* and *ICR* which are independent of the right-hand sides is also negligible (less than 1% of the total CPU-time) as we scale all systems such that *IGA* and *ICR* have to be applied to coefficient matrices of the form $(-1, D, -1)$. These operations are carried out before reactivating the two tasks for *IBU* because their results are needed in both tasks. We denote this algorithm by *M2-UL*.

Another possibility consists in the definition of tasks according to the block structure of M, i.e. that of *IBU*. Fig.1 illustrates the case $n = 3$, i.e. $q = 15$. Each line, from the top to the bottom, contains the blocks involved in the respective step r of *IBU*, $r := 1(1)n$, $r := n(-1)0$. The arrows indicate the data dependencies. The lack of horizontal arrows proves that there are no dependencies between the blocks in all steps r. This is valid for all informations needed or computed in a particular block, i.e. $p_j^{(r)}$, $q_j^{(r)}$ or *LES*. According to the data dependencies between the different steps we obtain an algorithm with three main steps carried out in the following order:

I :   reduction phase in parallel for the blocks $1,..,(q-1)/2$ and $(q+1)/2+1,..,q$, resp., for $r := 1(1)n-1$;

II :   reduction and solution phase in two parallel tasks for lower and upper bounds of block $(q+1)/2$
      for $r := 1(1)n$, $r := n$;

III :   solution phase in parallel for the blocks $1,..,(q-1)/2$ and $(q+1)/2+1,..,q$, resp., for $r := n-1(-1)0$.

The operations in step II on the single block $(q+1)/2$ have to be splitted into separate operations on the lower and the upper bounds. We denote this algorithm by *M2-BL*. In contrast to *M2-UL* there are two synchronization points in *IBU* (between I and II and between II and III). In the remaining parts of (3), however, we can at least save one synchronization point when compared to *M2-UL*.

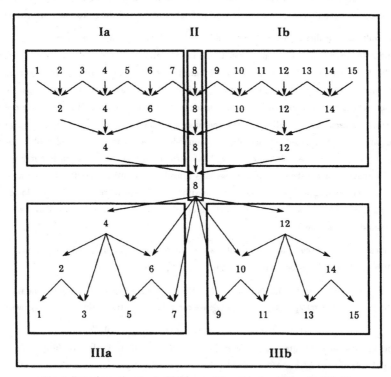

Fig. 1: Data dependencies in *IBU* for $q = 15$ and block splitting for *M2-BL*

The combination of the ideas leading to *M2-UL* and *M2-BL* almost immediately yields a 4-processor algorithm: first we create two tasks by separating upper and and lower bounds. Then we divide each task into two tasks according to the block structure. Some loops outside *IBU* in (3) for which a separation of the bounds is not possible, are splitted into four parts according to the block structure. This version *M4-1* has the drawback that for the block $(q+1)/2$ in *IBU*, i.e step II in Fig.1, only two tasks (for lower and upper bounds) are active. Although the computation time needed for II is not decisive (about 10% - 15% of the total computation time), it is important enough to reduce the speed-up factor measurably.

We consider a second 4-processor algorithm *M4-2* in which all 4 tasks also run in step II in *IBU*. Step II consists of vector additions, multiplications with T and sequences of consecutive applications of *LES*. Therefore, we have to split the applications of *LES* to lower and upper bounds, resp., a second time by splitting according to the blocks. In *ICR* in step II we encounter on the component level the same situation like in *IBU* on the block level illustrated in Fig.1. In each application of *LES* the computation of the component $(p+1)/2$ in block $(q+1)/2$ must be synchronized. In order to avoid a further synchronization and to create sufficiently large parallel portions of code, we always carry out in all four tasks the respective operations for the solution part of one application of *ICR* and the reduction part of the next application. We apply *ICR* independently on the lower and the upper bounds. Both applications are splitted similarly to Fig.1, but now at the component level for the components $1,..,(p-1)/2$ and $(p+1)/2+1,...,p$. We omit the details of this rather complicated algorithm in which several operations have to be splitted or computed twice or even deferred due to the necessary synchronization with respect to the component $(p+1)/2$. The granularity of the tasks decreases by orders of magnitude in step II. Satisfactory speed-up factors require a much larger problem size than for the 2-processor algorithms.

In all four multitasking algorithms we do not split inner loops, whenever possible, in order not to decrease the vector length. In the case of single loops or specific data dependencies like for $p<q$ this is obviously impossible. On the other hand, a similar effect occurs when lower and upper bounds are separated. In these cases loop bodies have to be splitted. Then vectors used in common by both bounds have to be loaded twice in separate loops. Also, overlapped or chained operations are separated. Due to the extensive use of COMMON blocks forced by the CRAY multitasking concept we only need a few and small additional arrays in the multitasked algorithms when compared to the 1-processor version. The program code, however, has to be considerably extended in our problem: we are able to create tasks which are well balanced, but whose code differs such that in several cases different subroutines have to be written. The necessity to avoid synchronizations often leads to another difficulty: the synchronization points do not coincide with the bounds of subroutines. The aim to keep processes busy as long as possible forces us to carry out portions of code in parallel which are spread over several, sometimes nested subroutines.

6. Numerical results: We consider the 9-point-discretization with central differential quotients and a mesh size $h=1/(p+1)$ in both directions of the nonlinear Dirichlet problem

$$u_{xx}+u_{yy}=e^{u/10} \text{ on } I=[0,1]\times[0,(q+1)/(p+1)], u(x,y)=(x+2y)/(q+1) \text{ on the boundary of } I$$

leading to $A=(-4, 20+m(D_k),-4)_p$, $T=(1,4,1)_p$. We control the iteration (3) by the convergence criterion

$$\max\{|||s(x^k)-s(x^{k-1})|||_\infty, |||i(x^k)-i(x^{k-1})|||_\infty\}<10^{-6}.$$

All examples have been computed with the compiler version CFT 1.14. In Table 1 we show results for the 2-processor algorithms *M2-BL* and *M2-UL* and for the corresponding 1-processor algorithm on a CRAY X-MP/22. The speed-up by multitasking is given in Col.4(9) by the quotient of the realtime (wall-clock time) for *M2-BL(-UL)* and the CPU-time for the 1-processor algorithm. In order to get further information on the speed-up we also note the accumulated CPU-times for *M2-BL(-UL)* indicating the CPU-time for these algorithms when executed on a single processor. Then, Col.5(10) show that $M2$-$BL($-$UL)$ are almost optimally balanced, i.e. the two processors are almost equally used. Due to the very small number of synchronisation points the SO is not measurable. Col.6(11) reveal the unevitable degradation of the vector performance caused by the transition from one-processor to two-processor algorithm. This seems to be the main reason for the difference between the overall speed-up factors in Col. 4(9) and the optimal factor of 2. The speed-up strongly depends on the vector performance of the algorithm. The performance increases for increasing p, i.e. decreasing q ($N = pq$), and if a version with (close to) optimal l is used. In $M2$-BL single or - because of data dependencies- even the innermost of nested loops have to be partitioned. In $M2$-UL where the tasks are defined by the separation of lower and upper bounds the effect of reduced vector lengths can mostly be avoided, but loop bodies have to be splitted by separating the operations concerning upper and lower bounds. The difference between $M2$-UL and $M2$-BL remains rather small. The speed-up is remarkably high for optimal and close to optimal l. We note the results for $l = 1$, $l = n + 1$ and optimal l.

p	q	l	ct 1-P (1)	rt M2-UL (2)	acc. ct M2-UL (3)	(1):(2) (4)	(3):(2) (5)	(3):(1) (6)	rt M2-BL (7)	acc. ct M2-BL (8)	(1):(7) (9)	(8):(7) (10)	(8):(1) (11)
255	255	1	3.08	1.67	3.30	1.84	1.97	1.09	1.64	3.19	1.88	1.95	1.04
		*2	3.03	1.65	3.25	1.84	1.97	1.07	1.61	3.13	1.89	1.95	1.03
		7	4.37	2.75	5.39	1.59	1.96	1.23	2.68	5.22	1.63	1.95	1.20
31	4095	1	10.44	5.90	11.65	1.76	1.98	1.12	5.77	11.37	1.79	1.97	1.10
		*8	9.62	5.39	10.68	1.77	1.98	1.12	5.39	10.18	1.80	1.97	1.09
		11	10.50	6.12	12.07	1.71	1.97	1.15	5.81	11.42	1.80	1.97	1.09
4095	31	*1	2.38	1.23	2.40	1.94	1.95	1.01	1.27	2.47	1.87	1.94	1.04
		4	3.75	2.41	4.69	1.56	1.95	1.25	2.33	4.37	1.61	1.88	1.17

Table 1: $M2$-BL and $M2$-UL on a CRAY X-MP/22 (*: optimal l, ct: CPU-time, rt: realtime, in sec)

In Table 2 we report results for a simulation of the 4-processor algorithms $M4$-1 and $M4$-2 on a CRAY X-MP/22 in single processor mode. Col.12(14) contain similarly to Col.3(8) the accumulated CPU-times for 4 processors, i.e. the CPU-time measured by two calls to the system function SECOND() before the start of the first and after the termination of the last task. This time also includes the SO. While the latter is negligible in $M2$-BL, $M2$-UL, $M4$-1 and, if $p > q$, $M4$-2, it becomes significant for $M4$-2 if $p < < q$. Therefore, we also note the accumulated CPU-time needed by the original algorithm $M4$-2 excluding the SO (Col.15). In order to obtain this time, we determine in all four tasks individually the CPU-times between each pair of consecutive synchronization points and add all these times. The comparison of the accumulated CPU-time in the Col.12(15) with the CPU-time of the 1-processor algorithm in Col.1 yields in Col.13(17) factors indicating the performance degradation for $M4$-1 ($M4$-2) similarly to Col.6(11) for $M2$-$BL($-$UL)$. The degradation grows from $M2$-$BL($-$UL)$ to $M4$-1 and then to $M4$-2 due to a further algorithmic overhead. The quotients of Col. 14 and 15 illustrate in Col.20 the SO for $M4$-2. The number of synchronizations in step II in IBU depends on q. For $p > > q$ this number is negligible; it remains small for $p = q$ and becomes important for $q > > p$. For the determination of the theoretically possible speed-up we compute the minimal theoretical CPU-time for $M4$-2 on four processors. We take the above mentioned CPU-times between each pair of consecutive synchronization points and compute in each case the

p	q	l	acc. ct $M4$-1 (12)	(12):(1) (13)	acc.ct $M4$-2 SO incl. (14)	acc.ct $M4$-2 SO excl. (15)	theor. min. ct $M4$-2 (16)	(15):(1) (17)	(16):(1) (18)	(15):(16) (19)	(14):(15) (20)
255	255	1	3.36	1.09	3.63	3.54	0.915	1.15	3.37	3.87	1.03
		*2	3.34	1.10	3.61	3.52	0.910	1.16	3.33	3.81	1.04
		7	6.82	1.56	7.09	6.99	1.792	1.60	3.15	3.90	1.01
31	4095	1	12.84	1.23	14.92	13.39	3.494	1.28	2.99	3.83	1.11
		*8	11.54	1.21	14.70	12.90	3.378	1.34	2.85	3.81	1.14
		11	12.93	1.23	16.10	14.27	3.734	1.36	2.81	3.82	1.12
4095	31	*1	2.57	1.08	2.62	2.61	0.690	1.10	3.45	3.78	1.00
		4	5.71	1.52	5.73	5.72	1.474	1.53	2.54	3.88	1.00

Table 2:   simulation of multitasking for $M4$-1 and $M4$-2 on a CRAY X-MP/22

(rt: real time, ct: CPU-time, in sec, *: optimal l)

maximum over all processors with respect to portions of code executed in parallel. The sum of the maxima yields the minimal CPU-time for $M4$-2, i.e. a lower bound for the realtime. This bound is independent of the SO. Col.19 indicates the load balance, i.e. the degree of parallel use of the four processors. A comparison with Col.5(10) shows, that the values have almost doubled, i.e. the load balance has been almost conserved when passing from two to four processors. Finally Col.18 shows the maximal possible speed-up factors (SO excluded). For $p > > q$ they are satisfactory in view of the fact that they are maintained in a rather complex algorithm.

In conclusion we remark that the efficiency of the multiprocessor algorithms strongly depends on the vector efficiency. The SO is negligible except for $M4$-2 when $p < < q$. It could be reduced by a mechanism like the microtasking on the loop level announced by CRAY [3]. The difference of Col.14 and 15 illustrates, however, the degree of a possible improvement. When the SO is reduced, it is also possible to work with a smaller granularity of the algorithm, i.e. to decrease the algorithmic overhead necessary to create parallel portions of code. The difference of Col. 15 and 12 illustrates the limits of this measure. A further significant speed-up by algorithmic means seems not to be possible as the algorithms are vectorized as far as possible and because they are almost optimally balanced (Col.5,10,19).

Theoretically, the above mentioned algorithms can be modified for larger numbers of vector processors if the problem size guarantees a sufficiently large granularity. Fig. 1 shows that the steps Ia and Ib have the same structure than the whole reduction phase. Similarly, the steps IIIa and IIIb have the structure of the whole solution phase. The subdivision can be recursively continued depending on the system size. In view of the limited parallelism in steps like II the speed-up factors decrease. On the other hand the program for $M4$-2 seems to be the limit for a program using multitasking in the presently available form and whose code has a reasonable complexity. For larger numbers of processors easier mechanisms like microtasking are necessary for the above mentioned problems.

Acknowledgements: I am indebted to Dr.F.Hossfeld, KFA Jülich, for providing me the access to the CRAY X-MP/22 .

References:

[1] B.L.Buzbee, G.H.Golub, C.W.Nielson: On DirectMethods for Solving Poisson's Equation,
     SIAM J.Num.Anal. 7(1970), 627-656.

[2] S.S.Chen, J.J.Dongarra, C.C.Hsiung: Multiprocessing for linear algebra algorithms on the CRAY X-MP-2:
     Experience with small granularity, J.Par.Distr.Comp. 1(1984), 22-31.

[3] CRAY Multitasking User's Guide, Ref. SN-0222 B, CRAY Research, Mendota Heights, 1986.

[4] R.W.Hockney: (r_∞, $n_{1/2}$, $s_{1/2}$) measurements on the 2-CPU CRAY X-MP, Par.Comp. 2(1985), 1-14.

[5] J.Ortega, W.C.Rheinboldt: Iterative Solution of Nonlinear Equations in Several
     Variables, Academic Press, New York, 1970.

[6] H.Schwandt: Almost globally convergent interval methods for discretizations of
     nonlinear elliptic partial differential equations, to appear in SIAM J.Num.Anal.

[7] Schwandt,H.: Newton-like interval methods for large systems of nonlinear equations on
     vector computers, Comp. Phys. Comm. 37(1985), 223-232.

[8] H.Schwandt: An interval arithmetic approach for the construction of an almost globally
     convergent method for the solution of the nonlinear Poisson equation on the unit square,
     SIAM J.Sc.St.Comp. 5(1984), 427-452.

[9] H.Schwandt: The solution of nonlinear elliptic Dirichlet problems on rectangles by
     almost globally convergent interval methods, SIAM J.Sc.St.Comp., 6(1985), 617-638.

FULL RECURSIVE FORM OF THE ALGORITHMS FOR FAST

GENERALIZED FOURIER TRANSFORMS

B.J. JECHEV
Center of Robotics, Higher Institute of Mechanical
and Electrical Engineering
Sofia 1156, Bulgaria

Abstract

In this paper the full recursive forms of the
discrete Fourier , Hadamard, Paley and Walsh
transforms are developed. The algebraic properties and computational complexity of the
GFT are investigated on the basis of a theoretical group approach and a matrix pseudoinversion. The approach considered reveals common
and sometimes unexpected features of these
transforms, the parallel realization of the
algorithms becoming thus possible.

The discrete Fourier and Hadamard-Walsh Transforms are among the
basic algorithms for digital signal processing. As shown in [1] they
are the extreme cases of decomposition through the characters of Abelian groups. If for instance, the dimension is N = 1024, there are
42 different groups, and hence 42 decompositions, which we shall call
Generalized Fourier Transforms (GFT).

The problem of performing any of the GFT is a typical autonomous
not-Π task [2]. The theoretical group approach makes it possible for
the symmetry of such a task to be analyzed and fast algorithms for parallel processing to be designed.

In this paper the techniques of abstract harmonic analysis
[3,4,5] and matrix pseudoinversion [6,9] are used to develop the full
recursive forms of some of the GFT for the most frequent case of transform dimension $N = 2^n$. The algebraic properties and the computation
complexity are investigated. All the algorithms are obtained through
a general design procedure and not as different independant problems,
solved by using specific approaches.

I. Discrete Fourier Transform and its Full Recursive form.

The standard cyclic convolution

$$y_k = \sum_{0 \leq l \leq N-1} x_l h_{k-1}; \quad k,l = 0,1,\ldots, (N-1)(\bmod N), \tag{1}$$

can be represented in the following matrix-vector form:

$$y_k = \vec{x}^T R_N^k S_N \vec{h}$$

$$\vec{x} = [x_0 \vdots x_1 \cdots x_{N-1}]^T, \quad \vec{h} = [h_0 \vdots h_1 \cdots h_{N-1}]^T, \quad \vec{y} = [y_0 \vdots y_1 \cdots y_{N-1}]^T$$

$$R_N = [\delta_{k-1,l}], \quad S_N = [\delta_{k,N-1}], \quad k,l = 0,1,\ldots,(N-1)(\bmod N) \tag{2}$$

δ_{ij} - Kronecker symbol.

The vectors $\vec{x}$, $\vec{h}$ and $\vec{y}$ are considered to be functions over the cyclic group $C_N = \langle r | r^N = 1 \rangle$. The orthogonal matrices R_N and S_N have a mirror image form:

$$R_4 = \begin{bmatrix} 0 & 0 & 0 & 1 \\ 1 & 0 & 0 & 0 \\ 0 & 1 & 0 & 0 \\ 0 & 0 & 1 & 0 \end{bmatrix}, \quad S_4 = \begin{bmatrix} 1 & 0 & 0 & 0 \\ 0 & 0 & 0 & 1 \\ 0 & 0 & 1 & 0 \\ 0 & 1 & 0 & 0 \end{bmatrix}, \quad N = 4. \tag{3}$$

If D_N is dehedral group [7,8] with generators ρ and σ,

$$D_N = \langle \rho,\sigma | \rho^N = \sigma^2 = 1, \rho^k \sigma = \sigma \rho^{-k} \rangle, \tag{4}$$

then R_N and S_N satisfy its defining relations and hence are a linear representation on D_N.

The discrete Fourier transform is given by the matrix $\mathcal{F}_N = [w_N^{kl}]$, $W_N = \exp(-j2\pi/N)$, $k,l = 0,1,\ldots, N-1$. A basic feature of $\mathcal{F}_N$ is to transform the cyclic convolution into an algebraic multiplication. So

$$\mathcal{F}_N^{-1} = \frac{1}{N} S_N \mathcal{F}_N = \frac{1}{N} \mathcal{F}_N S_N = \frac{1}{N} [w_N^{-kl}],$$

$$\mathcal{F}_N^{-1} R_N^k \mathcal{F}_N = \mathrm{diag}\,(1, w_N^{-k},\ldots, w_N^{-(N-1)k}). \tag{5}$$

Thus

$$y_k = \frac{1}{N} (\mathcal{F}_N \vec{x})^T \mathrm{diag}\,(1, w_N^{-k},\ldots, w_N^{-(N-1)k}) \mathcal{F}_N \vec{h}. \tag{6}$$

If $\mathcal{F}_N \vec{x} = [X_i]$, $\mathcal{F}_N \vec{h} = [H_i]$, then it follows from (6) that $y_k = 1/N \sum_i X_i H_i w_N^{-ik}$, and the number of active multiplications $\{X_i H_i\}$

when determining $\vec{y}$ from (1) and (2) equals N, i.e. the Winograd bound
[10].

The cyclic group characters C_N [4,5,7] are rows (and columns) of the symmetrical matrix $\mathcal{F}_N$. As shown in [1], they can be represented as an expansion of its cyclic N/2-th order subgroup characters

$$\mathcal{X}_{N,k} = [\mathcal{X}_{\frac{N}{2},k} \mid \mathcal{X}_{\frac{N}{2},k} . \mathcal{W}_N^k], \quad \mathcal{X}_{N,k+N} = [\mathcal{X}_{\frac{N}{2},k} \mid -\mathcal{X}_{\frac{N}{2},k} . \mathcal{W}_N^k], \tag{7}$$

$$k = 0, 1, \ldots, N/2 - 1$$

To preserve the result $\mathcal{F}_N\vec{x}$, when the columns of $\mathcal{F}_N$ are permutated in accordance with (7), it is necessary to transform $\vec{x}$ into a vector, whose first half is composed of the even coordinates of $\vec{x}$, and the second half of the odd ones. The selection of the coordinates can be represented in a matrix form:

$$\vec{x}_e = E_{\frac{N}{2}} \vec{x}, \quad \vec{x}_o = O_{\frac{N}{2}} \vec{x}, \tag{8}$$

where $E_{\frac{N}{2}}$ and $O_{\frac{N}{2}}$ are $\frac{N}{2}$ x N - dimensional matrices, obtained from the N x N unit matrix I_N by crossing out the odd rows 1, 3, 5, ..., and the even rows 0, 2, 4, ... Their elements are $e_{kl} = \delta_{2k,1}$ and $O_{kl} = \delta_{2k+1,1}$, $k = 0, 1, \ldots \frac{N}{2} - 1$, $1 = 0, 1, \ldots, N-1$ respectively.

Let U_N and L_N be $\frac{N}{2}$ x N matrices with elements $u_{ik} = \delta_{ik}$ and

$$1_{ik} = \delta_{i+\frac{N}{2},k}, \quad i = 0, 1, \ldots, \frac{N}{2} - 1, \quad k = 0, 1, \ldots, N-1,$$ i.e. the upper and lower "halves" of the unit matrix I_N.

If $\mathcal{R}(A)$ and $\mathcal{N}(A)$ are the space of columns of A and the null-space respectively, and $\mathcal{R}^{\perp}$ is the orthogonal complement of $\mathcal{R}$, then the following relation can be developed from the fundamental theorem of linear algebra [6,9]:

$$\mathcal{R}(L_{\frac{N}{2}}^T) = \mathcal{R}^{\perp}(U_{\frac{N}{2}}^T) = \mathcal{N}(U_{\frac{N}{2}}),$$

$$\mathcal{R}(E_{\frac{N}{2}}^T) = \mathcal{R}^{\perp}(O_{\frac{N}{2}}^T) = \mathcal{N}(O_{\frac{N}{2}}). \tag{9}$$

The orthogonality of the spaces in (9) is the most important item in paralleling the algorithm to determine $\mathcal{F}\vec{x}$. Let us denote by A^+ the pseudoinverse matrix of A [6,9]. The projectors on $\mathcal{R}(U_{\frac{N}{2}}^T)$ and $\mathcal{R}(L_{\frac{N}{2}}^T)$,

$$\hat{e}_1 = U_{\frac{N}{2}}^+ U_{\frac{N}{2}} \quad \text{and} \quad \hat{e}_2 = L_{\frac{N}{2}}^+ L_{\frac{N}{2}} \quad \text{respectively are mutually orthogonal} - e_1 e_2 = 0,$$

and they define a decomposition of the unit as follows: $e_1 + e_2 = I_N$. This refers to the projectors on $\mathcal{R}(E_{\frac{N}{2}}^T)$ and $\mathcal{R}(U_{\frac{N}{2}}^T)$ as well.

It follows from (7), (8) and (9) that

$$U_{\frac{N}{2}} \mathcal{F}_N = \mathcal{F}_{\frac{N}{2}} E_{\frac{N}{2}} + D_{\frac{N}{2}} \mathcal{F}_{\frac{N}{2}} O_{\frac{N}{2}} ,$$

$$L_{\frac{N}{2}} \mathcal{F}_N = \mathcal{F}_{\frac{N}{2}} E_{\frac{N}{2}} - D_{\frac{N}{2}} \mathcal{F}_{\frac{N}{2}} O_{\frac{N}{2}} , \tag{10}$$

$$D_{\frac{N}{2}} = \text{diag} (1, \omega_N, \ldots , \omega_N^{N/2-1}).$$

The following formula is obtained by multiplying (10) by $U_{\frac{N}{2}}^+ = U_{\frac{N}{2}}^T$ and $L_{\frac{N}{2}}^+ = L_{\frac{N}{2}}^T$, and then summing

$$\mathcal{F}_N = [U_{\frac{N}{2}}^T + L_{\frac{N}{2}}^T]\mathcal{F}_{\frac{N}{2}} E_{\frac{N}{2}} + [U_{\frac{N}{2}}^T - L_{\frac{N}{2}}^T]D_{\frac{N}{2}}\mathcal{F}_{\frac{N}{2}} O_{\frac{N}{2}} , \tag{11}$$

which represents the full recursive form of the FFT with time decimation (11). After transposing (11), the algorithm with frequency decimation is obtained:

$$\mathcal{F}_N = E_{\frac{N}{2}}^T \mathcal{F}_{\frac{N}{2}} [U_{\frac{N}{2}} + L_{\frac{N}{2}}] + O_{\frac{N}{2}}^T \mathcal{F}_{\frac{N}{2}} D_{\frac{N}{2}} [U_{\frac{N}{2}} - L_{\frac{N}{2}}] . \tag{12}$$

The imitial transform $\mathcal{F}_N$ is thus split into independent parallel transforms $\mathcal{F}_{\frac{N}{2}}$. If $(N/2-2)$ multiplications for D_N are assumed, the total number of multiplications m_N and additions s_N (on condition that $m_4 = s_1 = 0$) will be:

$$m_N = 2m_{\frac{N}{2}} + \frac{N-2}{2} = (n-3)\frac{N}{2}+2,$$

$$s_N = 2s_{\frac{N}{2}} + N = nN, \quad N = 2^n . \tag{13}$$

The real multiplications and additions are:

$$m_N^r = 3[(n-3)\frac{N}{2} + 2] ,$$

$$s_N^r = 2s_N + 3m_N = (7n-9)\frac{N}{2} + 6 . \tag{14}$$

This result can be improved. By using the equation $2 \cos(\frac{2\pi 1}{N})\omega_N^1 =$

$= 1 + W_{\frac{N}{2}}^{1}$ and (5), the following expressions are obtained:

$$\mathcal{F}_{\frac{N}{2}} D_{\frac{N}{2}} = (I_{\frac{N}{2}} + R_{\frac{N}{2}}^{T})\mathcal{F}_{\frac{N}{2}} \text{ diag}^{+} (c_0, c_1, \ldots, c_{\frac{N}{2}-1}) + V_{\frac{N}{2}}, \tag{15}$$

$$c_k = 2\cos(2\pi k/N), \quad V_{\frac{N}{2}} = [v_{ik}], \quad v_{ik} = -j(-1)^{i}\delta_{\frac{N}{4},k} .$$

In that way (12) obtains the form:

$$\mathcal{F}_N = E_{\frac{N}{2}}^{T} \mathcal{F}_{\frac{N}{2}} [U_{\frac{N}{2}} + L_{\frac{N}{2}}] + 0_{\frac{N}{2}}^{T} \left\{ (I_{\frac{N}{2}} + R_{\frac{N}{2}}^{T}) \times \right.$$

$$\left. \times \mathcal{F}_{\frac{N}{2}} \text{ diag}^{+}(c_0, c_1, \ldots, c_{\frac{N}{2}-1}) + V_{\frac{N}{2}} \right\} [U_{\frac{N}{2}} - L_{\frac{N}{2}}].$$

This is the full recursive form of the Rader-Brenner algorithm [12]. The complex multiplications in (12) by $D_{\frac{N}{2}}$ are reduced to multiplications by real constants $\left\{ C_k \right\}$. Hence

$$m_N^{r} = 2[(n-3)\frac{N}{2} + 2], \quad s_N^{r} = 4nN . \tag{17}$$

Since a symmetrical matrix Q_N exists, for which $E_{\frac{N}{2}} = U_N Q_N$, and $0_{\frac{N}{2}} = L_{\frac{N}{2}} Q_N$, the following N x N permutation matrix $P_{N,n}$ is formed:

$$P_{N,0} = Q_N = \begin{bmatrix} E_{\frac{N}{2}} \\ 0_{\frac{N}{2}} \end{bmatrix}, \quad P_{N,k} = \text{diag } (\underset{1}{Q_{\frac{N}{2}k}}, \underset{2}{Q_{\frac{N}{2}k}}, \ldots, \underset{2^k}{Q_{\frac{N}{2}k}}) P_{N,k-1}, \tag{18}$$

which makes it possible for the calculations in place to be carried out [10,11]. $P_{N,n}$ permutates the coordinates of the input or output vector, all the matrices $E_{\frac{N}{2}}$ and $0_{\frac{N}{2}}$ being changed into $U_{\frac{N}{2}}$ and $L_{\frac{N}{2}}$ in the above full recursive forms. The permutation is equivalent to a binary inversion of the coordinate's index [11]. In such a way, (11), for instance is transformed into:

$$\mathcal{F}_N = \mathcal{F}_N^{0} P_{N,n}, \mathcal{F}_2^{0} = \begin{bmatrix} 1 & 1 \\ 1 & -1 \end{bmatrix},$$

$$\mathcal{F}_N^{0} = [U_{\frac{N}{2}}^{T} + L_{\frac{N}{2}}^{T}] \mathcal{F}_N^{0} U_{\frac{N}{2}} + [U_{\frac{N}{2}}^{T} - L_{\frac{N}{2}}^{T}] D_{\frac{N}{2}} \mathcal{F}_{\frac{N}{2}}^{0} L_{\frac{N}{2}} . \tag{19}$$

2. Full Forms of the Hadamard, Paley and Walsh Transforms

The Hadamard, Paley and Walsh transforms are decompositions through characters of the dyadical group, which is a direct product of cyclic groups: $C_2^n = C_2 \times C_2 \times \ldots \times C_2$ [1,7,8]. They differ in ordering the characters in the rows of the corresponding symmetrical matrices.

The short exact sequences [7] of the dyadical group C_2^n and its group of characters $\hat{C}_2^n$,

$$1 \to C_2 \xrightarrow{\alpha} C_2^n \xrightarrow{\beta} C_2^{n-1} \to 1; \quad 1 \to \hat{C}_2^{n-1} \xrightarrow{\hat{\beta}} \hat{C}_2^n \xrightarrow{\hat{\alpha}} \hat{C}_2 \to 1 , \tag{20}$$

make it possible for the following full recursive forms to be obtained:

a) Hadamard's transform

$$\mathcal{H}_N = [U_{\frac{N}{2}}^T + L_{\frac{N}{2}}^T] \mathcal{H}_{\frac{N}{2}} U_{\frac{N}{2}} + [U_{\frac{N}{2}}^T - L_{\frac{N}{2}}^T] \mathcal{H}_{\frac{N}{2}} L_{\frac{N}{2}}. \tag{21}$$

b) Paley's transform

$$P_N = E_{\frac{N}{2}}^T P_{\frac{N}{2}} [U_{\frac{N}{2}} + L_{\frac{N}{2}}] + O_{\frac{N}{2}}^T P_{\frac{N}{2}} [U_{\frac{N}{2}} - L_{\frac{N}{2}}] . \tag{22}$$

c) Walsh's transform

$$W_N = G_N P_N; \quad G_N = \text{diag}\ (G_{\frac{N}{2}}, D_{\frac{N}{2}}^r G_{\frac{N}{2}}); \quad G_2 = I_2 ,$$

$$D_{\frac{N}{2}}^r = Id_{ij}^r I, \quad d_{ij}^r = \delta_{i, \frac{N}{2}-1-j}, i,j = 0, 1, \ldots, \frac{N}{2} - 1 , \tag{23}$$

$$W_N = E_{\frac{N}{2}}^T W_{\frac{N}{2}} [U_{\frac{N}{2}} + L_{\frac{N}{2}}^r] + O_{\frac{N}{2}}^T W_{\frac{N}{2}} [U_{\frac{N}{2}} - L_{\frac{N}{2}}^r]$$

$$L_{\frac{N}{2}}^r = D_N^r L_{\frac{N}{2}} = [1_{ij}^r], \quad 1_{ij}^r = \delta_{i,N-1-j}, \quad i = 0,1,\ldots,$$

$$\frac{N}{2} - 1, \quad j = 0,1,\ldots, N-1.$$

New algorithms are obtained if the right sides of (22) and (23) for P_N and W_N are transposed (like (12), obtained by (11). The transposition of (21) does not lead to any new algorithm.

3. Structural Implementation of Parallel Computations

Different parallel architectures can be elaborated to realize the above algorithms. Those design decisions should be accepted, which tally with the graph of information connections.

It follows from (11), (12), (16), (19), (21), (22) and (23), that the graph has the same structure for each GFT. In can be seen from (19), for instance, that the operator $\mathcal{F}_N^0$ splits into two operators of a smaller dimension $\mathcal{F}_N^0$, which are independent and can be executed in parallel. The Z level of loading of each parallel working processor depends on the depth of recursion.

4. Conclusion

In this paper the full recursive forms of the fast algorithms for discrete Fourier, Hadamard, Paley and Walch transforms were obtained by a generalized technique. They are a part of the GFT for a given value of N, i.e. the decomposition through characters of the finite Abelian groups.

The theory of group approach reveals the symmetry of the task and hence, the possibilities for reducing the computation complexity and its parallel implementation.

REFERENCES

1. Kasabov, N.K., G.T. Bijev. B.J. Jechev, Hierarchical Discrete Systems and the Realisation of Parallel Algorithms, Lecture Notes in Computer Science, CONPAR 81, Springer Verlag, Berlin, Heidelberg, New York.

2. Wallach Y., Alternating Sequential /Parallel Processing, Springer-Verlag, Berlin, Heid., New York, 1982.

3. Morris, S.A., Pontryagin Duality and the Structure of Locally Compact Abelian Groups, Cambridge University Press, London, New York, 1977.

4. Hewitt E., K. Ross, Abstract Harmonic Analysis, v. II, Springer Verlag, Berlin, Heidelberg, New York, 1970

5. Serre J.- P., Representations Lineaires des Groupes Finis, Herman Paris, 1967.

6. Albert A., Regression and the Moor-Pentrouse Pseudoinverse, Academic Press, New York and London, 1972.

7. Curtis C.W., I. Reiner, Represantation Theory of Finite Groups and Associative Algebras, Int. Publ., John Wiley and Sons, New York, London, 1962.

8. Grossman I., W. Magnus, Group and Their Graphs, Random House, 1964.

9. Strang G., Linear Algebra and its applications, Academic Press New York, 1976.

10. McClellan, J.H., C.M. Rader, Number Theory in Digital Signal Processing, Prentice-Hall, Inc. Englewood Cliffs, New Jersey 07632.

11. Oppenheim A.V., R.W. Schafer, Digital Signal Processing, Prentice Hall, Inc. Englewood Cliffs, New Jersey.

12. Nussbaumer H.J., Fast Fourier Transform and Convolution Algorithms, Springer-Verlag, 1982

SISAL: Initial MIMD Performance Results

R. R. Oldehoeft, D. C. Cann and S. J. Allan
Computer Science Department
Colorado State University
Fort Collins, CO 80523 USA

Abstract

SISAL is a parallel functional language developed for use on a variety of parallel processing architectures. In this report we discuss the implementation strategies that have allowed quick development of a reasonably portable system that can effectively exploit features of common target architectures. We outline the run time management software. Speedup data from a few representative benchmarks demonstrates that SISAL uses the available concurrency of the Denelcor HEP multiprocessor well via completely automatic detection and implementation of parallelism.

1 Introduction

SISAL (Streams and Iteration in a Single-Assignment Language) [MSA*85] is a language for expressing algorithms to execute on highly concurrent computers. Like other functional languages, SISAL displays freedom from side effects, single assignment, and locality of effect. These characteristics allow compilers to detect and easily exploit the underlying architectural parallelism and the potential for parallelism in the program.

Four groups associated with different organizations and with different original target architectures cooperated to define SISAL. The organizations (and architectures) are: Lawrence Livermore National Laboratory (Cray vector processors), Digital Equipment Corporation (VAX[1] processor clusters), the University of Manchester (Manchester data flow machine), and Colorado State University (Denelcor HEP multiprocessor). SISAL descends from VAL [AD79,McG82] and retains its functional, single assignment character. SISAL differs from VAL in possessing simpler error types, general recursion, a stream data type, and improved iteration forms. The SISAL project has also benefited from earlier work described in [GP79] and [KLP79].

SISAL offers several advantages for use on a multiprocessor system. The user need not (and cannot) manage or express parallelism in a program. The compiler detects parallelism, decides how much to exploit, and generates code to take advantage of the parallelism and manage it. Users express algorithms without expressing or implementing parallelism. Language syntax is Pascal-like. A familiar syntax decreases the time it takes to learn the language and aids in program readability. For a SISAL language overview see [AO85].

---

[1]VAX is a trademark of Digital Equipment Corporation

	Input		Translator		Output
(1)	SISAL program	$\rightarrow$	SISAL parser	$\rightarrow$	IF1
(2)	IF1	$\rightarrow$	IF1 optimizer	$\rightarrow$	IF1 (optional)
(3)	IF1	$\rightarrow$	IFPCC generator	$\rightarrow$	IFPCC
(4)	IFPCC	$\rightarrow$	C code generator	$\rightarrow$	Native code

Figure 1: SISAL Programming System at CSU

The SISAL groups have formed a pool of benchmark programs typical of those that programmers would actually write using SISAL. Many are short, but there are some over 1,500 lines long. Thus they often represent actual codes run in the "real world."

At CSU we implemented SISAL on the Denelcor HEP and evaluated the performance of the initial implementation.[2] Work proceeds to port the software to other MIMD systems. The sections below briefly discuss the compiler implementation with emphasis on portability considerations, describe the run time support system, and survey performance results. See [AO86] for a more complete description of the SISAL implementation at CSU.

2 Compiler

The SISAL compiler, designed for flexibility and portability, consists of several phases. We use a parser that produces a machine-independent intermediate form, "IF1" [SW85], along with optimizers that improve this intermediate form [SW85]; both were developed at LLNL. The next phase [CAO84a] translates to another intermediate form acceptable to the second pass (code generation and optimization) of the portable C compiler [Joh78], used almost universally in Unix [3] systems. This approach has saved a great deal of effort and promises to ease the porting of the translator system to other parallel processors that support C, or facilitate its use as a cross-compiler. A recent survey [Joh85] has found that, among 24 standalone systems for concurrent computing, 17 run a version of Unix. Because of its portability and built-in networking software, Unix is an attractive operating system for new supercomputers. A diagram of the CSU SISAL compiler appears in Figure 1.

3 Run Time System

Most SISAL run time software is written in C, with a few assembly language routines. This aids in system portability to other machines running Unix. The major responsibilities of the run time routines are managing processes, arrays, streams, and dynamic storage.

Parallel execution units in MIMD SISAL are function bodies, parallel loop "stripes," and multi-expression components. Execution of parallel loops and multi-expression components is performed by daemon processes that interact closely with SISAL process management in low-overhead ways. (For these tests, this had to be emulated by packaging loop slices as explicit

[2]U. S. Army Research Office Contract DAAG29-82-K-0108 supported this research.

[3]Unix is a trademark of AT&T Bell Laboratories.

functions; the automatic capability is now fully implemented.) So mapping SISAL processes onto the hardware resources is the major concern. If each function reference occupied a processor, then either the number of available processors would be overrun, or deadlock would result as parent processes held processors waiting for completion of child functions who cannot execute. We eliminate processor deadlock by requiring that a parent process waiting for value(s) from children relinquish its processor and suspend execution. This can be done more efficiently than in a general-purpose operating system because of the specialized nature of the SISAL environment. See [BAO84] and [VAO85] for more complete discussions of process management.

Multi-dimensional arrays in SISAL are "arrays of arrays" and are dynamic. At compile time we know only the dimensionality and element type; bounds are in general determined only at run time. Necessary resulting run time tasks include adding an element to an array, fetching a value from an array, etc. [CAO84b] has a complete discussion on array implementation.

Streams are an important data structure because they provide pipelined parallelism among stream producer and consumer functions. Both the stream producer and consumers execute simultaneously so that SISAL processes can form generalized parallel pipelines. Only a contiguous substream of a stream needs to be extant at any time because values that the slowest associated stream consumer no longer will reference need not remain. In this way programs can execute that produce and consume (finite prefixes of) infinite streams; these programs terminate normally. See, for example, the Sieve program in Figure 4. For a further discussion of streams see [AO83].

SISAL run time support relies on dynamic storage allocation for process descriptors, streams, and arrays. An adapted boundary tag method is in place that allows multiple concurrent allocations and deallocations [BAO85]. Also, we include a "front end" caching scheme for exactly matching request sizes that can greatly speed up dynamic storage management under the conditions that obtain during SISAL execution [OA85a]. It is possible for SISAL processes to deadlock in competing for dynamic storage. The run time software detects and reports deadlock if it occurs. For a complete discussion of dynamic storage management in SISAL, as well as other run time support details, see [OA85b].

Note that in these tests array storage is not properly recycled, adversely affecting performance. We anticipate that a new intermediate form under development at LLNL will help all SISAL implementations to optimize storage management.

Various parameters may be supplied at execution time that control how the run time routines work; many of these influence some aspect of storage management. To prevent fast stream producers from using up available storage with stream elements, a parameter limits the number of extant elements in a stream. To reduce the number of process state changes, a blocked stream producer or consumer remains blocked until a fraction of the maximum number have been consumed, or an empty stream has been replenished to a fraction of the maximum size. This hysteresis fraction is a run time parameter. Other parameters control the working set size of the exact-fit cache, and the conditions under which processes become blocked due to lack of storage. All parameters have default values.

The run time software is instrumented to measure some performance values that help to interpret speedup results. These include the number of assignments to previously idle processors, the number of times a blocking process found other work (another process) for its processor, and the number of times processes blocked for various reasons. In conjunction

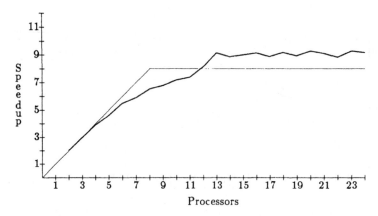

Figure 2: Numerical Integration Performance Results

with the run time parameters, these have been helpful in performance tuning.

4 Performance

We briefly describe the performance of a few benchmark programs as measured on a single-PEM Denelcor HEP processor; unfortunately this machine is no longer available. Because of the implementation restrictions mentioned in the previous section, we believe these results represent a baseline for enhanced performance on other shared-memory systems. Overall, the speedup curves display performance similar to those of HEP programs written in imperative languages with explicit, low-level process synchronization mechanisms. Further, these curves follow the general form predicted for this architecture in [Jor85]: a maximum speedup higher than eight but bounded above by twelve indicates that the machine is being fully utilized. In this section a "processor" is a hardware supported thread of execution within a HEP PEM.

4.1 Scalar Processing

The performance of a simple numeric integration program is seen in Figure 2. The speedup curve is typical of programs that operate on scalars. Process management among SISAL functions that exchange simple values (or scalar multi-expressions) is being tested here.

To further investigate the overhead of SISAL process management versus the process management software provided by the vendor, a C program was written that computes the same result as the SISAL integration program using the same process structure. The resulting speedup curve (omitted) is nearly identical with its SISAL counterpart.

4.2 Array Manipulation

Figure 3 shows the speed up curve for a matrix multiplication program. The sawtooth effect seen in the speedup curve comes from varying the number of processors against a fixed size for the data. The periodic degradations are due to the lack of array space recycling. The

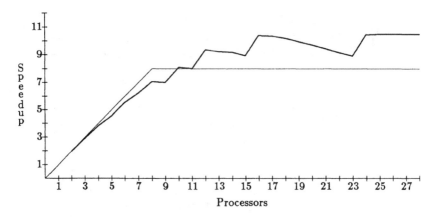

Figure 3: Matrix Multiplication Performance Results

dynamic storage exact-fit cache is unable to operate because no storage blocks for arrays are being freed.

4.3 Stream Processing

Finally, the performance of a sieve method for prime number generation was examined. Figure 4 shows the SISAL program. The speedup curve obtained is given in Figure 5. This graph shows the best speedup among the benchmarks discussed for small numbers of processors. Beyond 13 processors there is not enough work to keep SISAL functions running and offset the cost of frequently idling processors; performance actually degrades. It is beyond the highest point in the curve that we see a large increase in the number of times idle processors are detected. That is, from this point a blocking SISAL process will frequently find no other ready process to use the hardware it is vacating. The smoothness of the curve shows that stream run time support operates in a predictable fashion.

5 Conclusions

These experiments show that the SISAL implementation successfully exploits the underlying HEP architecture to automatically provide speedups competitive with those obtained from manually constructed, imperative parallel programs. In fact, we are led to believe that the granularity of parallelism could be made smaller with increased speedup. That is, we were initially too pessimistic about the cost of automatic run time management. We also learned that it is dangerous to use vendor-supplied, general purpose process management software, as exemplified in Figure 5. The generality leads inevitably to execution costs that can be reduced by taking advantage of what is known about the SISAL environment. Our early considerations for portability have resulted in a system that should be easily moved to other MIMD systems with a C compiler.

```
type Ints = stream[ integer ];

function Filter( S: Ints; M: integer returns Ints )
    for I in S
    returns stream of I unless mod(I,M) = 0
    end for
end function

function Integers( returns Ints )
    for initial
        I := 3
    while true repeat
        I := old I + 2
    returns stream of I
    end for
end function

function Primesupto( Limit: integer returns Ints )
    let Maxt := integer( sqrt( real( Limit ) ) )
    in
        for initial
            S := Integers(); T := 2;
        while T < Limit repeat
            T := first( old S );
            S := if T <= Maxt then Filter( rest( old S ), T )
                else rest( old S ) end if
        returns stream of T
        end for
    end let
end function
```

Figure 4: Sieve of Eratosthenes in SISAL

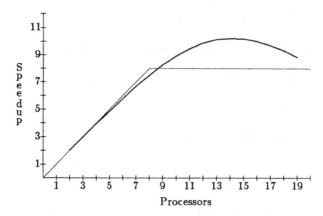

Figure 5: Sieve of Eratosthneses Performance Results

References

[AD79]   William B. Ackerman and Jack B. Dennis. *VAL – A value-oriented algorithmic language.* Technical Report LCS/TR-218, MIT, June 1979.

[AO83]   Stephen J. Allan and R. R. Oldehoeft. A stream definition for von Neumann multiprocessors. In *Proceedings of the 1983 International Conference on Parallel Processing*, pages 303–306, August 1983.

[AO85]   Stephen J. Allan and R. R. Oldehoeft. HEP SISAL: parallel functional programming. In J. Kowalik, editor, *Parallel MIMD Computation: The HEP Supercomputer and Its Applications*, pages 123–150, MIT Press, Cambridge, MA, 1985.

[AO86]   Stephen J. Allan and R. R. Oldehoeft. Parallelism in SISAL: exploiting the HEP architecture. In *19th Hawaii International Conference on System Sciences*, pages 538–548, 1986.

[BAO84]   Larry W. Booker, Stephen J. Allan, and R. R. Oldehoeft. *Process management for HEP SISAL.* Technical Report CS-84-05, Colorado State University Computer Science Department, Fort Collins, CO, June 1984.

[BAO85]   Bruce Bigler, Stephen J. Allan, and R. R. Oldehoeft. Parallel dynamic storage allocation. In *Proceedings of the 1985 International Conference on Parallel Processing*, pages 276–279, August 1985.

[CAO84a]   David C. Cann, Stephen J. Allan, and R. R. Oldehoeft. *An IF1 driven portable code generator.* Technical Report CS-84-15, Colorado State University Computer Science Department, Fort Collins, CO, December 1984.

[CAO84b]   Steven Cobb, Stephen J. Allan, and R. R. Oldehoeft. *Arrays in SISAL.* Technical Report CS-84-04, Colorado State University Computer Science Department, Fort Collins, CO, June 1984.

[GP79]   D. Grit and R. Page. *A multiprocessor model for parallel evaluation of applicative programs.* Technical Report, Colorado State University, Fort Collins, CO, September 1979.

[Joh78]   S.C. Johnson. A portable compiler: theory and practice. In *Conference Record of the 5th ACM Symposium on the Principles of Programming Languages*, pages 97–104, ACM, New York, January 1978.

[Joh85]   H. L. Johnson. *Characteristics of various contemporary products for high speed computing*. Technical Report, Information Intelligence Sciences, Aurora, CO, October 1985.

[Jor85]   Harry F. Jordan. HEP architecture, programming and performance. In J. Kowalik, editor, *Parallel MIMD Computation: The HEP Supercomputer and Its Applications*, pages 1–40, MIT Press, Cambridge, MA, 1985.

[KLP79]   R. Keller, G. Lindstrom, and S. Patil. A loosely-coupled applicative multiprocessing system. In *Proceedings of the 1979 AFIPS National Computer Conference*, pages 613–622, 1979.

[McG82]   James R. McGraw. The VAL language: description and analysis. *ACM Transactions on Programming Languages and Systems*, 4(1):44–82, 1982.

[MSA*85] James McGraw, Stephen Skedzielewski, Stephen Allan, Rod Oldehoeft, John Glauert, Chris Kirkham, Bill Noyce, and Robert Thomas. *SISAL: streams and iteration in a single assignment language: reference manual, Version 1.2.* Lawrence Livermore National Laboratory, Livermore, CA, M-146, rev. 1 edition, March 1985.

[OA85a]   R. R. Oldehoeft and S. J. Allan. Adaptive exact-fit storage management. *Communications of the ACM*, 28(5):506–511, 1985.

[OA85b]   R. R. Oldehoeft and Stephen J. Allan. Execution support for HEP SISAL. In J. Kowalik, editor, *Parallel MIMD Computation: The HEP Supercomputer and Its Applications*, pages 151–180, MIT Press, Cambridge, MA, 1985.

[SW85]   S. K. Skedzielewski and M. L. Welcome. Data flow graph optimization in IF1. In Jean-Pierre Jouannaud, editor, *Functional Programming Languages and Computer Architecture*, pages 17–34, Springer-Verlag, New York, NY, September 1985.

[VAO85]   Bruce Votipka, Stephen J. Allan, and R. R. Oldehoeft. *HEP SISAL process management*. Technical Report CS-85-08, Colorado State University Computer Science Department, Fort Collins, CO, May 1985.

CALTECH HYPERCUBE MIMD COMPUTER PERFORMANCES

MEASUREMENTS IN A PHYSICAL MATHEMATICAL APPLICATION

Claudio Martini, Mauro Morando, Sandro Ridella

Istituto per i Circuiti Elettronici

Consiglio Nazionale delle Ricerche

Genova, Italy

ABSTRACT

A Caltech Hypercube has been characterized using known methods to obtain performance figures from a MIMD computer. Speed-up, efficiency and communication cost have been evaluated versus the number of used processors and the physical problem dimensions.

INTRODUCTION

In recent years, a lot of new computers, composed by many processors interconnected and working together on the same problem, have been proposed. Caltech Hypercube [1] is one of them: this machine is interesting for two reasons. The first one is that it's not a theoretical speculation but it has been realized from Caltech researchers and from some industries (e.g. Intel), that commercialize it. The second one, is that Fox and his collaborators have shown that a lot of important physical-mathematical problems find a satisfactory solution in the hypercube implementation.

The aim of this work is to study the computer performances when it works on a well known application, rather then to suggest a hypercube solution to a new problem.

At this purpose, Hockney's work [2] has been used for the definition of $s_{\frac{1}{2}}$ parameter (task syncronization cost). The cost of interprocessors communications, besides, has been evaluated, whereas the load balancing hasn't been considered, because the problem has a natural equal work distribution between the processors (Ep = 1 following Hockney [2]).

The problem has been studied on a simulator, in C-language, kindly supplied from Caltech, and installed on a VAX 11/730 with VMS 3.4 . The P hypercube processors have been mapped on a square, two-dimensional lattice, in order to obtain an "Illiac IV - like" configuration.

THE PROBLEM

The considered problem consists in the solution of the discretized Laplace's equation, with assigned boundary potential, on a square with sides equal to $N*\sqrt{P}$, where $N*N$ is the number of points assigned to each processor. The linear equation system has been carried on by the traditional Gauss-Jacobi method, with a prefixed number of iterations: at each internal point the potential is computed as the average of the four nearest neighbours (north, south, east, west) and this requires four floating point operations. The number of internal points is $(N-2)*(N-2)$, considering an $N*N$ mattrix. Finally the number of iterations, in which this procedure is repeated, is I.

THE METHOD

The hypercube performances have been obtained with the following three steps:
1. one processor solution time evaluation $(Ts(\sqrt{P}*N))$;
2. P processors solution, with interprocessors communications suppressed, time evaluation $(To(P,N))$;
3. P processors solution time evaluation $(T(P,N))$.
It's important to note that, regarding this specific algorithm, it is possible to calibrate the time response of the simulator in order to valuate the response of the real machine: to do this, we used Caltech memos informations [3,4].
It' possible to write:

$$S.U.(P,N) = \frac{Ts(\sqrt{P*N})}{T(P,N)} \qquad [1]$$

$$T(P,N) = \frac{Ts(\sqrt{P*N})}{P} + Toh(P) + Tc(P,N) \qquad [2]$$

$$To(P,N) = \frac{Ts(\sqrt{P*N})}{P} + Toh(P) \qquad [3]$$

where:

S.U.(P,N) = speed-up

Toh(P)   = overhead time

Tc(P,N)   = interprocessor communication time

moreover:

$$O.C.(P,N) = \frac{Toh(P)}{T(P,N)} \qquad [4]$$

$$C.C.(P,N) = \frac{Tc(P,N)}{T(P,N)} \qquad [5]$$

$$\eta(P,N) = \frac{S.U.(P,N)}{P} = 1 - O.C.(P,N) - C.C.(P,N) \qquad [6]$$

where:

O.C.(P,N) = overhead cost

C.C.(P,N) = communication cost

η (P,N) = efficiency

EVALUATIONS

The following evaluation applies at the studied problem:

$$Ts(\sqrt{P*N}) = \frac{4*I*(\sqrt{P*N})**2}{r_\infty} \qquad [7]$$

where:

r_∞ = peak ops/sec per processor

I = number of iterations

So, it's possible to write from (3) and following Hockney [2]:

$$To(P,N) = \frac{4*I*N**2}{r_\infty} + Toh(P) = \frac{4*I*(N**2 + s_{\frac{1}{2}}**2)}{r_\infty} \qquad [8]$$

and, finally

$$s_{\frac{1}{2}} = \frac{r_\infty*Toh(P)}{4*I} \qquad [9]$$

Similarly, for the communications

$$Tc(P,N) = 4*I*N*tc \qquad [10]$$

where:

tc = time to perform a single packet (64 bits) transmission and a single packet reception

It's impssible to evaluate the hypercube overhead using the simulator. From [3] and [4], and using the Mark II - 8 MHz model data, it's known that

$$r_\infty = 27 \text{ Kops/sec}$$

and

$$tc = 149 \, \mu sec$$

In this situation, the communication time became equal to the computation time

$$Tc(P,N) = Ts(\sqrt{P}*N)/P \qquad [11]$$

when N=4. Using a multiple packets communication protocol, r_∞ is, obvsiouly, unchanged but Tc(P,N) becames

$$Tc(P,N) = 4*I*(tc1+tc2*N) \qquad [12]$$

where:

tc1 = 90 μsec ;   tc2 = 80 μsec from [3] and [4].

Solution of (11) gives N = 3.

Unconsidering the overhead time (Toh(P)=0), it's possible to made, for the two communication protocols, the following evaluations.

Single packet:

$$S.U.(P,N) = \eta(N) * P = \frac{P * N}{N + 4} \qquad [13]$$

$$\eta(P,N) = \eta(N) = 1 - C.C.(N) = \frac{N}{N + 4} \qquad [14]$$

$$C.C.(P,N) = C.C.(N) = (r_\infty*tc)/(N+r_\infty*tc) = 4/(N+4) \qquad [15]$$

Multiple packets:

$$S.U.(P,N) = \eta(N) * P = \frac{P*N**2}{N**2+2.2*N+2.5} \qquad [16]$$

$$\eta(P,N) = \eta(N) = 1 - C.C.(N) = \frac{N**2}{N**2+2.2*N+2.5} \qquad [17]$$

$$C.C.(P,N) = C.C.(N) = \frac{r_{\infty}*(tc1+tc2*N)}{N**2+r_{\infty}*(tc1+tc2*N)} =$$

$$= \frac{2.2*N+2.5}{N**2+2.2*N+2.5} \qquad [18]$$

ACKNOWLEDGEMENT

We thank very much Shirley Enguehard, Caltech Concurrent Computation Program Application Coordinator, for the hypercube simulator and for the support given to Mauro Morando and Claudio Martini when they was visiting researchers at the Caltech.

REFERENCES

1. G.C.Fox, S.W.Otto, Algorithms for Concurrent Processors, Physics Today, May 1984.
2. R.W.Hockney, (r , $n_\frac{1}{2}$, $s_\frac{1}{2}$) Measurements on the 2-cpu Cray X-MP, Parallel Computing, vol.2, n.1, March 1985.
3. S.Otto, A.Kolawa, A.Hey, Performance of the Mark II Hypercube, Caltech memo/paper HM188, August 1985.
4. G.C.Fox, A.Hey, D.Nicole, Communication Overhead for MIMD Computers, Caltech memo/paper HM221, December 1985.

A NEW APPROACH TO DECENTRALIZED CONTROL OF JOB SCHEDULING

Guoqing Zhang, Yueming Hu, Zhiliang Xie
Department of Computer Science and Engineering
Shanghai Jiao Tong University
Shanghai, People's Republic of China

Abstract This paper proposes a new approach to improve the existing techniques and algorithms for decentralized control of a multiprocessor system. Each processor in the model proposed can either be a controller or a controllee and resides in one of the following statuses: User, System, Blocked and Idle, similar to a process in an operating system. Job scheduling strategies are based on the concept of confliction vectors stored in a shared memory. Conventional task scheduling strategies such as that with MINIMAX criterion can still be employed to achieve both interprocessor communication minimization and processor load balancing. The new approach combines the idea concerning distributed processing and pipelining. It has extensibility and strong fault-tolerant capacity, and shows to be of practical use.

I. INTRODUCTION

Very fast computers are in high demand in many scientific and engineering applications such as computer simulation, image processing, automation and artificial intelligence etc. Multiprocessor systems are shown to be very attractive and effective for fulfilment of these requirements. Being an instance of MIMD systems, a multiprocessor system has many advantages over SIMD array processor systems in its structure flexibility, high reliability, high modularity and cost effectiveness. The most difficult problems associated with multiprocessor approach include job scheduling and task assignment. The strategy of job scheduling and its overhead are among the main barriers in the development of multiprocessor system. This paper proposes an effective way to solve this problem.

The common feature of computing in the applications mentioned above is that they include huge amount of calculations of few basic computing types. So large amount of jobs or subjobs can be divided into small number of job types. There are many scheduling strategies, including graph theoretic approaches[1][2], mathematical programming [3][4], queueing theory[5][6], and heuristic methods [7][8]. The scheduling strategy proposed in this paper combines the above methods and the scheduling methods used in pipelined computers to introduce the control of job initiation time. This strategy can be decentrally controlled. Every processor in the system can act either as a controller or as a controllee. The control information is stored in a shared memory. The processor status can be in one of the four states, that is,

1. User state, when a processor is executing a user task.

2. System state, when it is running operating system process including job scheduler.

3. Idle state, when it is waiting for jobs to arrive. If more than one processor in the system are in this state, they form a queue.

4. Blocked state, when a fault occurs, it is logically disconnected from the system.

Scheduling in a multiprocessor system can be divided into two layers. The job scheduling layer concerns the initiation of job or subjobs and aims to maximize the non-conflict initiations for the given jobs. The task scheduling layer deals with the assignment or mapping of tasks to processors and aims to optimize the tradeoff between load balancing and interprocessor communication minimization. This paper discusses the strategy of job scheduling.

In the scheduling model proposed, the job scheduler performs its function each time when there is a processor in system state. The scheduler per se can reside either in the shared memory or in every processor's local memory. The scheduling strategy classifies the arriving jobs into several job types or subjob types and creats a conflict table(CT), mutual conflict table(MCT), conflict vector(CV) and mutual conflict vector(MCV) for each type of job or subjobs. Every job is an instance of a certain job type. Its scheduling vector is represented by Ji.

When a job of new type arrives, the system establishes its conflict table according to some task scheduling strategies. Based on the conflict table, conflict vectors and mutual conflict vectors can be generated and then stored in the shared memory for further scheduling. If the job is very large, it can be divided into subjobs, each of which is also an initiation unit. All this can be done at compile time. Details of the strategy will be explained in section III. While in section II, a number of assumptions are made to simplify discussion. Section IV will go into further analysis of the approach.

II. ASSUMPTIONS

Before going into detail, it is necessary to make some assumptions on the environment of the system.

  1. The processors in the system are heterogeneous. But each of them can act as a controller and execute scheduling functions. This assumption is not a real restriction. Since the homogeneous system is a special case of a heterogeneous system. But in homogeneous systems more effective ways can be employed.

  2. The interconnection network of the multiprocessor system can be of any type. It is not necessary to have the processors fully connected. But each processor does have a communication path to any other processor in the system.

  3. Every processor can access the shared memory. A time interrupt signal is available.

  4. The resource requirement of a job and the inter-task communication, if they exist, can be determined before scheduling, this is the so called deterministic scheduling.

  The basic motivation of conflict vector scheduling is to simplify the distributed control, to reduce the scheduling overhead and support processor synchronization and finally to avoid deadlocks to occur. Tasks having communication links tend to be assigned to the same processor to reduce communication costs. But in order to balance the processor loading and to minimize the execution time, we tend to distribute the tasks evenly among all processors. In the later case, it would be better to initiate tasks having communication links at the same time. System resources should also be arranged to avoid conflict.

III. DESCRIPTION AND ALGORITHM OF THE SCHEDULING METHOD

  First we present some concepts of the scheduling system. The correspondent concepts for scheduling of pipelined computers can be found in P. Kogge[9].

  Conflict Table(CT) Each conflict table corresponds to a certain type of job and its resource requirements(Fig.1). The symbol "*" in certain slots depicted on the table indicates that a task, once dispatched, needs the resource of that same row at that same time shown in the corresponding column.

resource

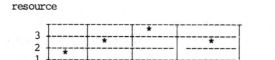

Fig.1 Conflict table of job type i

<u>Mutual</u> <u>Conflict</u> <u>Table(MCT)</u> There are several types of jobs existing in the system. Every two different types of jobs form a mutual conflict table. CT of job type j is shown in Fig.2. MCT of job type i and job type j can be seen in Fig.3. Obviously, MCT is formed by overlapping two CT's onto a single table.

resource   resource

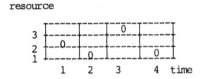
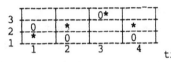

Fig.2 Job type j's CT   Fig.3 MCT of job type i
                               and job type j

<u>Conflict</u> <u>Vector(CV)</u> Let $V(i)$ be a bit vector of ith type of job. Depending on the contents of respective CT, the Kth bit from left to right of vector $V(i)$ is 1 if and only if there is at least one pair of "*" with distance K betwen them at the same row of the corresponding CT, otherwise a 0 is assigned to that bit (K=1,2,...,N).

<u>Mutual</u> <u>Conflict</u> <u>Vector(MCV)</u> A MCV $V(i,j)$ is deduced from the corresponding MCT similar to $V(i)$ from CT. The Kth bit of $V(i,j)$ is 1 if and only if there exists a time latency K from task of job type i to job type j at the same row of the MCT. For the above examples we have.$V(i)=0100$ $V(j)=0100$ $V(i,j)=V(j,i)=1010$.

Note that two jobs can share the same CV but fall into two different job types. They are distinguished by MCV which tacitly represents the relations between two types of jobs. Also note that $V(i)=V(i,i)$.

When a new job arrives, the system also sets up a job scheduling vector Ji. The initial value of Ji is zero. The difference between $V(i)$ and Ji is that $V(i)$ is a static value for a given job type while Ji is a variable for the job type. It varies from time to time during the scheduling procedure.

Initially, all processors are in Idle state. Upon receipt of GO command from either system operator or an active processor in System state, the processor changes to User state. Whenever possible, a processor in System state continually finds a job in the queue. Whenever a task to be executed in the next time slice is assigned to a processor in Idle state, the processor changes to User state to execute the task.

The job scheduling algorithm consists of two procedures. The first is job initiation procedure, another is time interrupt handler. Each processor has a task execution list which specifies the tasks to be executed at each time slice. The job initiation procedure is to assign each task to a processor to insure no conflict. This is fulfilled by updating all the Ji values whenever a task assignment is done. The

time interruption handler is to update the Ji's by shift one bit to the left each
time a time slice is over. These can be shown in the following two algorithms.

Algorithm 1. Job Initiation

1. change the present processor to be a scheduler;

2. find a job type with the first bit of V(i) being 0;

3. fetch a job item of that job type from the job queue;

4. assign the tasks of that job to respective processors;

5. FOR every Ji

    DO

6.   Ji:=Ji U V(j,i); (Where U is a bit OR operation.)

    END;

7. Change the present processor back to its original state.

Algorithm 2. Time Interrupt Handler

    FOR every Ji

        DO

            Ji left shift one bit with 0 append to the rightmost;

        END;

    RETURN.

The correctness of above algorithms means that whenever a task assignment is done,
no conflict will occur in its execution. This follows directly from the definition
of the conflict vector. If at time t a conflict vector has a 1 in bit i, then at time
t+i initiation of that job must be avoided. Once a job is initiated, every job scheduling vector in the system is updated in algorithm 1 to avoid its conflict with that
job.

IV. ANALYSIS AND IMPLEMENTATION PROBLEMS

As can be seen from the above algorithms, the proposed scheduling method is a
time sliced method. This simplifies the complexity of the problem and has the advantages that task synchronization and task execution sequence can be easily managed.

One feature of the proposed scheduling method is that it schedules a whole job or
a subjob rather than a task at a time, thus increasing the scheduling efficiency and
reducing the overhead. This kind of scheduling is called the group scheduling by K.
Hwang[10], which has several advantages. First, if closely related tasks run in
parallel, blocking due to synchronization and frequency of context switching may be
reduced. Second, if placement decisions are made in combination with the scheduling
method, the "distance" betwen various tasks and their referenced objects might be

minimized, thus effective memory management is easier.

Since job scheduling is an operating system function, algorithms implementing job scheduling must run as quickly as possible. It is trivial to prove that the time complexity of algorithm 1 is $O(n+m)$, where m is the number of job types in the system, n is the average number of tasks within a job. The time complexity of algorithm 2 is $O(m)$.

The interrelationship of tasks within a job can be divided into three basic types or combinations of these basic types.

1. Tasks that have mutual communications. It is better to execute these tasks concurrently.

2. Tasks that have sequential dependencies. One task should be executed after another task. This relationship can be represented by a precedence graph.

3. Tasks that are independent from each other.

In the first case, task scheduling can be carried out using a graph theoretic approach. The graph matching method of C.C.Shen and W.H.Tsai[11] can well be adapted here. Based on that approach both minimization of interprocessor communication and load balancing between processors can be achieved.

In the second case, Hu's algorithm[12] represents an optimal task scheduling for the rooted tree precedence graph. Detailed discussion about this problem can also be found in reference[15].

The third case is a special case of both case 1 and case 2, so there exist many methods for its scheduling.

Another feature of conflict vector scheduling is that system deadlock can be effectively prevented. This is because in the conflict table, system resources can either be processors or memory, I/O access rights etc. These resources can be arranged properly using this scheduling method. Moreover it is just the time slice that a job uses certain resource is that resource be "locked" to a task of that job, instead of being "locked" to the whole job, thus both deadlock prevention and resource utilization maximization can be achieved.

From algorithm 1, we can see that only one job scheduling is done in a time slice. If there are many processors in the system, this is not enough. In that case, we can let the scheduler occupy a whole time slice on a processor or a special processor can be employed to scheduling. In the case that many jobs can be scheduled in one time slice, the CV and MCV should include bit 0 to show the conflicting situation of present time slice.

The algorithm 1 represents the Greedy strategy of scheduling which is a control strategy that always picks the minimum possible latency between one initiation and the last initiation without regard to any further initiations. Other strategies include priority scheduling in which jobs may have a priority value. Algorithm 1 can be changed into priority one by changing the phase 2 so that when there are more than one job to be initiated in the same time slice, the job with the highest priority is selected first. The optimization of job scheduling is a complex problem. But an easy way to achieve good scheduling is to generate compatible initiation sets according to bit 0. First consider maximally compatible initiation sets. For any initation set S a subset C is maximally compatible with respect to S if and only if C is compatible and the addition of any other CV in S but not in C causes the result set to be noncompatible. Initiation of jobs in the compatible set will maximize the initiation of nonconflicting jobs[9].

The algorithm can be described with the following example. Suppose there are three processors available for execution, two jobs of different types, e.g. job i and job j as shown in Fig.1 and Fig.2. If a processor in system state finds out that there exists a job to be executed and subsequently works as a controller to assign job i to processors. Because only one assignment operation is permitted at a time according to algorithm 1, job j can not be assigned at once. After one cycle of time a processor looks at Ji and Ji to find if there exists a value 0 at the first bit of the vectors. Before going on, it should be reminded that initially Ji=Jj=0000 and at present Ji=0100 Jj=1101 so job j can not be initiated. Then Ji and Ji are left shifted by one bit with 0 appending to the rightmost bit and the process goes on.

By optimal scheduling strategy we mean that the queueing job can be fulfilled in minimum time. In many applications such as cited at the begining of this paper, there are few types of jobs existing in the system. Then optimization is not very difficult using state diagram methods. Assume V(i)=V(j)=0010 V(i,j)=V(j,i)=1101 and if the number of jobs of type i is approximatly the same as that of type j, then the optimal scheduling is as shown in blackened lines of Fig.4. Where the arrows represent the transition of states, numbers besides every arrow means the time latency to initiate the task from the pressent state, following which a job number is presented.

V. CONCLUSION

The job scheduling strategy proposed in this paper, like other job scheduling techniques as wave scheduling [13] and bidding scheme approach[14], has the advan-

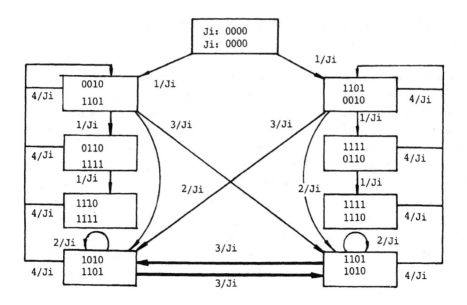

Fig.4   State diagram of scheduling

tages of system extensibility and fault-tolerance capacity, but unlike others this
method is relatively simple and can achieve optimal scheduling.

The system described in this paper can also be looked as a task flow machine,which
integrates the concept of data flow machine. All tasks of a job are initiated whenever
they are ready to run and are dispatched randomly. This is a strong support for parallel languages and an exploitation of maximum parallelism.

REFERENCES

[1] H.S.Stone and S.H.Bokhari, "Control of Distributed Processes," Computer, vol.11,
pp.97-106, July 1978.
[2] T.C.K.Chow and J.A.Abraham. "Load Balancing in Distributed Systems," IEEE Trans.
Software Eng,vol. SE-8, July 1982.
[3] W.W.Chu, L.J.Holloway, M.T.Lan and K.Efe, "Task Allocation in Distributed Data
Processing," Computer, vol.13, pp.57-69, Nov. 1980.
[4] P.P.Ma, E.Y.S.Lee and M.Tsuchiya. "A Task Allocation Model for Distributed
computing systems," IEEE Trans. Computer, vol C-31, pp.41-47, Jan. 1982.

[5] Y.C.Chow and W.Kohler, "Models for Dynamic Load Balancing in a Heterogeneous Multiple processor system," IEEE Trans. Computer. vol. C-28, May 1979.

[6] L.Kleinrock and A.Nilsson. "On Optimal Scheduling Algorithms for time-shared systems," J.ACM, vol.28, No.3, pp.477-486, July 1981.

[7] K.Efe. "Heuristic Models of Task Assignment Scheduling in Distributed Systems," Computer, vol.15, pp.50-56, June 1982.

[8] O.I.El-Dossouki and W.Huen, "Distributed Enumeration on Beteen Computers," IEEE Trans. Computer, vol. C-29, pp.818-825, Sept. 1980.

[9] P.Kogge, "The Architecture of Pipelined Computers," 1981.

[10] K.Hwang and F.A.Briggs, "Computer Architecture and Parallel Processing," McGraw-Hill Inc., 1984.

[11] C.C.Shen and W.H.Tsai, "A Graph Matching Approach to Optimal Tast Assignment in Distributed Computing Systems Using a Minimax Criterion," IEEE Trans. Computer, vol.C-34, No.3, March 1985.

[12] M.J.Gonzalez, "Deterministic Processor Scheduling," Computing Surveys, vol.9, No.3, pp.173-204, Sept. 1977.

[13] A.M.Van Tilborg and L.D.Wittie, "Wave Scheduling -- Decentralized Scheduling of Task Forces in Multicomputers," IEEE Trans. Computer, vol.C-33, No.9, Sept. 1984.

[14] R.G.Smith, "The Contract Net Protocol: High-level Communication and Control in a Distributed Problem Solver," IEEE Trans. Computer, vol. C-29, No.12, December 1980.

[15] E.G.Coffman, JR. et al, "Computer and Job-shop Scheduling Theory". 1976, John Wiley & sons. inc.

Synchronous Communication of Cooperating Processes in the M^{5}PS Multiprocessor

J. Milde[*], T. Plückebaum, W. Ameling

Aachen Technical University, Department of Electrical Engineering and Computer Science, Schinkelstraße 2,
D-5100 Aachen, W.-Germany

[*]Brown Boveri Research Center, Dept. KLR-CF, CH-5405 Baden/ Switzerland

Abstract

The M^{5}PS[*] multiprocessor consists of a loosely coupled set of tightly coupled subsystems. Because of this heterogeneous interconnection network, transparent communication between cooperating processes is only possible by message passing. The communication mechanism implemented in the M^{5}PS system supports port-addressed synchronous message passing of cooperating processes independently of the interconnection network. This paper discusses the implementation of this mechanism and presents execution times for communication primitives for different interconnection devices. The results are compared to communication of processes with shared variables. The comparsion reveals a significant overhead of transparent message passing as against synchronized communication via shared variables.

[*]M^{5}PS := modular multi mode multi micro processor system

Introduction

With the development of highly integrated microprocessors the interest increased in using many of these processors within one system. The goal was to build modular flexible systems, which can be easily adapted to different performance requirements by adding new processor elements, and to yield a better ratio of price and performance than conventional single-processor systems. To operate such multiprocessor systems by a single user it is necessary to split one task into several subtasks, which can be executed by different processors in parallel. Two principles are known for the cooperation of these subtasks or processes:

- *Cooperation by shared variables* which needs some address space common to all processes and can only be implemented in systems with shared memory (tightly coupled systems).

- *Cooperation by message passing* which can be used also in systems without shared memory (loosely coupled systems).

Although both principles are equivalent in theory /LAUE78/, there are some important differences in practice. Message passing is often preferred because of its independence of the interconnection network and the absence of side effects. This advantage is reduced by more overhead for communication within loosely coupled systems.

Today it is possible to join the two directions of development of systems with more than one processor. The development of tightly coupled multiprocessor systems is state-of-the-art but the number of processors within those systems is limited by the bandwidth of the common memory bus and does not normally exceed 16 processors. The development of more general interconnection networks (like serial links) have reached a level where these networks can not only be used for file transfer between different user jobs but also allow for communication between cooperating processes of a single task. The combination of these interconnection structures results in systems where several clusters of tightly coupled processors are connected by a more universal network. These systems overcome the restrictions on the number of processors in tightly coupled systems but preserve the advantages in a local environment.

Examples of systems with this structure are the CEDAR system, the HAMA structure and the SUPREMUM architecture, which are more or less in a planning phase. The M^{5}PS is one of the few systems, developed to an extent where it is possible to measure the execution times of basic communication primitives.

Measurements in the M^{5}PS are used to answer the question of whether it is possible to efficiently hide the heteregeneous interconnection network by a communication scheme based on message passing or whether the user should be able to communicate via shared variables within tightly coupled processor clusters to preserve the advantages of this hardware feature.

Hardware Structure of the M^{5}PS

The M^{5}PS multiprocessor was designed, built, and evaluated during the last 10 years to study performance characteristics of parallel processor systems and to complete the theoretical investigations on parallel processing by experimental results. The goal of the project was to build a flexible modular multiprocessor system using off-the-shelf microprocessors, components for memory and interconnection network, which means that the interconnection network was designed as a hierarchical system of buses.

The basic building block of the system is the processor module consisting of an 8-bit microprocessor Z80 connected to private memory and private peripherals by a local bus. Up to 8 processor modules may be connected to shared memory and shared peripherals by a cluster bus in order to build a cluster of tightly coupled processors.

Several processor clusters can be interconnected by an intercluster bus, which provides a common address space for all connected clusters. It is possible to connect one cluster to several intercluster buses simultaneously. This allows systems to be built with different interconnection topologies and with any number of processors. It should however be mentioned, that clusters, which are not connected to the same bus, do not share any address space and therefore are only loosely coupled.

While isolated processor clusters have been running for several years, the intercluster bus was finished as a prototype only, to allow some experiments with a global operating system. The memory access times of the three bus hierarchy levels (local, cluster, intercluster) are in the ratio of 1:1:2 for writing and 1:1:3 for reading. Besides the prototype of the intercluster bus a serial CSMA/CD-link has been developed with a data transmission rate of 250 KBd. This serial bus is also used to couple different processor clusters. The entire system is described in more detail in /KRIN84/.

Operating System of the M^{5}PS

The operating system of the M^{5}PS is divided into two different levels. Within a cluster the operating system is procedure-oriented. It supports the user to define parallel processes in a dynamic way, to communicate between processes via shared variables, and to synchronize the processes by spinlocks and semaphores. On a higher level Concurrent Pascal is implemeted, which supports process cooperation by monitors and was extended by shared classes. There exists no master processor in the system. All operating system functions are executed by the processor in need of them.

The performance of such clusters of tightly coupled processors with this operating system was evaluated for different applications. The results can be found in /KRIN84/. The execution times of the important functions for process management are summarized in table 1.

The global operating system is process-oriented. The different system functions are performed by system processes, which are located at a special cluster or replicated in all clusters. The interface between user processes and the operating system is implemented by remote procedure calls, which hide the difference between the local procedure-oriented and the global process-oriented operating system levels.

The global system supports the user to spread his programs over different clusters and to communicate between the processes. It also defines an universal interface to the peripheral devices within the whole system and hides the location of a particular device to the user. The system manages the actual configuration of the system hardware with respect to the available processor clusters and communication links as well as the actual number of processors in a cluster, the extent of memory and the connected peripherals. A detailed description of the operating system and the associated communication system is given in /MILD85/.

Table 1: Execution times of system functions for process management

System function	Execution time	Comment
spinlock		
unlock	25 µs	
lock	(26 + n•14) µs	n tests with result false
semaphore		
initialize	74 µs	
signal	0.63 ms 3.25 - 13.63 ms	no waiting process activation of a waiting process
wait	0.55 ms 2.28 - 5.22 ms	no blocking of the process blocking of the process
process management		
start	5.31 - 17.1 ms	regarding to the number of processes
put in ready queue	2.28 - 5.22 ms	"
stop	2.6 ms	
32-bit floating point multiplication	6 ms	software function for comparision

Communication System of the M^5PS

Many proposals for process cooperation by message passing can be found in the literature. An overview of the most important ones and their features is given in /ANDR83/. They can be classified by the addressing scheme of the sender and the receiver, their possible interactions and synchronization and the structure of the messages. The advantages and shortcomings of these proposals and their combinations are discussed in /MILD85/ and will not be repeated here. Only the results of this investigation are described here as implemented in the M^{5}PS.

Within the M^{5}PS a synchronous communication mechanism is used, where the sender is blocked until the receiver has given an acknowledgment for the received message. It is also possible to define a timeout for the sender as well as for the receiver to prevent blocking. This synchronous communication allows for very good fault handling, simplifies flow control of messages, and supports the user for process synchronization. The blocking of the sender can be tolerated in a multiprocessor system, if the degree of parallelism at the application level is high.

The concept of ports is used to address a communication channel, which is defined by several senders and a simple receiver. Using ports a sender sends its message to a particular port of a particular receiver, while the receiver accepts messages from any sender. This addressing mechanism is well suited to client-server applications often found in parallel systems. In the M^{5}PS it is possible to distinguish between different ports of a receiver and to use this for message typing. The communication system also allows multicast addressing beside the direct addressing scheme.

The length of a message is variable but limited to 140 bytes (128 bytes for user data). This concept was chosen to avoid segmentation of messages within the communication system. Segmentation results in large amount of protocol overhead, while a variable message length almost does not influence the performance of message passing. The limit of 128 bytes is reasonable, because most messages in a parallel program and the operating system are only a few bytes long and the sector length of the mass storage used is 128 bytes.

Results of Measurement and Conclusions

In table 2 the measured and computed times for different kinds of synchronous communication in the M^{5}PS system are given.

The communication by message passing within the memory of one cluster takes nearly twice as much time as synchronization by semaphores. This difference is mainly explained by the more general communication system, which is able to deal with different physical interconnection structures and to hide these structures to the user.

The same factor of performance degradation must be expected, if a serial bus at a speed of 10 MBd is used for cluster interconnection instead of shared memory. This result is calculated by an extrapolation of the times measured for the slow serial bus in the M^{5}PS.

Table 2: Execution times for synchronous exchange of a 140 byte message

Implemetation	Execution time
DMA-block transfer	0.5 ms
programmed block transfer	1.5 ms
communication via shared variables	
synchronization with spinlocks (2 processors)	2.2 ms
synchronization with semaphores (1 processor)	21.5 ms
synchronization with semaphores (2 processors)	16.2 ms
time for pure data transfer	~ 10%
communication by message passing within a common address space	
send - receive (1 processor)	55.0 ms
send - receive (2 processors)	46.4 ms
time for pure data transfer	~ 5%
communication by message passing using a serial bus	
data transfer to communication controller programmed, 250 KBd	173.8 ms
time for pure data transfer	~ 7%
data transfer to communication controller with DMA, 250KBd, (calculated)	109.2 ms
time for pure data transfer	~ 11%
data transfer to communication controller with DMA, 10 MBd, (calculated)	97.4 ms
time for pure data transfer	~ 0.3%

The absolute values for the communication primitives are related to the hardware of the M^5PS, which is built of rather slow 8-bit processors with a 2 MHz clock. It should however be mentioned, that at least 95% of the communication time is used to execute procedures of the communication system. This percentage will not change significantly even if faster processors are considered in such systems.

The measured communication times must be considered a lower limit for protocol overhead in systems which implement a transparent communication system on top of a heterogeneous interconnection network, because the communication protocols used in the M^{5}PS system are extremely optimized.

The values in table 2 also show another result. The overhead for process cooperation is reduced by a factor of 10 if spinlocks are used for process synchronization. In many cases of process communication synchronization is also not necessary. Compared to the overhead for message passing the communication can be done in these cases with reduced overhead, if shared variables are used in a tightly coupled system. Using message passing the measured overhead is needed, even if only 1 bit has to be exchanged and no synchronization is necessary. With respect to this result and the experience with clusters of tightly coupled processors in the M^{5}PS project, a communication scheme should be chosen for systems of this type which does not hide the shared memory and supports the user to benefit from this efficient communication concept at least for local communication.

Literature

/AND83/ Andrews, G.R.; Schneider, F.B.
Concepts and notations for concurrent programming
ACM Computing Surveys, 15,1 (1983), pp3-44

/KRIN84/ Krings, L.; Milde, J.; Ameling, W.
Das Multiprozessorsystem M5PS
W.E. Proebster, R. Remshardt (eds.), Entwicklungsperspektiven mittlerer
Rechnersysteme
Oldenbourg Verlag, München Wien, 1984, pp83-110

/LAUE78/ Lauer, H.C.; Needham, R.M.
On the duality of operating system structures
Proc. 2nd Int. Symp. Operating Systems, Paris, Oct. 1978

/MILD85/ Milde, J.
Überlegungen zur Organisation verteilter Mehrrechnersysteme
Dissertation am Lehrstuhl für Allgemeine Elektrotechnik und Datenverarbeitungs
Systeme der RWTH Aachen, 1985

PARALLEL IMPLEMENTATION OF THE ALGEBRAIC PATH PROBLEM

Yves ROBERT[+] & Denis TRYSTRAM[++]

[+] CNRS, Laboratoire TIM3, BP 68, 38402 St Martin d'Hères Cedex, France

[++] Ecole Centrale Paris, 92295 Chatenay Malabry Cedex, France

Abstract: The Algebraic Path Problem is a general framework which unifies several algorithms arising from various fields of computer science. Rote [11] introduces a general algorithm to solve any instance of the APP, as well as a hexagonal systolic array of $(n+1)^2$ elementary processors which can solve the problem in $7n-2$ time steps. We propose a new algorithm to solve the APP, and demonstrate its equivalence with Rote's algorithm. The new algorithm is more suitable to parallelization: we propose an orthogonal systolic array of $n(n+1)$ processors which solves the APP within only $5n-2$ steps. Finally, we give some experiments on the implementation of our new algorithm in the parallel environment developped by IBM at ECSEC in Roma.

INTRODUCTION

In a recent paper [11], Rote introduces the Gauss-Jordan elimination algorithm for the Algebraic Path Problem (APP for short), a general framework which unifies several algorithms arising from various fields of computer science. The Algebraic Path Problem is defined as follows [11] [14]: given a weighted graph G = (V,E,w) where V is a finite vertex set, E an arc set, a function w : E -> H with weights from a semiring $(H,(+),(x),*)$ with zero 0 and unity 1, find for all pairs of vertices (i,j) the quantities d_{ij} = (+) { w(p), $p \in M_{ij}$ } where M_{ij} denotes the set of all paths from i to j. With the weighted graph (V,E,w) we associate the n by n weigth matrix A = (a_{ij}), where a_{ij} = w(i,j) if (i,j)$\in$E and a_{ij}=0 otherwise. We denote $M_{ij}^{(k)}$ the set of all paths from i to j which contain only vertices x with $1 \leq x \leq k$ as intermediate vertices. In practice, $a_{ij}^{(k)}$ = (+) { w(p), $p \in M_{ij}^{(k)}$ } is equal to the successive values of a_{ij} which we want to compute, starting from the initial value $a_{ij}^{(0)}$ = a_{ij} up to $a_{ij}^{(n)}$ = d_{ij}. Applications of the APP are obtained by specializing the operations (+), (x), and * in the appropriate semirings. We detail three of them:

- (i) determination of the inverse of a real matrix: A is a real matrix, (+) and (x) are the usual arithmetic operations in $\mathbb{R}$, and the *-operation is the following: if $c \neq 1$ then c^* := 1/(1-c)). The algorithm computes $(I-A)^{-1}$. Of course, straightforward modifications permit to compute directly A^{-1}.

Support from the IBM European Center for Scientific and Engineering Computing in Roma and the Coordinated Research Program C3 of CNRS is gratefully acknowledged.

- (ii) shortest distances in a weighted graph: the weights a_{ij} are taken in $H=\mathbb{R}\cup\{-\infty,+\infty\}$ (we let $a_{ij} = +\infty$ if the arc (i,j) is missing), (+) is the minimum in H, (x) is the addition in $\mathbb{R}$ extended to H (with $-\infty$ (+) $+\infty = +\infty$) and * is defined by (**if** $c\geq0$ **then** $c^*:=0$ **else** $c^* := -\infty$)

- (iii) transitive and reflexive closure of a binary relation: the a_{ij} are boolean, (+) et (x) are respectively the "and" and "or" operations, and * is defined by ($c^* :=$ true for all c).

We do not assume the multiplication in the semiring to be commutative: this permits to easily implement blocks schemes. Rote [11] presents a hexagonally connected systolic array of $(n+1)^2$ processors which can solve any instance of size n of the APP in 7n-2 time steps, each time being the time necessary to achieve a multiply-and-add in the underlying algebra. In section 2, we introduce a new algorithm to solve any instance of the APP, which is more suitable to parallelization.

A NEW ALGORITHM FOR THE ALGEBRAIC PATH PROBLEM

```
{ The new algorithm) }
for k := 1 to n
    akk(k) := (akk(k-1))*
    for i := 1 to n, i ≠ k
        aik(k) := aik(k-1) (x) akk(k)
    for j := 1 to n, j ≠ k
    begin
        for i := 1 to n, i ≠ k
            aij(k) := aij(k-1) (+) aik(k) (x) akj(k-1) ;
        akj(k) := akk(k) (x) akj(k-1) ;
    end ;
end ;
```

The following lemma (which can be easily proven using induction on k) demonstrates the equivalence of the new algorithm with Rote's one [11]:

Lemma : given a n by n matrix $A^0 = (a_{ij}^{(0)})$, the new algorithm computes the solution matrix $A^n = (a_{ij}^{(n)}) = D$ of the APP.

THE SYSTOLIC ARRAY

We use a two-dimensional array of orthogonally connected processors (see figure 1). The array is composed of n rows, each row k including n+1 processors numbered from left to right $P_{k,1}$, ... , $P_{k,n+1}$. The operation of each processor is detailed in the figure 2. There are three types of processors:

• type 1: circle processors perform the * operation on their first input data. Afterwards they simply act as delay cells.

• type 2: square processors first initialize their current register by storing after modification their first input data; then they act as multiply-and-add cells (when (+) and (x) are the standard operations on real numbers, they become classical IPS cells [5] [6] [8] [9]).

• type 3: double-square processors actually operate as square processors, with the exception that their current register is not initialized in the same way (remember that (x) is not commutative).

In the k-th row of the array, the leftmost processor $P_{k,1}$ is of type 1 and the rightmost processor $P_{k,n+1}$ is of type 3. All the other processors $P_{k,2}, ..., P_{k,n}$ are of type 2.

The matrix A, followed by I, the identity matrix of order n, is fed into the array row by row. More specifically, row k of the n by 2n matrix (A,I) is input to processor P_{1k}, one new element each time-step, beginning at time t=k. This input format is depicted in the figure 1. We can state the

Theorem : given a dense nonsingular n x n matrix $A^{(0)}$ = A, the orthogonal systolic array of n(n+1) processors computes the solution $A^{(n)}$ of the APP within 5n-2 time-steps.

Rote's hexagonal array [11] involves $(n+1)^2$ processors and solves the APP in 7n-2 time-steps. As pointed out in [11], the value of 5n-2 time-steps achieved by our orthogonal array is optimal within one step, provided that each of the n^2 data elements is used only once in each step. We point out that the performances of our array overcome those of the array of [3] for computing the transitive closure (n^2 processors and 6n-2 time-steps) and those of the array of [8] for matrix inversion (n(3n+1)/2 processors and 5n-2 time-steps). Moreover, the solution of a new instance of the APP can begin every 2n steps. Finally, in the case of matrix inversion, if we input the matrix A followed by a n by n matrix B instead of I, it can be seen that the array delivers $(I-A)^{-1}B$ (or $A^{-1}B$ with straighforward modifications) in the same number of steps.

IMPLEMENTATION IN THE VM/EPEX ENVIRONMENT

In this section, we deal with the implementation of the new algorithm 2 using the VM/EPEX environment at ECSEC in IBM Roma. The Experimental Software for Parallel FORTRAN Programming VM/EPEX has been developed at the IBM T.J. Watson Research Center [13] and runs under the Virtual Machine/Conversational Monitor System (VM/CMS).

The general philosophy of the VM/EPEX software is to provide the user with facilities to run a program on several Virtual Machines (VMs for short) rather than one, hence allowing parallelism [1] [2] [13]. The problem of communication and synchronisation between the VMs where pieces of programs run (tasks with the definition of [7]) has been solved in two different ways [2]:

• shared memory : the user has the possibility to create a shared memory which can be accessed by all the VMs

• message passing : the VMs can exchange messages and data through communication subroutines (VMFACS).

The Algorithm 2 that we want to implement requires an amount of $O(n^3)$ arithmetic operations; it consists of $O(n)$ iteration steps, each step being composed of $O(n)$ independent tasks, which are identical but operate on different data. Each task has an execution time of $O(n)$. A full synchronisation is needed at the end of each step. Thus a shared-memory approach is better suited to such a synchronisation-intensive problem.

The programmer writes his program using an extension of standard IBM FORTRAN that specifically includes a few new keywords for multitasking handling [2] [13]:

- creating shared data : **@Shared** (statement equivalent to COMMONs in sequential FORTRAN programs)

- distributing the instances of a parallel loop among the VMs : **@Do** and **@Enddo** with the **Wait** and **Nowait** options. Successive values of the loop index will be randomly distributed among the VMs. The default option **Wait** specifies that a process must wait for the completion of all the iterations of the loop before proceeding, whereas the **Nowait** option permits the process to continue as soon as all the work of the loop has assigned, even though other processes may still be completing some of the loop iterations

- executing serial pieces of code on a single VM : **@Serial begin** and **@Serial end**, with the same options and the possibility of specifying the VM where the piece of code is to be executed (**Process=**)

- each VM is identified by its own number **@Mynum**. The total number of Vms is **@Numprocs**.

We do not detail further here the use of these extensions (see [13]). We concentrate now on the problem of the parallelization of our new algorithm. The algorithm will be executed by several VMs, which communicate through the shared memory. We have the following conceptual scheme:

```
        { Algorithm 2 }
        Do 1 k = 1, n
                execute task T_kk  { updating of column k }
                execute in parallel the tasks T_kj, j≠k, 1≤j≤n
1       Continue

        { Task T_kk }
        A(k,k) = Star(A(k,k))
        Do 11 i = 1,k-1
                A(i,k) = A(i,k) (x) A(k,k)
11      Continue
        Do 12 i = k+1,n
                A(i,k) = A(i,k) (x) A(k,k)
12      Continue

        { Task T_kj (j≠k) }
        Do 21 i = 1,k-1
                A(i,j) = A(i,j) (+) A(i,k) (x) A(k,j)
21      Continue
        Do 22 i = k+1,n
                A(i,j) = A(i,j) (+) A(i,k) (x) A(k,j)
22      Continue
        A(k,j) = A(k,k) (x) A(k,j)
```

Here Star(x) is the function which computes x^* for an input data x. Notice that task T_{kk} vanishes when computing the transitive closure of a binary relation

The task T_{kk} must be executed by a single processor (say the first one) and must be completed before it is possible to start the execution of any task T_{kj}, $j \neq k$. This leads to the following implementation (we omit the lecture of the matrix A):

```
{ create shared memory }
@Shared  /MATRIX/A(n,n)
Do 1 k = 1, n
        { serial piece of code to be executed by Processor 1 }
        @Serial begin  process=1
                execute task Tkk
        @Serial end
        { execute in parallel the tasks Tkj, j≠k }
        @Do j = 1, k-1
                execute task Tkj
        @Endo  nowait
        @Do j = k+1, n
                execute task Tkj
        @Endo
1       Continue
```

After the @Serial end, the default option is Wait, hence all the processors 2, ..., p are waiting at this synchronization point for processor 1 to complete the execution of T_{kk}. In the contrary, the Nowait option is used after the first @Enddo to ensure that some processors can start the execution of the tasks $T_{k,k+1}$, $T_{k,k+2}$, ... before all the tasks T_{kj} with j<k are completed.

Now we have to measure the performances of our parallel algorithm. Considering an algorithm executed on a parallel computer with p (identical) processors in time T_p, and letting TSEQ be its sequential execution time (with 1 processor), we define the speed-up factor as the ratio $S_p = $ TSEQ/T_p, and the efficiency is given by $e_p = S_p/p < 1$ [4] [12].

The first idea is to use the available Fortran procedure CPUT to compute the CPU time of each virtual machine. The interest is twofold (i) this will permit to check whether the tasks have been evenly distributed among the VMs, and (ii) we can compute the overhead due to the parallelization. However, this does not permit to evaluate PARTIME, the execution time of the parallel algorithm. We have to know whether the tasks have been well distributed among the VMs inside each instance of the outer sequential Do loop on k. A global measure of the task repartition is not sufficient. For instance, one can imagine an execution scheme where every instance on k is executed by a single processor (not always the same) which performs all the tasks T_{kj}, $j \neq k$, whereas the global repartition of the work is still good. Therefore, we declare a two-dimensional array in the shared memory:

@Shared/TIME_ARRAY/TIME(@Numprocs,#steps)

and we store at each step k the virtual CPU time of a given VM in TIME(@Mynum,k). We can now compute the efficiency

$$e_p = TSEQ / (@Numprocs * PARTIME)$$

The results of some experiments are given in the figure 3. For each of the three aformentioned instances of the APP, the efficiency was computed for various sizes of matrix, ranging from 128 to 640. The curves are presented for 2 and 8 processors. With 2 processors (□ on the curves), the efficiency varies beetween 0.5 and 0.8, whereas for 8 processors (+ on the curves), it varies between 0.15 and 0.3. In the figure 4, the efficiency obtained for the three instances are compared, with 2, 4, 6 and 8 processors. □ refers to shortest distances, + to matrix inversion, and o to the transitive closure. The sequential time for 512 x 512 matrices is 842 seconds for shortest distances, 648 seconds for matrix inversion, and 533 seconds for the transitive closure. This shows that the elementary tasks are more costly for shortest distances than for matrix inversion and, in turn, than for the transitive closure. Since the number of tasks is the same in each of the three instances of the APP, this explains why the best efficiency is obtained for shortest distances, and the worst for the transitive closure.

The relatively low efficiency obtained with 4 processors or more is due both to the synchronization-intensity of our algorithm, and to the fact that the granularity of our tasks is relatively small (a few milliseconds in average). Nevertheless, our approach demonstrates that the VM/EPEX environment with the shared-memory option offers full possibilities to analyze the performance of parallel programs.

REFERENCES

[1] E. CLEMENTI, Progress report on our experimentation with parallel supercomputers ICAP1 and ICAP2, Conf. "Le Calcul ... Demain", P. Chenin et al. eds, Masson 1985

[2] P. DI CHIO, V. ZECCA, IBM ECSEC facilities: user's guide, IBM ECSEC Report, Roma 1985

[3] L.J. GUIBAS, H.T. KUNG, C.D. THOMPSON, Direct VLSI implementation of combinatorial algorithms, Proc. Caltech Conf. on VLSI, California Inst. Technology, Pasadena 1979, 509-525

[4] K. HWANG et F. BRIGGS, Parallel processing and computer architecture, Mc Graw Hill, 1984

[5] H.T. KUNG, Why systolic architectures, Computer 15, 1 (1982), 37-46

[6] H.T. KUNG, C.E. LEISERSON, Systolic arrays for (VLSI), Proc. of the Symposium on Sparse Matrices Computations, I.S. Duff and G.W. Stewart eds, Knoxville, Tenn. (1978), 256-282

[7] R.E. LORD, J.S. KOWALIK, S.P. KUMAR, Solving linear algebraic equations on an MIMD computer, J. ACM 30 (1), (1983), p 103-117

[8] J.G. NASH, S. HANSEN, G.R. NUDD, VLSI processor arrays for matrix manipulation, VLSI Systems & Computations, H.T.Kung et al. eds, Computer Science Press (1981), 367-378

[9] Y. ROBERT, Block LU decomposition of a band matrix on a systolic array, Int. J. Computer Math. 17 (1985), 295-315

[10] Y. ROBERT, D. TRYSTRAM, Un réseau systolique pour le problème du chemin algébrique, C.R.A.S. Paris 302, I, 6 (1986), 241-244

[11] G. ROTE, A systolic array algorithm for the algebraic path problem (shortest paths; matrix inversion), Computing 34 (1985), 191-219

[12] U. SCHENDEL, Introduction to numerical methods for parallel computers, E. Horwood 1984

[13] J.M. STONE, V.A. NORTON, F.D. ROGERS, E.A. MELTON, G.F. PFISTER, The VM/EPEX FORTRAN preprocessor reference, IBM Report, Yorktown Heights, NY, USA (1985)

[14] U. ZIMMERMANN, Linear and combinatorial optimization in ordered algebraic structures, Ann. Discrete Math. 10, 1 (1981), 1-380

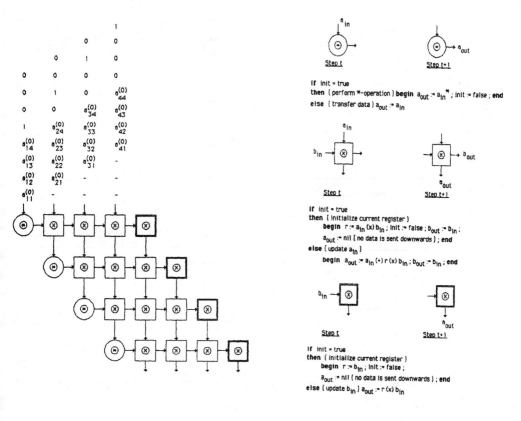

155

if init = true
then (perform *-operation) **begin** $a_{out} := a_{in}^*$; init := false ; **end**
else (transfer data) $a_{out} := a_{in}$

if init = true
then (initialize current register)
    begin $r := a_{in}$ (x) b_{in} ; init := false ; $b_{out} := b_{in}$;
    $a_{out} :=$ nil (no data is sent downwards) ; **end**
else (update a_{in})
    begin $a_{out} := a_{in}$ (+) r (x) b_{in} ; $b_{out} := b_{in}$; **end**

if init = true
then (initialize current register)
    begin $r := b_{in}$; init := false ;
    $a_{out} :=$ nil (no data is sent downwards) ; **end**
else (update b_{in}) $a_{out} := r$ (x) b_{in}

Figure 1
The systolic array

Figure 2
Operation of the processors

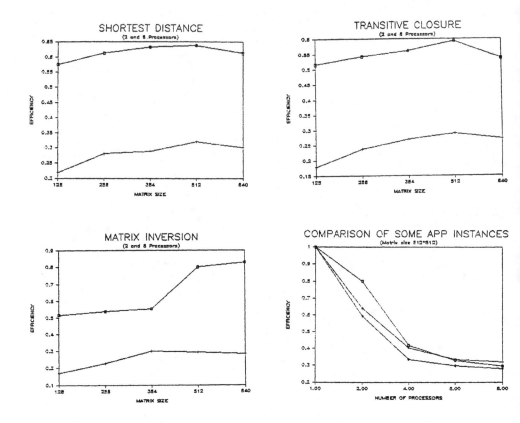

Figure 3
Efficiency for the three selected instances of the APP

IMPLEMENTING BRANCH-AND-BOUND
IN A RING OF PROCESSORS

OLIVER VORNBERGER
Dept. of Mathematics & Computer Science
University of Paderborn
West - Germany

Abstract

A set of personal computers is connected to form a ring structured parallel system:
Each processor has access to its local memory and can exchange messages with its two
ring neighbors.

A branch-and-bound procedure is implemented in Pascal to run in parallel on the ring
and solve the Travelling-Salesman-Problem. Heuristics are developed to maintain a
priority queue in a distributed heap. The computing times and speedups for 25 random graphs obtained with up to 16 ring members are discussed.

1. Introduction

Branch-and-Bound is a popular algorithm design technique that has been used successfully for the solution of combinatorial problems in the area of artificial intelligence and operations research. Many theoretical and practical problems such as travelling salesman, job-shop scheduling, knapsack, vertex cover and graph coloring can
be formulated as combinatorial optimization problems where we are required to find
a solution vector x that minimizes some criterion function f(x) subject to a set C
of constraints. Exhaustive search is usually too time consuming for solving large
combinatorial problems, especially when they are NP-complete [2]. In a branch-and-
bound approach the search through the solution space is organized by a partitioning
algorithm that repeatedly decomposes a problem into smaller subproblems until the
best solution is found.

One approach to enhance the efficiency of branch-and-bound algorithms is to exploit
parallelism. The design and anlysis of algorithms for parallel computer architectures has become a central research area for theoretical and applied computer scientists. There are mainly two reasons for this:

1.) the performance of sequential computers can not be improved with up-to-date
    technologies because of electronic principles

2.) processing and memory units can be produced in a standardized manner and the
    cost per hardware unit has, due to mass production, gone down substantially.

As a result computer architectures evolve that consist of a system of identical processing units which are connected by a communication network.

In this paper we design a very simple multiprocessor system and a parallel search
strategy to handle branch-and-bound algorithms for NP-complete problems. Heuristics
are developed to cope with the distributed memory: a single priority queue is simulated in several local heaps with very little synchronization overhead. As an example
we have implemented the strategy for the travelling-salesman problem. Our system is
formed by a set of personal computers. Aside from some cables, no extra hardware is
needed. A comprehensive description can be found in the full paper [1o] and in [8,9]
where the issue of parallel backtracking is adressed.

Parallelism for branch-and-bound has been studied by several authors. J. Mohan [7]
solved the travelling-salesman problem on the CM*, a multiprocessor system built at
Carnegie-Mellon University, consisting of a hierarchical networks of LSI-11 computers.
Using 16 processors, Mohan got 1/8 of the one-processor running time for 3o node instances. R. Finkel and U. Manber [1] proposed DIB, a general purpose package for distributed backtracking implementations on the Christal multicomputer, a collection
of 16 VAX-11/75o computers connected by a 1o Mb/sec token ring. MANIP, a parallel
machine for processing NP-hard problems was introduced by Wah and Ma [11]. Their
theoretical analysis for a suitable interconnection network was confirmed by simulation results. Wah also studied the behaviour of parallel approximate branch-and-
bound algorithms [6]. Lai and Sahni [4] considered anomalies in parallel branch-and-
bound algorithms by presenting conditions under which k > 1 processors need more
time than 1 processor.

The common point to the implementations of Mohan, Finkel and Wah is a multicomputer,
i.e. a special designed hardware that provides global memory to all processors or
allows fast communication between the processors. Both is neccessary for a parallel
branch-and-bound algorithm, that uses a single subproblem list. Our attempt, on the
other hand will start from standard hardware: the personal computer, a mass product,
available at low rates and powerful enough to act as an integrated part of a (loosely
coupled) parallel system. Since we have neither global memory nor fast communication
we have to provide a mechanism that simulates on distributed memory the typical data
structures used in branch-and-bound algorithms.

2. The Hardware

The basic ingredients of any multiprocessor network are processing units (called nodes) and connections between them (called links). Most universities, banks and insurance companies are equipped with a lot of personal computers that are used for programming tasks and administration work.

Each personal computer (like the SIRIUS I at the University of Paderborn) has

-   its own microprocessor (Intel 8o88)
-   its own main memory for program code & data (256 KB)
-   two serial ports (RS 232) to the outside world:
    Each port can send one byte, receive one byte.

These properties obviously qualify such a personal computer to act as a processing unit in our parallel system. How do we design the connections? There are mainly two possibilities:

Centralized version: A supervisor (with special hardware and software) is introduced. He is connected to all the nodes, acts as an operating system and is responsible for balancing the work load.

Decentralized version: All nodes form a ring by connecting the left port of a computer to its left neighbor and its right port to its right neighbor.

There are several advantages inherent to the decentralized version:

-   simple concept
-   no special designed hardware for supervisor
-   not only parallel computation but also parallel communication (in the centralized version the supervisor forms a bottleneck, since he can manage only one pair of nodes talking to each other at a time).

We will see later that the main disadvantage, namely the very restrictive communication pattern, will take effect only partly when this network is running our branch-and-bound strategy.

3. Sequential branch-and-bound

A survey of branch-and-bound methods in general was presented by Lawler and Wood [5]. For our purpose it is more convenient to choose as an example the travelling salesman problem and describe a typical branch-and-bound strategy to solve this problem.

The travelling salesman problem is to find a minimum cost roundtrip tour that visits each of N cities once, given the costs of travelling from one city to another of those N cities. In other words: We are given an undirected, weighted graph $G = (V,E,c)$ with node set V, representing the cities, edge set E, representing the roads between the cities and cost function $c:E \rightarrow \mathbb{N} \cup \{\infty\}$, representing the length of a raod ($\mathbb{N}$ denotes the nonnegative integers; if there is no road between city i and j the cost of edge (i,j) will be ∞=infinity.) Among all hamiltonian cycles, i.e. cycles that visit each node exactly once, we have to find the shortest. If the graph F forms a clique then there is always such a cycle; if the graph is sparse, i.e. several edges are missing, there may not be a hamiltonian cycle of finite length.

The following is a simplified version of a branch-and-bound strategy of Held and Karp [3].

Let $L = (W,b)$ be a subtour, i.e. W is a path in G, starting at node 1, b is a lower bound for W meaning, that every hamiltonian cycle that contains W will cost at least b. (The computation of the bound b is done by constructing a spanning tree. See [1o] for details).

Let us organize the subtours in a heap H, which allows us quick access to the cheapest subtour (i.e. the subtour with the smallest lower bound). Let $L_0 = (W_0, b_0)$ be a temporary (not necessarily optimum) solution, i.e. W_0 represents a hamiltonian cycle with cost b_0. Call a subtour $L = (W,b)$ reasonable, if $b < b_0$, i.e. if its bound is smaller than the bound of the temporary solution. Then the algorithm reads:

Compute an initial temporary solution $L_0 = (W_0, b_0)$, e.g. with an approximation algorithm "nearest neighbor".

Put $L = (\{1\}, 0)$ as first subtour into the heap H.

While H contains reasonable subtours do
begin
    Remove $L = (W, b)$ the cheapest subtour from the heap.
    Form from L new subtours $L_1, \ldots L_k$ by expanding W at its last vertex x to all
    neighbors of x that do not already occur in W and compute the corresponding
    lower bounds $b_1, \ldots, b_k$

    If one of the new subtours forms a hamiltonian cycle that is shorter than the
    current cycle W_0 then replace L_0 by this new temporary solution.

    For i: = 1 to k do if L_i is reasonable put L_i into the heap (i.e. only tours
    that can improve the current solution L_0 are stored for further examination)
end;

The optimal solution, i.e. the shortest hamiltonian cycle, is W_0 and has length b_0.

4. Parallel Branch-and-bound

Let us now consider the simultaneous use of several heaps. Remember that our ring members do not have access to a global memory that could distribute subproblems to idle processors. Instead they will all work with their own local heaps as long as possible.

Let us define the following

procedure communicate
begin
    if heap contains no reasonable subtours then ask the left neighbor for a subtour.
    if right neighbor asks for a subtour and the heap contains a reasonable subtour
    then send it.
    if a new (shorter) temporary solution is found, inform the left neighbor.
    if the right neighbor sends a new (shorter) solution then update, if necessary,
    the temporary solution L_0.
end;

Now if we distribute the input graph to all processors and incorporate the procedure communication into the main while-loop of our sequential branch & bound algorithm we are almost ready to run it in parallel on the ring. What still has to be changed is the while-condition, because we have to go on as long as there are reasonable subtours somewhere in the ring. We have managed this by delegating the task of detecting the end of the computation to one special node, called the master. At the beginning the master is the only one having the initial subtour $L = (\{1\}, 0)$ in its heap, all other heaps (at the slaves) are empty. A request for a subtour is expressed by the master with a "master request". A request for a subtour by the slaves is expressed as a "slave request" unless the slave was itself asked for a subtour and could not provide one: in this case it formulates its need by a "master request". Clearly, when the master receives a "master request" he can conclude that all slaves (and he himself) are idle and therefore initiate a stop signal and collect the optimum solution.

What has been desribed so far had been the first version of our parallel branch-and-bound algorithm. After we had conducted several experiments it turned out that some tuning was necessary, mainly to compensate the following three effects:

1. Initially the work is distributed extremely uneven: the master has the whole input problem, all slaves have empty heaps. So they all start at the same time to ask their neighbors for work and it takes quite a while until the first subproblem (stored at the master) is split   over and over again and spread to all ring members. Even then the individual start problems for the slaves are not of equal size since slave i constructs his work by restricting a subproblem of slave i-1.

2. When a processor runs out of work he gets a new subproblem from his neighbor. However in most cases it takes only a few iterations to completely solve this subproblem and so the processor is again idle and disturbs his neighbor once more. This leads to high interaction and results in loss of performance since each time the processors have to synchronize for their communication.

3. As long as a processor has subproblems in his heap he sees no reason to demand work from his neighbor. However, it often can be observed that the lower bound of the cheapest problem in one of the heaps is much higher than this bound in other heaps. In fact it could be higher than a solution that is still to be found. So it is clear that the processor working on these "relative expensive" subproblems does superfluous work.

So in order to support a better balanced work load our implementation is augmented by three heuristics:

1. At the beginning all k processors (not only the master) put the initial subtour $W = (\{1\},0)$ into the heap, then iterate the while loop until at least k subtours are in the heap and then processor with number i deletes from its heap all subtours but the i-th cheapest. This guarantees a fast distribution of disjoint roughly equal sized subtours to all processors.

2. Upon a request, not only one problem is sent but several, depending on some heuristic arguments such as the total number of subproblems in the heap and the difference between the lowest bound in the heap and the cost of the temporary solution.

3. The processor A asks his neighbor B for work not only with an "unconditional request" when A has run out of reasonable subtours but also, at certain intervalls (depending on an increase of the smallest lower bound in his heap by a certain constant) with a "conditional request". Such a request is only granted by B, if B detects that his own smallest lower bound is smaller than A's smallest lower bound by more than this constant.

   At a first glance , this "precautious data transfer" seems to contradict our aim to minimize communication. However, it is not a good idea to have several processors work at subproblems with too high lower bounds. Since the lower bound for a subproblem represents the likelyness that this subproblem will, upon expanding, turn into a new and better solution, it makes sense to work on these subproblems first. In a multiprocessor system with a single subproblem list the k processors always work on the k smallest subproblems. So the additional expense for transmission is justified by a (logically) better balanced work load.

Let us summarize the main philosophy of our implementation. Parallelism is organized by a ring of independent stand alone computers, each of which can exchange data with its 2 immediate neighbors at a low transmission rate. If it is possible to reduce the need of communication by keeping the ring members busy (i.e. keep them working on their local heap) sending a few slow bytes once in a while will not affect the total efficiency too much.

5. Experimental results

Due to lack of space we can not present our experiments in detail. For a comprehensive discussion see [1o]. Several sets of undirected graphs have been randomly generated and then solved on configurations of 1,2,4,8,16 ring members. As an example, we present results from a set of 25 graphs having 3o vertices of degree 4, the costs of the edges ranging from 1 to 2oo.

One of the most important criterions to measure the performance of a multicomputer system is the speedup: the ratio between the 1-processor solution time and the k-processor solution time. Table 1 shows execution time and speedup. The execution time covers the total work period, beginning with the distribution of the graph and ending with the display of the solution. So included are communication overhead and idle times. It can be seen that for up to 8 ring members we have a speedup close to optimum. The 16-processor ring however shows a significant loss of performance: the average speedup drops to 12.13. Careful study of communication protocolls revealed that these effects are produced by the fact that towards the end of the computation only a few processors have still subproblems and can not distribute them fast enough to idle processors.

	Number of processors						Number of processors				
	1	2	4	8	16		1	2	4	8	16
Graph No. 01	1714	902	470	267	180		1.00	1.90	3.65	6.42	9.52
Graph No. 02	2878	1505	780	407	240		1.00	1.91	3.69	7.07	11.99
Graph No. 03	5680	2875	1498	769	461		1.00	1.98	3.79	7.39	12.32
Graph No. 04	5380	3002	1534	821	510		1.00	1.99	3.90	7.28	11.73
Graph No. 05	603	340	190	117	92		1.00	1.77	3.17	5.15	6.55
Graph No. 06	2688	1389	740	395	232		1.00	1.94	3.63	6.81	11.59
Graph No. 07	10866	5509	2780	1459	814		1.00	1.97	3.91	7.45	13.35
Graph No. 08	5060	2575	1311	699	391		1.00	1.97	3.86	7.24	12.94
Graph No. 09	3314	1700	870	465	291		1.00	1.95	3.81	7.13	11.39
Graph No. 10	5785	2950	1494	805	473		1.00	1.96	3.87	7.19	12.23
Graph No. 11	4079	2091	1078	575	357		1.00	1.95	3.78	7.09	11.43
Graph No. 12	8507	4287	2203	1144	658		1.00	1.98	3.86	7.44	12.93
Graph No. 13	7557	3851	1947	1016	586		1.00	1.96	3.88	7.44	12.90
Graph No. 14	2820	1455	767	404	248		1.00	1.94	3.68	6.98	11.37
Graph No. 15	2810	1438	749	405	238		1.00	1.95	3.75	6.94	11.81
Graph No. 16	3847	1982	1029	538	315		1.00	1.94	3.74	7.15	12.21
Graph No. 17	2878	1505	770	412	242		1.00	1.91	3.74	6.99	11.89
Graph No. 18	3262	1674	854	464	282		1.00	1.95	3.82	7.03	11.57
Graph No. 19	4670	2393	1212	643	370		1.00	1.95	3.85	7.26	12.62
Graph No. 20	1671	873	452	260	169		1.00	1.91	3.70	6.43	9.89
Graph No. 21	4537	2326	1198	629	382		1.00	1.95	3.79	7.21	11.88
Graph No. 22	2646	1359	711	382	237		1.00	1.95	3.72	6.93	11.16
Graph No. 23	5397	2759	1396	739	414		1.00	1.96	3.87	7.30	13.04
Graph No. 24	4340	2219	1129	602	372		1.00	1.96	3.84	7.21	11.67
Graph No. 25	5154	2630	1343	704	412		1.00	1.96	3.84	7.32	12.51
Average:	4349	2223	1140	604	358		1.00	1.96	3.81	7.19	12.13

Table 1: Execution times and speedup

Table 2 shows statistical data for the computation of graph No 7 with 16 processors. The columns have the following meaning:

CPU   time in seconds spent on working on the graph
TRANS   time in seconds spent on waiting for a problem or transmitting a problem
TOTAL   total time in seconds, i.e. CPU + TRANS
%   work load in percent , i.e.1oo * CPU/TOTAL
>0   first moment that the node has run out of work
>5   first moment that the node has to wait more than 5 seconds to get work from his neighbor
WAIT   maximal time period the node has spent for waiting to get work
REQ   number of requests
IN   number of problems received from left neighbor
OUT   number of problems sent to right neighbor
HEAP   maximal heap size in bytes
ITERAT   number of iterations of the while-loop

Graph No 7 is an example for a good performance. The sum of all iterations has decreased from 61437 (single processor) to 612o9 (16 processors). This is possible because in the 16-member-ring subproblems are expanded in a different order than in the 1-member-ring. So a temporary solution could be found at a time where it can cut off from the heap a lot of (now unreasonable) subproblems. Most processors run out of work for the first time after more than 7oo seconds and had to wait more than 5 seconds only very close to the end. This results in an average work load of 82%. Both, reduced iterations and little communication overhead, causes a speedup of 13.35.

	CPU	TRANS	TOTAL	%	>0	>5	WAIT	REQ	IN	OUT	HEAP	ITERAT
Master	671	143	814	82	742	814	27	228	615	654	48578	3767
Slave 1	653	160	813	80	728	813	46	253	654	648	50118	3746
Slave 2	650	163	813	79	710	767	45	262	648	664	47786	3678
Slave 3	625	187	812	76	706	756	56	269	664	625	53064	3606
Slave 4	630	181	811	77	693	811	77	276	625	429	49942	3647
Slave 5	633	178	811	78	691	717	76	264	429	268	41398	3621
Slave 6	638	172	810	78	692	717	92	255	268	173	34422	3616
Slave 7	640	169	809	79	705	809	104	223	173	187	28528	3585
Slave 8	653	155	808	80	714	808	94	214	187	171	28574	3682
Slave 9	687	121	808	85	753	808	55	172	171	174	27802	3881
Slave 10	742	66	808	91	799	808	9	129	174	129	27618	4197
Slave 11	726	80	806	90	796	806	6	131	129	215	24906	4169
Slave 12	726	81	807	89	786	807	5	126	215	363	25556	4127
Slave 13	703	102	805	87	777	805	5	158	363	511	34226	4013
Slave 14	715	90	805	88	763	805	7	177	511	581	40166	3960
Slave 15	691	113	804	85	750	796	8	216	581	615	45188	3914
Total	10783	2161	12944					3353	6407	6407	607864	61209
Average	673	135	809	82	737	790	44	209	400	400	37991	3825
Single	10859										226976	61437

Table 2: Statistical data for computation of graph No. 7, 16 processors.

6. Conclusion

We have presented an implementation of a parallel branch-and-bound strategy for a set of personal computers. This strategy was tuned to the specific requirements of the hardware environment: no global memory, restricted routing (ring), slow transmission. Our experimental results show that suitable software can cope with these handicaps and produce astonishing high speedup.

With the more and more intense use of personal computers LANs (local area networks) become commercially available. Via a common bus they allow clique-like connections. It is the goal of our next project to use communication routines of such a LAN to handle requests for subproblems more effective: the donator can be any network member and the transmission is much faster (1 Megabit/sec).

7. Acknowledgements

Many thanks to B. Monien for inspiring discussions and to R. Feldmann and P. Mysliwietz for intelligent programming.

8. References

[1] Finkel, R. and U. Manber, 1983, "DIB - A Distributed Implementation of Backtracking", Computer Science Technical Report # 583, University of Wisconsin, Madison

[2] Garey, M.R. and D.S. Johnson, 1979, "Computers and Intractability: A Guide to the Theory of NP-Completeness", Freeman, San Francisco, Calif.

[3] Held, M. and R. Karp, 1971, "The Travelling Salesman Problem and Minimum Spanning Trees: Part II", Math. Prog. 1, pp. 6 - 25

[4] Lai. T.-H. and S. Sahni, 1984, "Anomalies in Parallel Branch-and-Bound Algorithms", Communications of the ACM, Vol. 27, No. 6, pp. 594 - 6o2

[5] Lawler, E.-L. and D.E. Wood, 1966, "Branch-and-Bound Methods: A survey", Operations Research 14, pp. 699 - 719

[6] Li, G. and B.W. Wah, 1984, "Computational Efficiency of Parallel Approximate Branch-and-Bound Algorithms", Proc. of the 1984 International Conference on Parallel Processing, pp. 473 - 48o

[7] Mohan, J. 1983, "A study in Parallel Computations: the Travelling Saelsman Problem", Technical Report CMU-CS-82-136(R), Dept. of Computer Science, Carnegie-Mellon University, Pittsburgh

[8] Monien, B., E. Speckenmeyer, O. Vornberger, 1986, "Superlinear Speedup for parallel Backtracking", submitted for publication

[9] Monien, B., O. Vornberger, 1986, "The Ring Machine", submitted for publication

[1o] Vornberger, O., 1986, "Implementing Branch-and-Bound in a Ring of Processors", Technical Report Nr. 29, Dept. of Mathematics and Computer Science, University of Paderborn, W.-Germany

[11] Wah, B.W. and Y.W. Eva Ma, 1984, "MANIP - A Multicomputer Architecture for Solving Combinatorial Extremum-Search Problems", IEEE Transactions on Computers, Vol. C-33, No. 5, pp. 377 - 39o

SYNTHESIS OF SYSTOLIC ALGORITHMS AND PROCESSOR ARRAYS

Nikolay Petkov Turkedjiev

Technische Universität Dresden

Sektion Informationstechnik

DDR-8027 Dresden, Mommsenstr. 13

ABSTRACT

A formal definition of a systolic array and a systolic algorithm is
given. The design of a systolic array and the necessary input-output
relations for a given computational problem include the design of
an algorithm expressed in terms of a functional graph as an intermediate level. A discipline is introduced in the design process by
identifying the features of a class of algorithms which can be embedded in systolic arrays. Cluster-homogeneous functional graphs
with cluster-independent data dependences are shown to represent
systolic algorithms. The proof of the theorem given is a realization
procedure at the same time. The approach used is illustrated on the
1-D-convolution. The transformations used to obtain different designs
are more general than those used elsewhere /4/ and have a larger
field of application. The set of the linear 1-D systolic designs
for the 1-D-convolution is shown to be enumerable and the different
designs are grouped together in 7 classes and 42 groups (36 in case
of symmetry in two of the classes). A minimal (in some sense) design
can be given for each of the 42 groups. Eight of these designs, however, were given by H. T. Kung elsewhere /3/.

INTRODUCTION

In the present paper we are conserned with the design scheme in Fig.1.

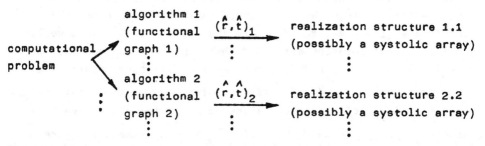

Fig. 1

Algorithms are described in terms of functional graphs /1,2/. Fig.2

gives a notion of a functional graph for the addition of four numbers.

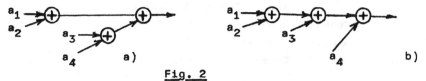

Fig. 2

The mapping pair $(\hat{r},\hat{t}): K_f \rightarrow R{\times}T$ consists of a task allocation function $\hat{r}$ and a task scheduling function $\hat{t}$ (K_f - the set of the nodes of the functional graph $\underline{G}_f$, $\underline{G}_f = (K_f, \underline{Z}_f)$, R - the set of the processor locations, T - the discrete time scale). The design scheme in Fig. 1 is a general one but not that formal. In order to make it a practical tool for the creation of systolic arrays a certain discipline must be introduced in it by identifying the kind of algorithms (functional graphs) and the mappings $(\hat{r},\hat{t})$ at the intermediate design levels.

In this paper, a class of algorithms suitable for systolic implementation as well as the corresponding mappings $(\hat{r},\hat{t})$ are identified. The theorem given is a realization procedure at the same time.

SYSTOLIC ARRAYS

A hardware structure is called a <u>systolic array</u>, if
1) The processor elements are positioned regularly:

$$R \equiv \left\{ (i,\underline{r})/ \ i \in I, \ \underline{r} \in \mathbb{R}^n, \ \underline{r} = \sum_{k=1}^{n} c_k \underline{e}^{*(k)}, \ c_k \in \mathbb{Z}, \ \underline{e}^{*(k)} \in \mathbb{Z}^n \right\},$$

and the processors $P_{i,\underline{r}}$ and $P_{i,\underline{r}'}$ execute the same function $f_{i,\underline{r}} = f_{i,\underline{r}'}$ during all clock periods.(The processor elements are positioned in processor cells with coordinates $\underline{r}$ and i denotes the different processor elements in one cell. All cells have the same structure. A processor element can be as simple as a connecting path. I is an index set for denoting the different PE's in a cell.)
2) The processor interconnections do not depend on the position of the cell: Input $E_{j,i,\underline{r}}$ ($j \in J$, j denotes the different inputs of a processor element, I and J are finite sets) receives input data units from output $A_{i;\underline{r}'}$ of processor (element) $P_{i;\underline{r}'}$ (each processor has a single output) through a chain of $n^{(j,i)}$ delay elements, where $i' = \hat{i}'(i,j)$, $\underline{r}' = \underline{r} - \underline{a}^{(j,i)}$, $\underline{a}^{(j,i)} = \sum_{k=1}^{n} a_k^{(j,i)} \underline{e}^{*(k)}$, $a_k^{(j,i)} \in \mathbb{Z}$

$n^{(j,i)} \in \mathbb{N} \cup \{0\}$. A processor can possibly receive external input data units at certain clock periods.

3) There is at least one pipeline cell connection. An interprocessor connection is called to be a pipeline cell connection, if

a) $\underline{a}^{(j,i)} \neq \underline{0}$ (i.e. $\underline{a}^{(j,i)}$ specifies a connection between different cells),

b) $n^{(j,i)} \neq 0$ (a pipeline connection, i.e. not a direct connection, but a connection through a number of delay elements).

A processor array is called to be <u>full-systolic</u>, if all connections between different cells are pipelined.

Only special kinds of algorithms can be embedded in systolic arrays. We refer to these as to <u>systolic algorithms</u>.

A CLASS OF SYSTOLIC ALGORITHMS

The nodes of a functional graph can be combined in groups, which are called <u>clusters</u>, if they form clusters in RxT under a certain mapping pair $(\hat{r}, \hat{t})$ called a cluster realization /2/. Functional graphs constituting of identical clusters are called <u>cluster-homogeneous</u> graphs. A necessary condition for a functional graph to be embedded in a systolic array is that it is or can be extended to a cluster-homogeneous graph.

<u>Theorem</u>: Let G_f be a realizable /2/ functional graph, so that:

1) $K_f \subset I \times \mathbf{Z}^n$, I - a finite set, ($k \in K_f$, $k = (i, \underline{c})$, $i \in I$, $\underline{c} \in \mathbf{Z}^n$, $\underline{c}$ denotes a cluster and i a certain node in that cluster) and
$$\underline{e} \in \mathbf{Z}^n: |\underline{c} - (\underline{c}.\underline{e}/e^2)\underline{e}| \leqslant C, \; C \in \mathbb{N}$$

2) The arcs of $\underline{G}_f$, i.e. the so called data dependences , are independent of the position $\underline{c}$ of the cluster in $\mathbf{Z}^n$:
$(A_{i,\underline{c}}, \; E_{j,i,\underline{c}}) \in \underline{Z}_f \Rightarrow \underline{c}' = \underline{c} - \underline{d}^{(j,i)}$, $i' = \hat{i}'(i,j)$, $\hat{i}': I \times J \to I$, and $\underline{d}^{(j,i)}.\underline{e} \geqslant 0$. (A and E denote node outputs, inputs respectively; j is an index denoting different inputs of a node.)

3) The functional graph is cluster-homogeneous:
$$\forall (i,\underline{c}), \; (i,\underline{c}) \in K_f \quad f_{i,\underline{c}} = f_{i,\underline{c}'}$$

The functional graph $\underline{G}_f$ with the properties 1-3 above can be embedded in a systolic array.

<u>Proof</u>: Let us consider the processor location set
$$R^{(n)} = \left\{ (i,\underline{r})/ \; i \in I, \; \underline{r} \in \mathbb{R}^n, \; \underline{r} = \underline{c} - (\underline{c}.\underline{e}/e^2)\underline{e}, \; (i,\underline{c}) \in K_f \right\}$$
and specify the function of the processor (element) $P_{i,\underline{r}}$ by $f_{i,\underline{r}} = f_{i,\underline{c}}$. It can be shown that $R^{(n)}$ is finite.

Let the processor output $A_{i,r}$, be connected to the processor input $E_{j,i,r}$, $i' = \hat{i}'(i,j)$, $r' = r - (\underline{d}^{(j,i)} - (\underline{d}^{(j,i)}.\underline{e}/e^2)\underline{e})$ through a chain of $\underline{d}^{(j,i)}.\underline{e}$ delay elements.

The relations above specify a processor array for which the properties 1 and 2 of a systolic array become evident, if we introduce the denotions $\underline{e}^{*(k)} = \underline{e}^{(k)} - (\underline{e}^{(k)}.\underline{e}/e^2)\underline{e}$, where $\underline{e}^{(k)}$, k = 1,2...n, are the unit basis vectors in $\mathbb{R}^n$, $\underline{a}^{(j,i)} = \underline{d}^{(j,i)} - (\underline{d}^{(j,i)}.\underline{e}/e^2)\underline{e}$, $n^{(j,i)} = \underline{d}^{(j,i)}.\underline{e}$.

By means of a linear injective transformation, it is always possible to achieve that for at least one data dependence vector $\underline{d}^{(j,i)}$ holds $\underline{d}^{(j,i)}.\underline{e} \neq 0$ and $\underline{d}^{(j,i)} - (\underline{d}^{(j,i)}.\underline{e}/e^2)\underline{e} \neq \underline{0}$, so that property 3 of a systolic array can also be satisfied. In particular applications the above procedure is applied to as many data dependence vectors as possible, in order to get a full-systolic array or a systolic array with desired structure and properties /2,4/. The case n > 3 can be transformed in a case n $\leq$ 3 by means of a similar linear injective transformation of the coordinates of the processor cells. The properties 1-3 of a systolic array are retained by the linearity of the transformation.

The functional graph $\underline{G}_f$ can now be embedded in the processor array specified above by means of a task allocation function $\hat{r}(i,\underline{c}) =$ $= (i, \underline{c} - (\underline{c}.\underline{e}/e^2)\underline{e})$ and a task scheduling function $\hat{t}(i,\underline{c}) = \underline{c}.\underline{e}$. Details can be found in /2/. $\square$

DESIGNING SYSTOLIC ALGORITHMS AND ARRAYS FOR 1-D-CONVOLUTION

The 1-D-convolution $\quad y_m = \sum_{i=0}^{2} a_i x_{m-i}$, m = 0, 1, 2, ... , $\qquad$ (1)

can readily be identified as a computational problem for which a systolic algorithm exists. We rewrite (1) in the form

$$y_m = \sum_{\substack{c_2=0 \\ c_1=m-c_2}}^{2} a_{c_2} x_{c_1} \qquad (2)$$

and attach the multiplication $a_{c_2} x_{c_1}$ to the point (c_1, c_2) in $\mathbb{Z}^2$, c_1 = 0, 1, 2,... , c_2 = 0, 1, 2. The results of all multiplications lying on $c_1 = m - c_2$ belong to one convolution output data unit y_m. The additions necessary to build y_m can be carried out along $c_1 = m - c_2$ — the operation at point (c_1, c_2) is extended with an addition of the result coming from (c_1-1, c_2+1) and the result of the operation is sent to point (c_1+1, c_2-1). Since all points lying on $c_1=$ const and $c_2 =$ const receive the same x_{c_1}, a_{c_2} respectively, the number of external input operations (open arcs) can be reduced by means of supplying point (c_1,c_2) with the data unit x_{c_1}, a_{c_2} respectively, from its neighbour (c_1,c_2-1), (c_1-1,c_2) respectively. The cluster graph in Fig. 3 results from the procedure described. The points in Fig. 3.a) are clusters and input data is assigned to the open arcs. The structure of one cluster is shown in Fig. 3.b).

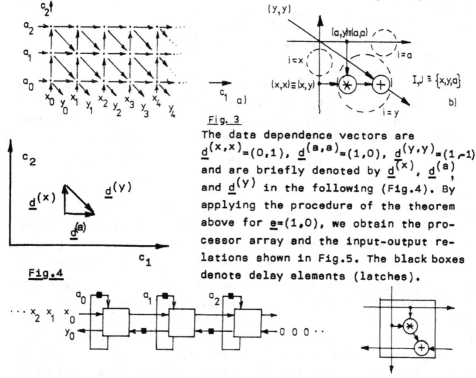

Fig. 3

The data dependence vectors are $\underline{d}^{(x,x)}=(0,1)$, $\underline{d}^{(a,a)}=(1,0)$, $\underline{d}^{(y,y)}=(1,-1)$ and are briefly denoted by $\underline{d}^{(x)}$, $\underline{d}^{(a)}$, and $\underline{d}^{(y)}$ in the following (Fig.4). By applying the procedure of the theorem above for $\underline{e}=(1,0)$, we obtain the processor array and the input-output relations shown in Fig.5. The black boxes denote delay elements (latches).

Fig.4

Fig.5

Characteristic for that design is that one of the data dependence vectors corresponds to broadcasting ($\underline{d}^{(x)}.\underline{e} = 0$), one to pure storage (staying) without movement from cell to cell ($\underline{d}^{(a)}-(\underline{d}^{(a)}.\underline{e}/e^2)\underline{e}=\underline{0}$) and one to a pipelined movement of data ($\underline{d}^{(y)}.\underline{e} \neq 0$, $\underline{d}^{(y)}-(\underline{d}^{(y)}.\underline{e}/e^2)\underline{e} \neq \underline{0}$). Another 5 designs have the same characteristics. They are obtained by permutation of the data type assignments to the data dependence vectors (Fig.6).

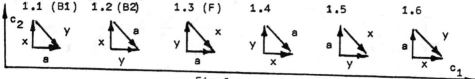

1.1 (B1) 1.2 (B2) 1.3 (F) 1.4 1.5 1.6

Fig.6

The denotions B1, B2, and F are from /3/. It is supposed that $\underline{e} = (1,0)$ is used for the building of $(\hat{r},\hat{t})$.

We show further how the algorithm for design 1.6 can be obtained from the algorithm for design 1.1 (Fig.3, Fig.5). By means of a linear transformation $\hat{L}: \mathbf{Z}^2 \to \mathbf{Z}^2$ of the coordinates, a new point $\underline{c}'$, $\underline{c}' = \hat{L}.\underline{c}$, is assigned to the multiplication in point $\underline{c}$. The matrix by which the transformation is performed is determined from the equations

$$\underline{d}'^{(x)} = v^{(x)}\hat{L}.\underline{d}^{(x)} \ , \quad v^{(x)} = \pm 1 \ , \quad d_1^{(x)} \geq 0,$$

$$\underline{d}'^{(y)} = v^{(y)}\hat{L}.\underline{d}^{(y)}, \quad v^{(y)} = \pm 1 \ , \quad d_1^{(y)} \geq 0,$$

$$\underline{d}'^{(a)} = v^{(a)}\hat{L}.\underline{d}^{(a)}, \quad v^{(a)} = \pm 1 \ , \quad d_1^{(a)} \geq 0,$$

where $\underline{d}'^{(x)}$, $\underline{d}'^{(y)}$, and $\underline{d}'^{(a)}$ are the data dependence vectors of the design 1.6: $\underline{d}'^{(a)} = (0,1)$, $\underline{d}'^{(x)} = (1,0)$, $\underline{d}'^{(y)} = (1,-1)$, and $\underline{d}^{(x)}$, $\underline{d}^{(a)}$, and $\underline{d}^{(y)}$ those of design 1.1, which are given above. From the equations for x- and a-data, the transformation matrix is found to be

$$\hat{L} = \begin{pmatrix} 0 & 1 \\ 1 & 0 \end{pmatrix} \ , \quad \underline{c}' = \hat{L}.\underline{c} \ , \text{ and the equation for y-data is satisfied}$$

by $v^{(y)} = -1$.

<u>Remark</u>: The corresponding Diophantine equations used in /4/ for the determination of the linear transformation matrix have no solution in this case and, that is why, the approach used here is more general. After the transformation the multiplication $a_{c_1'} \times c_2'$ is assigned to point (c_1', c_2') in $\mathbf{Z}^2$. Carrying out the steps used in the construction of the cluster graph in Fig. 3, we obtain the cluster graph in Fig.7.a). The structure of one cluster is the same as in Fig. 3.b). If we build $\hat{r}$ and $\hat{t}$ with $\underline{e} = (1,0)$ for this cluster graph, an infinite processor array arises (R - infinite). This is circumvented by carrying out a second transformation $\hat{T}: \mathbf{Z}^2 \to \mathbf{Z}^2$ (translation):

$$\hat{T}: \quad c_1^{\sim} = c_1' + c_2' - (c_2')_{\text{mod } 3} \ , \quad c_2'^{\sim} = (c_2')_{\text{mod } 3}$$

Using the same procedure as for the construction of the cluster graph in Fig.3, the cluster graph in Fig. 7.b) is obtained.

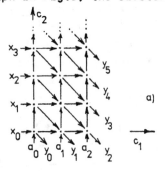

a)

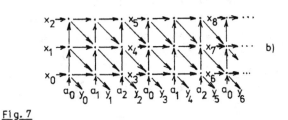

b)

<u>Fig. 7</u>

The corresponding processor array and input-output relations (Fig.8) are obtained after building $\hat{r}$ and $\hat{t}$ with $\underline{e} = (1,0)$.

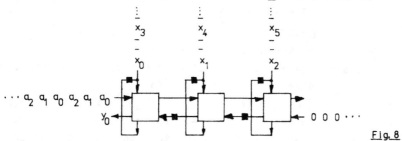

Fig. 8

It is proceeded similarly for all other designs /2/.

CLASSIFICATION OF THE SYSTOLIC DESIGNS FOR 1-D-CONVOLUTION

A triangle in Fig.6 represents in fact not a single design, but a group of designs. Different designs can be obtained for each group by varying the length of the data dependence vectors. For example, a design with the data dependence vectors
$$\underline{d}^{(x)}=(0,1), \quad \underline{d}^{(a)} = (2,0), \quad \underline{d}^{(y)} = (2,-1)$$
falls in group 1.1: broadcasting of x-data, pipelined movement of y-data, and staying of a-data. The set of designs falling in one group is enumerable — it can be described by the coordinates of two of the triangle's corners, the third corner is fixed.
We introduce a norm
$$\| \cdot \| = \sum_{\substack{i=x,y,a \\ l=1,2}} \left| d_l^{(i)} \right|$$
for the comparison of the different designs in one group. This norm is reasonable, because it represents the number of delay elements and the total length of cell interconnections per cell. The rest hardware of a cell is common for all designs of one group. The designs are otherwise equal as far as data flows and input-output relations are concerned. In that sense, the designs represented are minimal for the respective groups 1.1 and 1.6 .
All design groups in Fig.6 fall in one class, the class of designs in which one data flow is broadcasted, one stays,and one is moved in a pipelined fashion . All other possible classes are showed below. The corresponding groups in one class is obtained by permutation of data type assignments to the different data dependence vectors. A triangle of the data dependence vectors in space-time domain can be given for any systolic algorithm for 1-D-convolution represented in $\mathbb{Z}^2$. In that way, any such algorithm falls in one of the 7 classes and

42 (36 by symmetry in two of the classes) groups described below.

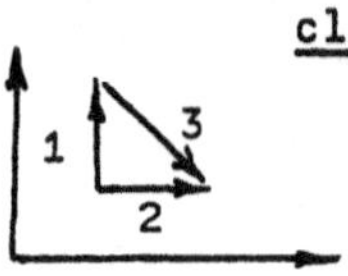

class 1: broadcasting of (1), staying of (2), pipelined movement of (3)

$\|\cdot\|_{min}=4$ for $\underline{d}^{(1)}=(0,1)$, $\underline{d}^{(2)}=(1,0)$, $\underline{d}^{(3)}=(1,-1)$

number of groups - 6

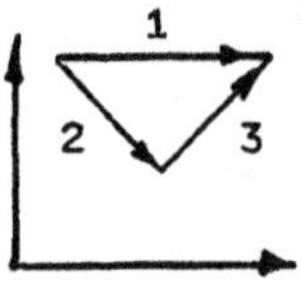

class 2: staying of (1), pipelined movement in opposite directions of (2) and (3)

$\|\cdot\|_{min}=6$ for $\underline{d}^{(1)}=(2,0)$, $\underline{d}^{(2)}=(1,-1)$, $\underline{d}^{(3)}=(1,1)$

number of groups - 6 (3 in case of symmetry)

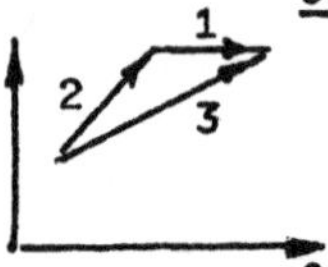

class 3: staying of (1), pipelined movement of (2) and (3) in the same direction

$\|\cdot\|_{min}=6$ for $\underline{d}^{(1)}=(1,0)$, $\underline{d}^{(2)}=(1,1)$, $\underline{d}^{(3)}=(2,1)$

number of groups - 6

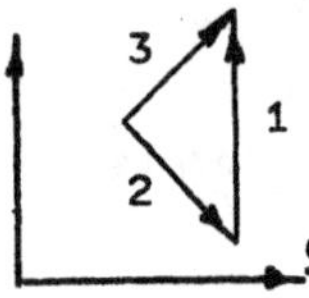

class 4: broadcasting of (1), pipelined movement of (2) and (3) in opposite directions

$\|\cdot\|_{min}=6$ for $\underline{d}^{(1)}=(0,2)$, $\underline{d}^{(2)}=(1,-1)$, $\underline{d}^{(3)}=(1,1)$

number of groups - 6 (3 in case of symmetry)

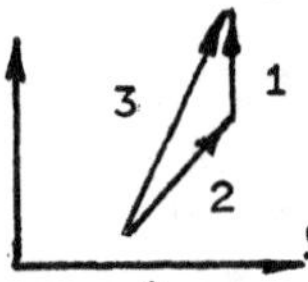

class 5: broadcasting of (1), pipelined movement of (2) and (3) in the same direction

$\|\cdot\|_{min}=6$ for $\underline{d}^{(1)}=(0,1)$, $\underline{d}^{(2)}=(1,1)$, $\underline{d}^{(3)}=(1,2)$

number of groups - 6

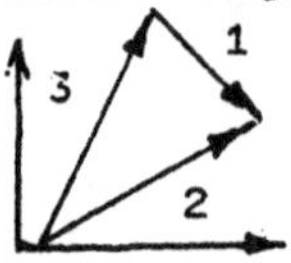

class 6: pipelined movement of (1), (2), and (3), two of them in the same direction

$\|\cdot\|_{min}=8$ for $\underline{d}^{(1)}=(1,-1)$, $\underline{d}^{(2)}=(2,1)$, $\underline{d}^{(3)}=(1,2)$

number of groups - 6

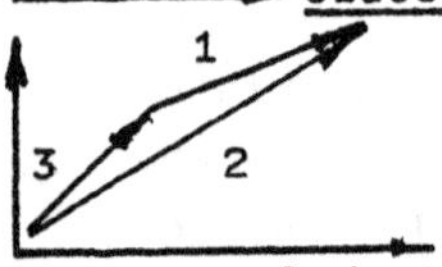

class 7: pipelined movement of (1), (2), and (3) in the same direction

$\|\cdot\|_{min}=10$ for $\underline{d}^{(1)}=(2,1)$, $\underline{d}^{(2)}=(3,2)$, $\underline{d}^{(3)}=(1,1)$

number of groups - 6

The minimal designs for 8 of the 42 groups were described in /3/.

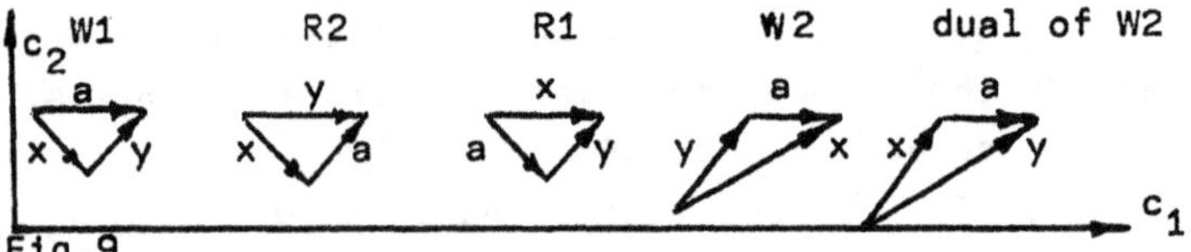

W1   R2   R1   W2   dual of W2   B1, B2, F

see Fig.6

Fig.9

REFERENCES

/1/ Harao, M., Lomtong, P.: A cellular reconfigurable data flow computing system. PARCELLA 84, Berlin, Sept. 84. Akademie-Verlag, Berlin 1985, pp.63-72.

/2/ Petkov-Turkedjiev, N.: Beitrag zur Synthese systolischer Algorithmen und Prozessorfelder. Dissertation A, TU Dresden, 1986.

/3/ Kung, H.T.: Why systolic architectures. Computer (IEEE) 15 (1981) 1, pp. 37-46.

/4/ Moldovan, D.I.: On the design of algorithms for VLSI systolic arrays. Proc. IEEE 71 (1983).

Fraktale und ihre Untersuchung
mit Parallelrechnung

Dr.rer.nat. R. Böhm, Dipl.-Inf. D. Homeister
Institut für Informatik der Universität Stuttgart
D-7000 Stuttgart 1

Graphical representation of fractals (recursive complex difference equations) is done by uncoupled, pointwise calculation in the complex plane. Method: as there is one task for each pixel, asynchronous task switching is needed because of different execution times. For this reason a MIMD architecture is appropriate. Scheduling and optimizing strategy are done by the host, whereas the time consuming arithmetic operations (iteration of sequences) runs on the parallel processor elements (PPE's). All asynchronous running PPE's work on an identical short program. The minimal configuration of PPE's could be: a CPU, an arithmetic coprocessor, and a minimal local store.

Grafische Darstellung von Fraktalen (rückgekoppelte komplexe Differenzengleichungen) über entkoppelte, punktweise Berechnung in der komplexen Ebene. Vorgehensweise: eine Task pro Rasterpunkt, durch unterschiedliche Rechenzeiten muß der Taskwechsel asynchron erfolgen. Dafür ist eine MIMD-Architektur zweckmäßig. Prozessorzuteilung und Optimierungsstrategie erfolgen im Host, während die zeitintensive Berechnung der Folge auf den Parallelrechner verlagert wird. Auf allen Prozessorelementen läuft ein identisches kurzes Programm zeitlich unabhängig ab. Die Prozessorelemente bestehen nur aus CPU, Arithmetik-Coprozessor und minimalem Speicher.

1. Berechnung der Fraktale

Stellvertretend für alle von uns behandelten Fraktale sei hier nur das Mandelbrot-Set [MAN82] beschrieben, da das Verhalten dieser Funktion am besten bekannt ist. Zum Set gehören alle Punkte der komplexen Ebene, deren Folgen nicht divergieren, wobei die jeweilige Koordinate der komplexen Ebene als c in die Iterationsgleichung eingeht. Die Iterationsvorschrift hat die Form

$$z_0 = 0$$
$$z_{n+1} = (z_n)^2 + c \qquad \text{(z und c komplex)}$$

Divergiert die Folge an einem Punkt nicht, so bedeutet dies in den wenigsten Fällen echte Konvergenz auf *einen* Grenzwert. Meistens oszilliert die Folge um mehrere Werte. Zur Veranschaulichung sind in *Tabelle 1* einige charakteristische Fälle dargestellt.

Die Ergebnisse der Iteration kann man auf einem entsprechenden Ausgabemedium graphisch in Farbe darstellen. Konvergente, also zum Mandelbrot-Set gehörende Bereiche werden dabei gewöhnlich schwarz dargestellt. Die restlichen Farben werden auf die außerhalb des Mandelbrot-Sets liegenden Punkte verteilt, sie geben in ihrer Abstufung die Geschwindigkeit der Divergenz an.

Die graphische Ausgabe bietet den großen Vorteil, daß selbst geringfügige Fehler im Programm und in der Arithmetik sofort sichtbar werden. Bei Arithmetikfehlern verschwindet z.B. bei starker Ausschnittsvergrößerung die "Selbstähnlichkeit" ganz oder teilweise.

Die farbige Darstellung entstand daraus, daß an den divergenten Punkten die Folge abgebrochen werden muß, bevor ein arithmetischer Überlauf auftritt (*Bild 1*). Die Folgen steigen mitunter sehr schnell an, so daß eine relativ niedrige Grenze nötig ist, bei der die Berechnung an den jeweiligen Punkten abgebrochen werden muß. Die erreichte Schleifenzahl beim Abbruch wird als Maß für die Geschwindigkeit der Divergenz genommen und dem Punkt als entsprechende Farbe zugeordnet.

	c	2	-2	-1	-0.1300 +0.7400i
	z_0	0	0	0	0
	z_1	2	-2	-1	-0.1300 +0.7400i
	z_2	6	2	0	-0.6607 +0.5476i
Tabelle 1	z_3	38	2	-1	0.0067 +0.0164i
	z_4	1446	2	0	-0.1302 +0.7402i
	z_5	2090918	2	-1	-0.6610 +0.5472i
	z_6	$4.37*10^{12}$	2	0	0.0067 +0.0164i
		divergent	echt konvergent	oszillierend (um 2 Werte)	oszillierend (um 3 Werte)

Eine weitere Abbruchbedingung der Berechnung ist die maximale Schleifenzahl. Mit Erhöhung dieses Wertes steigt die benötigte Rechenzeit an, der Anstieg ist im ungünstigen Fall quadratisch und liegt in der Praxis meist nur knapp darunter. Gelangt die Berechnung an diese Abbruchbedingung, wird der Punkt als stabil angenommen und schwarz gezeichnet. Bei einer zu niedrigen maximalen Schleifenzahl wird die Berechnung ungenau, es werden dann Punkte dem Set zugerechnet, die in Wirklichkeit divergent sind. Mit steigender Schleifenzahl ist also eine genauere Aussage möglich. Für die Interpretation eines als konvergent berechneten Punktes gibt es somit drei Möglichkeiten :
- echte Konvergenz (*Bild 2*)
- oszillierende Konvergenz, die Funktion oszilliert um zwei oder mehrere Punkte (*Bild 3*)
- die Folge divergiert "zu langsam" und die Schleifenzahl ist zu niedrig, so daß ein divergenter Punkt irrtümlich als konvergent eingestuft wird (*Bild 4*). Hier wurde die zweite Abbruchbedingung (die Begrenzung der Schleifenzahl) vor der ersten (Grenze für den Betrag der Folgeglieder) erreicht.

Der Grenzwert für den Betrag der Folgeglieder muß so hoch gewählt werden, daß beim Oszillieren ein Überschreiten des Grenzwertes sicher ausgeschlossen werden kann. Die maximale Schleifenzahl muß so groß sein, daß auch eine sehr langsame Divergenz noch erkannt werden kann.

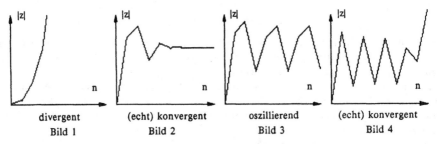

divergent	(echt) konvergent	oszillierend	(echt) konvergent
Bild 1	Bild 2	Bild 3	Bild 4

Die Vermutung, daß die Selbstähnlichkeit, also die Wiederholung fast gleicher Formen in verschiedenen Größen an anderen Stellen auf der komplexen Ebene, nur das Resultat numerischer Effekte ist, kann leicht widerlegt werden. In diesem Fall würde sich bei Berechnung mit halber Genauigkeit ein anderes Bild ergeben. Dies ist aber nicht der Fall, es sei denn, die Genauigkeit der halbgenauen Berechnung reicht bei starker Vergrößerung nicht mehr aus.

2. Optimierung

Die hier verwendete Optimierung [HOM86] nutzt einige in [DOU82] beschriebene Eigenschaften des Mandelbrot-Sets aus, um die Rechenzeit drastisch zu verringern. Alle zum Set gehörende Punkte hängen wie durch Nabelschnüre verbunden zusammen. Das Mandelbrot-Set bildet eine baumartig verästelte Struktur aus, deshalb entstehen nie geschlossene Ringe. Daraus folgt, daß divergente Gebiete in keinem Fall vollständig von Punkten des Sets umschlossen sein können. Es genügt also, zusammenhängende, zum Set gehörende Gebiete nur an den Rändern zu berechnen, die Berechnung des eingeschlossenen Teils erübrigt sich, wenn nur der Rand genau bekannt ist. Der innere Teil enthält keine zusätzliche Information.

Dieses optimierte Verfahren funktioniert außer beim Mandelbrot-Set auch bei vielen ähnlichen Funktionen, im Einzelfall muß theoretisch oder experimentell untersucht werden, ob divergente "Inseln" vorkommen, die von konvergenten Bereichen eingeschlossen sind.

Durch die Ungenauigkeit, die durch die Rasterung bei der Berechnung entsteht, können scheinbare Inseln aus sehr "dünnen" Bereichen entstehen. *Bild 5* zeigt diesen Effekt bei einer Verringerung des Rasters um den Faktor 3.

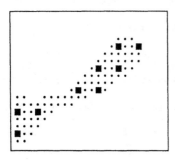

Bild 5

konvergente Punkte im feinen Raster: • und ■,
konvergente Punkte im groben Raster: nur ■,
divergente Punkte sind nicht gezeichnet

Es genügt also nicht, die unmittelbar benachbarten Rasterpunkte zu untersuchen. Im bisher implementierten Programmsystem werden deshalb wahlweise Punkte bis zu einem Abstand von zwei bzw. drei berücksichtigt. Die Lage der Nachbarpunkte ist aus *Bild 6* zu ersehen.

```
 .  .  .  .  .  .  .  .  .        .  .  .  .  .  .  .  .  .
 .  .  .  .  .  .  .  .  .        .  .  .  ¤  ¤  ¤  .  .  .     Bild 6
 .  .  .  .  ¤  .  .  .  .        .  .  ¤  ¤  ¤  ¤  ¤  .  .
 .  .  .  ¤  ¤  ¤  .  .  .        .  ¤  ¤  ¤  ¤  ¤  ¤  ¤  .
 .  .  ¤  ¤  ■  ¤  ¤  .  .        .  ¤  ¤  ¤  ■  ¤  ¤  ¤  .     ■ = aktueller Bildpunkt
 .  .  .  ¤  ¤  ¤  .  .  .        .  ¤  ¤  ¤  ¤  ¤  ¤  ¤  .     ¤ = berücksichtigte Nachbarpunkte
 .  .  .  .  ¤  .  .  .  .        .  .  ¤  ¤  ¤  ¤  ¤  .  .     • = in dieser Rekursionsebene
 .  .  .  .  .  .  .  .  .        .  .  .  ¤  ¤  ¤  .  .  .          unberücksichtigte Bildpunkte
 .  .  .  .  .  .  .  .  .        .  .  .  .  .  .  .  .  .
         Abstand 2                        Abstand 3
```

3. Verfahren der Optimierung

Vor Beginn der eigentlichen Berechnung wird ein zweidimensionales Feld zum Ablegen der Ergebnisse angelegt. Dieses Feld dient gleichzeitig dazu, berechnete Punkte zu markieren, um eine Doppelberechnung auszuschließen. Ein positiver Wert oder Null bedeutet dabei "schon berechnet". Die Berechnung der einzelnen Punkte unterscheidet sich nicht vom Standard-Verfahren. Es wird das gleiche

Unterprogramm aufgerufen, nur die Reihenfolge der Aufrufe ist geändert. Beim normalen Verfahren werden die Bildpunkte zeilenweise abgetastet. Beim optimierten Verfahren werden zunächst alle Randpunkte des Bildausschnittes berechnet, weil von jeder Stelle der vier Bildränder divergente Bereiche in das Bild hineinragen können.

Bei einem divergenten Punkt wird im Ergebnisfeld die Schleifenzahl beim Abbruch (der Farbwert) abgelegt, mit dem positiven Wert ist der Punkt gleichzeitig als berechnet markiert. Dann werden die 12 bzw. 36 Nachbarpunkte rekursiv demselben Verfahren unterworfen, falls der jeweilige Nachbarpunkt nicht schon berechnet wurde. Bei konvergenten Punkten wird in das Ergebnisfeld 0 eingetragen und damit der Punkt als berechnet markiert. In dieser Situation werden keine Nachbarpunkte untersucht, um nicht ins Innere des konvergenten Bereiches vorzudringen. Die Rekursion ist beendet, wenn alle Nachbarpunkte eines Punktes schon als berechnet markiert sind. Das Verfahren ist abgeschlossen, wenn die Rekursion von allen Randpunkten aus vollständig durchgeführt wurde.

Auf diese Art wird jedes konvergente Gebiet von allen Seiten eingegrenzt. Damit sind alle divergenten Punkte berechnet. Von zusammenhängenden konvergenten Flächen werden nur die Randpunkte echt berechnet, der innere Teil bleibt mit -1 markiert, um die Optimierung zu dokumentieren. Jetzt kann das Ergebnisfeld auf die externe Datei geschrieben werden.

Das folgende Programmstück in Pascal zeigt die prinzipielle Funktion:

```
procedure sucherekursiv ( x,y : short_integer );
begin {sucherekursiv}
if feld [ x,y ] < 0 then  {noch nicht berechnet und nicht außerhalb}
      {alle Feldelemente wurden mit -1 initialisiert}
      {Bremse: außerhalb des Bildes liegende Feldelemente sind mit 1 vorbesetzt}
   begin
   farbe := berechne_punkt ( x,y );  {innerste Schleife in FORTRAN }
   feld [ x,y ] := farbe;
   if farbe>0 then { 12 Umgebungspunkte rekursiv berechnen, falls nicht konvergent}
      begin
      sucherekursiv(x+2,y);
      sucherekursiv(x-2,y);
      sucherekursiv(x,y+2);
      sucherekursiv(x,y-2);      {           ^            }
      sucherekursiv(x+1,y);      {         ^ ^ ^          }
      sucherekursiv(x-1,y);      {       < < * > >        }
      sucherekursiv(x,y+1);      {         v v v          }
      sucherekursiv(x,y-1);      {           v            }
      sucherekursiv(x+1,y+1);
      sucherekursiv(x+1,y-1);
      sucherekursiv(x-1,y+1);
      sucherekursiv(x-1,y-1);
      end;
   end;
end; {sucherekursiv}
```

Der Speicherplatzbedarf des Verfahrens ist extrem hoch, für das Ergebnisfeld sind zwei Byte pro Bildpunkt nötig. Die Rekursionstiefe ist im ungünstigsten Fall gleich der Zahl der Bildpunkte. Die Rekursion wurde deshalb aufgelöst und der Stack manuell verwaltet. Dadurch konnte die Information, die im Stack abgelegt wird, auf ein Byte pro Rekursionsebene reduziert werden.

Die erzielbare Geschwindigkeitssteigerung hängt stark vom berechneten Gebiet ab. Günstig für eine Berechnung nach dem optimierten Verfahren sind Bildausschnitte, die große zusammenhängende konvergente Gebiete beinhalten. Bei solchen Gebieten wurden Geschwindigkeitssteigerungen um einen Faktor 200 beobachtet. Meist verringert sich die Rechenzeit um einen Faktor 2 bis 10.

4. Möglichkeiten der Parallelisierung

Die Parallelisierung der Berechnung von rückgekoppelten Differenzengleichungen mit einem Multiprozessor-Rechner erscheint sehr effizient in Hinblick auf die Rechenzeit und auf die Kosten, weil hierbei viele gleichartige Prozessoren ohne Peripherie verwendet werden können. Falls die Parallelisierung so weit geht, daß einzelne Bildpunkte parallel berechnet werden, kommen die einzelnen Prozessorelemente sogar mit einem Minimum an Programm- und Datenspeicherplatz aus. Denkbar wäre hier beispielsweise ein preiswertes Minimalsystem für jedes Prozessorelement mit einer 16-Bit-CPU, einem Arithmetik-Coprozessor und 64 KByte Speicher.

Ein großer Anteil der Berechnungen bei Fraktalen besteht aus *entkoppelten* Einzelberechnungen der Punkte in einem zweidimensionalen Feld. Unter diesen Randbedingungen bietet sich eine Parallelisierung dieser Berechnung geradezu an. Dabei kann der Verwaltungsteil dem Front-End-Rechner übergeben werden. Dieser Teil beinhaltet den Benutzerdialog, den externen Datentransfer und die äußeren beiden verschachtelten Schleifen, die das Feld in zwei Dimensionen abarbeiten. Die serielle Berechnung der innersten Schleife, welche die Iteration an jedem Punkt berechnet, kann den Prozessorelementen eines Parallelrechners übertragen werden.

Die Problemstellung unterscheidet sich von vielen *stark gekoppelten* Berechnungen wie Fourier-Analyse oder Simulationen in der Atomphysik vor allem dadurch, daß die einzelnen Teilberechnungen verschieden lange Rechenzeiten benötigen (*Bild 8*), obwohl auf allen Prozessoren das gleiche Programm läuft. Die Teilberechnungen unterscheiden sich nur durch die unterschiedliche Koordinate des jeweiligen Bildpunktes, der in die Berechnung eingeht.

Um den Zeitvorteil eines Parallelrechners voll auszuschöpfen, ist ein Rechner mit MIMD-Architektur mit entsprechender Betriebssoftware nötig, also eine Anordnung aus völlig unabhängig arbeitenden Prozessorelementen. Bei der Verwendung von Vektorrechnern oder anderen SIMD-Rechnern entsteht *implizit* ein *stärkerer Kopplungsgrad*, weil ein großer Teil der Einzelberechnungen vor Erreichen der maximalen Schleifenzahl beendet werden darf. Bei einem SIMD-Rechner müssen aber *alle* Berechnungen, die in einem Zeitabschnitt parallel bearbeitet werden, mit der maximalen Schleifenzahl ausgeführt werden, obwohl dies für viele der Einzelpunkte unnötig ist. Eine gewisse Optimierung ist dabei noch möglich, die Berechnung aller Punkte kann beendet werden, sobald die letzte Einzelberechnung beendet ist.

Der Zeitvorteil eines Vektorrechners wie der CRAY I würde bei dieser speziellen Problemstellung also durch seine SIMD-Architektur teilweise zunichte gemacht. Viele Elemente der parallelen Berechnung verbringen lange Zeit mit Warteschleifen!

Die Anforderungen an ein Parallelrechner-Betriebssystem für einen MIMD-Rechner sind unter diesen Gesichtspunkten nicht sehr hoch. Es ist lediglich nötig, die zeitlich linearen Aufrufe in der vorliegenden (nichtparallelisierten) Implementierung in eine verteilte Abarbeitung auf mehreren unabhängigen Prozessorelementen umzuwandeln. Das Betriebssystem muß dazu nur bei jedem "Unterprogrammaufruf" ein freies Prozessorelement suchen und bei Beendigung jedes Teilprozesses den jeweiligen Prozessor als frei markieren und das Ergebnis ablegen.

Wird aber das optimierte Verfahren verwendet, entsteht eine *begrenzte Kopplung* zwischen den Bildpunkten, da einige Punkte in Abhängigkeit ihrer Nachbarpunkte überhaupt nicht berechnet werden. Bei Verwendung dieses rekursiven Verfahrens benötigt ein Rekursionsaufruf möglicherweise das Ergebnis eines anderen, wodurch Wartezustände entstehen. Eine Systemverklemmung ist aber ausgeschlossen, weil durch die baumartige Verzweigungsstruktur der Rekursionsaufrufe keine gegenseitige Abhängigkeit der Berechnungsergebnisse vorkommen kann. In ungünstigen Fällen ist es nur möglich, daß alle Prozessorelemente auf das Ergebnis eines Elementes warten. Durch eine günstige Verteilung der Startwerte der Rekursion können solche Wartezustände voraussichtlich stark reduziert werden. Im bisherigen (linearen) Verfahren wird von einem Startwert ausgehend rekursiv das ganze Feld berechnet. Bei n Prozessoren können n Startwerte gleichmäßig am Rand des Bildausschnittes verteilt werden, so daß es erst in einer späten Phase der Berechnung zu Überschneidungen kommen

178

kann. In diesem Fall müssen allerdings mehrere Stacks verwaltet werden, da bei dem optimierten Verfahren jeder Startpunkt mit einer unabhängigen Rekursion berechnet werden muß.

Zur Zeitersparnis sollte bei der Parallelberechnung der Algorithmus der Optimierung an einer Stelle abgeändert werden. Bisher wird am Ende jeder Berechnung eines Punktes in einem gemeinsamen Feld das Ergebnis *und* die Information, daß der Punkt berechnet wurde, abgelegt, um einen Zugriff einzusparen. Bei der optimierten Berechnung auf einem Parallelrechner sollte jeder Punkt erst vom Front-End-Rechner als berechnet markiert werden, und danach die eigentliche Berechnung gestartet werden. Andernfalls könnte die Berechnung an einem Punkt mehrfach von verschiedenen Nachbarpunkten aus gestartet werden, bevor der erste Prozeß, der den Punkt bereits bearbeitet, diesen Punkt als berechnet markiert.

5. Gegenüberstellung der verschiedenen Verfahren

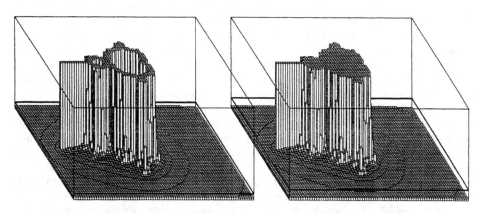

Bild 7: Optimierte Berechnung mit unabhängigen Prozessorelementen Durchschnitt: 7.7%

Bild 8: Nichtoptimierte Berechnung mit unabhängigen Prozessorelementen Durchschnitt: 12.2%

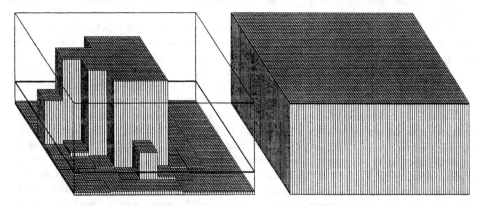

Bild 9: Partiell gekoppelte Berechnung Durchschnitt: 23.7%

Bild 10: Vollständig gekoppelte Berechnung Durchschnitt: 100%

Rechenzeit pro Punkt (Höhe der Quader) und mittlere Rechenzeit (dicke schwarze Linie)

Verfahren 1: Serielle Berechnung

Die Berechnung erfolgt bei diesem Verfahren auf einem Prozessor zeitlich seriell Punkt für Punkt. Der Arbeitsspeicherbedarf ist sehr niedrig.

Die Berechnungszeit ist dabei die Summe der Berechnungszeiten aller Punkte, bei hoher Schleifenzahl ist der Verwaltungsaufwand zu vernachlässigen (*Bild 8*).

Verfahren 2: Serielle optimierte Berechnung

Hier berechnet ein Prozessor zeitlich seriell alle divergenten und einen Teil der konvergenten Punkte. Der Speicherplatzbedarf ist dabei extrem hoch.

Es entsteht ein erheblicher Verwaltungsaufwand, der aber bei großen konvergenten Bereichen und hoher maximaler Schleifenzahl von den eingesparten Schleifendurchläufe aufgewogen wird. Die gesamte Berechnungszeit ist im ungünstigsten Fall länger als im Verfahren 1, im günstigsten Fall aber weniger als 1% davon. Im Mittel beträgt sie 10 bis 40% der Zeit des 1. Verfahrens (*Bild 7*).

Verfahren 3: Berechnung mit einem Vektorrechner

Die Zahl der Bildpunkte übersteigt in der Regel die Zahl der maximal möglichen parallelen Berechnungen. Die gesamte zu berechnende Fläche muß also segmentiert werden. Es ist dabei günstig, nicht ganze Zeilen oder Teile von Zeilen parallel zu berechnen, sondern kleine Flächen. Dadurch wird eine gleichmäßigere Verteilung innerhalb eines parallel berechneten "Vektors" erreicht, dies begünstigt das nachfolgend beschriebene Verfahren. Zur Veranschaulichung wurden im *Bild 7* quadratische Flächen mit einer Kantenlänge von 8 dargestellt, was einer Vektorlänge von 64 entspricht.

Anstatt wie im *Bild 10* alle Bildpunkte bis zur maximalen Schleifenzahl zu berechnen, kann die Berechnung schon dann abgebrochen werden, wenn der letzte Bildpunkt einer parallel bearbeiteten Gruppe berechnet ist. Eine andere Abbruchbedingung wäre, wenn bei allen Bildpunkten einer Gruppe ein arithmetischer Überlauf aufgetreten ist. Hier wird also die innerste Schleife parallelisiert und mit einer geänderten Abbruchbedingung ausgeführt. Dadurch werden viele unnötige Durchläufe durch die innerste Schleife vermieden, der Zeitbedarf sinkt (s. *Bild 9* gegenüber *Bild 10*).

Tritt bei einzelnen Punkten ein Overflow auf, muß trotzdem weitergerechnet werden. Dabei geht die Information verloren, bei welcher Schleifenzahl der Betrag der Folge den vorgegebenen Grenzwert überschreitet. Das Ergebnis besagt nur, ob ein Punkt divergent ist oder nicht, die Farbinformation geht verloren. Um die Farbinformation zu erhalten, müssen einige oder alle der Zwischenergebnisse abgespeichert und später ausgewertet werden.

Durch die gegenseitige Abhängigkeit aller Berechnungen innerhalb eines Vektors verliert dieses Verfahren stark an Effizienz. Es erscheint nur sinnvoll, andere Eigenschaften von Vektorrechnern zu nutzen, z.B. hochgenaue Arithmetik. Die Vektorrechner Siemens 7·800 VP x00 bieten z.B. bei serieller Abarbeitung eine schnelle Arithmetik mit Zahlen von 128 Bit Länge an [SIE85].

Die Berechnungszeit kann etwa aus *Bild 9* abgelesen werden, dividiert durch die Vektorlänge. Der Verwaltungsaufwand ist bei hoher Schleifenzahl zu vernachlässigen. Falls die Farbwerte berechnet werden sollen, steigt die Zeit allerdings nochmals an.

Verfahren 4: Parallele Einzelpunktberechnung auf unabhängigen Prozessoren

Diese Lösung basiert auf dem Verfahren 1. Nach Ende einer Berechnung meldet sich der Prozessor beim Front-End-Rechner zurück, liefert das Ergebnis ab und erhält einen neuen Berechnungsauftrag. Der Prozessorwechsel erfolgt hier asynchron, deshalb entstehen keine Wartezeiten wie bei einem Vektorrechner.

Der Speicherbedarf für Daten und Programm ist sehr gering. Jedes Prozessorelement enthält nur die innerste Schleife als Programm. Organisation und Benutzerdialog bleiben im Front-End-Rechner.

Der Zeitbedarf liegt hier knapp über dem Durchschnittwert der Berechnungen aller Einzelpunkte (*Bild 8*), dividiert durch die Zahl der unabhängigen Prozessorelemente. Es müssen zwar nur wenige Daten transportiert werden (zwei Koordinaten und ein Ergebniswert pro Punkt), aber die Datenübertragung kann in extrem kurzen Zeitabständen stattfinden. Bei Verwendung eines Front-End-Rechners mit Time-Sharing entstehen möglicherweise Verzögerungen, weil die Prozessorzuteilung dann um die Reaktionszeit des Front-End-Rechners verlangsamt wird. In diesem Fall könnte ein kleiner Echtzeitprozessor für die Zuteilung zwischengeschaltet werden. Dann entsteht eine dreistufige Arbeitsteilung:

Front-End-Rechner:	Benutzerdialog, Verwaltung, File-Handling
Zuteilungsrechner:	Zuteilung der Prozessorelemente in Echtzeit
Prozessor-Array:	Parallele Berechnung der Einzelpunkte

Verfahren 5: Parallele Berechnung von ganzen Bildzeilen

Dieses Verfahren modifiziert das Verfahren 4, um die Kommunikationshäufigkeit zu senken. Statt der innersten Schleife werden hier die beiden inneren Schleifen in jeden Prozessor des Parallelrechners verlagert. Dadurch entfällt die Notwendigkkeit des Zuteilungsrechners. Die Kommunikation kann dann sogar problemlos über einen seriellen Bus abgewickelt werden.

Das Zeitverhalten ähnelt dem des Verfahrens 4. Die Wartezeiten verringern sich, dafür kann am Ende der Berechnung eine Zeile mit hoher Gesamtschleifenzahl übrigbleiben, die von einem Prozessorelement berechnet wird, während alle anderen warten. Es könnte sich daher als besser erweisen, nur Teile von Zeilen an die Prozessorelemente zu vergeben.

Verfahren 6: Parallele optimierte Berechnung auf unabhängigen Prozessoren

Eine Kombination der Verfahren 2 und 4 vereinigt die Vorteile beider Verfahren. Ein hoher Speicherplatzbedarf entsteht nur im Front-End-Rechner, nicht aber auf den Prozessorelementen des Parallelrechners.

Der Zeitbedarf beträgt etwas mehr als der Mittelwert bei der optimierten Berechnung (*Bild 7*), dividiert durch die Zahl der Prozessorelemente. Verwaltungaufwand und Wartezeiten werden hier merklich ins Gewicht fallen. Bei ungünstiger Organisation kann der Fall eintreten, daß alle Prozessorelemente bis auf eines warten müssen. Falls dieser Zustand oft auftritt, sollte das Feld in zwei oder vier unabhängig zu optimierende Teilfelder zerlegt werden (bei freier Prozessorverteilung). Die freie Kapazität wartender Prozessoren würde dann anderen Teilfeldern zufließen. Die Erfahrungen mit dem (nichtparallelisierten) Verfahren 2 zeigen, daß die Optimierung auch einen erheblichen Verwaltungsaufwand aufwiegt.

Verfahren 7: Parallele Berechnung von Teilflächen.

Bei diesem Verfahren wird die Verwaltung vom Front-End-Rechner zu den Prozessorelementen verlagert. Nur der Benutzerdialog und die Dateiverwaltung bleibt im Front-End-Rechner. Das zu berechnende Feld wird in eine Anzahl von Unterfeldern aufgeteilt, die größer als die Prozessorzahl sein soll. Jeder Prozessor arbeitet sein aktuell zugeteiltes Teilfeld dabei seriell ab. Die Bildteile können auch nach dem optimierten Verfahren berechnet werden.

Dieses Verfahren bietet gegenüber den bisher aufgeführten keine Zeitvorteile. Beim optimierten Verfahren entsteht sogar ein Verlust an Effizienz, weil zur Optimierung ein möglichst großes Feld nötig ist. Der Speicherbedarf für Daten und für das Programm in den Prozessorelementen ist wesentlich höher als bei allen anderen Verfahren. Möglicherweise stehen für den jeweiligen Parallelrechner auch keine Compiler zur Verfügung, die andere als arithmetische Operationen realisieren können, die Verwaltungsaufgaben können dann nur von Front-End-Rechnern übernommen werden.

6. Rechenzeit-Abschätzung

Anhand zweier Beispiele soll die benötigte Rechenzeit der im letzten Kapitel beschriebenen Verfahren abgeschätzt werden. Bei *Bild 11* fallen stark ungleich verteilte Rechenzeiten an, während bei dem inneren Bildausschnitt (Kasten in *Bild 11*) die Rechenzeiten gleichmäßiger verteilt sind. Durch den hohen Anteil konvergenter Bildpunkte (etwa 52%) müssen beim optimierten Verfahren die meisten der rechenzeitintensiven Punkte überhaupt nicht berechnet werden.

Daten zu *Bild 11* (in Klammern Werte bei optimierter Berechnung) :

	gesamtes Bild	innerer Ausschnitt
Maximale Schleifenzahl:	4000	4000
Raster:	560 * 455	560 * 455
Zahl der Bildpunkte:	254800	254800
Durchläufe durch die innerste Schleife:	$72.4*10^6$ $(60.1*10^6)$	$610*10^6$ $(176*10^6)$
Mittlere Schleifenzahl pro Punkt:	284 (236)	2312 (638)
Anteil Punkte mit maximaler Schleifenzahl:	1.48% (0.27%)	52.1% (1.22%)

Tabelle 2 zeigt geschätzte Zeiten bei Voraussetzung einer Vektorlänge bzw. Prozessorzahl von 64. Zum Vergleich sind auch die Meßergebnisse der nichtparallelisierten Berechnungen mit ausgeführt. Die Zeiten beinhalten Rechenzeit und Verwaltungszeit.

Tabelle 2

Verfahren	gesamtes Bild 11	innerer Teil
Verfahren 1: seriell	32000 sek. [1]	267000 sek. [1]
Verfahren 2: seriell optimiert	27131 sek. [2]	78000 sek. [1]
Verfahren 3a: vollständig gekoppelt	8000 sek. [3]	8000 sek. [3]
Verfahren 3b: 8*8-Felder gekoppelt	1500 sek. [3]	5300 sek. [3]
Verfahren 4: entkoppelte Einzelpunkte	500 sek.	4000 sek.
Verfahren 5: entkoppelte Zeilen	600 sek.	4200 sek.
Verfahren 6: entkoppelte Punkte, optimiert	425 sek.	1200 sek.
Verfahren 7a: entkoppelte Teilflächen (8*8)	600 sek.	4200 sek.
Verfahren 7b: entkoppelte Teilfl., optimiert	600 sek.	3000 sek.

Anmerkungen zur Tabelle:
- Zugrundegelegte Zeit pro Schleifendurchlauf: 440 µs
- Wenn nicht anders angegeben, geschätzte Zeiten
- [1] Zeit aus Berechnungen mit geringerer Punktezahl extrapoliert
- [2] Messung auf Hewlett-Packard System 9000/520 (ca. 1 Mips)
- [3] falls nur Information über Divergenz bzw. Konvergenz berechnet werden soll (d.h. keine Farbwerte), sind etwa 1000 Sekunden weniger nötig

Bild 11: Ausschnitt des Mandelbrot-Sets

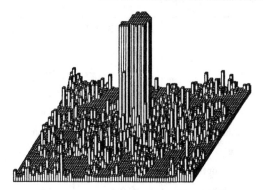

Bild 12: Balkendiagramm der Rechenzeiten in Bild 11

Literatur

[DOU82]   A. Douady, J. Hubbard: *Itérations des polynômes quadratiques complexes*,
          C. R. Acad. Sci. Paris 294, 123-126, 1982

[HOM86]   Dieter Homeister: *Software-Werkzeuge für die effiziente Untersuchung von rückgekoppel-
          ten komplexen Differenzengleichungen*,
          Diplomarbeit Nr. 538, Institut für Informatik, Universität Stuttgart, 1986

[MAN82]   Benoit B. Mandelbrot: *The Fractal Geometry of Nature*,
          Freeman, New York, 1982

[SIE85]   *Vector Processor System VP100/VP200*,
          Siemens, Order No. U1917-J-Z64-1-7600, ca. 1985

A parallel processing algorithm for Thinning Digitised Pictures

R H Perrott
C Holt
M Clint
A Stewart

Department of Computer Science
Queen's University of Belfast
Northern Ireland BT7 1NN

Abstract

A digitised picture can be represented as a two dimensional array of Boolean values.
An iterative thinning algorithm reduces each connected pattern of such a picture to
a corresponding skeleton of unitary thickness ensuring that:

(1)   spurious branches are not present in the final skeleton;

(2)   the thinned pattern is approximately in the centre of the original pattern.

A new algorithm is presented which is designed to exploit the computing potential of
array processors.   In particular, the algorithm can be efficiently implemented on
the ICL Distributed Array Processor.

1   Introduction

A digitised picture can be represented by a Boolean matrix in which each element is
either true (represented as one) or false (represented as zero).   A thinning
algorithm [1,2] has the task of determining a line which represents the picture,
that is, a skeleton of unit thickness.   This skeleton can then be used to facilitate
pattern recognition.

Most algorithms work by peeling off a layer of the picture on each iteration until a

skeleton is obtained. This can be achieved by applying a 3 X 3 window to each
element and using the values of the eight neighbours to determine whether or not the
central element survives to the next iteration. The usual method for identifying
the neighbours of any element P is by using the points of the compass as in

```
NW  N   NE
W   P   E
SW  S   SE
```

In general, an element may be removed when it is on the edge of a stroke. In most
situations this occurs when the element has from 2 to 6 connected neighbours, where
connectedness is defined as the existence of a path between any two true neighbours
that passes only through true neighbours.

Examples of situations in which an element has between 2 and 6 connected neighbours
are the following:

```
1 1 0            1 1 1            1 1 1
0 P 0            0 P 0            0 P 1
0 0 0            0 0 0            0 1 1
```

It is therefore safe to remove the element P in each of these three cases.

The following are examples of elements which do not satisfy the above conditions and
should not be removed

```
0 0 0            0 0 0
0 P 1            1 P 1
0 0 0            0 0 0
```

In the first case P is an endpoint and in the second case P is an interior point of
a skeleton line. If P is removed in the first case then all lines are thinned down
to points and if P is removed in the second case the overall continuity of the
pattern is broken.

The conditions under which an element can be removed can be determined by examining
pairs of neighbours of an element proceeding clockwise. There are between two and
six connected neighbours when at least one (0,0) pair is found, at least one (1,1)
pair is found, and exactly one (0,1) pair is found.

The detection of such a situation can be carried out in a function called edge which
is given in the Appendix.

Hence the condition for removing an element is that the expression

v(P) and edge(P) is true   (1)

where

v(P) is the value of the element P and

edge(P) is a function that ensures the above conditions are true for the element P.

Conversely an element survives to the next iteration if the expression

$$v(P) \text{ and not } edge(P) \tag{2}$$

is true.

If applied in a sequential fashion this technique will produce a skeleton of unit thickness. However with a parallel algorithm which considers many elements at the same time additional constraints are required, namely,
(1)   the removal of the edges of a stroke should not remove the entire stroke;
(2)   all four elements of an isolated 2 X 2 square should not be removed;
(3)   the connectedness of the overall structure should not be affected by the simultaneous removal of a number of elements.

The second case can be illustrated as follows. Given

```
0 0 0 0
0 1 1 0
0 1 1 0
0 0 0 0
```

then each present element has 2 pairs of connected neighbours and if the edge condition is applied in parallel then all of the present elements are simultaneously removed – which is, clearly, an undesirable effect.

Such problems can be avoided by introducing a directional bias to the algorithm by, for example, favouring North over South and West over East and associating a subiteration with each directional bias.

The first subiteration may result in the removal of an element if it is on a South or East edge or if it is a North-West corner element. The condition for this to be true is

$$\text{not } v(E) \text{ or not } v(S) \text{ or } (\text{not } v(N) \text{ and not } v(W)) \tag{3}$$

Hence the element survives if the expression

$$v(E) \text{ and } v(S) \text{ and } (v(N) \text{ or } v(W)) \tag{4}$$

is true.

In the second subiteration the element may be removed if it is on a North or West edge or if it is a South-East corner element. The condition for this to happen is

$$\text{not } v(W) \text{ or not } v(N) \text{ or } (\text{not } v(S) \text{ and not } v(E)) \tag{5}$$

Hence the complete expression for survival of an element on the first subiteration is obtained by combining expressions (2) and (4) giving

v(P) and (not edge(P) or (v(E) and v(S) and (v(N) or v(W))))   (6)

On the second subiteration the complete expression for survival of an element is

v(P) and (not edge(P) or (v(W) and v(N) and (v(S) or v(E))))

(7)

This result has been applied successfully as shown by Zhang and Suen [3].

2 An improved algorithm

It has been shown that it is possible to remove one of the subiterations if edge information is provided about the neighbours of an element [4]. For example, in a 2 X 2 square the removal of each element can be avoided if a check is made about the East, South and South-East neighbours using the edge function. The function edge(E) determines the value of an element's East neighbour. If the three neighbouring elements of an element P is on a corner the expression

edge(E) and edge(SE) and edge(S)   (8)

is true and the element P should not be removed. Hence only the North-West element of an isolated 2 x 2 square is preserved as shown in the following example.

```
before        after
0 0 0 0       0 0 0 0
0 1 1 0       0 1 0 0
0 1 1 0       0 0 0 0
0 0 0 0       0 0 0 0
```

Another situation which must be checked is the presence of a vertical stroke of width 2 - one of whose edges must be retained. Maintaining the westward bias of the algorithm, an element on a West edge is preserved if it is not on a corner and its East neighbour is on an edge. This condition can be expressed in the above notation as

edge(E) and v(N) and v(S)   (9)

if this expression is true the element is preserved. This is shown in the following example

```
before        after
0 0 0 0       0 0 0 0
0 1 1 0       0 0 0 0
0 1 1 0       0 1 0 0
0 1 1 0       0 1 0 0
```

```
0 1 1 0      0 0 0 0
0 0 0 0      0 0 0 0
```

By similar analysis the North edge of a horizontal 2-stroke is preserved if the expression

$$\text{edge}(S) \text{ and } v(E) \text{ and } v(W) \tag{10}$$

is true.

Hence, an element survives an iteration if the combined conditions represented by the expression

$$
\begin{aligned}
v(P) \text{ and } \quad &(\text{not edge }(P) \text{ or} \\
&(\text{edge}(E) \text{ and } v(N) \text{ and } v(S)) \text{ or} \\
&(\text{edge}(S) \text{ and } v(E) \text{ and } v(W)) \text{ or} \\
&(\text{edge}(E) \text{ and edge}(SE) \text{ and edge}(S)))
\end{aligned}
\tag{11}
$$

is true.

3 Complexity of the algorithm

It is assumed that each element of the picture has its own processing element and that elements can communicate with their neighbours.
Let

S be the time to shift a value between two neighbours, and

T the time to perform a logical operation and an assignment.

In addition assume that an *if* - *then* statement can be determined as one logical operation.

The edge function therefore requires

84T + 8S units of time.

Using the original algorithm based on two subiterations means that in addition to the edge time we require

7T units of time.

Hence one complete iteration requires twice the sum of these times giving a total time of

182T + 16S per iteration.

The new algorithm requires an additional cost of

12T + 3S

after the edge condition has been removed. Thus the total time is

97T + 11S.

units per iteration

4 Implementation

The algorithm has been implemented on an ICL DAP, a 64 x 64 array processor [5]. The original Zhang and Suen algorithm [3] was modified as described above. The results of applying the original and modified algorithms to a digital moving body are given below and are typical. They include the total time used, the number of iterations for the pattern, and the time per iteration (a constant over any kind of pattern). Times are given in milliseconds; the total time includes an initial overhead of 1.58 milliseconds.

Algorithm	Time	Its.	T/it.
Zhang and Suen	4.74	8	.39
Improved version	2.84	6	.21

The basic improvement in time is 40 percent, partly due to the reduced time per iteration and partly due to the reduced number of iterations.

5 Summary

It is possible to remove the need for alternating subiterations of a thinning algorithm by expanding the window for each element to include edge information about its neighbours. This reduces the time required for thinning substantially. This assertion has been confirmed by tests on the ICL Distributed Array Processor in which neighbouring processors are able to communicate in two dimensions.

Acknowledgement

This work was supported by the Science and Engineering Research Council under grant GR/B/42343

References

(1)   Hilditch, C J, "Linear Skeletons from Square Cupboards", Machine Intelligence IV, B Meltzer and D Michie Eds, American Elsevier, New York, 1969, pp 403-420
(2)   Stefanelli, R and Rosenfeld, A, "Some Parallel Thinning Algorithms for Digital Pictures", JACM, Vol 18, No 2, April 1971, pp 255-264.
(3)   Zhang, T Y and Suen, C Y, "A Fast Parallel Algorithm for Thinning Digital Patterns", CACM, Vol.27, No.3, March 1984, pp. 236-239.
(4)   Holt, C, Stewart, A, Clint, M, Perrott, R H, "An improved thinning algorithm" (to appear CACM).
(5)   Stewart, A, Holt, C, Clint, M, Perrott, R H, "A DAP Fortran Subroutine for Thinning Digitised Pictures" (submitted to the Computer Journal - Algorithms section).

Appendix. The edge function

The basic approach in implementing the edge function is to take pairs of neighbours
around the centre element. There are between two and six connected neighbours when
at least one (0,0) pair is found, at least one (1,1) pair is found, and exactly one
(0,1) pair is found. To minimize logical operations, these tests are performed on
one side at a time. The local variables in the program code below take the value
True if their specified pairs have been found. For example, t00 is assigned the
value true if a (0,0) pair has been found; t01s is assigned the value True if more
than one (0,1) pair is present etc.

```
Function edge:  Boolean;
   Var t00, t01, t01s, t11: Boolean;
   Procedure check(vl,v2,v3:Boolean);
     Begin
       If Not v2 And (Not vl Or Not v3)  Then t00 := True;
       If  v2 And (  vl Or  v3)  Then t11 := True;
       If (Not vl And v2) Or (Not v2 And v3) Then
           Begin  t01s := t01;  t01 := True  End
     End;

   Begin {edge}
     t00:=False; t01:=False; t01s:=False; t11:=False;
     check(vNW,vN,vNE);          check(vNE,vE,vSE);
     check(vSE,vS,vSW);          check(vSW,vW,vNW);
     edge := t00 And t11 And Not t01s;
   End;
```

This pseudo-code can be translated easily into DAP or standard Fortran.

FAULT-TOLERANT HARDWARE CONFIGURATION MANAGEMENT ON THE
MULTIPROCESSOR SYSTEM DIRMU 25

E. Maehle, K. Moritzen and K. Wirl

Department of Computer Science (IMMD)
University of Erlangen-Nuremberg
Martensstr. 3, D-8520 Erlangen
Federal Republic of Germany

ABSTRACT: This paper describes fault tolerance techniques which have been developed and implemented for the multiprocessor system DIRMU 25 - a 25-processor system which is operational at the University of Erlangen-Nuremberg. First a short overview of the DIRMU hardware architecture, programming environment and parallel application programs is given. Fault-diagnosis and reconfiguration are implemented in a layer of the DIRMOS operating system: the hardware configuration management. The concept of this configuration management is described in general (based on a graph model) and its application for the fault-tolerant execution of parallel programs is discussed.

0. Introduction

Multiprocessor systems with a large number of processors do not only offer high performance by parallel processing [1], but also have the potential for fault-tolerant operation [2]. Though individual VLSI components are very reliable by themselves, large multiprocessors are reaching a hardware complexity that makes fault tolerance a necessity (systems with hundreds or even thousands of processors become feasable today).

In general it is desirable to make fault tolerance as user-transparent as possible, i.e. the ideal situation is to offer a perfect reliable machine at the user interface which tolerates all kinds of faults at lower levels. On the other hand for economical reasons the cost for redundant hardware and software for fault tolerance must be kept as low as possible. For example it will not be practical to use triplication and voting (TMR - Triple Modular Redundancy) for all hardware modules in a large high-performance multiprocessor system - a technique that is usual in critical control applications like aircraft control [3].

For many applications (e.g. multiprocessors for future supercomputer systems) a reasonable level of fault-tolerance can be achieved by making use of the 'natural' redundancy in multiprocessors as much as possible. In the following paper we will present such a fault tolerance concept for the multiprocessor system DIRMU 25 [4,5] which currently is operational with 25 processors (plus one spare) in Erlangen. In DIRMU 25 fault tolerance is implemented in the configuration management layer of the DIRMOS operating system. The basic idea is to offer an intact virtual configuration which is mapped onto the potentially faulty physical configuration. This concept can formally be described by a graph model [6-9] and is general enough to be applied to other multiprocessor architectures as well.

1. Multiprocessor System DIRMU 25

1.1 Hardware Architecture

The DIRMU (DIstributed Reconfigurable MUltiprocessor kit) system which has been developed at the University of Erlangen-Nuremberg has already been described in more detail elsewhere [4,5]. So, here we will only concentrate on those aspects which are relevant for the configuration management.

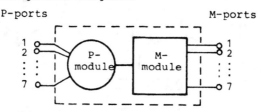

Fig. 1. DIRMU building block.

The DIRMU 25 system is based on an universal microcomputer building block (Fig. 1) consisting of a processor module (P-module) with 8086 microprocessor and 8087 arithmetic coprocessor, 320 K bytes of private RAM, 16 K bytes of private ROM and some I/O interfaces (disks, terminals etc.) as well as a multiport memory (M-module) with 64 K bytes. By pluggable cables between P- and M-ports several DIRMU building blocks can be interconnected to a DIRMU multiprocessor configuration.

Fig. 2. shows the addressing of shared data objects in DIRMU configurations. For example data object A in the M-module of building block B0 can be accessed not only by its own P-module P0 but also by the neighbouring P-modules P1 and P2 over pluggable cables. Note that shared data in the M-modules are accessed with the same speed from all connected processors. Only the addresses differ (depending on the P-port number). Access conflicts are resolved by a hardware arbiter in the multiport logic. The number of building blocks in a DIRMU configuration is in principle unlimited. However, the number of P- and M-ports is restricted (currently to eight), i.e. DIRMU configurations usually have a restricted neighbourhood interconnection structure (e.g. rings, nearest neighbour arrays, cubes, pyramids, trees). It is up to the system designer to select a configuration that fits his performance (parallel processing) and fault tolerance requirements (redundancy) best.

1.2 Programming Environment

Parallel programs for DIRMU 25 consist of a set of communicating concurrent processes with at least one process per processor. Program code and private data objects are always stored in the private memory within the P-modules. Communication between processes on the same processor uses private memory, communication between processes on neighbouring processors uses common memory in the M-modules.

Our preferred programming language is Modula-2 [10], which we use for system programming as well as for application programming. Multiprocessor support (e.g. communication and synchronization primitives) are contained in a special library which can be

imported by application programs. This multiprocessor library is built on top of the
hardware configuration management. The development of parallel programs (editing,
compiling, linking) is done on DIRMU building blocks which are equipped with terminal

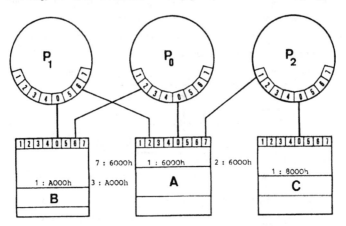

Fig.2. Addressing shared data objects in DIRMU multiprocessor configurations.

and disk (MASTERS) in monoprocessor operation (CP/M-86 operating system). A distributed loader allows to load parallel programs from the MASTER's disk into other
building blocks (SLAVES) of a configuration (Fig. 3). The reservation of the SLAVES
and the assignment of processes to processors is controlled by the configuration
management. All I/O is usually done by the MASTER. Multi-user operation in DIRMU 25
is achieved by space-sharing, i.e. there is a MASTER for each user in the system. For
the execution of parallel programs different MASTERS are competing for SLAVES. Note
that we do not allow that a building block is assigned to more than one user at the
same time (no time-sharing). The role of a MASTER or SLAVE is purely logical, i.e.
the MASTER building block in the current configuration can play the role of a SLAVE
in the next one. Note that I/O-devices are not shared but dedicated to single
building blocks. Currently 16 building blocks are equipped with terminals and disks
and thus are potential MASTERS.

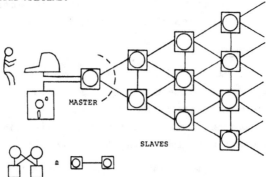

Fig. 3. Programming DIRMU configurations. Note that a single link represents a
'crossed' interconnection between P- and M-modules.

1.3 Parallel Application Programs

Several parallel application programs have already successfully been implemented on DIRMU 25. Table 1 gives some examples. As can be seen high speedups in respect to the corresponding monoprocessor programs have been measured for a broad spectrum of applications (see [4,5,11,12] for more details). For the discussion of the configuration management in the next section it should be mentioned that some programs are written such that they adapt themselves to the numbers of available processors. For example the programs for ring configurations (e.g. Laplace PDE) can run on rings with 2 to p building blocks.

DIRMU APPLICATION PROGRAMS

* LAPLACE PDE (WAVEFRONT GAUSS-SEIDEL METHOD)
  Configuration: Ring
  Speedup   : 23.3 (25 procs, 100x100 grid)

* MULTI-GRID SOLUTION OF POISSON EQUATION WITH DIRICHLET BOUNDARY CONDITIONS (MG00D)
  Configuration: 2x4 nearest-neighbour array
  Speedup   : 7.5 (8 procs, 7 grids)

* MEDIAN FILTERING OF DIGITAL IMAGES
  Configuration: Ring
  Speedup   : 22.8 (26 procs, 128x128 image, 3x3 window)

* EDGE DETECTION IN A SEQUENCE OF MEDICAL IMAGES
  Configuration: Ring
  Speedup   : 6.3 (7 procs, 12+1 images)/12.5 (13 procs, 12+1 images, estimated)

* PARALLEL SORTING (QUICKSORT + PIPELINED MERGE)
  Configuration: Ring
  Speedup   : 8.5 (15 procs)

* FAST-FOURIER TRANSFORM (FFT)
  Configuration: 4-cube
  Speedup   : 14.3 (16 procs, 4096 points)

Tab. 1. Configurations and speedups for some DIRMU sample applications.

2. Fault-Tolerant Hardware Configuration Management

2.1 Basic Concepts

In the following we will model DIRMU configurations by so-called K-graphs (from German 'Konfigurationsgraphen') $K = (V, E)$. The nodes from node set V correspond to the building blocks and the (undirected) edges from edge set E correspond to a 'crossed' interconnection between the P- and M-modules of two neighbouring building blocks in a DIRMU configuration (Fig.2, Fig.3). The exact formal definition of the K-graph model is given in [7]. Here, we will only give a short informal introduction to explain the basic concepts of the configuration management.

Assume, the physical machine configuration is described by K-graph MK. At a given time some of the nodes and/or edges in MK may be in the state 'defective' (corresponding to failed building blocks and links). The K-graph that results after the deletion of defective nodes and edges from MK is called PK (potential K-graph).

The configuration, required by an application program, is modeled by another K-graph AK (application K-graph). In order to allow fault-tolerant operation AK is mapped by a mapping g onto MK. Mapping g must map different nodes of AK onto different intact nodes of MK such that each edge of AK is mapped onto the corresponding intact edge in MK (i.e. AK must be isomorphic to a subgraph of PK). Fig. 4 shows some examples. Note that the MK can easily be configured with DIRMU building blocks. The computation of mapping g (e.g. by a backtracking algorithm) is carried out by the configuration management. Unfortunately the computation of mapping g in general can become very inefficient (the subgraph isomorphism problem is known to be NP-complete [13]). However, it could be shown in [9] that efficient reconfiguration algorithms can be found for important special classes of AK (e.g. rings, nearest-neighbour arrays, hierarchical symmetric trees and shuffle/exchange graphs). These algorithms make use of the special properties of their AK and thus reduce the search tree which the backtracking algorithm has to traverse in order to find mapping g.

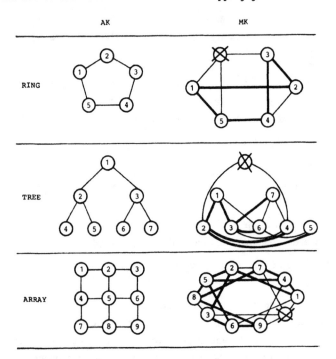

Fig. 4. Reconfiguration by mapping AK onto MK.

An important precondition for a successful reconfiguration is that faulty building blocks and links are automatically identified. In DIRMU this is achieved by distributed self-diagnosis [7,8] which consists of three basic steps: (1) intra-building block diagnosis (hardware fault detectors, self-test programs), (2) neighbourhood diagnosis, (3) system-level diagnosis. A fault in a building block is first detected by step (1). Then in step (2) its immediate neighbours will be informed. By message passing (step (3)) this information is passed to all intact building blocks in the configuration (including the current MASTER). Based on the diagnosis information (current PK) the reconfiguration algorithm can compute a new mapping g. Note that repaired modules can be handled in a similar way. Formally distributed self-diagnosis can also be described by the K-graph model [7]. The diagnosis algorithm can be found in [8].

2.2 Interprocessor Communication

Interprocessor communication plays an important role for the DIRMU configuration management. Two different standard communication mechanisms are supported: message passing and shared data plus spin locks [14]. Message passing is based on 'send no-wait' and provides SEND/RECEIVE primitives for arbitrary data objects. Though this message system is rather comfortable it is also rather slow and does not exploit the full bandwidth of the multiport memories. An alternative approach is to place common data objects directly in the M-modules and to synchronize by WAIT/SIGNAL operations on shared synchronization variables (semaphores, spin locks). In our Modula-2 programs data objects in the multiport memories are accessed via pointer variables whose values point to the physical addresses of the common data objects. Note that in general different processors access the same data objects under different physical addresses (Fig. 2). The user does not have to care about the values of these pointers, he simply allocates common data objects by giving them identical names in the participating processes. The pointers are then set by calls to the configuration management [9].

If a process is assigned to a different physical processor (e.g. after a reconfiguration in case of a failure) the configuration management simply changes the values of the pointers. In this way parallel programs for DIRMU can easily be written for a logical configuration with logical neighbours identified by names. The binding of logical neighbours to physical ones is done at run time by the configuration management. Of course a similar concept can also be applied to message passing communication.

2.3 Implementation

The DIRMU configuration management consist of the following main components which are part of the DIRMOS operating system: finder, configurator, distributed loader, memory manager.

An idle building block is in the state 'FREE SLAVE' and executes self-test programs. By pressing a key on its terminal a FREE SLAVE is turned into a MASTER and a dialogue with the configuration manager begins. First the user is told which building blocks and links currently are intact and available. This is known from the distributed self-diagnosis (current PK). Note that building blocks which are reserved by other MASTERs in space-sharing mode are considered as 'faulty'. Then the user is asked for the desired AK (e.g. ring of length 16 or 4x4 nearest-neighbour array). The finder then tries to map this AK on the current PK. If a mapping has been found, the distributed loader computes a load tree that connects the mapped nodes and links of

PK (spanning tree) with the MASTER as the root node. Next a reservation is made by the configurator starting from the root to the leaves of the spanning tree turning the affected building blocks from FREE SLAVES into RESERVED SLAVES.

As mentioned earlier self-adapting programs can run on a _class_ of AK (e.g. rings of different length). In this case the user can ask the finder to search for the maximum AK from this class that currently can be found. In this way fail-soft operation is possible. If the reservation has been completed successfully, the parallel program is loaded from the MASTER's disk into the private memories of the corresponding P-modules along the edges of the load tree. Then the pointers for the interprocessor communication of the application program are set according to the physical neighbour-hood. The user program can now run on the established configuration.

2.4 Restart and Checkpointing

If a hardware failure occurs during the execution of a parallel application program, the state of the distributed computation usually becomes inconsistent. Therefore, after diagnosis and after establishment of a new intact configuration by the configuration management, the application program must be restarted. For short application programs a complete restart may be acceptable. For longer programs we have provided a simple checkpointing facility. At appropriate points in the computation the user can call a library routine to checkpoint relevant data objects on disk. Checkpointing is under user control because only the user knows the best time for a consistent check-point (e.g. after a global synchronization) and the relevant data in this state. 'Brute force' checkpointing which dumps the whole memory contents to disk would become too inefficient (DIRMU 25 has about 10 M bytes of physical memory!).

As the MASTER and its disk can themselves be subject to failure, a copy of the checkpoint data will also be made on at least one SLAVE disk. If a SLAVE fails, reconfiguration and restart from the last checkpoint on disk is carried out by the MASTER. If the MASTER itself fails, one of the SLAVES with a valid checkpoint on its disk becomes the new MASTER and executes the same steps. Note that with this concept no central critical component exists.

3. Concluding Remarks

It has been described how fault-tolerant operation can be achieved in a multiprocessor system with a restricted neighbourhood interconnection structure by embedding diagnosis and reconfiguration in the configuration management layer of the multiprocessor operating system. This concept makes as much use of the 'natural' redundancy of the physical machine configuration as possible. Depending on the machine and application program structure standby sparing as well as fail-soft operation can be supported. Also multi-user operation by space sharing is possible. As the general concept is based on a formal graph model it applies to other multiprocessor architectures with a restricted neighbourhood as well.

The implementation aspects have been discussed in connection with the DIRMOS operating system on DIRMU 25. Practical experience which has been gained so far with ring configurations shows that the system works as desired. Future work will consist in the support of more application graphs (e.g. nearest-neighbour arrays, trees, N-cubes, pyramids) and experiments with the fault-tolerant execution of corresponding parallel application programs. Another area of future investigations will be a more user-transparent support of efficient checkpointing and restart techniques.

Acknowlegement

The authors wish to thank Prof. Dr. W. Handler for his continuous support of this work. The project DIRMU has been supported by the DFG (Deutsche Forschungsgemeinschaft), BMFT (Bundesministerium fuer Forschung und Technologie) and Siemens, Munich. CP/M-86 is a trademark of Digital Research.

References

[1] Hwang, K., Briggs, F.A.: Computer Architecture and Parallel Processing, McGraw Hill 1984.

[2] Siewiorek, D.P., Swarz, R.S.: The Theory and Practice of Reliable System Design, Digital Press 1982.

[3] Hopkins, Jr, A. L., Smith, III, T.B., Lala, J.H.: FTMP - A Highly Reliable Fault-Tolerant Multiprocessor for Aircraft, Proc. of the IEEE, Vol. 66, No. 10, 1221-1239.

[4] Handler, W., Maehle, E., Wirl, K.: DIRMU Multiprocessor Configurations, Proc. 1985 Int. Conf. on Parallel Processing, St. Charles, Ill., 1985, 652-656.

[5] Handler, W., Maehle, E., Wirl, K.: The DIRMU Testbed for High-Performance Multiprocessor Configurations, Proc. Int. Conf. on Supercomputing Systems, St. Petersburg, Fl., 1985, 468-475.

[6] Hayes, J.P.: A Graph Model for Fault-Tolerant Computing Systems. IEEE Trans. on Computers, Vol. C-25, No. 9, Sept. 1976, 875-884.

[7] Maehle, E., Fehlertolerantes Verhalten in Multiprozessoren - Untersuchungen zur Diagnose und Rekonfiguration, Dissertation, Arbeitsberichte des IMMD, Vol. 15, No. 2, Univ. of Erlangen-Nuremberg 1982.

[8] Moritzen, K.: System-Level Fault-Diagnosis in Distributed Systems, 2nd GI/NTG/GMR Conf. 'Fault-Tolerant Computing Systems', Informatik-Fachberichte 84, Springer, Berlin Heidelberg New York Tokyo 1984, 301-312.

[9] Moritzen, K.: Softwarewerkzeuge zur Programmierung von Multiprozessoren mit begrenzten Nachbarschaften - ein Beitrag zur Konfigurationsverwaltung, Dissertation, Univ. of Erlangen-Nuremberg (to appear).

[10] Wirth, N.: Programming in Modula-2, Springer, Berlin, Heidelberg New York Tokyo 1982.

[11] Maehle, E., Wirl, K., Japel, D.: Experiments with Parallel Programs on the DIRMU Multiprocessor Kit, Proc. 'Parallel Computing 85', Berlin 1985, 515-520.

[12] Bode, A., Fritsch, G., Henning, W., Volkert, J.: High Performance Multiprocessor Systems for Numerical Simulation, Proc. First Int. Conf. on Supercomputing Systems, St.Petersburg, Fl., 1985, 460-467.

[13] Cook, S.A.: The Complexity of Theorem Proving Procedures, Proc. 3rd Annual Symp. on Theory of Computing, 1971, 151-158.

[14] Andrews, G.R., Schneider, F.B.: Concepts and Notations of Parallel Programming, ACM Computing Surveys, Vol. 15, No. 1, March 1983, 3-43.

A GENERAL PURPOSE PIPELINED RING ARCHITECTURE

K. von der Heide, FFM / FGAN, 5307 Werthhoven, Germany

Abstract: A new high-performance object-oriented architecture is proposed. The main features are: (i) Vectors, buffers, stacks and program loops are basic object types implemented in hardware; (ii) control flow on machine level is procedural but GOTO-less and event-driven (with priority over procedural control); (iii) the machine does not use registers, there is no allocation of processes to the processor; (iv) the machine offers exceptional high speed in running procedural and applicative higher level laguages; (v) most semantic software errors and all one bit hardware faults are detected at run time.

1. Introduction

Conventional digital computers are advanced evolutions of a very simple model called the von Neumann computer. A basic feature of this model is the use of a memory with addresses counting from zero up to a certain limit. These addresses are directly used in the instructions in order to access stored data. As a consequence of this linear address space, structured data objects and control structures like loops have to be simulated by additional instructions. Object codes generated by today's compilers usually contain only about 10 per cent user-specified data operations. The rest is governed by the simulations just mentioned. Even sophisticated assembly programs of inner loops hardly reduce the simulation overhead to 50 per cent.

Astonishingly, all effort to make the computer faster concentrated on ways to run the given code faster, but not to change the code. Two accelerating extensions of the von Neumann model are generally adopted today: registers and overlapped instruction execution. The net gain of registers is application-dependent and not very large [3]. In most cases registers help to accelerate the simulations mentioned above by their use as index registers, but not to accelerate the user-specified data operations. Thus eliminating these simulations would by far be better. Another drawback of registers is the costly context switch. It prevents fine grain parallelism on parallel processors of this type from being efficient. Overlapped instruction execution on the other hand suffers from the well known problems caused by data dependencies and conditional program branches. If a processor would not contain any register it could execute instructions of different processes in a pipelined fashion which guarantees an always filled pipeline.

From this introduction it is clear what we intend to do:

1. Implementation of basic data structures by hardware

2. Implementation of basic control structures (e.g. "loop") by hardware

3. Omission of conventional registers that transfer information from one instruction to the next (including the program counter)

2. The Puma-architecture

2.1. The memory architecture

In Puma a conventional physical storage device is used for the main memory. But there is no way to address the memory cells directly. Any data, instruction or what so ever must be stored in an object. These objects are the entities the processor addresses by their physical object identifier. The physical object identifier is the concatenation of a process identifier and the logical object identifier. It is directly used as the absolute address of the object descriptor in a special descriptor memory (Figure 1). The address translation is performed by a device called the address generator.

Figure 2 gives an overview of an object descriptor. It contains a describing part, a reference part, and a protection part. In contrast to other object oriented architectures (the Intel 432 for example) the Puma processor only issues the object identifier and a specific access function code to the memory block, but not a displacement. This would implement a linear address space within an object visible to the programmer. In Puma the displacement is part of the descriptor and called the read index and the write index. These indexes always point to the cells that were accessed last. The normal access mode (defined by the access function code) is 'read the next element of the object' or 'write into the next cell of the object'. What is meant by 'next' is defined by the descriptor fields 'element type' and 'increment'. Thus, rows and collumns and diagonals of matrices are simply vectors, and the processor can step through them without realizing any difference, because the difference is hidden in the object descriptor.

The address generator has the following tasks:

checking the access rights,

computing the new read index or write index and checking
whether it is out of bounds,

updating the read index or the write index in the descriptor,

computing the address for the main memory.

Additionally there are some access functions for descriptor manipulation and descriptor transport between main memory and descriptor memory.

The physical representation of an object in the main memory consists of the object header and the data. The header holds general information about the object that must be accessed only in special cases (making the object accessible for another process for example). The header of structured objects also includes two descriptors of exception handlers (objects containing code). Any event of the type 'index < lower bound', 'index > upper bound', 'buffer empty', 'buffer full', etc. will cause the execution of the corresponding exception handler defined individual-

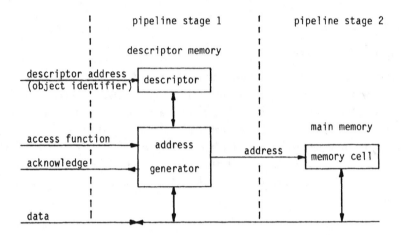

Figure 1. The architecture of a memory block. The address generator contains logic to compute the actual address and to perform the
implicit linear indexing. The acknowledge signal offers a very
specific information on the state of the access.

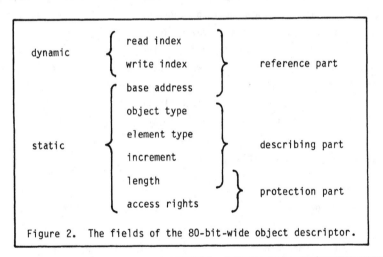

Figure 2. The fields of the 80-bit-wide object descriptor.

the undefined object

the scalar object

the linear object

the cyclic object

the stack

the buffer

Figure 3. The basic object types implemented by the address generator hardware.

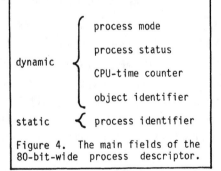

Figure 4. The main fields of the
80-bit-wide process descriptor.

ly for each object. This event-driven control will be discussed in Chapter 2.3. Accesses to the object header are possible by special access function codes.

The address generator is a piece of hardware that fits into one large gate array. The descriptor memory is twice as fast as the main memory. So address generator and main memory can be arranged in a static two-stage pipeline as indicated by Figure 1.

Such data structure architectures are not new. Probably the best known examples are the Starlet concept of Giloi [1] and the Intel 432 (see for example Myers [3]). The Puma concept differs in many details from these. The main differences are:

* In Puma any access to code or data is performed only in one way through the address generator no matter if the object is structured or a scalar.

* In Puma the address generation takes just the time of one main memory access cycle.

* In Puma an unusual set of basic object types is implemented by the address generator hardware (see Figure 3). The most important basic object type is the type buffer (it gives the machine its name: Puma stands for the German Puffer-Maschine). This type renders possible very efficient implementations of the multiprogramming concept (see Chapter 2.3), of process communication and many other things like memory management that will not be discussed in this paper.

2.2. The instruction format

There exists only one simple instruction format in Puma. It contains the operational code and three object identifiers for the operands. The access modes for the operands are uniquely defined by the operational code. An example is

          ADDR   A   B   C
The semantic of this instruction is:

               fetch the next element of the object A,

               fetch the next element of the object B,

               add the two operands,

               and store the result into the next cell of the object C.

The instruction works with any object structure as long as A and B deliver integers or reals and C takes the results.

2.3. The control

A main feature of Puma is the absence of a program counter register. Similar to object descriptors that contain static and dynamic information about objects, process descriptors are introduced to describe processes. Figure 4 shows the several fields of such a process descriptor. The main fields are 'process identifier' and 'object identifier'. The concatenation of these two logical identifiers yields the physical address of the descriptor of the object from where the next instruction of this process should be read.

In order to eliminate any allocation between processors and processes for longer than one instruction cycle, the location of control was moved from the processor to the main memory. There an object of object type 'buffer' and of element type 'process descriptor' is generated at initial operating system loading. A process is started by pushing its process descriptor into this process descriptor buffer. It should be noted that the process descriptor buffer is not an extra piece of hardware as the program counter register is in a von Neumann computer.

The instruction cycle of the processor begins by fetching a process descriptor from the process descriptor buffer. With this information the instruction can be fetched, and the execution is performed quite conventionally. The instruction cycle ends by writing the updated process descriptor back into the process descriptor buffer. If there are more than one process descriptor in the process descriptor buffer, then the corresponding processes are executed in an interlaced manner. Thus, by simple utilization of the data structure memory, Puma realizes the multiprogramming concept in hardware.

Pieces of code that have to be executed sequentially are stored in objects of object type 'linear' and element type 'instruction' (and access right 'execute' only). An equivalent to the conventional program counter is the read index within the object descriptor of such an object. Instead of implementing GOTO-instructions that act on these indexes, we decided to eliminate the GOTO-concept generally. The only explicit control instructions are unconditional and conditional DO-instructions and a loop exit instruction.

DO-instructions simply force the processor to insert the execution of another object before the current object is executed further. Instead of an explicit RETURN-instruction the acknowledge signal 'index > upper bound' when reading an instruction is interpreted as a RETURN. The DO and the automatic RETURN act on a subroutine stack which is an object of object type 'stack' and element type 'process descriptor'. Program loops are stored in objects of object type 'cyclic'. The code then will be repeated indefinitely if not stopped by some control operation. There are two possibilities in Puma: the explicit conditional loop exit instruction can be included in the code of the loop or an appropriate event can be chosen to cause the exit of the loop.

The event-driven control is a specific feature of Puma. If, for example, an instruction cannot orderly be processed because the acknowledge signal when fetching an operand from object X says 'index > upper bound', then this event will be recorded in detail in the status field of the process descriptor. As mentioned in

Chapter 2.1., the header of each structured object includes two descriptors of exception handlers. Whenever the processor fetches a process descriptor the status of which indicates that the preceeding instruction could not orderly be processed because of the event that now is recorded in the status, then the processor does not fetch the next instruction but implicitely performs a DO-instruction that inserts the handler for this event.

In contrast to the automatic RETURN at the end of normal code objects, handlers must be left by an explicit EXIT-statement. The most important EXIT-instructions are:

'exit the handler and repeat the instruction that recorded the event',

'exit the handler and return without repetition of the last instruction',

'exit the handler and exit the loop where the event occurred'.

2.4 The hardware structure

There are many ways for a realization of a von Neumann computer spanning the space from a single board microcomputer to a super computer. This is also true for the Puma architecture. If we want to run a benchmark we have to select a specific hardware structure. For comparison, we select three different but related structures.

Structure A uses a 7-stage processor pipeline as shown in Figure 5. Each stage performs a dedicated function, and each instruction runs through exactly these seven stages. To reach the necessary high memory bandwidth, a virtual pipeline of memory blocks steps synchronously along the processor stages as indicated by Figure 6. This optimizes the utilization of the processor at the cost of a very fast 10-by-10-crossbar switch. Because the memory block itself is a two-stage pipeline, each of the seven processor stages is a two-stage sub-pipeline.

Structure B performs logically the same as Structure A. But the seven processor stages are realized by one hardware stage that executes exactly the seven stages sequentially. The processor is coupled to one private memory block. The utilization of the ALU is by a factor 7 lower than in Structure A. Instead of a fast crossbar switch here a slower I/O-channel is sufficient. I/O-devices and processor cannot access the memory in parallel in contrast to Structure A.

Structure C is similar to Structure B. But the number of steps necessary to execute an instruction is arbitrary. This allows the implementation of vector instructions. These vector instructions use specific acknowledge signals from the address generator to control the micro program loop (loop exit when 'index > upper bound' at one of the operands for example).

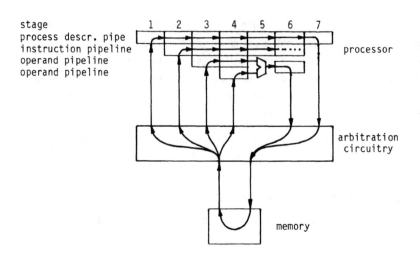

Figure 5. The pipelined ring architecture of Puma. The first stage
of the processor addresses the object 'process descriptor buffer'
and gets a process descriptor that contains the following fields:
'desciptor address of the object the instruction should be read
from', 'process status' and 'CPU-cycle counter'. The second stage
fetches the instruction, and so on. The seventh stage writes the
new process descriptor into the process descriptor buffer. The pipelined ring is closed via the memory. There is no other feedback in
this architecture.

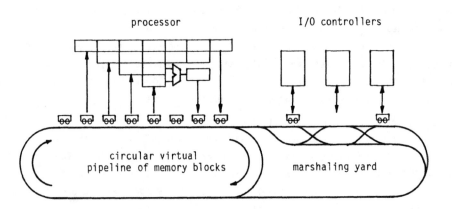

Figure 6. The principle of the virtual pipeline of memory blocks.
The memory shown in Figure 5 is partitioned into several independent memory blocks indicated here as carriages. The arbitration
circuitry is a special cross bar switch that shifts the memory
blocks along the processor stages in synchronism with the pipeline
of the processor. For I/O-operations memory blocks are taken out of
the virtual chain and are privately allocated to one of the I/O
controllers.

3. Benchmarks

Structure A was designed down to the gate level and simulated on this level. A sophisticated software-controlled timing guarantees a pipeline clock cycle of 50 ns. Structure B was not simulated. Its timing is less critical because of the absence of the arbitration circuitry between processor and memory block. Also a clock cycle of 50 ns was assumed. Since both, Structure A and Structure B, run the same code with the same clock, there is no difference in the turn around time of a job. The only difference is the parallel utilization of the CPU in Structure A by 14 processes instead of 2 in the case of Structure B. Structure C also runs with a clock of 50 ns, but this time a vector instruction was used. Benchmark results for the inner product and for matrix multiplication are presented in Figure 7.

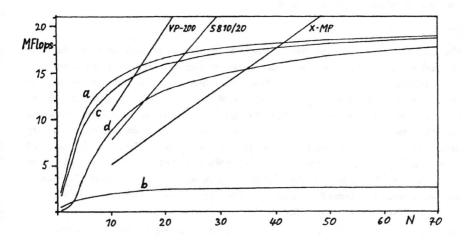

Figure 7. Benchmark results for the inner product of two vectors of length N.

a: 14 processes running in parallel on Structure A

b: 2 processes running in parallel on Structure B

c: 2 processes running in parallel on Structure C

d: 2 processes running closed procedures for multiplication of N*N-matrices on Structure C including parameter transfer and context switch

For comparison, the results of Lubeck et al. [2] for three super computers are also shown. While Puma allows any increment, increments other than 1 can cause memory bank conflicts in these super computers.

4. References

[1] Giloi,W.K., Berg,H.K.: Introducing the Concept of Data Structure Architectures, Proc. 1977 International Conference on Parallel Processing, IEEE Cat. No. 77CH1253-4C, pp. 44-51.

[2] Lubeck,O., Moore,J., Mendez,R.: À Benchmark Comparison of Three Supercomputers: Fujitsu VP-200, Hitachi S810/20 and Cray X-MP/2, Computer, Dec. 1985, pp 10-23.

[3] Myers,G.J.: Advances in Computer Architecture, 2nd ed., J. Wiley, New York, 1982.

An Adaptive Parallel Algorithm for Display of CSG Objects

David T Morris and *Peter M Dew*

Departments of Computer Studies and Mechanical Engineering
The University,
Leeds LS2 9JT,
England.

ABSTRACT

This paper presents a parallel algorithm for the direct display of solid objects represented by Constructive Solid Geometry. The algorithm overcomes many of the limitations of previous approaches by using an
adaptive technique that ensures a high degree of parallelism. Performance estimates have been obtained by
simulation, and a parallel architecture is proposed.

1. INTRODUCTION

With the advent of modern CAD/CAM systems based around solid modelling techniques there is a
need for extremely high performance workstations to allow the engineer to manipulate and display solid
models at interactive speeds. Conventional Von-Neumann architectures need minutes and even hours to
produce an image of a complex solid model, hence the need for parallelism. For example, A real time
display of a 1000 primitive object at 512 by 512 resolution would need around 150 MFLOPS per second
using the algorithms described below. This paper presents a new version of an algorithm for drawing
solids defined by means of Constructive Solid Geometry (CSG) that is suitable for execution on a parallel
architecture. The original serial algorithm was developed by Woodwark [WOOD82], and extended by Peter
Quarendon at the IBM UK Scientific Centre. It is based on the use of recursive spatial subdivision to
determine visible surfaces. A detailed discussion of the basic algorithm can be found in [MORR85], and a
discussion of the CSG representation in [REQU77].

For the purposes of this paper we will assume a CSG solid representation consists of a binary tree
whose leaf nodes represent instances of halfspaces (defined by a quadratic function $f(p) \le 0$, where p is
a point in 3D-space) and non-leaf nodes represent set theoretic combinations of two sub-solids. The set
operators are UNION ($\cup$), INTERSECTION($\cap$), and DIFFERENCE (–). A 2-dimensional example is
given in Figure 1 below. A, B and C are discs corresponding to the halfspaces which are the *primitives* of
the tree. The intersection and difference nodes are referred to as *composite nodes*.

Figure 1 - An Example of a CSG Object in 2-D

The basic objective is to produce a shaded image of a complex CSG object (defined by 100 or more primitives) at near real time speeds. The total drawing time should be under half a second to allow swift interaction with the object, and should preferably be less than 1/30 second to allow real time manipulation.

2. THE POTENTIAL FOR PARALLELISM

2.1. The Drawing Algorithm

The object to be drawn is assumed to be contained in a cubic *Universe Cell* whose front face corresponds to the image to be produced. The basic task of the drawing algorithm is to *simplify* the CSG tree with respect to a cubic cell by pruning those parts of the tree which lie outside it and retaining those parts lying wholly or partially inside. If the resulting tree consists of one primitive intersecting the cell it can be displayed immediately, by computing intensities for the pixels in the square region of image in front of the cell. Otherwise the cell is subdivided orthogonally into eight cubic sub cells. The drawing algorithm is called recursively to process each of the four frontmost sub cells, and is then called to draw each of the four rearmost ones that have not been hidden. The front four are processed first so that the parts of the object which are visible are shaded and the hidden parts in the cells behind can be ignored (hidden surface elimination).

Subdivision proceeds until a cell contains only one primitive or its front face is the size of a single pixel. In the latter case (which is relatively infrequent for any reasonable resolution) the visible surface must be determined by ray tracing or some other technique. A quadtree (see [SAMET86]) is used to maintain information about the shaded screen areas so that the cell visibility test can be implemented efficiently. A description of the drawing algorithm is given below.

```
procedure Draw_Tree ( Tree : CSG_Tree ; Cell : Cube ) is
New_Tree : CSG_Tree;
begin
    if not hidden( Cell ) then -- front face is not shaded
        New_Tree := Simplify_Tree( Tree, Cell );
        if Empty ( New_Tree ) then return;
        else if Cell has reached limiting resolution ( is pixel_sized )  or
            New_Tree contains only one primitive then
            Shade( New_Tree, Cell ) --shade tree onto the front of the cell
        else  -- subdivide the current cell into eight
            for all front cells in parallel
                Draw_Tree( New_tree, one front subcell ).
            for all back cells in parallel
                Draw_Tree( New_tree, one back subcell ).
        end if; -- subdivide
    end if; -- not hidden
end; -- Draw_Tree;
```

The recursive nature of the drawing algorithm makes it difficult to exploit spatial parallelism. One solution adopted by Woodwark [WOOD84] is to allocate fixed volumes of image space to each processor. The processors can each run the drawing algorithm independently without the need to communicate with any others. This enables us to exploit a limited amount of parallelism but as Woodwark's analysis shows we only obtain around 50% efficiency with 16 processors. The efficiency drops rapidly as we increase the number of processors because objects are rarely distributed evenly throughout space,leading to uneven loading and loss of coherence. Therefore a more adaptive approach is needed for highly parallel systems. A method must be found of allocating processors to cells as they are generated so that processing power is concentrated where it is needed. In particular we must ensure that frontmost cells are fully processed before starting the ones that lie behind. This avoids processing cells that are hidden from view and ensures that the image will be correct.

There are inherent limits to the amount of spatial parallelism available. Initially there is no parallelism possible because there is only the universe cell to process. At the next level of subdivision there are four cells that may be processed in parallel. Each descendant of the four may also generate four further cells, leading to an exponential growth in potential parallelism as subdivision proceeds.

2.2.   The Simplify Algorithm

We will now discuss the "divide and conquer" algorithm used to prune a tree to a cell. It recurses down the tree to primitive level and then classifies the cell with respect to each primitive as either full, empty or partially occupied. These classifications are then combined at composite nodes in accordance with set theory to produce a *simplified* or pruned tree. For instance if either of the trees to be combined at an intersection node is empty the combined tree will be empty. The algorithm is given below.

```
function Simplify_Tree ( Tree : CSG_tree ; Cell : Cube ) return  CSG_Tree  is
    Left, Right: CSG_Tree;
begin
  case kind_of ( Tree ) is
      when COMPOSITE  =>
              par -- evaluate two operands in parallel
                    Left    :=  Simplify_Tree( left_of ( Tree ), Cell );
                    Right   :=  Simplify_Tree( right_of ( Tree ), Cell );
              return combine( operator_of( Tree ), Left, Right );
      when PRIMITIVE  =>
              return classify_primitive( Cell, primitive_of( Tree ));
  end case;
end Simplify;
```

The two operands of a composite CSG tree node may be classified in parallel; hence at any level in the tree we can perform all the Combine operations and all the primitive classifications simultaneously. Parallelism for the overall tree classification is therefore governed by both the size and structure (in particular depth) of the tree. Allocation of processors to nodes in the CSG tree to perform parallel CSG

classification will be referred to as *Structural Parallelism*, because it is the structure of the tree that is being exploited. For large trees substantial speed-ups can be obtained by this technique.

Kedem and Ellis [KEDEM84] have proposed an architecture for parallel CSG ray tracing which uses a rectangular grid of processors into which the CSG tree is embedded. Simulations by the authors indicate that the trees generated by spatial subdivision are badly matched in size and structure to a fixed grid of processors. In particular they are either unbalanced or generally small in size, resulting in very low usage of the processors used to perform the combine operations..

3. ADAPTIVE PARALLELISM FOR THE ALGORITHM

The drawing algorithm can be seen to be doubly recursive, yielding two ways of exploiting parallelism. Either many tree simplifications may be performed in parallel or the simplification algorithm itself may be done concurrently. Our aim is to devise a highly parallel algorithm that decomposes the initial problem into a large number of independent subproblems at all phases of execution. Both of the approaches considered above have limitations in this respect. At the start of spatial subdivision there is no spatial parallelism available because the universe cell is the only cell being processed. However it is possible to exploit a large amount of structural parallelism because the initial trees are large. Conversely the amount of spatial parallelism grows exponentially as subdivision proceeds because the number of cells to be processed grows eightfold at each level. However due to *spatial locality* in the object, the trees inside the small cells produced by fine subdivision are likely to be fairly small, thereby limiting the potential structural parallelism.

The authors have obtained statistics (discussed in [MORR86]) on the complexity of the CSG tree/cell classifications for a range of objects, including two mechanical parts, a molecular model, and an artistic image. On average around 80% of primitive and composite node classifications are executed when processing trees with 5 primitives or fewer. This seems to be relatively insensitive to the kind of object being displayed. The implication is that hardware which exploits structural parallelism will be used efficiently during the initial cell subdivision when trees are large but will be under utilised near pixel resolution. In addition, it is possible to construct a more efficient processor for small trees because they are bounded in size, and structurally dense.

On the other hand hardware designed to exploit spatial parallelism will perform badly at the start of subdivision because the trees are large and will have to be classified serially. In addition there are relatively few cells to classify. For these reasons the following hybrid approach has been devised to combine spatial and structural parallelism.

We will now define a *Small Tree Classification* (STC) as a cell/tree classification in which the number of primitives in the tree is less than or equal to P. The parameter P is typically 5, and is chosen to allow efficient implementation of the STC. A very small value of P will result in most of the tree combine operations being processed serially. In contrast, a large value of P will produce the problems outlined above when classifying large trees. A *Large Tree* is any tree that is composed of two or more small trees.

We conclude from the above discussion that it is beneficial to build special purpose hardware to implement the *Small Tree Classifications* (STC's) efficiently. Now the problem is to develop an algorithm which will generate many *independent* STC's to be executed in parallel. Near pixel resolution this is not a problem due to the exponential growth in spatial parallelism at each subdivision level. In contrast, spatial parallelism is limited at the initial levels of subdivision when the trees are large. We propose an algorithm that performs classifications on large trees by splitting them into a set of STC's which are done in parallel, and then recombined to form the pruned tree. This means that at all stages in the algorithm the STC

computation is a basic building block which could be executed on special purpose hardware.

We will now consider the algorithm used to generate small tree classifications. Due to limited space we can give only a brief overview, interested readers are referred to [MORR86]. There are four logical sections in the algorithm, all of which run in parallel. Figure 2 shows how they communicate.

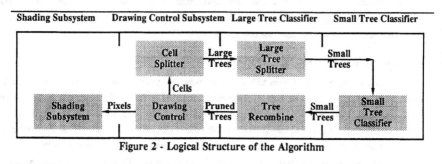

Figure 2 - Logical Structure of the Algorithm

3.1. The Drawing Controller

The *Drawing Control Subsystem* (DCS) controls spatial parallelism by arranging the simultaneous execution of many cell/tree classifications, while ensuring hidden surface elimination. Every cell that is currently being processed has a corresponding *Draw Request* which invokes a parallel version of the Draw_Tree routine given in section 2. The DCS issues commands to the and the Shading subsystem in order to draw each cell.. Every request to the *Large Tree Classifier* (LTC) is identified by the draw request that issued it, so that results can be generated in arbitrary order. The DCS consists of two main modules: (i) a *Cell Splitter* which generates Draw Requests and instructs the LTC to perform classifications, and (ii) a *Drawing Controller* which reads results from the LTC and processes them.

The Cell Splitter reads its input from a stack of Draw Requests which need to be subdivided. It splits each "parent" request into eight child cells and arranges for them to be drawn. It initially creates Draw Requests for the frontmost four "children" cells of the parent that are not completely hidden from view. When all the front cells have been evaluated, requests to draw the four rearmost cells are created. This strategy ensures that no cell may be drawn before any of the ones lying in front of it have been completed, so that hidden surface elimination is performed correctly. (As in the serial algorithm a quadtree is used to determine whether a cell is hidden). As a new request is created a Large Tree Classification Request (LTCR) is sent to the LTC to ask it to classify the new cell against the parent tree. The request is then suspended until the result returns from the LTC.

The draw control process repeatedly reads pruned (simplified) trees from the LTC and performs one of three actions:

(1) If the pruned tree is empty the draw request is deleted, as there is nothing further to do.

(2) If the cell being classified is at limiting resolution (e.g the size of a single pixel on the screen) then the shading subsystem is instructed to draw the pixel. The quadtree is updated to reflect the fact that a pixel is to be hidden and the draw request is deleted. (Note that in this case the result returned from the LTC is the colour and intensity of the pixel in front of the cell. It is more efficient to compute the surface normals and lighting calculations in the STC subsystem because the geometric

information needed is already available once the tree/cell classification has been done.

(3) If there are many primitives in the cell and the cell is not at limiting resolution the request is pushed onto the input stack for the Cell Splitter, so that it can be subdivided.

An important property of this algorithm is that pruned trees do not have to be transmitted to and from the LTC . All that is required is to know what the root node of the pruned tree actually is, so that it can be subdivided at a later date.

3.2.   The Large Tree Classifier (LTC)

The Large Tree Classifier has two processes : (i) a *Tree Splitter* that continuously decomposes large trees into small trees to be processed by the Small Tree Classifiers and (ii) a Tree Recombiner that builds Large Trees from the small trees returned from the STC processors.

The Tree Splitter copies each large tree, replacing all subtrees less than a given size (usually 5) by a special small tree classification node. The reason the tree is copied is to ensure that a unique simplified tree is generated for each of the eight requests to simplify the same tree. All of the small trees are then sent to the STC subsystem.

The Tree Recombination algorithm is data driven. It reads the results from the STC subsystem, each of which consists of a simplified small tree, the parent Draw Request, and the parent node in the tree that the small tree must be attached to. It then attaches the tree to the parent node and performs as many simplifications as possible until a node is found with either one of its operands unevaluated, or the root node is reached. In the latter case the root node of the simplified tree can be sent to the DCS together with the parent Draw Request.

4. A RING ARCHITECTURE FOR THE PARALLEL SMALL TREE CLASSIFIER

The algorithm presented above generates a large number of small tree classifications which can be executed in parallel. We will now present an architecture which is capable of exploiting this parallelism. Our aim is to use a large number of simple and relatively cheap processors (e.g Inmos Transputers) to gain maximum parallelism. In addition, we must be careful to ensure that I/O operations do not dominate the total computation time. Global communication between processors is to be avoided so that shared memory and I/O buses do not become a bottleneck. We believe the following ring structure (Figure 3) satisfies these aims, while also providing expandability and fault tolerance. (Note that it can be replicated several times to process disjoint areas of screen).

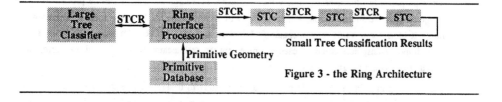

Figure 3 - the Ring Architecture

The Ring Interface Processor (RIP) is responsible for reading the STC requests from the Large Tree Classifier, and putting them onto the ring where they continuously circulate until a STC processor is free to classify them. The free processor then becomes busy and will pass requests through unchanged until it has finished processing. On completion, it inserts the result onto the ring where it is read by the RIP and passed back to the Large Tree Classifier.

The I/O bandwidth of the ring processors limits the performance of the whole system, hence it is important to minimise the size of the STC requests. Since most of the size of a CSG tree is in the descriptions of primitive geometry, (e.g 28 bytes are needed for a Cylindrical halfspace represented by 32 bit coordinates) separating the CSG tree structure from its primitive geometry would reduce the I/O needed for an STC request by an order of magnitude. Therefore a STC request is encoded as a postfix representation of the tree with pointers to the primitives.

It is, of course, necessary to make the primitive geometry descriptions available to the STC processors. It is too costly and wasteful in memory to store copies of all the primitives in every STC. We have been investigating the use of a LRU cache to store the last few primitives most recently classified. The success of this approach relies on the fact that there is *Spatial Coherence* in the object, that is cells that are near to each other in space are likely to contain a similar set of primitives. The above algorithms are designed to ensure that cells that are spatially close are also processed together. Simulations by the authors, [MORR86], have shown that this technique works well, with consistently high hit rates with relatively small numbers of primitives in the cache. For instance, a CSG tree with 1500 half spaces obtained a 75% hit rate with only 50 primitives in the cache when using an essentially random allocation of STC's to processors. More intelligent scheduling algorithms should be able to increase this further. The use of a LRU cache alleviates two problems by minimising the I/O bandwidth for transmitting primitives, and bounding the amount of memory used for storing primitives in each STC.

The RIP stores the database of all the primitive descriptions and is responsible for allocating STC requests to processors and providing primitive descriptions when needed. The architecture satisfies the goal of minimising I/O bandwidth because every transmission of a primitive description by the RIP is shared by every processor in the ring, albeit at the expense of increased *Latency*. The bandwidth to and from the LTC is also minimised by passing pointers to data objects, maintaining the philosophy of only allowing local communication between processors.

5. CONCLUSIONS AND FUTURE WORK

This paper presents an algorithm that decomposes a complex data dependent problem into a large number of regular Small Tree Classifications that can be executed in parallel. Spatial locality is used to bound the amount of memory needed in an STC processor and to reduce the I/O bandwidth needed. The architecture proposed has the useful property that it consists of a large number of similar processors which do not require global communication, a large amount of local storage, or large computational bandwidth. This makes it ideal for a VLSI implementation. Initial studies (see [MORR86]) have shown that a large network of Inmos Transputers could be used to implement the architecture. It is estimated that a ring of up to 100 Transputers could be used effectively.

The work reported in this paper is part of a larger study to design high performance algorithms and architectures for the display and manipulation of CSG objects using a spatially divided solid model (SDSM). An SDSM can be generated using a slight modification to the above algorithms. Applications such as ray tracing into the divided model also generate many independent small tree classifications which are ideal for processing in the proposed ring architecture.

It appears that the STC processor is a primitive building block in many CSG algorithms, and is therefore worthy of special purpose hardware. Studies are in progress to define carefully its functionality. The architecture outlined above is currently being simulated.

6. ACKNOWLEDGEMENTS

The authors would like to acknowledge the help and guidance given by Professor A de Pennington. They are grateful to Gordon Oliver for his help in drafting this paper. We would also like to thank Tom Heywood, Steven Todd and Peter Quarendon of the IBM UK Scientific Centre (UKSC) for many helpful discussions. David Morris is supported by a SERC CASE studentship in conjunction with the IBM UKSC.

7. REFERENCES

[WOOD84]   J.R Woodwark, *A Multiprocessor Display Architecture for Viewing Solid Models*,
            Displays, April 1984.

[WOOD82]   J.R Woodwark and K.M Quinlan, *Reducing the Effects of Complexity on Volume Model Evaluation*,
            CAD Journal 14(2) pp 85-95 (1982).

[REQU77]   A.A.G Requicha and H.B. Voelker, *Constructive Solid Geometry*, published as Technical Memorandum 25,
            Production Automation Project, University of Rochester, Rochester, NY 14627 (1977).

[KEDEM84]   G Kedem and J.Ellis, *Computer Structures for Curve-Solid Classification in Geometric modelling*,
            Production Automation Project, University of Rochester, Rochester, NY 14627 (1984).

[MORR85]   D.T Morris and P.Quarendon, *An Algorithm for the Direct Display of CSG objects by Spatial Subdivision*,
            Nato ASI series Vol f17, Fundamental Algorithms for Computer Graphics. Springer Verlag. (1985).

[MORR86]   D.T Morris and P.M Dew, *Adaptive Parallel Algorithms for Constructive Solid Geometry*,
            Technical Report no 206, Dept of Computer Studies, University of Leeds, England.(1986).

[SAMET86]   H Samet and R.E Webber, *Hierarchical Data Structures*
            Proceedings of the Second International Electronic Image Week, Nice, France (1986).

A PACKET BASED DEMAND/DATA DRIVEN REDUCTION MODEL
FOR THE
PARALLEL EXECUTION OF LOGIC PROGRAMS

Matthew K. O. Lee
Department of Computer Science
University of Manchester
Manchester M13 9PL
United Kingdom

ABSTRACT

This paper presents a computational model for Horn-clause logic programs. OR parallelism and a restricted kind of AND parallelism inherent in such programs are exploited. The model is reduction based and utilizes both data driven and demand driven mechanisms for the efficient use of computational resources and control of parallelism. The binding environment of logical variables in a clause is distributed in nature and a form of back-unification is used to reduce communication traffic in a parallel machine architecture. The model is described in a packet reduction framework which makes it possible for implementation on the range of existing parallel machines supporting packet based reduction model for functional programs.

1. Introduction

Following the boost given by the Japanese fifth generation computer research programme[1], logic programming has gradually established itself as one of the major formalisms for programming the next generation of very powerful parallel computers. There are at least three major reasons for its widespread acceptance in this context. First, it is because of its strong mathematical foundation (i.e. predicate calculus) and clear semantics which facilitate the (possibly automatic) construction of correct programs and their proof. Secondly, because of its close relationship with logic it is a good formalism for writing artificial intelligence programs involving semantic information processing. The third reason, which is at least as important, is because parallelism is inherent in such formalism and transparent to the programmer. This greatly facilitates the programming of parallel machines. The next generation of computers will be composed typically of a large number of cooperating processors working in parallel. It will be very difficult indeed to program them generally if the programmer has to deal with low level synchronization and communication of the processors explicitly. It is desirable to have a programming formalism which can make efficient use of parallel machine resources without forcing the programmer to deal with low level details of actually organizing the parallel computation.

At least two major forms of parallelisms, AND and OR, are inherent in a logic programming language. Throughout this paper, the term logic programming language is used with the understanding that it refers to the Horn-clause variety of which PROLOG[2] is a prime example. A program written in PROLOG is basically a set of Horn-clauses and its execution conceptually entails a search of the AND-OR tree representing the program clauses[5]. Resolution[4] is the main inference mechanism used in such evaluator. During program execution, OR parallelism corresponds to parallel search of the OR branches in the conceptual AND-OR tree whereas AND parallelism results from searching AND branches in parallel. Other forms of inherent parallelism include stream parallelism, search parallelism, goal-list parallelism and unification parallelism[5].

Data-flow techniques[6] are now widely recognized as effective in making use of parallel machine resources[7]. Basically, data-flow execution strategy dictates that an instruction is executed when it has received all its operands. There isn't any concept of a program counter as in a conventional machine and hence no explicit sequencing is imposed upon a computation. A computation can then be represented as a two-dimensional graph and execution can progress along various paths simultaneously and hence achieving inherent parallelism. However, it is desirable to have some mechanism for controlling the parallelism obtained for various obvious reasons. Not least because too much parallelism can easily swamp available machine resources, clog up communication bandwidth, increase processing overhead and severely downgrade machine performance. A demand-driven mechanism[8] with which a branch of the computation will start only if there is a demand for it seems a good candidate for this purpose. In other words, data-flow is a mechanism for raw parallelism while demand-driven mechanism is a way of moderating it. The model described in this paper makes use of both mechanisms.

2. Logic programming with Horn-clauses

A Horn-clause logic program consists of a set of procedures and a goal statement. A procedure is a clause of the form $P :- Q_1, \ldots, Q_n$ which is called a definite clause if $n > 0$, or a unit clause if $n = 0$. P is the clause head and $Q_1, \ldots, Q_n$ forms the clause body. Declaratively it can be read as P is true if $Q_1, \ldots, Q_n$ are true. Procedurally it may be interpreted as: in order to solve goal P, all the subgoals $Q_1, \ldots, Q_n$ must be solved. A goal statement has the form of a degenerated clause with no head $:- Q_1, \ldots, Q_m$ $(m > 0)$ which is also called a goal clause. P and Q_1 are called literals. A literal is composed of a predicate name and a tuple of terms placed in juxtaposition. Terms are either constants, variables, or composite terms of the form $f(t_1, \ldots, t_k)$ where f is a function symbol and t_k, $k > 0$, are terms again. Following the convention of PROLOG, capital letters are used for variables and literals while lower case letters are used for all others.

Given a logic program LP with a goal statement $:- G_1, \ldots, G_n$, a PROLOG interpreter tries to solve this goal statement by first selecting the leftmost subgoal G_1 and then the LP is searched to find a clause which unifies with G_1. Suppose such a clause exists and it is a definite clause of the form $Q :- Q_1, \ldots, Q_m$ and the resulting unifier is Θ, i.e. $(G_1)\Theta = (Q)\Theta$, then the body of the definite clause replaces G_1 and a new goal statement is formed $(Q_1, \ldots, Q_m, G_2, \ldots, G_n)\Theta$.

However, if G_1 matches with a unit clause Q_u from the LP producing an unifier Θ_u then G_1 is deleted from the original goal statement and the new goal statement becomes :- $(G_2,\ldots,G_n)\Theta_u$.   Of course, variables appearing in a unifying clause must be renamed if necessary so that they are distinct from those in the goal statement before unification is performed to avoid confusion caused by name clashes. This problem will be discussed in more detail later. This process is repeated until either the empty clause () remains, implying success with results embedded in the sequence of unifiers obtained, or until no clauses in the LP unify with the selected subgoal, signifying failure. Upon failure a process of backtracking is triggered on, and execution backtracks to the last unified clause choice and unification is attempted with the next unifiable clause at that point. Backtracking is necessary in PROLOG interpreters because the goal tree is searched in a depth-first fashion. If the search is performed in parallel (i.e. OR parallel), backtracking as it is will not be necessary.

As program execution progresses, a sequence of unifiers (call it Θ) are obtained as each successful unification adds a unifier to the previously obtained sequence. Whenever a subgoal is selected it has to access Θ in order to instantiate itself before unification with a clause from the LP. Since any selected subgoal in the goal statement will have to access Θ, it conceptually implies some kind of global storage for storing Θ as program execution progresses. In a distributed environment it is more appropriate to avoid a global storage concept. This can be achieved by either instantiating all the subgoals in the goal statement with a unifier whenever one is obtained, or distributing a copy of Θ to be stored in each subgoal as execution proceeds. In practice, it is only necessary to make sure that once a subgoal is selected it has access to a copy of Θ. Even if some form of AND parallelism is provided, not all subgoals will be selected simultaneously because together with OR-parallelism it implies combinatorial explosive growth of the search space and raises the difficulty of resolving binding conflicts resulting from variables shared by subgoals.

Viewed within a reduction framework, the problem of solving a subgoal G_1 can be regarded as a process of reducing G_1, viewed as a non-deterministic function (relation, or a function returning a set-value), using the matching clauses from the LP. As mentioned in the last paragraph, a selected subgoal G_1 needs to access Θ (call it the initializing environment Θ_{int}) before it can be solved. Using data-flow terminology G_1 can be regarded as an instruction and Θ_{int} its operand, and the process of reducing G_1 is activated once it has received its operand Θ_{int}. The clauses in the LP provide the reduction-rules for reducible subgoal in much the same way as in a functional programming system[7]. The difference is, of course, that many different reduction-rules may be applied to a subgoal, each yielding one or more different solutions. Thus a reduction system as such has not the Church-Rosser property[10] as found in many functional programming systems.

3. A Packet Reduction Model for Logic Programming

In this model, it is assumed that execution always starts at the leftmost subgoal of a goal statement. A goal statement $:- G_1, G_2, \ldots, G_n$ is represented as a list of linked nodes $G_1(\quad)-->G_2(\quad)-->\ldots G_n(\quad)$. Each node is represented by a packet having four fields: pac(literal,env,ctl,ptr). The literal field corresponds directly to a subgoal G_i, the env field holds the binding environment for logical variables appearing in the literal, the ctl field contains various control information such as the state of a packet and counters for garbage collection purpose. A packet may be in one of three states: active, suspended, or dormant[11]. In active state a packet has its operand ready and can be processed at any time. A packet in a suspended state is waiting to receive its operand; and once it is received the packet becomes active again. A dormant packet is one which may have already received its operand, but execution is delayed until a demand is sent to it turning it into an active state. The ptr field simply holds a pointer to the next subgoal G_{i+1} in the goal statement. A node such as $G_i(\quad)$ denotes the corresponding packet having an empty env field and in a suspended state waiting for an initializing environment. It is assumed that each processor in a parallel machine has a reduction-rule store which holds a copy of an executing LP in reduction-rule form. A distributed packet pool for holding packets is also assumed much the same as in Alice[7]. In a reduction-rule store a definite clause $Q :- Q_1, \ldots, Q_n$ is represented as:

$$G(\Theta_{int}) => comp(\Theta_{int}, Q_n(Q_{n-1}(\ldots(Q_1(unify((G)\Theta_{int}, Q)))\ldots)$$
$$\text{where } G = q(t_1, \ldots, t_n)$$
$$Q = q(t_1', \ldots, t_n')$$

A unit clause $:- Q$ is simply expressed as:

$$G(\Theta_{int}) => comp(\Theta_{int}, unify((G)\Theta_{int}, Q))$$
$$\text{where } G = q(t_1, \ldots, t_n)$$
$$Q = q(t_1', \ldots, t_n')$$

where $(G)\Theta_{int}$ means producing an instance of G using Θ_{int} and unify is a function which takes two unifiable literals as arguments and produces their most general unifier as result. For the sake of brevity all control informations are left out. The body of the first rule (called a 'definite rule') corresponds to a graph of the form:

$$comp(\Theta_{int}, \quad)$$
$$\text{\textffi}--Q_n(\quad) <--\ldots Q_1(\quad)$$
$$\text{\textffi}--unify((G)\Theta_{int}, Q)$$

Similarly, the graph for the second rule (a 'unit rule') is expressed as:

$$comp(\Theta_{int}, \quad)$$
$$\text{\textffi}--unify((G)\Theta_{int}, Q)$$

In this model, the notion of reduction is not restricted only to a sub-expression being transformed into a simpler entity which is in some way closer to its normal form. The computational graph in this model continuously expands and collapses in the course of its computation. An expansion takes place whenever a reducible subgoal node is reduced by a definite rule. A branch of the graph starts to collapse whenever one of its tip nodes is reduced by a unit rule or unification failure is encountered. The dynamic garbage collection mechanism[12] employed in this model automatically reduces the size of a graph whenever possible. Eventually a computational graph will be reduced to only a stream of result environments.

When a subgoal Gi has received its initializing environment and hence becomes active (i.e. reducible), the reduction-rule store of the processor processing this subgoal is searched for all rules which has the same predicate name as the subgoal. A simple unifiability test is then performed between the subgoal and the selected rule-heads to screen out some of the more obvious non-unifiable rule-heads. Only those successful in the test will have their rule bodies activated. These activated rule bodies now points to the next subgoal G_{i+1} for returning results. OR parallelism arises when at least two rule-bodies are activated simultaneously as a result of subgoal reduction. A simple test for unifiability (e.g. testing for arity, data type etc.) consumes little processing power, especially if some form of indexing is used in representing rule argument data structures. This helps towards decreasing communication bandwidth and the number of useless packets in the packet pool. It also reduces the burden of garbage collection. The results of solving the rule bodies are composed with θ_{int} before passing back to the next subgoal. This can be regarded as a process of back-unification whereby the unification results of solving a subgoal is communicated back to the next selected subgoal. This mechanism saves the need of having to instantiate the goal statement every time a successful unification step occurs in the process of solving a subgoal. Instead, subgoal variables are instantiated by $comp(\theta_{int}, G(\theta))$ once only when a complete solution of solving a subgoal is returned. Other subgoals in the goal statement are not informed of the instantiation instantly; only those selected for the next execution will be sent a copy of the instantiation result by $comp(\theta_{int}, G(\theta))$. An arrangement such as this saves a lot of needless communication, especially in a parallel machine.

Consider a rule body: $comp(\theta_{int}, G(\theta))$, it should produce a solution composition with every result environment it receives from the evaluation of $G(\theta)$. Therefore it must not lose its own identity after receiving the first solution from $G(\theta)$. In general, applying a reduction-rule to a node should not cause the node to be destroyed or overwritten. Instead, a properly instantiated rule-body should be activated, which points to the parent of a reduction node, each time a reduction takes place. In the case of $comp(\theta_{int}, G(\theta))$; suppose $G(\theta)$ produces n solutions, eventually n copies of $comp(\theta int, \theta_i)$, where $0 < i < n+1$, and each θ_i denotes one of the n solutions returned by $G(\theta)$, each copy being a deterministic function pointing to the same parent as those of the original node, will be created and activated. Note that for instance if a subgoal G_i is being reduced, its corresponding rule-bodies will return result environments to the next subgoal (G_{i+1}) in the goal statement eagerly which means that G_{i+1} may be reduced while other rule-bodies are at the same time trying to produce the remaining solutions corresponding to G_i. In effect, more than one subgoal may be active simultaneously, albeit each one is working on a different solution to a query. Since a goal statement is composed of the conjunction of subgoal literals, it can be said that a kind of pipelined AND parallelism exists in this model.

To get a closer look at the working of the model, the ubiquitous 'append' program shown below serves as a good example. The notation [A¦X] is equivalent to cons(A, X) in Lisp.

a) append(nil, X, X).
b) append([A¦X], Y, [A¦Z]) :- append(X, Y, Z).

In reduction-rule form they are represented as:

a) $G(\theta_{int})$ => comp(θ_{int}, unify((G)θ_{int}, append(nil, X, X)))
b) $G(\theta_{int})$
   => comp(θ_{int},
      append(X, Y, Z)(unify((G)θ_{int}, append([A¦X], Y, [A¦Z]))))

        where G = append(t_1, t_2, t_3)

A goal statement :- append([1], [2], Z) is represented as
      append([1], [2], Z) {Z/Z}
      +----+----------+ +--+-+
            G θ_{int}

An environment is expressed simply as a set of bindings (i.e. {variable/binding term}) for the logical variables in the corresponding literal. An unbound variable is represented as an identity mapping in the initializing environment. When $G(\theta_{int})$ is reduced, the reduction-rule store is searched and rule b is found applicable producing:

      comp({Z/Z}, append(X, Y, Z){A/1, X/nil, Y/[2], Z/[1¦Z]})

Here the well known variable name-clash arises because the variable Z appears in both the goal and the invoked rule. To prevent the variables in an invoked rule from being erroneously captured by bindings of variables in the goal statement, variables in the invoked rule should be consistently renamed before unification so that they are unique from those in the goal statement. So the application of rule b should actually produce

      comp({Z/Z}, append(X, Y, Z'){A/1, X/nil, Y/[2], Z/[1¦Z']})

Now the second argument in comp becomes reducible using rule a producing:

      comp({Z/Z},
          comp({A/1, X/nil, Y/[2], Z/[1¦Z']},
              unify(append(nil, [2], Z'), append(nil, X', X'))))
and the following reductions follow:
i) comp({Z/Z},
          comp({A/1, X/nil, Y/[2], Z/[1¦Z']}, {X'/[2], Z'/[2]}))
ii) comp({Z/Z}, {A/1, X/nil, Y/[2], Z/[1¦[2]]})

The result binding {Z/[1¦[2]]} is returned as expected. The comp function performs the composition of two environments rather akin to functional composition. Its exact behaviour is described in a separate document[12].

4. OR Parallelism Control

When a subgoal is being reduced, a set of reduction-rules may be applicable and the simultaneous activation of them forms the basis of OR parallelism in this model. A way of controlling this kind of parallelism can be achieved by constraining this process of simultaneous activation. A subgoal is prefixed by an asterisk if the parallelism resulting from its evaluation is to be constrained. When such a subgoal (e.g. *G) is to be reduced, it is, as usual, given its θ_{int} rendering it active for reduction. As the reduction of *G(θ_{int}) takes place, although all the applicable rule-bodies are created and copied into the packet pool with their operands (i.e. θ_{int}) ready, only one of them is made active while all others are put into a dormant state. A rule-body in a dormant state, despite having its operand ready, cannot be further processed until a demand is made for it. If the first activated rule-body eventually fails to deliver any result, a demand is then sent to one of the dormant rule-bodies. Upon receiving a demand, a dormant rule-body becomes active again. If this rule-body does not turn out a solution, a demand is then sent to another dormant rule-body and so forth. Note that although at the top level only one rule-body is made active at a time, there is no parallelism restriction in solving the subgoals in that rule-body. Hence parallelism at a smaller scale still exists and multiple solutions may be returned. This mechanism corresponds to searching the goal tree sequentially only at the top level while still maintaining an OR parallel search at the lower levels.

Clearly, this mechanism can be generalized so that one can specify the level of the search tree from which parallelism should start. For example, a subgoal G prefixed by n* specifies that parallel exploration of the branches of the search tree corresponding to subgoal G can only start at level n, where the level of a node in a tree is assigned in the usual way, with the root node assigned level 0 and its immediate children assigned level 1 and so forth.

5. Some Concluding Remarks

In this paper an abstract computational model for the parallel execution of Horn-clause type logic programs is proposed. The presentation is not precise and many questions of concrete implementation are left untouched. The intention here is only to convey the central ideas of the model and show how data-driven and demand-driven principles can be exploited in designing a parallel computation model to support logic programming. A characteristic of this model is the total absence of any concept of common physical storage for the storage of bindings for logical variables. This clearly has considerable advantage in the context of a parallel machine, although the von Neumann storage economy of structure sharing is therefore not achieved here. Since the model can be conceptually described within a packet based reduction framework, it is conceivable that existing parallel packet reduction machines (such as Alice[7]) can be used for its implementation.

An important aspect of the model left unaddressed to in this paper is in the area of garbage collection and subgoal failure reporting. In this model an activated rule-body will become garbage once it has delivered all its solutions. The problem is mainly one of deciding when the last solution belonging to a rule-body has arrived, or, when the rule-body is first activated deciding how many solutions it will deliver. Recognizing the last solution is difficult because solutions may be returned in any temporal order. Deciding in advance the number of solutions a rule-body will return is not straightforward because of the dynamic nature of rule activation. A novel counting scheme for solving these problems has been devised together with an efficient environment management scheme which minimizes the cost of context copying in OR-parallel evaluation[12].

Finally, a formal specification of the model in the style of CSP[13] is under construction. This will help towards clarifying some aspects of the model.

References

1. Moto-oka et al, Challenge for Knowledge Information-Processing Systems, Proceedings of the International Conference on Fifth Generation Systems, North-Holland, Amsterdam, 1982.
2. Clocksin, W. F. and Mellish, C. S.,'Programming in PROLOG', Springer-Verlag, Berlin, 1981.
3. Kowalski, R. A., Logic for Problem Solving, Elsevier-North Holland, New York, 1979.
4. Robinson, J. A., A Machine-oriented Logic based on the Resolution Principle, Journal of the ACM(12), PP.23-41, 1965.
5. Conery, J. S., The AND/OR Process Model for Parallel Interpretation of Logic Programs, Technical Report 204, University of California, Irvine, June 1983.
6. Dennis, J. B., First Version of a Data Flow Procedure Language, in Lecture Notes in Computer Science, Vol.19, pp.362-376, Springer-Verlag, 1974.
7. Gurd, J. R. and Watson, I., Preliminary Evaluation of a Prototype Dataflow Computer, Proceedings of IFIP 83, Sept 1983.
8. Treleaven, P. C., Brownbridge, D. R., and Hopkins, R. C., Data-Driven and Demand-Driven Computer Architecture, ACM Computing Surveys, 14(1), pp.93-143, March 1982.
9. Darlington, J. and Reeve, M., ALICE: A Multiprocessor Reduction Machine for the Parallel Evaluation of Applicative Languages, Proceedings of the 1981 ACM Conference on Functional Programming and Computer Architecture.
10. Bundy, A., 'The Computer Modelling of Mathematical Reasoning', Academic Press, 1983.
11. Watson, I., Watson, P., and Woods, V., Parallel Data-Driven Graph Reduction, Proceedings of IFIP 85, Sept. 1985.
12. Lee, M.K.O., A Packet Based Demand/Data Driven Reduction Model for the Parallel Execution of Logic Programs, Internal Working Paper, Declarative Systems Group, Dept. of Computer Science, The University, Manchester, April, 1986.
13. Hoare, C. A. R., Communicating Sequential Process, Communication of ACM 21(8), pp.666-677, 1978.

Information Processing with Associative Processors *

Hans-Albert Schneider
Universität Kaiserslautern
Fachbereich Informatik
D-6750 Kaiserslautern

Werner Dilger
FhG-IITB
Sebastian-Kneipp-Str. 12
D-7500 Karlsruhe

ABSTRACT

Associative processors keep their data in content addressable memories (CAMs) accessing them by content, not address. Our interest concentrates on how associative processors can be used for inference processes.

We have developed the model of an associative processor based on the Deduction Plan theorem proving method. Our approach also includes a unification algorithm which provides information about all causes of unification conflicts (if any) and allows simple backtracking of the unification graph.

1. Introduction

The idea to store data in memory cells which are accessed by their contents instead of their addresses is rather convenient because this is more similar to the way humans access data in their mind. Memories with this property are called content addressable memories (CAMs for short) or associative memories. There are different models of CAMs which differ in their degree of parallelity and the operational abilities of their cells.

In a restricted sense, associativity is achieved in high level programming languages by the ability to choose expressive identifiers. However, it often is necessary to access e.g. the elements of a list not as "the fifth entry in list PERSONS" but as "the entry in PERSONS where NAME='Smith'". This normally results in a lot of search time and/or management overhead, and the attempt to find a good compromise between both is classically known as time/space tradeoff. CAMs, however, can deal with this problem by operating on all cells (or a selected subset of cells) in parallel.

Although the idea of CAMs came up in the middle fifties, there are only few applications where they are used.

---

* Project sponsored by the Deutsche Forschungsgemeinschaft (DFG) under grant number Ma 581/4-1

The property to access cells by content makes CAMs well suited for applications where pattern directed retrieval plays an important role. There are a lot of pattern directed deductions in artificial intelligence (AI), thus associative processors (processors that store their data in a CAM) seem to have a good application domain there. We have picked out a special area of AI, namely automated theorem proving, to develop the model of an associative processor for it.

This paper is organized as follows: The second section gives a brief overview on the structure of CAMs and associative processors. The third section then sketches the theorem proving method we use, and the fourth section gives some idea of the model and how it would operate.

2. Associative Processors

For an overview on CAMs see also [4].

A content addressable memory is a storage unit that stores data in a number of cells such that those cells can be accessed by their content. The smallest unit of a CAM is the bit cell. It is able to

1) store one bit of information
2) read out one bit of information
3) compare its content with given information.

Searching is done using masks and the comparison operations of the cells.

An associative processor is a processor that uses a CAM as its data store. It therefore essentially consists of

1) a CAM
2) an arithmetic and logic unit (ALU)
3) a control system with an instruction store.

3. Deduction Plans and UwC

For the standard definitions of the terms used in automated theorem proving, such as clause, literal, or term, cf. [1].

The deduction plan theorem proving method is a graph based approach, that is, the proof is done by manipulation of a graph. This inference graph will be called a deduction plan throughout this paper (however, the terminology is slightly different in [3]). Its nodes are variants of input clauses (i.e. sets of literals). Its edges are directed and labelled by tripels (t,u,v) where u and v are the literals of interest of the incident clauses (u of the starting node and v of the ending node), and t is the type of the edge which indicates the kind of deduction step by which it was introduced. There are two possible types: SUB and RED. Edges of type SUB are added to the graph due to a SUBstitution step (which is similar to a resolution step), and those of type RED are added due to a REDuction step (similar to C-literal reduction in [5]).

A major idea of the deduction plan method is to separate deduction from unification, that is, no test for unifiability of the whole graph is done when adding a new edge; unification is performed using a separate graph. If unification conflicts occur, then this allows to locate their source(s) and to reset the 'bad' deduction step(s) immediately. Exhaustive (also called blind) backtracking instead would try to revise the last deduction step, then the previous one, and so on, until it were successful.

Note that this separation has a second effect: because clauses are not instantiated in the graph, there are no dependencies between the literals of a clause which would diminish the degree of AND-parallelism.

As mentioned above, unification is done by manipulation of a second graph, called unification graph with constraints (UwC for short). The idea of this graph was first published in [2]. Its nodes are terms (precisely all subterms of the literals in the deduction plan) and its edges are labelled with sets of deduction steps (i.e. their numbers). E.g., if an edge (t,u,v) is added in the nth step, and (omitting the sign)

$$u = P (s_1,\ldots,s_m),$$
$$v = P (t_1,\ldots,t_m),$$

then t_1 must be unified with s_1, t_2 with s_2, and so on. This is recorded by the notion of constraint. A constraint is a pair of terms. For simpler reference we add an identifier to it. For our purpose this "identifier" need not indicate the exact constraint but just the deduction step(s) responsible for it. A set of constraints is assigned to each edge of the deduction plan. The constraint set of the above edge would be

$$\{ (t_1, s_1, \{n\}), \ldots, (t_m, s_m, \{n\}) \} .$$

The constraint set of a deduction plan G is the union of the constraint sets of all edges of G.

If (s, t, d) is a constraint, then the UwC will contain an (undirected) edge between s and t labelled d. d is called the value of this edge. The value of a path w in the UwC is obtained as the union of the values of all edges of w. If s and t are terms starting with the same function symbol, say

$$s = f (s_1, \ldots, s_n),$$
$$t = f (t_1, \ldots, t_n),$$

and they are connected in UwC, then their corresponding arguments have to be unified, too. Therefore, for all paths w between s and t, new constraints

$$(s_1, t_1, val(w)), \ldots, (s_n, t_n, val(w)),$$

where val(w) is the value of w, have to be processed.

When processing is complete, then, in the case of conflicts, the UwC allows to find out all reasons of all unification conflicts (clashes as well as cycles), and to compute minimal conflict sets. A clash is indicated by two different leading function symbols in the same connectivity component of the UwC. To locate cyclic conflicts we add directed edges to the UwC leading from a term to its arguments (we are able to confine the number of the directed edges to those really contributing to cyclic conflicts).

One of the minimal conflict sets has to be selected and all the deduction steps indicated by it have to be removed. This will remove all unification conflicts from the deduction plan. As a consequence of this removal some nodes and edges might render unreachable from the top node; they will be removed, too. Note that the structure of the UwC also allows simple backtracking of the unification graph: if deduction step n is removed then all edges of UwC containing n in their label are removed; if a clause is removed then all its subterms which contain variables are removed (the others might be subterms of another clause; however, different clauses do not have variables in common).

If there is no unification conflict, then a most general unifier of the deduction plan can be derived from the UwC.

4. ASSIP-T

The previous chapter has shown that there are a lot of associative operations in the context of the sketched deduction, unification, and backtracking procedures (e.g., removing edges and nodes, or searching for a partner literal). This gave reason to us to develop the model of an associative processor, ASSIP-T, which supports this deduction method. The structure of ASSIP-T is shown in figure 1. ASSIP-T consists of two CAMs to store the clauses (CAM1) and terms (CAM2), respectively.

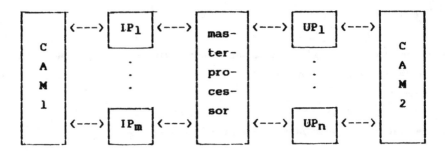

Figure 1 : Structure of ASSIP-T

There are several inference processors (IP_1, ..., IP_m) which operate on CAM1, searching for and selecting partner literals for a given literal, adding edges to the deduction plan and computing the resulting constraints. It is also possible to use one or more of them to check the structure of the plan (there are some restrictions on the structure) which would allow simpler processing for the other inference processors.

Similarly, unification is performed by a set of unification processors, UP_1, ..., UP_n, which process the constraints by adding edges to the UwC and computing the resulting constraints. Again it is possible to have one or more of them checking the structure, i.e. testing for clashes or cycles. However, we think it will be more efficient having the master processor test for cycles by means of a reachability matrix.

The master processor's job is to control the inference process (it determines e.g. which literals to resolve next), to accept the constraints computed by both inference and unification processors, and to distribute them to the unification processors. This distribution must be done in a way that avoids wellknown faults of parallel processing (like lost update). In addition, we want the master processor to maintain a reachability matrix for easier location of cycles. The graph represented by this matrix is not just the UwC but an abstraction of it.

In the case of unification conflicts the master processor instructs the unification processors to search for paths contributing to those conflicts and to deliver their values. From these values, it computes the conflict sets, chooses one and initializes the backtracking processes for both inference and unification graph.

The structure of CAM1 and CAM2 realizes a two level associativity: their cells are no memory words but can be looked at as small associative processors each of which stores a clause (or term, respectively) together with its variants and the incident edges. The variants (remember that they form the nodes) are implemented by indexing the variables of the respective expressions. Due to the properties of the CAM, the edges incident to a node need not be stored in an array or linked list: it is sufficient to store them in the same cell and add a field indicating the variant to which they belong. Thus, a cell contains two sorts of entries: nodes and edges.

To give an idea of the operation, let us suppose the following clauses (the example is taken from [3]):

```
1)   P(x), Q(y), R(x,y), V(a,x)
2)   -P(a)
3)   -V(y,a)
4)   -P(c)
5)   -Q(w), U(v,w)
6)   -R(z,z)
7)   -R(u,v), S(u)
8)   -S(a)
9)   -U(b,b)
10)  -U(c,c)
```

Suppose this deduction plan:

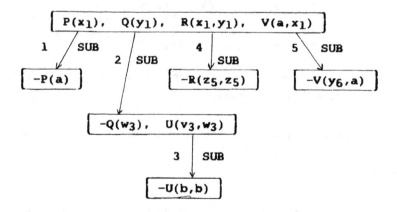

A UwC of this plan is

$$x_1 \xrightarrow{\{4\}} z_5 \xrightarrow{\{4\}} y_1 \xrightarrow{\{2\}} w_3 \xrightarrow{\{3\}} b$$

with $\{1\},\{5\}$ below x_1 connecting to $a \xrightarrow{\{5\}} y_6$, and $\{3\}$ below b connecting to v_3.

Obviously, there is a unification conflict, namely a clash between a and b, caused by the deduction steps 2, 3, 4, and 1 or 5. The minimal conflict sets here are $\{1,5\}$, $\{2\}$, $\{3\}$, and $\{4\}$.

We encourage the reader to imagine the backtracking process and to check that removal of any of the minimal conflict sets will remove the conflict.

The cells of CAM2 have the following contents :

term	variants' indices	edges (index, label, partner)
a	-.-	$(0, \{1\}, x_1)$, $(0, \{5\}, x_1)$, $(0, \{5\}, x_6)$
b	-.-	$(0, \{3\}, v_3)$, $(0, \{3\}, w_3)$
c	-.-	-.-
u	-.-	-.-
v	3	$(3, \{3\}, b)$
w	3	$(3, \{2\}, y_1)$, $(3, \{3\}, b)$
x	1	$(1, \{1\}, a)$, $(1, \{5\}, a)$, $(1, \{4\}, z_5)$
y	1, 6	$(1, \{2\}, w_3)$, $(1, \{4\}, z_5)$, $(6, \{5\}, a)$
z	5	$(5, \{4\}, x_1)$, $(5, \{4\}, y_1)$

Note that there are no variants of the constants a, b, and c; the "index" entries of their edges are dummy values.

CAM1 is structured similarly to CAM2 and therefore will be omitted here.

5. Conclusion

This paper described the model of an associative processor for theorem proving which has been developed for the deduction plan method. However, it should be applicable to other graph based theorem proving procedures as well which do not create completely new clauses but simply copy input clauses, and, in addition, allow the separation of deduction and unification.

As far as we know, there is no other approach which tries to use associative processors for theorem proving or other inference processes. Our model, ASSIP-T, is not yet realized; a simulation program using parallel processes instead of processors is actually being implemented.

6. References

[1]   C.-L. Chang, R. C.-T. Lee :
Symbolic Logic and Mechanical Theorem Proving.
Academic Press, New York 1973

[2]   W. Dilger, A. Janson :
Unifikationsgraphen für intelligentes Backtracking in Deduktionssystemen.
Proc. GWAI-83, Informatik-Fachberichte 76, Springer Verlag Berlin 1983, 189-196.

[3]   S. Matwin, T. Pietrzykowski :
Intelligent Backtracking in Plan-Based Deduction.
IEEE Trans. on Pattern Analysis and Machine Intelligence, vol. PAMI-7 (1985), 682-692.

[4]   B. Parhami :
Associative Memories and Processors. An Overview and Selected Bibliography.
Proc. IEEE 61 (1973), 722-730.

[5]   R.E. Shostak :
Refutation graphs.
Artificial Intelligence, vol. 7 (1976), 51-64.

A HIGH PERFORMANCE INTERCONNECTION CONCEPT FOR DATAFLOW- OR OTHER CLOSELY COUPLED MULTIPROCESSORS

R. E. Buehrer
Institut fuer Elektronik, ETH- Zentrum
CH - 8092 Zurich, Switzerland

Abstract

The interconnection network is a crucial part in many existing or proposed multiprocessor systems. Generalized cube- or crossbar-type networks featuring packet-switching [Sieg85] are often proposed if the bandwith demand exceeds the limited capacity of common-bus solutions.
The paper outlines an upgraded version of the intercommunication memory Intercom being successfully implemented in the ETH- Multiprocessor Empress [Bueh82]. This n-way multiport memory type concept is well suited to realize a high bandwith packet-switched network at reasonable cost despite the fact that its complexity is of the order $n*n$ (n equals the number of connected processors) rather than $n*\log n$ as in a generalized cube network. Key properties are particularily congestion- (i.e. collision) elimination and minimal network latency. The Intercom technique avoids, therefore, the potential network bottleneck in many multiprocessor concepts as long as the number of connected processors is not exceeding an upper limit.

1. Introduction

Success or failure of any innovative computer architecture and implementation is dictated by many factors: the power of the available programming language and its user acceptance, software development tools, hardware component feasibility, system reliability and availability [Levi81], etc.; the key attribute, however, is usually system performance, usually expressed in terms of Mips (Million instructions per second) or Mflops (Million floating point operations per second). Comparing performance figures turns out to be strongly controversial as long as one relies on pure numbers of instructions per time unit only without giving e.g. any references to the richness of the instruction-set of the machine [Gurd85] or the kind of applications being executed. We will not elaborate this problem in more detail, as a consequence, however, we will use the term performance in a more informal way: a computer is said to have a superior performance compared to another one if a particular program or set of programs is executed faster; in other words, if the response time is smaller.
Good performance in this sense can be achieved by means of applying a powerful strategy to exploit the parallelism in the programs (i.e. parallel processing) and, secondly, by means of providing sound architectural and implementational support. We will concentrate mainly on the second aspect. The particular question to be answered is how to improve the performance of a particular class of parallel processor systems by means of

optimizing the interconnection network.

The processor systems we are refering to belong to the group of closely coupled multiprocessors being connected via a packed-switched network [Sieg85] as depicted in figure 1; their field of application is mainly in technical/ scientific computing. Examples of parallel processors which fit into this category are MIMD or SIMD systems of various kinds; refer e.g. to [Sieg85], and dataflow machines [Denn80], [Ager82], [Gurd85].

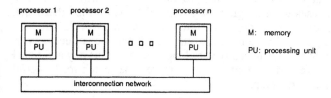

Figure 1: The closely coupled multiprocessor

The most widely proposed network concepts for either architecture are versions of the generalized cube network [Sieg85], (e.g. Omega-, flip-, SW-banyan-, shuffle-exchange-, multi-stage switching-, delta networks, etc.) as outlined in figure 2. (We are not considering the common-bus concept [Sieg85] since the multiprocessor systems on which we are concentrating usually consist of too many processors with a network bandwith demand exceeding the limits of such a solution.)

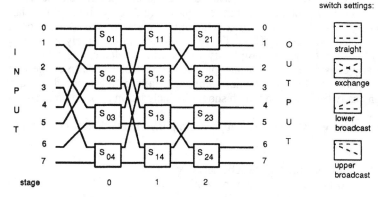

Figure 2: The generalized cube network

Generalized cube networks are featuring relatively high bandwith at reasonable cost since their complexity grows on the order of n * log n, where n is the number of connected processors. The major drawback, however, is the well-known congestion (or collision) problem [Sieg85] occuring whenever two information packets collide because they are sent at the same time to the same communication channel; refer e.g. to [Pfis85]. There are two basic solutions to this problem. The first method is based on a handshaking mechanism in the network: a switch element S_i cannot send a data packet to the input of switch S_j of the next stage as long as no idle-signal is sent back from S_j to S_i. The second solution relies on the implementation of sufficient storage in each switch element to temporarily store data packets in case of congestion. The price one has to pay is a potentially significant network latency increase if the first solution is applied, or a significant increase of complexity in the switch element [Pfis85] in the second case.

A word has to be added on network-latency. Multistage cube networks have a latency on the order of log n time units, and it is a common understanding that, provided enough inherent parallelism exists in the program(s), the performance of the system should not be considerably affected. This is particularly true in dataflow machines because network latency has almost no influence at all provided that the program contains sufficient inherent parallelism [Ager82]. In those cases were program parallelism is low, on the other hand, network latency can become very cumbersome. Dataflow machines in particular are very sensitive to this effect since their pipeline length (i.e. the number of steps necessary to execute two succeeding instructions) is intrinsically very long [Gais82]; thus any additional delay in the network aggravates the performance loss even more. The search for powerful network concepts is therefore an important topic.

After looking at some network complexity issues in the next chapter we will describe in chapter 3 the upgraded version of an intercommunication memory concept which indeed avoids many drawbacks of the generalized cube networks described above. In chapter 4 some implementation details will be given. Final conclusions will be drawn in chapter 5.

2. Network complexity aspects

If multistage cube networks are compared with e.g. crossbar-type switch networks [Hwan84], [Sieg85] it is usually concluded that the complexity and cost of both approaches are related approximately as $n / 2 * \log n$ (2-by-2 switching element) versus $n * n$, where n is the number of connected processors. These figures represent an extremely simplified comparison model because neither the complexity of the switch element is taken into account, nor is there any consideration of throughput relations. "Costs" due to congestion and packet routing activities or due to potential component failures are ignored. In fact, even more criteria can easily be identified which should be included in a sound comparison formula.

To avoid lenghty discussions we will therefore apply a simplified network cost criterium C_i as follows:

$C_1 := P_1 * n / 2 * \log n;$ cost for a multistage cube network.
$C_2 := P_2 * n * n;$ cost for a crossbar-type network.

P_1 and P_2 are constants reflecting all additional factors, some of which are mentioned above. Depending on their individual weight, various cost estimates can be plotted with respect to the network type and the number of connected processors (refer to figure 3). Note that the crossbar-type network curve in fact reflects any network architecture with $n * n$ growth. It turns out that in those cases where P_1 is significantly larger than P_2 a crossbar-type network is more cost-effective than a multistage cube network or at least comparable as long as the number of connected processors does not exceeded a certain limit.

The Intercom concept described in the following features a relatively small constant P_2 because it can be implemented in a very cost-effective manner. In addition, most other cost factors mentioned above are also low. The relations shown in figure 3 are thus by no means unrealistic.

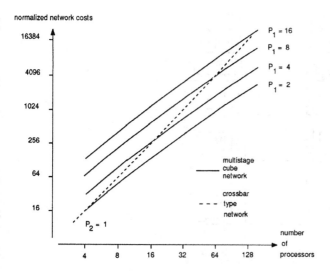

Figure 3: Comparison of network cost

3. The intercommunication memory Intercom

3.1. Architecture

Although the Intercom approach is similar to a conventional crossbar-type switch network, it is a completly different concept (refer to figure 4).

(Note: An Intercom concept was successfully implemented in the ETH- Multiprocessor EMPRESS [Bueh82] which consists of 17 processors. The version which was built is used as a conflict-free 17-port memory with a memory block size of 12k * 16 bit words in the blocks assigned to the first processor (for writing) and 256 words in the remaining blocks; it is optimized for the initial application area of the Empress machine (parallel simulation of ordinary differential equations [Hali80]). The Intercom is featuring powerful virtual addressing modes to optimize reads within groups of cooperating processors. No optimizations were made, however, to use it as an alternative to a generalized cube network for packet-switching.)

Rather than having n * n switching elements it is consisting of a quadratic organized matrix of memory blocks MB_{ij} (i, j = 1,..,n). The basic operation principle is such that processor k ($1 \leq k \leq n$) can simultaneously write (i.e. duplicate) data into a single one, a selected subrange, or all MB_{kj} (j = 1,..,n) memory block(s) of its associated row. Processor k is able to read out data of all MB_{ik} (i = 1,..,n) memory blocks of its associated column. (Note that the size of each memory block is implementation dependent, it may contain from several bytes up to many words of a certain length). Duplication of data, as mentioned above, can individually be enabled by means of setting a specific write-enable-mask WEM in the transmitting processor. This provides an easy means for various types of message broadcasts as partially indicated in figure 2.

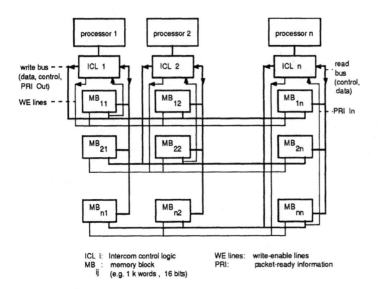

Figure 4: The Intercom concept

Since the memory blocks in the Intercom consist of passive memory modules requesting explicit write- and read operations, provisions have to be made to achieve the dynamic behavior of a packed-switched network. The solution we propose is based on the introduction of additional logic to forward "packet-ready" information PRI upon completion of the transfer of a full data package to invoke data collection at the target processor(s).

3.2. Data transfer concept

For simplicity reasons we restrict the description of the Intercom transfer concept to the very basic mechanism. We assume that initially either the operating system (in case of e.g. an MIMD multiprocessor system) or the output section (in case of a dataflow system; refer to [Arvi83]) of the sending processor is providing a data package being available in a queue which is implemented in some local memory of the processor. This data package consists of a header for transfer control and identification purposes and a body with the data values (refer to chapter 4 for further details).

Packet transmission is initiated by means of sending an appropriate request to the Intercom control logic ICL. This device will read all necessary transfer parameters such as target processor(s) identification, word count etc. and subsequently copy the package into all relevant memory blocks of the corresponding Intercom row using the write bus. Upon completion a "packet-ready" information PRI will be generated and forwarded to the ICLs of all receiving processors. This message, in turn, will initialize the transfer of the local copy of the data package either to the operating system (in von Neumann applications) or to the input section in case of a dataflow machine.

4. Implementation aspects

4.1. Data packet format

The data packages to be transmitted contain the following information (subsets or extensions may be applicable):
header:
target processor(s) identification (i.e. write-enable-mask WEM), word count (i.e. length of data packet), type, target within the receiving processer (i.e. process identification, context etc.), identification of sending processor and process priority, etc.
body:
an arbitrary number of bytes or words

4.2. Memory blocks

The individual processing units of the multiprocessor are operating asynchronously; writes to and reads from a particular Intercom memory block may thus occur at the same time. As a consequence, the memory implementation has to provide decoupled input and output access. Dual-port memories with this property are commercially available, refer e.g. to [Pope83] or [Texa84]. We propose a slightly modified implementation.
Since the Intercom is used as a packet-switched network, the memory cells can be implemented as temporary buffers with separate write- and read ports as in a first-in-first-

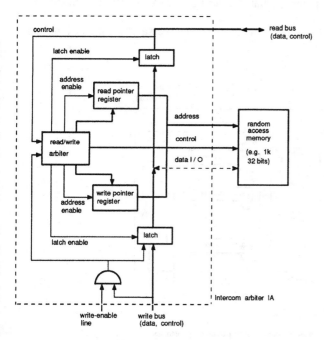

Figure 5: Intercom memory block

out (FIFO) logic. As a consequence, neither the sending nor the receiving ICLs do have to provide the actual addresses within the memory cell.

The memory block concept consists of a combination of an Intercom arbiter IA in conjunction with a conventional random-access-memory RAM, as depicted in figure 5. The RAM is operating as a cyclic buffer. The IA which can be implemented as a separate chip or as an extension within a conventional RAM-chip, is in charge of alternating between write and read cycles. Writes to and reads from a matrix cell can thus be performed at approximately half the speed specified for the RAM. Note that this cycling between input and output is completely hidden from the outside logic. The address lines for the RAM are provided either by the write- or the read pointer register; each of it is individually incremented after a write- or a read operation, respectively.

According to the setting of the corresponding write-enable line, data arriving on the write bus are either ignored or accepted and copied in the memory block.

4.3. Intercom control logic ICL

The ICL, as depicted in figure 6, consists of two basic subunits:

a) Control and transfer logic CTL

The CTL provides the logic for all data transfers between a processor and its attached Intercom memory modules. It has also control over the WEM Register which holds the state of all write-enable lines for partial duplication in the memory blocks of a corresponding Intercom row.

Data transfers between processor and Intercom and vice-versa are done by means of

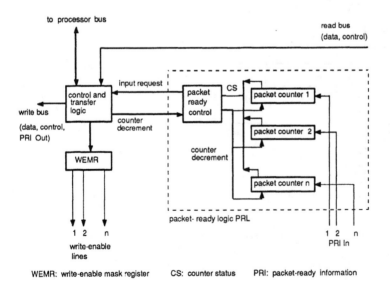

Figure 6: The Intercom control logic ICL

direct-memory-accesses; standardized protocols are used in either direction. They are invoked by the processor (output request) for data output or by the <u>packet-ready control PRC</u> (input request) for data input; refer to b).

b) Packet-ready logic PRL

The PRL is in charge of keeping book of the packet-ready information PRI In and of invoking the CTL for input data transmission. A particular <u>package counter PCi</u> is incremented upon arrival of PRI In i (provided by the sending processor's ICL as PRI Out) and decremented after the corresponding data packet is forwarded to the processor. The packet-ready control PRC monitors the state of all counters and generates the input request to the CTL depending on a priority basis. Since counter increments and decrements may occur asynchronously provisions have to be made to decouple these inputs.

5. Conclusions

The implementation of the Intercom as described above is relatively straightforward. Considering realistic cost comparison formulae for n * n and n * log n networks, strong evidence leads to the conclusion that up to a certain number of processors (e.g. ≤ 32) an Intercom may indeed be superior to a generalized cube network.
It is still not clear today which parallel architecture will perform best for a particular application e.g. in the field of technical/ scientific computing. One conclusion can already be drawn however: in those cases where the parallelism of the program is below a certain limit, a multiprocessor consisting of relatively few high-performance processors (e.g. 20 50-Mips machines) will always outperform a system consisting of many low-performance processors (e.g. 1000 1-Mips machines).
The Intercom as a powerful interconnection concept is thus well suited to support the necessary bandwith demand of such a system. Detailed implementation and simulation studies are under way to substantiate the above findings by providing sound quantitative results.

Acknowledgements

The author acknowledges the stimulus provided by his colleagues of the computer architecture group. Many thanks also to H.T. Auerbach and the referees for their helpful comments on the draft of this paper.

References

[Ager82]   Agerwala T. and Arvind, "Data Flow Systems. Guest Editors' Introduction", IEEE Computer, Vol. 15, No. 2, Feb. 1982, pp. 10-13. [Arvi83] Arvind and members of the Functional Languages and Architectures Group, "The Tagged Token Dataflow Architecure", Memo, Computation Structures Group, Laboratory for Computer Science, MIT, Cambridge, Mass., March 1983.

[Bueh82]   Buehrer R.E., Brundiers H.J., Benz H., Bron B., Friess H.M., Haelg W., Halin H.J., Isacson A., and Tadjan M., "The ETH- Multiprocessor Empress: A Dynamically Configurable MIMD System", IEEE Transactions on Computers, Vol. 31, No. 11, Nov. 1982, pp. 1035-1044.

[Denn80]   Dennis J.B., "Data Flow Supercomputers", IEEE Computer, Vol. 13, No. 4, Nov. 1980, pp. 48-56.

[Gais82]   Gajski D.D, Padua D.A., Kuck D.J., and Kuhn R.H., "A Second Opinion on Data Flow Machines and Languages", IEEE Computer, February 1982, pp. 58-69.

[Gurd85]   Gurd J.R., Kirkham C.C., and Watson I., "The Manchester Prototype Dataflow Machine", Communications of the ACM, Vol. 28, No. 1, Jan. 1985, pp. 34-52.

[Hali80]   Halin H.J., Buehrer R., Haelg W., Benz H., Bron B., Brundiers H.J., Isacson A., and Tadjan M., "The ETH- Multiprocessor Project: Parallel Simulation of Continuous Systems", Simulation, Oct. 1980, pp. 109-123.

[Hwan84]   Hwang K. and Briggs F.A., "Computer Architecture and Parallel Processing" McGraw-Hill, Inc., U.S.A., 1984

[Levi81]   Levi P., "Betriebssystem für Realzeitanwendungen", CCG Texte 3, Datakontext-Verlag, Koeln, Germany, 1981.

[Pope83]   Pope K.W., "Asynchronous dual-port RAM simplifies multiprocessor systems", EDN, September 1983, pp. 147-154.

[Pfis85]   Pfister G.F., Norton V.A., "'Hot Spot' Contention and Combining in Multistage Interconnection Networks", Proceedings of the 1985 International Conference on Parallel Processing, August 1985, pp.790-797.

[Sieg85]   Siegel H.J., "Interconnection Networks for Large-Scale Parallel Processing", Lexington Books, Lexington, U.S.A., 1985.

[Texa84]   Texas Instruments, "TMS 9650, Multiprocessor Interface (MPIF) Data Manual", Texas Instruments Inc., May 1984.

Parallel Solution of Eigenvalue Problems in Acoustics on the

Distributed Array Processor (DAP)

Dipl. Math. A. Polster
Universität Erlangen
IMMD 7
Martensstr. 3
852 Erlangen
West Germany

Abstract:

The paper deals with the parallel solution of the partial differential equation $-\Delta u = u$ in an 2- or 3-dimensional domain on the **Distributed Arrary Processor (DAP)**. We want to find the eigenfunctions corresponding to the two or three smallest eigenvalues. A discretisation leads to a system of linear equations $Ax = \lambda\, Bx$, $A, B \in R^{n \times n}, x \in R^n$, A and B large and sparse.

λ and x are determined by minimising the Rayleigh quotient $f(x) = \dfrac{(x, Ax)}{(x, Bx)}$ using a modified conjugate gradient method. We describe the implementation of the algorithm and show how to generate the linear systems automatically for arbitrary domains. We show results of 2- and 3-dimensional calculations, where we looked for the resonance swings in the interior of a car by solving linear systems with up to 263144 unknowns.

Keywords: PDE, Rayleigh Quotient, Conjugate Gradient Method, DAP, arbitrary domains, 3-dimensional calculations.

1. The Partial Differential Equation and its Discretisation

The starting point of the work is the PDE

(1.1) $\qquad -\Delta u = \lambda\, u \quad$ in $\Omega \subset R^n$

(1.2) $\qquad \dfrac{\partial u}{\partial n} = 0 \quad$ in $\partial\Omega$

(1.1) describes the resonance swings of a string (n=1), a membrane (n=2), or a medium filling an interior space (n=3).

We want to find the eigenfunctions corresponding to the two or three smallest eigenvalues. We started using the unit square as initial domain : We cover Ω with a rectangular grid of m knots per spatial direction and number the knots starting from 1 to $m^2 := n$. The Finite Element Method (FEM) or an Finite Difference approach leads to the discrete problem

(1.3) $\qquad Ax = \lambda\, Bx, \quad A, B \in R^{n \times n}, x \in R^n.$

This results in large sparse matrices with nonzero values only in five diagonals:

Example:

$$A = \begin{bmatrix} \end{bmatrix} \qquad B = c \cdot I \;,\; c \in \mathbb{R}^{+}$$

The eigenvector x of (1.3) gives the desired approximation of the values of the oscillation in the knots.

2. Solution of (1.3) with a Conjugate Gradient Method

In order not to destroy the sparcity of our matrices we used the Rayleigh quotient

$$(2.1) \qquad f(x) = \frac{(x, Ax)}{(x, Bx)}$$

to formulate an equivalent minimisation problem

$$(2.2) \qquad \lambda_1 = \min f(x)$$

The minimum of f is the smallest eigenvalue λ_1 of (1.4) and the corresponding vector x is the eigenvector . We modified the Conjugate Gradient (cg-) Method of Fletcher/Reeves [FLE].

Our algorithm: Choose an arbitrary starting point $x \in R^n$ and set

$$h_0 = -g_0 = -grad\ f(x_0)$$

Iteration :

$$(2.3) \quad \dot{x}_{k+1} = x_k + \alpha_k d_k,$$

$$(2.4) \quad \hat{x}_{k+1} = \frac{\dot{x}_{k+1}}{|\dot{x}_{k+1}|},$$

$$(2.5) \quad x_{k+1} = \hat{x}_{k+1} - \frac{\sum_{i=1}^{n} \hat{x}_{k+1_i}}{n} I, \quad I = (1,...,1)$$

$$(2.6) \quad g_{k+1} = -grad f(x_{k+1}) = \frac{2(Ax_{k+1} - f(x_{k+1})Bx_{k+1})}{(x_{k+1}, Bx_{k+1})},$$

$$(2.7) \quad d_{k+1} = g_{k+1} + \beta_k d_k, \text{ where } \beta_k = \frac{(g_{k+1}, g_{k+1})}{(g_k, g_k)}.$$

Comments:

(2.3)   performs a line search, i.e. α_k is chosen so that f is minimized in the direction d_k.

(2.4)   Improving a proposal of Bradbury and Fletcher [BRAD] we minimised f on the n-dimensional unit cube, i.e. we divided every $\dot{x}_k$ by $\|\dot{x}_k\|$ (Euclidean norm).

(2.5)   The smallest eigenvalue of the PDE (1.1)/(1.3) is zero with a constant eigenfunction. As we are interested in the smallest nontrivial eigenvalue we have to use the fact that one can get the second smallest eigenvalue by minimising the Rayleigh Quotient on a subspace that is orthogonal to the eigenspace of the smallest eigenvalue. So for every step of the iteration we need an $x \in R^n$ that fulfils

$$(x,c) = 0 \quad \Longleftrightarrow \quad \sum_{i=1}^{n} x_i = 0.$$

We need vectors x_k with mean value zero which is achieved by adding (2.3) to the cg-method.

3. Taking Advantage of the structure of the Matrices

3.1 Mapping of Vectors and Matrices on the DAP-Store

We cover Ω with a rectangular grid of 64 knots per spatial direction and number the knots from 1 to 4096. They can also be identified by the pair (i,j) of their row- and column- numbers. Every vector $x \in R^{4096}$ contains the values of some function in these 4096 knots. We store the component (i,j) of such a vector in a DAP-matrix at the location (i,j).

The five nonzero diagonals of A represent the coefficients belonging to the knots themselves or their neighbours in the north,south, east and west . And so every diagonal is stored in a separate DAP-matrix. Since A is symmetrical we only need to store the main diagonal and the two upper diagonals. So these DAP-matrices contain at the point (i,j) the coefficients of the knot (i,j) or of its neighbour in the south or east .

3.2 Realisation of the Multiplication

The product of the quindiagonal matrix A with the vector x is evaluated by five multiplications of its diagonals with x. Appropriate shifts are necessary to obtain the correct result. So the product of a 4096x4096 matrix with a vector is reduced to 5 DAP- multiplications and 4 DAP-additions. This requires only 17 msec on the DAP.

This scheme is easyly modified for matrices with more nonzero diagonals (resulting perhaps from FE- approaches of higher accuracy). So we were able to evaluate the eigenvalue of (1.3) in 17 sec by 100 iterations with an accuracy of 10^{-4}. So the DAP is faster by a factor of 100 than the serial CYBER 173 where it took almost half an hour.

4. Two-Dimensional Calculations on Arbitrary Domains

4.1 Generation of the Linear Systems

Up to now we solved the PDE (1.1/1.2) on the unit square. This led to the matrices A and B described in 1. . Arbitrary domains can be generated by starting with the unit square and "cutting of" unnecessary parts by logical masks until we have a domain of the desired shape.
This approach requires modifications of the matrices A and B in two steps:

1. In all diagonals of A and B those elements must be set to zero that correspond to knots outside the new domain or to knots on its border.

2. The values of the components belonging to the new boundary must be updated.

So we can generate domains that consist not only of vertical and horizontal borders of the initial rectangular grid but also of edges that stand in a 45 degree angle to the others:

1.Step: The user defines via a logical matrix OMEGA the new domain. OMEGA(I,J) = 1 if knot (i,j) belongs to the new domain or its border, OMEGA(I,J) = 0 else.

2.Step: Different types of knots are characterised by evaluating their neighbourhood. All knots of one type are collected simultaneously in a logical matrix. This matrix contains .true. in the location (i,j) when the knot (i,j) is of that type.

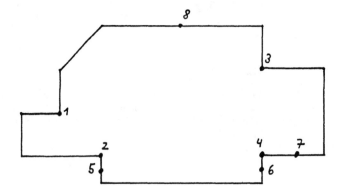

• = knot inside the domain
o = knot outside the domain

type of the knot	characterisation		number
horizontal border		or	8,7
vertical border		or	5,6
upper left			1
lower left			2
upper right	reentrant corner		3
lower right			4

and so on.

3.Step: The diagonals of A and B are now modified. All elements (i,j) of the diagonals belonging to gridpoints of the same type are simultaneously set to the correct value.

4.2 Numerical Results

Our goal was the calculation of the resonance swings of the interior of the car Schwarz used in [Schw]. This domain contains boundaries that are neither rectangular nor stand in a 45 degree angle to our initial grid. So we approximated these borders by rectangular ones. This resulted in ca. 2000 grid points for the different domains compared to only 185 Schwarz used. We stopped the calculation when the eigenvalues differed by less than 10^{-4}. We needed 120 to 137 iterations for that accuracy, it took 12.9 to 14.7 seconds DAP - time.

The figure shows the size of the oscillations' amplitudes, the biggest being normed to the value 100. A big number corresponds to a big amplitude, i.e. change of pressure, i.e. sound volume.

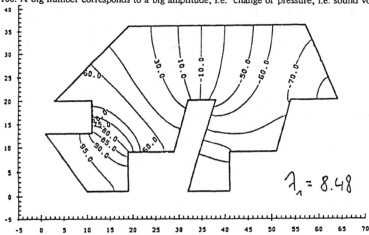

$\lambda_1 = 8.48$

5. Three Dimensional Calculations

5.1 Mapping of Vectors and Matrices on the DAP-Store

We used the same approach as in the 2 - dimensional problem and started with an equidistant grid of 64 knots in the x- and y- direction and 40 knots in the z- direction. We organized the grid as a number of vertical planes put behind each others. A vector $x \in R^{4096 \times 40}$ is stored in an array of 40 DAP-matrices whose i-th component belongs to the i-th plane of the grid. We again have to solve the discrete problem (1.3).

The resulting matrices are:

$$A = \begin{bmatrix} C & D & & & \\ D & 2C & & & \\ & & \ddots & & \\ & & 2C & D \\ & & & D & C \end{bmatrix}$$

where C is a quindiagonal matrix like A in the two-dimensional case; B and D are diagonal matrices, dim D = 4096, dim B = 4096x40. A is a block-tridiagonal matrix, every block corresponds to one plane of the grid. We have 4 diagonals per plane to store, 40 planes, so we need 200 DAP - matrices for A. The diagonalmatrix B needs only 40 DAP- matrices.

5.2 The Multiplication of the Matrix A with a Vector

Using the blockstructure of A we realised the multiplication by

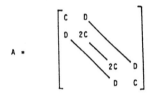

$$\begin{bmatrix} C_1 & D_1 & & & \\ D_1 & & \ddots & & \\ & & & D_{39} & \\ & & & D_{39} & C_{40} \end{bmatrix} \cdot \begin{bmatrix} X_1 \\ \vdots \\ X_{40} \end{bmatrix} = \begin{bmatrix} C_1 X_1 + D_1 X_2 \\ D_1 X_1 + C_2 X_2 + D_2 X_3 \\ \vdots \\ D_{39} X_{39} + C_{40} X_{40} \end{bmatrix}$$

The products $D_i X_j$, $C_i X_i$ are calculated as described earlier.

5.3 Treatment of Arbitrary Domains

Using the same method like before we start with the 64x64x40 grid and cut off unnecessary parts. All parts of A belonging to knots outside the new domain are set to zero. Then successively for every plane we must first determine the types of the knots and then update A in that plane according to the new boundary. Here we must distinguish 64 different types of knots by their neighbourhood.

Examples:
● = knot inside the domain
o = knot outside the domain

Reentrant corner from top front left:

Reentrant edge from top back:

Salient corner:

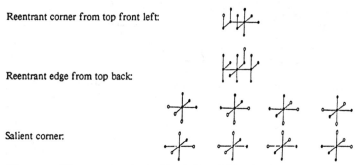

Other types of knots are characterised by similar neighbourhoods.

5.4 Results

We used following domain:
View from the front: View from the top:

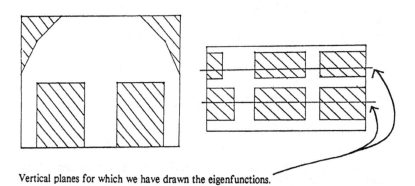

Vertical planes for which we have drawn the eigenfunctions.

These planes were choosen because they show the oscilations that the driver and his passengers hear.

Here we solved system (1.3) with approx. 160000 unknowns. It took ca 170 iterations and ca 800 seconds on the DAP to calculate the eigenfunctions. The results do not differ very much from the two dimensional calculations since the interior of a car doesn't change too much in the third dimension.

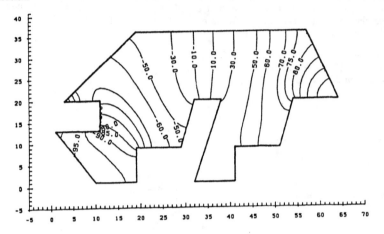

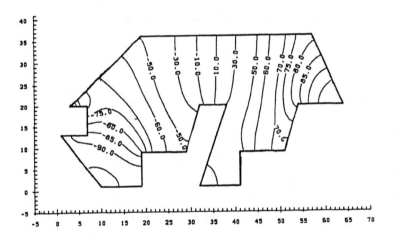

References:

[BRAD] W.W. Bradbury and R.Fletcher: New Iterative Methods for Solution of the Eigenproblem; Numer. Math. 9 (1966) , 256 - 267.

[SCHW] H.R. Schwarz : Methode der finiten Elemente; Teubner (Studienbuch Mathematik) : Stuttgart 1980.

GAUSS ELIMINATION ALGORITHMS FOR MIMD COMPUTERS

M. Cosnard[+], M. Marrakchi[+], Y. Robert[+] and D. Trystram[#]
[+] CNRS, Laboratoire TIM3, BP 68, 38402 St Martin d'Hères Cedex, France
[#] Ecole Centrale PARIS, 92295 Chatenay Malabry Cedex, France

ABSTRACT : This paper uses a graph-theoretic approach to analyse the performances of several parallel variations of the Gaussian triangularization algorithm on an MIMD computer. Dongarra et al. [DGK] have studied various parallel implementations of this method for a vector pipeline machine. We obtain complexity results permitting to select among these parallel algorithms.

INTRODUCTION

The most commonly used algorithm to solve linear systems of equations on sequential computers is the well-known Gaussian elimination method. Six different versions for a vector pipeline machine have been considered in [DGK]. Three implementations where data are accessed columnwise have been discussed in detail, each of them corresponding to a given permutation of the loop indices i,j,k of the sequential algorithm: namely the SAXPY version (form kji), the GAXPY version (form jki) and the DOT version (form ijk). In this paper, we deal with the design of MIMD versions of these algorithms (see [Fly], [GP], [HJ] and [HB] for a classification of parallel computers).

A parallel MIMD version of the Gaussian elimination algorithm with partial pivoting has been discussed in [Kum] and [LKK], and an implementation of the LDL^t decomposition algorithm in [KK]. The performance analysis is based on the task graph model presented in [Kum]. Informally, algorithms are splitted into elementary tasks, whose execution ordering is directed by precedence constraints. The task graph model which can be constructed directly from these precedence constraints, is the basic tool of our theoretical analysis. Together with MIMD versions of the [DGK] algorithms, we analyse a modified version of the KJI-SAXPY and the Doolittle algorithm.

We assume a system which is capable of supporting multiple instruction streams executing independently and in parallel on multiple data streams [GP], [HJ], [HB] and [Sch], and that there are means to impose temporal precedence constraints between the tasks of the implemented algorithms [KK]. Moreover we suppose that each processor can perform any of the four arithmetic operations in an unit of time and that there are no memory conflicts nor data communication delays. Throughout the paper, p denotes the number of processors, and E_p is the efficiency of the parallel algorithm under study. When triangularizing a dense n by n matrix, we set $p=\alpha n$, with $\alpha<1$, in order that processors communications costs do not overcome arithmetic [Saa]. Elementary tasks will be of length $O(n)$, so that synchronization and data communication do not predomine.

A model where communication delays are neglected could appear unrealistic. However, we deal with pointwise methods for which the elements of a given matrix are accessed columnwise or rowwise, depending on the storage mechanism and programming environment. Hence we can assume a stride-one accessing of data as prevalent in vector machines and cache-based architectures, so that data loading and unloading can be pipelined, and overlapped with arithmetic. In the following we assume that data is accessed columnwise, to be close to a FORTRAN programming style environment.

This work has been supported by the CNRS through the GRECO C^3.

If data loading and unloading cannot be overlapped with arithmetic, communications should not be neglected any longer. It is shown in [CMRT] that block methods should be used in such a case.

Most often, pivoting of rows or columns is used for stability reasons. We shall not consider here the overhead due to pivoting, taking into account the remarks of [DGK] who state that the pivoting procedure is just some additional overhead and does not significantly affect the performance. However, partial pivoting could be very easily included in our analysis: simply consider that comparing and interchanging two reals takes one unit of time, which only modifies the granularity of the tasks.

Once the constraints defined, the first step in the parallelization of a method is the definition of the elementary tasks and their precedence graph. This graph shows the temporal dependency of the operations of the algorithm. The tasks are then assigned to the available processors according to the precedence graph. Throughout the paper, the relation T<<T' denotes the precedence constraint and means that task T is to be completed before task T' can start its execution [Kum], [LKK].

THE ALGORITHMS

Five sequential algorithms will be considered which are variations of Gaussian elimination. Like this one, they all need the same number of arithmetic operations: $2n^3/3+O(N^2)$

(A)   { Generic Gaussian elimination algorithm. Form KJI - SAXPY of [DGK] }

> **For** k := 1 to n-1
> T_{kk} : < **For** i := k+1 to n
> do $a_{ik} := -a_{ik}/a_{kk}$ >   n-k arithmetic operations
> **For** j := k+1 to n
> T_{kj} : < **For** i := k+1 to n
> do $a_{ij} := a_{ij} + a_{ik}*a_{kj}$ >   2(n-k) arithmetic operations

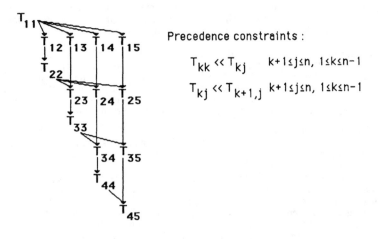

Precedence constraints :

$$T_{kk} << T_{kj} \quad k+1 \le j \le n, \ 1 \le k \le n-1$$

$$T_{kj} << T_{k+1,j} \quad k+1 \le j \le n, \ 1 \le k \le n-1$$

Figure 1 : Precedence graph of Gaussian elimination (form KJI)

(B)   { Generic Gaussian elimination algorithm. Form JKI - GAXPY of [DGK] }

For j := 1 to n
    For k := 1 to j-1
        T_{kj} : < For i := k+1 to n
                do $a_{ij} := a_{ij} + a_{ik}*a_{kj}$ >   2(n-k) arithmetic operations
        T_{jj} : < For i := j+1 to n
            do $a_{ij} := -a_{ij}/a_{jj}$ >   n-j arithmetic operations

Precedence constraints : $T_{kj} << T_{k+1,j}$ $1 \leq k \leq j-1,\ 1 \leq j \leq n$
                          $T_{jj} << T_{jk}$ $j+1 \leq k \leq n-1,\ 1 \leq j \leq n$

Remark that the precedence graph is the same as this of the form KJI-SAXPY (A). This is due to the fact that for a given j, the tasks T_{kj}, $1 \leq k \leq j$, are to be processed sequentially. In the contrary, for a given k, the tasks T_{kj}, $k+1 \leq j \leq n$, can be processed in parallel.

(C)   { Generic Gaussian elimination algorithm. Form IJK - DOT of [DGK] }

For i := 2 to n
    For j := 2 to i
        T_{ij} : < $a_{i,j-1} := - a_{i,j-1}/a_{j-1,j-1}$
            For k := 1 to j-1
            do $a_{ij} := a_{ij} + a_{ik}*a_{kj}$ >   2j-1 arithmetic operations
    For j := i+1 to n
        U_{ij} : < For k := 1 to i-1
            do $a_{ij} := a_{ij} + a_{ik}*a_{kj}$ >   2(k-1) arithmetic operations

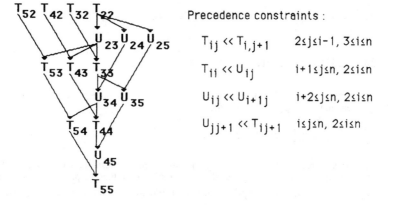

Precedence constraints :

$T_{ij} << T_{i,j+1}$ $2 \leq j \leq i-1,\ 3 \leq i \leq n$

$T_{ii} << U_{ij}$ $i+1 \leq j \leq n,\ 2 \leq i \leq n$

$U_{ij} << U_{i+1j}$ $i+2 \leq j \leq n,\ 2 \leq i \leq n$

$U_{jj+1} << T_{ij+1}$ $i \leq j \leq n,\ 2 \leq i \leq n$

Figure 2 : Precedence graph of Gaussian elimination (form IJK)

(D)   { Generic Gaussian elimination algorithm. Form KJI - SAXPY modified }

For k := 1 to n-1
    For j := k+1 to n
        T_{kj} : < $a_{kj} := -a_{kj}/a_{kk}$
            For i := k+1 to n
            do $a_{ij} := a_{ij} + a_{ik}*a_{kj}$ >   2(n-k)+1 arithmetic operations

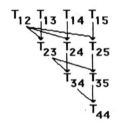

Precedence constraints :

$$T_{k,k+1} \ll T_{k+1,j} \quad k+2 \leq j \leq n, \ 1 \leq k \leq n-1$$

$$T_{kj} \ll T_{k+1,j} \quad k+2 \leq j \leq n, \ 1 \leq k \leq n-1$$

Figure 3 : Precedence graph of Gaussian elimination (form KJI modified)

(E) { Doolittle reduction [GV] }

> For k := 1 to n
>> For j := k to n
>>> T_{jk} : < **For** p := 1 to k-1
>>>> do $a_{kj} := a_{kj} - a_{kp}{}^{*}a_{pj}$ >   2(k-1) arithmetic operations
>> For i := k+1 to n
>>> U_{ki} : < **For** p := 1 to k-1
>>>> do $a_{ik} := a_{ik} - a_{ip}{}^{*}a_{pk}$
>>>> $a_{ik} := a_{ik}/a_{kk}$ >   2k-1 arithmetic operations

Precedence constraints : $T_{jk} \ll T_{j,k+1}$ $k+1 \leq j \leq n, \ 2 \leq k \leq n$
$T_{kk} \ll U_{k,j}$ $k+1 \leq j \leq n, \ 2 \leq k \leq n$
$U_{ki} \ll U_{k+1,i}$ $k+2 \leq i \leq n, \ 2 \leq k \leq n$
$U_{kk+1} \ll T_{j,k+1}$ $k+1 \leq j \leq n, \ 2 \leq k \leq n$

The precedence graph is the same as this of the form IJK-DOT (C).

GRAPH-THEORETICAL ANALYSIS

These five algorithms lead to three task graphs which shows that two different sequential versions of an algorithm can lead to the same parallel implementation:
• the task graph of the algorithm (D)
• the task graph of the algorithms (A) and (B)
• the task graph of the algorithms (C) and (E).

In this section we design parallel algorithms and establish complexity results for these graphs. We let $T_{(X)}$ denote the asymptotic execution time of the parallel algorithm that we propose for the version (X), and $T_{(X)opt}$ denote the time of an optimal algorithm. We point out that comparing the execution times is equivalent to comparing the efficiency in this case, since the number of arithmetic operations is the same in all the versions.

The task graph of the algorithm (D)

Such a graph is also encountered when solving linear systems by diagonalization methods [CRT1] and [CRT2]. For a given value of k, there are n-k tasks to be executed. Let $T \leqslant T'$ denote the following precedence constraint: the execution of T' cannot begin before that of T (but a simultaneous execution is allowed). We have the

Lemma 1 [CRT1] : There exist optimal algorithms which satisfy to the additional precedence constraint
(*): $T_{k,j} \lesssim T_{k,j+1}$ ($j \geq k+2$)

The greedy algorithm G executes the tasks from one level of the precedence graph to another, from left to right in each level, and it starts the maximum number of tasks at each time (hence the name of greedy). More precisely, the algorithm G executes the tasks in the following order:
$$T_{12} \lesssim T_{13} \lesssim ... \lesssim T_{1n} \lesssim T_{23} \lesssim T_{24} \lesssim T_{2n} \lesssim T_{34} \lesssim ... \lesssim T_{n-1,n}$$

At time t=1, the algorithm G starts the execution of the tasks T_{12}, T_{13}, ..., T_{1p}. For any $t \geq 1$, if $q \leq p$ processors are idle, the algorithm G assigns these q processors to the execution of the following maximum number of tasks.

Proposition 1 : The greedy algorithm G is asymptotically optimal. Its execution time is
$$T_{(D)opt} = [\ 2/(3\alpha) + \alpha^2/3\ ]\ n^2 + O(n) \text{ and } E_\alpha = 1/(1+\alpha^3/2)$$

Proof : Using proposition 1, we show that G is asymptotically optimal in the class of the algorithms which satisfy to (*). Since we know that a task T_{kj} is to be executed before a task $T_{k,j+1}$ in this particular class of algorithms, we can prove by induction that the greedy algorithm starts the execution of the tasks T_{1n}, T_{2n}, ..., $T_{n-1,n}$ as early as possible, up to a linear factor O(n).

To compute the execution time of the greedy algorithm, we notice that the p processors are activated without any latency until the execution of the task $T_{n-p,n}$. Therefore the execution time up to $T_{n-p,n}$ is equal to the sequential execution time of all the precedings tasks, divided by p. We add to this value the execution time of the tasks $T_{n+1-p,n}$, $T_{n+2-p,n}$, ..., $T_{n-1,n}$ which concludes the proof.

Contrarily to the intuitive feeling, the greedy algorithm is *not* always optimal. For some values of n and p, we can design algorithms gaining a linear factor O(n) over the greedy scheme [Rot].

The task graph of the algorithms (A) and (B)

Contrary to the preceding case, we do not know any optimal algorithm for the graph of the algorithms (A) and (B). We propose an algorithm whose execution is divided into three different parts. In order to simplify the presentation, we assume the existence of an extra processor denoted P_0. Since the total number of processors is proportional to n, this hypothesis does not modify our asymptotic performance evaluation.

The first part of the algorithm corresponds to the execution of level 1 up to level n-2p. We assign all the tasks T_{kk}, $2 \leq k \leq n-2p$, to the processor P_0. The remaining processors will execute the tasks T_{ki}, $i \geq k+1$, in a greedy manner, level by level and in each level from left to right. We let P_0 begin the execution of the task $T_{k+1,k+1}$ as soon as the task $T_{k,k+1}$ is completed. In order to obtain an asymptotic efficiency equal to 1 in this phase, we can show that there is enough tasks to be executed at each time-step so that no processor P_i, $i \geq 1$, is idle.

Let us now consider the second phase of the algorithm: from level n-2p to n-p. In this phase, the algorithm has not asymptotic efficiency 1. We choose to synchronize the processors so that they all begin simulta- neously the execution of new tasks. The algorithm proceeds level by level.

Let us detail the execution of level k, which is composed of n-k tasks $T_{k,k+1}$, ..., $T_{k,n}$. At time t, P_1, ..., P_p start the execution of $T_{k,k+1}$, $T_{k,k+2}$, ..., $T_{k,k+p}$. At time t+2(n-k), P_1, ..., P_{n-k-p} start the execution of the last n-k-p tasks and terminate at time t+4(n-k). P_0 starts the execution of $T_{k+1,k+1}$ when $T_{k,k+1}$ is completed. The execution of $T_{k+1,k+1}$ is completed at time t+3(n-k).

In the last phase: from level n-p to level n, the processors operate in a very similar fashion as in phase 2, the only difference lies in the fact that $P_1, ..., P_p$ complete the execution of a given level k before P_0 completes the execution of $T_{k+1,k+1}$. Hence the processing of level k+1 starts only when P_0 has finished its work.

We point out that if p=n, the first two phases of the algorithm are empty. The precedence constraints imply that our algorithm is optimal in this case, since its execution time corresponds to the longest path of the tasks graph.

Proposition 2 : The execution time $T_{(A)}$ of the previous algorithm is:

$$T_{(A)} = T_{(B)} = [\, 2/(3\alpha) + 13\alpha^2/6 \,] \, n^2 + O(n) \text{ if } \alpha \leq 1/2$$

$$T_{(A)} = T_{(B)} = [\, 2 - \alpha^2/2 \,] \, n^2 \text{ otherwise}$$

$$E_a = 1/(1 + 13\alpha^3/4) \text{ if } \alpha \leq 1/2 \text{ and } E_a = 4/(12\alpha - 3\alpha^3) \text{ otherwise}$$

We compare the performances of optimal algorithms for the two preceding graphs. Remark that we know neither how to design an optimal algorithm, nor how to compute the optimal time for version (B).

Proposition 3 : $T_{(A)opt} = T_{(B)opt} \geq T_{(D)opt} - O(n)$

Proof : Let t be the time where the greedy algorithm completes the level n-p. When an optimal algorithm for the graph of (A) completes the level n-p at time t', it must have executed all the tasks of previous levels (due to the precedence constraints). Since the number of operations from level 1 to level n-p is the same in the two graphs (up to a linear factor), and since the greedy algorithm works with efficiency 1, we deduce that t'≥t-O(n).

Let $T_{n-p,j}$ be the last executed task of level n-p by the optimal algorithm of version (A). The path $\{T_{(n-p)+1,j}, T_{(n-p)+2,j}, ..., T_{jj}, T_{j,j+1}, T_{j+1,j+1}, ..., T_{n,n}\}$ is composed of tasks that must be processed sequentially. The shortest path is obtained for j=n. Using proposition 1, we deduce the result.

<u>The task graph of the algorithms (C) and (E)</u>

The design and analysis of parallel algorithms for versions (C) and (E) are derived from the previous results in a very straightforward manner. The key-idea is to gather $T_{j,k+1}$ and $U_{k,j}$ into a single task, leading to a graph that we have already studied. It can be easily verified that the new graph is similar to the one of version (A): the precedence constraints are the same as in section 3.1. However, we point out that we cannot prove here the optimality of this greedy algorithm, since there could exist more efficient algorithms which do not gather the tasks. But we can obtain a lower bound for the execution time in a similar way as in section 3.2.

Proposition 4 : The execution time of the preceding algorithm is:

$$T_{(C)} = T_{(E)} = [\, 2/(3\alpha) + 4/3 \,] \, n^2 + O(n)$$

$$T_{(C)opt} = T_{(E)opt} \geq [\, 2 + 2\alpha - 7\alpha^2 + 4\alpha^3)/(3\alpha) \,] \, n^2 + O(n)$$

COMPARING THE PERFORMANCES

Proposition 5 :   (i) $T_{(C)} \geq T_{(A)} \geq T_{(D)}$

               (ii) $T_{(A)opt} \geq T_{(D)opt}$

               (iii) $T_{(C)opt} \geq T_{(D)opt}$ for $\alpha \leq 1/3$

Among the five algorithms, the form KJI-greedy SAXPY (D) has the best performances, followed by the form KJI-SAXPY (A) and JKI-GAXPY (B), whatever the number of processors. The least parallelizable versions are IJK-DOT and Doolittle reduction. Regarding optimal algorithms, we conjecture that version (D) is the most efficient for any α.

CONCLUDING REMARKS

We have presented five parallel versions of Gaussian elimination algorithm for solving dense linear systems. We have used a graph-theoretical approach to analyse and compare their performances. Using $p = \alpha n$ processors, where $\alpha \leq 1$, we design for each version a parallel algorithm and obtain either asymptotically optimal execution times or lower bounds thereof.

It is worth pointing out that designing parallel algorithms is quite different from designing vector pipeline algorithms. For instance, the vector versions KJI-SAXPY and JKI-GAXPY of [DGK] lead to the same task graph, hence to the same parallel implementation. Contrarily to the vector case where the JKI-GAXPY appears to be the best form, the KJI-greedy SAXPY is the most suitable for parallelization on an MIMD machine.

REFERENCES

[CRT1] M. COSNARD, Y. ROBERT, D. TRYSTRAM, Résolution parallèle de systèmes linéaires denses par diagonalisation, Bulletin EDF série C, n° 2, 1986

[CRT2] M. COSNARD, Y. ROBERT, D. TRYSTRAM, Comparaison des méthodes parallèles de diagonalisation pour la résolution de systèmes linéaires denses, C. R. A. S. Paris 301, I, 16, 1985, 781-784

[CMRT] M. COSNARD, J.M. MULLER, Y. ROBERT, D. TRYSTRAM, Communication costs versus computation costs in parallel Gaussian elimination, Proc. of Conf. Parallel Algorithms and Architectures, M. Cosnard et al. eds, North Holland, to appear

[DGK] J.J. DONGARRA, F.G. GUSTAVSON, A. KARP, Implementing linear algebra algorithms for dense matrices on a vector pipeline machine, SIAM Review 26, 1, 1984, 91-112

[Fei] M. FEILMEIER, Parallel computers - Parallel mathematics, IMACS North Holland, 1977

[Fly] M.J. FLYNN, Very high-speed computing systems, Proc. IEEE 54,1966, 1901-1909

[GP] D.D. GAJSKI, J.K. PEIR, Essential issues in multiprocessors systems, IEEE Computer, June 1985, 9-27

[GV] G. H. GOLUB, C. F. VAN LOAN, Matrix computation, The Johns Hopkins University Press, 1983

[Hel] D. HELLER, A survey of parallel algorithms in numerical linear algebra, SIAM Review 20, 1978, 740-777

[HJ] R.W. HOCKNEY, C.R. JESSHOPE, Parallel computers: architectures, programming and algorithms, Adam Helger, Bristol, 1981

[HB] K. HWANG, F. BRIGGS, Parallel processing and computer architecture, MC Graw Hill, 1984

[Kum] S.P. KUMAR, Parallel algorithms for solving linear equations on MIMD computers, PhD. Thesis, Washington State University, 1982

[KK] S.P. KUMAR, J.S. KOWALIK, Parallel factorization of a positive definite matrix on an MIMD computer, Proc. ICCD 84, 410-416

[LKK] R.E. LORD, J.S. KOWALIK, S.P. KUMAR, Solving linear algebraic equations on an MIMD computer, J. ACM 30, 1, 1983, 103-117

[Rot] G. ROTE, Personnal Communication

[Saa] Y. SAAD, Communication complexity of the Gaussian elimination algorithm on multiprocessors, Report DCS/348, Yale University, 1985

[Sam] A. SAMEH, An overview of parallel algorithms, Bulletin EDF, 1983, 129-134

[Sch] U. SCHENDEL, Introduction to Numerical Methods for Parallel Computers, Ellis Horwood Series, J. Wiley & Sons, New York, 1984

FAST PARALLEL ALGORITHMS FOR EIGENVALUE AND SINGULAR VALUE COMPUTATIONS

Marian Vajteršic
Institute of Technical Cybernetis
Slovak Academy of Sciences
Bratislava, Czechoslovakia

Abstract

Three parallel algorithms for the eigensolution of real symmetric matrices of order n on a SIMD-type parallel computer with an associative
memory are considered. The algorithms realize various parallel orderings of the Jacobi orthogonalization procedure. A detailed description
of the parallel computational process is given which allows the power
of the machine to be exploited. The arithmetic parallel complexity
achieved for the complete solution is $O(n)$, the number of parallel
data transfers is $O(n \log n)$. The results of algorithm simulations
are included.

1. Introduction

In last years, the availability of highly parallel machines has
influenced the development of algorithms which can exploit effectively
a concurrency in solving numerical as well as non-numerical problems.

This paper brings an implementation of three parallel orthogonalization schemes for solving the eigenproblem for real symmetric matrices and the singular value decomposition (SVD) on the associative
parallel computer [3]. Our parallel scheme defined in [6], the Sameh's
second scheme of [5] and Modi-Price's scheme [2] are tailored to exploit the advantages of this type of parallel machine where shifts and
cyclic data permutations are realizable easily.

This computer is composed of associative modules (one-module version of the computer will be considered throughout this paper). Each
module contains an orthogonal associative memory block, a vector of
processor units and a permutation network block. The role of permutation network is to realize data transfers required. The processor
units operate on a bit slice of a vector of data in parallel. The location of data in the memory will be considered in fields of length
n^2, where $n = 2^r$ is the order of the matrix to be transformed. Thus,
each field (R) can be seen as composed of n blocks R_i, $i = 1,...,n$ of
n elements $(R_i)_j$, $j = 1,...,n$. A parallel execution of operation Ⓐ on
memory fields R1, R2 with a result in R3 can be expressed as R3 ← R1 Ⓐ

R2(M) where 1's (0's) in the boolean vector M (mask) indicate those elements in R3 where the result of $\emptyset$ is (not) written in. (The mask M or its complement $\overline{M}$ can be omitted when no masking is necessary). The following data transfer functions will be defined for $k = 0, 1, \ldots, r-1$:

$$\text{SHUP2}^k R = (R_{2^k+1}, R_{2k+2}, \ldots, R_n, R_1, \ldots, R_{2^k})$$

$$\text{SHDOWN2}^k R = (R_{n-2^k+1}, \ldots, R_n, R_1, \ldots, R_{n-2^k})$$

$$\text{shup } 2^k R = (\text{SHUP2}^k R_1, \text{SHUP2}^k R_2, \ldots, \text{SHUP2}^k R_n) \tag{1}$$

$$\text{shdown2}^k R = (\text{SHDOWN2}^k R_1, \text{SHDOWN2}^k R_2, \ldots, \text{SHODWN2}^k R_n)$$

$$P2^k R = (R_{1'}, R_{2'}, \ldots, R_{n'}), \quad 1' = (1-1+2^k) \bmod 2^{k+1} + (\lceil 1/2^{k+1} \rceil - 1) 2^{k+1} + 1,$$

$$p2^k R = (P2^k R_1, P2^k R_2, \ldots, P2^k R_n) \qquad 1 = 1, \ldots, n .$$

The eigenvalue and SVD problems can be solved by the Jacobi-like algorithms. The Jacobi method for a real symmetric matrix A generates a sequence of rotation matrices $Q^{(p)}$, $p = 1, 2, \ldots$ with non-zero elements $q_{ii}^{(p)} = q_{jj}^{(p)} = c_{ij}$, $q_{ij}^{(p)} = s_{ij}$, $q_{ji}^{(p)} = -s_{ij}$ which annihilate off diagonal elements $a_{ij}^{(p)}, a_{ji}^{(p)}$ $(i < j)$ of a matrix $A^{(p)}$ by constructing

$$A^{(p+1)} = \left[Q^{(p)} \right]^T A^{(p)} Q^{(p)} \tag{2}$$

from $A^{(1)} = A$. The rotation coefficients c_{ij} and s_{ij} are computed for given i,j as proposed in [4]:

$$x_{ij} = (a_{jj}^{(p)} - a_{ii}^{(p)})/2a_{ij}^{(p)}, \quad y_{ij} = \text{sign}(x_{ij})/(|x_{ij}| + \sqrt{1+x_{ij}^2}) \tag{3}$$

$$c_{ij} = 1/(\sqrt{1+y_{ij}^2}), \quad s_{ij} = y_{ij} c_{ij} \tag{4}$$

The formulas for the modified values are:

$$a_{ii}^{(p+1)} = a_{ii}^{(p)} - y_{ij} a_{ij}^{(p)} \qquad a_{jj}^{(p+1)} = a_{jj}^{(p)} + y_{ij} a_{ij}^{(p)} \tag{5}$$

$$a_{ij}^{(p+1)} = a_{ji}^{(p+1)} = 0$$

$$a_{iq}^{(p+1)} = c_{ij} a_{iq}^{(p)} - s_{ij} a_{jq}^{(p)} \qquad a_{jq}^{(p+1)} = c_{ij} a_{jq}^{(p)} + s_{ij} a_{iq}^{(p)} \qquad q \neq i,j \tag{6}$$

$$a_{qi}^{(p+1)} = c_{ij} a_{qi}^{(p)} - s_{ij} a_{qj}^{(p)} \qquad a_{qj}^{(p)} = c_{ij} a_{qj}^{(p)} + s_{ij} a_{qi}^{(p)} \qquad q \neq i,j . \tag{7}$$

The efficiency of the algorithm depends on the annihilation ordering. One of the schemes for sequential computation (scheme PERSEQ) is defined by

$$(i,j) = \{(1,2), (1,3), \ldots, (1,n), (2,3), \ldots, (2,n), (3,4), \ldots, (n-1,n)\} \tag{8}$$

The number of iterations (2) in one annithilation cycle is $n(n-1)/2$ for PERSEQ.

It was observed that more than one orthogonalizations can be performed in one iteration [5]. In the next section, three parallel schemes are formulated in terms of operations (1).

How to use these schemes in parallel algorithms, an explanation is given in section 3 on an example of one iteration for the Sameh's scheme. In each algorithm, $0(n)$ matrix transpose operations are saved in one annihilation cycle on ground of efficient performance of rotations (6), (7).

The results obtained by a simulation of the algorithms developed and their comparisons to a sequential process based on the scheme (8) are given in the last section.

2. Parallel orthogonalization schemes

The first scheme was developed by Sameh in [5]. For $n = 8$, the illustration is given in fig. 1. The row index i and column index j respectively of elements $a_{ij}^{(k)}$, $a_{ji}^{(k)}$ annihilated in k-th iteration, $k = 1,2,\ldots,n-1$ are represented for corresponding k by the left and right column of permuted integers. (Further, instead of $a_{ij}^{(k)}$ only the index pair ij will be used).

k	0	1		2		3		4		5		6		7		0
1		1	2	1	4	1	6	1	8	1	3	1	7	1	5	1
2		2	1	4	1	6	1	8	1	2	4	2	8	2	6	2
3		3	4	3	6	3	8	3	2	3	1	7	1	3	7	3
4		4	3	6	3	8	3	2	3	4	2	8	2	4	8	4
5		5	6	5	8	5	2	5	4	5	7	5	3	5	1	5
6		6	5	8	5	2	5	4	5	6	8	6	4	6	2	6
7		7	8	7	2	7	4	7	6	7	5	3	5	7	3	7
8		8	7	2	7	4	7	6	7	8	6	4	6	8	4	8
		$P2^0$		$P2^0$		$P2^0$		$P2^0$		$P2^1$		$P2^1$		$P2^2$		
		$SHUP2^0$		$SHUP2^0$		$SHUP2^0$		$SHUP2^0$		$SHUP2^1$		$SHUP2^1$		$SHUP2^2$		

Fig. 1

According to the permutation functions given in fig. 1 below, the scheme PERSAM can be defined for an arbitrary $n = 2^r$ by $n-1$ steps $PERSAM_k$, $k = 1,2,\ldots,n-1$ as follows:

$$
\text{PERSAM}_k \begin{cases} P2^0 & \text{SHUP2}^0 & k=1,2,\ldots,n/2 \\ P2^1 & \text{SHUP2}^1 & k=n/2+1,\ldots,n-n/4 \\ \vdots & \\ P2^{r-1} & \text{SHUP2}^{r-1} & k = n-1 \end{cases} \tag{9}
$$

One of schemes where one annihilation cycle is divided into n iterations [2] can be shown in a form given by fig. 2.

k	0	1	2	3	4	5	6	7	8	0
1		2 3	1 3	1 5	3 5	3 7	5 7	5 8	7 8	8
2		3 2	3 1	5 1	5 3	7 3	7 5	8 5	8 7	7
3		4 5	2 5	2 7	1 7	1 8	3 8	3 6	5 6	6
4		5 4	5 2	7 2	7 1	8 1	8 3	6 3	6 5	5
5		6 7	4 7	4 8	2 8	2 6	1 6	1 4	3 4	4
6		7 6	7 4	8 4	8 2	6 2	6 1	4 1	4 3	3
7		[8] 8	6 8	[6] 6	4 6	[4] 4	2 4	[2] 2	1 2	2
8		[1] 1	8 6	[3] 3	6 4	[5] 5	4 2	[7] 7	2 1	1
		TO	TE	TO	TE	TO	TE	TO	TE	

Fig. 2

The numbers in brackets correspond to elements ij not annihilated in odd iterations. TO and TE respectively denote transformation strings for odd and even iterations. Then the scheme PERMOPRY can be formulated using definitions of TO and TE as follows:

$$
\text{PERMOPRY}_k \begin{cases} \text{SHUP2}^0 \quad P2^0 \ (\text{masked 2 last terms}) \ \text{SHDOWN2}^0 (=\text{TO}) \\ \qquad\qquad\qquad\qquad\qquad\quad k = 1,3,\ldots,n-1 \\ \text{SHUP2}^0 \quad P2^0 \quad \text{SHDOWN2}^0 \ (=\text{TE}) \quad k = 2,4,\ldots,n \end{cases} \tag{10}
$$

It is to note that after n-th permutation the even cycles start with reversed ordering of elements. However, it does not cause any difficulty because the permutations in even cycles can ramain as defined.

We have developed a parallel scheme in which permutaions $P2^k$ and $p2^k$ occur only.

Its diagram for n = 8 is shown in fig. 3. Its formulation for $n = 2^r$ is

$$
\text{PERORD}_k \begin{cases} P2^0 & k = 1,3,5,\ldots,n-1 \\ P2^1 & k = 2,6,\ldots,n-2 \\ \vdots & \vdots \\ P2^r & k = n/2 \end{cases} \tag{11}
$$

As seen, the column index j of annihilated elements is permuted only whereby the row index i remains without any change.

k	0	1		2		3		4		5		6		7		0
1	1	1	2	1	4	1	3	1	7	1	8	1	6	1	5	1
2	2	2	1	2	3	2	4	2	8	2	7	2	5	2	6	2
3	3	3	4	3	2	3	1	3	5	3	6	3	8	3	7	3
4	4	4	3	4	1	4	2	4	6	4	5	4	7	4	8	4
5	5	5	6	5	8	5	7	5	3	5	4	5	2	5	1	5
6	6	6	5	6	7	6	8	6	4	6	3	6	1	6	2	6
7	7	7	8	7	6	7	5	7	1	7	2	7	4	7	3	7
8	8	8	7	8	5	8	6	8	2	8	1	8	3	8	4	8
		$P2^0$		$P2^1$		$P2^0$		$P2^2$		$P2^0$		$P2^1$		$P2^0$		$P2^2$

Fig. 3

As shown by the illustrations in fig. 1-3, the transformation rules prescribed by (9)-(11) in fact realize the schemes under consideration.

3. The transformation strategy

The aim is to perform all arithmetic operations required by the process (3)-(7) on vectors in parallel. Therefore, the matrix A to be orthogonalized will be located row-wise in the associative memory.

The programming structures of these algorithms are fundamentally similar. Each iteration consists of following parts:
- permutation of elements for a given iteration according to corresponding step of given permutation scheme
   - evaluation of c_{ij} and $\pm s_{ij}$ values for given pairs i,j
   - orthogonal transformation on rows
   - orthogonal transformation on columns.

For a simplicity of explanation, the evaluation of one iteration will be shown on the second iteration for the scheme PERSAM. Then assuming n = 4, elements ij, ji for i = 1,3 and j = 2,4 are annihilated. As a result of the previous iteration, the matrix elements are ordered in field A of the memory (see fig. 4) according to the first step of PERSAM.

As given by $PERSAM_2$, elements of the field A are shifted: $A \leftarrow shup2^0 A$, $A \leftarrow SHUP2^0 A$ (fig. 4). Elements ii, i = 1,...,4 are obtained in field D by $D \leftarrow A(M)$ where M is a mask with 1's in positions ii. The blocks of A and M are then permuted with the factor 2^0 which corresponds to the second step of PERSAM. The results $B \leftarrow P2^0 A$, $MB \leftarrow P2^0 M$ are shown in fig. 4. From B, one can obtain respectively in fields E and

1.iter 2. iter. 3.iter.

A	A	M	D	B	MB	E	F	F	X	Y	C	S	A	CR	SR	MC	A	B	A	CC	SC	A	A
22	11	1	11	41	1	41		44	x_{14}	y_{14}	c_{14}	s_{14}	11	c_{14}	s_{14}	0	11	0	44	c_{14}	s_{14}	44	11
21	14			44			44						0	c_{14}	s_{14}	0	0	44	0	c_{14}	$-s_{14}$	0	12
24	13			43									13	c_{14}	s_{14}	1	13	43'	42'	c_{23}	$-s_{23}$	42	13
23	12			42									12	c_{14}	s_{14}	1	12	42'	43'	c_{23}	s_{23}	43	14
12	41	1	44	11	1	14	11	11	$-x_{14}$	$-y_{14}$	c_{14}	$-s_{14}$	0	c_{14}	$-s_{14}$	0	0	11	0	c_{14}	s_{14}	0	21
11	44			14									44	c_{14}	$-s_{14}$	0	44	0	11	c_{14}	$-s_{14}$	11	22
14	43			13									43	c_{14}	$-s_{14}$	1	43	13'	12'	c_{23}	$-s_{23}$	12	23
13	42			12									42	c_{14}	$-s_{14}$	1	42	12'	13'	c_{23}	s_{23}	13	24
42	31	1	33	21	1	23	22	22	$-x_{23}$	$-y_{23}$	c_{23}	$-s_{23}$	31	c_{23}	$-s_{23}$	1	31	21'	24'	c_{14}	s_{14}	24	31
41	34			24									34	c_{23}	$-s_{23}$	1	34	24'	21'	c_{14}	$-s_{14}$	21	32
44	33			23									33	c_{23}	$-s_{23}$	0	33	0	22	c_{23}	$-s_{23}$	22	33
43	32			22									0	c_{23}	$-s_{23}$	0	0	22	0	c_{23}	s_{23}	0	34
32	21	1	22	31	1	32	33	33	x_{23}	y_{23}	c_{23}	s_{23}	21	c_{23}	s_{23}	1	21	31'	34'	c_{14}	s_{14}	34	41
31	24			34									24	c_{23}	s_{23}	1	24	34'	31'	c_{14}	$-s_{14}$	31	42
34	23			33									0	c_{23}	s_{23}	0	0	33	0	c_{23}	$-s_{23}$	0	43
33	22			32									22	c_{23}	s_{23}	0	22	0	33	c_{23}	s_{23}	33	44

Fig. 4

F elements ij and jj (i = 1,3; j = 2,4) by E ← B(M) and F ← B(MB). In order to get the non-zero elements of F on positions which correspond to
the non-zero elements of fields D and E (fig. 4), the field F has to
be permuted within blocks by the factor 2^0 assigned to the step
PERSAM$_2$, i.e. F ← p2^0F. The operation X ← (F-D)/2*E on fields D, E, F gives respectively values x_{ij} and $-x_{ij}$ on those positions in X, where
elements jj and ii are located in A. Hence, according to (3), the values of $\pm y_{ij}$ are obtained on the same positions in a field Y. Performing functions prescribed by (4) on fields, we get the values c_{ij} in a
field C on positions of $\pm y_{ij}$. The values respectively s_{ij} and $-s_{ij}$ are
obtained in a field S on positions of y_{ij} and $-y_{ij}$ (fig. 4).

The transformation (5) of diagonal elements is computed by
A ← D-Y*E(M). The annihilations in A are done with mask MB by A ← φ(MB),
where φ is a zero vector. In order to transform the rows a A by (6) in
parallel, it is necessary to spread the non-zero values of fields C
and S within their blocks. It is done in log n steps where for
k = 0,1,...,log n-1 operations

$$CR \leftarrow CR + p2^k CR \qquad SR \leftarrow SR + p2^k SR \qquad (12)$$

are realized from starting vectors CR = C, SR = S (fig. 4). Then the
row transformation can be obtained as A ← (CR*A - SR*B) (MC), where
MC = $\overline{M + MB}$.

In a straightforward realization of (7) a transpose of the field
A would be required. However, it can be done without this operation
which is rather complicated and expensive on this type of parallel computer. For this reason, the field A is permuted by the given permutation factor in blocks as well as within the blocks, i.e. B ← P2^0A,
A ← p2^0B (fig. 4). The components of the fields C and S are spread
block - wise in fields CC and SC. These fields can be created by

$$CC \leftarrow CC + P2^k CC \qquad SC \leftarrow SC + P2^k SC, \quad k = 0,1,...,\log n-1, \qquad (13)$$

where the process starts with CC = C, SC = S. Then the transformation
follows from A ← (CC*A + SC*B)(MC). The next iteration begins with shift
operations on A according to the factor prescribed by the third step of
the permutation scheme PERSAM. All further operational steps are performed in the same fashion as described above except the new value of
the permutation factor is 2^1 instead of 2^0.

As seen, the number of vector operations if 0(1) for the evaluation of one iteration. On ground of log n steps in (12) and (13), the
parallel data transfer complexity is 0 (log n) for one iteration.

The algorithm which realizes the scheme PERMOPRY is structured analogically as the above algorithm whereby the permutations required are prescribed by (10). The difference is only in evaluating the odd numbered iterations where always one pair of elements is not annihilated.

The arithmetic complexity remains the same as in the proceeding algorithm, while the data transfer complexity is increased only by the cost of one additional shift operation.

The advantage of the parallel associative algorithm for the last scheme PERORD is that no shift operations are needed. However, in order to overcome the necessity to transpose the matrix, this algorithm requires to compute the orthogonalizations from both sides on four vectors instead of one as it was the case in the two preceeding algorithms.

The orthogonalization computations of k-th iteration, $k = 1,2,\ldots,$ n-1 will be performed on elements of (k-1)-st iteration which are located in four fields AO, AR, AC, ARC ordered as follows:

AO - original ordering in blocks and within the blocks

AR - permutation of blocks corresponding to $PERSAM_{k-1}$, original odering within the blocks   (14)

AC - permutation within the blocks according to $PERSAM_{k-1}$, original ordering in blocks

ARC - permutation in blocks and also within the blocks according to $PERSAM_{k-1}$.

Then the orthogonalization coefficients (5) can be obtained in fields C and S analogically as in the algorithm formulated above. Their placement in respectively fields CR, SR and CC, SC is as given by (12) and (13) where a given permutation factor is used. The transformation of vectors (14) from the left is done easily in a vector-like manner by AO' ← CR*AO - SR*AR, AR' ← CR*AR + SR*AO, AC' ← CR*AC - SR*ARC, ARC' ← CR*ARC + SR*AC. Similarly, the column transformation does not require additional data transport operations because it can be done by AO ← CC*AO' + SC*AC', AR ← CC*AR'- SC*ARC' AC ← CC*AC' + SC*AO', ARC ← CC*ARC' + SC*AR'.

The number of parallel arithmetic operations remains 0 (1) for one iteration. As mentioned above, the number of data manipulations has been reduced and its value is 0 (log n).

Finally, let us mention that the all three above strategies can be implemented also for solving the singular value problem (SVD) on the associative machine considered as follows from the approaches for parallel solving this problem reported in [1] and [6]. For n not being a power of 2, the blocks can be filled up with zero elements and the process can be performed without any essential change. For a very large value of n there will arise a problem of dividing the data between more associative modules and also the communication strategy will play an important role.

4. Simulation results

The parallel algorithms of the proceeding section have been simulated on the PDP 11/40 computer.

The eigenvalue problem was solved for real symmetric matrices of order n for n = 4, 8, 16. The matrix elements were uniformly and independently distributed in <0,1>. The orthogonalization process was terminated after the initial sum of squares of off-diagonal elements was reduced to 10^{-12} times. The following table summarizes the results for the schemes PERSAM, PERMOPRY and PERORD for t = 100, 10, 5 where t gives the number of trials. As an illustrative comparison also the results for the classical scheme PERSEQ are given. The values in the table are mean numbers of iterations required to satisfy the stopping criterion. The simulation results are promising concerning the convergence of our algorithms.

n	t	PERSAM	PERMOPRY	PERORD	PERSEQ
4	100	3.11	3.40	3.11	3.20
8	10	4.10	4.30	4.50	3.90
16	5	5.00	5.20	5.20	4.40

Table 1

Acknowledgement.

The author is indebted to Mr. Z. Žambor for the simulation results.

References

[1] Brent, R.P., Luk, F.T., A systolic architecture for the singular value decomposition. Tech. Rep. TR-CS-92-09, Aust. Nat. Univ. (1982).

[2] Modi, J.J., Pryce, J.D., Efficient implementation of Jacobi's diagonalization method on the DAP. Numer. Math. 46, 3 (1985), 443-454.

[3] Richter, K., Parallel computer system SIMD. In: Artif. Intelligence and Inf.-Control Syst. of Robots, I. Plander, Ed., North-Holland, Amsterdam, 1984.

[4] Rutishauser, H., The Jacobi method for real symmetric matrices. In: Handbook for Automatic Computation 2, J.H. Wilkinson and C. Reinsch, Eds., Springer-Verlag, Berlin, 1971.

[5] Sameh, A.H., On Jacobi and Jacobi-like algorithms for a parallel computer. Math. Comput. 25 (1971), 579-590.

[6] Vajteršic, M., Some linear algebra algorithms proposed for a parallel associative computer. In: Proc. Algorithms 85, JSMF Bratisava, 1985.

A New Parallel Algorithm for Solving General Linear Systems of Equations

Liao Qui-wei

Chang Sha Computer Co., Hunan Province, China

Abstract

A new parallel direct algorithm for solving general linear systems of equations ist proposed in this paper. For sparse systems our algorithm requires less computations than the classical Jordan algorithm. Particularly we have also derived two related algorithms for linear recurrence problems of order 1 and tridiagonal systems. Each of the two algorithms has the same computational complexity as that of the corresponding recursive doubling algorithm or Even/Odd elimination algorithm, but requires half of the processors required by the corresponding algorithm.

The numerical experiments on the vector computer YH-1 indicate that, as the number of equations of a tridiagonal system increases, the speedup of our algorithm over the Even/Odd algorithm increases, and the maximum speedup is more than 3.

1. Introduction

There exists an inherent parallelism in the classical Jordan elimination algorithm for solving a general linear system of equations $\bar{A}x=b$. With this method, each elimination step can only make one column, except the diagonal element, become zero.

The idea of our new method is that each elimination step, which can be executed in parallel, is wished to make as many columns of $\bar{A}$ as possible, except the elements on the diagonal, become zero.

In section 2,3 and 4 we shall give our parallel elimination algorithms for general systems, linear recurrence problems of order 1 and tridiagonal systems respectively.

In section 5 we shall compare the efficiency of our algorithm with that of the Even/Odd algorithm for solving tridiagonal systems on the YH-1 vector computer.

Throughout section 2, 3 and 4 it is assumed that there are always enough processors available and all the processors can complete arithmetic operations of the same kind in the same time.

For convenience, we let t_+, t_*, $t_:$ denote the times of a parallel addition (or subtraction), multiplication and division.

2. The Parallel Algorithm for General Systems

We wish to solve the linear system

$$\bar{A}x=b \tag{1}$$

where $\bar{A}=(a_{i,j})_{N\times N}$, $x=(x_1, x_2,\ldots,x_n)^T$, $b=(b_1,b_2,\ldots,b_N)^T$.
Letting $A=(\bar{A}|b)$, then (1) can be defined by A.
First, we give the following definition and theorem.

Definition 1: The elimination operator $E^{(M)}$, where $M\subset\{1,2,\ldots,N\}$, is a transition from matrix A to A'. Letting $A'=(a'_{i,j})_{N\times(N+1)}=E^{(M)}(A)$, then A' is defined as

$$a'_{i,j}=\begin{cases} a_{i,j}-\sum_{q=1}^{k}a_{i,i_q}*a_{i_q,j}/a_{i_q,i_q} & \text{for } i\notin M \\[2em] a_{i,j}-\sum_{\substack{q=1\\i_q\neq i}}^{k}a_{i,i_q}*a_{i_q,j}/a_{i_q,i_q} & \text{for } i\in M \end{cases} \qquad (1\le i\le N, 1\le j\le N+1)$$

It is clear that A' is related to the set M, and the two linear systems defined by A and A' are equivalent.
The elimination step $A'=E^{(M)}(A)$ can be executed parallely in $(t_*+t_:+\log_2(k+1)t_+)$.

Theorem 1: If $M\subseteq\{1,2,\ldots N\}$ satisfy that for any i_{q_1}, $i_{q_2}\in M$, $a_{i_{q_1},i_{q_2}}\neq 0$, iff $i_{q_1}=i_{q_2}$; then letting $A'=E^{(M)}(A)=(a'_{i,j})_{N\times(N+1)}$, we have that for any $i_{q_0}\in M$ and $i\in\{1,2,\ldots,N\}$, $a'_{i,i_{q_0}}\neq 0$, iff $i=i_{q_0}$.

Proof: Let $M=\{i_1,i_2,\ldots,i_k\}$. For $1\le i\le N$, we have from Definition 1
(1): if $i\notin M$, then

$$a'_{i,i_{q_0}}=a_{i,i_{q_0}}-\sum_{q=1}^{k}a_{i,i_q}*a_{i_q,i_{q_0}}/a_{i_q,i_q}$$

since for $i_q\neq i_{q_0}$, $a_{i_q,i_{q_0}}=0$,
therefore $a'_{i,i_{q_0}}=a_{i,i_{q_0}}-a_{i,i_{q_0}}*a_{i_{q_0},i_{q_0}}/a_{i_{q_0},i_{q_0}}=0$

(2): if $i\in M$, then

$$a'_{i,i_{q_0}}=a_{i,i_{q_0}}-\sum_{\substack{q=1\\i_q\neq i}}^{k}a_{i,i_q}*a_{i_q,i_{q_0}}/a_{i_q,i_q}$$

if $i \neq i_{q_0}$, we have similarly that

$$a'_{i,i_{q_0}} = a_{i,i_{q_0}} - a_{i,i_{q_0}} * a_{i_{q_0},i_{q_0}} / a_{i_{q_0},i_{q_0}} = 0$$

if $i = i_{q_0}$, then

$$a'_{i,i_{q_0}} = a_{i,i_{q_0}} - 0 = a_{i_{q_0},i_{q_0}} \neq 0. \rfloor$$

From Definition 1 and Theorem 1, we know that if $M \subset \{1,2,...N\}$, which satisfies the condition of Theorem 1, is found, the parallel elimination step $A = E^{(M)}(A)$ requires only $(t_* + t_: + \log_2(k+1)t_+)$ to make k columns of A, except the elements on the diagonal, become zero, but $k(t_* + t_: + t_+)$ is required by the Jordan algorithm.

Letting $S = \{s_1, s_2, ..., s_L\}$, $M = \{m_1, m_2, ..., m_k\} \subset \{1,2,...,N\}$, then we can easily obtain the following algorithm for solving (1) from Definition 1 and Theorem 1.

Algorithm 1:

1. $S = \{1,2,...,N\}$; $L = N$ /* initialize */

2. while $L \geq 1$ do   /* if A is not a diagonal matrix then execute an elimination step */
   a. call CM $(A,S,M,1,k)$; /* find M satisfying the condition of Theorem 1 */
   b. $A = E^{(M)}(A)$;
   c. $S = S - M$; $L = L - k$

3. $x_i = a_{i,N+1}/a_{i,i}$ $(1 \leq i \leq N)$

where, the procedure which returns M and k can easily be given from Theorem 1.

procedure CM $(A,S,M,1,k)$

1. $M = \{s_1\}$; $k = 1$;

2. for $i = 2$ step 1 to L do
   a. if for $m \in M$, $a_{m,s_i} = a_{s_i,m} = 0$
      then $M = M \cup \{s_i\}$;

3. return;

When $\bar{A}$ is dense, $k = 1$, Algorithm 1 is just the Jordan algorithm; When $\bar{A}$ is sparse, k is generally bigger than 1, Algorithm 1 requires less computation than the Jordan algorithm.

Algorithm 1 requires additional time to find the set M, but when the non-zero elements of $\bar{A}$ arrange regularly, such as in the coefficent matrices of linear recurrence problems, tridiagonal systems, quindiagonal systems, Toeplitz Quindiagonal systems and so on, M is also regular. In this case, we need not find M in our algorithm, and its related algorithm can be obtained directly from Algorithm 1.

3. The Parallel Algorithm for Linear Recurrence Problems of Order 1

A linear recurrence problem of order 1 can be written in

$$\bar{A}x = b \qquad (2)$$

where,

$$\bar{A} = \begin{pmatrix} 1 & & & & & & \\ a_2 & 1 & & & & & \\ & a_3 & 1 & & & & \\ & & a_4 & 1 & & & \\ & & & \cdot & \cdot & \cdot & \\ & & & & \cdot & \cdot & \cdot \\ & & & & & a_{N-1} & 1 \\ & & & & & & a_N & 1 \end{pmatrix}$$

$$x = (x_1, x_2, \ldots, x_N)^\mathsf{T}, \quad b = (b_1, b_2, \ldots, b_N)^\mathsf{T}$$

we let $A = (\bar{A} \mid b)$, too.

For convenience, we assume, that N is a power of 2.

Using Algorithm 1 to solve (2), we can find that at the i-th elimination step, $\bar{A}$ has the following form

Letting $S^{(i)}$ and $M^{(i)}$, where $S^{(i)} = \{s_1^{(i)}, s_2^{(i)}, \ldots, s_{L(i)}^{(i)}\}$, $M^{(i)} = \{m_1^{(i)}, m_2^{(i)}, \ldots, m_{k(i)}^{(i)}\}$, are values of S and M at the i-th elimination step, then we have

$$\begin{cases} S^{(i)} = \{1,2,\ldots N\}, \\ S^{(i+1)} = \{s_2^{(i)}, s_4^{(i)}, \ldots, s_{L(i)/2}^{(i)}\}, \end{cases} \quad \begin{array}{ll} L(i) = N & i=1 \\ L(i+1) = L(i)/2 & i=2,3,\ldots \end{array} \quad (3)$$

$$M^{(i)} = \{s_1^{(i)}, s_3^{(i)}, \ldots, s_{L(i)-1}^{(i)}\}, \qquad k(i) = L(i)/2 \tag{4}$$

from (3) and (4), we have

$$\begin{cases} S^{(i)} = \{2^{(i-1)}, 2*2^{(i-1)}, \ldots, L(i)*2^{(i-1)}\}, & L(i) = N/2^{i-1} \\ M^{(i)} = \{2^{(i-1)}, 3*2^{(i-1)}, \ldots, (L(i)-1)*2^{(i-1)}\} \end{cases} \tag{5}$$

where $i=1,2,3,\ldots$

Thus, the following algorithm for solving (2) is directly obtained from Algorithm 1.

Algorithm 2:

```
1. for K=1 step K to N do                    /* K=2^(i-1) */
   a. a(2j-1)k+i = 0 - a(2j-1)k+i * a(2j-1)k
      b(2j-1)k+i = b(2j-1)k+i + a(2j-1)k+i * b(2j-1)k
                (1≤i≤K, 1≤j≤N/(2K))     /* A=E^(M)(A) */

2. x=b;  (1≤i≤N)
```

In Algorithm 2, if N processors are available, $(\log N)(t_+ + t_*)$ is required to solve (2).

If the recursive doubling algorithm [1] is used to solve (2), then if N processors are available, $(\log N)(2t_* + t_+)$ is required, and if 2N processors are available, $(\log N)(t_* + t_+)$ is required. So either the required computation time or the required number of processors for algorithm 2 is less than that for the recursive doubling algorithm.

4. The Parallel Algorithm for Solving Tridiagonal Systems

Considering a tridiagonal system

$$\bar{A}x=b \tag{6}$$

where,

$$\bar{A}= \begin{pmatrix} c_1 & d_1 & & & & & \\ a_2 & c_2 & d_2 & & & & \\ & a_3 & c_3 & d_3 & & & \\ & & \cdot & \cdot & \cdot & & \\ & & & \cdot & \cdot & \cdot & \\ & & & & a_{N-1} & c_{N-1} & d_{N-1} \\ & & & & & a_N & c_N \end{pmatrix} = (a_{i,j})_{N \times N}$$

$x=(x_1,x_2,\ldots,x_N)^T$, $b=(b_1,b_2,\ldots,b_N)^T$, let $A=(\bar{A} \mid b)$.
Using algorithm 1 to solve (6), we can find that at the i-th
$(i=1,2,\ldots)$ elimination step, $\bar{A}$ has the following form:

Letting $S^{(i)}$ and $M^{(i)}$, where $S^{(i)}=\{s_1^{(i)},s_2^{(i)},\ldots,s_{L(i)}^{(i)}\}$,
$M^{(i)}=\{m_1^{(i)},m_2^{(i)},\ldots,m_{k(i)}^{(i)}\}$, then we have

$$\begin{cases} S^{(i)} =\{1,2,\ldots,N\}, & L(i) =N & \text{for } i=1 \\ S^{(i+1)}=\{s_2^{(i)},s_4^{(i)},\ldots,s_{2L(i+1)}^{(i)}\}, & L(i+1)=\lfloor L(i)/2 \rfloor & \text{for } i=2,3,\ldots \end{cases} \quad (7)$$

$$M^{(i)} =\{s_1^{(i)},s_3^{(i)},\ldots,s_{2k(i)-1}^{(i)}\}, \quad k(i) =\lceil L(i)/2 \rceil \quad (8)$$

From (7) and (8), we have

$$S^{(i)}=\{K,2*K,\ldots,L(i)*K\}$$
$$M^{(i)}=\{K,3*K,\ldots,((2\lceil L(I)/2\rceil-1)*K)\} \quad \text{for } i=1,2,\ldots \quad (9)$$

where $K=2^{(i-1)}$.
   Thus Algorithm 1 for solving (6) can be rewritten in

Algorithm 3:

1. K=1; L=N;   /* initialize */

2. while L≥1 do
   a.   row(k) = row(k) / $a_{k,k}$;   /* normalize */
        (k=K,3K,5K,...(2⌈L/2⌉-1)K)

   b.   row(j) = row(j) - $a_{j,k}$ * row(k)
        (k-K<j<k+K, j≠K, k=K,3K,5K,...(2⌈L/2⌉-1)K)
        row(k) = row(k) - $a_{k,k-K}$ * row(k-K) - $a_{k,k+K}$ * row(k+K);
        (k=2K,4K,6K,...,2⌊L/2⌋K)
                                        /* A=E$^{(M)}$(A) */
   c.   K = K+K;   L=⌊L/2⌋;

3. x_i = $a_{i,N+1}$ (1≤i≤N);

where, row(i) (for 1≤i≤N) denotes the i-th row of A.

If 3N processors are available, ⌈log₂ N⌉(2t₊+t₊+t:) is required
to solve (6) by Algorithm 3.
   The Even/Odd elimination algorithm [2] can also solve (6) in
⌈log₂ N⌉(2t₊+t₊+t:), but the required number of processors is 6N.
Therefore, if the number of processors available is less than 6N,
then more parallel computation time is required to solve (6) by
the Even/Odd algorithm.
   Note that the total computation count for Algorithm 3 is less
than half of the Even/Odd's. Therefore, on the pipeline vector
computer YH-1, on which computation time is proportional to the
length of the vector operations, Algorithm 3 requires less computation time than the Even/Odd algorithm (see section 5).

5. Numerical Experiments

   We have compared the effiency of our Algorithm 3 with that of
the Even/Odd algorithm on the pipeline vector computer YH-1. The
results of the experiments are shown in table 1.

N	Time for Even/Odd	Time for Algorithm 3	speedup over Even/Odd
63	0.3863 ms	0.3635 ms	1.063
127	0.7270 ms	0.5955 ms	1.221
1023	8.0110 ms	3.0345 ms	2.640
4095	38.465 ms	12.3420 ms	3.117
32767	380.908 ms	111.095 ms	3.429

Table 1: The comparison of Algorithm 3 with the Even/Odd
          Algorithm on YH-1.

From table 1, we can see that when N ranges from 63 to 32767, Algorithm 3 runs faster than the Even/Odd algorithm, and the speedup of Algorithm 3 over Even/Odd increases as N increases, the maximum speedup is more than 3.

Acknowledgements

The author expresses his appreciation to Li Xiao-mei, He Nan-zhong, Yin Jian-pin of the Computer Department, Changsha Institute of Technology, China, for their many conversations, comments and criticism on this paper.

References

[1]: Peter M. Kogge and Harold S. Stone, "A parallel algorithm for the efficient solution of a general class of recurrence equations", IEEE Transactions on Computer Vol. C--22, No.8, August 1973.

[2]: AD-A024792, "A survey of parallel algorithms in numerical linear algebra".

[3]: UCRL-76993, "A comparison of direct methods for tridiagonal systems on the CDC-STAR-100".

GENERALIZED ASYNCHRONOUS ITERATIONS

Aydin Uresin and Michel Dubois

Computer Research Institute
Department of Electrical Engineering-Systems
University of Southern California
Los Angeles, CA90077 USA

ABSTRACT

Asynchronous iterative methods for multiprocessors are generalized to relaxation techniques involving discrete variables. Asynchronous algorithms are more efficient than synchronized algorithms in multiprocessors because processes do not have to wait on each other at synchronization points. Sufficient conditions for the convergence of generalized asynchronous iterations are given and proved. Applications of the theory presented in this paper include asynchronous relaxation algorithms for scene labeling in image processing applications.

1. INTRODUCTION

Asynchronous iterative methods are very attractive for multiprocessors because they remove the need for synchronization between the processors cooperating in the algorithm. It has been shown [ROB79, DUB82] that synchronization between processes is a major source of performance degradation in multiprocessor algorithms. The reason is that the processes that synchronize have to wait for the *slowest* among them [KUN76]. Randomness in execution time of the different processes between two successive synchronization points is caused by the difference in the computation time of each process because they perform different functions or because they perform the same function on different input data sets, and by conflicts for shared resources such as an interconnection link or a shared-memory module. When the iteration is asynchronous, the processors never wait on each other and they can compute at full speed.

Asynchronous iterative methods have been applied so far to the solution of systems of equations. The variables manipulated in the chaotic relaxation scheme of Chazan and Miranker [CHA69] and in the purely asynchronous algorithm described by Baudet [BAU78] are continuous and defined in the vectorial space R^n. The definition that is given in Baudet's paper of a contracting operator is based on a metric defined in R^n. Since all his proofs are based on the definition of contracting operators, they cannot be applied as such to relaxation techniques in discrete fields.

Many relaxation techniques involve the manipulation of symbolic or discrete-valued data. One major example is scene labeling relaxation used in image understanding applications to define features of a digital pictures [ROS76]. In the general formulation of the problem, a set of labels is associated with objects (objects may be pixels in a digitized picture); labels are related to objects by compatibility relations. Certain labels may be incompatible with some objects; also for each pair of objects some pair of labels may not be compatible. The scene labeling algorithm finds the greatest consistent labeling. "Consistent" means that the compatibility relations are respected and "greatest" means that the maximum number of compatible labels has been associated with each object. In this paper, we also consider the case of fuzzy labeling.

In the following, we first define the generalization of asynchronous iterative algorithms in which the relaxed variables belong to an arbitrary set S. In this context, the generalized definition of a contracting operator is introduced. Then the convergence is proved for the general case. The theory is applied to the scene labeling problem, including fuzzy labeling.

2. CONVERGENCE OF ASYNCHRONOUS ITERATIONS

The following definition of asynchronous iterations is similar to the one given by Baudet [BAU78]. In Baudet's paper, only operators from R^n to R^n are considered. The following is the generalization of asynchronous iterations for the case of an operator F from S^n to S^n, where S is any set, finite or infinite, countable or not.

Definition 2.1: Generalized Asynchronous Iteration

Let F be an operator from S^n to S^n. An asynchronous iteration corresponding to the operator F and starting with a given vector $x(0)$ is a sequence $x(j)$, $j = 0, 1,...$ of vectors of S^n and defined recursively by :

$$x_i(j) = \begin{cases} x_i(j-1) & \text{if } i \notin J_j \\ F_i(x_1(s_1(j)),..., x_n(s_n(j))) & \text{if } i \in J_j, \end{cases} \tag{1}$$

where $J = \{ J_j \mid j = 1,2,...\}$ is a sequence of nonempty subsets of $\{1,2,...,n\}$,

$C = \{s_1(j),..., s_n(j)) \mid j = 1,2,...\}$ is a sequence of elements in N^n and S is a set.

In addition, J and C are subject to the following conditions, for each $i = 1,...,n$:

(a) $s_i(j) \leq j-1, j = 1,2,...$;

(b) $s_i(j)$, considered as a function of j, tends to infinity as j tends to infinity;

(c) i occurs infinitely many often in the sets J_j, $j = 1,2,...$

An asynchronous iteration corresponding to F, starting with $x(0)$, and defined by J and C, will be denoted by $(F, x(0), J, C)$.

The above definition is a straightforward generalization of Baudet's definition for asynchronous iterative algorithms. An asynchronous algorithm is easily obtained by deriving first a synchronized multitasked algorithm, and by removing the synchronizations. Critical sections may still be necessary in order to preserve the integrity of shared data. In Baudet's paper, the significance and implications of definition 2.1 are further discussed in the context of numerical problems.

Definition 2.2 : Generalized Contracting Operator

An operator F from S^n to S^n is a generalized contracting operator on a subset

$$D = D_1 \times D_2 \times ... \times D_n \text{ of } S^n \text{ iff } \lim_{k \to \infty} F^k(D) = \{ \varsigma \}, \tag{2}$$

where ς is the point of convergence, and $F(D)$ is defined as

$$F(D) = \{F_1(x) \mid x \in D \} \times \{F_2(x) \mid x \in D\} \times ... \times \{F_n(x) \mid x \in D \}, \tag{3}$$

and F^k is the set obtained by applying this operator k times on D.

The above definition is a generalization of the two conditions given by Baudet for the convergence of an asynchronous iteration on R^n in the case where the domain D is a rectangle in n dimension. These conditions are that the operator F is contracting and that $F(D) \subseteq D$. It is clear that in the case of iterations defined in R^n, these conditions are equivalent to (2). It is also clear that condition (2) is a sufficient condition for convergence of the synchronous algorithm defined on any set. The following two lemmas and theorem demonstrate that the condition is also sufficient for the asynchronous counterpart, and for any sequences J and C satisfying the conditions of definition 2.1.

Lemma 2.1 : If an operator F from S^n to S^n is a generalized contracting operator on a subset $D = D_1 x D_2 x ... x D_n$ of S^n, then

$$\{ \varsigma \} \subseteq F^{p+1}(D) \subseteq F^p(D), \text{for all } p = 0,1,2,... \tag{4}$$

Proof :

Definition 2.2 implies that for each subset E of D such that $E = E_1 x E_2 x ... x E_n$ and $\{ \varsigma \} \subset E$, there is an integer n which satisfies:

$$\{ \varsigma \} \subseteq F^k(D) \subset E, \text{ for all } k \geq n \tag{5}$$

Now, suppose that there is an integer p such that $F^p(D) \subset F^{p+1}(D)$. Then,

$$F^{p+1}(D) = F^p(D) \cup R$$

$\rightarrow \qquad F\{F^{p+1}(D)\} = F\{F^p(D) \cup R\}$

$\rightarrow \qquad F^{p+2}(D) \subseteq F^{p+1}(D)$

$\rightarrow \qquad F^p(D) \subset F^{p+2}(D)$

Similarly, by mathematical induction,

$$F^p(D) \subset F^q(D), q > p. \tag{6}$$

If we choose $E = D \cap F^p(D)$, we cannot find an integer n such that

$$F^k(D) \subset E, \text{ for all } k \geq n,$$

which leads to a contradiction and proves

$$F^{p+1}(D) \subseteq F^p(D), p = 0,1,2,....$$

On the other hand, (5) implies that

$$\{ \varsigma \} \subseteq F^p(D), p = 0,1,2,...$$

Therefore, we obtain

$$\{ \varsigma \} \subseteq F^{p+1}(D) \subseteq F^p(D), p = 0,1,2,...$$

Lemma 2.2 : If F is a generalized contracting operator from S^n to S^n on a subset $D = D_1 x D_2 x ... x D_n$ of S^n, then

$$F_i^{p+1}(D) \subseteq F_i^p(D), i = 1,2,...,n, \tag{7}$$

where $F_i^p(D)$ is defined by

$$F^p(D) = F_1^p(D) x F_2^p(D) x ... x F_n^p(D) \tag{8}$$

Proof:

Let $E = F^p(D)$. Since $E = E_1 x E_2 x ... x E_n$, we have $F(E) = F_1(E) x F_2(E) x ... x F_n(E)$,

and, from lemma 2.1, $F(E) \subseteq E$.

The claim of the lemma follows.

The following theorem proves the convergence of generalized asynchronous iterations when the operator is a generalized contracting operator.

Theorem 2.1 : If F is a generalized contracting operator on a subset $D = D_1 x D_2 x ... x D_n$ of S^n, then an asynchronous iteration $(F, x(0), J, C)$ corresponding to F and starting with a vector $x(0)$ in D converges to a unique fixed point of F in D.

Proof:

We will show that for any $p \in \{0,1,2,...\}$, an integer j_p can be obtained such that the sequence of iterates of $(F, x(0), J, C)$ satisfies

$$x(j) \in F^p(D), \text{ for } j \geq j_p \qquad (9)$$

We first show that (9) holds for $p = 0$. If we let $j_0 = 0$, then for $j \geq 0$, we have:

$$x(j) \in D \qquad (10)$$

(10) is true for $j = 0$, since $x(0)$ is in D. Assume that it is true for $0 \leq j < k$ and consider $x(k)$. Let z denote the vector with components $z_i = x_i(s_i(k))$, for $i = 1,2,...,n$. From definition 2.1, the components of $x(k)$ are given either by $x_i(k) = x_i(k-1)$ if $i \notin J_k$, in which case $x_i(k) = x_i(k-1) \in D_i$, or by $x_i(k) = F_i(z)$ if $i \in J_k$. In this latter case, we note that, as $s_i(k) < k$ and $z \in D$, we have $F(z) \in D$.

This result in turn implies that $x_i(k) = F_i(z) \in D_i$, and that $x(k) \in D$. (10) is proved by induction, which shows that (9) is true for $p = 0$ if we choose $j_0 = 0$. Assume now that a j_p has been found to satisfy (9) for $0 \leq p < q$. First, define r by :

$$r = \text{Min } \{ k \mid \text{for all } j \geq k, s_i(j) \geq j_{q-1}, i = 1,...,n \}$$

We see from condition (b) of definition 2.1 that this number exists, and we note that, from condition (a), we have $r > j_{q-1}$ which shows in particular that $x(r) \in F^{q-1}(D)$.

Then, take $j \geq r$ and consider the components of $x(j)$. As above, let z be the vector with components $z_i = x_i(s_i(j))$. From the choice of r, we have $s_i(j) \geq j_{q-1}$, for $i = 1,...,n$ and this shows that $z \in F^{q-1}(D)$, and $F(z) \in F^q(D)$. This shows that, if $i \in J_j$, $F_i(z)$ satisfies $F_i(z) \in F_i^q(D)$, $i = 1,2,...n$, and we obtain

$$x_i(j) \in F_i^q(D), i = 1,2,...,n \qquad (11)$$

This result means that as soon as the ith component is updated between the rth and the jth iteration we have (11). On the other hand, if $i \notin J_j$, the ith component is not modified.

Now, define j_q as:

$$j_q = \text{Min} \{j \mid j \geq r, \text{ and } \{1,...,n\} = J_r \cup ... \cup J_j\}$$

This number exists by condition (c) of definition 2.1, and for any $j \geq j_q$ every component is updated at least once between the rth and the jth iterations and therefore (11) holds for $i = 1,...,n$. This shows that (9) holds for $p = q$, and by induction (9) holds for

$p = 0,1,....$ Since p can be chosen arbitrarily large, and therefore $F^p(D)$ can be made arbitrarily small, we obtain

$$\lim_{j \to \infty} x(j) = \varsigma,$$

which is the desired result.

The following section illustrates the application of theorem 2.1 to the problems of the discrete and fuzzy scene labeling described in [ROS76].

3. SCENE LABELING (DISCRETE MODEL)

The following definitions are drawn from [ROS76].

Let $A = \{a_1,...,a_n\}$ be the set of objects to be labeled and $\Lambda = \{\lambda_1,..., \lambda_n\}$, the set of possible labels. For any given object a_i, not every label in Λ may be appropriate. Let $\Lambda_{.i}$, be the set of labels which are compatible with object a_i, $i = 1,...,n$. For each pair of objects (a_i, a_j) some labels may be compatible, while others are not.

Let $\Lambda_{..} \subseteq \Lambda_{.i} \times \Lambda_{.j}$ be the set of compatible pairs of labels; thus $(\lambda, \lambda') \in \Lambda_{..}$ means that it is possible to label a_i with label λ and a_j with label λ'. If a_i and a_j are irrelevant to one another, then there are no restrictions on the possible pairs of labels that they can have, so that $\Lambda_{ij} = \Lambda_i \times \Lambda_j$.

By a labeling $L = (L_1,...,L_n)$ of A, we mean an assignement of a set of labels $L_i \subseteq \Lambda$ to each $a_i \in A$. The labeling is consistent if for all i,j we have $(\{\lambda\} \times \Lambda_j) \cap \Lambda_{..} \neq \phi$, for all $\lambda \in L_i$.

We say that a labeling $L = \{L_1,...,L_n\}$ contains another labeling L' if $L_i' \subseteq L_i$ for $i=1,...,n$. The greatest labeling L^∞ is a consistent labeling such that any other consistent labeling is contained in L^∞.

According to this model, the discrete relaxation procedure operates as follows. It starts with the initial labeling $L(0) = \{\Lambda_1,..., \Lambda_n\}$. During each step, we eliminate from each L_i all labels λ, such that $(\{\lambda\} \times L_j) \cap \Lambda_{..} = \phi$ for some j. Thus we discard a label λ from object a_i if there exists an object a_j such that no label compatible with λ is assigned to (a_i, a_j). If for all j's, such that $j = 1,...,n$, and $j \neq i$ there exists a label $\lambda' \in L_j$ and λ' is compatible with λ, then we keep the label λ in L_i. We shall refer to the operation executed at each iteration as Δ.

Lemma 3.1 : [ROS76]

$$L^\infty \subseteq ... \subseteq L(k) \subseteq ... \subseteq L(0). \tag{12}$$

Theorem 3.1 : [ROS76]

$$\lim_{k \to \infty} L(k) = L^\infty \tag{13}$$

The following lemma and theorem prove the convergence of the discrete labelling relaxation implemented as an asynchronous iteration.

Lemma 3.2 : If L and L' are labelings such that $L \subseteq L'$ then $\Delta(L) \subseteq \Delta(L')$

Proof:

Let $E = L - \Delta (L)$, $E' = L - \Delta (L')$ and suppose that $\Delta (L') \subset \Delta (L)$. Then, from Lemma 3.1, $\Delta (L) \subseteq L$ and therefore $E \subset E'$, which implies that there exists a $\lambda \in L_i$ such that

$$(\{\lambda\} \times L_j') \cap \Lambda_{ij} = \phi, \text{ and}$$

$$(\{\lambda\} \times L_j) \cap \Lambda_{ij} = \phi,$$

for some i,j pair. However, this is not possible, since $L_j \subseteq L_j'$. This contradiction completes the proof.

Theorem 3.2 : An asynchronous iteration $(\Delta, L(0), J, C)$ converges to L^∞.

Proof :

Let $D(k) = \{ L \mid L^\infty \subseteq L \subseteq L(k) \}$. From Lemma 3.2, $\Delta (D(k)) \subseteq D(k+1)$.

Assume $\Delta^k (D(0)) \subseteq D(k)$ (14)

Then, $\Delta^{k+1} (D(0)) \subseteq D(k+1)$

since (14) is true for k=0, and therefore, by mathematical induction, it is also true for k=1,2,...

On the other hand, from theorem 3.1, $\lim\limits_{k \to \infty} L(k) = L^\infty$.

As a result, $\lim\limits_{k \to \infty} D(k) = \{L^\infty\}$ (15)

Therefore, $\lim\limits_{k \to \infty} \Delta^k (D(0)) = \{L^\infty\}$ (16)

which proves that Δ is a contracting operator on $D(0)$. Since the initial labeling, $L(0)$, is in $D(0)$, from Theorem 2.1, the sequence $L(k)$ converges to L^∞.

In an asynchronous multiprocessor implementation of the scene labeling algorithm, each processor is assigned a subset of the objects to classify. The relaxation process does not require any synchronization. A process can freely access the set of label currently associated with objects processed by different processors. Critical sections may be needed to access the label set.

4. SCENE LABELING (FUZZY MODEL)

In this model, A and Λ are defined as in the discrete case, and for each i we are given a fuzzy label set Λ_i associated with the object a_i. This Λ_i is a fuzzy subset of Λ, i.e., a mapping from Λ into the interval [0,1]. In addition, for each pair of objects (a_i, a_j), where $i \neq j$, we are given a fuzzy set Λ_{ij} of pairs of labels; this is a mapping from $\Lambda \times \Lambda$ into [0,1]. Here, we assume that

$$\Lambda_{ij} (\lambda, \lambda') \leq \inf (\Lambda_i (\lambda), \Lambda_j (\lambda'))$$

for all i,j,λ,λ'. By a fuzzy labeling $L = (L_1,...,L_n)$ of A we mean an assignement of a fuzzy subset L_i of Λ to each a_i, i=1,...,n. We say that $L \leq L'$ if $L_i \leq L_i'$, i=1,...,n (i.e., $L_i(\lambda) \leq L_i'(\lambda)$. We also define sup $(L, L') = (\sup (L_1, L_1'), ..., \sup (L_n, L_n'))$. The fuzzy labeling L is called consistent if, for all i,j, and λ, we have

$$\sup [\inf (L_j (\lambda'), \Lambda_j (\lambda, \lambda')] \geq L_i (\lambda) \text{ over all } \lambda'$$

The label weakening algorithm is defined as follows. We start with the initial fuzzy labeling $L(0) = (\Lambda_1, ..., \Lambda_n)$. At each iteration, we apply the operation Ω, defined as follows:

$$\Omega_i(L(\lambda)) = \inf \{ \sup [\inf (L_j(\lambda'), \Lambda_{ij}(\lambda,\lambda'))] \} \text{ over all } \lambda' \text{ and } j \tag{17}$$

Lemma 4.1 [ROS76]

$$L^\infty \leq \cdots \leq L(k+1) \leq L(k) \leq \cdots < L(0), \tag{18}$$

where L^∞ is the greatest consistent labeling.

Theorem 4.1 [ROS76]

$$\lim_{k \to \infty} L(k) = L^\infty \tag{19}$$

Lemma 4.1

If L and L' are fuzzy labelings such that $L \leq L'$ then $\Omega(L) \leq \Omega(L')$.

Proof:

The proof is obvious from (17)

Theorem 4.2

An asynchronous iteration $(\Omega, L(0), J, C)$ converges to L^∞.

Proof:

If we substitute $\subseteq$ with $\leq$ and Δ with Ω, the proof of theorem 4.2 is exactly the same as the proof of theorem 3.2

5. CONCLUSION

In this paper, we have introduced a sufficient condition for the convergence of asynchronous parallel relaxation of discrete data in multiprocessors systems. To illustrate the algorithm, we have applied the main theorem (theorem 2.1) to the cases of discrete and fuzzy labelings of a set of objects. These algorithms are important algorithms in image processing and understanding. The results presented here are extensions of results published in [BAU78] and [ROS76].

6. REFERENCES

[BAU78] G.M Baudet,"Asynchronous Iterative Methods," JACM, April 1978.

[CHA69] D. Chazan, and W. Miranker,"Chaotic Relaxation," *Linear Algebra and Applications*, 1969, pp.199-222.

[DUB82] M. Dubois and F.A. Briggs,"Performance of Synchronized Iterative Processes in Multiprocessor Systems," *IEEE Transactions on Software*, Vol. SE-8, No.4, July 1982, pp.419-432.

[KUN76] H.T. Kung,"Synchronized and Asynchronous Parallel Algorithms for Multiprocessors," *Algorithms and Complexity: New Directions and Recent Results*, J.F. Traub Ed., New York: Academic Press, 1976.

[ROB79] J.T. Robinson,"Some Analysis Techniques for Asynchronous Multiprocessor Algorithms," *IEEE Transactions on Software Engineering*, Vol. SE-5, Jan. 1979, pp24-30.

[ROS76] A. Rosenfeld, *et al.* "Scene Labeling by Relaxation Operations," *IEEE Transactions on Systems, Man and Cybernetics*, June 1976.

PARALLEL COMPILATION ON A MULTIPROCESSOR SYSTEM

Peter Brezány
Department of Cybernetics
Slovak Technical University Bratislava
Gottwaldovo nám. 17
812 43 Bratislava
Czechoslovakia

Abstract

To date few serious attempts have been made to study the development
of compilers capable of fully exploiting architectures of multiprocessor systems. This paper describes one such effort based on the existing multiprocessor system DIRMU-25 developed at the University of
Erlangen-Nürnberg. A parallel compiling scheme is proposed and implementation of its parts is discussed. Finally, the achieved results and
experiences are summarized and directions for further research are indicated.

INTRODUCTION

Considerable research and investments have been devoted to the development of programming languages that enable to produce software for
multiprocessor systems. However, compilation of programs written in
these languages is still executed as a serial process. Thus the advantage of new architecture innovations is not taken into consideration.

In literature we find only few attempts studying the possibilities
of the development of compilers which would be capable of maximally
exploiting parallel architectures of multiprocessor systems. No published work mentions a compiler design or implementation of its parts
in relation to a concrete multiprocessor system.

This paper deals with parallel compilation on multiprocessor systems having a multiport memory organization. In part 1, the parallel compiling scheme oriented on the multiprocessor system DIRMU-25 is proposed. The author of this paper had opportunity to work with this system during his stay at the University of Erlangen-Nürnberg /FRG/. Part 2 deals with the implementation of a parallel algorithm for lexical and syntactic analyses on DIRMU-25. In part 3, results and experiences achieved at implementation and experiments are summarized.

1. A COMPILATION SCHEME AND A SUITABLE MULTIPROCESSOR ARCHITECTURE

The design of an appropriate multiprocessor architecture, that reflects the structure of the computational problems plays a very important role also at compilation.

A compilation scheme is usually split up into several cooperating processes, e.g. lexical analysis, syntactic analysis, production of the object code, etc.

By now, only two works [1], [4] appeared dealing with syntactic analysis in a multiprocessor environment. Both assume the basic configuration and communications of processors in the form of Fig. 1.

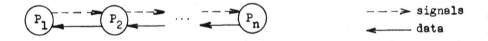

Figure 1. Basic configuration and communications of processors

The syntactic analysis drives the compilation in most compilers. Therefore by seeking the suitable multiprocessor architectures, we must take into account the configuration in Fig. 1.

We can imagine the parallel compilation implemented as a pipeline /Fig. 2/ consisting of the following processes: lexical analysis /LA/, syntactic, semantic analysis /SSA/ and code generation /CG/. Each stage can be refined into substages or can be analysed with the aim to implement it as a set of parallel processes. However, by now no method for parallel code generation has been published.

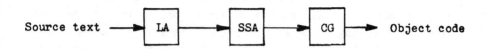

Figure 2. Parallel compilation implemented as a pipeline

For the parallel compilation on the multiprocessor system DIRMU-25 we proposed the structure in Fig. 3.

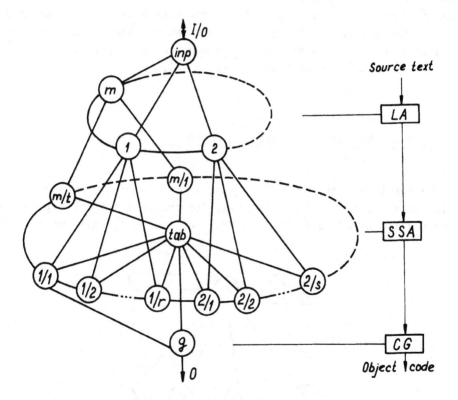

Figure 3. DIRMU-25 configuration proposed for the parallel compilation

The DIRMU-25 /Distributed Reconfigurable Multiprocessor Kit/ has been developed at the University of Erlangen. The reader can find more information about this system e.g. in [2].

The source program text is divided by some criteria into n parts. The integer number n equals to the number of processors at the level SSA, without including processor tab. Processors at the level LA perform lexical analysis. Processor inp provides them with input source characters which are taken from the appropriate parts. Further they provide the n processors at the level SSA with lexical tokens and receive eventual error messages from them. These processors

$$1/1, \ 1/2, \ \ldots, \ 1/r, \ \ldots, \ m/t$$

perform syntactic and semantic analyses, transform the source text into an intermediate form, build their local tables and global ones; according to the method proposed in [4]. The global tables are sited in the multiport memory of processor tab, that performs table manipulation operations. The produced intermediate code is continually shifted to the multiport memory of the lefmost processor 1/1. Processor g can start object code generation as soon as the first entry of the intermediate code appears at processor 1/1.

2. PARALLEL SYNTACTIC ANALYSIS ON DIRMU-25

The parallel variant of LR parser, we implemented, is based on parsing models introduced in [1], [4]. For the experimental implementation the smaller DIRMU configuration /Fig. 4/ was used, which represents

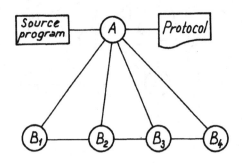

Figure 4. DIRMU configuration used for experiments

part of the structure of Fig. 3. As implementation programming language we used MODULA-2.

The main role of processor A is lexical analysis /LA/ and of processors marked B_i syntactic analysis /SA/. Processor A views the source program as if it were divided into n parts /n equals to the number of processors B_i/ in such a way that it can start LA of each part /except the first/ at the character immediately following a semicolon. Processor A sends each B_i messages about analysed lexical tokens in the i-th source text part through the i-th buffer, that is placed in its multiport memory. Each message can be looked upon as a triple (lexical type, lexical value, position in the input text).
The third item is used by error processing. Processors B_i take lexical tokens from appropriate buffers and perform SA. Each processor B_i, except B_1, starts parsing at the token immediately following a semicolon, B_1 at the first token of the first input part. Therefore the LR-table for B_1 will be different from the one that controls the parsing process in other B_i's. Complication arises if a processor does not have context enough in its stack to perform a reduction. As a simple example, assume that we use two processors B_1, B_2 and the parsed input string is

$$\ldots \underline{\text{begin}} \text{ I:=K; } \underline{\text{begin}} \text{ J:=O;} | \text{ L:=M } \underline{\text{end}} \ \underline{\text{end}}; \text{ L:=A; } \ldots$$

parsed by B_1 | parsed by B_2

When processor B_2 processes the token corresponding to the second <u>end</u>, it could have on the top of its stack the configuration

...	entry corresponding to the first <u>end</u>	t_i

t_i is the parser's state

If according to the LR-table, the parser's action is to be e.g. the reduction associated with the rule

Statement ::= <u>begin</u> Statement_List <u>end</u>

this reduction couldn't be done, because processor B_2 has not the corresponding begin within its stack. Therefore it signals to processor A, it wants to begin with parsing a new construction, that begins after the next semicolon. Then it puts a flag on the stack top, to notice this event and transfers the content of the stack from bottom upwards to the buffer in its multiport memory. Through this buffer it communicates with its left neighbour, which will use this stack information later, by parsing the part of the input string bypassed now.

After recognizing the signal from processor B_2, processor A will prepare the starting token /result of analysis of 'L' in our case/ of the next construction into buffer$_2$, from which the signalling processor takes messages. Before the above operation, processor A transferred the two tokens /results of analysis of the bypassed part 'end;'/ in a queu, localized in its private memory. From there they will be transferred to the buffer$_1$ when the lexical analysis of the first part has been finished. When the token corresponding to 'L' appears in the buffer$_2$, processor A signals it to processor B_2, which can resume parsing. In this way we achieve that from processor A to processors B_i's only messages are transferred they really will use in parsing.

When B_1 has finished parsing its portion, it waits until B_2 prepares in its multiport memory the appropriate stack part for merging. Then it transfers stack elements into its own parsing stack until a flag is found and resumes parsing of the part /tokens corresponding to 'end;'/ bypassed by processor B_2.

The described interactions between parsing processors rely on the method designed by Cohonen and Kolodner [1]; also the idea to divide the source program text at semicolons. For the construction of LR-tables for parallel parsing we have adapted the technique developed by Mickunas and Schell [4].

We used the error processing scheme with local syntax error recovery mechanisms described in [3]. When the parser finds out some error, it sends a message to a special buffer in the multiport memory of processor A. This message consists of the error number and the reference to the position in the input string where the incorrect token occurs /this information is connected with each processed token/. Processor A uses these error messages by producing the protocol of compilation.

3. RESULTS

For experimentation we used input programs written in a language derived from the language PL/0 [5]. The time spent by processor A on the division of the input source program file on appropriate parts and on printing protocol was not included into the measured time. The observed speed-ups depended on the length of input programs and on the language constructions used in them. By analyses of statistical control prints, we found out that at some input program structures processor A did not succeed to provide communications buffers with appropriate lexical tokens in time. However, this would change when processors B_i perform also semantic analyses.

The speed-ups measured by syntax analysis of two syntactic correct input programs of the lengths of L=374 and L=505 tokens we can see in Table 1.

Table 1

Number of processors B_i	Speed-up L=374	Speed-up L=505
2	1.6	1.8
3	2.5	2.7
4	3.3	3.6

This partly confirms the results obtained by monoprocessor simulation of the parallel parsing algorithm published in [1]. However, Cohen and Kolodner suppose tens or hundreds parsing processors and predict upper bounds for speedup as well. Therefore it would be useful to use for similar experiments the whole DIRMU-25 configuration according to the structure in Fig. 3. Then we could approach to the design and implementation of parallel semantic analysis and code generation.

We found the implemented error recovery mechanisms [3] as not very effective for using in multiprocessor environment. We think that the development of mechanisms for parallel syntactic analysis that would be comparable with ones used in serial syntactic analysis will still require considerable research.

The method of separating text is rather specific to the Pascal-like languages. Problems can arise e.g. at programs with many declarations where too many tokens could be between semicolons. Therefore, it would be useful to develope a more general parallel parsing method based on a set of text separating symbols.

REFERENCES

[1] Cohen, J., Kolodner, S.: Estimating the Speedup in Parallel Parsing. IEEE Trans. on Soft. Eng., Vol. 11, Jan. 1985, pp. 114-124.

[2] Händler, W., Maehle, E., Wirl, K.: The DIRMU Testbed for High-Performance Multiprocessor Configurations. In Proceedings of the 1-st International Conference on Supercomputing Systems, St. Petersburg, Dec. 1985, pp. 468-475.

[3] Lewis, M.P., Rosenkrantz, D.J., Stearns, R.E.: Compiler Design Theory. Addison-Wesley Publ. Comp., Reading, 1976.

[4] Mickunas, M.D., Schell, M.R.: Parallel Compilation in a Multiprocessor Environment. In Proceedings 1978 Annual Conference, ACM, Dec. 1978, Washington, D.C., pp. 241-246.

[5] Wirth, N.: Algorithms + Data Structures = Programs. Prentice-Hall, Inc., Englewood Cliffs, New York, 1976.

SEMI-AUTOMATIC PARALLELIZATION OF FORTRAN PROGRAMS*

Hans P. Zima, Heinz-J. Bast, Michael Gerndt, Peter J. Hoppen

Universität Bonn
Institut für Informatik III
Bertha-von-Suttner-Platz 6
D-5300 Bonn 1
Federal Republic of Germany

In this paper we describe the design of an interactive, knowledge-based
system for the semi-automatic transformation of Fortran 77 programs into
parallel programs for a new supercomputer. The system is characterized by
a powerful analysis component, a catalog of MIMD and SIMD transformations,
and a flexible dialog facility. It contains specific knowledge about the
parallelization of an important class of numerical algorithms.

Keywords: Multiprocessors, analysis of algorithms, program transformations

1 INTRODUCTION

The objective of the German supercomputer project SUPRENUM is the development of a machine capable of solving very large numerical simulation problems which cannot be handled by current computer systems. This objective
is being pursued in two ways: firstly, by designing a highly parallel architecture, and secondly, by providing a powerful and efficient software
environment, in particular with regard to application languages, tools,
and parallel algorithms for the primary application areas.

The architecture of the SUPRENUM machine is characterized by a hierarchical multiprocessing structure whose essential components are nodes and
clusters. The basic processing node is a single board computer, consisting of a 32-bit microprocessor connected to an 8 Mbyte dynamic memory, a
4 MFLOPS vector unit, and a dedicated communication processor. Each node
has a local operating system which schedules the processes of the node,
supports the communication with other nodes, and manages the local resources. A cluster consists of up to 16 nodes which communicate via
an ultra-fast parallel bus with a bandwidth of 256 Mbits per second. The
structure of an overall system is characterized by a matrix of clusters
whose rows and columns are connected by one slotted ring bus (Fig. 1). A
separate operating system machine manages the global resources, the distribution of the workload, and system recovery. Program execution is handled by the set of local node operating systems.

---

* The work described in this paper is being performed within the German
Supercomputer project SUPRENUM and is supported by the Federal Ministry
for Research and Technology (BMFT), F. R. Germany

The main application envisaged for the SUPRENUM machine is the numerical simulation of very large problems. Highly specialized algorithms are being developed for these problems, with a particular emphasis on the multigrid method [Stüb 82] which provides one of the fastest known disciplines for solving partial differential equations on general bounded domains. The differential equations are discretized on a grid with a fine mesh size; the solution process is a combination of standard relaxation methods and the computation of corrections on coarser grids. The computations at each grid point are usually local, a typical program will have from 10^6 to 10^9 grid points.

The SUPRENUM software environment includes optimizing compilers for extensions of the languages Fortran 77 (this extension will be called C-Fortran in the following) and Modula-2. These language versions specify a process concept, message-based synchronization and communication facilities, and array handling in the style of Fortran 8x [ANSI 86]. In addition, the software environment includes a very high-level specification language, an interactive program development facility and a simulation system.

An important criterion for the acceptance of the new machine by the user community is a software tool that supports the transformation of existing Fortran programs into parallel programs that can be efficiently executed on the SUPRENUM computer. This paper describes the design of a semi-automatic parallelization system that solves this problem.

The paper is organized as follows: Section 2 gives an overview of the parallelization system, describes the main properties of its principal components, and relates the design to previous work. The set of all program transformations used in the system is called the catalog; it is treated in Section 3. Section 4 discusses the interactive component, outlining the main mechanisms used for the dialog-controlled analysis and transformation of programs. Our concluding remarks are to be found in Section 5.

2 SYSTEM STRUCTURE AND COMPONENTS

The structure of the parallelization system is shown in Fig. 2. Let P denote a Fortran source program. The overall task of the system, applied to P, is the transformation of P into a semantically equivalent parallelized program P* in C-Fortran. This process can be outlined as follows: First, the Front End is applied to P, creating an intermediate program representation. Then, by a coordinated repetitive application of analysis processes and catalog transformations a representation is obtained which can be used by the Back End to generate P*. The whole process can be interactively controlled by the user. In order to provide maximum flexibility, the system may be applied to arbitrary C-Fortran programs including programs that have already been (partially) parallelized.

We now discuss the individual components in more detail: The Front End, applied to a C-Fortran program P, creates an intermediate representation consisting of two parts: structural information and analysis information. The structural information specifies the abstract syntax of P together with the results of conventional semantic analysis, auxiliary control information, and a decomposition of the program into segments which are to be executed as processes at run time*. It includes [Aho 86, Hecht 77,
----

* This is the decomposition initially present in P immediately after application of the Front End; for a sequential program P, it will be trivial.

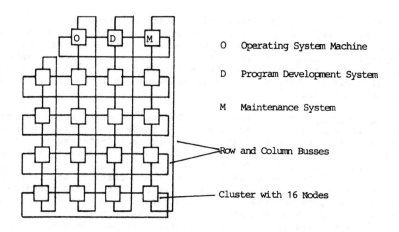

Fig.1: SUPRENUM Machine Architecture

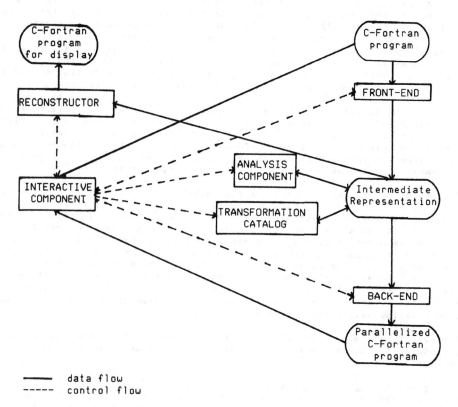

Fig.2: Structure of the Parallelization System

Zima 82, Zima 83] the attributed abstract tree, an associated symbol table, the interprocedural call graph and the intraprocedural program flow graphs. The second part of the intermediate representation, the _analysis information_, stores the results of the analysis processes applied to the program during its parallelization. Examples for such information sets are definition-use chains, available expressions and live variables associated with a program unit.

The _Analysis Component_ furnishes a collection of data flow analysis services that can be applied to selected parts of the program (such as expressions, elementary statements, basic blocks, DO-statements, and subprograms) or to the whole program. The role of analysis in the parallelization system is twofold: first, it verifies the existence of preconditions necessary for the application of transformations and helps to establish criteria for a selection from a number of valid transformations; secondly, it provides the information required to clean up after a transformation sequence has been applied. Analysis operates on the second part of the intermediate program representation without changing the structural information. Two categories of analysis services can be distinguished: (1) _data flow analysis_, performed on the basis of the call graph and the flow graphs associated with subprograms [Hecht 77, Much 81], and (2) _Dependence Analysis_. For intraprocedural analysis a general frame work will be provided using the Monotone Data Flow Analysis Systems introduced by Kildall, Kam and Ullman [Kild 73, Kam 76], together with a general iterative algorithm for arbitrary flow graphs. The interactive nature of the overall system allows the selective use of arbitrary analysis services; in addition a facility for user-defined specification of data flow problems will be supplied. _Dependence Analysis_ is based on the following concept [Kuck 80]: A statement S2 _depends_ on a statement S1 iff (i) there is an execution path from S1 to S2, and (ii) S1 and S2 access the same memory cell c, with at least one of the statements writing into c. This concept is crucial for parallelization since, apart from transformations eliminating semantically irrelevant dependences, the dependence relation must remain invariant under the transformations of the catalog. The results of dependence analysis are stored in the dependence graph which is part of the analysis information in the intermediate representation.

Corresponding to the machine architecture which, from a global point of view, is MIMD [Flynn 72], but, on the level of the basic processing node, contains a vector processing unit, parallelization is performed in two steps: First, an attempt is made to determine coarse grained parallelism and to decompose a program into disjoint segments that can be executed as processes (_MIMD parallelization_); second, every segment is analyzed for statements in loops that can be rewritten as vector operations (SIMD [Flynn 72] parallelization or _vectorization_). While a large body of knowledge exists about automatic vectorization [Kuck 80, Allen 82, Arno 82], MIMD parallelization has for practical purposes been carried out up to now almost exclusively manually [Adams 84, Holt 85, Mühl 85].

Beside these two major classes of transformations the _Catalog_ provides procedures for normalization and cleanup. It will be further discussed in Section 3.

The _Interactive Component_ plays a central role in the system. It allows flexible control of the other system services by establishing a two-way communication link between the user and the modules of the system. Details are discussed in Section 4.

The <u>Back End</u> uses the information in the intermediate representation to create a parallelized C-Fortran program. An instrumentation module attached to this component provides a facility for dynamic efficiency tests. We omit the details here.

3 THE TRANSFORMATION CATALOG

Due to the distributed architecture of the SUPRENUM machine, the limited memory in every node and the communication network structure, the problem of implementing MIMD parallelization can be restated as the task of translating a sequential program into a parallel program with coarse grained parallelism and minimal communication and synchronization overhead. It is in general extremely difficult to automatize MIMD parallelization because analysis usually unveils only the semantics of rather low-level components of algorithms and cannot grasp the underlying idea. Early work begun in this field in the late 60's [Bern 66, Rama 69, Russ 69] has only very limited significance for our problem because loops - the only sources of massive parallelism - were not adequately taken into account. More recent proposals [Cytr 84] do not seem to be directly applicable to the highly specialized problem under discussion.
Our approach is knowledge based: attention is focussed on numerical algorithms, in particular the multigrid method (see Section 1). The system provides specific knowledge about the structure of these algorithms and methods for their parallelization. The class of programs considered in this context can be characterized as follows: (1) The programs work on a mesh or mesh-like data domain, (2) the computations at the mesh points are local, i.e. depend only on the values of a small number of points in the neighborhood, and (3) the problems to be solved are very large. There are three steps in the MIMD parallelization of such programs: (1) Determination of the data domains, (2) decomposition of the data domains into data segments, and, (3) decomposition of the code into segments that can be executed as processes; this partitioning is done in accordance with the decomposition of the data domains and depends upon the problem size and the number of processing nodes available in an actual configuration. In the current practice of application program development, these steps are performed manually. In contrast to this, our system provides the user with analysis information and knowledge to support the transformation. As an example, information about loop variables and the use of COMMON objects may facilitate step 1, and knowledge about the method, the hardware (e.g. communication delays), control and data flow, and the dependence graph can significantly improve steps 2 and 3 of the MIMD parallelization.

The modular structure of the system allows easy subsequent extension to accommodate knowledge about new classes of algorithms.

The segments of a program obtained by MIMD parallelization can be subjected to vectorization. Its objective is the detection of statements in loops that can be rewritten as vector operations. For example, the loop below can be translated into the C-Fortran statement on the right, because the statement in the body does not depend on itself:

```
DO 10 I = 1, 100
A(I) = B(I) + C(I)          ===>     A(1:100) = B(1:100) + C(1:100)
10 CONTINUE
```

In contrast to this, the loop

```
DO 10 I = 1, 100
A(I+1) = A(I) + B(I)
10 CONTINUE
```

cannot be vectorized because for I = 2, 3,...100 the occurrence of A(I) in
the right hand side of the statement in the body refers to a value computed in the previous iteration, i.e. the statement depends cyclically on
itself. Such a dependence prevents vectorization. Vectorization transformations are described in detail in the abundant literature on the subject (see e.g. [Kuck 80, Allen 82]). Examples include the normalization
of subscripted variables, with the objective of obtaining linear index expressions in the loop variables wherever possible (induction variable substitution, scalar forward substitution), the translation of IF-statements
into WHERE statements (which correspond to masked vector operations), and
the elimination of semantically irrelevant dependences by the renaming of
variables or the expansion of a scalar temporary variable into an array.

The dependence concept used in our system is a generalization of Kuck's
version [Kuck 80] proposed by Allen and Kennedy [Allen 82]. It classifies
dependences according to the level of a loop in which they occur and allows parallelization across all levels of a loop.

4 THE INTERACTIVE COMPONENT

The Interactive Component is an essential part of the parallelization system since some of the transformations discussed in the previous section -
in particular the MIMD transformations - cannot in general be completely
automatized but are inherently dependent on human interaction. The principal tasks of the Interactive Component are as follows:

(1) Displaying information about the program

By using the Reconstructor (see Fig.2) the abstract program tree of the
intermediate representation can at any time be reconverted into a Fortran
source program and displayed to the user. The properties of the original
program text are preserved as far as possible. In addition, the auxiliary
control information stored in the call graph and the program flow graphs
can be made visible, and special routines will exist for the intelligible
display of analysis information and its association to program units.

(2) Executing user queries and commands

Both the Analysis Component and the Catalog can be viewed as program modules providing a set of services that may be selectively activated during
a dialog session. In this way, built-in mechanisms of the system (i.e.,
sequences of analysis processes and transformations representing some
standard approach to parallelization) can be overriden by the user. The
user may send a query to the Analysis Component to obtain information
about the use of variables, expressions, and other objects in selected
parts of the program; this information can in turn provide a rational basis for manual application of transformations, in particular for MIMD parallelization. The user may enforce transformations by explicit commands
if the system has insufficient information and thus cannot reach a decision, and, conversely, he may prevent the application of transformations
whose preconditions are satisfied.

(3) Accepting information from the user

Some of the static analysis processes employed in the system are constrained by inherent limitations due to the undecidability or impractical
computational complexity of the problems. As a result, analysis in general produces only a safe approximation of the data flow information requested, but not a precise solution [Hecht 77, Much 81, Zima 83]. In the
absence of sufficient information, worst-case assumptions must be made,
leading to a suboptimal operation of the transformation system. For example, the dependence graph is defined in such a way that dependence between
statements is assumed whenever independence cannot be established with
certainty. Consider the following DO-loop:

```
DO 10 I = 1, 10
A(I+C) = A(I) * B(I)
10 CONTINUE
```

The statement in the body of the loop depends on itself if and only if the
value of C is in the range -10 < C < 0 or 0 < C < 10. If dependence analysis cannot negate this condition, a cyclic dependence must be assumed. In
situations like this the user may supply information - frequently in the
form of assertions about the values of variables or their value ranges -
that increases the system's knowledge about the program to be transformed
and thereby permits closer control of the parallelization process.

In addition to the basic features of the Interactive Component discussed
above, a number of more advanced concepts are being considered for long-
term inclusion. They include a macro facility for user-defined parameter-
ized transformation strategies, differentiated behavior according to different user profiles, and automated learning by analyzing the effects of
transformation strategies applied to certain classes of problems. Finally,
it seems to be possible to define the transformations in the catalog as
rules in a rule-based system, and to introduce mechanisms for the modification of existing rules and the inclusion of new ones. This topic will
be the subject of future research.

5 CONCLUSION

In this paper the design of a semi-automatic parallelization system for
Fortran programs was described. Its distinctive features in relation to
previous work are the following: First, the system gives support for the
MIMD parallelization of a large class of numerical algorithms; second, an
extensive interprocedural data flow analysis subsystem yields a broad
range of information about the behavior of programs, and third, a dialog
facility provides the user with flexible control over the analysis and
transformation components.

The implementation of these features will lead to a system that can act as
an intelligent partner for the complex problem of parallelization.

ACKNOWLEDGEMENT We would like to thank Barbara M. Chapman for her helpful
comments on an earlier version of the paper.

REFERENCES

[Adams 84] Adams, L. M. , Voigt, R. G. : A Methodology for Exploiting Parallelism
in the Finite Element Process
In: Kowalik, J. S. (Ed.): High-Speed Computation, NATO ASI Series,
373-392, Springer Verlag (1984)

[Aho 86] Aho, A. V. , Sethi, R. , Ullman, J. D. : Compilers. Principles,
Techniques, and Tools
Addison-Wesley (1986)

[Allen 82] Allen, J. R. , Kennedy, K. :   PFC: A Program to Convert Fortran to
Parallel Form
Proc. IBM Conf. Parallel Comp. and Scientific Computations (1982)

[ANSI 86] American National Standards Institute X3J3:   Fortran 8X Version
98 (Jan 1986)

[Arno 82] Arnold, C. N. :   Performance Evaluation of Three Automatic
Vectorization Packages
Proc. 1979 Internat. Conf. Parallel Processing, 235-242 (1982)

[Bern 66] Bernstein, A. J. : Analysis of Programs for Parallel Processing
IEEE Trans. Electronic Computers EC-15, 757-762 (Oct 1966)

[Cytr 84] Cytron, R. G. : Compile-Time Scheduling and Optimization for
Asynchronous Machines
Ph. D. Dissertation, Dept. of Computer Science, University of
Illinois at Urbana-Champaign (1984)

[Flynn 72] Flynn, M. J. : Some Computer Organizations and Their Effectiveness
IEEE Trans. Computers, C-21, No. 9, 948-960 (Sep 1972)

[Hecht 77] Hecht, M. S. : Flow Analysis of Computer Programs
North Holland (1977)

[Holt 85] Holter, W. H. : A Vectorized Multigrid Solver for the
Three-Dimensional Poisson Equation
In: Emmen, A. H. L. (Ed.): Supercomputer Applications, Elsevier(1985)

[Kam 76] Kam, J. B. , Ullman, J. D. : Global Data Flow Analysis and Iterative
Algorithms
Journal ACM 23, 158-171 (1976)

[Kild 73] Kildall, G. A. : A Unified Approach to Global Program Optimization
Conf. Rec. ACM Symp. on Principles of Prog. Lang. , 194-206 (1973)

[Kuck 80] Kuck, D. J. , Kuhn, R. H. , Leasure, B. , Wolfe, M. : The Structure of an
Advanced Retargetable Vectorizer
Proc. COMPSAC ' 80 (1980)

[Much 81] Muchnick, S. S. , Jones, N. D. (Eds.): Program Flow Analysis. Theory
and Applications
Prentice Hall (1981)

[Mühl 85] Mühlenbein, H. , Warhaut, S. : Concurrent Multigrid Methods in an
Object-Oriented Environment - A Case Study
Proc. 1985 Internat. Conf. Parallel Processing, 143-146 (Aug 1985)

[Rama 69] Ramamoorthy, C. V. , Gonzalez, M. J. : A Survey of Techniques for
Recognizing Parallel Processable Streams in Computer Programs
In: Proc. AFIPS 1969 Fall Joint Comp. Conf. , 1-15 (1969)

[Russ 69] Russell, E. C. : Automatic Program Analysis
Ph. D. Dissertation, Dept. of Electrical Engineering, University
of California, Los Angeles, California (1969)

[Stüb 82] Stüben, K. , Trottenberg, U. : Multigrid Methods: Fundamental
Algorithms, Model Problem Analysis and Applications
Proc. Conf. Multigrid Methods, Lecture Notes in Mathematics,
Vol. 960, Springer Verlag (1982)

[Zima 82] Zima, H. : Compilerbau I: Analyse
Reihe Informatik Band 36, Bibliographisches Institut (1982)

[Zima 83] Zima, H. : Compilerbau II: Synthese und Optimierung
Reihe Informatik Band 37, Bibliographisches Institut (1983)

Code Generation for Partially Vectorizable Loops in the Vectorizing Pascal-XT Compiler

C. Hammer, G. Raebel
Siemens AG, ZTI SOF 222
Otto-Hahn-Ring 6
8000 München 83, West Germany

Abstract. Automatic vectorization of loops by investigation of data access dependences is known from literature. But the algorithms almost only describe the vectorization of fully vectorizable loops. A loop is judged to be nonvectorizable, if some data access dependences form a cycle. However, practical programs often contain loops with cyclic data access dependences where not all variables are included in the cyclic dependence. If cyclic dependences can be isolated, variables not encountered in the cyclic dependence are vectorizable. Thus, in vectorizing compilers not only full loop vectorization but also partial vectorization should be done. Here, the code generation for partially vectorizable loops is described for the vectorizing Pascal-XT compiler. The effect is compared to the vectorizing Fortran compilers of CDC, Cray and Fujitsu.

Key words: Automatic vectorization, dependence, partial vectorization, Pascal-XT.

Introduction. The vectorizing Pascal-XT compiler Pascal-XT(VSP) is part of the Siemens Pascal-XT compiler family. Pascal-XT (= Extended Pascal) is an extension of Pascal, Level 1, of the Pascal standard ISO 7185. The major extensions with respect to ISO Pascal are packages, separate compilation, exception handling, inline procedures, string handling, static expressions and aggregates, and interfaces to other programming languages. The Pascal-XT compiler family comprises a common front end and a set of back ends. Back ends are available for personal computers, process control computers and mainframes. The presently being developed vectorizing Pascal-XT compiler Pascal-XT(VSP) consists of the common front end, and a back end that generates code for the supercomputers VP50 to VP400 of the Siemens Vector Processor Series, whose most interesting feature may be the peak performance rate of 1.14 GFLOPS for the VP400 [1]. The overall structure of the Pascal-XT compiler family is described in [2].

Pascal-XT(VSP) regenerates parallelism from for-loops of a sequential Pascal-XT program by analysing the dependences between variable accesses (based on [3]). The basic idea will be sketched in the next section. Information obtained by dependence analysis is used to control code generation. How this is done even for statements that contain both vectorizable and not vectorizable parts is described in this paper. Constraints imposed on the code generation by the vector processor hardware are that vector registers cannot be accessed by scalar instructions, and that two occurrences of the same array variable that have different index expressions need different vector registers.

The Dependence Analysis. For the explanation of the dependence analysis consider the following for-loop:

```
for i := 2 to 100 do
    begin
        a[i-1] := b[i];
        c [i]  := a[i]
    end
```

When this loop is executed on a scalar computer, an arbitrary element of a (say a[5]) is first read by the second occurrence of a in the loop. In the next iteration of the loop (i = 6) this element a[5] is written by the first occurrence of a in the loop. (We denote the first occurrence of a by a_1 and the second one by a_2. Nevertheless, they denote the *same* variable a.) Thus, every element of a is first accessed by a_2 and then by a_1. This access order is written $a_2 \rightarrow a_1$. If the loop is vectorized line by line without paying attention to this dependence, all values of a are first written by a_1 in the first assignment and then read by a_2 in the second assignment, leading of course to a different result. The original access sequence can be restored, if we use the access dependence $a_2 \rightarrow a_1$ to execute the statement containing a_2 before the statement containing a_1. By this, the results of the scalar loop and the vectorized loop are the same. In general, the central idea is to analyse the data access dependences and to preserve these dependences on vectorization by statement reordering. In fact, this principle cannot only be used to reorder statements but also to break off assignment statements or even expressions and to reorder the fractions.

The dependences among variables can form cycles due to so called data recurrences. Operations on variables contained in these cycles cannot be vectorized except some special cases. Three types of recurrence handling are possible:

- The unit of vectorization is the whole loop. If a cyclic recurrence is found, the loop is judged nonvectorizable.
- The unit of vectorization is a statement. Dependences between variables are treated as dependences between statements. On one hand this permits a simple and straight-forward code generation, but on the other hand statements having only variables not included in a cyclic dependence may be attracted by a cycle, decreasing the vectorization ratio. The example given at the end of this paper shows such a situation.
- The unit of vectorization is a single variable occurrence. Only the variable occurrences contained in a cyclic dependence are accessed in a scalar loop, the rest is vectorized.

The last approach is chosen in the Pascal-XT(VSP) compiler to extract parallelism as much as possible from a given program.

For simplicity we shall assume here that the loop to be vectorized contains only assignment statements, and that the variables in these statements are array variables indexed by simple expressions depending on the loop control variable, as shown in the examples. Nevertheless, vectorizable and nonvectorizable scalar variables can be treated by the following algorithm as well as dependences originating from control structures (e.g. if-statements).

The Dependence Graph. The dependences computed by the dependence analysis are used to construct the dependence graph. This graph is then topologically sorted, thus delivering an access order of the variable occurrences. The sorting process extracts the cyclic parts of the dependence graph corresponding to recurrences, and joins the variables of each cycle into a single node of the sorted graph. Thus, the sorted dependence graph becomes an ordered list of variable accesses whose elements are either single (vectorizable) variable occurrences or sets of (nonvectorizable) variable occurrences.

Fully Vectorizable Loops. In a fully vectorizable loop, every node of the sorted dependence graph represents a single variable access. In this case an instruction selection could proceed as follows. As long as no variable occurrence with write access is found, the instruction selection generates load instructions for the variables in the sorted dependence graph (assuming an unlimited number of registers). When a write access is found in the list, the instruction selection accesses the right hand side expression of the corresponding assignment statement, and generates code for the arithmetic operations of the expression. The order of the sorted dependence graph assures that all variables of that expression are already loaded. Finally, the vector store operation for the write access in the list is generated.

As a simple optimization, the arithmetic instructions and the store instruction can be moved backwards in the list of already generated instructions until an instruction is found that loads or computes a value used by the moved instruction. This optimization reduces register lifetimes and improves pipeline parallelism. (In the Pascal-XT(VSP) compiler more sophisticated optimizations will be used.)

After this, the instruction selection proceeds with the next list entries in the same way as described above.

Partially Vectorizable Loops. As already mentioned, in a partially vectorizable loop the vectorizable variable accesses appear in single element nodes of the sorted dependence graph whereas the nonvectorizable variable accesses form a set node. These set nodes are used to flag every variable access that occurs in a cyclic dependence. Moreover, a list of the statements containing at least one variable access in a cyclic dependence is constructed. The statements must appear in the list in the same order as in the source program, and code for the variable accesses in the scalar loop must be generated in just this sequence. For the code generation for a single statement in this list we make the following observations:

- If the left hand side (LHS) of the statement is flagged, it is assured by the sorted dependence graph that every unflagged variable occurrence of the right hand side (RHS) is already loaded before the scalar loop.
- If the LHS is flagged, the whole RHS must obviously be computed before the result is assigned scalar to the LHS.

It follows that the arithmetic instructions for vectorizable (not flagged) subexpressions of the RHS must be generated and moved immediately before the scalar loop. Furthermore, the vector result of such a subexpression must be stored into a temporary vector area, where it can be accessed by scalar instructions. This store instruction must also be moved immediately before the loop. (The backward move optimization described in the last section can then be applied to these instructions.) Thus, a vectorizable subexpression is replaced by a scalar access to a temporary vector in storage computed before the loop.

The case where the LHS is not flagged remains:
- If the LHS is not flagged, no statement can be made about the relative order of unflagged RHS subexpressions with respect to the LHS, because dependences may require that subexpressions are to be executed before resp. after the scalar loop.
- If the LHS is not flagged, the LHS access appears in the sorted dependence graph after the variables in the cyclic dependence.

Thus, if the LHS is not flagged, only subexpressions with flagged operands can be computed scalar, the results must be stored into a temporary vector area. Immediately after the scalar loop these temporary vectors must be loaded into vector registers in order to be available for subsequent vector operations. This influences the generation of vector instructions for the single element nodes of the sorted dependence graph. In the last section we have generated code for the whole RHS expression except the load operations. Now the code generator must pay attention that no code is generated for subexpressions whose operands are flagged and are thus already computed in a scalar loop.

With these explanations the algorithm can be summarized as follows.

The dependence analysis constructs a data dependence graph for every for-loop under scan. After topological sorting the graph is passed to the code generation. The sorted graph contains the order in which variables must be accessed to preserve data accesses as seen by the programmer (i.e. the graph is an ordered list of variable occurrences). Each element of the list is either a single variable (which can be accessed by a vector instruction) or a set of variables (which are enclosed in a data dependence cycle and must be accessed in a scalar loop).

The appropriate action to be taken for each element of this list is:
- If the element is a single variable, and the variable has read access, generate a vector load instruction.
- If the element is a single variable, and the variable has write access, generate vector instructions for the corresponding RHS except for loading variables and except for flagged subexpressions, and generate a vector store instruction for the write access variable.
- If the element is a set of variables,
  - flag in the program all variables contained in the set,
  - generate the initial part of a scalar loop control,
  - construct a sorted list of all statements that contain at least one flagged variable. For each statement in the list do:
    - If the LHS of the statement is flagged, generate scalar instructions for the corresponding RHS expression. If subexpressions with unflagged operands are

encountered, generate vector instructions except for loading variables and move these instructions before the scalar loop. Generate a vector store instruction into a temporary vector for the result of that subexpression and move this instruction before the loop. Use this temporary vector instead of the sub-expression in the scalar code. Generate a scalar store instruction for the LHS.

- If the LHS of the statement is not flagged, generate scalar instructions for sub-expressions with flagged operands. Store the result of such a subexpression into a temporary vector. Retain a vector load instruction for this temporary vector that must be generated directly after the final part of the scalar loop control.
- Generate the final part of the scalar loop control.
- Generate the retained vector load instructions for the temporary vectors.

This completes the algorithm.

Example. The code generator of the Pascal-XT(VSP) compiler translates a tree like high level intermediate language into an assembler like low level intermediate language. For clarity, translation is described here in terms of the source language and mostly self explanatory mnemonic instructions. Instruction mnemonics starting with a "V" are vector instructions. An unlimited number of pseudo registers is assumed, each register being unique-ly defined as the result register of an instruction. The register allocation phase maps these pseudo registers onto real registers. Scalar registers are denoted by "s(...)", vector registers by "v(...)". Thus the register $v(a[i-1])$ is the vector register that holds the values $a[i-1]$ for all i, $s(a[i-1])$ is the scalar register containing the value of $a[i-1]$ for the current value of i.

Consider now the following for-loop (the arrays are supposed to be declared from 1 to 1000):

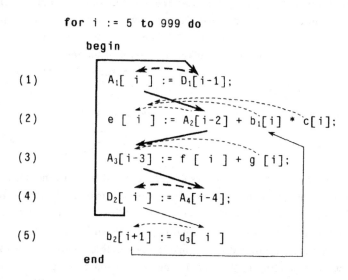

```
for i := 5 to 999 do
      begin
(1)       A₁[ i ] := D₁[ i-1 ];
(2)       e [ i ] := A₂[ i-2 ] + b₁[ i ] * c[ i ];
(3)       A₃[ i-3 ] := f [ i ] + g [ i ];
(4)       D₂[ i ] := A₄[ i-4 ];
(5)       b₂[ i+1 ] := d₃[ i ]
      end
```

In this example, different occurrences of a variable are again distinguished by subscripts. Variable occurrences written in upper case letters form a cyclic dependence, whereas

```
( 1)  VLOAD   v(f[i])        := f[i]                             i = 5..999
( 2)  VLOAD   v(g[i])        := g[i]                             i = 5..999
(10)  VADD    v(f[i]+g[i]) := v(f[i]) + v(g[i])                  i = 5..999
(11)  VSTORE  v(f[i]+g[i]) =: vtemp_f_g[i]                       i = 5..999
( 3)  VLOAD   v(c[i])        := c[i]                             i = 5..999
( 4)  loop start control for loop with control variable i
( 5)      LOAD   s(D[i-1])       := D[i-1]
( 6)      STORE  s(D[i-1])       =: A[i]
( 7)      LOAD   s(A[i-2])       := A[i-2]
( 8)      STORE  s(A[i-2])       =: vtemp_A[i-2]
(12)      LOAD   s(f[i]+g[i])    := vtemp_f_g[i]
(13)      STORE  s(f[i]+g[i])    =: A[i-3]
(14)      LOAD   s(A[i-4])       := A[i-4]
(15)      STORE  s(A[i-4])       =: D[i]
(16)  loop end control for loop with control variable i
( 9)  VLOAD   v(A[i-2])      := vtemp_A[i-2]                     i = 5..999
(17)  VLOAD   v(d[i])        := d[i]                             i = 5..999
(18)  VSTORE  v(d[i])        =: b[i+1]                           i = 5..999
(19)  VLOAD   v(b[i])        := b[i]                             i = 5..999
(20)  VMULT   v(b[i]*c[i]) := v(b[i]) * v(c[i])                  i = 5..999
(21)  VADD    v(A[i-2]+b[i]*c[i]) := v(A[i-2]) + v(b[i]*c[i])    i = 5..999
(22)  VSTORE  v(A[i-2]+b[i]*c[i]) =: e[i]                        i = 5..999
```

Generated code for the example loop

variable occurrences written in lower case do not. Dependences originating from the given access order in index space are indicated by solid arrows. Broken arrows indicate the dependences that RHS occurrences must be accessed before the LHS in the same statement. The cyclic dependence is drawn with bold arrows. Note that we have a dependence sequence $D_2 \to d_3 \to b_2 \to b_1$. Thus b_1 must not be used in line (2) before it is written by b_2 in line (5) after execution of the scalar loop. If statements were taken as units of vectorization, the statement in line (5) would become part of the cycle and had to be added to the scalar loop. Here, it can be executed with vector instructions.

One sorted dependence graph for our example (the sorting is not unique) is

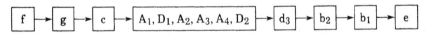

The first three elements of the sorted dependence graph are variable occurrences with read access. Thus, f, g and c will be loaded into vector registers (lines (1) to (3) in the code sequence above). The next element is a set of variable occurrences contained in a cyclic dependence. The corresponding variable occurrences in the program are flagged (here written in upper case letters), the statements containing at least one of these variable occurrences are sorted into a statement list corresponding to their occurrence in the source program (here this statement list is (1)-(2)-(3)-(4)), and the initial part of the scalar loop control is generated (line (4) of the code, the loop end control will be generated after the last statement in the cyclic dependence).

The LHS of the first statement of the statement list is flagged. The RHS expression consists only of a flagged variable, thus it is loaded (line (5) of the code, the abbreviated form in this line stands for a sequence of scalar instructions needed to access an array element). After this code generation for the RHS the store instruction for the LHS is generated (6). In the second statement of the list, the LHS is not flagged. Thus only code for the flagged RHS subexpressions will be generated and stored into a temporary vector (the flagged subexpression consists only of a single variable, (7, 8)). The corresponding vector load instruction (9) is retained and will be inserted after the loop end control (16). The third statement of the list has again a flagged LHS. Because the RHS expression has unflagged operands, vector operations for these operands are generated and inserted before the loop (and moved backwards, (10, 11)). The temporary vector is used on evaluation of the RHS and the result is stored to the LHS (12, 13). The last statement of the list can be treated the same way as the first one (14, 15). This completes the statement list. The final part of the scalar loop control is generated (16), and the retained vector instruction is inserted (9).

The next element in the sorted dependence graph is a read access, resulting in a vector load operation (17). The following element contains a write access. The corresponding RHS has no flagged variables and the expression consists of only one unflagged variable. So only the store instruction for the write access need to be generated (18). The last but one element is again a read access (19) which is followed by a write access in the last element. Thus the code for the corresponding RHS must be generated which is a vector multiply operation (20) (the vector operands are already loaded) and an addition with a subexpression with flagged operands (consisting only of a single variable). This subexpression must already have been computed and loaded. The computation of the RHS is thus completed by the vector addition (21), and the result is then stored to the LHS (22).

Comparison to other compilers. Up to now, vectorizing compilers mean almost only vectorizing Fortran compilers. There are also vectorizing compilers for C [4] and Pascal [5] for the CDC Cyber 205 but these compilers translate only extended language constructs for arrays into vector instructions. The example given above has been directly translated into Fortran and compiled by the vectorizing Fortran compilers for the CDC Cyber 205, the Cray 1, the Cray X-MP (both Cray Fortran compiler CFT 1.14), and for the Fujitsu/Siemens VP Series (Fortran77/VP compiler [6]).

The Cray compiler does not vectorize the program at all, it complains a "dependency involving array D" between lines (1) and (4), and a "dependency involving array B" between lines (2) and (5). Indeed, CFT cannot vectorize partially vectorizable loops.

The Cyber Fortran compiler does not vectorize the loop, too. The compiler provides only full loop vectorization in a simple form.

The Fujitsu compiler does the best job (it is said to be the best vectorizing compiler today) and vectorizes lines (1) - (4) partially, but does not vectorize statement (5). Instead, the assignment to b_2 is included in the scalar loop as a store operation from the register containing A_4. This seems to be an optimization because the compiler vectorizes the statement (5) completely if it contains an additional vectorizable operation. Unfortunately, the Fujitsu optimization results in slower code, the vectorized load/store operations are about 8 times faster than the scalar store operation in the scalar loop (on the VP200). But in general, the code generated by the Fujitsu compiler is very similiar to ours.

Time measurements on the Siemens VP200 show that the partially vectorized loop of the example where about 50 percent is vectorized, needs only about 60 percent of the time of the fully scalar executed loop. This meets the expected speedup.

Conclusion. Dependence graph controlled code generation can effectively be used to regenerate a maximum of parallelism from a program, if single variable occurrences are chosen as units of vectorization.

References

[1]   Vector Processor System. Siemens System 7.800 - System Description. Order no. U1889-J-Z62-2-7600 (1985).

[2]   Pascal-XT(BS2000/SINIX), Brief Description. Siemens. Order no. U2491-J-Z52-1-7600 (1985).

[3]   L. Lamport: The Parallel Execution of DO Loops. Communications of the ACM 17, 2 (1974), 83-93.

[4]   K.-C. Li: A Note on the Vector C Language. ACM SIGPLAN Notices 21, 1(1986), 49-57.

[5]   H. Ehlich: PASCALV - Der PASCAL Compiler für den Vektorrechner CYBER205. Bochumer Schriften zur Parallelen Datenverarbeitung 5. RZ Ruhr Universität Bochum (1984).

[6]   S. Kamiya, F. Isobe, H. Takashima, M. Takiuchi: Practical Vectorization Techniques for the "FACOM VP". Information Processing 83, R. Mason (ed.), Elsevier Science Publishers B. V. (North-Holland).

Automatic Vectorisation for High Level Languages based on an Expert System

Thomas Brandes

FB Mathematik/Informatik, Philipps-Universität

3550 Marburg, Lahnberge

Abstract:

New hardware architecture use vector operations and parallelism for high speed computation; existing software has mostly to be rewritten. The automation of the adaptation of existing software to the new hardware is unsatisfactory, especially when using high level languages, as the vectorisation and parallelisation process needs a knowledge of the hardware, of convenient transformations and of semantic properties of the program to take advantage of the hardware possibilities. The expert system SAVER will be the basis to accelerate and automate thoroughly the vectorisation process. The most interesting features of the Saver system will be presented in this paper.

1. Introduction

The importance of modern hardware providing high speed computation by the use of vector processing, massively parallel processors and MIMD architecture ([1],[2],[20]) is increasing. This paper refers to vector processors but can be generalised easily for all kinds of parallel hardware.

High level languages are provided for "sequential" programming. They can be used for such parallel hardware, if there is
▸ a compiler for an extended language with vector operations ([3],[4])
▸ a possibility to include assembler routines (perhaps machine code insertion [6])
▸ an autovectorising compiler ([7],[8]).
There is, however, no standardisation, either for extended languages and the kind of assembler routines, or for the requirements of an autovectorising compiler.

The adaptation of existing software and the production of new software for parallel hardware usually require exact knowledge of this hardware. Preprocessors and interactive vectorisers ([9],[12],[13]) may give information about the possibilities of vectorisation and produce hints for program transformations to obtain a better vectorisation. But they are unsatisfactory, as they identify only some special cases. In addition, they are not available for high level languages such as Pascal, Modula or ADA, which are used not only for numerical programming and array manipulating as is FORTRAN, but also for dynamic programming and manipulating dynamic data structures like lists and trees.

Furthermore it has been discovered, that "sequential" algorithms seldom obtain a relevant speedup (see [20]). New "parallel" algorithms are required, which are often considerably different from their "sequential" counterparts. What is needed to get a good "parallel" algorithm is not only an exact knowledge of the algorithm, but also a familiarity with parallel thinking and useful transformations.

Therefore an expert system for vectorisation is required containing the following types of knowledge:

- Knowledge of vectorisation in principle
- Knowledge of the hardware architecture
- Knowledge of the possibilities for using the hardware, i.e. knowledge of extended languages, assembler routines and autovectorising compilers, which are available
- Knowledge of transformation possibilities to get "parallel" algorithms from "sequential" ones

Compared with a preprocessor or an interactive vectoriser the expert system SAVER (**S**uper **A**uto-**V**ectorising **E**xpert System) has the following advantages:

- Automatic vectorisation will be easier to understand
- The expansion of the knowledge base with new vectorisation issues is easy
- Little knowledge of the underlying hardware architecture is needed
- Applying semantic properties to parallelisation (properties can be given by the user or by the rules of the system)
- Interactive assistance for an inexperienced user and learning from an experienced one
  ‣ Building a database of successful applied transformations
  ‣ Setting up heuristics for useful transformation
  ‣ Generalisation of specific knowledge

2. Structure of the expert system SAVER

The entire expert system SAVER looks like a preprocessor; an existing "sequential" program will be analysed (lexical, syntactic and semantic analysis) and translated into an intermediate language. After vectorisation at this intermediate level it will be transformed back into a "parallel" program-text (unparsing), which will be compiled by a compiler with vectorisation facilities into a high speed machine program.

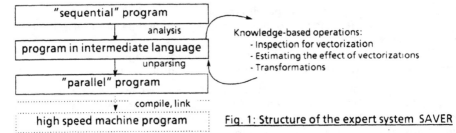

Fig. 1: Structure of the expert system SAVER

Analysis and unparsing are also "knowledge-based" operations, because they will only be specified by structures like a finite automaton, a grammar, an initial symbol table, a type compatibility table and attribute grammars (for semantic analysis and unparsing), which form the knowledge of these operations. Error handling is neglected, because it is assumed that only correct programs will be vectorised.

Code generation immediately after vectorisation is also possible but not desirable, because on the one hand after each change of the old program vectorisation has to be repeated, on the other hand machine dependent optimisations (register allocation, peephole optimisation, pipeline optimisation) ought to be done preferably by the compiler.

An InterLisp environment ([14]) supporting an Ethernet communications network and graphic representations is used for realising the expert system SAVER. The Ethernet network makes vectorisation of programs from host processors possible, the graphics makes the dialogue with an user easier (e. g. graphic representation of dependencies). The functional programming language LISP, extended by the object oriented programming language LOOPS ([15]), makes an efficient realisation of algorithmic components possible (functions for analysis, unparsing, detection of vectorisable statements, determination of simultaneous access to variables, etc.) and a reasonable knowledge representation ([16],[17],[18],[19]).

The knowledge of the expert system, which is represented in the first instance as rules, is composed of knowledge of how to determine semantic properties, knowledge of how to estimate the effects of vectorisations as well as knowledge and heuristics of transformations. Quality and structure of this knowledge will be presented in the next four chapters. Although SAVER contains knowledge for multi-dimensional loops, in this paper rules and knowledge are presented for one-dimensional loops.

3. A knowledge base for vectorisation in principle

A set of statements, which are executed several times, has generally to be vectorised; these may be statements within a loop or statements of a repeatedly called procedure or function.

If the execution of several statements is parallelised, attention has to be paid to the variable-accesses to the same place in the memory; they must not conflict with the sequence as defined by the statements and by the semantics of the language.

Conflicts can always arise if there are concurrent accesses to the same variable or if one access is needed before another. For this some definitions are brought in:

Def.: i) $P_{v,j}$: access to the variable v during the j. execution

ii) $P_{v_1,j_1} \rightleftharpoons P_{v_2,j_2}$ (is in conflict with) :$\Leftrightarrow P_{v_1,j_1}$ and P_{v_2,j_2} have to be accessed according to the sequential order

iii) $P_v := \{P_{v,j}\}_j$: simultaneous access to v for all executions

iv) $P_{v_1} < P_{v_2}$:$\Leftrightarrow$ $\exists$ i,j: $P_{v_1,i} \rightleftharpoons P_{v_2,j} \wedge P_{v_1,i}$ must be accessed before $P_{v_2,j}$ according to the sequential order

(a simultaneous access P_{v_2} has to follow a simultaneous access P_{v_1})

v) $\ll$: the transitive hull of the relation <

vi) P_v has a cyclic dependency :$\Leftrightarrow P_v \ll P_v$

If some accesses are in conflict, there will be a dependency for the simultaneous accesses. These dependencies can be classified:

Assumption: v_1 lies before v_2 according to the sequential execution order.

Def.: P_{v_1} BEFORE P_{v_2} :$\Leftrightarrow$ $\exists$ i,j: i$\leq$j $\wedge P_{v_1,i} \rightleftharpoons P_{v_2,i}$
($\Rightarrow$ $P_{v_1} < P_{v_2}$)

Def.: P_{v_1} AFTER P_{v_2} :$\Leftrightarrow$ $\exists$ i,j: i>j $\wedge P_{v_1,i} \rightleftharpoons P_{v_2,j}$
($\Rightarrow$ $P_{v_2} < P_{v_1}$)

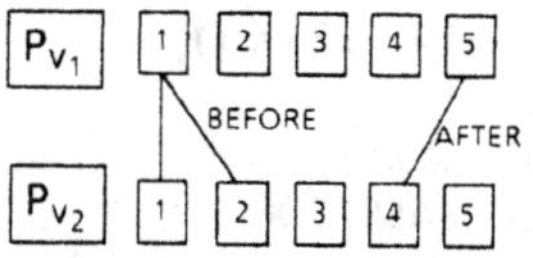

Fig. 2: BEFORE, AFTER-conflicts

The first step of a vectorisation is to establish all the dependencies (the relation <). With this information it will be decided whether full vectorisation is possible (no P_v has a cyclic dependency). If full vectorisation is not possible, the information will be used to select transformations (see chapter 6).

One kind of dependency for simultaneous accesses in a set of statements results from the dependencies of the accesses given by the program; these dependencies can generally be determinated by an algorithm.

$v_1 := \ldots \ v_2 \ \ldots$ $\Rightarrow P_{v_2}$ BEFORE P_{v_1}
$v_1[\ \ldots \ v_2 \ \ldots]$ $\Rightarrow P_{v_2}$ BEFORE P_{v_1}
if v_1 then $\ldots \ v_2 := \ldots$ (else $\ldots v_2 := \ldots$) $\Rightarrow P_{v_1}$ BEFORE P_{v_2}
$p(v_1, v_2, \ldots v_n) \Rightarrow$ dependencies are those within the procedure but only for parameters

The other kind of dependencies are given by concurrent accesses to one place in the memory and at least one access is a write access. Each access will be considered as an indexed access to determine these dependencies; this is also possible for selections and dereferences $(v\uparrow \doteq \$HEAP[v], \ v.x \doteq v[offset(x)])$.

For every write access v $P_v < P_v$ is assumed, and for each two accesses v_1 and v_2 to the same variable, at least one is a write access, $P_{v_1} < P_{v_2}$ and $P_{v_2} < P_{v_1}$ (BEFORE and AFTER) are assumed, until a dependency can be disproved.

<u>Rules for dependencies:</u>

P_{v_1}, P_{v_2} are different accesses to the same variable, one is a write access:
       NOTBEFORE(P_{v_1}, P_{v_2}) can't be proved $\Rightarrow P_{v_1}$ BEFORE P_{v_2}
       NOTAFTER(P_{v_1}, P_{v_2}) can't be proved $\Rightarrow P_{v_1}$ AFTER P_{v_2}
P_v is a write access and NOCONFLICTS(P_v) can't be proved $\Rightarrow P_v < P_v$
P_{v_1} BEFORE P_{v_2} $\Rightarrow P_{v_1} < P_{v_2}$
P_{v_1} AFTER P_{v_2} $\Rightarrow P_{v_2} < P_{v_1}$
$P_{v_1} < P_{v_2}$ $\Rightarrow P_{v_1} \lll P_{v_2}$
$P_{v_1} < P_{v_2}, P_{v_2} \lll P_{v_3}$ $\Rightarrow P_{v_1} \lll P_{v_3}$

Disproving can be done if there is enough information about the indexes of the accesses, like "the values of the indexes of v are all different" or "an index of v_1 never appears as an index of v_2" or "an index of v_1 doesn't appear 'before' or 'after' an index of v_2". Indexes can't be compared by an algorithm, because the values of these indexes are a semantic property, which isn't decidable. But assertions can be made for many special cases to disprove dependencies. The rules for such assertions are one kind of knowledge in SAVER.

Let v be an access to a variable, then the following notation is used:

INDEXES(v) : Indexes of v (syntactic)   INDEX(v,k) : k. index of v (syntactic)

The following (syntactic) predicates describe semantic properties of accesses, expressions, indexes or statements (for all executions); big letters stand for syntactic structures of the statements to be vectorised:

NEVERBEFORE (X,Y)	: $X = (x_1, x_2, \ldots, x_n), Y = (y_1, y_2, \ldots, y_n), \forall i,j : i \leqq j \Rightarrow x_i \neq y_j$
NEVERAFTER (X,Y)	: $X = (x_1, x_2, \ldots, x_n), Y = (y_1, y_2, \ldots, y_n), \forall i,j : i > j \Rightarrow x_i \neq y_j$
INJECTIVE (X)	: $X = (x_1, x_2, \ldots, x_n), \forall i,j : x_i = x_j \Rightarrow i = j$
INCREASING (X)	: $X = (x_1, x_2, \ldots, x_n), \forall i,j : i < j \Rightarrow x_i < x_j$
DECREASING (X)	: $X = (x_1, x_2, \ldots, x_n), \forall i,j : i < j \Rightarrow x_i > x_j$
SAMEDIFFERENCE (X,Y,c)	: $X = (x_1, x_2, \ldots, x_n), Y = (y_1, y_2, \ldots, y_n), \forall i : x_i - y_i = c$
EQUAL (X,Y)	: $X = (x_1, x_2, \ldots, x_n), Y = (y_1, y_2, \ldots, y_n), \forall i : x_i = y_i$
DIFFERENT (X,Y)	: $X = (x_1, x_2, \ldots, x_n), Y = (y_1, y_2, \ldots, y_n), \forall i,j : x_i \neq y_j$
MODULO (X,m,k)	: $X = (x_1, x_2, \ldots, x_n), \forall i : x_i \bmod m = k$
CONSTANT (X,c)	: $X = (x_1, x_2, \ldots, x_n), \forall i : x_i = c$
ISCONSTANT (X)	: $X = (x_1, x_2, \ldots, x_n), \forall i,j : x_i = x_j$
LINEAR (X,c)	: $X = (x_1, x_2, \ldots, x_n), \forall i < n : x_{i+1} - x_i = c$
UPPERBOUND (X,k)	: $X = (x_1, x_2, \ldots, x_n), \forall i : x_i \leqq k$
LOWERBOUND (X,k)	: $X = (x_1, x_2, \ldots, x_n), \forall i : x_i \geqq k$

Rules to disprove dependencies:

$NEVERBEFORE(INDEXES(V_1),INDEXES(V_2)) \Rightarrow NOTBEFORE(P_{v_1},P_{v_2})$

$NEVERAFTER(INDEXES(V_1),INDEXES(V_2)) \Rightarrow NOTAFTER(P_{v_1},P_{v_2})$

$INJECTIVE(INDEXES(V)) \Rightarrow NOCONFLICTS(P_v)$

$NEVERBEFORE(INDEX(V_1,k),INDEX(V_2,k)) \Rightarrow NEVERBEFORE(INDEXES(V_1),INDEXES(V_2))$

$NEVERAFTER(INDEX(V_1,k),INDEX(V_2,k)) \Rightarrow NEVERAFTER(INDEXES(V_1),INDEXES(V_2))$

$INJECTIVE(INDEX(V,k)) \Rightarrow INJECTIVE(INDEXES(V))$

$INCREASING(E_1) \wedge SAMEDIFFERENCE(E_1,E_2,c) \wedge c \geqq 0 \Rightarrow NEVERAFTER (E_1,E_2)$

$INCREASING(E_1) \wedge SAMEDIFFERENCE(E_1,E_2,c) \wedge c < 0 \Rightarrow NEVERBEFORE (E_1,E_2)$

$DECREASING(E_1) \wedge SAMEDIFFERENCE(E_1,E_2,c) \wedge c > 0 \Rightarrow NEVERAFTER (E_1,E_2)$

$DECREASING(E_1) \wedge SAMEDIFFERENCE(E_1,E_2,c) \wedge c \leqq 0 \Rightarrow NEVERBEFORE (E_1,E_2)$

$DIFFERENT(E_1,E_2) \Rightarrow NEVERBEFORE (E_1,E_2)$

$DIFFERENT(E_1,E_2) \Rightarrow NEVERAFTER (E_1,E_2)$

Rules to get semantic properties from the syntax;

for I: = a to b do anw; $\Rightarrow LINEAR(I,1) \{$ for every I in anw$\}$

for I: = a downto b do anw; $\Rightarrow LINEAR(I,-1) \{$ for every I in anw$\}$

$LINEAR(X,c) \wedge c > 0 \Rightarrow INCREASING(X)$

$LINEAR(X,c) \wedge c < 0 \Rightarrow DECREASING(X)$

$INCREASING(X) \Rightarrow INJECTIVE(X)$

$DECREASING(X) \Rightarrow INJECTIVE(X)$

$MODULO(E_1,m,k_1) \wedge MODULO (E_2,m,k_2) \wedge k_1 \neq k_2 \Rightarrow DIFFERENT (E_1,E_2)$

$UPPERBOUND(E_1,k_1) \wedge LOWERBOUND (E_2,k_2) \wedge k_1 < k_2 \Rightarrow DIFFERENT (E_1,E_2)$

V_1, V_2 accesses to the same variable, for which is meanwhile
no write access $\wedge \forall k: EQUAL(INDEX(V_1,k),INDEX(V_2,k)) \Rightarrow EQUAL(V_1,V_2)$

$EQUAL(I_1,I_2) \wedge CONSTANT(C_1-C_2, c) \Rightarrow SAMEDIFFERENCE(I_1 + C_1,I_2 + C_2,c)$

$CONSTANT(M,m) \Rightarrow MODULO(M*X,m,0)$

$MODULO(X,m,j) \wedge CONSTANT(C,c) \Rightarrow MODULO(X + C,m, (c + j) \bmod m)$

$INCREASING(I) \wedge ISCONSTANT(C) \wedge op \in \{ +,- \} \Rightarrow INCREASING(I op C)$

$DECREASING(I) \wedge ISCONSTANT(C) \wedge op \in \{ +,- \} \Rightarrow DECREASING(I op C)$

$INCREASING(I) \wedge ISCONSTANT(C,c) \wedge c > 0 \Rightarrow INCREASING(I*C)$

$CONSTANT(C,c) \Rightarrow UPPERBOUND(C,c)$

....

Example:

Dependencies for simultaneous accesses (see also [10])

```
for I:=2 to N do
   begin
   ③A[I] := ①B[I]+②C[I];
   ⑤B[I] := ④A[I+1];
   ⑦C[I] := ⑥C[I-1]+2.5;
   end;
```

①②③④⑤⑥⑦ are the simultaneous accesses (note: the simultaneous accesses to I are irrelevant, because there is no write access to I)

<u>Dependencies of the program:</u> ① BEFORE ③, ② BEFORE ③, ④ BEFORE ⑤ and ⑥ BEFORE ⑦

<u>Dependencies for same variables:</u> ③ AFTER ④ , ① BEFORE ⑤, ⑥ AFTER ⑦

Note: a) ③ < ③, ⑤ < ⑤, ⑦ < ⑦ are not valid, because INJECTIVE(I)

b) ③ NOTBEFORE ④, because $INCREASING(I) \wedge SAMEDIFFERENCE(I,I + 1,-1) \wedge -1 < 0$
$\Rightarrow NEVERBEFORE(I,I + 1)$

c) ① NOTAFTER ⑤, because $INCREASING(I) \wedge SAMEDIFFERENCE(I,I,0) \wedge 0 \geq 0$
$\Rightarrow NEVERAFTER(I,I)$

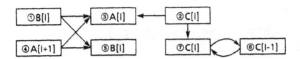

Only accesses ⑥ and ⑦ are cyclic dependent, the other accesses can be vectorised; that includes all operations in which they appear (sometimes a help vector is needed).

Statements (partly) vectorised:

```
$H[I] := A[I+1];     I=2(1)N
A[I]  := B[I]+C[I];  I=2(1)N
B[I]  := $H[I];      I=2(1)N
for I:=2 to N do C[I] := C[I-1]+2.5;
```

4. A knowledge base for the hardware architecture

The way statements about dependencies on simultaneous accesses and statements about vectorisation and parallelisation in principle are used depends mainly on the possibilities of the existent hardware architecture.

Issues:

a) Are there commands like 'Vector Indirect Load' and 'Vector Indirect Store' (to access A[B[I]])?

b) If the number of iterations of a loop is known only at run time, it is important to know the maximum vector-length for vector-operations.

c) What kind of vector-reductions are supported by the hardware architecture (vector add, vector minimum, vector compress, vector expand)?

d) How many pipelines and what kind of pipelines are there? Can the pipelines be used in parallel, e.g. can a vector-multiplication (B*C) and a vector-load (D) (e.g. in the statement A[I]:=B[I]*C[I]+D[I]) be executed in parallel?

e) How many elements should have a vector to take advantage of the use of a pipeline?

f) Which possibilities are there to execute conditional vector-operations (see [8]: masked operation method, gather-scatter method, list vector method)?

Each issue evaluates a qualitative, sometimes even a quantitative measure of the potential use of the hardware or a measure of the speedup. This measure may give a decision about whether to look for further vectorisations, and if there are several possibilities for vectorisation (see chapter 6), it can be decided which is the best option.

Determination of predicates for operations and variables (here for VP200 hardware, [8])

$\forall k$:ISCONSTANT(INDEX(V,k)) $\Rightarrow$ IS-A-SCALAR (V)

$\neg(V \triangleleft V) \wedge \neg$IS-A-SCALAR(V) $\Rightarrow$ IS-A-VECTOR (V)

$\forall k$:LINEAR(INDEX(V,k),c) $\wedge$ IS-A-VECTOR (V) $\Rightarrow$ SIMPLE-VECTOR (V)

IS-A-VECTOR(V$_1$) $\wedge$ IS-A-VECTOR(V$_2$) $\Rightarrow$ IS-A-VECTOR(V1 op V2)

$\neg(V_1 \triangleleft V_2) \wedge \neg(V_2 \triangleleft V_1)$ $\Rightarrow$ INDEPENDENT(V$_1$,V$_2$)

INDEPENDENT(V$_1$,V$_2$) $\wedge$ SIMPLE-VECTOR (V$_1$)
$\wedge$ SIMPLE-VECTOR (V$_2$) $\Rightarrow$ PARALLEL(LOAD(V$_1$),LOAD(V$_2$))

INDEPENDENT(V,V$_1$) $\wedge$ INDEPENDENT(V,V$_2$) $\Rightarrow$ INDEPENDENT(V,V$_1$ op V$_2$)

INDEPENDENT(V,V$_1$ op V$_2$) $\Rightarrow$ PARALLEL(LOAD(V),Vop(V$_1$,V$_2$,op))

...

5. A knowledge base for the possibities for using the hardware

With this kind of knowledge a vectorisation strategy will lead to program transformation that can afterwards be compiled by an available compiler into a high speed machine program. The possibility for using the hardware may raise the following problems:

a) autovectorising compiler / extended language

It is important to know which kind of dependencies the autovectorising compiler realises and what directives are accepted by the compiler; vectorisable operations have to be translated into vector-operations of the extended language. But not every vectorisation can be described by the existing resources (see also [12]).

b) subroutines

It doesn't make sense to transform vectorised operations into a sequence of subroutine calls realising single vector-operations, because machine dependent optimisation can only be done locally for each subroutine. Machine code insertion is a possibility, but is only useful if machine dependent optimisation is done afterwards (see [6]). If an assembler subroutine realises a complex operation using vector-operations (such as sorting), they should be used, as such routines achieve generally a high performance.

The effective use of a subroutine library is generally a problem; an expert system may help the user to select appropriate subroutines and may advise the user how and where they can be used.

The expert system should also be able to recognise, whether a procedure called for each element of a vector can be extended for vectors. This means that the entire procedure should also be realised by vector operations and then be used.

Knowledge:

IS-A-VECTOR(V) ∧ IS-A-SCALAR(A)   ⇒ USE(A: = A*V,VECTORMULT(A,V))
IS-A-VECTOR(V)   ⇒ VECTORISABLE (sin(V))
...

6. A knowledge base for transformations

There are series of transformations for a program which don't change the semantics of the program, but can change immensely the possibilities for vectorisation. This is possible for control structures as well as for data structures.

- Permutation of inner and outer loops for better vectorisation ([10], [13])
- Choosing of new index variables (Hyperplane Method [10])
- Detection, Classification and Resolving of Recurrences ([11], [12], [13])
- Detection of vector reductions (vector add, vector minimum etc.)
- Replacing linked lists by pointer-arrays to get simultaneous access to the elements

The knowledge of transformations is the most important knowledge of the expert system; it is based on experience and heuristics. Uncertain knowledge should only be used when confirmed by the user, especially when it is suspected that a transformation may change the semantics of the program.

The properties and dependencies of concurrent memory accesses and pattern recognition become the most important part of the application of program transformations.

7. Conclusion

The use of an expert system depends mainly on the size and on the quality of the available knowledge and on the time which may be used for autovectorisation. Therefore much knowledge must be acquired. The knowledge must be reasonably structured and must be generalised cleverly.

The state of the development up to now shows that the expert system SAVER compared with an interactive vectoriser (e.g. [8]) is a clear winner on account of the graphical representation of dependencies and as a consequence of the more powerful usage and better maintenance, and in addition, SAVER allows (for the first time) the use of high level languages other than Fortran such as for example Pascal, Modula and ADA.

In what way the expert system distinctly improves the process of vectorisation has to be discovered in future.

Acknowledgements

The author is indebted to Prof. M. Sommer, H. Gasiorowski and G. Völksen for many valuable comments on this paper and on the development of SAVER.

8. Bibliography

[1] Hwang,K.; Shun-Piao,S.; Noi,L.M:Vector Computer Architecture and Processing Techniques; Advances in Computers, Vol. 20

[2] Kowalik,S.J.: High Speed Computation; Springer Verlag 1984; Series F: Computer and Systems Sciences, Vol. 7, Part 1

[3] Perrott,R.H.; Crookes,D.; Milligan,P.; Purdy,M.: A Compiler for an Array and Vector Processing Language; IEEE - Transactions on SE, Vol. 11, No.5, May 1985

[4] Li,K.C.; Schwetmann,H.: VectorC: A Vector Processing Language; Journal of Parallel and Distributed Computing 2

[5] Ehlich,H.: PASCALV: Der Pascal-Compiler für den Vektorrechner CYBER 205; Bochumer Schriften zur Parallelen Datenverarbeitung

[6] Völksen,G.; Wehrum, P.: Transition to ADA for Super Computers; ADA-Europe Conference Edinburgh, May 1986; Cambridge University Press

[7] Peterson,W.P.: Vector Fortran for Numerical Problems on CRAY-1; Comm. of the ACM: November 1983, Vol. 26, No. 11

[8] Siemens: Vector Processor System VP100,VP200; Siemens 7-800 System Description

[9] Nagel,W.: Ein Preprocessor zur Unterstützung vektorisierender Compiler; Diplomarbeit am Institut für Allgemeine Elektrotechnik und DV-Systeme der Rheinisch-Westfälischen Technischen Hochschule Aachen

[10] Lamport,L.: The Parallel Execution of DO Loops; Comm. of the ACM: Feb. 1974, Vol. 17, No.2

[11] Kogge, P.M.: Parallel Solution of Recurrence Problems; IBM J.Res. Development, March 1974

[12] Lee,G.; Kruskal,C.; Kuck,D.: An Empirical Study of Automatic Restructuring of Nonnumerical Programs for Parallel Processors; IEEE Transactions on Computers Vol C-34, No10, Oct. 85

[13] Allen,J.R.: Kennedy,K.: A Parallel Programming Environment; IEEE Software, July 1985

[14] Teitelman, W.: Interlisp Reference Manual; Technical Report Xerox PARC

[15] Bobrow,D.; Stefik,M.: The LOOPS Manual;Technical Report Xerox PARC

[16] Steels, L.: Design Requirements for Knowledge Base Representation Systems; 8th German Workshop on Artifical Intelligence Wingst/Stade 1984; Springer Verlag

[17] E.Rich: Artifical Intelligence; Mc Graw-Hill Book Company

[18] Stefik,M.; Bobrow,D.G.; Mittal,S.; Conway,L.: Knowledge Programming in LOOPS: Report on an experimental course; Artifical Intelligence 4,3 (Fall 1983), pp. 3-14

[19] Fikes,R.; Kehler,T.: The Role of Frame-Based Representation in Reasoning; Comm. of the ACM: September 1985, Vol. 28, No. 9

[20] Sommer,M.: Vektorisierung von Algorithmen; Siemens Forschungs- und Entwicklungsberichte, Heft 5/86

HIERARCHICAL ARRAY PROCESSOR SYSTEM (HAP)

Shigeharu Momoi, Shigeo Shimada, Masamitsu Kobayashi, Tsutomu Ishikawa
NTT Electrical Communications Laboratories,
Musashino-shi, Tokyo, Japan.

Abstract

A MIMD type highly parallel processor comprising 4096 processing elements (PEs) with a nearest neighbor mesh connection is studied. The system realizes more than 100MB/S initial data transfer capability by multi-layering PE arrays, transmitting data from each upper layer PE to dependent lower layer PEs simultaneously. This configuration reduces the maximum internode distance and the inter-PE data transfer delay by relaying inter-PE data via upper layer PEs. High speed inter-PE synchronizations, for instance, synchronization of all PEs and local synchronization within any layer, have been realized (less than one microsecond for all PEs). A small scale system with 256 PEs is now under fabrication. Each PE consists of a 16-bit micro-processor, DRAMs and two newly developed types of LSIs. The size of a PE is 9cm x 6cm x 3cm.

1. Introduction

Research into parallel processors is being carried out on a worldwide scale [1]-[4], to meet the increasing needs for high performance computers. Especially approaches that use $10^3 \sim 10^4$ or more processing elements (PE) are receiving attention [5][6]. This is being stimulated by recent progress in LSI technology. In such a highly parallel processor, upgrading data transfer capability appears to hold the most promise for developing a practical machine, though, development of a parallel processing algorithm for each application is presupposed.

The system performance of a parallel processor is evaluated on the total time from initial data supply to processed data output. It is progressively limited by the data transfer time to and from all the PEs, rather than their processing time, as the number of PEs, and therewith the overall processing power, increases. Accordingly, the most important performance problem concerns data transfer to and from all PEs. The next most important problem is the data transfer delay between PEs. This is because the maximum internode distance (1 + the number of PEs used as a relay) increases with the number of PEs in any network-type parallel processor[7], and the data transfer delay increases accordingly.

Conventional research rarely touches on the aforementioned problems. To cope with them, we researched the architecture of a system that uses a nearest neighbor mesh (NNM) connection selected to be suitable for a highly parallel structure. From those studies, we have developed a highly parallel processor, the hierarchical array processor system (HAP). The HAP is a MIMD type processor with 4096 PEs designed for scientific calculation and speech, picture and other recognition processing applications. The previously mentioned problems are handled with a hierarhical PE array structure that utilizes its upper layer for data transfer.

2. System Architecture

In order to cope with the inherent data transfer problems, we adopted a hierarchial PE array structure similar to the EGPA [8], namely a large scale array with a small scale array above it. The number of PEs in the smaller array is approximately the square root of the number in the large one. By making use of the small array to accomplish data transfer to and from the large PE array and between PEs in the array, realization of a data transfer rate that matches the large array's processing power and reduction of the inter-PE data transfer delay are attempted. Hence, even if there is an increase in the number of PEs, a high performance system that is not limited by data transfer capability can be realized.

2.1 System Configuration

In the HAP, multiple users are assumed in order to make full use of the processing power of all the PEs. It is most properly used as the back-end processor for a number of user computers. Figure 1 shows the system configuration of the HAP. It consists of a PE array, a control PE array and a system management processor that are hierarchially coupled, and a data I/O mechanism.

1) Configurations and Roles of Each Block

The PE array consists of a maximum of 4096 (64 x 64) PEs, and it can execute parallel tasks. The control PE array (cPE array) has a maximum of 64 (8 x 8) control PEs (cPE). Together with the data I/O mechanism, it performs the input-output of data to the PE array. It also relays the inter-PE data transfers. Besides these, hierarchical parallel tasks can also be executed. A system management processor (SMP), using a general purpose computer, controls the whole system.

The data I/O mechanism performs the input-output of data to user computers and cPEs, and also data buffering.

2) Physical Connection among PEs

The PEs inside the PE array are physically NNM and torus-connected in consideration of the total data transfer capability / hardware quantity for connection between PEs and easy expansion to a physical structure. Therefore, each PE is connected with its four nearest neighbor (north, south, east and west) PEs. Although torus-connection slightly increases the inter-PE wiring length, it has the merit of reducing the maximum internode distance to half, compared to that of only an NNM, and it is used. The cPE array also has the same connection scheme as the PE array. In inter-layer connection, such as the connection between PEs and cPEs, called lower PEs and upper PEs, respectively, a bus is used to reduce the amount of connecting hardware. The connection between the cPE array and the SMP is the similar.

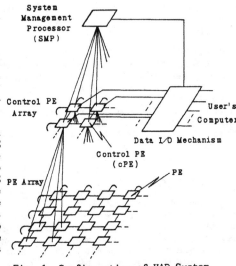

Fig. 1　Configuration of HAP System

2.2　Data Transfer

In the operation of a parallel processor, the program and the required initial data are supplied to the PEs in the first phase. Then, tasks expanded in parallel are executed in the PEs with necessary data transfer between the PEs. Finally, the processed data are collected by the user computer. That is, there are usually four types of data transfer in a parallel processor, namely, program load, initial data supply, inter-PE data transfer and result collecting. Since system preformance is evaluated by the total processing time, which includes these data transfers, improvement in its transfer capabilities increases the value of a parallel processor. In the HAP, rapid data transfer is realized through the following approach:

1) Program Load

Load distribution, instead of function distribution, is used to improve the performance in highly parallel processors. The programs for all PEs are basically identical, so they are broadcast to all cPEs and PEs by the SMP. Moreover, independent program load to each PE is also possible, in consideration of occasions when the programs are different for part of the PEs. These are realized through memory accesses (write operations) to the lower PEs or PE by the upper PE.

2) Initial Data Supply and Result Collecting

Since the data to be processed by each PE is different, it is transferred from the SMP in serial fashion. This is a potential bottleneck in system performance. Therefore, in the HAP, data elements are supplied in parallel through the cPEs. Specifically the initial data buffered in the data I/O mechanism is transfered simultaneously to all the cPEs, then each cPE transfers it to the PEs that are coupled to it. Result collecting is basically similar, except the direction of data flow is reversed. These data transfers are DMA transfers by the cPEs.

3) Inter-PE Data Transfer

A parallel processor with NNM connection is very suitable for processing problems where inter-PE data transfer occurs locally or regularly (e.g. solving Poisson's equation by the ODD-EVEN SOR method)[4][9]. However, it is not suitable for problems where transfers occur irregularly between PEs with large internode distances, e.g., logic simulation. This is because the maximum internode distarce is still as large as N, where N equals the number of PEs, in this kind of parallel processor even if torus connection is employed together with the NNM; therefore, much time is needed for these data transfers in such a problem.

To make it more suitable for the latter type of problem, a new data transfer mode, hierarchical relaying, utilizing the cPE (Table 1d) in addition to the usual modes (Tables 1a-1c) is provided to reduce the maximum internode distance and the inter-PE data transfer delay in the HAP. This mode is used for data transfers between PEs where the internode distance is greater than Nc, where Nc equals the number of cPEs. Hence, for the HAP, wherein N=4096 and Nc=64, shown Fig. 1, the maximum internode distance is 10. This is less than the 12 of a hyper cube type [7] parallel processor with an equal number of PEs. Moreover, this mode can be used together with array relaying (table 1b), thus helping to improve the transfer rate.

In the HAP, any of the several data transfer modes shown in Table 1 can be used, depending on the type of problem. These data transfers are realized through the repetition of memory accesses to neighboring PEs, memory accesses to the lower PEs by the upper PE or both.

Table 1 Inter-PE Data Transfer Method

Method	Summary	Maximum Internode Distance	Maximum Transfer Parallelization
a) Routing	Same directional transfer in PE Array repeated by all PE's	$2\sqrt{N}-2$	N
b) Array Relaying	Transfer relaying other PE's in PE Array	$\sqrt{N}$	N
c) SMP Relaying	Transfer relaying the SMP (cPEs are bypassed)	2	1
d) Hierarchical Relaying	Transfer from PE to cPE, relaying in cPE array, and then from cPE to PE	$\sqrt{\dfrac{N}{Nc}}+2$	Nc

N : Number of PEs , Nc : Number of cPEs

3. Practical Application (Solving the Diffrential Equation)

A procedure for a hierarchical structure to solve first order simultaneous equations having M unknowns using Gauss' elimination method is considered in the next section.

1) Algorithm

It was explained by Kung [10] that an algorithm concerned with NNM needs B squared number of PEs, where B is the half band width and each PE occupies one element of the coefficient matrix. In this algorithm, the initial data is a sub-matrix of the matrix for all PE arrays. On the other hand, we applied an algorithm more suitable for MIMD type parallelism in which every PE processes multiple elements of the matrix. The algorithm is actualized by sub-steps called forward-elimination and backward-substition.

Figure 2 shows an example of the assignment of initial data to PEs and an outline of the forward-elimination process. The difference between this the algorithm and Kung's is that the neighbouring elements of the matrix are scattered among neighbour PEs so that the amount of calculation is similar for each PE. The degree of paralellism obtained in our algorithm is equivalent to the number of PEs determined in the forward-elimination step, and square root number of PE on backward-substition.

As mentioned above, it is necessary for our algorithm to select the address number of the PE for each element of the matrix when the SMP supplies the initial data to the PE array. The period for supplying all data to the PE array (Ts), and the period for forward-elimination (Tc), which is the biggest term affecting the calculation period, are given by the dimensions of the matrix represented by M as follows:

$Ts=((2M+1-B)\cdot B\cdot W)/(S\cdot M)$. $Tc=2B\cdot M/(A\cdot N)$.

Here, B is the half band width of the matrix, W is the width of the tranfer data, S is the capabilty of data tranfer from the SMP to the PE array, N is the number of PEs, and A is the calculation capability of one PE.

As it is possible for Ts to be greater than the PE array calculation period if M is greater than $(W\cdot A\cdot N/S)$, we introduced a paralellized distributing method wherein the SMP serially supplies streamly the data for all cPEs. In this broadcast method, each cPE selects the PE addresses of dependent lower-layer PEs rather than having the SMP select them.

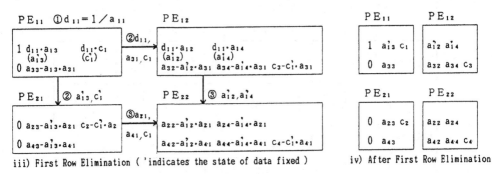

$$\begin{bmatrix} a_{11} & a_{12} & a_{13} & a_{14} \\ a_{21} & a_{22} & a_{23} & a_{24} \\ a_{31} & a_{32} & a_{33} & a_{34} \\ a_{41} & a_{42} & a_{43} & a_{44} \end{bmatrix} \begin{bmatrix} x_1 \\ x_2 \\ x_3 \\ x_4 \end{bmatrix} = \begin{bmatrix} c_1 \\ c_2 \\ c_3 \\ c_4 \end{bmatrix}$$

Coefficient Matrix   Constant Vector

i) Matrix Expresion of Differential Equation

ii) Initial Data Asignment

iii) First Row Elimination ('indicates the state of data fixed)

iv) After First Row Elimination

Fig. 2   Outline of Forward Elimination Process

2) Experimental Result

Figure 3 shows an example of the experimental results obtained by the SSI version prototype system comrising 16 PEs, and 4 cPEs. This system utilizes 8086 and 8087 micro-processors, and an 80KB memory. It is confirmed that the hierarchical structure is effective during initial data supply, because the period for supplying data was reduced to one-half compared with that of the no cPE structure.

Additionally, using our algorithm, calculation by the PE array can begin before the data supplying process is complete. Accordingly, the data supply and the PE calculation operations can overlap. The result is shown in Fig. 3. The data supplying and calculating processes are overlapped by about 70%. This reduces the data suppling period to only one-quarter of that of the no cPE structure.

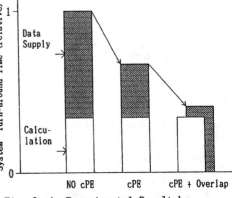

Fig. 3   An Experimental Result by Prototype Hierarchical Structure

4. Inter-PE Data Transfer Performance

In evaluating transfer performance, the average of data transfer delay, i.e., expected delay, is taken from the point of total system turn around time. The data transfer model is shown in Fig. 4. In this model:

1) All PEs are processing in syncronization.

2) The data transfer pattern and the amount of data to each PE is random.

Here, the transfer rate, K, corresponds to the ratio of the number of PEs which generate a data transfer, versus the total number of PEs in the array. Moreover, K can be regarded as approximatly equal the ratio of the number of machine cycles that the CPU processed versus the number of data transfers that occurred. The value of K is only a few percent on a MIMD type parallel processor.

Figure 5 shows the data transfer performance corresponding to the transfer modes mentioned in 2.2 for inter-PE data transfers. The cPE transitting mode is effective within a large range (0.003~0.1) by the number of inter-PE data transfers versus the total number of PEs in the array. Furthermore, in the region of the K less than 0.003, SMP relaying is applied to reduce the transfer delay, and int region of K nearly equal to 1, PE relaying is also applied. Accordingly, in practical application, these inter-PE tranfer modes are used properly in relationship to the existing problem. Hence, the HAP can be expected to have a higher system performance than current NNM models on a number of problems, including the aforementioned ones.

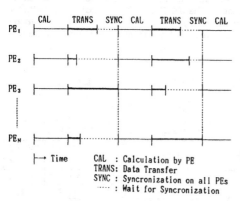

├──→ Time
CAL : Calculation by PE
TRANS: Data Transfer
SYNC : Syncronization on all PEs
····· : Wait for Syncronization

Fig. 4 Inter-PE Transfer Model

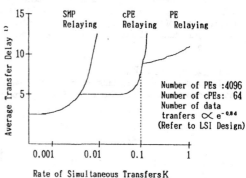

Rate of Simultaneous Transfers K

[1] one corresponds to the one nearest-neighbor PE transfer delay

Fig. 5 Theoretical Result of Inter-PE Transfer Delay

5. Implementation

In the following paragraphs, the practical implementation of the PEs, the control method for the PEs, and programming the HAP are considered.

5.1 PE Configuration and Function

The PEs must be miniaturized in order to realize a practical parallel processor utilizing 4096 PEs. Although it would be ideal to fabricate the whole PE on a single LSI chip, market-available micro-processors, RAMs and gate arrays are used for the following reasons:

i) It is difficult to fabricate the PE for a MIMD machine, in which large memory is essential, on one LSI chip, even with the present advanced LSI technology.

ii) Fabrication of a memory-less PE on one LSI chip does not have much effect on miniaturization.

iii) Existing compilers and other software can be utilized, when market-available microprocessors are used, without having to develop them.

Moreover, PEs and cPEs have the same configuration thus reducing the number of LSI types that need to be developed for the HAP.

Figure 6 shows the configuration and table 2 shows the specification of the PE.

1) Communication Control Unit (CCU)

The CCU performs the data transfers between PEs, cPEs and the SMP, and it provides the control that is needed for them. Packeted information is asynchronously time-divided and bidirectionally transfered. Every interface, namely, north, south, east, west, upper and lower, has four bus structured data lines. Moreover, taking application to various problems into consideration, all the interfaces between the PEs possess a bus-arbiter function so that any PE, cPE or SMP can operate as a master or as a slave. Additionally, the CCU also performs the control concerning the synchronization of PEs and the start, stop or other relevant control when they are used as a cPE.

The CCU is realized on a 1-chip gate array packaged in a pin grid array (PGA) case with 176 pins.

2) Memory Control Unit (MCU)

The MCU arbitrates the contention between memory accesses of the CPU and APU, and memory accesses due to data transfers, and it transmits data transfer requests and the several control

316

requests to the CCU. In addition, it provides the interface between the microprocessors and the memory, namely, the CPU and the APU and the MEM.
The MCU is realized by the same type of gate array as the CCU.

3) Memory (MEM)

Besides the storage of PE programs and data, the MEM is used for various types of data transfer. From the point of view of upgrading PE performance, the MEM should be configured as two independent memory banks to avoid contention between CPU and APU memory accesses and data transfer memory accesses. However, in the PE of a MIMD machine, there is a much smaller number of accesses on the latter type than the former (e.g. only a few percent in the ODD-EVEN SOR method). Accordingly, degradation of PE performance due to contention can be ignored and the MEM is configured as one bank. This makes miniaturization of the PE and expansion of the memory area used for data transfer possible.

4) Bus Interface (B.INT)

It is used for interfacing general busses such as the multi-bus, the VME bus and others. The cPE is connected to the data I/O mechanism through it.

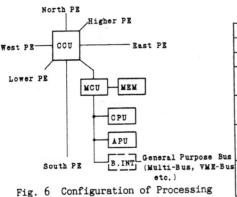

Fig. 6 Configuration of Processing Element (PE)

Table 2 PE Specification

		TYPE1	TYPE2	TYPE3
CPU		80186	80286	80386
APU		8087	80287	80387
MEM	256Kb Device	256KB	512KB	1MB
	1Mb Device	—	2MB	4MB
Performance of PE	General Operation	0.8 MIPS	1.6 MIPS	3.5 4 MIPS
	Floating Point Op.	0.04MFLOPS	0.08MFLOPS	0.45MFLOPS
Interface Between PEs	in Array and Inter-Layer	4bits x 4		and 4bits x 2
	I/O Bus	16bits x 1		32bits x 1
Data Transfer Rate	in Array and Inter-Layer	2 MB/S	2 MB/S	4 MB/S
	I/O Bus	2 MB/S	8 MB/S	3 2 MB/S

5.2 System performance

The peak system performance of the HAP, using an 80386 and an 80387 as the CPU and the APU respectively, is:
P = 4 MIPS x 4096 ≈ 16GIPS   (for fixed point arithmtic or general data processing).
P = 0.45 MFLOPS x 4096 ≈ 1.8 GFLOPS   (for floating point arithmetic).
For initial data supply, the HAP with 64 cPEs will realize more than 100MB/S (2MB/S for each cPE).

5.3 Control Method

It is necessary to have controls for starting, stopping, data transfer and synchronization of PEs in a parallel processor. These controls are each initiated by a single instruction to ease program development, and are realized in hardware to provide high speed execution in the HAP.

1) Fundamental Control Scheme

Table 3 shows the fundamental control scheme where all the control requests of the controlling PE (including the SMP and the cPE) are done in the form of a label access to variables. These become pseudo memory accesses during processor operation. Based on this access information, the control circuits recognize the control request and generate the necessary control information.
The control information is transfered to the controlled PE (or PEs) through a physical link such as data lines or control lines. The control lines are provided, only in case that it is impossible to utilize the data lines, for the reduction of interface lines. The controled PE uses this control information to realize the various control operations through the generation of interrupt vectors, interrupt operations and execution of the required interruption handling routines.

Table 3 Fundamental Control Scheme

Function Realized Control Level	(Controlling PE)		(Controlled PE)		
	Control Request	PE Start or Stop	Synchronization	Data Transfer* Control
Software	Label Access	Interruption Handling	Next Process	Interruption Handling
Processor Operation	Psuedo Memory Access	Interrupt Operation	Excution of Next Instruction	Interrupt Operation
Control Circuit	Decoding of Address or Data	Interrupt Detection	"Ready" Generation	Generation of Interrupt Vector
Physical Link	Data Lines	Control Lines	Data Lines	Control Lines

*Detection of data transfer request from the lower PE

2) Flexible Synchronization Mechanism

A flexible synchronization mechanism utilizing the hierarchial structure is realized in the HAP. Figure 7 shows the sync-mask-register specifying the return of the synchronous signal to its own layer or its propagation to the upper layers. The propagation of synchronous signals is controlled with this register, and the synchronization of all PEs, including the cPEs and the SMP, local synchronization of PEs that are connected to the cPE, and other functions are possible. This mechanism is expected to be highly useful processing, especially in some recognition in pattern matching, such as character recognition, speech recognition where hierarchical parallel algorithms are often used. Furthermore, the synchronization between neighboring PEs (or cPEs) can easily be realized through the setting and referring of shared variables such as flags and semaphores, since the couplings are via memory.

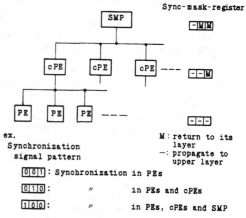

Sync-mask-register

ex.
Synchronization signal pattern

M: return to its layer
—: propagate to upper layer

|0|0|1| : Synchronization in PEs
|0|1|0| :   "   in PEs and cPEs
|1|0|0| :   "   in PEs, cPEs and SMP

Fig. 7 Flexible Syncronization Mechanism

5.4 Programming

A lot of research [11-13] has been done to develop a parallel processing oriented language that makes abstraction of parallelism in a problem easy. However, the present automatic abstraction of parallelism tends to be at low levels, such as the instruction level or the DO loop level. We believe that to achieve an effective improvement in performance, which is the primary goal of a parallel processor, attention must be paid to the higher level of parallelism in the MIND machine, but that the abstraction of these parallelisms still requires the involvement of man. Consequently, in the HAP, the programmer must be conscious of the parallel structure corresponding to the level of the program written.

1) Software Structure

Only writing the program for his computer by utilizing the library program, without being conscious of the HAP hardware, is required by the HAP user. This is in order to allow performance improvement and ease-of-use, and also in consideration of the utilization of the HAP as a back-end processor. That is, the user's job is expanded to parallel tasks and subroutined at the library level.

Specifically, a parallel processing algorithm suitable to the job is developed at the library level, and then the programs for executing the algorithm, divided into a PE program and an SMP program, are written. The main function of the PE program is the parallel alogrithm, and the SMP program is for program load, control of PEs and other functions. When assigning general processing to the cPE, aside from data transfer and synchronization, which are written into the control program, the writing of a cPE program is necessary too. However, this programming is easy since it can use the subroutined control programs, and the fundamental controls are described by single instructions, as mentioned in 5.2. The control programs, supplied together with the HAP hardware as a whole, are written to meet the various control requirements.

2) Program Development Environment

In consideration of library program development using a general computer (not parallel), procedure calls and function calls are used instead of macro instructions in this order to reduce dependency on the machine and language used. A simple operating system (OS) is stored in every PE for ease of software debugging using the HAP. The PE is assumed to have an I/O device, though I/O requests and operations are actually detected and performed by the SMP (or cPE). Hence symbolic debugging of a PE program is possible. For programming, high level languages such as PASCAL, C, Ada, FORTRAN and others can be used without any modification.

6. Conclusion

The configuration of a MIMD type highly parallel processor, the HAP, with 4096 PEs is discussed. The HAP appears capable of ensuring practical data transfer capability that matches the processing capability of its PEs, which is considered the main problem in high parallelization.

The data transfer problem is solved by adopting a hierarchial PE array structure, namely, a large scale array with a small scale array above it, and utilizing the latter to transfer data. Specifically, the small PE array is used to parallel the data transfer to and from the large PE array and to reduce the inter-PE data transfer delay by relaying the data. With these approaches, the HAP is expected to attain a system performance near a peak value of 16 GIPS and 1.8 GFLOPS over a broad range of applications when using 80386 and 80387 processors.

PE miniaturization is also a necessary condition for such a high parallelization. This is handled by using Intel's microprocessor family, DRAMs and newly developed gate arrays in the HAP, after taking development time and economic factors into consideration.

A small scale LSI version of the HAP with 256 PEs and 16 cPEs is under fabrication. Each PE consists of 13 LSIs, namely 80186 and 8087 type processors, 9 DRAMs (256kbits/chip) and 2 gate arrays. The PE's dimensions are 9cm x 6cm x 3cm. Testing of its capability for general scientific calculation and various types of recognition together with an overall evaluation is scheduled.

References

[1] Charles L. Seitz "The Cosmic Cube" Commun. ACM 1 (January 1985), 22-33

[2] H. F. Jordan "Performance Measurements on HEP - A Pipelined MIMD Computer" The 10th Annual Symp. on Computer Architecture, (1983), 207-212

[3] S. J. Stolfo and D. P. Miranker "DADO" A Parallel Processor for Expert Systems" 1984 Int. Conf. Parallel Processing, (August 1984), 74-82

[4] T. Hoshino, T. Kawai, T. Shirakawa, K. Higashino, A. Yamaoka, H. Ito, T. Sato and K. Sawada "PACS: A Parallel Microprocessor Array for Scientific Caluculations" ACM Trans. Computer System Vol. 1, No. 3, (August 1983), 195-221

[5] D. Gajski, D. Kuck., D. Lawrie and A. Sameh "Cedar - A Large Scale Multiprocessor" 1983 Int. Conf. Parallel Processing, (August 1983), 524-529

[6] L. Snyder "Introduction to the Configurable, Highly Parallel Computer" Computer, (January 1982), 47-56

[7] L. D. Writtie, "Communication Structures for Large Networks of Microcomputers" IEEE Trans. Computer, vol. C-30, NO.4, (April 1981), 264-273

[8] M. Vajteršie "Parallel Poisson and Biharmonic Solvers Implemented on the EGPA Multiprocessor" 1982 Int. Conf. Parallel Processing (August 1982), 72-81

[9] T. Hoshino, T. Kamimura, T. Kageyama, K. Takenouchi and H. Abe "Highly Parallel Processor Array "PAX" for Wide Scientific Applications" 1983 Int. Conf. Parallel Processing, (August 1983), 95-105

[10] H. T. Kung, "Why Systolic Architective ?" Computer, Vol 15, No.1, (January 1978), 47-64

[11] C. A. R. Hoare "Communicating Sequential Processes" Commun. ACM 8 (August 1978), 666-677

[12] P. B. Hansen "Distributed Processes: A Concurrent Programming Concept" Commun. ACM/1 (November 1978), 934-941

[13] E. Shapiro "System Programming in Concurrent PROLOG" ACM Symp. on principles of Programming Languages, (January 1984), 93-105

OCSAMO

A SYSTOLIC ARRAY FOR MATRIX OPERATIONS

A. A. Abdel Kader *

Fachbereich Informatik

Universität Hamburg

D-2000 Hamburg 13

Abstract

A new orthogonally connected systolic array for matrix operations called **OCSAMO** is proposed in this paper. This array is a two dimensional orthogonally connected array. It consists of interconnected simple and identical processors. This makes it suitable for VLSI implementation.

The OCSAMO is able to decompose a matrix into its upper and lower triangular matrices and to solve a system of linear equations . These operations are done in shorter time compared with other systolic arrays doing the same functions. The elements of the matrix to be processed can be fetched from the outside of the array which is the case in all other known systolic arrays. They can also be preloaded in the corresponding processing elements. Further advantages of the OCSAMO and comparison with other systolic arrays are discussed in the paper.

1- Introduction

The achievement of higher computing speed is one of the main requirements in some real time computations. Unfortunately, the architectures of conventional computers suffer from some difficulties limiting their speed [2],[5]. Concurrency makes it possible,

---

* A. A. Abdel Kader is now with Faculty of Engineering, Port Said, Egypt

using a large amount of hardware, to increase the computing speed.

In designing computing devices for practical applications, one is faced not only with the high throughput requirement but also with the need for low cost hardware implementation of the device.

Nowadays the technology of Very Large Scale Integration (VLSI) allows the use of a large amount of hardware with very low cost, reduced power consumption and physical size [3],[4]. On the other hand, the VLSI technology has its problem, which put constraints on its use. To avoid these constraints [1], the systolic arrays are suggested to achieve concurrency using this new technology.

However, the concurrency has been applied mostly to those problems that are well defined or where use of partitioning is evident. This limits the computational flexibility of all concurrent computers to a specified class (wide or narrow) of problems. One important class of these problems is the solution of a system of linear equations.

Selection of many scientific and engineering problems requires the ability to solve various systems of linear equations. This means that a special purpose device capable to solve such systems very fast would have enormously many applications. Such a device would be even more useful if it would be able to perform some other matrix calculations.

This paper considers the problem of designing a homogeneous systolic array for some matrix operations including solving a system of linear equations. The LU decomposition technique will be used in solving a system of linear equations. One of the most important reasons for its use is due to the inherent parallelism in the nature of the problem. The recurrence evaluation of the L and U matrices is given in section 2, while the systolic array performing this operation is described in section 3. The use of the array in solving a system of linear equation is explained in section 4.. Finally, the array is analysed in section 5 to make a comparison between it and other known arrays.

2- Recurrence evaluation of the L and U matrices

The problem of factoring a square matrix A_{n*n} into a product of lower and upper triangular matrices L_{n*n} and U_{n*n} respectively is called the LU decomposition of A.

Fig.(1) illustrates the LU decomposition of a matrix A.

$$
\begin{bmatrix}
a_{11} & a_{12}\cdots & a_{1j}\cdots & a_{1n} \\
a_{21} & a_{22}\cdots & a_{2j}\cdots & a_{2n} \\
\hline
a_{i1} & a_{i2}\cdots & a_{ij}\cdots & a_{in} \\
\hline
a_{n1} & a_{n2} & a_{nj}\cdots & a_{nn}
\end{bmatrix}
=
\begin{bmatrix}
1 & 0 & \cdots 0 & 0 \\
l_{21} & 1 & \cdots 0 & 0 \\
\hline
l_{i1} & & l_{ik} & 0 \\
\hline
l_{n1} & & & 1
\end{bmatrix}
*
\begin{bmatrix}
u_{11} & u_{12}\cdots & u_{1j}\cdots & u_{1n} \\
0 & u_{22}\cdots & u_{2j}\cdots & u_{2n} \\
\hline
0 & & u_{kj}\cdots & u_{kn} \\
\hline
0 & & & u_{nn}
\end{bmatrix}
$$

Fig.(1)

LU decomposition of a square matrix A

From fig.(1), it is seen that

$$a_{ij} = \sum_{k=1}^{\min(i,j)} l_{ik} * u_{kj} \qquad (1)$$

Depending on the values of i and j there are two different cases:-

case 1

IF i ≤ j then

$$a_{ij} = \sum_{k=1}^{i} l_{ik} * u_{kj}$$

which implies

$$a_{ij} = l_{ii} * u_{ij} + \sum_{k=1}^{i-1} l_{ik} * u_{kj}$$

and because of $l_{ii} = 1$

$$u_{ij} = a_{ij} - \sum_{k=1}^{i-1} l_{ik} * u_{kj} \qquad (2)$$

case 2

IF i > j then

$$a_{ij} = \sum_{k=1}^{j} l_{ik} * u_{kj}$$

and hence

$$l_{ij} = (a_{ij} - \sum_{k=1}^{j-1} l_{ik} * u_{kj}) / u_{jj} \qquad (3)$$

Assume

$$a_{ij}^{(0)} = a_{ij} \qquad\qquad (4.1)$$

then set

$$a_{ij}^{(k)} = a_{ij}^{(k-1)} - l_{ik} * u_{kj} \qquad (4.2)$$

From equation (2) we get

$$u_{ij} = a_{ij}^{(i-1)} \qquad\qquad \text{for } i \le j \quad (5.1)$$

and from (3)

$$l_{ij} = a_{ij}^{(j-1)} / u_{jj} \qquad \text{for } i > j \quad (5.2)$$

The triangular matrices L and U can be evaluated from fig. (1) and the equations (4) and (5) according to the following recurrences:-

$$a_{ij}^{(0)} = a_{ij} \qquad\qquad (6.1)$$

$$a_{ij}^{(k)} = a_{ij}^{(k-1)} - l_{ik} * u_{kj} \qquad (6.2)$$

$$l_{ij} = \begin{cases} 0 & \text{if } i < j \\ 1 & \text{if } i = j \quad (6.3) \\ a_{ij}^{(j-1)} / u_{jj} & \text{if } i > j \end{cases}$$

$$u_{ij} = \begin{cases} 0 & \text{if } i > j \\ & \qquad\qquad (6.4) \\ a_{ij}^{(i-1)} & \text{if } i \le j \end{cases}$$

3- LU decomposition of a matrix on homogeneous orthogonally connected systolic array

3-1 The basic idea

In order to compute

1- u_{ij}: equation 2 implies that one needs $l_{i1}, \dots l_{i(i-2)}, l_{i(i-1)}$ and $u_{1j}, \dots u_{(i-2)j}, u_{(i-1)j}$

2- l_{ij}: equation 3 implies that one needs $l_{i1}, l_{i(j-2)}, l_{i(j-1)}$ and $u_{1j}, \dots u_{(j-1)j}, u_{jj}$.

This suggests that to compute all u- and l- values, an array of processors P_{ij} is used, where $1 \leq i \leq n$, $1 \leq j \leq n$. Processor P_{ij} computes u_{ij} if $i \leq j$ or l_{ij} if $i > j$. It sends the computed values to all processors which need them in such a way (pipelining u_{ij} and l_{ij}) that all values come to all these processors exactly when needed.

The array consists of n^2 processors. Each of them has two input registers and two output registers. The output registers are the input to its neighbour processors. It needs also a memory (an internal register) to store the computed value at any step, which is needed at the next step (eq.(6.2)). Each processor is able to compute the inner product (eq. (6.3) and eq. (6.4)) as well as the division (eq. (6.3)).

3-2 Description of the array

If the LU decomposition of a square matrix A of dimension n*n can be computed using Gaussian elimination without pivoting, then

1- It can be computed on a homogeneous rectangular array of processors n^2 with area $F = O(n^2)$ and the total processing time $T = 3n - 2$.

2- The topology and the distribution of the stored elements of the matrix processor are shown in fig.(2).

3- The control function (ß1 and ß2) of the array are supplied to the boundary. The arrangement of the control function with respect to time is shown in fig.(2).

4- The function of the processor is shown in fig.(3), where S is its internal state and S′ is its next state.

In the present array ß1 and ß2 are fed to the left and upper boundaries of the array in the sequence shown in fig.(2). Each processor is preloaded with the corresponding element of the matrix A (fig.(2)). The array operates synchronously in time units (T) which will be called steps. Each processor computes the inner product of its input and the content of its internal register. It stores the new computed value in its internal register and put s out its input until a certain step depending on its location in the array. At this step, the output of the processor is either its internal content (S) or S/Y. The combinations of ß1 and ß2 determine the different operations of the processor.

Four steps of the LU decomposition of A performed by this new array are shown in fig.(4).

324

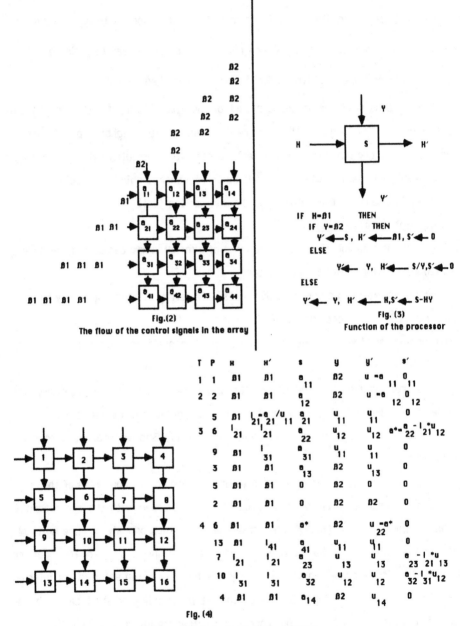

Fig.(2)
The flow of the control signals in the array

IF H=ß1 THEN
  IF Y=ß2 THEN
    Y' ← S , H' ← ß1, S' ← 0
  ELSE
    Y' ← Y, H' ← S/Y, S' ← 0
ELSE
  Y' ← Y, H' ← H, S' ← S-HY

Fig. (3)
Function of the processor

T	P	H	H'	s	y	y'	s'
1	1	ß1	ß1	a_{11}	ß2	$u_{11}=a_{11}$	0_{11}
2	2	ß1	ß1	a_{12}	ß2	$u_{12}=a_{12}$	0_{12}
	5	ß1	$l_{21}=a_{21}/u_{11}$	a_{21}	u_{11}	u_{11}	0
3	6	l_{21}	l_{21}	a_{22}	u_{12}	u_{12}	$a^*=a_{22}-l_{21}^*u_{12}$
	9	ß1	l_{31}	a_{31}	u_{11}	u_{11}	0
	3	ß1	ß1	a_{13}	ß2	u_{13}	0
	5	ß1	ß1	0	ß2	0	0
	2	ß1	ß1	0	ß2	ß2	0
4	6	ß1	ß1	a^*	ß2	$u_{22}=a^*$	0
	13	ß1	l_{41}	a_{41}	u_{11}	l_{41}	0
	7	l_{21}	l_{21}	a_{23}	u_{13}	u_{13}	$a_{23}-l_{21}^*u_{13}$
	10	l_{31}	l_{31}	a_{32}	u_{12}	u_{12}	$a_{32}-l_{31}^*u_{12}$
	4	ß1	ß1	a_{14}	ß2	u_{14}	0

Fig. (4)

Some steps in the LU decomposition using OCSAMO

4- Solution of system of linear equations

Assume the system equation is

$$A*x = d \qquad\qquad (7.1)$$

Decomposing A into its L and U matrices gives

$$L*U*x = d$$

$$L*v = d \qquad\qquad (7.2)$$

Equations (7.1) and (7.2) can be written as

$$\begin{bmatrix} L & 01 \\ 02 & 1 \end{bmatrix} * \begin{bmatrix} U & v \\ 02 & \pounds \end{bmatrix} = \begin{bmatrix} A & d \\ 02 & \pounds \end{bmatrix} \qquad\qquad (7.3)$$

or

$$L1 \qquad * \qquad U1 \qquad = \qquad A1$$

where,

01 is a column, whose elements are zero

, 02 is a row, whose elements are zero

and £ is selected to maintain A1 suitable for LU decomposition. In this case, v is the first n outputs of the column n+1 of the array employed by A1. £ is not needed in the computation until this moment. Therefore the estimation of its value is not required.

From this fact, it can be said that using only one column of n processors, one can solve a lower triangular system of equations $Lv = d$ in a time $T = [\, 3(n+1) - 2\,] - 1 - n = 2n - 1$

where,

$3(n+1) - 2$ is the time required to process A1

, 1   is the time required to process £

and n   is the time spent from the beginning of processing in A untill the beginning of processing in d column.

Some steps during the solution of lower triangular system $Lv=d$ are shown in fig.(5). From this figure, it is shown that the solution does not depend on the value of l_{ii}. Therefore the upper triangular system $U*x=v$, which can be written as lower triangular system, can be solved using a similar column. Because the solution of the lower triangular system begins after $T=n$ (see fig.(4) and fig.(5)), the total time required to solve a system of linear equations is $T = n + (2n-1) + (2n-1) = 5n-2$

The processing of u-values begins after 3n-1 units of time, while all u-values are available after 3n-2 units of time. This allows the transformation of the U matrix to the lower triangular form.

5- Analysis of the OCSAMO

The systolic arrays introduced by Kung and Leiserson [2] performs the LU decomposition of a square matrix of n dimension in 4n units of time and solve a lower triangular system in 3n units of time. The unit of time is the time required for division allowing all processors to give their output at the same time.

The OCSAMO can be used to decompose a square matrix of dimension n in 3n-2 units of time and solve a lower triangular system in 2n-1 units of time. The time needed for division is the unit of time, which ensure that the OCSAMO is faster than the other system. Moreover, the OCSAMO is homogeneous array and all processors have the same orientation (no rotation as in [2]). This helps to use one type (but a few number) of chips for larger matrix dimension.

The OCSAMO is suitable for practical applications, in which the elements of the system matrix A is constant. However, the elements of A, if they are variable can be fetched from the outside of the array as shown in fig.(6). This does not need an extra time because the fetching is done parallel to the processing of the matrix.

The new systolic array uses only one type of processor. Each one of them has 4 I/O terminals and three registers, one of them is internal.

Conclusion

The OCSAMO is suitable to multiply two matrices due to its capability to do the inner product computation. The processing element of the OCSAMO is designed and simulated. It is now in the implementation phase using gate array technique.

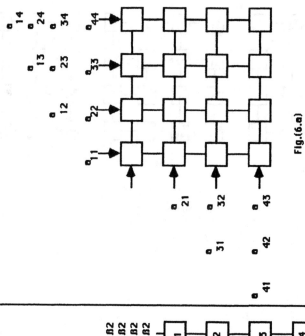

Fig.(6.a)

The sequence of input data to the OCSAMO
in the case of regular input data flow

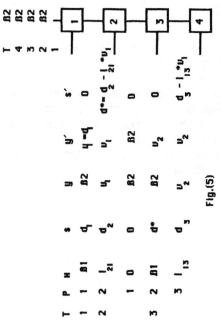

Fig.(5)

Some steps in solving lower triangular system using OCSAMO

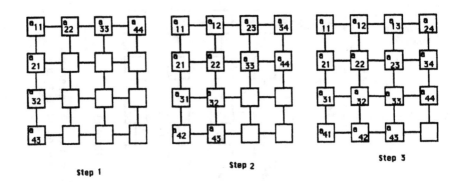

Step 1

Step 2

Step 3

Fig.(6.b)

Data March in the OCSAMO

References

1-H. T. Kung, "Why Systolic Architectures",Computer vol.15,1982, pp.37-46
2-C. A. Mead and L. A. Conway, "Introduction to VLSI Systems", Readings, MA:
Addison-Wesley,1980
3-D. I. Moldovan, "On the Anaysis and Synthesis of VLSI algorithms", IEEE
Trans. on Comp. vol. c-31,1982,pp.1121-1125
4-D. I. Moldovan, "On the Design of Algorithms for VLSI Systolic Arrays", Proceedings of
IEEE vol. 71,1983, pp. 113-120
5- V. Zakharov, "Parallelism and Array Processing", IEEE Trans. on Comp. vol.
c-33,1984, pp.45-78

A GENERAL APPROACH TO SORTING ON 3-DIMENSIONALLY MESH–CONNECTED ARRAYS

Manfred Kunde[*]
Institut für Informatik
Technische Universität München
Arcisstr. 21
D–8000 München 2, W. Germany

Abstract

A general method for generating 3–dimensional sorting algorithms by using 2–dimensional algorithms is presented. The main advantage is that from a large class of sorting algorithms suitable for mesh-connected rectangles of processors we efficiently obtain sorting algorithms suitable for 3–dimensional meshes. It is shown that by using the s^2–way merge sort of Thompson and Kung sorting n^3 elements can be performed on an $n \times n \times n$ cube with $12n + 0(n^{2/3} \log n)$ data interchange steps. Further improvements lead to an algorithm for an $n/2 \times n \times 2n$ mesh sorting n^3 items within $10.5n + O (n^{2/3}\log n)$ interchange steps. By a generalization of the method to r–dimensional cubes one can obtain algorithms sorting n^r elements with $0(r^3 n)$ interchange steps.

1. Introduction

The design and analysis of fast parallel algorithms has become more and more important by the advancements of VLSI-technology. Especially for VLSI-architectures, where a regular net of simple processing cells and local communication between these cells are required [FK,KL] , several parallel algorithms for fundamental problems as matrix arithmetic, signal and image processing, sorting and searching etc. have been proposed [U].

In this paper a general method for generating 3–dimensional sorting algorithms by using 2–dimensional algorithms is presented. The advantage compared with former research [TK,NS] is that from a large class of sorting algorithms suitable for mesh-connected rectangles of processors [KH,NS,LSSS,SI,TK] we efficiently obtain sorting algorithms suitable for 3–dimensional meshes.

[*]This work was partially done at the Institut für Informatik, University of Kiel, and partially supported by the Siemens AG, München.

A mesh–connected $n_1 \times n_2 \times \ldots \times n_r$ array of processors is a set of $N = n_1 n_2 \ldots n_r$ identical processors where each processor $P = (p_1,\ldots,p_r)$, $1 \leq p_i \leq n_i$, is directly interconnected to all its nearest neighbours only. A processor $Q = (q_1,\ldots,q_r)$ is called a nearest neighbour of P if and only if the distance fulfills $d(P,Q) = \sum_{i=1}^{r} | p_i - q_i | = 1$. For example, for $r = 2$, that is in the plane, every processor has at most 4 nearest neighbours. Note that no "wrap–around" connections are allowed. At each time step each processor can only communicate with one of its nearest neighbours. That is, at most $N/2$ communications can simultaneously be performed. For the sorting problem we assume that N elements from a linearly ordered set are loaded in the N processors, each receiving exactly one element. The processors are thought to be indexed by a certain one–to–one mapping from $\{1,\ldots,n_1\} \times \ldots \times \{1,\ldots,n_r\}$ onto $\{1,\ldots,N\}$. With respect to this function the sorting problem is to move the i-th smallest element to the processor indexed by i for all $i = 1, \ldots, N$.

In the following for the 3–dimensional case we assume an index function f with $f(p_1,p_2,p_3)$ $= n_1 n_2 (p_3 - 1) + g(p_1,p_2)$, where g is either a pure or a snake–like or a shuffled row–major indexing for an $n_1 \times n_2$ mesh [TK] (Figure 1). If g is a (pure) row–major index function, then one might call f a plane–major–row–major indexing [S] (Figure 2).

Clearly, the sorting problem can be solved by a sequence of comparison and interchange steps. It is well–known that data movement is a significant performance measure for sorting algorithms on mesh–connected architectures. Therefore, in this paper we concentrate on the number of data interchange steps which may be caused by a comparison or not. Note that one interchange step is equivalent to two routings in [TK].

For the 3–dimensional case sorting algorithms for an $n \times n \times n$ mesh–connected cube have already been proposed in [TK,NS]. Both algorithms asymptotically need 15n interchange steps whereas Schimmler [S] recently developed a simpler sorting algorithm on a cube with 19n interchange steps. All the algorithms are generalizations of special 2–dimensional sorting algorithms and use recursion steps where eight presorted $n/2 \times n/2 \times n/2$ cubes are merged to one sorted $n \times n \times n$ array.

In the second section of this paper we present a method (called 3BY2) for obtaining sorting algorithms on arbitrary $a \times b \times c$ arrays based on arbitrary sorting algorithms for mesh–connected rectangles with row–major indexing. For a 2–dimensional mesh–connected $u \times v$ rectangle let SORT(u,v) denote the number of interchange steps needed by the underlying sorting algorithm SORT. If for an $a \times b \times c$ mesh 3D–SORT(a,b,c) denotes the corresponding number for that 3–dimensional algorithm which have been obtained by an application of the mehtod 3BY2 to algorithm SORT, then it is shown that

$$3D\text{–}SORT(a,b,c) \leq SORT(a,c) + SORT(b,c) + 2 \cdot SORT(a,b) + 2 .$$

<u>Figure 1</u>   4 x 3 mesh

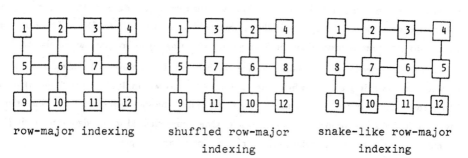

row-major indexing   shuffled row-major   snake-like row-major
                                indexing   indexing

<u>Figure 2</u>

3 x 3 x 3 mesh-connected
cube

plane-major-row-major
indexing

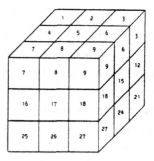

<u>Figure 3</u>   a x b x c mesh-connected array

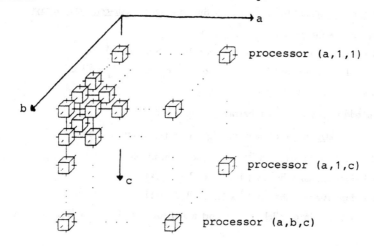

Hence, by using the s^2-way merge sort of Thompson and Kung [KT] a sorting algorithm for an n x n x n cube, n a power of 2, can be constructed needing only $12n + O(n^{2/3}\log n)$ interchange steps, which is asymptotically optimal within a factor of 2.4 [Ku]. Therefore, for large n this algorithm is faster than the 3-dimensional sorting algorithms mentioned above.

In the third section it is shown how the method can be improved. An algorithm for an n/2 x n x 2n mesh is presented which one sorts n^3 elements within $10.5n + O(n^{2/3}\log n)$ interchange steps. Furthermore, it is indicated how to generalize the sorting method for r-dimensional meshes, r≥4. This can be done in several ways. One approach lead to an algorithm sorting n^r elements on an r-dimensional cube within $O(r^{2.71}n)$ interchange steps.

2. A general 3-dimensional sorting method

For the rest of the paper let a, b and c denote the side lengths of an arbitrarily given a x b x c mesh-connected array (Figure 3) . For the beginning let us assume that the N = abc elements have to be sorted with respect to an index function f defined by $f(i,j,k) = i + a(j - 1) + ab(k - 1)$ for all i = 1,...,a, j = 1,...,b, and k = 1,...,c. As an illustration imagine a container where the heavy (large) elements have to sink to the bottom, while the light (small) ones must go up to the top. Various 2-dimensional u x v subarrays, u,v ∈ {a,b,c}, are used in the below given 3-dimensional sorting method. They are thought to be indexed by functions $g_{u,v}$ defined by $g_{u,v}(i,j) = i + u(j - 1)$, i = 1,...,u , j = 1,...,v , which is equivalent to (pure) row-major indexing. However, following the later given proof of correctness it is easily seen that the proposed method also works for snake-like and shuffled row-major index functions. Furthermore, let us say that a u x v array is sorted in reversed order with respect to an index function g iff it is sorted with respect to the reversed index function $\overline{g}$ given by $\overline{g}(i,j) = uv + 1 - g(i,j)$.

3BY2 - a general method for sorting on 3-dimensionally mesh-connected arrays:

For a positive integer x let $I_x = \{1,...,x\}$.

1. For all i = 1,...,a in parallel :   sort b x c subarray {i} x I_b x I_c

2. For all j = 1,...,b in parallel :   sort a x c subarray I_a x {j} x I_c

3. For all k = 1,...,c in parallel :

   if k is odd then sort a x b subarray I_a x I_b x {k}

   else sort a x b subarray I_a x I_b x {k} in reversed order

4. For all i = 1,...,a , j = 1,...,b , k = 1,..., ⌊c/2⌋ in parallel :

   1. sort 1-dimensional subarray {i} x {j} x {2k - 1,2k}

   2. sort 1-dimensional subarray {i} x {j} x {2k,2k + 1}

5. For all k = 1,...,c in parallel: sort a x b subarray I_a x I_b x {k}.

Before going in details of the proof of correctness we should mention that in step 4 the greater elements have to be sorted in those processors with greater third components. Moreover, if c is an even integer, then neglect the step 4.2 for the non−existent subarrays $\{i\} \times \{j\} \times \{c, c + 1\}$.

In the following the proof for the validity of 3BY2 will be done by extensive use of the zero−one principle [Kn]. That is, instead of proving that the generated algorithms sort arbitrary initial loadings of arbitrary integers it is sufficient to show that all initial loadings only consisting of zeros and ones are sorted correctly.

Let cont_t (i,j,k) , $1 \leq i \leq a$, $1 \leq j \leq b$, $1 \leq k \leq c$, denote the contents of processor (i,j,k) at time t. At the starting time let cont_0 be an arbitrary function from $I_a \times I_b \times I_c$ into $\{0, 1\}$. For every column of processors $\{i\} \times \{j\} \times I_c$ let $m_t(i,j)$ denote the number of ones contained in the corresponding column. That is, $m_t(i,j) = \text{cont}_t(i,j,1) + \ldots + \text{cont}_t(i,j,c)$. (In the following the time index t is omitted, since it is clear which time point is meant in each case.) Then we can observe the following situations:

Situation after step 1 (Figure 4a):

For all $i = 1,\ldots,a$ let $\min(i) = \min \{ m(i,j) \mid 1 \leq j \leq b \}$. Since all the subarrays $\{i\} \times I_b \times I_c$ are sorted, the ones must have sunk to the bottom in each b x c slice. Hence for all $j = 1,\ldots,b$ we get $\min(i) \leq m(i,j) \leq \min (i) + 1$. Note that at this moment the number of ones in each subarray $I_a \times \{j\} \times I_c$, $1 \leq j \leq b$, is $\text{sum}(j) = m(1,j) + \ldots + m(a,j)$. Hence

$$(1) \quad x = \sum_{i=1}^{a} \min(i) \leq \text{sum}(j) \leq \sum_{i=1}^{a} \min(i) + a = x + a \quad \text{for all } j = 1,\ldots,b .$$

Situation after step 2 (Figure 4b):

Since for all $j = 1,\ldots,b$ the corresponding subarrays $I_a \times \{j\} \times I_c$ are sorted and contain sum(j) ones, only subrow $I_a \times \{j\} \times \{c - \lfloor \text{sum}(j)/a \rfloor \}$ can obtain both zeros and ones. By (1) we know that $\lfloor x/a \rfloor \leq \lfloor \text{sum}(j)/a \rfloor \leq \lfloor x/a \rfloor + 1$ for all $j = 1,\ldots,b$. Therefore, at most two unsorted a x b planes have remained, namely $I_a \times I_b \times \{c - \lfloor x/a \rfloor - 1\}$ and $I_a \times I_b \times \{c - \lfloor x/a \rfloor \}$.

Situation after step 3 (Figure 4c):

Since $\lfloor x/a \rfloor$ and $\lfloor x/a \rfloor + 1$ differ by 1, one of the critical a x b planes is sorted with respect to the index function g, while the other is sorted in reversed order. Let y be the number of ones in the upper critical plane and z be the corresponding number of the lower one. Without loss of generality we assume that the upper plane is sorted in reversed order, that is, the ones are contained in the processors indexed by 1 to y with respect to the original, not reversed index function g. Then in the lower plane the zeros are contained in the processors 1 to ab − z.

Situation after step 4 (Figure 4d):

(a)

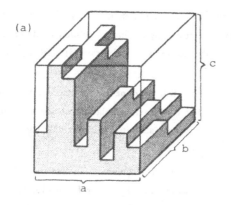

b × c slices sorted

(b)

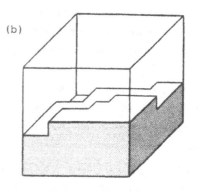

a × c slices sorted

(c)

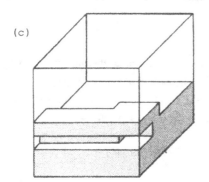

two critical a × b planes
sorted in opposite directions

(d)

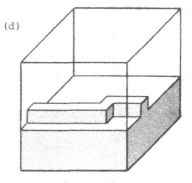

one critical a × b plane

(e)

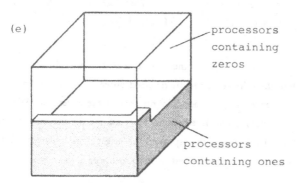

processors
containing
zeros

processors
containing ones

a × b × c mesh sorted

If $y + z \geq ab$, then $y \geq ab - z$. In this case all of the zeros of the lower plane have inter-changed their position with the corresponding ones from the upper plane. Therefore, only the upper plane possibly has remained unsorted. If $y + z < ab$, then all the ones of the upper plane have sunk to the lower plane, meaning that only the lower plane is left unsorted. Thus at most a single a x b plane still might contain both zeros and ones.

Situation after step 5 (Figure 4e):

The total a x b x c mesh is sorted.

Hence we have shown the following theorem:

Theorem 1

For all 2-dimensional sorting algorithms SORT the method 3BY2 generates 3-dimensional algorithms 3D-SORT sorting abc elements on a mesh-connected a x b x c array with

3D-SORT(a,b,c) = SORT(a,c) + SORT(b,c) + 2 · SORT(a,b) + 2 interchange steps.

One of the main advantages of the method 3BY2 is that in contrast to former results one can use arbitrary 2-dimensional sorting algorithms in order to obtain 3-dimensional algorithms. Although the algorithms generated by 3BY2 might be slower than the special algorithms in [TK,NS,S], if the same 2-dimensional method is taken as a basis, a very good result can be obtained by an application of 3BY2 to the until now not generalized s^2-way merge sort [TK].

Theorem 2

Sorting on a mesh-connected n x n x n cube, n a power of 2, can be done with $12n + 0(n^{2/3}\log n)$ intergchange steps, which is asymptotically optimal within a factor of 2.4.

Proof: An n x n array can be sorted with $3n + 0(n^{2/3}\log n)$ interchanges by the s^2-way merge sort [TK]. Hence the first part of our claim is proven by theorem 1. In [Ku] it is shown that sorting on an n x n x n mesh asymptotically needs at least 5n interchange steps, whereby the second part is shown.

3. Extensions

Looked at more closely one can detect that the correctness proof of 3BY2 does not really use the fact that in step 1 and 2 the corresponding subarrays are totally sorted. In the following we will utilize this observation for an improvement of our method. Let us say that an algorithm mixsorts uv elements on a u x v mesh iff it transforms all initial zero-one loadings into final loadings where the number of zeros (ones) in all columns $\{i\} \times I_v$ and $\{k\} \times I_v$, $1 \leq i, k \leq u$, differ from each other at most by 1. Furthermore, an algorithm presorts the mesh iff it transforms an arbitrary initial zero-one loading into a presorted loading. A zero-one loading is presorted iff there is a j, $1 \leq j \leq v$, such that $I_u \times \{1,...,j-1\}$ only contains zeros, $I_u \times \{j+1,...,v\}$ only contains ones, whereas in $I_u \times \{j\}$ you may find both zeros and ones.

Improved 3BY2 - method:

1. For all $i = 1,...,a$ in parallel: mixsort $\{i\} \times I_b \times I_c$

2. For all $j = 1,...,b$ in parallel: presort $I_a \times \{j\} \times I_c$

Step 3. to 5. as before.

Proving this method to be correct can be done in the same way as for the proof of the original 3BY2.

Theorem 3

Sorting n^3 elements on an $n \times n/2 \times 2n$ mesh, n a power of 2, can be done with $10.5n + O(n^{2/3}\log n)$ interchange steps, which is asymptotically optimal within a factor of 2.1.

Sketch of a proof: For the first step of the improved 3BY2 divide the $n/2 \times 2n$ subarrays into upper and lower $n/2 \times n$ subarrays and sort these half subarrays. Then sort all rows in the upper half to the right and all rows in the lower half to the left. This kind of mixsorting can be done with the help of the generalized s^2-way merge sort [TK] and costs asymptotically $2.5n$ interchanges. Step 2. to 5. can also be performed with suitable applications of the generalized s^2-way merge sort and need $8n + O(n^{2/3}\log n)$ interchange steps. Since at least approximately $5n$ interchange steps are necessary [Ku], we obtain the asymptotic factor of 2.1.

It should be mentioned that some more improvements exist (e.g. for step 5) and that a lot of other modifications of the general method are also possible. For example, note that different 2-dimensional sorting algorithms are allowed for each of the five steps. Hence algorithms suitable for a number of VLSI-chips stacked on top of each other can be obtained. Furthermore, sorting algorithms developed for the 2-dimensional instruction systolic array [KLSSS,L] can be used as fundamental units for a 3-dimensional instruction systolic architecture.

Finally, extensions of the 3BY2-method to the r-dimensional case, $r \geq 4$, can be done in several ways. For example, for an $n_1 \times ... \times n_r$ mesh let $A = (n_1,...,n_{i_A})$, $B = (n_{i_A}+1,...,n_{i_B})$, and $C = (n_{i_B}+1,...,n_r)$, $1 \leq i_A < i_B \leq r$, and let $I_Y = I_{y_1} \times ... \times I_{y_n}$ for an arbitrary integer vector $Y = (y_1,...,y_k)$, $k \geq 1$. Then we can generate r-dimensional sorting algorithms by using i_A-, $(i_B - i_A)$- and $(r - i_B)$-dimensional algorithms as a basis for the slightly altered 3BY2 method where the integer vectors A,B and C take the places of the integers a,b and c. Such an approach needs $SORT_1(A,B,C) = SORT_1(A,C) + SORT_1(B,C) + 2 \cdot SORT_1(A,B) + 2$ interchange steps. Similar observations as in the above mentioned improved 3BY2 lead to algorithms with complexity of $SORT_2(A,B,C) \leq SORT_2(A,C) + SORT_2(B,C) + SORT_2(A,B) + 2(n_1 + ... + n_{i_A})$. For an r-dimensional cube with side length n and $r = 3i_B/2 = 3i_A$ one can obtain a sorting algorithm sorting n^r elements by approximately less than $2r^{2.71}n/3$ interchange steps. A more detailed discussion of the r–dimensional case and the improvements for the 3–dimensional case can be found in a full version of this paper which is available by the author.

Acknowledgement

I wish to thank M. Schimmler for putting my attention to 3–dimensional sorting and H.W. Lang for helpfull discussions.

References

[FK]   Foster, M.J., Kung, H.T., The design of special–purpose VLSI–chips. IEEE Computer (1980), 26–40.

[KH]   M. Kumar and D.S. Hirschberg, An efficient implementation of Batcher's odd–even merge algorithm and its application in parrallel sorting schemes, IEEE Trans. Comp., Vol. C–32, 254–264 (1983)

[KL]   Kung, H.T., Leiserson, C.E., Systolic arrays for VLSI. Symposium on Sparse Matrix Computation 1978, Proceedings, eds: I.S. Duff, C.G. Stewart, (1978).

[KLSSS] M. Kunde, H.–W. Lang, M. Schimmler, H. Schmeck and H. Schroeder, The instruction systolic array and its relation to other models of parallel computers, in Proc. Parallel Computing '85, (1985)

[Kn]   D.E. Knuth, The art of computer programming, Vol. 3: Sorting and Searching, Addison Wesley, Reading, 1973, pp 224–225.

[Ku]   M. Kunde, Lower bounds for sorting on mesh–connected architectures, Proceedings AWOC 86 VLSI Algorithms and Architectures, LNCS 227, Springer, Berlin, 1986, 84–95.

[L]   H.–W. Lang, The instruction systolic array, a parallel architecture for VLSI, to appear in Integration

[LSSS] H.–W. Lang, M. Schimmler, H. Schmeck and H. Schroeder, Systolic sorting on a mesh–connected network, IEEE Trans. Comp., Vol. C–34, 652–658 (1985)

[NS]   D. Nassimi and S. Sahni, Bitonic sort on a mesh–connected parallel computer, IEEE Trans. Comp., Vol. C–28, 2–7 (1979)

[S]   M. Schimmler, Fast sorting on a three dimensional cube grid, Bericht 8604, Institut fuer Informatik, University of Kiel, Germany, 1986

[SI]   K. Sado and Y. Igarashi, A fast parallel pesudo–merge sort algorithm, Technical Report, Gunma University Japan, 1985

[TK]   C.D. Thompson and H.T. Kung, Sorting on a mesh–connected parallel computer, CACM, vol. 20, 263–271 (1977)

[U]   J.D. Ullmann, Computational aspects of VLSI, Computer Science Press, Rockville, 1984

COMPLEXITY OF PARALLEL PARTITIONED ALGORITHMS

Thula Vogell

Kernforschungsanlage Jülich GmbH

Zentralinstitut für Angewandte Mathematik

Postfach 1913

D-5170 Jülich

Abstract

A general concept for the description of partitioned algorithms is presented. It is based on a partitioning of the occurring data in datablocks of equal size. For a class of partitioned algorithms including matrix multiplication, LU-decomposition of a matrix, solving a linear system of equations it is proved: using a fixed number p of processing elements (PEs) the time complexity of a parallel partitioned algorithm is minimal if either all p PEs or if only one PE is used for executing one operation on datablocks.

0. Introduction

Usually a parallel algorithm solving a problem of size n is developed for p(n) processing elements (PEs), that is the number of PEs is assumed to be a function of the problem size. But in reality only a constant number p of PEs will be available. So one is forced to "partition" the algorithm.

One approach is to distribute the programs of the p(n) theoretical PEs among the p real PEs. This corresponds to a partitioning of the operationset of the algorithm. Another possibility is to develop new algorithms which work on partitioned data. In the literature no rigid distinction between these approaches is made; the term "partitioning of algorithms" is used in both cases. As an example for the first approach see [4].

We are interested in the second kind of partitioned algorithms. Examples for such algorithms are partitioned versions of sorting algorithms ([1]), LU-decomposition of a matrix, inversion of a nonsingular triangular matrix and back substitution ([3]), matrix multiplication, matrix transposition, the Fast Fourier transform and an algorithm for determining the minimum spanning tree of a graph represented by its adjacency matrix.

In the first section we develop a formal definition of partitioned algorithms which not only models known examples but could also be useful for constructing new partitioned algorithms. There are several possibilities for parallelization of a partitioned algorithm. In section 2 we compare the efficiencies and execution times of these different parallelizations. Under certain assumptions which hold for all examples listed above we prove that using p PEs a minimal execution time is achieved if one chooses the simplest parallelization, which means that the partitioned structure of the algorithm is *not* mapped onto the set of PEs. Finally as a typical example we explain the partitioned Gaussian elimination algorithm.

1. General concepts

What in general is understood by a partitioned algorithm is essentially an algorithm operating on partitioned data. To describe easily the necessary data partitioning we consider matrices (or vectors) as input/output data. To avoid confusion by using too much indices we only regard the case of k $(n \times n)$-matrices $A(1), \ldots, A(k)$ as input and one $(n \times n)$-matrix as output.

All definitions and results may be generalized for different matrix sizes and more than one output matrix.

In what follows, $m \in \mathbb{N}$ is assumed to divide n.

DEFINITION 1:

Let $A = (a_{ij})_{1 \leq i, j \leq n}$ be an $(n \times n)$-matrix. The *partitioning $\bar{A}$ of A with blocksize m* is defined as the matrix

$$\bar{A} = (\bar{a}_{ij})_{1 \leq i, j \leq n/m} \quad , \quad \text{where}$$

$$\bar{a}_{ij} := \begin{pmatrix} a_{(i-1)m+1,(j-1)m+1} & \cdots & a_{(i-1)m+1,jm} \\ \vdots & & \vdots \\ a_{im,(j-1)m+1} & \cdots & a_{im,jm} \end{pmatrix}$$

□

DEFINITION 2:

Let $f: (\mathbb{R}^n \times \mathbb{R}^n)^k \to \mathbb{R}^n \times \mathbb{R}^n$ be a function, $R := \mathbb{R}^m \times \mathbb{R}^m$.

A *partitioning of f* is a function

$$\bar{f}_m : (R^{n/m} \times R^{n/m})^k \to R^{n/m} \times R^{n/m} \quad \text{with}$$

$$\bar{f}_m(\overline{A(1)}, \ldots, \overline{A(k)}) = \overline{f(A(1), \ldots, A(k))}.$$

□

By a parallel algorithm computing f we understand a PRAM (parallel RAM) $M(n)$ with $p(n)$ PEs computing f as defined for example in [2]. We allow each register of $M(n)$ to store one element of $\mathbb{R}$. Any fixed set S of arithmetic operations is permitted, usually $S = \{+,-,*,/\}$. $p(n)$ is assumed to be polynomially bounded.

Based on this concept we define a functional PRAM $\bar{M}(n/m)$ (computing $\bar{f}_m$):

DEFINITION 3:

A *functional PRAM $\bar{M}(n/m)$* consists of

- $p_0(n/m)$ PEs , $p_0 \in \mathbb{R}[X]$.
- An unlimited number of registers $1,2,\ldots$. Each register can store one element of $\mathbb{R}^m \times \mathbb{R}^m$ or an element of $\mathbb{N}$ (addresses!).
- $p_0(n/m)$ accumulators $01,\ldots,0p_0(n/m)$.
- $p_0(n/m)$ programs attached to the different PEs.

Let S_1 be a fixed set of unary matrix-operations and S_2 a fixed set of binary matrix-operations. Then every program is a finite sequence of instructions. Denoting the content of register k by <k> the possible instructions and their effects are:

c-load (X)	$<0i> := X$, $X \varepsilon R^m \times R^m$
load (k)	$<0i> := <k>$, $k \varepsilon N$
store (k)	$<k> := <0i>$, $k \varepsilon N$
i-load (k)	$<0i> := <<k>>$, $<k> \varepsilon N$
i-store (k)	$<<k>> := <0i>$, $<k> \varepsilon N$
f	$<0i> := f(<0i>)$, $f \varepsilon S_1$, $k \varepsilon N$
g(k)	$<0i> := g(<0i>,<k>)$, $g \varepsilon S_2$, $k \varepsilon N$
stop	machine stops

$\overline{M}(n/m)$ computes $\overline{f}_m$:<=> $\overline{M}(n/m)$ started with input $\overline{A(1)},\ldots,\overline{A(k)}$ stops with output $\overline{f}_m(\overline{A(1)},\ldots,\overline{A(k)})$.

□

Typically $S_1 = \{$LU-decomposition, inversion, transposition$\}$ and $S_2 = \{$multiplication, addition, subtraction, multiplication by coefficients$\}$.

For $p_1 \varepsilon R[X]$ let $M(n,m)$ be a PRAM with $p_0(n/m)p_1(m)$ PEs computing f which simulates $\overline{M}(n/m)$ in the following way:

Let $M_1(m),\ldots,M_q(m)$ be PRAMs with $p_1(m)$ PEs computing the functions in S_1 and S_2. $M(n,m)$ simulates $\overline{M}(n/m)$ stepwise by using $p_1(m)$ PEs for each instruction in the programs of $\overline{M}(n/m)$. An arithmetic instruction of $\overline{M}(n/m)$ is simulated in such a way that a group of $p_1(m)$ PEs of $M(n,m)$ works like the corresponding $M_i(m)$, $1\leq i\leq q$. $M(n,m)$ works synchronized. That is, the simulation of one (parallel) step of $\overline{M}(n/m)$ is started after the simulation of the foregoing step has been finished.

We call $M(n,m)$ a *partitioned PRAM* computing f. Given a PRAM $M(n)$ computing f we say $M(n,m)$ is a *partitioning of* $M(n)$:<=> $M(n,1) = M(n)$.

We also speak of partitioned algorithms instead of partitioned PRAMs. In terms of algorithms we call $\overline{M}(n/m)$ the *external* algorithm and $M_1(m),\ldots,M_q(m)$ the *internal* algorithms.

Clearly each partitioned algorithm $M(n,m)$ is also a partitioning of some algorithm $M(n)$: $M(n):= M(n,1)$.

2. Execution time

By the execution time of one PE of a PRAM $M(n)$ computing f we mean the number of arithmetic operations in the program of that PE. The *execution time* $t(n)$ of $M(n)$ is then defined by the maximum of all its PE execution times.

We restrict ourselves to the case of only one internal algorithm. Let $t_0(n/m)$, $t_1(m)$ be the execution times of $\overline{M}(n/m)$, $M_1(m)$ resp.. The execution time of $M(n,m)$ then is given by $t_0(n/m)t_1(m)$.

Given a functional PRAM $\overline{M}(n/m)$ computing $\overline{f}_m$ there might be several partitioned algorithms $M(j)(n,m)$ simulating $\overline{M}(n/m)$ depending on the different possibilities for parallelization of the internal algorithm.

On the other hand there will be several possibilities for parallelization of the external algorithm with corresponding functional PRAMs $\overline{M(i)}(n/m)$ all computing $\overline{f}_m$.

So altogether there are partitioned algorithms $M(i,j)(n,m) =: M(i,j)$ corresponding to the PE number functions $p_0(i)$, $p_1(j)$ and the execution times $t_0(i)(n/m)$, $t_1(j)(m)$ all computing f.

Let $p_0(1) \equiv 1$, $p_1(1) \equiv 1$.

We ask: which of these partitioned algorithms $M(i,j)$ works with maximal efficiency?

Sequential execution of the external *and* the internal algorithm leads to a sequential algorithm computing f. Let $t_0(1)(n/m)$ and $t_1(1)(m)$ be the execution times of sequential algorithms computing $\overline{f}_m$ and the internal function. We consider *efficiencies* of the parallel partitioned algorithms with respect to the sequential execution time

$$t(1)(n) := \min_m (t_0(1)(n/m) t_1(1)(m)).$$

We write "$E_p(M)$" to indicate the efficiency of the parallel algorithm M using p PEs.

In general the product $t_0(1)(n/m) t_1(1)(m)$ of sequential execution times depends on m. We define a function $q(m) \leq 1$ by

$$t(1)(n) = q(m) t_0(1)(n/m) t_1(1)(m).$$

LEMMA 1:

$$E_{p_0(i)p_1(j)}(M(i,j)) = q(m) E_{p_0(i)}(\overline{M(i)}) E_{p_1(j)}(M(j)).$$

$\square$

THEOREM 1:

$$E_{p_1(j)}(M(1,j)) \geq E_{p_0(i)p_1(j)}(M(i,j)).$$

$$E_{p_0(i)}(M(i,1)) \geq E_{p_0(i)p_1(j)}(M(i,j)).$$

PROOF:

$$E_{p_0(i)p_1(j)}(M(i,j)) = q(m) E_{p_0(i)}(\overline{M(i)}) E_{p_1(j)}(M(j)) \text{ and}$$

$$E_{p_1(j)}(M(1,j)) = q(m) E_{p_1(j)}(M(j)).$$

Because $E_{p_0(i)}(\overline{M(i)}) \leq 1$ the assertion of the theorem follows. (Part two is shown in the same way.)

$\square$

So the most efficient partitioned algorithm amongst all $M(i,j)(n,m)$ must be one which executes either the external or the internal algorithm in a sequential mode.

We are interested in the execution time of partitioned algorithms on more realistic machines. The essential restriction made now in considering a real machine M is that M possesses only a constant number p of PEs. One wishes to use all p PEs, therefore one has to choose m so that

$$p_0(n/m) p_1(m) = p.$$

Working with fixed p one must be more careful, because the efficiencies to be compared will depend on m.

For fixed n let $p_0(i)(n/m) p_1(j)(m) = p_0(i)(n/m') = p_1(j)(m'') = p$.

Naturally $p_0(i)$ and $p_1(j)$ are increasing functions, so we have $m' \leq m$ and $m'' \geq m$.

Assuming all occurring execution times to be polynomially bounded we distinguish two cases:

- $q(m)$ is an increasing function of m. ("$t_1(1)$ grows faster than $t_0(1)$".)
- $q(m)$ is a decreasing function of m. ("$t_0(1)$ grows faster than $t_1(1)$".)

In the following we index the algorithms in the terms for the efficiencies only if this is necessary for understanding.

LEMMA 2:

Let $E_{p_0(i)(x)}$, $E_{p_1(j)(x)}$ ε $\{O(1), O((\log x)^{-r}), O(x^{-s})\}$, $r,s \varepsilon \mathbb{R}^+$, and

$h(\alpha) := E_{p_0(i)(n^{1-\alpha})} E_{p_1(j)(n^{\alpha})}$, $\alpha \varepsilon [0,1]$.

Then there exists a ε $[0,1]$ so that in $[0,a]$ h is a monotone decreasing function and in $[a,1]$ h is a monotone increasing function. That is: In $[0,1]$ h is either constant or achieves exactly one local minimum.

$\square$

In the next theorem and corollaries we assume the efficiencies of the internal and external algorithm to be as in lemma 2. It is proved for a class of partitioned algorithms that the result of theorem 1 holds in the case of a constant number of PEs, too.

THEOREM 2:

Let $m = n^{\alpha}$, $\alpha \varepsilon [0,1]$. If q is increasing and $\alpha \varepsilon [a,1]$, then

$$E_p(M(1,j))(n,m'')) \geq E_p(M(i,j)(n,m)).$$

If q is decreasing and $\alpha \varepsilon [0,a]$, then

$$E_p(M(i,1)(n,m')) \geq E_p(M(i,j)(n,m)).$$

PROOF:

Part one: Let $m'' = n^{\alpha''}$, $\alpha'' \varepsilon [a,1]$. Then $h(\alpha'') \geq h(\alpha)$, in other terms:

$E_{p_0(i)(n/m'')} E_{p_1(j)(m''')} \geq E_{p_0(i)(n/m)} E_{p_1(j)(m)}$.

Together with lemma 1 and theorem 1 we get:

$E_p(M(i,j)) = E_{p_0(i)(n/m)p_1(j)(m)}(M(i,j))$

$= q(m)E_{p_0(i)(n/m)} E_{p_1(j)(m)}$

$\leq q(m'')E_{p_0(i)(n/m'')} E_{p_1(j)(m'')}$

$= E_{p_0(i)(n/m'')p_1(j)(m'')}$

$\leq E_{p_1(j)(m'')}(M(1,j)) = E_p(M(1,j))$.

Part two of the theorem is shown in the same way.

$\square$

Let $t(i,j)$ be the execution time of $M(i,j)$ using p PEs. Then we get as a direct consequence of the last theorem:

COROLLARY 1:

For q increasing and $\alpha \varepsilon [a,1]$:

$$\min_i(t(i,j)) = t(1,j).$$

For q decreasing and $\alpha \varepsilon [0,a]$:

$$\min_j(t(i,j)) = t(i,1).$$

COROLLARY 2:

For q increasing and $E_{p_1}(j) = O(1)$:

$$\min_i(t(i,j)) = t(1,j).$$

For q decreasing and $E_{p_0}(i) = O(1)$:

$$\min_j(t(i,j)) = t(i,1).$$

$\square$

In nearly all examples of partitioned algorithms we have more than one internal function. But one can think of each external algorithm as built up by "subalgorithms", where each subalgorithm contains only functions from S_1 and S_2 needing the same execution time $t_1(m)$. Then the above results hold for every subalgorithm.

3. Example

One should notice that there might be algorithms to which the above corollaries can not be applied depending on the behaviour of q. Nevertheless in all listed examples from linear algebra we have $q(m) = 1$, so there won't be any difficulties.

Further the condition $p_0(n/m)p_1(m) = p$ implies boundaries for p. If for example $p_0(n/m) = n/m$ and $p_1(m) = m^2$ condition $nm = p$ leads to $n \leq p \leq n^2$.

As a typical example we now examine the partitioned Gaussian elimination algorithm for an $(n \times n)$-matrix A.

$S_1 = \{$inversion of a triangular matrix, LU-decomposition of a matrix$\}$

$S_2 = \{$matrix-multiplication, matrix-addition$\}$

The algorithm may be described in pseudo code by

```
begin
  for i = 1,...,n/m do
    begin
    a̅_ii = l̅_ii u̅_ii;
    l̅_ii := l̅_ii^{-1}; u̅_ii := u̅_ii^{-1};
    for k = i,...,n/m do
      begin
      a̅_ik := l̅_ii a̅_ik;
      for j = i+1,...,n/m do
        begin
        a̅_ji := a̅_ji u̅_ii;
        a̅_jk := a̅_jk - a̅_ji a̅_ik
        end
      end
    end
end
```

Looking at the subalgorithm consisting of the multiplication steps and taking into account only the leading terms of the execution time polynomials we have:

$p_0(1)(n/m) = 1$ $t_0(1)(n/m) = 2/3(n/m)^3$

$p_0(2)(n/m) = n/m$ $t_0(2)(n/m) = (n/m)^2$

$p_0(3)(n/m) = (n/m)^2$ $t_0(3)(n/m) = 3n/m$

$p_1(1) = 1$ $t_1(1)(m) = 2m^3$

$p_1(2)(m) = m$ $t_1(2)(m) = 2m^2$

$p_1(3)(m) = m^2$ $t_1(3)(m) = 2m$

$p_1(4)(m) = m^3$ $t_1(4)(m) = \log m$

The execution times of the 12 possible partitionings are summarized in the following table. The second term corresponds to the condition $p_0(i)(n/m)p_1(j)(m) = p$. These times are to be compared by the corrolaries.

	1	m	m^2	m^3
1	$(4/3)n^3$	$(4/3)(n^3/m)$	$(4/3)(n^3/m^2)$	$(2n^3/3m^3)\log m$
		$(4/3)(n^3/p)$	$(4/3)(n^3/p)$	$(2n^3/9p)\log p$
n/m	$2n^2m$	$2n^2$	$2n^2/m$	$(n^2/m)\log m$
	$2n^3/p$	$2n^3/p$	$2n^3/p$	$(n^3/2p)\log(p/n)$
$(n/m)^2$	$6nm^2$	$6nm$	$6n$	$3(n/m)\log m$
	$6n^3/p$	$6n^3/p$	$6n^3/p$	$3(n^3/p)\log(p/n^2)$

$q(m) = 1$ and constant efficiencies allow the application of corollary 2 for all partitionings. In case of $p_1(m) = m^3$ part two of the corollary has to be used (a = 1 !). Obviously the best execution times are achieved for either the internal or the external algorithm executed sequentially.

Literature

[1] Bitton,D., DeWitt,D.J., Hsaio,D.K., Menon,J., A taxonomy of parallel sorting, ACM Comp. Surv. 16,3 , 287-318 (1984)

[2] Fortune,S., Wyllie,J., Parallelism in random access machines, Proc. of the 10th ACM STOC, 114-118 (1978)

[3] Hwang,K., Cheng,Y.-H., Partitioned matrix algorithms for VLSI arithmetic systems, IEEE Trans. Comp. C-31,12 , 1215-1224 (1982)

[4] Moldovan,D.I., Fortes, J.A.B., Partitioning and mapping algorithms into fixed size systolic arrays, IEEE Trans. Comp. C-35,1 , 1-12 (1986)

Shuffle/Exchange is the natural interconnection scheme for the parallel Fast Fourier Transform

Frank Wagner
Lehrstuhl für angewandte Mathematik
insbesondere Informatik
RWTH Aachen
Templergraben 64
5100 Aachen

Abstract

It is known, that the Shuffle/Exchange-Network (S/E) is well suited to perform the parallel Fast Fourier Transform (FFT). In this paper we show, that it is *optimal* for this purpose in a quite general sense:
We assume, that a parallel FFT consists of a sequence of (parallel) *butterfly*-operations on and permutations of the given data vector . It is shown, that only the S/E and a slight variation thereof guarantee a maximum of regularity of the data flow. It follows, that the S/E is best suited for a realisation of a parallel FFT by specialized hardware.

Introduction

The *Discrete Fourier Transform* of a complex vector of length $n = 2^k$ is defined as:

$$\mathrm{DFT}(p_0, \ldots, p_{n-1}) := (P_0, \ldots, P_{n-1})$$

$$\text{with } P_k := \sum_{i=0}^{n-1} p_i \omega_n^{ki}$$

$$\text{with } \omega_n := e^{2\pi i/n}$$

$$\text{with } i := \sqrt{-1}$$

The naive computation of the DFT requires $O(n^2)$ arithmetical operations. Fortunately there is a better algorithm, the *Fast Fourier Transform*, for the first time explicitly stated by [Cooley and Tukey, 1965], which needs only $O(n \log n)$ operations. Everything, which is used but not defined in the rest of this paper, can be found in [Nussbaumer, 1981].

Two sequential algorithms

To motivate the following assumptions about the general structure of a FFT algorithm, we present two essentially sequential standard algorithms.
The *Straight-Forward Manner* of executing the FFT is visualized best by presenting the corresponding data flow graph for the size $n = 2^3$:

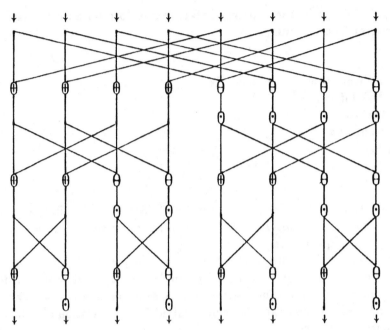

The ⊕- and ⊖-symbols are intuitively clear, the ⊙ means multiplication by appropriate n-th roots of unity.

The output is not in the correct but in the *bit-reversed order*. To avoid this disadvantage one can design a *Correct-Order Output* algorithm, described for $n = 2^3$ again:

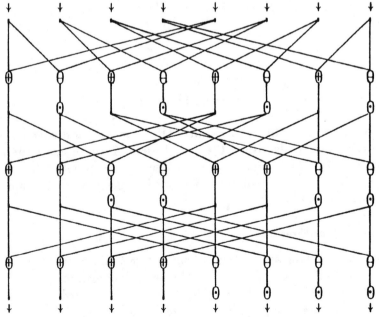

A unified description

The log n stages of both algorithms are pairwise unequal, but they have the common property, that each stage consists of $\frac{n}{2}$ so-called *butterfly* operations:

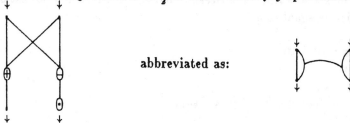

abbreviated as:

The butterflies in one stage are independent and therefore parallely executable. Using the abbreviating style above, the two algorithms have the following shape:

SFM:

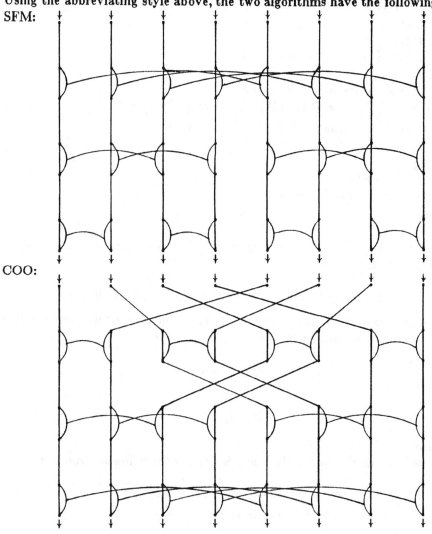

COO:

For general size $n = 2^k$ the two algorithms can be described in pseudo-PASCAL: $BFLY\ S$ denotes the parallel execution of butterflies at the places given by the elements of S.

b_i denotes the set of numbers between 0 and $n-1$, whose i-th lowest bit in binary representation is equal to b.

SFM:
for $i := 1$ **to** k **do**
   begin
      $P := \pi(P)$
      $BFLY\{(a, a + 2^{k-i}) \mid a \in 0_{k-i}\}$
   end
COO:
for $i := 1$ **to** k **do**
   begin
      $P := \pi'_i(P)$
      $BFLY\{(a, a + 2^{i-1}) \mid a \in 0_{i-1}\}$
   end

π_i and π'_i are elements of S_n. For $n = 2^3$:

$\pi_i = id\ (i = 1, 2, 3);\ \ \pi'_1 = (124)(356);\ \ \pi'_2 = (24)(35);\ \ \pi'_3 = id.$

In general we assume, that a FFT Algorithm has the form G :

for $i := 1$ **to** k **do**
   begin
      $P := \pi_i(P)$
      $BFLY\{(a, f_i(a)) \mid a \in A_i\}$
   end

where:
$\pi_i \in S_n,\ A_i \subset \{0, \ldots, n-1\}$ with $|A_i| = \frac{n}{2}$ and f_i is a bijection between A_i and $\{0, \ldots, n-1\} \setminus A_i$.

Requirements on a really parallelizable algorithm and their fulfillment

A parallel prozessor, suited to perform the FFT, should have the structure described by three regularity conditions RC:

(1) $$\pi_i = \pi_j = \pi$$
(2) $$A_i = A_j = A$$
(3) $$f_i = f_j = f$$

Theorem
An FFT-algorithm of type G, which fulfills RC has the following properties:

(A) $$\pi = PS,\ A = 0_0 \text{ and } f(a) = a + 1 \quad \text{or}$$
(B) $$\pi = \tilde{P}S,\ A = 1_0 \text{ and } f(a) = a - 1$$

PS and $\tilde{PS}$ are elements of S_n, with

$$PS(a) := \begin{cases} 2a, & \text{if } a \in \{0, \ldots, \frac{n}{2} - 1\}; \\ 2a + 1 - n, & \text{otherwise.} \end{cases}$$

and

$$\tilde{PS} := (01)(23) \ldots (n - 2 \ n - 1) \circ PS.$$

PS means *Perfect Shuffle*.

Proof:

Step 1: Each algorithm of the described form has to execute the same arithmetical operations, i.e. the permutations π_i and the arrangement of the butterflies, defined by the A_i's and f_i's, determine only the structure of the algorithm with respect to the data flow and the order of the arithmetical operations. On the other hand for example all of these algorithms have to perform the butterflies

$$BFLY\{(\pi_1(a), \pi_1(a + 2^{k-1})) \mid a \in 0_{k-1}\}$$

in the first stage, after permuting the input for the first time, in order to carry out the same arithmetic as SFM, whose permutations are all equal to identity. Analogously it can be seen, that in the i-th stage the butterflies

$$BFLY\{(\pi_i(\pi_{i-1} \ldots (\pi_1(a)) \ldots)), (\pi_i(\pi_{i-1} \ldots (\pi_1(a + 2^{k-i})) \ldots)) \mid a \in 0_{k-i}\}$$

have to be executed. Fulfilling RC(1) this means, that in the i-th stage

$$BFLY\{(\pi^i(a), \pi^i(a + 2^{k-i})) \mid a \in 0_{k-i}\} \tag{a}$$

has to be carried out. It follows, that

$$A_i = \{(\pi^i(a) \mid a \in 0_{k-i}\} =: \pi^i(0_{k-i}) \text{ for } i \in \{1, \ldots, k\}.$$

Fulfilling RC(2) this means:

$$\pi^i(0_{k-i}) = A \text{ for } i \in \{1, \ldots, k\}$$
$$\Rightarrow \pi^{k-j}(0_j) = \pi^{k-j-1}(0_{j+1}) \text{ for } i \in \{1, \ldots, k-2\}$$
$$\Rightarrow \pi(0_j) = 0_{j+1} \text{ for } i \in \{1, \ldots, k-2\} \tag{b}$$

π is a bijection, so

$$\pi\left(\bigcap_{j=0}^{k-2} 0_j\right) = \bigcap_{j=0}^{k-2} \pi(0_j) = (\text{by (b)}) \bigcap_{j=1}^{k-1} 0_j$$

$$\Rightarrow \pi\left(\{0, \frac{n}{2}\}\right) = \{0, 1\} \tag{c}$$

Step 2: According to RC(2) and (3) the arrangements of the butterflies in two different stages are identical. So, by (a):

$$\{(\pi^i(a), \pi^i(a + 2^{k-i})) \mid a \in 0_{k-i}\} = \{(\pi^j(a'), \pi^j(a' + 2^{k-j})) \mid a \in 0_{k-j}\} \text{ for } i, j \in$$
$$\{1, \ldots, k\}$$

$\Rightarrow (i := j + 1)$

$$\{(\pi^{j+1}(a), \pi^{j+1}(a + 2^{k-j-1})) \mid a \in 0_{k-j-1}\} = \{(\pi^j(a'), \pi^j(a' + 2^{k-j})) \mid a \in 0_{k-j}\}$$
for $j \in \{1, \ldots, k-1\}$

$\Rightarrow (a' := \pi(a);$ this choice of a' is possible, because by (b) $\pi(0_{k-j-1}) = 0_{k-j}$ for $j \in \{1, \ldots, k-1\})$

$$\{(\pi^{j+1}(a), \pi^{j+1}(a + 2^{k-j-1}) \mid a \in 0_{k-j-1}\} = \{(\pi^{j+1}(a), \pi^j(\pi(a) + 2^{k-j}) \mid a \in$$
$$0_{k-j-1}\} \text{ for } j \in \{1, \ldots, k-1\}$$

$\Rightarrow$ (Pairs with the same first component have to be equal in the second component too, to fulfill the demanded set equality)

$$\pi^{j+1}(a + 2^{k-j-1}) = \pi^j(\pi(a) + 2^{k-j}) \text{ for } a \in 0_{k-j-1} \text{ and } j \in \{1, \ldots, k-1\}$$
$$\Rightarrow \pi(a + 2^{k-j-1}) = \pi(a) + 2^{k-j} \text{ for } a \in 0_{k-j-1} \text{ and } j \in \{1, \ldots, k-1\}$$

This means in detail particularly: The values of π at even points determine those at the odd ones.

The values of π at the points, which are divisible by four, determine those, which are even but not divisible by four.

The values of π at the points, which are divisible by eight, determine those, which are divisible by four but not by eight. And so on.

The completing of this recursion shows, that all values of π are determined by $\pi(0)$ and $\pi(\frac{n}{2})$. By (c) there are only two possibilities of defining π at these two points:

$$\pi(0) = 0 \text{ and } \pi\left(\frac{n}{2}\right) = 1 \tag{1}$$

$$\pi(0) = 1 \text{ and } \pi\left(\frac{n}{2}\right) = 0 \tag{2}$$

By using the recursion above the two possible permutations are given by:

$$PS(a) = \begin{cases} 2a, & \text{if } a \in \{0, \ldots, \frac{n}{2} - 1\}; \\ 2a + 1 - n, & \text{otherwise.} \end{cases} \tag{1}$$

$$\tilde{PS}(a) = \begin{cases} 2a + 1, & \text{if } a \in \{0, \ldots, \frac{n}{2} - 1\}; \\ 2a - n, & \text{otherwise.} \end{cases} \tag{2}$$

The claimed values of A and f are a direct consequence. q.e.d

The description of PS and $\tilde{PS}$ becomes more elegant, if one uses the binary representation of a:

$$PS((a_{k-1} \ldots a_0)_2) = (a_{k-2} \ldots a_0 a_{k-1})_2$$
$$\tilde{PS}((a_{k-1} \ldots a_0)_2) = (a_{k-2} \ldots a_0 \overline{a_{k-1}})_2$$

The Perfect Shuffle was already suggested for the parallel FFT. The permutation PS is only a slight variation thereof. For $n = 2^3$ the two dataflow graphs are:

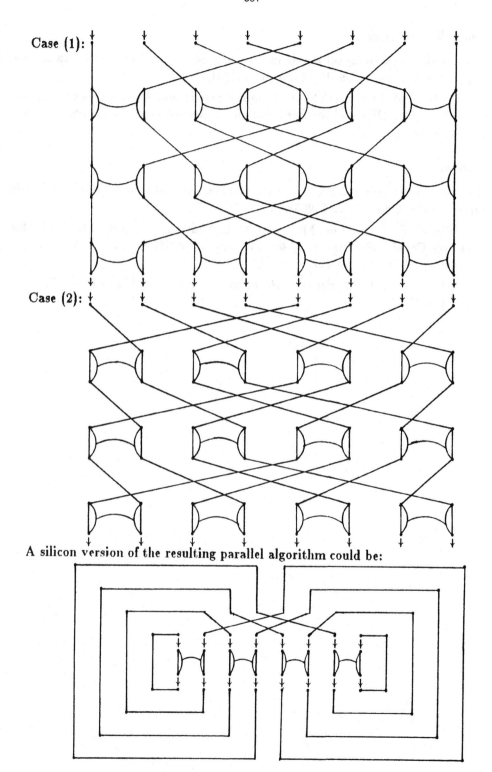

Case (1):

Case (2):

A silicon version of the resulting parallel algorithm could be:

352

Concluding Remarks

The question, how to layout the demanded S/E on a VLSI-Chip with area as small as possible, was solved by [Kleitman et al.,1981].

The fixed size of the network above is no real restriction, because it is easy, to split a long DFT into DFT's of the fixed size, or to execute short DFT's parallely with the fixed-sized network.

References

J. Cooley, J. Tukey: An algorithm for machine computation of complex Fourier Series. *Math. Comput.* **19** (1965), p. 297-301.

D. Kleitman, F. T. Leighton, M. Lepley, G. L. Miller: New Layouts for the Shuffle-Exchange Graph. *Proceedings of the 13th Annual ACM Symp. on the Theory of Computing* (1981), p. 278-292.

H.Nussbaumer: Fast Fourier Transform and Convolution Algorithms. *Springer, Berlin* (1981).

Kronecker Products of Matrices
and their Implementation on Shuffle/Exchange-Type Processor Networks

Otto Lange

Allgemeine Elektrotechnik und Datenverarbeitungssysteme, RWTH Aachen

Abstract - In generalized spectral analysis an orthogonal transformation provides a set of spectral coefficients by a vector-matrix-multiplication. If the $p^n \times p^n$-transformation matrix H_n is a Kronecker product of n pxp-matrices M_r, $r = 0,1,\ldots,n-1$, then - as has been shown by Good - there exists a factorization $\prod_{r=0}^{n-1} G_r$ of the transformation matrix H_n in such a way that the vector-matrix-multiplication can be reduced from $O(N^2)$ to $O(N\log N)$ operations, where $N = p^n$. The specific structure of the matrix factors G_r, $r = 0,1\ldots,n-1$, permits an implementation of the multiplication on processor networks, in case of $p = 2$ on permutation networks of the Shuffle/Exchange-type.

1.0 Introduction

The Kronecker product of matrices is a well known tool in digital signal processing /AN70/, /AK70/. Its use is based on the fact, that signals can be represented as a set of coefficients of orthogonal waveforms, which is the general process of spectral decomposition using vector-matrix products.

The transformation can be implemented using a reduced number of operations, provided that the transformation matrix can be suitably factorized. Good /GO58/ has shown, that a significant reduction of vector-matrix multiplications can be achieved if the matrix H_n is a $p^n \times p^n$-matrix which is the Kronecker product of n pxp-matrices M_r, $r = 0,1,\ldots,n-1$. The matrix H_n can then also be represented as the product of n $p^n \times p^n$-matrices G_r resulting in a structure that only requires $O(N\log N)$ operations instead of $O(N^2)$, $N = p^n$, required for the straightforeward procedure.

The special structure of the matrices G_r allows the realization of the multiplications in processor networks, which are of the Shuffle/Exchange type for the binary case of $p = 2$ /ST71/, /LA76/.

Examples are transformations which result from Kronecker products of a single orthogonal symmetric corematrix. A multitude of transformations can be represented in this form, which results in many unanswered questions regarding importance and usefullness of such transformations. So far few have been shown to be of practical importance, e. g. the discrete Walsh-transform.

2.0 Kronecker Product

2.1 Definition and Properties

Let A and B be matrices over a field K, where A is an mxn-matrix, $A = (a_{ik})$, $i = 0,1,\ldots,m-1$, $k = 0,1,\ldots,n-1$, and B is a pxq-matrix, $B = (b_{jl})$, $j = 0,1,\ldots,p-1$, l=0,1,...,q-1. The set of all products a_{ik} b_{jl} can be arranged in a mpxnq-matrix where

(1) all products a_{ik} b_{jl} with the same indexpair (i,j) are placed in the same row, and

(2) all products a_{ik} b_{jl} with the same indexpair (k,l) are placed in the same column.

The rows and columns are arranged in lexicographic order according to the indices (i,j) and (k,l), respectively. The resulting productmatrix is the Kronecker product A O B of the matrices A and B. The following properties of the Kronecker product are important in the context of this paper:

(i)   The product A O B is a regular matrix, if A, B are regular matrices.

(ii)   If A, B are quadratic matrices then the product A O B will also be a quadratic matrix.

(iii) If A, B are orthogonal matrices then the product A O B will also be an ortho-gonal matrix.

2.2 Successive Kronecker Multiplications

We shall now examine those Kronecker products, which result from successive Kronecker multiplications of a matrix M_0 with matrices M_r, r = 1,2,...,n-1, where all M_r, r = 0,1,...,n-1 are quadratic matrices of order p. This yields the following system of equations:

$$H_1 := M_0; \quad H_2 := M_1 \, O \, H_1; \quad ...; \quad H_n := M_{n-1} \, O \, H_{n-1}.$$

Since M_r is a pxp-matrix, H_r will be a $p^r x p^r$-matrix and H_n will be a $p^n x p^n$-matrix. Subsequently, we will define N to be N = p^n.

2.3 Closed Product Form

Let $H_r(x,y)$ denote the entry with the indexpair (x,y), thus positioned in the intersection of row x and column y. Since H_r is a $p^r x p^r$-matrix the indices x and y will assume all values 0 through p^r - 1 and can be considered as numbers in the p-nary radix representation:

$$x = x_{r-1} \, x_{r-2} \, ... \, x_1 \, x_0; \qquad y = y_{r-1} \, y_{r-2} \, ... \, y_1 \, y_0,$$
$$x_i, y_i \in \{0, 1, ..., p - 1\}, \quad i = 0, 1, ..., r - 1.$$

The entries of the matrix H_1 can be expressed as products. We shall require the matrixelement m_{0ij} of the matrix $H_1 = M_0$ to be placed in the position defined by the indices (i,j) for all i, j = 0,1,...,p-1. Using the Kronecker symbol $\delta(u-v) = 1$ for u = v and $\delta(u-v) = 0$ for u $\neq$ v the matrix H_1 can be defined as:

$$H_1(x,y) = \prod_{i=0}^{p-1} \prod_{j=0}^{p-1} m_{0ij}^{\delta(x_0-i) \, \delta(y_0-j)}$$

which through successive application of the above relations finally yields the alternative definition of the matrix H_n as:

$$H_n(x,y) = \prod_{r=0}^{n-1} \prod_{i=0}^{p-1} \prod_{j=0}^{p-1} m_{rij}^{\delta(x_r-i)\ \delta(y_r-j)} . \tag{2.1}$$

The importance of this notation is the fact that each entry of the matrix H_n can be obtained without the need to store all $(p^n)^2$ entries of the matrix. Only $n \cdot p^2$ entries m_{rij}, $r = 0,1,....,n-1$ are required for the above calculations. Even larger savings can be realized if for all $r = 0,1,....,n-1$: $M_r = M$. The number of entries to be stored will then be reduced to p^2.

2.4 Vectormultiplications using Kronecker Matrices

The closed product representation of $H_n(x,y)$ demonstrates, that each entry of H_n can be expressed as the product of n values of m_{rij}, $r = 0,1,....,n-1$, where m_{rij} is an entry of the r-th step in the Kronecker multiplication process.

One needs to examine, whether H_n can also be expressed as the product of n matrices G_{n-1}, G_{n-2}, ..., G_0, where each matrix G_r is of order $N = p^n$. This question has been answered positively by Good /GO58/ for Kronecker matrices described by eq. (2.1). The matrix G_r can be described as

$$
\begin{bmatrix}
m_{r00} & \cdots & m_{r0(p-1)} & & & & & & \\
& & & m_{r00} & \cdots & m_{r0(p-1)} & & & \\
& & & & & & m_{r00} & \cdots & m_{r0(p-1)} \\
m_{r10} & \cdots & m_{r1(p-1)} & & & & & & \\
\vdots & & & m_{r10} & \cdots & m_{r1(p-1)} & & & \\
\vdots & & & & & & m_{r10} & \cdots & m_{r1(p-1)} \\
m_{r(p-1)0} & \cdots & m_{r(p-1)(p-1)} & & & & & & \\
& & & m_{r(p-1)0} & \cdots & m_{r(p-1)(p-1)} & & & \\
& & & & & & m_{r(p-1)0} & \cdots & m_{r(p-1)(p-1)}
\end{bmatrix} \tag{2.2}
$$

Each row and column contains p non-zero entries, where the m_{rij} are arranged according to eq. (2.1). Thus each matrix G_r, $r = 0,1,....,n-1$, contains $p^n \cdot p$ non-zero elements of which only p^2 are non-redundant, i. e. the m_{rij} of the matrix M_r.

Expressing the Kronecker product $H_n = M_{n-1} \ 0 \ M_{n-2} \ 0 \ ... \ 0 \ M_0$ as a matrix product of Good matrices allows a vector-matrix multiplication $A \cdot H_n$ to be performed using only $O(p \cdot N \cdot \log_p N)$ arithmetic operations instead of the $O(N^2)$ otherwise required.

3.0 Calculation of Kronecker Products Using Permutation Networks

We will restrict our analysis to quadratic orthogonal matrices of order $N = p^n$; $p, n \in \mathbb{N}$.

Let $A = (A(0), A(1), ..., A(N-1))$ be the input vector and

$H_n = (H_n(x,y)) = M_{n-1} \ 0 \ M_{n-2} \ 0 \ ... \ 0 \ M_1 \ 0 \ M_0 = G_{n-1} \cdot G_{n-2} \cdot ... \cdot G_1 \cdot G_0$

be the Kronecker product of the matrices M_r.

It will then be necessary to differentiate between the right hand side multiplication $A \cdot H_n$ (Sec. 3.1) and the left hand side multiplication $H_n \cdot A$ (Sec. 3.2). These two cases are identical for symmetric matrices H_n, and the corresponding networks will produce the same results.

3.1 The Right Hand Side Multiplication

The right hand side multiplication yields the resulting vector E,

$$E = A \cdot H_n = \underbrace{A \cdot \underbrace{\underbrace{G_{n-1}}_{E_{n-1}} \cdot G_{n-2} \cdot \ldots \cdot G_0}_{E_0}}_{E_{n-2}}.$$

Let $E_n := A$, $E_r := E_{r+1} \cdot G_r$, $r = n - 1, n - 2, \ldots, 1, 0$, then E_0 corresponds to the resulting vector E. Using this result the product $E = A \cdot H_n$ according to

$$E(y) = \sum_{x=0}^{N-1} A(x) H_n(x,y)$$

can successively be calculated as $E_r = E_{r+1} \cdot G_r$ according to

$$E_r(y) = \sum_{x=0}^{N-1} E_{r+1}(x) G_r(x,y), \quad r = n-1, n-2, \ldots, 1, 0. \tag{3.1}$$

Due to the special structure of G_r consideration must be given to which components $E_{r+1}(x)$ will be weighted by which entries m_{rij} of the matrix M_r to yield the linear combinations of the component $E_r(y)$. The following system of equations can be derived from eqs. (3.1) and (2.2)

$$
\begin{aligned}
E_r(0) &= m_{r00} \; E_{r+1}(0) &&+ m_{r10} \; E_{r+1}(p^{n-1}) &&+ \ldots + m_{r(p-1)0} \; E_{r+1}((p-1)p^{n-1}) \\
E_r(1) &= m_{r01} \; E_{r+1}(0) &&+ m_{r11} \; E_{r+1}(p^{n-1}) &&+ \ldots + m_{r(p-1)1} \; E_{r+1}((p-1)p^{n-1}) \\
\end{aligned}
$$

$$E_r(p-1) = m_{r0(p-1)} \; E_{r+1}(0) + m_{r1(p-1)} \; E_{r+1}(p^{n-1}) + \ldots + m_{r(p-1)(p-1)} \; E_{r+1}((p-1)p^{n-1})$$

$$
\begin{aligned}
E_r(p) &= m_{r00} \; E_{r+1}(1) &&+ m_{r10} \; E_{r+1}(p^{n-1}+1) &&+ \ldots + m_{r(p-1)0} \; E_{r+1}((p-1)p^{n-1}+1) \\
E_r(p+1) &= m_{r01} \; E_{r+1}(1) &&+ m_{r11} \; E_{r+1}(p^{n-1}+1) &&+ \ldots + m_{r(p-1)1} \; E_{r+1}((p-1)p^{n-1}+1) \\
\end{aligned}
$$

$$E_r(2p-1) = m_{r0(p-1)} \; E_{r+1}(1) + m_{r1(p-1)} \; E_{r+1}(p^{n-1}+1) + \ldots + m_{r(p-1)(p-1)} \; E_{r+1}((p-1)p^{n-1}+1)$$

$$\tag{3.2}$$

$$E_r(p^{n-1}) = m_{r0(p-1)} \; E_{r+1}(p^{n-1}-1) + m_{r1(p-1)} \; E_{r+1}((p-1)p^{n-1}-1) + \ldots + m_{r(p-1)(p-1)} \; E_{r+1}(p^{n-1})$$

p components of the vector E_r at a time are comprised of linear combinations of the same p components of the vector E_{r+1} weighted differently by the p^2 entries m_{rij} of the matrix M_r for all $r = n-1, n-2, \ldots, 1, 0$. Therefore, the computation $E_r = E_{r+1} \cdot G_r$ can be performed using p^n/p processors. Each of these p^{n-1} processors will be assigned p components of E_{r+1} and will perform p different linear combinations of these elements using the weights m_{rij} to yield the p components of the resulting vector E_r.

Eq. (3.2) illustrates that a specific processor will be assigned the components $E_{r+1}(0)$, $E_{r+1}(p^{n-1})$, $\ldots$, $E_{r+1}((p-1) \cdot p^{n-1})$ and will generate the components $E_r(0)$, $E_r(1)$, $\ldots$, $E_r(p-1)$.

A single stage of p^{n-1} processors will perform a single multiplication $E_r = E_{r+1} \cdot G_r$. If n of such stages are arranged sequentially, where the inputs of a stage are connected to the outputs of the previous stage, the multiplication of $A \cdot H_n$ can be implemented using $n \cdot p^{n-1}$ processor elements. Each of these processors must consist of p inputs and p outputs and all p^2 entries m_{rij} of the corresponding r must be made available to this processor.

The special case $N = 2^n$:

In comparison with the general case $N = p^n$ the special case of $N = 2^n$ results in a significant reduction. The computation of $E_r = E_{r+1} \cdot G_r$ requires the evaluation of the following expressions:

$$
\begin{aligned}
E_r(0) &= m_{r00}\, E_{r+1}(0) &&+ m_{r10}\, E_{r+1}(2^{n-1}) \\
E_r(1) &= m_{r01}\, E_{r+1}(0) &&+ m_{r11}\, E_{r+1}(2^{n-1}) \\
E_r(2) &= m_{r00}\, E_{r+1}(1) &&+ m_{r10}\, E_{r+1}(2^{n-1}+1) \\
E_r(3) &= m_{r01}\, E_{r+1}(1) &&+ m_{r11}\, E_{r+1}(2^{n-1}+1)
\end{aligned}
\qquad (3.3)
$$

$$
\begin{aligned}
E_r(2^n-2) &= m_{r00}\, E_{r+1}(2^{n-1}-1) &&+ m_{r10}\, E_{r+1}(2^{n-1}) \\
E_r(2^n-1) &= m_{r01}\, E_{r+1}(2^{n-1}-1) &&+ m_{r11}\, E_{r+1}(2^{n-1})
\end{aligned}
$$

This evaluation shall be performed in a single stage using 2^{n-1} processors in parallel as shown in Fig. 3-1. In this example the processor P_0 of this stage uses the components $E_{r+1}(0)$ and $E_{r+1}(2^{n-1})$ as inputs to generate the results $E_r(0)$ and $E_r(1)$ as linear combinations of these inputs.

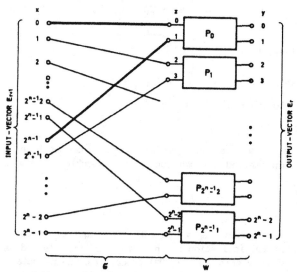

Fig. 3-1 Stage r of the processor network

The input x, $x = 0,1,...,2^n-1$, of the r-th stage is associated with the index x of the components of the input vector E_{r+1} and the output y, $y = 0,1,...,2^n-1$, of this stage is associated with the index y of the components of the output vector, which are identical to the inputs z, $z = 0,1,\ldots,2^{n-1}$, of the processors belonging to this stage. These conventions allow two basic choices for mapping the inputs x of this stage onto the inputs z of the corresponding processors:

$$\pi_1 = (0 \to 0, \ 2^{n-1} \to 1) \text{ or } \pi_2 = (0 \to 1, \ 2^{n-1} \to 0)$$

However, we will use the mapping π_1 and we will extend this choice to all other (x,z) according to eq. (3.3), which gives the Perfect-Shuffle permutation σ.

The total of all operations to be performed by a single processor at this stage (two additions and four multiplications) can be considered to be the mapping W of the inputs z onto the outputs y of this processor, thus the computation of E_r by E_{r+1} at this stage is the sequential implementation of the mappings σ and W:

$$E_{r+1} \xrightarrow{\sigma W} E_r{}^{*)}.$$

The computation $E = E_0 = E_n \cdot G_{n-1} \cdot G_{n-2} \cdot \ldots \cdot G_0$ requires n such stages (σW) and the vector-matrix multiplication $E = A \cdot H_n$ can be implemented as a permutation network $PSW = (\sigma W)^n$ consisting of $n \cdot 2^{n-1}$ processors. The permutation network PSW is isomorphic to the Omega-Network $\Omega = (\sigma E)^n$ /PA80/.

3.2 Left Hand Side Multiplication

The left hand side multiplication yields the resulting vector

$$E = H_n \cdot A = G_{n-1} \cdot G_{n-2} \cdot \ldots \cdot G_1 \cdot \underbrace{G_0 \cdot A}_{E_1} \, .$$

$$\underbrace{}_{E_2}$$

$$\underbrace{\phantom{G_{n-1} \cdot G_{n-2}}}_{E_n}$$

Let $E_0 := A$, $E_r := E_{r-1} \cdot G_r$, $r = n-1,n-2,\ldots,1,0$

then E_n corresponds to the resulting vector E.

The special case $N = 2^n$:

Analysis of the underlying equations reveals, that the computation of E_{r+1} by E_r at this stage can be implemented through successive execution of the mappings W and σ^{-1}, thus

$$E_r \xrightarrow{W\sigma^{-1}} E_{r+1}.$$

The computation $E = E_n = G_{n-1} \cdot G_{n-2} \cdot \ldots \cdot G_0 \cdot E_0$ requires n such stages ($W\sigma^{-1}$) and the vector-matrix multiplication $E = H_n \cdot A$ can be implemented as a permutation network $PSW = (W\sigma^{-1})^n$ consisting of $n \cdot 2^{n-1}$ processors. The permutation network PSW is isomorphic to the inverse Omega-network $\Omega^{-1} = (E\sigma^{-1})^n$.

---

*) The composition σW denotes that σ is to be performed first and W is then applied to the result of the mapping σ.

4.0 Examples of Kronecker Products

Consider the quadratic matrices M_r, $r = 0,1,...,n-1$, of order $p = 2$, where:

$$M_r = \begin{vmatrix} A_r & B_r \\ C_r & D_r \end{vmatrix}$$

Restricting M_r to $M_r = M$ for all r gives $A_r = A$, $B_r = B$, $C_r = C$, $D_r = D$.

If the corematrix M is an orthogonal matrix then the Kronecker product H_n will also be orthogonal and can be considered a transformation for spectral decomposition. For M to be an orthogonal corematrix the conditions:

$$A^2 + B^2 = 1, \quad C^2 + D^2 = 1, \quad AC + DB = 0$$

must hold. In addition the conditions of symmetry $B = C$ must be satisfied in order for the orthogonal transformation to yield the original input if applied twice successively.

There exists a multitude of orthogonal transformations which allow the representation in Kronecker form. Due to this multitude many questions concerning the importance and usefullness of these transformations need yet to be answered. Only few of these transformations have actualy been used and implemented thus far.

The generalized Walsh-transform /AN70/ of order p can be expressed as Kronecker product of the corematrix $M = (W(x,y))$ where $W(x,y) = \exp(2\pi ix \cdot y/p)$. Although the corematrix $(W(x,y))$ of the generalized Walsh-transform implements a Fourier-transform, the Kronecker product of these corematrices itself does not represent a Fourier-transform.

In the discrete domain the orthogonal Walsh-functions /WA23/ take the roll of the corresponding orthogonal sine- and cosine functions of the Fourier-transform. For the special case of $N = 2^n$ the discrete Walsh-transform can be expressed as n times the Kronecker product of the corematrix

$$M = \begin{vmatrix} 1 & 1 \\ 1 & -1 \end{vmatrix}.$$

The discrete Fourier-transform F_n, $N = p^n$, can in a similar fashion be expressed as the product of matrices according to Good, but not as the Kronecker product of a corematrix M. The matrices G_r of the factorization according to Good will in addition be multiplied by diagonal matrices D_r.

$$F_n = I \cdot G_0 \cdot D_1 \cdot G_1 \cdot \ldots \cdot D_{n-1} \, G_{n-1}.$$

The G_r and D_r are related through permutations as described by Whelchel and Guinn /WG68/. It is well known that Pease /PE68/ has shown that the Fourier-transform can be implemented with a network of the type $(\sigma W)^n \sigma$. Such a network consists only of Shuffle permutations and a bit-reversal permutation as the last step.

5.0 Conclusion

This paper has analyzed several properties of Kronecker products of matrices representing orthogonal transforms. It has turned out that the factorization of these Kronecker products according to Good leads to vector-matrix-multiplications which can be implemented on processor networks of the Shuffle/Exchange-type. With this established, the universality of this network-type - its ability to realize all kinds of transforms based on Kronecker products - was examined.

Acknowledgement

The author is indebted to Mrs. S. C. Roder without whom this work would not have been done. He is also grateful to Dipl.-Ing. G. Hölling for his assistance in preparing the English version of this paper.

References

/AK70/ Andrews, H. C., Kane, J.: Kronecker Matrices, Computer Implementation and Generalized Spectra
J. ACM, Vol. 17, No. 2, April 1970.

/AN70/ Andrews, H. C.: Computer Techniques in Image Processing
Academic Press, New York/London, 1970.

/GO58/ Good, I. J.: The Interaction Algorithm and Practical Fourier Analysis
J. Roy. Statist. Soc. London, B 20, 1958.

/LA70/ Lawrie, D. H.: Access and Alignment of Data in an Array Processor
IEEE Transactions on Computers, Vol. C-25, No. 12, Dec. 1976.

/PA80/ Parker, D. S.: Notes on Shuffle/Exchange-Type Switching Networks
IEEE Transactions on Computers, Vol. C-29, No. 3, March 1980.

/PE68/ Pease, M. C.: An Adaption of the Fast Fourier Transform for Parallel Processing
J. ACM, Vol. 15, April 1968.

/WA23/ Walsh, J. L.: A Closed Set of Normal Orthogonal Functions
Ann. J. Math. 55, 1923.

/WG68/ Whelchel, J. E., Guinn, D. F.: The Fast Fourier Hadamard Transform and its Use in Signal Representation and Classification
The Electronic and Aerospace Systems Convention Record (EASCON),
IEEE New York, 1968.

/ST71/ Stone, H. S.: Parallel Processing with the Perfect Shuffle
IEEE Transaction on Computers, Vol. C-20, No. 2, Feb. 1971.

LISA: A PARALLEL PROCESSING ARCHITECTURE

G.M. Megson & D.J. Evans
Department of Computer Studies
Loughborough University of Technology

Loughborough, Leicestershire,
U.K.

The purpose of this paper is two-fold. Firstly, it introduces and develops the ideas of the Linear Instruction Systolic Array (LISA), and shows that it can simulate MIMD, SIMD and Systolic Wavefront Processor Algorithms involving no-backtracking.

Secondly, we show that it can be used to develop a powerful Parallel Architecture based on LISA chips, which should be expandable and area efficient.

As a subsidiary argument we can also demonstrate that there is real evidence for the role of Systolic Computation particularly pipelining in the development of parallel computations.

INTRODUCTION

Before introducing the concept of the Linear Instruction Systolic Array (LISA), we consider the results from the work of Kunde, Lang, Schimmler, Schmeck, and Schroder [1] and Lang [4]. In [1] the idea of the Instruction Systolic Array (ISA), a 2-D mesh of computing processors was developed. In comparing a Processor Array (PA) an MIMD-array of independent processors and Instruction Broadcast Array (IBA) (with instructions broadcast to all the processors in one column, and executed according, to selector information broadcast to all the processors of a row), and the ISA with instructions pumped through the array row by row with selectors pumped column by column, we can discern certain correlations. These relations indicate that programs on a PA could be transformed into equivalent programs on an ISA either directly or via the IBA; each transformation being achieved by adding extra instructions to the existing program. Hence simple program transformations indicate larger and slower programs. However each architecture or model could also have a more efficient program written directly for that architecture than the equivalent but transformed version. The result of these transformations show that the ISA is at least as powerful as SIMD machines from Flynn's classification, and can also simulate many MIMD programs. Umeo [7],[8] has also investigated systolic implementation of SIMD programs.

Since our starting point is the ISA, we can take the results of [1] that apply

to the ISA and extend them by a further program transformation to the LISA implying
that the Linear Systolic Array Pipeline can perform programs from a PA including SIMD
and MIMD programs.

INSTRUCTION SYSTOLIC ARRAY (ISA)

The structure of an ISA is as follows:

(i)   An n*n array of $N=n^2$ identical processors

(ii)   Each processor has a simple control unit without a control store

(iii)   Instructions and processor selector information are pumped through
the mesh,

    a)   Instructions top to bottom (vertically) from the set I

    b)   Selectors left to right (horizontally) from the set $\{0,1\}$

(iv)   A processor is capable of performing any of a finite number of simple
operations from a set I

(v)   Some local memory, with one register designated the communication
register

(vi)   A register R and a flag F to prevent the overwriting of the
communication register before all the processors neighbours have had
the chance to read it.

(vii)   Instruction cycle:

    a)   first half communication

    b)   second half computation

The 2-D arrangement of the ISA is given in Figure 1.

A program P on an ISA consists of a pair $P=(<>,<>)$ $<>$=sequence

$$P = \{ <P^{(1)},P^{(2)},\ldots,P^{(r)}>, <S^{(1)},S^{(2)},\ldots,S^{(r)}> \},$$

with $P^{(i)}$ and $S^{(i)}$ the n-tuples

$$P^{(i)} = (P_1^{(i)},P_2^{(i)},\ldots,P_n^{(i)}) \quad P_j^{(i)} \in I \ , \ j=1(1)n, \ i=1(1)r$$

and

$$S^{(i)} = (S_1^{(i)},S_2^{(i)},\ldots,S_n^{(i)}) \quad S_j^{(i)} \in \{0,1\} \ , \ j=1(1)n, \ i=1(1)r.$$

For every $i,j \leq n$ and $t \leq r$, $P^{(t)}$ is the row of instructions which enters the ith row at
time $t+i-1$ and $S(t)$ the column selector information enters the jth column at time
$t+j-1$, i.e., the instruction executed by processor (i,j) at time t is $P_j^{(t-i+1)}$ if
$S_i^{(t-j+1)}=1$, and 0 otherwise. The lower portion of the array not in use performs
no-op instructions. The program terminates when the last instruction $P^{(r)}$ has
entered the first row. See Figure 2.

REMARK: $I=I_u' \{c,\text{no-op}\}$, where c=copy command to transfer contents of R to the
communication register when F is set, then reset F. No-op is a null
operation and I'=set of arithmetic operations.

Instructions

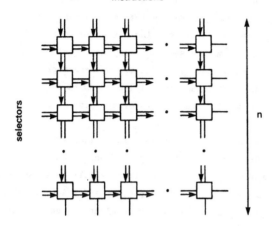

Figure 1: Instruction Systolic Array (ISA)

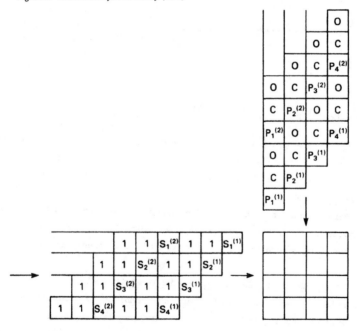

Figure 2: Control Flow in an ISA Program

THE WAVEFRONT ARRAY PROCESSOR

The wavefront array processor introduced by Kung [3], is a 2-D matrix of processing elements (PE's). Each PE communicates with its neighbours as shown in

Figure 3. The order of activation and subsequent computation of processors act like waves, propagating across the array. We consider only algorithms which contain multiple wavefronts acting on Huygen's principle where no two waves can pass or interfere with each other from the same source, this precludes any back-tracking of waves. Kung has also noted in [3] that the wavefront processor is a trade-off between the general purpose data flow multi-processors and the dedicated systolic array. This implies that the wavefront processor is related strongly to the ISA.

The ISA can easily be made to simulate any wavefront algorithm (from above), first notice that the pumping of the instructions and selectors in the ISA forms a set of wavefronts propagating out along the matrix from PE(1,1) as shown in Fig.3, (i.e. PE(1,1) is a point source). Setting $I=\{no\text{-}op, c, I_1\}$ and selectors=1, with $I_1=$ simple arithmetic operation such as an inner product evaluation, each instruction in the ISA program has the form,

$$
\left.
\begin{aligned}
P^{(i)} &= \langle I_1, I_1, \ldots, I_1 \rangle \\
P^{(i+1)} &= \langle c, c, \ldots, c \rangle \\
P^{(i+2)} &= \langle 0, 0, \ldots, 0 \rangle
\end{aligned}
\right\} \quad i=1(3)r-3
$$

$$\longleftarrow n \longrightarrow$$

$$O = no\text{-}op$$

$$S^{(i)} = \langle 1, 1, \ldots, 1 \rangle \qquad i=1(1)r$$

$$\longleftarrow n \longrightarrow$$

$$P = \{\langle P^{(1)}, P^{(2)}, \ldots, P^{(r)} \rangle, \langle S^{(1)}, S^{(2)}, \ldots, S^{(r)} \rangle\}$$

Thus, if $T(Q)$ is the cost of executing r wavefronts on the wavefront processor, then the cost on the ISA is given by $T(p) \leqslant 3rT(Q)+2n-1$. As each instruction is converted to 3 instructions on the ISA, we add an extra $2n-1$ steps to propagate the last wavefront off the grid.

The converse argument that all ISA programs can be converted to specialised wavefront processor algorithms does not apply, since for an MIMD simulation the instruction set I in general cannot be limited to just three operations.

THE MAPPING OF 2-D ARRAY PROCESSORS TO 1-D ARRAY PROCESSORS

In [2] Yang and Lee, introduced a mapping technique to transform a wavefront processor algorithm and architecture into a 1-D (i.e. linear) array. The mapping technique was applied to single-wavefront algorithms, where at time cycle i, only the PE's on the diagonal $W(i)$ are activated as in Figure 3.

We extend Yang and Lee's technique to multiple wavefront processor algorithms via the ISA, forming the basis of a more general mapping technique of ISA programs/algorithms to linear systolic arrays.

The mapping proceeds in two phases as follows:-

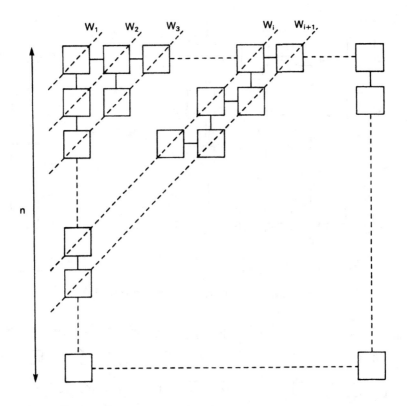

Figure 3: Wavefront Array Processor

    a)   convert the wavefront processor to an equivalent ISA

    b)   map the ISA into a linear or 1-D array

First, consider single wavefront algorithms, at any time t there is at most 1 active wavefront on the wavefront processor. The single wavefront algorithm is coded as a ISA with only one instruction triple followed by 2n-1 no-op instructions to push the wavefront through the array

$$P^{(1)} = \langle I_1, I_1, I_1, \ldots, I_1 \rangle \qquad S^{(1)} = \langle 1, 1, \ldots, 1 \rangle$$
$$P^{(2)} = \langle c, c, c, \ldots, c \rangle \qquad S^{(2)} = \langle 1, 1, \ldots, 1 \rangle$$
$$P^{(3)} = \langle 0, 0, 0, \ldots, 0 \rangle \qquad S^{(3)} = \langle 1, 1, \ldots, 1 \rangle$$
$$P^{(3+i)} = \langle 0, 0, \ldots, 0 \rangle \qquad S^{(3+i)} = \langle 1, 1, \ldots, 1 \rangle \qquad i=1(1)2n-1$$

Single Wavefront Program for ISA

The multiple wavefronts (Fig. 4b) for the single wavefront ISA program on an ISA for n=4, are shown at times t=1,4,8. The array will receive 3 more inputs to push out the $P^{(3)}$ wavefront at which time the ISA program will terminate. In order to

(a)

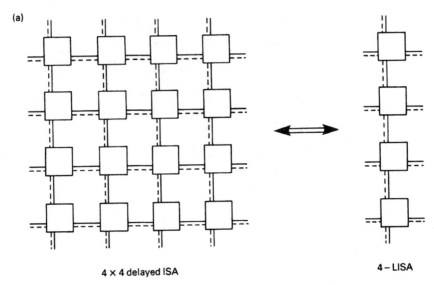

4 × 4 delayed ISA

4 – LISA

Equivalence of (4 × 4) mesh and 4 processor LISA

(b)

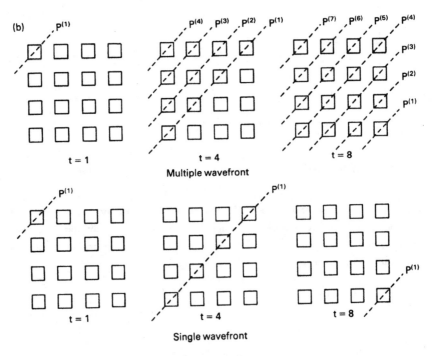

Multiple wavefront

Single wavefront

Figure 4: ISA→LISA Mapping

apply Yang and Lee's mapping technique to the Multiple case the ISA program needs to be converted to a Delayed Wavefront Program (DWP).

The DWP ensures that only one wavefront is active at t=1,4,8 is shown in Fig. 4b for $P^{(1)}$. This implies that the processors behind the wave have to execute a no-op instruction, or be de-selected for 2n-1 cycles between instructions making the program extremely large. However the LISA mapping controls this problem.

Next convert the ISA into a Linear Instruction Systolic Array (LISA) simulating the DWP (see Fig. 4a). For the conversion define a new basic processor structure called the LISA cell, for the simulation of an n*n, $N=n^2$, 2-D ISA array. We use n LISA cells linearly connected (see Fig. 5). Each LISA cell contains 4 bi-directional input/output lines for data, a select line passing horizontally through the cell from west to east, and the instruction line from north to south.

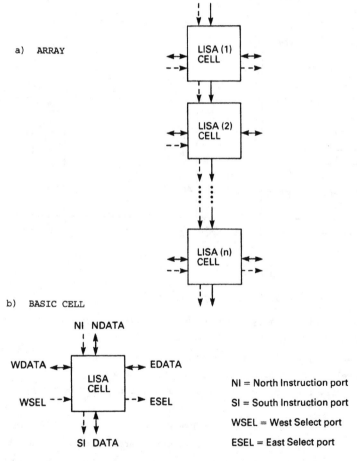

a) ARRAY

LISA (1) CELL

LISA (2) CELL

LISA (n) CELL

b) BASIC CELL

NI NDATA

WDATA — EDATA

LISA CELL

WSEL — ESEL

SI DATA

NI = North Instruction port
SI = South Instruction port
WSEL = West Select port
ESEL = East Select port

Figure 5: Linear Instruction Systolic Array

Immediately we see that:

(1) LISA(i) corresponds to the ith row of the original 2-D ISA array

(2) If LISA(i) acts as the (i,j)th ISA processor then LISA(i-1) and LISA(i+1) act as the (i-1,j+1)th and (i+1,j-1)th ISA processors respectively.

(3) If LISA(i) acts as (i,j)th processor of ISA at time t, then at time step t+1 this processor acts as (i,j+1)th ISA processor.

(4) Since each ISA cell can communicate in four directions, we consider the problem of communication on the linear array. The north direction is omitted because the processor there is executing no-op commands (behind the wavefront). Since LISA(i) simulates row i of the ISA east and west communication is no problem. This leaves communication south, as LISA(i) acts as (i,j)th ISA processor at time t, the data is moved to LISA(i+1) which at time t+1 acts as the (i+1,j)th processor.

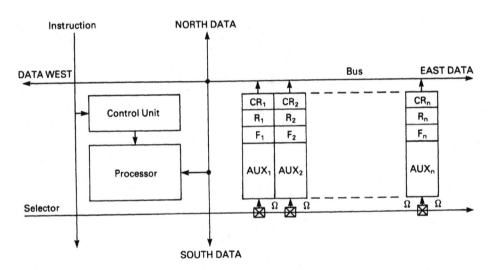

Figure 6: General LISA cell for n*n mesh

The cell contains sufficient memory for each cell in a row of the ISA array.

CR_j = communication register of jth cell in row

R_j = computation save register of jth cell in row

F_j = flag of jth cell in row to indicate CR_j has to be changed

Aux_j = Auxiliary memory for storing any extra data values required by the row (e.g. Yang & Lee Data Storage)

The Lisa cell is a simple arrangement. From DWP Fig.4b and Yang & Lee [2] only one section of memory (CR_i, R_i, F_i, AUX_i) is in use at any particular time, hence bus selection can be performed by the selector signal. The instruction is used to enable the direction of communication and its compass direction.

The resulting LISA array is area efficient, as only n processors and control units are used, rather than N as required by ISA, the memory requirements remain the same. Thus, we save more area than the ISA (and the IBA) itself by removing the processors from n-1 cells reducing the area involved with the mesh connected (PA). The selector information is also pipelined inside each LISA cell, ensuring that each section of memory is activated in a mutually exclusive fashion.

Returning to the mapping problem it is trivial to see that the single wavefront considered in Fig. 4b is simulated by the LISA array, leaving the problem of placing the next wavefront into the array, while it still holds the correct values. Clearly at time $t+1=n+1$ the wavefront has passed the anti-diagonal of processors and LISA(1) of the LISA array must be free. Rather than wait for the current wavefront to leave the array altogether we can start the next instruction. This is $P^{(2)}$ which is the copy command, after another $n+1$ time cycles we can enter the $P^{(3)}$ or no-op command, etc. This leaves the problem of how to produce a delay of $n+1$ cycles between ISA array instructions to produce the DWP. The DWP can be produced simply by considering the dataflow in the LISA pipeline, and the instruction and the selector information.

The whole LISA pipeline has only one instruction input register/path, hence the input sequence of Figure 7.

This format clearly shows that any ISA program can be translated into a DWP for the LISA pipeline. Here we show for $n=4$, hence 4 LISA cells, the pipeline above executes DWP's derived from ISA programs executed on the 4*4 matrix of Fig. 4a.

Clearly if we have a large mesh (n) and a long program (size r) the length of the input becomes very large and could slow programs down sufficiently to make the method impractical. From a theoretical point of view it is important to point out that in principle SIMD and MIMD programs can be transformed from PA to LISA by a sequence of at most four program transformations.

$$\text{PA} \Rightarrow \text{IBA} \Rightarrow \text{ISA} \Rightarrow \text{LISA} \quad \left\{ \begin{array}{l} \Rightarrow \text{Transformation, by a single or no} \\ \quad \text{transformation} \\ \stackrel{*}{\Rightarrow} \text{By one or more transformations} \end{array} \right.$$

Hence if q is a program on PA, and p is a program on LISA then,

$$q \stackrel{*}{\Rightarrow} p$$ means that q is equivalent to p as a transformation

is possible, i.e., $q \Rightarrow P_0 \Rightarrow P_1 \Rightarrow P$, P_0=IBA version of q, P_1=ISA version of q.

Thus, if MIMD=set of all MIMD programs, and SIMD=set of all SIMD programs then for $q \in \{\text{MIMD}_u\text{SIMD}\}$ then $q \stackrel{*}{\Rightarrow} p$ such that $p \in$ LISA programs.

From these results we can ask if LISA is a feasible parallel architecture for parallel computing?

THE LISA ARCHITECTURE

The theoretical construction of LISA pipelines has two undesirable features:

    (i)   The transformation from a ISA program to a LISA program introduces a large number of instructions and selectors related to the size of the mesh.

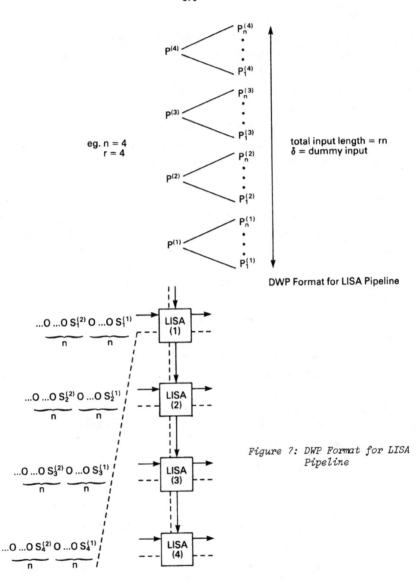

eg. n = 4
r = 4

total input length = rn
δ = dummy input

DWP Format for LISA Pipeline

Figure 7: DWP Format for LISA Pipeline

(ii) The size of the LISA cell is also dependent upon the mesh size. Both (i) and (ii) make the design of a flexible and expandable architecture difficult. However we can approach the design of a flexible and area efficient ISA based on LISA building blocks, by introducing the principle block partitioning to the ISA and forming a block-ISA. Considering the ISA mesh as a matrix of processor elements, we choose a block size k such that the ISA is partitioned into k*k blocks.

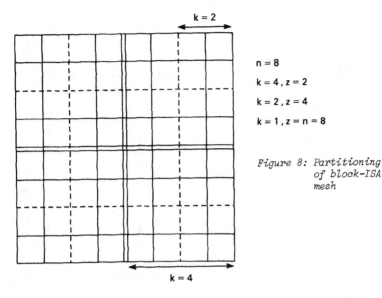

n = 8

k = 4 , z = 2

k = 2 , z = 4

k = 1 , z = n = 8

Figure 8: Partitioning of block-ISA mesh

The idea is to maximise the size of the block, while trying to minimise the number of additional instructions required to produce the DWP from the ISA program. The size of the block k is also the length of the LISA pipeline required to simulate the block. Clearly we have the problem of trading-off increased program size (hence program execution time) with the area required by a LISA cell, and the length of the pipe.

Notice that the size of the blocks is independent of the horizontal connections but not of the vertical connections an additional constraint. Here we will choose k=4, so that the LISA pipeline contains 4-cells and each cell simulates 4 ISA processors. An N=64 processor array can now be constructed as a BLOCK-ISA using only 4 LISA pipelines of length 4. The choice of k=4 is arbitrary, but based on the fact that the memory in each LISA cell is relatively small, we still save quite a lot of area by removing 12 processors and control units per block, while retaining possibilities of implementing the LISA pipeline as a chip.

NOTE: We use only one input and one output data line both horizontally and vertically, why? The immediate objection is that perhaps more than 1 ISA node/processor requests information from an adjacent block via a boundary. Analysis shows that at most two ISA processors can be active across either a horizontal or block boundary at the same time, and are always in adjacent rows or columns. Hence all data can be communicated in two communication steps using only one data line, and save chip pins.

Each LISA chip has a linear array of LISA cells like Fig. 4a. The design is expandable, as the LISA chip is of fixed area and we can add a row and column of LISA chips to upgrade the design to a 144 processor array without changes to the cycle time. Fig. 11 shows the simulated block ISA wavefront movement. Notice that the maximum delay between instructions is now dependent on the block size k, not the

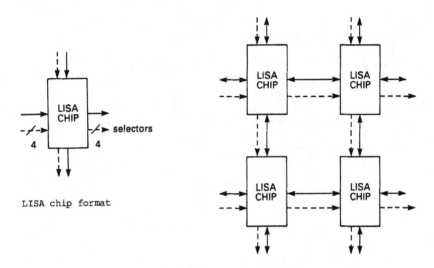

Figure 9: k=4 4-chips to implement 64-processor ISA

size of the ISA array.

Any program on the ISA has an equivalent DWP on the BLOCK ISA which is at most k times as long as the ISA program (in this example 4 times as long). For n=8 k=4 (block size). The instructions $P^{(1)} = (P_1^{(1)}, P_2^{(1)}, \dots, P_8^{(1)})$ is partitioned into r-sized components and input into the two chips of row 1 as shown in Fig.10.

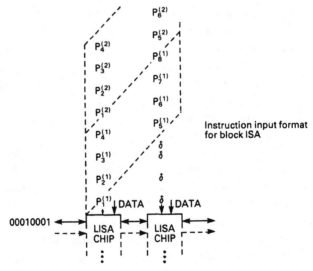

Figure 10: Instruction input format for block ISA

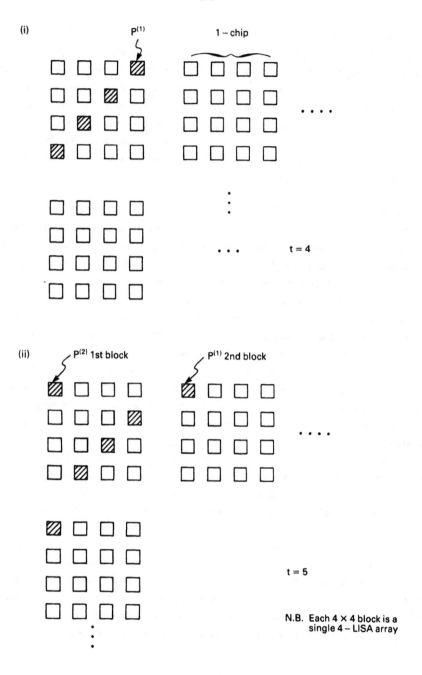

Figure 11: Block-ISA Wavefronts

Thus if we required a 4096 ISA, we could construct a block ISA with 16*16=256 LISA chips (with block size k=4), and still have no problems with broadcasting. In fact although the transformation process for producing DWP's to run on the block ISA introduces larger problems, the larger the array the less significant this becomes, when comparing it with broadcasting type machines which would be forced to change the cycle time of the machine for each upgrade, here we just tag on the extra chips (in matrix notation we can add either an extra row and column of blocks or just single chips - we suggest that a block size should be a power of two to allow suitable sized expansions.

CONCLUSION

This **paper** has indicated that the pipeline can be used to simulate MIMD and SIMD programs, on a systolic pipeline like the Linear Instruction Systolic Array. This indicates that the systolic pipeline has a much wider potential than has yet been exploited. Although our mapping technique shows that the ISA can be simulated by LISA it is more theoretical than practical for large mesh sizes.

We also showed that the so-called wavefront processor algorithms involving no backtracking can also be simulated as pipelines (LISA again) which supports the view that pipeline computation is fundamentally important, to computing.

Finally, the paper shows that although the simulation of ISA's by LISA is theoretical for large arrays, by applying the divide and conquer principle and the idea of block matrix calculation to derive a block-ISA utilises the mapping concept into a full parallel architecture proposal, using the LISA pipeline as its main building block.

A quantitive analysis of the LISA system in relation to other structures is not appropriate at this time, due to the problem of analysing transformed programs or dedicated LISA algorithms. Work is progressing in the development of algorithms and the authors have implemented a soft-systolic program simulator (SSPS) executed as a virtual machine in OCCAM which allows ISA programs specified in a special language RISAL (Replicating ISA language) to be designed and tested see [9]. Problems such as Matrix Product, LU Factorisation, Gaussian Elimination and some sorting algorithms have been implemented. For instance a 4*4 LU factorization can be executed on a 4*4 ISA with a RISAL program of r=39 statements and a transformation of a hex-systolic array [6] requires r=32 RISAL statements (about twice as many as the dedicated hex). Details of SSPS, RISAL and algorithms will be reported elsewhere.

REFERENCES
[1] M. Kinde, H.W. Lang, M. Schimmler, M. Schmeck, M. Schroder, "The Instruction Systolic Array and Its Relation to Other Models of Parallel Computers", Proc. International Conference Parallel Computing 85, North-Holland, 1986, eds. Schendel, Joubert, Fielmeier.

[2] C.B. Yang & R.C.T. Lee, "The Mapping of 2-D Array Processors to 1-D Array Processors", Parallel Computing, 1986, 3 (in press).

[3] S.Y. Kung, "Wavefront Array Processor: Language, Architecture & Applications", IEEE Trans. on Computers, Vol. C-31, No. 11, p.1054-1066, Nov. 1982.

[4] H.W. Lang, "The Instruction Systolic Array, A Parallel Architecture for VLSI", Report 8502, Institute Fur Informatik Und Praktische Mathematik.

[5] H.T. Kung, "The Structure of Parallel Algorithms", Advances in Computers, Vol. 19, 1980.

[6] C.E. Leiserson, "Area Efficient VLSI Computation", Ph.D. Thesis 1981, Carnegie Mellon University.

[7] Hiroshi Umeo, "A Class of SIMD Machines Simulated by Systolic VLSI Arrays", Proc. International Workshop on Parallel Computing & VLSI 1984, edits. P. Bertolazzi, F. Luccio, North-Holland Publishers.

[8] Hiroshi Umeo, "Two-Dimensional Systolic Implementation of Array Algorithms", Report AL82-32, Faculty of Engineering, Osaka-Electro-Communication Univ.

[9] G.M. Megson & D.J. Evans, "The Soft-Systolic Program Simulation System (SSPS)", Loughborough University of Technology, Comp.Stud. Rep. 272 (1986).

A Classification of Algorithms which Are
Well Suited for Implementations on the DAP
as a Basis for Further Research
on Parallel Programming

Klaus D. Thalhofer
Karl D. Reinartz

Universität Erlangen-Nürnberg
Institut für Mathematische Maschinen
und Datenverarbeitung
D-8520 Erlangen

Abstract

Considering the programs which have been written for the DAP (Distributed Array Processor) by members of our research group or other institutes we are in contact with, one sees quickly that there are a few classes of algorithms which cover nearly all the work done on the DAP.

These classes are:

— Operations from Linear Algebra (matrix multiplication, matrix inversion, solution of large systems of linear equations)
— Bit-algorithms for the fast computation of function values
— Arithmetic on numbers with variable lengths of representation
— Simulations or similar computations on two-dimensional structures taking advantage of the north-east-south-west neighbourhood facilities of the DAP
— "Large scale"-pipelining (in contrast to: "small scale"-pipelining, i.e. pipeline architectures)

In addition to the original DAP facilities some very tricky programming techniques have been developed. With the examples of "linear routing" and "recursive doubling" we shall point out how these techniques can be made available to all users by supplying them with "algorithm patterns" at a somewhat higher language level than provided by DAP-FORTRAN.

Key Words and Phrases

Parallel programming, SIMD-principle, algorithm patterns, preprocessors, recursive doubling, routing, binary decomposition, large scale pipelining.

Introduction

Since 1982 we are concerned with the research project PARCOMP* (**Parallel Computing**) which offers us an access to the ICL-DAP with 64 x 64 processing elements (PEs) at the *Queen Mary Collage* (QMC), London (A description of this computer is given by Hockney and Jesshope [3]). During these four years the members of our research group introduced many scientists and students of several institutes of our university to the use of the DAP for solving special computing problems. Now in 1986 we have been supplied with a DAP2 (32 x 32 = 1024 PEs) at our institute. This event - a cut in our work - is a motive for reviewing the programs written for the DAP in the past years and so establishing a good basis for planning the future work. The main results of this review and planning phase are published within this paper.

I. Classification of the Programs Run on the DAP so Far

The users of the DAP at our university and their main application fields are

---

* sponsored by the Deutsche Forschungsgemeinschaft (DFG)

Fluid mechanics Theoretical physics	} } }	Solution of partial differential equations, resulting in large systems of linear equations (operations from **Linear Algebra**); 2D-Simulations; grid relaxation methods
Applied mathematics		Operation research; transport problems (often described by the means of **Graph Theory**)
Computer science		Bit-algorithms (Reinartz [6]); modular arithmetic; arithmetic on numbers with various lengths of representation; and as a service for all the users: "asynchronous" in-/output

But more interesting than this kind of classification - especially from a computer scientist's point of view - is the following "hierarchical" classification. Table 1 shows the fields of application together with the most important techniques used for them and their relation to the hardware and system software facilities of the DAP making those possible.

Table 1.

DAP-Facilities	provided by	supported algorithms	used techniques

matrix mode
component-wise arithmetic/
    logical operations
nearest neighbourhood
    communication
	hardware
	system software
	DAP-FORTRAN
		2D-simulations
		grid relaxation
		modular arithmetic
		bit-algorithms
			"vertical storage" of data
			bit-sequential computation

activity control / masking
   (esp. alternating masks)
 	
shift facilities
	hardware
	system software
		individual mask generation
		special (horizontal)
		    data transports
		"recursive doubling"
		    algorithms (in principle)	

vector mode	system software DAP-FORTRAN	bit-algorithms	"horizontal storage" of data bit-parallel computation

(fast) summation, maximum,
   minimum, AND, OR etc.
 	
reversion, transposition
	system software
	DAP-FORTRAN
		linear algebra
		   (esp. scalar product,
		   matrix multiplication)
		graph theory
			special recursive doubling
			special binary decomposition
			   (used by system software;
			   hidden from the programmer)

macros, subroutines, control structures	APAL-assembler DAP-FORTRAN RATFOR	a l l	structured programming
input before start of DAP-job output after termination	operating system	a l l	

(Techniques shown at a certain level can be performed using only facilities of the same level or levels above.
DAP-FORTRAN is a FORTRAN dialect which allows to use the DAP-facilities in a rather transparent way ([1]).
RATFOR is a programming language (FORTRAN augmented by control structures, IF-THEN-ELSE constructs, compound statements etc.). RATFOR programs are translated into FORTRAN by a preprocessor. This tool can be used to enrich DAP-FORTRAN without any modification of the preprocessor ([7]).)

Although the list of facilities contained in table 1 covers all the essential features of the DAP, the list of techniques which can *immediately* be performed with those facilities is remarkably incomplete with respect to the parallel programs we have studied for our classification. Among the additional techniques we have detected there is a considerable number of very special applications, but there are also some very general ones which are the subject of the following paragraphs.

II. General Techniques not Originally Supported by Special Functions

In this part of the paper the techniques and their applications are introduced. Examples of language constructs to describe them and their equivalents in DAP-FORTRAN show how programmers even when not familiar with these techniques can use them nevertheless correctly and efficiently.

II.1 Generalization of the DAP-FORTRAN routines for vectors and matrices of arbitrary size

In the past many of the users did not mind to get restricted to a "64-by-64-world". It seemed very convenient to most of them to map the real problem onto the DAP-size by varying mesh widths or by adding or discarding some elements and so on. Others have been interested in the solution of their problem "in principle", have chosen one model size and "accidentally" taken an example of dimension 64 by 64.

When they finally tried to transfer their very efficient and easily gained solution to a real problem of fixed but different size or to generalize the algorithm for an arbitrary problem size they had to recognize that this generalization takes a considerable lot of work, too. Sometimes the total loss of the feeling of convenience when working on the DAP was the consequence.

The recognition of this fact gave us the idea of writing support software. From that time we have tried to remedy such problems in general rather than assist the programmers in particular.

In this case, we regard as the best solution to leave the language DAP-FORTRAN unchanged in its syntax, but allow the programmer to do as if he is using a "DAP of his size", i.e. to call the routines with vectors of arbitrary length and rectangular (not necessarily quadratic) matrices of any size (declared as 1- resp. 2-dimensional arrays).

Example: (large DAP: 64 x 64)
When a source file contains the lines

REAL X(64,128), EX(64,128)   {the sizes need not be multiples of 64;
                                      eventually masking is necessary in addition}

. . .
EX = EXP(X)   {element-wise exponential function}

the preprocessor will produce the following DAP-FORTRAN (RATFOR) lines

REAL X(,,1,2), EX(,,1,2)   {two-dimensional arrays of matrices}

. . .
DO K_GENSIZE = 1,2
{
  EX(,,1,K_GENSIZE) = EXP(X(,,1,K_GENSIZE))   {the two DAP-matrices are computed separately}
}

II.2 The linear routing problem

II.2.1 Description of the problem

One of the most frequently occurring problems is the transport of data within a matrix or vector or the permutation of their components. This so called *routing* problem arises, for example, when a processing element has to perform an arithmetical/logical operation with at least one operand residing in another processing element's memory.

There may be applications with very general routing demands, but of really great importance is the class of *linear routing* problems, i.e. - considering vectors - the class of assignments

$$V1(A*I + B) = V2(C*I + D), \quad I = LB,...,UB,$$

where all identifiers within the parentheses and the lower and upper bounds (LB, UB) represent integer scalars (in most applications constants). The assignments are to be understood as **collateral**.

The index expression on the *left hand side* is thought to perform masking (as usual in DAP-FORTRAN), i.e. only those components will be changed that are met by the value of the index expression after evaluating it with an I in the specified interval. On the *right hand side* the index expression denotes the components to be routed (as well-known from nearly all programming languages). In both cases indices which exceed the vector length (VECLEN $\in$ {32, 1024} resp. {64, 4096}) are to cause no effect.

The vector V2, when different from V1 is to be left unchanged. Therefore the routing problem should be solved by three steps:
- copy V2 to a temporary vector variable
- perform the actual routing on this temporary vector

- copy the result to V1 under usage of appropriate masks.

During the following considerations we will restrict ourselves to the second step, the actual routing "in place". This routing can again be decomposed into the following partial tasks:

a) translation: $V(I) = V(I + D), \ D \in Z$

b) reversion: $V(I) = V((VECLEN + 1) - I)$

c) linear contraction: $V(A^*I) = V(C^*A^*I), \ A,C \in N, C > 1$

d) linear extension: $V(A^*C^*I) = V(C^*I), \ A,C \in N, A > 1$

II.2.2 The influence of the SIMD-principle on the solution of the linear routing problem

The consideration of the decomposition above gives a good opportunity of reflecting the general *SIMD*-principle of the DAP (Single Instruction, Multiple Data). Its importance for parallelizing large arithmetical expressions is well known from literature: at a single program execution step one can perform at most one single arithmetical/logical operation on all the processing elements (with the additional possibility of masking certain processing elements to prevent them from storing the result).

The great influence of the *SIMD*-principle on the execution of routing tasks, however, has - as far as we know - not been reflected as well. Now we inspect the partial problems of linear routing from this point of view:

Translation (a) is a pure *SIMD*-operation: all processing elements get data out of another processing element's memory with the same distance D.

Pure reversion (b) is available from DAP-FORTRAN. A programmer can make use of efficient system software routines. We suppose that these also use the technique of *binary decomposition* we shall introduce in the next paragraph.

Finally there is the task of **contraction** and **extension** (c,d). These operations are not available from DAP-FORTRAN. Looking at the shift distances that are needed here one will find out that they all are different. Consider the contraction example (suppose $\{1,2\} \subseteq \{LB,...,UB\}$): To get the desired (new) $V(A)$ $(I = 1)$ one has to shift the (old) element $V(C^*A)$ by $(C - 1) \cdot A$ to the left, to get $V(A^*2)$ $(I = 2)$ one has to shift (old) $V(C^*A^*2)$ by $2 \cdot (C - 1) \cdot A$ and so on. This is not very well suited for a *SIMD*-computer, but can be handled rather efficiently, though, as we shall explain below.

II.2.3 The technique of binary decomposition

For an elegant solution of the linear contraction/extension problem one proceeds as the following figure shows:

Example: linear contraction $V(I) = V(C^*I), \ I = 1,...,N$

(displayed for C=5; d_i represents the value to be shifted when considering I=i)

Figure 1.

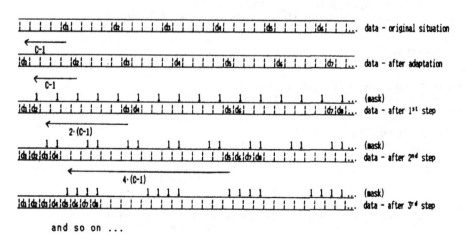

and so on ...

As one sees the task has once again been decomposed. The adaptation step prepares the vector so that in the following process the masks with alternately 2^{k-1} FALSE- resp. TRUE-values can be used. These masks are available from DAP-FORTRAN (function ALT) and very quickly built up by the DAP.

Then at the first step only the data belonging to even (destination) indices are shifted by C-1, at the second the data whose destination indices are equivalent to 3 or 0 modulo 4 are shifted by $2 \cdot (C - 1)$. In general: at the k-th step those data whose destination indices are equivalent to $2^{k-1} + 1, \ldots, 2^k - 1, 0$ modulo 2^k are shifted by $2^{k-1} \cdot (C - 1)$ ($k \in \{1,2,\ldots, \lceil \log_2 N \rceil \}$).

This sequence of steps induced us to call this technique *binary decomposition*. We have formally proved that this algorithm is correct, especially that data needed at later steps are not overwritten at earlier steps, independently of the contraction scale C.

If the factor A (in the general contraction scheme) is greater than 1, both the masks to be used and the shift widths have to be "zoomed" by A.

The reverse task of extension is performed by using the same ideas with a reversed order of steps.

It has already been mentioned that - for vector lengths which are powers of two - reversion can be performed by binary decomposition, too. An even more interesting fact, however, is that reversion and contraction can be combined to one binary-decomposition-algorithm.

The following example explains the combination of several binary decomposition steps for the solution of a more complex linear routing problem.

Example: The input

ROUTE (V(4*I + 2) = V(-6*I + 32), I = 0,...,5)

(assume VECLEN = 32, V of type REAL) will cause the routing preprocessor to produce the output

LOGICAL ROUTE_MASK()
REAL ROUTE_DATA()   (declaration of temporary variables)

. . .


```
#     "ROUTE" - Linear routing preprocessor:
#     Solution of
#        V(4*I + 2) = V(-6*I + 32), I = 0,...,5

#     A) CONTRACTION and REVERSION
#        ROUTE_DATA(2*I + 2) = V(-6*I + 32),  I = 0,...,5
```

ROUTE_DATA = SHRC(V,2)   (adjust and copy to temporary vector)
ROUTE_DATA(ALT(2)) = SHRC(ROUTE_DATA,8)
ROUTE_DATA(ALT(4)) = SHRC(ROUTE_DATA,16)   (cyclic right-shifts and storage
                                                    according to alternating masks)


```
#     B) EXTENSION
#        ROUTE_DATA(4*I + 2) = ROUTE_DATA(2*I + 2),  I = 0,...,5
```

ROUTE_DATA(ALT(16)) = SHRC(ROUTE_DATA,8)
ROUTE_DATA(ALT(8)) = SHRC(ROUTE_DATA,4)
ROUTE_DATA(ALT(4)) = SHRC(ROUTE_DATA,2)


```
#     C) MASKED STORAGE
#        V(4*I + 2) = ROUTE_DATA(4*I + 2),  I = 0,...,5
```
                                        (normally an additional shift is necessary
                                         for correction; this step can be omitted
                                         for this special example)

ROUTE_MASK = SHLP(ALT(4),2)
V((ROUTE_MASK .LNEQ. ROUTE_MASK(+)) .AND. ELS(2,22)) = ROUTE_DATA
                                        (the mask within the parantheses exactly

 # END "ROUTE"   indicates the components to be stored)

(The comments on the right hand side are added for this presentation.)

The proceeding is illustrated by the following figure

Figure 2.

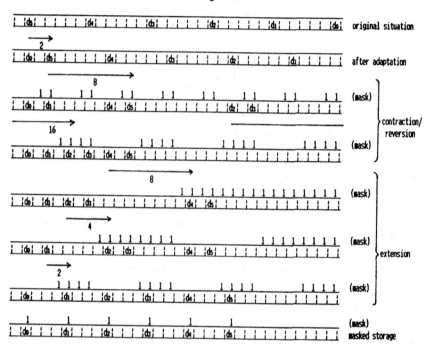

We have to restrict ourselves to the introduction of the principle of binary decomposition for this paper. Unfortunately we cannot discuss all the details of the algorithm, nor the design decisions for our preprocessor. But we should mention that the routing preprocessor can handle linear routing requirements for matrices, too, i.e. collateral assignments of the very general shape

$$M1(A1^*I + B1^*J + C1, A2^*I + B2^*J + C2) = M2(D1^*I + E1^*J + F1, D2^*I + E2^*J + F2),$$
$$I = LBI,...,UBI, \quad J = LBJ,...,UBJ .$$

Linear routing problems which are of practical interest can be considered as special cases of this class of assignments. Most of the scale factors will be 0 or 1 in many cases, a fact that considerably simplifies the task to be performed. The preprocessor is designed to make use of this chance of simplification and to yield an efficient program in every case. For the solution the principal ideas of binary decomposition are applied both in north-south and in east-west direction.

II.3 Recursive doubling for the solution of recurrence relations

The idea of *recursive doubling* is well known from literature and widely used for *rank reduction* purposes, i.e. functions which map a matrix onto a vector/scalar or a vector on a scalar value, e.g. for the built-in DAP-functions like (row-wise, column-wise, total) summation, maximum, minimum etc. It can be used for connecting N operands by an associative operation. The time-complexity of this kind of algorithms is $O(\log_2 N)$, if the associative operation can be performed in constant time. Kogge and Stone [4] show how to employ recursive doubling for the solution of m-th order linear recurrences, i.e. systems of equations of the shape

$$x_i = a_{i1}{\cdot}x_{i-1} + a_{i2}{\cdot}x_{i-2} + \ldots + a_{im}{\cdot}x_{i-m} + b_i \; ; \quad i=1,\ldots,N$$
$$x_i = 0 \, , \; i \le 0.$$

In the following example we use their ideas and a very closely related formalism for transforming the problem of evaluating a polynomial into a recursive-doubling-algorithm.

Example:
The evaluation of a polynomial according to *Horner's scheme*

$$p(x) = (\ldots((a_n{\cdot}x + a_{n-1}){\cdot}x + \ldots + a_1){\cdot}x + a_0$$

can be written as a recurrence relation like

$$p_i = p_{i-1}{\cdot}x + a_{n+1-i} \, , \quad i=1,\ldots,n+1.$$

This relation can be transformed into

$$\begin{pmatrix} p_i \\ 1 \end{pmatrix} = \begin{pmatrix} x & a_{n+1-i} \\ 0 & 1 \end{pmatrix} \cdot \begin{pmatrix} p_{i-1} \\ 1 \end{pmatrix}$$

which is a "vector recurrence" like

$$P_i = A_i{\cdot}P_{i-1} .$$

Then the result of the polynomial evaluation is the first component of

$$P_{n+1} = A_{n+1} \cdot A_n \cdot \ldots \cdot A_1 \cdot \begin{pmatrix} 0 \\ 1 \end{pmatrix} .$$

Matrix multiplication is associative. The product of two adjacent matrices A_i and A_{i-1} is

$$\begin{pmatrix} x & a_{n+1-i} \\ 0 & 1 \end{pmatrix} \cdot \begin{pmatrix} x & a_{n+2-i} \\ 0 & 1 \end{pmatrix} = \begin{pmatrix} x^2 & a_{n+2-i}{\cdot}x+a_{n+1-i} \\ 0 & 1 \end{pmatrix} .$$

As one can see immediately, the second row does not change. So only the top row of the product matrix has to be computed and stored.
So the preprocessor for recurrence relations will generate from the source line

RECURRENCE (P(I) = P(I-1) * X + A(33-I), I=1,...,32)   {evaluate polynomial of degree 31}

the following pieces of a DAP-FORTRAN program with RATFOR constructs
(suppose X and A(I) are of type **REAL**):

REAL RECUR01(), RECUR02()   {declaration of two real vectors}
LOGICAL RECUR_MASK()   {and a mask vector}

. . .

```
#    "RECUR" - Recurrence Preprocessor:
#    Solution of
#        P(I) = P(I-1) * X + A(33-I), I=1,...,32
#    Chosen technique: RECURSIVE DOUBLING
```

RECUR01 = X   {set all components of RECUR01 to X}

ROUTE (RECUR02(I) = A(33 - I), I = 1,...,32)   {a task for the *routing* preprocessor}

K_RECUR = 1   {shift bias}

DO I_RECUR = 1, 5   {5 = $\log_2 32$}
```
{
  RECUR_MASK = .NOT. ELS(1,K_RECUR)
  RECUR02(RECUR_MASK) = RECUR01 * SHRP(RECUR02,K_RECUR) + SHRP(RECUR02,K_RECUR)
  RECUR01(RECUR_MASK) = RECUR01 * SHRP(RECUR01,K_RECUR)
```
                                             {perform rudimentary matrix multiplication;

right-shifts transport components
of left hand matrices to the place of operation}

K_RECUR = K_RECUR + K_RECUR   {double bias}
}

P(ELS(1,32)) = RECUR02   {store results}

 #   END "RECUR"

(The comments on the right hand side are added for this presentation.)

A reader who is familiar with programming the DAP will find that this is a quite 'normal' parallel program for polynomial evaluation. This fact demonstrates that the possibility of using high level *algorithm patterns* does not prevent the user from getting efficient programs, on the contrary, it shows that recurrence relations are very useful instruments for describing a great variety of algorithms. It has to be noted, however, that the recursive doubling approach with the necessity of multiplying matrices of size $(m+1) \times (m+1)$ can be of practical interest only when m is small (at least compared with N). For a relatively large m, however, one should choose an algorithm like the *column-sweep* algorithm proposed by Kuck [5]. We have written a preprocessor which tries to decide from the information given at preprocessing time which algorithm to choose. This is an efficient realization of a *poly-algorithm* (cf. III.).

II.4 Large-scale-pipelining

Many users want to have handled their problems in an assembly-line manner. We call this technique *large-scale-pipelining*, in contrast to "small-scale"-pipelining as performed by pipeline architectures (e.g. CYBER 205). We have evaluated two kinds of pipelining appearances:

a) "Asynchronous" in/output (Erhard [2]): Programs which have to handle large amounts of data not residing in working memory all the time can be run continuously, if the host computer performs all the in/output while the DAP does its computations. If the amount of data needed or produced by the DAP for a certain span of time is small in comparison to the total memory available to the job, the host and the DAP can work nearly *asynchronously*, i.e. there are synchronization points that are not critical for the host.

b) Pipelining within the processor array: There are also some (parts of) programs which are performed in certain steps that can overlap (also under consideration of the *SIMD*-restriction), and some of these steps together can be performed on the processor array of the DAP. This concept is quite closely related to recurrence equations, but it is unnecessary and inefficient to employ methods like recursive doubling whenever the utilization of the processor array induced by the "natural" algorithm is high (perhaps except of a warm-up- and a shut-down-phase).

We are searching for a description method for these applications in order to get a preprocessor which will be able to free the user from "organizing" work (esp. from typing all the operating system commands necessary for asynchronous in/output) in a similar way as with the other methods introduced before.

III. Preprocessors for the Realization of Algorithm Patterns

Our use of the term "algorithm patterns" is due to the experience that the application of the techniques described above results in programs of a special, obvious structure. Indeed, the work of detecting and generalizing the techniques - esp. binary decomposition and recursive doubling - first was a pattern matching process. The realization of our preprocessors conversely consists of supplying the patterns as a framework and filling it with program constructs like variable names and (sub)expressions introduced by the programmer.
The main aspects of our approach can be comprehended by the following items:

1. "Shorthand" notation
A short text contains all the information needed to generate considerably complex pieces of programs. Due to this fact the source text becomes shorter, more readable, and easier to be changed.

2. Adequate description
The inputs required quite well meet the original, problem specific way of describing the intended algorithm (**specification of the problem**, not of the **operation sequence**). The correctness of programs specified in this way

can be proved immediately.

3. Poly-algorithms with the choice of the best algorithm before run-time

So called *poly-algorithms* (a collection of various algorithms for the solution of different instances of the same problem in one program with the possibility of switching between the single algorithms depending on the actual input data) are rather widely used not only for parallel computers. Switching at run-time, however, causes inefficiencies both in execution time (evaluation of conditions, branching) and in storage requirement (the entire program with all its branches has to be kept in memory). Our preprocessors try to choose the most efficient algorithm at preprocessing time whenever possible.

4. Chance of getting the result of preprocessing as a DAP-FORTRAN program

We have chosen the way of preprocessing, because the two alternatives we have taken into account seemed to bring up great disadvantages:

A **complete compilation** into assembler code has been left out of consideration, because we want to make use of the memory allocation and arithmetic routines provided by the DAP-FORTRAN compiler.

The use of **DAP-FORTRAN subroutines** does not fulfil all requirements we have. Especially the unability of performing asynchronous in-/output and the fact that the language does not offer the opportunity of expressing compile-time decisions make its use inconvenient.

We have tried hard to make the output of the preprocessors as clear and instructive as possible by including comments in order to enable the user to learn parallelizing techniques and to check the quality of his specification. Reversely we are interested in a reasonable feed-back from the users. A hint how to improve or to complete our preprocessors is always welcome.

5. Machine independence

As pointed out under item 4. one can use the preprocessors to produce DAP-FORTRAN programs in order to learn how to use this computer efficiently. On the other hand a user can use the algorithm patterns without knowing anything about the DAP or about parallelizing techniques in general. This fact makes these language constructs a good interface to other perhaps more complicated parallel computers. The preprocessors must be changed, but the users' programs can be run on other machines without modification.

All the preprocessors have been developed by using the tools LEX (lexical analyser), M4 (macro generator), and YACC (compiler-compiler) supplied by the operating system UNIX (Trademark of Bell Laboratories; [7]) and therefore available on many machines.

Conclusion

We think that the DAP, its architecture together with the SIMD-principle, represents a very powerful approach to parallel programming. This estimation is supported by the fact that - as we have been told - the ICL company is expecting commercial success from a further development of this kind of computers. With our work we intend to make a contribution to a convenient software environment for SIMD-computers in general and the DAP in particular.

References

[1] DAP: FORTRAN Language, ICL Techn. Publ. 6918, 3rd Ed., 1981

[2] Erhard W.: Feldrechner DAP: Invertierung großer Matrizen, Arbeitsberichte des Instituts für Math. Maschinen und Datenverarbeitung, Erlangen, Bd. 19, Nr. 1, 1986

[3] Hockney R.W., Jesshope C.R.: Parallel Computers: Architecture, Programming and Algorithms, Bristol, 1981

[4] Kogge P.M., Stone H.S.: A Parallel Algorithm for the Efficient Solution of a General Class of Recurrence Equations, IEEE Trans. Comp., Vol. C-22, No. 8, 1973, pp. 786-793

[5] Kuck D.J.: The Structure of Computers and Computations, John Wiley & Sons, New York, 1978

[6] Reinartz K.D.: Bitalgorithmen zur schnellen Berechnung transzendenter Funktionen auf Parallelrechnern, in: Proceedings of "Parallel Computing 83", Elsevier, North-Holland, 1984, pp. 217-224

[7] UNIX Programmer's Manual, Vol. 2: Supplementary Documents, 7th Ed. (1979) in: ICL PERQ Manual, No. RP10126, 1983

Use of inherent parallelism in database operations

T. Härder, Ch. Hübel, B. Mitschang
University Kaiserslautern

Abstract
Non-standard applications of database systems (e.g. CAD) are characterized by complex objects and powerful user operations. Units of work decomposed from a single user operation are said to allow for inherent semantic parallelism when they do not conflict with each other at the level of decomposition. Hence, they can be scheduled concurrently. In order to support this processing scheme it is necessary to organize parallel execution by adequate control units. Therefore, client-server processes and nested transactions are applied to hierarchically structure the DBS-operations. On the other hand, the DBS-code itself has to be mapped onto a multiprocessor system to take advantage of multiple processing units.

1. Introduction
Parallel computer architectures of various kinds - often referred as super-computing - offer huge instruction rates for processing a special sort of applications. They are implicitly tailored to data-intensive numerical applications for which such a tremendous demand of processing power is necessary to yield the required precision of the solution (e.g. finite elements) or the mandatory response time (e.g. real time applications). For these numerical applications, the transformation of (parts of) a sequential program - the so-called vectorization - to an equivalent program, which can take advantage of parallel facilities, is comparably simple because of the homogeneous data structures used, e.g. the distribution of a large matrix operation to a SIMD-architecture.

Database operations are also data-intensive and must be executed fast enough to support an interactive environment - in particular in "future" applications like engineering (CAD, CAM), or geographic information systems. Their decomposition to exploit parallelism on complex objects within a single operation is by far more complicated compared to numerical applications. In the first place, heterogeneous data structures and their interfering operations appear to be responsible for this difficulty. Therefore, up to now almost no efforts are made to gain some kind of "inherent" parallelism. Nowadays commercial database systems (DBS) execute the operation of a user's transaction (DML-operation) in a strictly sequential manner. In this context, parallelism at the level of DML-operation is only achieved by concurrent execution of requests in a multi-user mode.

Database applications do not allow for arbitrary kinds of syntactic parallelism; they rather require logical serialization of all committed transactions whose results must be equivalent to the results obtained by some serial schedule. Hence, a transaction is defined to be a unit of application-oriented work, of synchronization and of recovery. Its properties can be summarized by the ACID-principle of [HR83] (Atomicity, Consistency, Isolation and Durability). These requirements usually lead to a processing concept as sketched in Fig. 1. Parallel execution is only achieved between transactions subject to conflict-free data references controlled by some synchronization algorithm e.g. locking.

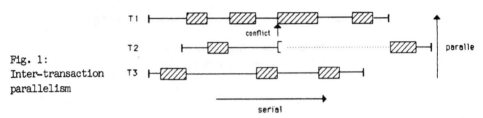

Fig. 1:
Inter-transaction
parallelism

The use of parallelism within a single DBS-operation mainly focusses on two approaches explored in research projects: data-oriented parallelism for disk search in SIMD-architectures and parallel processing of relational operators in MIMD-architectures [DW79]. Both approaches have not been particularly successful.

Non-standard applications of DBS manipulate complex objects by powerful operations (ADT's). These objects are represented by simpler data structures (sets of hetero-geneous tuples) handled by simpler operations. Hence, the decomposition of complex objects/operations to simpler ones offers a potential for parallelism to be investigated.

2. A new approach to parallel DBS-processing

2.1 Model of DBS-operation

Before sketching our approach we introduce a gross DBS-model to explain its operations. The architecture of a DBS may be conveniently represented by a multi-layer model describing the mapping hierarchy of data. A layer implements the objects and operations offered at its interface (level) to the above layer thereby using the services of the subordinate layer. For an NDBS (DBS for non-standard applications), the model may be illustrated by the type of operations and the level names indicating the type of objects:

levels	layers	operations
object level		ADT-operations
	application layer	
data model level		DML-operations
	data system	
record level		record/access path op.
	access system	
page level		page operations
	storage system	
disk level		disk accesses

An ADT-operation is processed in the application layer by using a number of DML-operations executed at the underlying layer which, in turn, are supported by primi-tive operations of the next subordinate layer. Each call at one level of implemen-tation invokes a set of primitives at a lower level of control. In current DBS, typically all (sub-)operations are synchronously called and serially executed.

2.2 Control structures for system operations

ADT-operations, however, may consume quite a lot of DML-operations for their execution. For example, we have measured ADT's which have issued more than 10^4 DML's in a CAD-application. In order to reduce response time, efforts should be made to call and distribute these operations in a <u>synchronous</u> or <u>asynchronous</u> manner and to execute them in <u>parallel</u>. Since the data structures are heterogeneous and dependent on the operations in quite complicated ways, such an approach must be planned carefully. Our idea is to decompose an ADT into a sequence of conflict-free operations. Then, sets of sequence-independent operations may be scheduled in parallel. Such decomposition units (DU's) are roughly equivalent to DML-operations of nowadays DBS. A set of DU's scheduled concurrently is called a parallel execution unit (PEU) (see Fig. 3). DU's are said to allow for <u>inherent</u> <u>semantic</u> parallelism when they do not conflict with each other at the level of decomposition. Currently, the decomposition is done "manually" (not supported by a compiler) by preparing sets of procedures for each ADT at the application layer. This job is facilitated by the fact that the DB-schema at the data model level is fixed for an application class.

For an ADT-operation, <u>atomicity</u> must be provided at the user interface ("all or nothing" has to be executed in case of arbitrary failures). Since the DBS processing is quite complex for an ADT (sometimes 10^7-10^8 instructions or more and lots of data references which may be serviced by disk accesses), there is a strong need for appropriate control structures. Nested system transactions have been proposed for this purpose [Wa84, WS84]. The nesting of sub-transactions (STA's) may be designed in accordance with the system layers. For example, at the application layer STA_1 is a proper structure to accept/return an ADT-call. The DU's used as primitives to the subordinate layer are, in turn, embedded into STA_{2i} ($1 \le i \le n$) to take care of the atomicity of the service calls. Again, a DU may require some services from the storage structure layer which are organized by STA_{3j} and so on. Obviously, the atomicity of STA's greatly facilitates the design of the DBS. Two additional properties are required for our purpose:

- The operations within an STA must be synchronized against operations of other users (transaction principle). Furthermore, they must be isolated against the operations (DU's) within a PEU. Since they run in parallel, they might conflict at the physical level (common page).
- A committed STA_{ij} may be rolled back if a parent STA_{kl} ($k<i$) fails in order to reach the "nothing" state.

2.3 Using semantic parallelism – an example

Until now, we have sketched some abstract concepts allowing for decomposition and parallelization of ADT-operations. In order to demonstrate the practical usefulness of these approaches, we are going to introduce a simple but illustrative example. For this purpose, we have chosen the area of geometric solid modeling, where the user interface is designed for the construction of 3D-workpieces. Each user operation refers to solids and is either binary (UNION, DIFFERENCE and INTERSECTION) or unary (TRANSLATION, ROTATION and SCALING).

One important representation of such solids, especially for graphical output, is the so-called boundary representation scheme (BREP). There, each solid is represented by its faces, which are, in turn, composed of its border-lines, whereof each line is limited by its endpoints.

Using this modeling approach, each workpiece is represented by a heterogeneous structure as depicted in Fig. 2. A generalization of a decomposed ADT-operation using the above modeled BREP-scheme is shown in Fig. 3, where each DU is represented by a rectangle and the PEU's are built by means of dotted line rectangles.

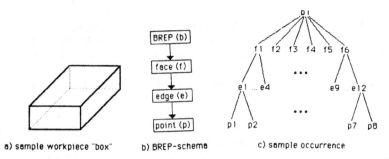

a) sample workpiece "box"   b) BREP-schema   c) sample occurrence

Fig. 2: Boundary representation

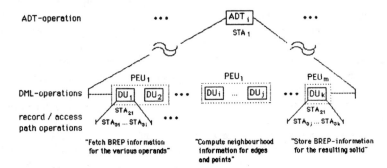

Fig. 3: Decomposition of an ADT-operation

3. Mapping of DBS-layers to software structures

Now we want to sketch some important concepts and constructs in the field of programming languages and operating systems necessary for the implementation of the ideas discussed above.

3.1 Use of process structures

The parallel execution of DU's anticipates the existence of concurrent processing units typically embodied by processes. From an OS point of view, they are the units of processor and resource allocation, protection and scheduling. Since these processes work together for a common job, there is an urgent need for effective cooperation which requires suitable mechanisms for communication and synchronization, e.g. service calls/results must be distributed/returned or access to shared data must be controlled efficiently. The concept of remote operations appears to be adequate for process communication when its semantics is extended for our purpose. A parallel activation of remote operations is a mandatory option for the concurrent execution of DU's within a PEU. An appropriate programming notation to express such a calling semantics is given by the **Parbegin...Parend** construct combined with the remote procedure call mechanism (Fig. 4a). **Parbegin** marks the begin of a set of parallel calls. **Parend** determines the "wait for result" point, i.e. the point of synchronization [AS83].

Our multi-layered architecture model describes the abstract mapping hierarchy of a DBS. Various ways for the DBS implementation are discussed in literature: object-, function- or layer-oriented. Here, we refer to the classic way of layer-oriented

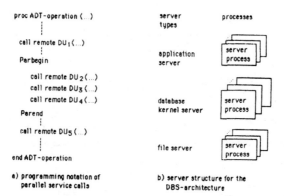

Fig. 4: Sample program and server structure

implementation. The system then has to be divided into parts and allocated to processes to appropriately support the anticipated parallel execution. We propose a separation of the mapping hierarchy into application, kernel and file server (Fig. 4b); their cooperation is performed by client-server relationships where a required service-call is directed to a task (generic processing structure for requests). In general, several client requests (from one or several processes) are issued concurrently (at each level). Hence, a suitable mapping of the above introduced tasks to their corresponding server processes must be provided. Among the conceivable solutions only multi-process/single-tasking (i.e. only one task within one process) or multi-process/multi-tasking (i.e. several tasks within one process) may be chosen for each of the three DBS components (Fig. 4b), when the full potential of parallelism in our hardware structure should be exploited (Fig. 6). Multi-tasking introduces an additional level of scheduling performed in a process. It is only justified for reasons of high process switching overhead or by the need to dynamically create cheap processing structures and tailored scheduling strategies. The application server offers ADT-operations to the user. An application server process includes the execution of some model mapping functions and the distribution of DU's by activating several DML-operations. DU's within PEU's may be performed by asynchronous service calls. The kernel server executes DML-operations thereby using primitive operations offered by the file server. This mapping involves functions of the data system, access path system and parts of the storage system. Finally, the file server manages the disc accesses. Each of those three server types can be represented by several processes.

The kernel server works on behalf of one or more users on common data structures (records, access paths, locking/logging informaton). Message-oriented exchange of data/control would have an heavy impact on system performance. Therefore, common memory for these data is an important implementation requirement. Then, some mutual exclusion mechanism has to be provided to control access to these shared resources. The frequency of these events makes it necessary to use direct protocols by the participating process (e.g. semaphore-based).

3.2 Use of functional parallelism

The proposed client-server model exhibits a very simple structure for the sake of reduced inter-server complexity. As a consequence, especially the kernel server has a significant internal complexity which may be reduced by introducing some further

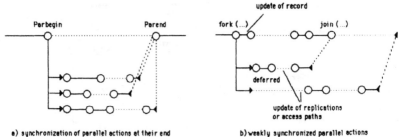

Fig. 5: Synchronization of parallel actions

server types. The expected gain of such subdivisions (e.g. simpler module structures) will often be paid off by increased communication costs. The intent to exploit parallelism, however, could be a strong motivation. On the other hand, a refined decomposition of operations and their parallel execution must be carefully considered for the kernel server, since shrinking operation granules coincide with a constant overhead for process communication and process switching.

Another use of parallelism, however, may be worth a closer look. Some DBS-functions and actions can be executed in parallel without the necessity of strict synchronization at their end (Fig. 5a). For example, locking and logging/recovery actions, integrity checking or access path/replica maintenance [HR85] are candidates for applying weakly synchronized parallel operations (Fig. 5b). Only at the end of the resp. STA or even later in case of deferred execution some acknowledgement has to be accepted. Obviously the price to pay is a new control structure for keeping track of such events. In addition, error detection and recovery become more complex. When a failure occurs, rollback is more difficult implying new and extended mechanisms for error recovery. This approach also allows for an optimistic attitude when concurrently calling functions. For example, record update can be initiated together with the request for the corresponding lock. If this asynchronous locking procedure does not succeed (lock is not granted), the depending record modifications must be undone. The rationale behind this optimistic idea is to try parallel actions with the (hopefully low) risk of bad luck.

Functional parallelism of this kind can be utilized to take advantage of refined server structures (or client-server relationships between kernel server processes) without being fully compensated by processing overhead. It requires some sort of inter-process communication to report the delayed end of operation. For this purpose, a less restrictive method (**FORK...JOIN** (AS83)) compared to Parbegin...Parend seems to be convenient. Nevertheless, the application of functional parallelism is less clear than the use of parallelism generated by semantic decomposition of operations. This idea deserves further attention.

4. Hardware architecture for parallel DBS-processing

Thus far, we have introduced the various levels and organizational concepts of our DBS-architecture, i.e. the computational model of the software system:
- the static view of the DBS-architecture expressed by hierarchic layers
- the organization of the execution by a nested transaction concept
- the mapping of the layers to server types
- the use of dynamic relationships (client-server) between process structures of the same or of different server types.

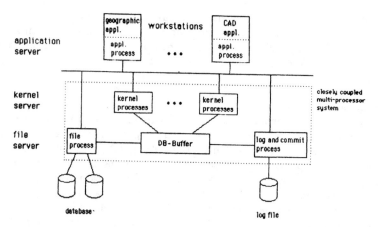

Fig. 6: Hardware architecture and server allocation

As a final step, mapping of processes to a multi-processor system must be accomplished adequately to preserve the inter-process parallelism as far as possible.

Our "ideal" hardware configuration and server allocation for the proposed type of parallel processing is illustrated in Fig. 6. This architecture is based on general purpose processors, for example of type MC 68020, each of them equipped with about 4 MBytes main memory. They are connected by a high bandwidth communication system (bus or ring) of about 10-100 MBits/sec. Some processors are <u>closely</u> coupled by a common memory partition. It is tailored to the particular processing needs of a DBS and serves as a common system buffer (having a size of preferably 10-? MBytes). All processors run an own copy of the OS and the DBS-components in their memory. The user process (e.g. for CAD/VLSI application) is allocated together with an application server process to a separate processor (e.g. workstation).

The prime mechanism for communication is message-based. Access to shared data by kernel server processes is extremely frequent; hence, a message protocol would have severe impact on performance. Therefore, shared data is located in a memory partition accessible for all kernel and file processes. Exclusive control is achieved by a semaphore protocol. File and commit processes are able to read/write pages (data and log information) to/from the system buffer. Kernel processes are directly referencing the contents of buffer pages by machine instructions.

Since data structures can be manipulated directly, DBS-algorithms for all important functions (e.g. buffer management, locking, logging) may be designed similar to the centralized case. Due to the server structure, service calls at various levels and granules must be distributed and assigned to processes in a suitable way. Hence, it is necessary to provide a load control function [Re86], in particular for the kernel server processes. Since these are accessing a common buffer, load control is comparably simple. Obviously, the use of special purpose processors would have complicated load control considerably.

All kernel server processes have the same view to the entire database – there is no need for distributing copies or dedicating processors to database partitions. Multi-processor database architectures without shared memory – e.g. DB-sharing vs. DB-distribution systems – are forced to use copies of data or are restricted to partitioned access [Hä86] – these properties make access to data and load control much more difficult. Of course, shared memory is then a limiting factor to system's growth. On the other hand, the potential parallelism gained by decomposing a single user operation is not unlimited (up to 3-5 DU's in a PEU). In addition, synchronization between DU's of a PEU (at the physical level) and between user operations does not allow for arbitrary degrees of parallelism.

5. Conclusions

We have discussed a new approach to exploit parallelism on heterogeneous data structures. As opposed to homogeneous data structures of numerical applications, the transformation of a user operation to allow for parallel execution is much more complicated. We have proposed a decomposition of ADT-operations into units to be executed concurrently thereby using the inherent semantic parallelism.

The parallel execution is aimed at suboperations of a powerful user operation rather than separate user operations. Therefore, the concept of nested transactions (within a single operation) is needed to organize the dynamic flow of control. Based on adequate process and communication concepts two different kinds of parallelism are considered – semantic and functional parallelism with strictly synchronized and weakly synchronized communication. To maximize parallel actions the DBS-code has to be mapped appropriately to processes which in turn have to be assigned to processors in a suitable way. For DBS-processing of the particular kind, a closely coupled hardware architecture seems to be mandatory because references to shared data are very frequent.

6. References

AS83   Andrews, G.R., Schneider, F.B.: Concepts and Notations for Concurrent Programming, in: ACM Computer Surveys, Vol. 15, No. 1, March 1983, S. 3-43.

DW79   DeWitt, D.J.: DIRECT – A Multiprocessor Organization for Supporting Relational Database Management Systems, in: IEEE Trans. on Computers, Vol. 28, No. 6, 1979, pp. 395-405.

Hä86   Härder, T.: DB-Sharing vs. DB-Distribution – die Frage nach dem Systemkonzept zukünftiger DB/DC-Systeme, in: Proc. 9. NTG/GI-Fachtagung "Architektur und Betrieb von Rechensystemen", Stuttgart, März 1986.

HR83   Härder, T., Reuter, A.: Principles of Transaction-Oriented Database Recovery, in: ACM Computing Surveys, Vol. 15, No. 4, Dec. 1983, pp. 287-317.

HR85   Härder, T., Reuter, A.: Architektur von Datenbanksystemen für Non-Standard-Anwendungen, in: Proc. GI-Fachtagung "Datenbanksysteme in Büro, Technik und Wissenschaft", März 1985, Karlsruhe (eingeladener Vortrag), IFB 94, S. 253-286.

Re86   Reuter, A.: Load Control and Load Balancing in a Shared Database Management System, in: Proc. Int. Conf. on Data Engineering, Los Angeles, Feb. 1986.

Wa84   Walter, B.: Nested Transactions with Multiple Commit Points: An Approach to the Structure of Advanced Database Applications, in: Proc. 10th Int. Conf. on VLDB, Singapore, 1984,, pp. 161-171.

WS84   Weikum, G., Schek, H.-J.: Architectural Issues of Transaction Management in Layered Systems, in: Proc. 10th Int. Conf. on VLDB, Singapore, 1984, pp. 454-465.

PARALLEL DYNAMIC PROGRAMMING ALGORITHMS

Marinus Veldhorst

Department of Computer Science, University of Utrecht,
P.O.Box 80.012, 3508 TA Utrecht, The Netherlands.

ABSTRACT

This paper presents a number of parallel algorithms for the dynamic programming problem

$$c(i,i) = 0 \quad (0 \leq i \leq n)$$
$$c(i,j) = w(i,j) + \min_{i < m \leq j} (c(i,m-1) + c(m,j))$$

Sequential algorithms run in $O(n^3)$ time or, if the quadrangle inequality holds (cf. [7]), in $O(n^2)$ time. For the former we design parallel algorithms that run in $O(n^3/p)$ time on $p < n^2$ processing elements (PEs). It is also shown that dynamic programming problems satisfying the quadrangle inequality can be solved in $O(n^2/p + n \log \log p)$ time using p $(1 < p \leq n)$ PEs. A global shared memory is assumed. Moreover, we design a systolic array for computing the $c(i,j)$'s that runs in linear time using $\Theta(n^2)$ PEs.

1. Introduction.

Many combinatorial optimization problems can be solved with the dynamic programming technique. Essential in it is the principle of optimality (cf. [2]): the optimal solution can be written as a recurrence relation in optimal solutions of subproblems. Computed optimal solutions (and possibly additional information) of subproblems are maintained in memory so that they are computed only once. This latter aspect creates also the difficulty of dynamic programming: storage requirements may become unacceptably high (the "curse of dimensionality" (cf. [2])).

In this paper we will consider the dynamic programming problem

Given values $w(i,j)$ $(0 \leq i \leq j \leq n)$; compute $c(0,n)$ defined as

$$c(i,i) = 0 \quad (0 \leq i \leq n)$$
$$c(i,j) = w(i,j) + \min_{i < m \leq j} (c(i,m-1) + c(m,j)) \quad \text{for } 0 \leq i < j \leq n \qquad (1)$$

A straightforward sequential algorithm to solve (1) is given in algorithm A. It runs in time $O(n^3)$.

Example 1. Optimal binary search trees (cf. [4]).

Given n keys $a_1, ..., a_n$ and $2n+1$ probabilities $p_1, ..., p_n$ and $q_0, ..., q_n$ where p_i $(1 \leq i \leq n)$ is the probability that a_i is the search argument and q_i $(0 \leq i \leq n)$ is the probability that the search argument is between a_i and a_{i+1}. The problem is to find a binary search tree which minimizes the expected

```
(1)    for  i := 0  to  n  do  c(i,i) := 0;
(2)    for  k := 1  to  n  do begin
(3)        for  i := 0  to  n−k  do begin
(4)            value := ∞;
(5)            for  m := i+1  to  i+k  do  value := min(value, c(i,m−1)+c(m,i+k));
(6)            c(i,i+k) := value + w(i,i+k)
(7)        enddo
(8)    enddo
```

algorithm A. program to solve dynamic programming problem (1).

---

number of comparisons during a search. Thus

$$\sum_{j=1}^{n} p_j \times (1+ \text{level of } a_j) + \sum_{k=0}^{n} q_k \times \left[\text{level of external node that corresponds to interval } (a_k,a_{k+1}) \right]$$

must be minimized (the root of a binary tree has level 0). Let $c(i,j)$ be the cost (i.e., the expected number of comparisons during a search) of the optimal subtree T_{ij} with probabilities for internal and external nodes $p_{i+1}, ..., p_j$ and $q_i, ..., q_j$. Then $c(i,j)$ satisfies (1) with $w(i,j) = p_{i+1} + ... + p_j + q_i + ... + q_j$.

In many applications (e.g. **example 1**) algorithm A can be accelerated to run in $O(n^2)$ time, namely when the cost function $c(i,j)$ satisfies the quadrangle inequality.

DEFINITION 1. (cf. [7]). A function $f(i,j)$ satisfies the *quadrangle inequality* if

$$f(i,j) + f(i',j') \le f(i',j) + f(i,j') \tag{2}$$

for all $i \le i' \le j \le j'$ for which it is defined.

THEOREM 1. (cf. [7]). If the cost function c in (1) satisfies the quadrangle inequality, then (1) can be solved in $O(n^2)$ time.

Moreover, if $w(i,j)$ is monotone increasing on the lattice of intervals and $w(i,j)$ satisfies the quadrangle inequality, then $c(i,j)$ satisfies the quadrangle inequality. The acceleration is due to the fact that the possible values m for which the right hand side of (1) attains its minimum, is restricted. Let

$$R_c(i,j) = \max\{ m : c(i,j) = w(i,j) + c(i,m-1) + c(m,j)\}$$

Then, if $c(i,j)$ satisfies the quadrangle inequality (2),

$$R_c(i,j-1) \le R_c(i,j) \le R_c(i+1,j)$$

In order to be able to assess parallel algorithms we will use the so-called speed-up and efficiency of processor utilization. Let X be an algorithm using p processing elements (PEs) to solve some problem. Then the speed-up is defined as:

$$S_p(X) = \frac{\text{Time used by the most efficient sequential algorithm}}{\text{Time used by algorithm } X \text{ on } p \text{ PEs}}$$

and the efficiency as: $E_p(X) = S_p(X)/p$.

Obviously we have $S_p(X) \leq p$ and $0 \leq E_p(X) \leq 1$. It is our purpose to design parallel algorithms for p PEs that have a speed-up near p and an efficiency near 1.

In dynamic programming one distinguishes between stages, state variables and control variables and similarly between a stage loop, a state loop and a control loop (cf. [2]). In algorithm A these loops consist of the lines 2-8, 3-7 and 5, respectively. The term *inspection* is used in this paper to denote the execution of the body of the control loop for some value of m. Observe that in algorithm A the number of inspections in the control loop is independent of the state i. This is not necessarily true for the modified algorithm (for the case the quadrangle inequality holds).

In the past results on parallel algorithms for dynamic programming problems used one of the following 3 ways (cf. [3], [1]):

(i)   divide the control loop among the PEs. Thus at each moment there is one state such that all PEs are performing inspections for this state.

(ii)   divide the state loop among the PEs. Each PE performs all inspections necessary for the state assigned to it. At any moment all PEs (some of which may be idle) are performing inspections in the same stage.

(iii)   divide the state loop and control loops among the PEs. In [3] and [1] the number of controls must be equal for all states. If this would not be the case some PEs may be idle. At any moment all PEs (some of which may be idle) are performing inspections for states in the same stage.

This paper is organized as follows. In **section 2** we consider algorithm A as a task system with some precedence constraints. In **section 3** we design a linear time systolic implementation of algorithm A using $\Theta(n^2)$ PEs. In **section 4** we prove that each parallel algorithm following strategy (ii) for solving (1) must run in $\Omega(n^2)$ time on any number of PEs even when the problem satisfies the quadrangle inequality. In this section we present $O(n^3/p)$ time algorithms that use $p (\leq n^2)$ PEs. In **section 5** we present a parallel algorithm to solve dynamic programming problems with the quadrangle inequality in $O(n \log \log n)$ time on a shared memory computer with n PEs. We generalize this result for shared memory computers with p $(1 < p \leq n)$ processors.

2. A precedence graph.

We consider algorithm A (and its modification in case the quadrangle inequality holds) to consist of a number of tasks J_{ij} $(0 \leq i \leq j \leq n)$ such that J_{ij} computes the cost $c(i,j)$. Because the task J_{ij} uses a number of other costs $c(i',j')$, we can define a precedence relation on the set $J_n = \{J_{ij} : 0 \leq i \leq j \leq n\}$

$$J_{ij} \ll J_{i'j'} \quad \text{if} \quad (i=i' \text{ and } j<j') \text{ or } (i>i' \text{ and } j=j')$$

Moreover define the relation $<$ as

$$J_{ij} < J_{i'j'} \quad \text{if} \quad (i=i' \text{ and } j=j'-1) \text{ or } (i=i'+1 \text{ and } j=j')$$

The relation $\ll$ includes the relation $<$ and moreover, if $J_{ij} \ll J_{i'j'}$, then there are $i = i_1,...,i_k = i'$ and $j = j_1,...,j_k = j'$ such that $J_{i_1 j_1} < J_{i_2 j_2} < ... < J_{i_k j_k}$. For our purposes it suffices to use the relation $<$ instead of $\ll$. Figure 1 shows graphically the relation $<$ in the form of a pyramid. In this pyramid, stage k consists of tasks $J_{m,m+k}$ $(0 \leq m \leq n-k)$, the jth left oriented diagonal and the ith right oriented diagonal consist of the tasks J_{mj} $(0 \leq m \leq j)$ and J_{im} $(i \leq m \leq n)$, respectively. We say that the ith right oriented and the jth left oriented diagonals cross at task J_{ij}.

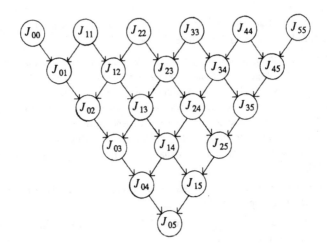

Figure 1. Precedence graph for the set J_5.

3. Systolic arrays.

In a systolic array of PEs the connectivity pattern between PEs is fixed. PEs may have a local memory, but there is no shared memory. The PEs run in lockstep and it is desirable that many PEs are identical (i.e., execute (a copy) of the same program code). For this reason systolic arrays tend to be well suited for implementation on silicon chips. Now we will design a systolic array for the dynamic programming problem (1). We will assume that when PE P_i sends a value to P_j at time t, P_j must read this value at time t, otherwise it would be lost.

Our systolic array consists of $(n+1)(n+2)/2$ PEs P_{ij} ($0 \le i \le j \le n$) arranged in a pyramid like the tasks J_{ij}. P_{ij} performs J_{ij}. We assume that P_{ij} contains the weight $w(i,j)$ in its register w (i.e., $w(i,j)$ is computed in advance). P_{ij} needs costs from PEs on both diagonals that cross at it and it must send them forward on the same diagonals. However, the cost $c(i,j)$ computed at P_{ij} must be sent in both directions. The obvious order to send the costs forward as they are received, appended by the newly computed $c(i,j)$, however, leads to an $\Omega(n^2)$ time systolic array: the order in which costs are received does not fit the order of computation of a new cost. Moreover, in this case $P_{i,i+k}$ needs $\Omega(k)$ memory.

In order to do better we have to find for each i,j a permutation π_{ij} of the numbers $1..j-i$ (i.e., the order in which P_{ij} receives the costs) such that

(1) $c(i,i+\pi_{ij}(k)-1)$ and $c(i+\pi_{ij}(k),j)$ are the kth number received from the right and left oriented diagonals, respectively;

(2) knowing permutation π_{ij}, the permutations $\pi_{i,j+1}$ and $\pi_{i-1,j}$ can be determined on-line using a constant amount of memory, i.e. P_{ij} can determine the order in which costs are sent forward easily from the order in which costs are received.

Such permutations exist but we have to distinguish between PEs of even and odd stages. Let $\pi_{i,i+2k}$ and $\pi_{i,i+2k+1}$ be defined as

$$\pi_{i,i+2k}(2m+1)=k-m \qquad 0\leq m\leq k \qquad\qquad \pi_{i,i+2k+1}(2m+1)=k+1+m \qquad 0\leq m\leq k$$

$$\pi_{i,i+2k}(2m)=k+m \qquad 1\leq m\leq k \qquad\qquad \pi_{i,i+2k+1}(2m)=k+1-m \qquad 1\leq m\leq k$$

Figure 2 shows in what order $P_{2,6}$ receives and sends forward cost values. Remind that the sending orders established by $P_{2,6}$ are the receiving order of $P_{1,6}$ and $P_{2,7}$. P_{ij} can easily modify the order in which costs are sent forward. $P_{i,i+2k}$ interchanges on the left oriented diagonal the 2nd and 3rd, the 4th and 5th, etc. values; $c(i,i+2k)$ and $c(i+2k,i+2k)$ are sent last. As for the right oriented diagonal $P_{i,i+2k}$ interchanges the 1st and 2nd, the 3rd and 4th, etc. values and finally sends forward $c(i,i+2k)$. Similar interchanges occur at PEs of odd stages. Obviously a PE can perform this receive/send pattern on-line using a constant amount of memory.

Now the question arises whether we can develop programs for all PEs such that this receive/send pattern is obtained while a value sent to a PE must be read by this PE at the same time. We may expect to find different programs for PEs on odd and even stages. Each value received by a PE will be used three times by it: it must be read, it must be used for an inspection, and it must be sent forward. In one unit of time two values from different diagonals can be used for an inspection. Thus, all the work for two values from both diagonals at one PE requires at least 10 units of time. In order to prevent loss of efficiency no values should be swapped from one register to another. Algorithm B shows programs for PEs that will do the job. It is assumed that all commands on one line can be done in one unit of time. Less than 7 memory locations are needed when different programs are written for PEs at stages $4k$, $4k+1$, $4k+2$ and $4k+3$ and the loops are untangled. The programs given in algorithm B satisfy all the requirements provided that each PE starts 6 units of time after the PEs at the previous stage started (except for PEs at stage 1, that must start 1 unit of time later than PEs at stage 0 do). All this leads to it that P_{0n} must wait at most $6n-5$ units of time before it can start execution and it needs $5n+9$ units of time itself. Observe that this systolic array does not adhere to the strategies mentioned in the introduction: computations for different stages are done simultaneously.

THEOREM 2. There is a systolic array for the dynamic programming problem (1) that runs in $O(n)$ time, using $p=(n+1)(n+2)/2$ PEs with a constant amount of memory for each PE, thus achieving a speed-up of $S_p=\Omega(p)$ and an efficiency of $E_p=\Omega(1)$.

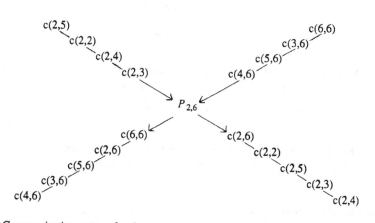

Figure 2. Communication pattern for the computation of costs.

$P_{i,i+2k}$ $(k \geq 1)$

```
read(ROD,R[0];
C := ∞,  F := 1;
read(LOD,L[F]);
wait;
C := min(C,R[1−F]+L[F]);
read(LOD,L[1−F]);
send(LOD,L[F]);
read(ROD,R[F]);
send(ROD,R[F]);
C := min(C,R[F]+L[1−F]);
to k−1 do begin
   read(ROD,R[F]);
   send(ROD,R[1−F]);
   read(LOD,L[F]);
   send(LOD,L[F]);
   C := min(C,R[F]+L[F]);
   read(LOD,L[F]);
   send(LOD,L[1−F]);
   read(ROD,R[1−F]);
   send(ROD,R[1−F]);
   C := min(C,R[1−F]+L[F]);  F := 1−F;
enddo;
C := C+W;
send(ROD,R[1−F]);
wait;
send(LOD,C);
wait;
wait;
send(LOD,L[1−F]);
wait;
send(ROD,C);
```

$P_{i,i+2k+1}$ $(k \geq 0)$

```
read(LOD,L[0];
C := ∞,  F := 1;
read(ROD,R[F]);
wait;
C := min(C,L[1−F]+R[F]);
to k do begin
   read(ROD,R[1−F]);
   send(ROD,R[F]);
   read(LOD,L[F]);
   send(LOD,L[F]);
   C := min(C,R[1−F]+L[F]);
   read(LOD,L[F]);
   send(LOD,L[1−F]);
   read(ROD,R[F]);
   send(ROD,R[F]);
   C := min(C,R[F]+L[F]);  F := 1−F
enddo;
C := C+W;
send(ROD,R[F]);
wait;
send(LOD,C);
wait;
wait;
send(LOD,L[1−F]);
wait;
send(ROD,C);
```

P_{ii}

```
C := 0;
send(LOD,C);
wait;
send(ROD,C);
```

Algorithm B. Programs for the systolic array for dynamic programming problem (1). LOD and ROD stand for left and right oriented diagonal, respectively.

However, when the dynamic programming problem satisfies the quadrangle inequality, these numbers are $S_p = \Omega(n) = \Omega(\sqrt{p})$ and $E_p = \Omega(1/\sqrt{p})$, which is not very satisfactory.

4. Using less than n^2 processors.

In this section we consider the case that $p < n^2$ PEs are available and design an algorithm that requires

$O(n^3/p)$ parallel time, which is the best possible. We will also develop some ideas important for the next section. As a machine model the PRAM model is used: PEs have a shared memory, may execute different programs and moreover can be synchronized, i.e., points in the program can be specified where the PE can only proceed when the other PEs have arrived at the corresponding synchronization points in their programs.

A first approach would be to divide the tasks of J_n among the PEs and to establish synchronization between two consecutive stages. However this may lead to an $\Omega(n^2)$ algorithm.

THEOREM 3. Let A be a scheduling of the task system J_n with precedence relation $<$ on a set of PEs such that (i) each J_{ij} is assigned to exactly one PE, and (ii) the execution of a task in stage k will only start when the execution of all tasks in stage $k-1$ are finished. Then the execution of A requires at least $\Omega(n^2)$ time.

Proof. We will construct an example of an optimal binary search tree problem. Suppose n (n even) keys $a_1 < ... < a_n$ are given. Let the search probabilities for the intervals between keys all be zero. Assign positive weights to $a_{n/2}$ and $a_{n/2+1}$ such that $a_{n/2+1}$ is the root of the optimal subtree $T_{n/2-1,n/2+1}$. Now suppose that weights are assigned to $a_{n/2-i+1}, ..., a_{n/2+i}$. Then weights can be assigned to $a_{n/2-i}$ and $a_{n/2+i+1}$ such that the optimal subtrees $T_{n/2-i-1,n/2+i}$, $T_{n/2-i,n/2+i+1}$ and $T_{n/2-i-1,n/2+i+1}$ are as shown in figure 3. Then we have

$$R(n/2-i, n/2+i) = n/2+i, \quad R(n/2-i-1, n/2+i) = n/2-i \quad \text{and} \quad R(n/2-i, n/2+i+1) = n/2+i+1.$$

and as a consequence task $J_{n/2-i,n/2-i+2i}$ requires at least $2i$ keys that must be inspected to be the root. Thus for each i ($1 \le i \le n/2$) there is a task at stage $2i$ whose execution requires at least $2i$ control values for inspection. Summing over all even stages leads to $\Omega(n^2)$ control values that are inspected sequentially. Hence, the overall parallel time is $\Omega(n^2)$. Q.E.D.

In order to obtain an upper bound $O(n^3/p)$ even with $p = O(n^{1+\epsilon})$ ($\epsilon > 0$) we must assign inspections of one task to different PEs. The main idea is to number all inspections of each stage k from $I_1^{(k)}, ..., I_{(n-k+1)k}^{(k)}$. Then inspection $I_x^{(k)}$ is used for task $J_{i,i+k}$ with $i = \lfloor (x-1)/k \rfloor$ and the involved control variable $uvar$ is $uvar = i+1+\mod(x-1,k)$. Thus, given the index of an inspection, we can easily determine the task it belongs to and the control variable involved. The total number of inspections in stage k is $(n-k+1)k$ ($0 \le k \le n$).

If at stage k $p > (n-k+1)k$, there are more PEs than inspections. All inspections can be done in parallel, hence in constant time. The results of the inspections must be used to find the $n-k+1$ optimal costs. With so many PEs the optimal costs can be found in $O(\log n)$ time.

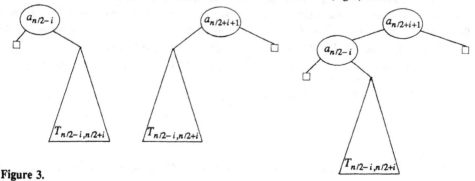

Figure 3.

If $n \leq p < (n-k+1)k$, each PE performs $\lceil (n-k+1)k/p \rceil$ inspections, belonging to at most two different tasks. It can already take the minimum of the inspections it performs and that belong to the same task (we will call such a minimum a *partial* minimum). Computation of the partial minima requires at most $O((n-k+1)k/p)$ parallel time. Suppose $P_{j_1}, \ldots, P_{j_m}$ compute partial minima for some task J. Then P_j $(j_1 < j < j_m)$ computes only one partial minimum. $P_{j_1}, \ldots, P_{j_m-1}$ can be used for the computation of the optimal cost for J. Hence, no PE is involved in the computation of more than one optimal cost and with m partial minima for one task, $m-1$ PEs are used to determine the optimal cost. Obviously this can be done in $O(\log p/(n-k+1))$ time.

Thus at stage k $(n \leq p < (n-k+1)k)$ the amount of time is $O(\frac{(n-k+1)k}{p} + \log\frac{p}{n-k+1})$.

THEOREM 4. With $p = \Theta(n^{1+\varepsilon})$ $(0 < \varepsilon < 1)$, the dynamic programming problem (1) can be solved in time $O(n^3/p)$.

Proof. At stage k $O(\log n)$ time is needed when $p > (n-k+1)k$ and $O(\frac{(n-k+1)k}{p} + \log\frac{p}{n-k+1})$ time otherwise. Taking the sum over all stages k $(1 \leq k \leq n)$ yields the time bound.   Q.E.D.

THEOREM 5. The dynamic programming problem (1) can be solved in $O(n^3/p)$ time on $p \leq n$ PEs.
Proof. Use strategy (ii) mentioned in the introduction.   Q.E.D.

Observe that in the latter two theorems most time is used for performing the inspections. Computation of the optimal costs out of the partial minima is only a minor term. **Theorem 5** still hold for a ring of PEs with local memories. It is an open question whether this is true for **theorem 4** also.

5. An $O(n^2/p + n \log\log p)$ algorithm.

Though **theorem 3** was proven for dynamic programming problems in general, it even holds in those cases that the quadrangle inequality is satisfied. In order to achieve an upper bound lower than $O(n^2)$ we must allow for assignments of parts of tasks to different PEs. When the quadrangle inequality holds, there are at most a linear (in n) number of inspections per stage (cf. [4]). With $p = \Omega(n)$ we could assign inspections to PEs in such a way that the number of inspections performed by one PE, is bounded by a constant. Unfortunately, the inspections can be divided very unevenly among the tasks of one stage (e.g. in the example used in the proof of **theorem 3**). As a consequence we must take more care of the computation of the optimal costs out of the partial minima.

Suppose that at stage $k-1$ the control variables at which the optimal costs are achieved, are stored in the array $R^{(k-1)}[0..n-k+1]$. Task $J_{q,q+k}$ consists only of inspections associated with control variable $R^{(k-1)}[q], \ldots, R^{(k-1)}[q+1]$. Let us therefore number the inspections as follows:

inspection		task	control variable
$I_i^{(k)}$	$1 \leq i \leq R^{(k-1)}[1]$	$J_{0,k}$	i
$I_i^{(k)}$	$R^{(k-1)}[1]+1 \leq i \leq R^{(k-1)}[2]+1$	$J_{1,k+1}$	$i-1$
$I_i^{(k)}$	$R^{(k-1)}[2]+2 \leq i \leq R^{(k-1)}[3]+2$	$J_{2,k+2}$	$i-2$
etc.			

Thus we have:

Given i $(1 \leq i \leq 2n-k)$; let q $(0 \leq q \leq n-k)$ satisfy $R^{(k-1)}[q]+q \leq i \leq R^{(k-1)}[q+1]+q$ (3)

Then inspection $I_i^{(k)}$ is used in task $J_{q,k+q}$ and involves control variable u_{i-q}.

A search on $R^{(k-1)}$ seems to be involved when for an arbitrary i the q satisfying (3) must be found. However, things are easier when several consecutive values for i or consecutive stages k are involved. Without proof we state the following two lemmas.

LEMMA 6. Let q_i satisfy (3) for a given value i. Then $q_i \leq q_{i+1} \leq q_i + 1$ and $q_i - 1 \leq q_{i-1} \leq q_i$.

LEMMA 7. Let inspection $I_i^{(k)}$ be used for task $J_{q,k+q}$. Then $I_i^{(k+1)}$ is used for either $J_{q-1,k+q}$ or $J_{q,k+q+1}$.

These two lemmas make the following assignment of inspections of stage k to PEs obvious.

P_j $(\mathrm{mod}(2n-k,p) \leq j \leq p)$ will perform $I_i^{(k)}$ for all i with

$$\lfloor \frac{2n-k}{p} \rfloor \times (j-1) + \mathrm{mod}(2n-k,p) + 1 \leq i \leq \lfloor \frac{2n-k}{p} \rfloor \times j + \mathrm{mod}(2n-k,p). \tag{4}$$

P_j $(1 \leq j \leq \mathrm{mod}(2n-k,p))$ will perform $I_i^{(k)}$ for all i with

$$\lceil \frac{2n-k}{p} \rceil \times (j-1) + 1 \leq i \leq \lceil \frac{2n-k}{p} \rceil \times j. \tag{5}$$

LEMMA 8. Given the above assignment of inspections to PEs. Given k, p, n and an arbitrary index x. Then we can determine in constant time which P_j performs $I_x^{(k)}$.
Proof. The following formula does the job.

if $x > \lceil (2n-k)/p \rceil \times \mathrm{mod}(2n-k,p)$ then $j := \lceil (x - \mathrm{mod}(2n-k,p)) / \lfloor \frac{2n-k}{p} \rfloor \rceil$

else $j := \lfloor x / \lceil \frac{2n-k}{p} \rceil \rfloor$

Q.E.D.

With this assignment we have that a PE that performs $I_s^{(k)}$, ..., $I_t^{(k)}$, performs also $I_s^{(k+1)}$, ..., $I_t^{(k+1)}$ or $I_{s-1}^{(k+1)}$, ..., $I_{t-1}^{(k+1)}$ or $I_s^{(k+1)}$, ..., $I_{t-1}^{(k+1)}$ but no other inspections of stage k and $k+1$.

Now the inspections of stage k are assigned very evenly to the PEs. Inspections of one task (state) can be assigned to different (consecutive) PEs. These PEs compute only partial minima for this task. Thus, the minimum (i.e., the optimal cost) of these partial minima must be computed. It even may happen that $\Omega(p)$ partial minima for one task are computed; (see the example in the proof of theorem 3). In [6] and [5] parallel algorithms are presented that compute the minimum of N numbers in $O(N/p + \log\log p)$ time if $1 < p \leq N$ PEs were available. We will use the algorithm of [5]. This algorithm uses the same PRAM model as we do, which explains our choice for a shared memory.

The parallel dynamic programming algorithm consists of the following steps for each stage k.

(1) Each P_j determines the indices of the inspections that it must perform (say $I_s^{(k)}$, ..., $I_t^{(k)}$), using (4) and (5).

(2) Each P_j determines the index qs such that $I_s^{(k)}$ belongs to task $J_{qs,qs+k}$, using lemmas 7 and 6.

(3) Each P_j determines the smallest index $firsts$ of all PEs that perform inspections for task $J_{qs,qs+k}$, using the formula in the proof of lemma 8.

(4) Each P_j performs its inspections $I_s^{(k)}$, ..., $I_t^{(k)}$ and computes as many partial minima as there are tasks in stage k of which inspections are performed by this P_j.

(5) Each P_j determines the index qt such that $I_t^{(k)}$ belongs to task $J_{qt,qt+k}$, using lemmas 7 and 6; each P_j determines the largest index $lastt$ of all PEs that perform inspections for task $J_{qt,qt+k}$,

using the formula in the proof of lemma 8.

(6) Find for each task in stage k its optimal cost, using the algorithm of [5].

THEOREM 9. With $p \leq n$ the algorithm runs in $O(n^2/p + n \log\log p)$ parallel time.

Proof. The initialization of all relevant data and stage 1 can be done in $O(n^2/p)$ time. Now consider stage k $(2 \leq k \leq n)$. Step (1) requires constant time. Step (2) can be done in constant time. In step (3) P_j computes which PE performs inspection $I_x^{(k)}$ with $x = R^{(k)}[qs]+qs$. According to lemma 9 this can be done in constant time. Each inspection in step (4) can be performed in constant time. With $O(n/p)$ inspections per PE per stage, step (4) needs at most $O(n/p)$ time. Step (5) can be done in constant time (similar to step (2) and (3)).

With step (6) we must be more careful. Observe that each PE computes at most two partial minima (for tasks $J_{qs,qs+k}$ and/or $J_{qt,qt+k}$) and at most $t-s+1$ optimal costs. These optimal costs can be stored in appropriate storage locations in $O(n/p)$ time. Now suppose that the partial minima for a task J have been computed by $P_{j_1}, ..., P_{j_m}$. With the same argument as used in section 4 $P_{j_1}, ..., P_{j_{m-1}}$ are used in the computation of the optimal cost for J only. Thus, when m $(m \leq p)$ partial minima must be composed to one optimal cost, there are $m-1$ PEs to do this. According to [5] it can be done in $O(\log\log p)$ time. Step (6) requires at most $O(n/p + \log\log p)$ time in each stage.

With n stages, the overall parallel time of the algorithm amounts to $O(n^2/p + n \log\log p)$.   Q.E.D.

COROLLARY 10. With n PEs the dynamic programming problem (1) satisfying the quadrangle inequality can be solved in $O(n \log\log n)$ time, thus achieving a speed-up of $S_n = \Omega(n/(\log\log n))$ and an efficiency of $E_n = \Omega(1/(\log\log n))$.

REFERENCES.

[1] Al-Dabass, D., Two methods for the solution of the algorithm on a multiprocessor cluster, Opt. Contr. Applic. & Methods 1 (1980), 227-238.

[2] Bertsekas, D.P., Distributed dynamic programming, IEEE Trans. Autom. Contr., AC-27 (1982), 610-616.

[3] Cati, J., M. Richardson and R. Larson, Dynamic programming and parallel computers, J. Opt. Theor. Applic. 12 (1973), 423-438.

[4] Knuth, D.E., Optimum binary search trees, Acta Inform. 1 (1971), 14-25.

[5] Shiloach, Y. and U. Vishkin, Finding the maximum, merging, and sorting in a parallel computation model, J. Algor. 2 (1981), 88-102.

[6] Valiant, L.G., Parallelism in comparison problems, SIAM J. Comput. 4 (1975), 348-355.

[7] Yao, F.F., Efficient dynamic programming using quadrangle inequalities, Proc. 12th Ann. ACM Symp. Theory of Comp., ACM, 1980, 429-435.

Multiprocessors: Main trends and dead ends

Wolfgang Händler
Institut für Mathematische Maschinen
und Datenverarbeitung (Informatik)
der Universität Erlangen-Nürnberg
Martenstr. 3, D-8520 Erlangen

The contributions of this Conference will be summarized, in particular in view of the following main trends:

- Growing importance of knowledge processing relatively to number crunching,

- Improvement of mutual fitting of topology and technology,

- Enhancement of realiability.

On the other hand, dead ends appear as for instance inhomogeneous architectures and some developments in the field of man-machine interface.

Toward the parallel inference machine

Shunichi UCHIDA

Fourth Research Laboratory
Institute for New Generation Computer Technology
Mita-kokusai Bldg. 21F, 1-4-28 Mita, Minatoku, Tokyo, JAPAN

Abstract

This paper describes an approach to the parallel inference machine (PIM) which provides a parallel programming environment to support AI applications. The importance of parallel software systems, especially parallel operating systems which control job allocation and resource management, has been recognized by many architecture researchers. However, research on these software systems is still in immatured status. This causes many problems for parallel inference machine research. In Japan's fifth generation computer systems project, parallel software research is now being emphasized and plans are conducted more systematically. The work is being pursued with one eye on parallel hardware research using a dedicated tool called a multi-PSI system consisting of several personal sequential inference machines. This paper describes research and development plans for the parallel inference machine in conjunction with the parallel software research.

1. Introduction

Research on parallel machines has a long history. Many parallel machines have been proposed and actually developed, but, they have been confined to only a small part of computer applications, mainly as special purpose machines. The reason for this is very obvious. Research on parallel software systems have not yet matured enough to make parallel machines sufficiently programmable for sophisticated applications.

Requirements for extremely powerful machines have increased recently in areas like AI. In most AI applications, computing power requirement is crucial. The power of computers often limits the scale of AI systems built on them. Furthermore, recent research on various knowledge representations has made it clearer that parallel computational models are suited to represent knowldge. Parallel machines are expected to be the best solution to fulfil these requirements.

Parallel machines for AI applications of course have to be powerful and they are also required to support knowledge programming environments where large scale AI systems can be efficiently developed and executed. The machines must be general purpose, with parallel operating system. This indicates the necessity of parallel machine research putting more weight on parallel software research, unsolved with more challenging research topics increasing many unknown problems. Vast application fields of AI will gurantee the value of conducting this difficult research.

In Japan's fifth genration computer (FGCS) project, parallel machine research is being conducted as one of the major research and development targets. The FGCS project aims at the research and development of new computer technology for knowledge information processing that will be required in the 1990's. Knowledge information processing is considered as a subset of AI technology which will be realized in the next decade.

In this project, knowledge information processing systems (KIPS) will have logical inference mechanisms using knowledge bases as their central functions. Its target computer system is defined as a parallel computer system having parallel software systems based on logic programming. This project was started in April, 1982, as one of the Japan's national projects. The work is being carried out by the institute for new generation computer technology (ICOT) and eight major computer manufactureres in cooperation with many people from universities and research institutes in Japan.

The project contains many research and development items on software and hardware systems. Software systems research includes such items as natural language understanding, program verification and synthesis, and expert systems. In addition to these systems, research on knowledge representations, knowledge acquisition, and knowledge base management is also being conducted as the bases for these systems.

Hardware and architecture research include such research items as parallel inference machines (PIM) and knowledge base machines (KBM). PIM research aims at the research and development of highly parallel machines supporting parallel logic programming languages and parallel programming environments.

In addition to these research and development items, development support systems are also being developed. One of these systems is a personal sequential inference machine (PSI) a logic programming workstation to provide software researchers with an efficient logic programming environment. A new machine language (KL0) and a system description language (ESP) were designed for this machine. ESP has a modularization mechnism based on the object-oriented concept and is used for writing PSI's programming and operating system (SIMPOS). Currently more than sixty PSI machines have already been distributed to researchers and are being used as main research tools.

In the past five years, PIM research was devoted to determining feasible architectures to execute logic programming languages in parallel, using reduction and dataflow mechanisms. Several software and hardware simulators were developed and used to collect data to evaluate various possible architectures of PIM.

In parallel with this PIM architecture reserach, parallel logic programming languages were also studied. This language research aimed at the design of a new parllel logic programming language with features appropriate to describe a parallel operating system and simple and efficient for hardware implementation. Starting from the studies on such languages as Concurrent Prolog and PARLOG, a new language named Gurded Horn Claulses (GHC) was developed as the base of the project's parallel language, Kernel Language Ver. 1 (KL1).

While these parallel languages and architectures are studied, AI software research such as natural language understading systems and CAD systems is also progressing. Some of them have been expermentally implemented on PSI using ESP. The researchers working these software systems have learned a lot about the the limitations of implementable functions on currently available machines including PSI machines. They feel that current workstations are too weak in computing power to implement expert systems having more than 1,000 rules. In natural languge understsnding, rough estimates of computing power have been made which indicate that machines 1,000 times faster than currently available will be required for sufficient context analysis in machine translation systems. They feel that they will need machines 100,000,000 times faster to perform sophisticated discourse understanding. For their knowledge representaion language, they have designed a new language, CIL, which is based on an event-driven type, parallel model. They are developing a pilot system called DUALS for discourse understanding using CIL. The progress of theis AI software research is greatly encouraging parallel machine research.

In addition to these requirements, PIM research in the past five years strongly indicated the importance of the parallel software research on language processors and operating systems. Effective combination of parallel software and hadware is essential to build the practical PIMs for AI applications.

The PIM research plan has been extended to augment parallel software research in more systematic way than in the past, providing more researchers and tools. The goal of this parallel software research is to develop an operating system for PIM called PIMOS. Currently, the main functions of PIMOS are considered to be the controls of job allocation, resource management and monitoring of parallel jobs. PIMOS must be written in KL1. The KL1 language processor is also included in PIMOS, however, the programming environment is not included. It is planned to build programming environment on a PSI machine.

Experimental construction of many PIMOS software modules is essential to perform the PIMOS research effectively making many feedbacks to parallel hardware research. For this purpose, a multi-PSI system is now being developed to provided software researchers with a realistic and stable environment. On the multi-PSI systems, such problems as job allocation, resource management and parallel job monitoring will be studied in the form of PIMOS development.

The goal of the hardware research is to develop a PIM consisting of 100 processing elements (100-PE PIM). Many problems remain to be solved, for example, the design of the high-speed processing element (PE) making full use of static optimization by compiler, garbage collection methods for parallel environments, and an interconnection mechanism including the clustering of PEs.

An approach to the PIM realizing an effective combination of parallel software and hardware systems is described in this paper.

2. PIM reserch and development guideline

To build PIMs which can flexiblly support AI applications, effective combination of parallel software and hardware systems is very important. In the ultimate PIM, all the hierarchical layers of the software and hardware systems must be built based on parallel computational models. These layers may be divided as follows.

L1) Application software

Natural language understanding systems and expert systems are representative application software included in this lanyer. From the architectural view point, knowledge programming systems including knowledge reperesentation languages and related software tools may be included in this layer. In this layer, research on parallel algorithms and parallel programming paradigms, etc. is very important.

L2) System software

Programming systems including such software modules as editors and debuggers are included in this layer. These modules must be written in a parallel programming language and need man-machine interface. Operating systems must be provided as a lower sublayer of this system software. Generally speaking, one of the main functions of operating systems is to map given parallel jobs to parallel hardware systems. This mapping from the model of a given job to the model of the hardware system is the key problem in realizing flexible parallel machines. This mapping function is to be implemented in software modules for job allocation and resource allocation.

L3) Languge

Languages are obviously important because they define the interface between software and hardware systems. Languages discussed here may be classified into at least two sublayers, namely, system description languages and machine languages.

System description languages must have modularization functions to build complex software systems such as operating systems. The object-oriented concept, which uses class and inheritance mechanisms is very efficient and expected to be used not only for sequential languages but also for parallel languages without any great loss in processing speed. Operating systems for parallel inference machines are complex and must be written in logic or functional languages which have efficient modularizaton functions.

For system description languages for parallel machines, one additianal function must be considered to permit programmers to specify the way of dividing one job into several subjobs to be processed in parallel. It is ideal that operaing systems and hardware systems can automatically divide one given job into several parallel subjobs well enough to exploit maximum prallelism, however, it must be difficult especially for most AI applications.

The practical way is to persuade programmers to estimate the behavior of their jobs and explicitly specify an estimated optimal way of dividing their jobs into parallel subjobs. However, this specified way of division may be incomplete in most cases. Thus, operating systems and hardware systems must compensate for this specified way of division depending on the dynamic behavior of the jobs and the load balancing of the PEs. In some cases, system programmers must have the capability to specify job division and job allocation explicitly to control load balancing.

Hardware people insist that machine languages be simple so that firmware and hardware systems can be simple and fast. Recently, static optimization techiques by compilers have advanced especially in such languages as Prolog and Smalltalk. For logic programming languages, this optimization is quite effective for deterministic parts of programs. This must be considered also for parallel inference machines. However, for nondeteministic parts and complex unification parts, this optimization is not effective and the execution speed greatly varies depending on the characteristic of programs. More firmware and hardware supports are necessary to attain higher speed for these parts Machine languages must be designed considering the trade-offs described above.

L4) Firmware

Firmware is often used to implement high level language machines like Lisp and Prolog machines. In these machines, machine language interpreters are inplemented in firmware. Firmware implementation is flexible and thus suitable to implement experimental machines. In parallel inference machines, firmware implementation is adequate especially to implement some of machine language primitives the specifications of which are not completely fixed. In the case of parallel machine languages, management of parallel processes have to be mainly implemented in firmware to attain higher speed. Conversion between local names and global names for inter-processor communications and garbage collection are also suitable for implemention using firmware. Micro diagnosis is also effective for maintenance.

L5) Hardware

Hardware for parallel inference machines may be roughly divided into two parts, namely, processing elements (PE) and inter-connection mechanisms. For the implementation of PE, there are several alternatives for architectures such as sequential based tag architecture and full dataflow based architecture. For the inter-connection mechanisms, there are also many alternatives such as a shared memory with parallel cache and a variety of packet switching networks.

One of the important decision factors may be the amount of hardware components to implement PEs. To encourage parallel software research, the greater number of PEs is important as well as the higher processing power of each PE.

Given higher priority for harmonized combination of software and hardware systems, the hardware must be designed to be simple making full use of static optimization techniques. However, it is also required to execute such functions so quickly that static optimization cannot improve processing speed. Examples of these functions are the process management and the inter-PE communications, such as the conversion of names and interruption handling. Their hardware supports necessarily increase the amount of hardware.

In addition to the above conditions, a stable and maintenable implementation is crutial to make the machines available for larger scale software development including the development of operating systems and large evaluation programs.

L6) Device

The trade-off between the number of PEs and the processing power of each PE heavily depend on device technology. Currently, CMOS is considered the most suitable device for logic circuits. However, there are still several alternatives such as gate arrays, standard cells and custom LSIs. They differ in such paremeters circuit density, design and production cost, and turn-around time.

The ideal way of promoting parallel machine research is to proceed on all these levels, but it is not practical because software research and hardware research are mutually related to each other.

Generally speaking, less practical software research has been done on parallel processing than on hardware. This is mainly because software researchers have never been provided with attractive parallel hardware environments stable and powerful enough to build large practical parallel software systems like operating systems.

The lack of practical software research and the experience of running practical parallel programs are imposing difficulty in dividing the required functions of PE into software functions and hardware functions. This problem happens in the design of a machine language.

One of practical approaches is to design a pure parallel language at first. This language must have the features required of both a system description language and a machine language. The design of both of these languages involves experimental construction of software and hardware modules to evaluate the design. This evaluation work is essential and often needs large scale experimental software and hardware systems as tools. The research and development of parallel inference machines may be regarded as the repitition of the design and evaluation cycle.

This repetition must be started on a small scale and proceed gradually to larger scale software and hardware systems. However, at the beginning, software researchers must be provided with parallel hardware environments which can hopefully attract them. The larger scale software experiments will produce more valuable information about the behavior of parallel programs. This information is essential to design better parallel inference machines.

3. The approach to PIM in FGCS project

3.1 Outline of PIM research plan

The FGCS project was planned as a ten-year project. It is divided into three stages, namely the initial stage (1982-1984), the intermediate stage (1985-1988) and the final stage (1989-1991). In each stage, research goals are roughly determined for each research and development item.

For PIM, the initial stage goal is to study basic mechanisms necessary to organize PIMs. The intermediate stage goal is to build a medium scale experimental PIM which consists of about 100 PEs. The final satge goal is to build a large scale experimental PIM which includes about 1,000 PEs. The processing speed of the final stage goal is expected to be around 100 MLIPS.

The research goal for the software system for PIM was not explicitly determined because it was too dificult for us to estimate the progress of the parallel software research when we planned FGCS project. At that time, we simply imagined that the hardware system of the final PIM could include most functions which we are now thinking that the software system, PIMOS, must have. The research and development items related to PIMOS and KL1 were recently added as a new part of the intermediate stage plan.

The research results of PIM and its related items in the initial stage are summurized in addition to their current status. They are PIM itself, kernel language (KL), and the sequential inference machine (SIM).

3.2 PIM research in the initial stage

PIM research in the initial stage was mainly intended to clarify problems by investigating various parallel processing mechanisms. We studied several PIM models such as reduction and dataflow for the parallel execution mechanisms of logic programming languages. Then we built several software simulators and three hardware simulators.

For dataflow, we designed a machine model which was named PIM-D. PIM-D executes logic programs in a goal-driven manner: the execution of a clause is initiated when a goal is given and it returns the results to the goal. In this execution, the PIM-D can exploit OR and AND prallelism as well as low-level parallelism in unification.

A hardware simulator of the PIM-D consists of 16 PEs and 15 structure memory (SM) modules, connected by an hierarchical bus network. Each PE and SM is made of bit-sliced microprogrammable processors (Am 2900 series) and TTL ICs.

A software simulator was developed in C on the VAX to confirm the detailed structure of the PIM-D. A Prolog or Concurrent Prolog program is compiled into a dataflow code, and runs on this simulator as well as on the PIM-D.

For reduction, we designed a machine model which was named PIM-R. Logic programs generate several pieces of resolvent from a body goal in a clause. This can be regarded as a reduction process. The PIM-R consists of two types of modules, inference modules and structure memory modules with networks connecting them. In each inference module, logic programs are executed based on the reduction mechanism.

A hardware simulator and two software simulators were built for the PIM-R. The hardware simulator consists of of 16 PEs (m68K boards) connected by a common bus with a shared memory.

In addition to these two models, we built an experimental hardware system to examine a hardware support mechanism for job division and allocation in a multiprocessor environment. This mechanism was named the Kabu-wake method in which idle processors issue requests for jobs to the busy processors. If one processor requests a job from another processor, it splits up its own job and passes one of the alternative clauses to the other processor. Then, they perform OR parallel execution of logic programs.

The experimental system consists of 16 PEs (m68K based computers) connected by two types of networks. One network is a high throughput swithing network for transferring a split job and the other is a ring network for job requesting packets.

We obtained the following conclusions through the software experiments using these simulators and the experimental system.

1) Logic progrmming is suitable for parallel processing. The programs can be processed in parallel if they contain parallelism in them.
2) The machine language must be simple to obtain a fast and compact PE.
3) A stream-based logic programming language like GHC is adequate for the base of the machine language.
4) Static optimization techniques must be introduced to make PEs faster and smaller.
5) Various hardware supports for inter-process communications are essential.
6) The total hardware system of PIM must be compact for stable implementation.

This conclusion implies the importance of parallel software research to make the hardware functions of PIM clearer and simpler.

3.3 Design of Kernel Languages

1) Design of KL0

The research on the kernel language (KLn, n=0, 1 or 2) was started for the design of KL0 which was the machine language for PSI. KL0 was designed in almost the same level as DEC-10 Prolog adding several control promitives and new data types.

A new language, ESP (Extended Self-contained Prolog) was designed for the system description language coresponding to KL0 adding the object-oriented modularization function using class and multiple inheritance mechanisms. The effectiveness of ESP, especially its modularization function has been proved in writing SIMPOS (PSI's programming and operating system). Software productivity has been greatly improved by ESP and its programming environment in SIMPOS.

In the intermediate stage, KL0 has been redesigned for the improvement of PSI to incorporate static optimization techniques more effectively by a compiler. The new KL0 is based on the abstract prolog machine instruction set proposed by D.H.D. Warren, however, many functions are added to keep the compatibility to the previous KL0. The introduction of static optimization is expected to improve the execution speed of the new PSI (PSI-II) two to three times. This language design experience and usage has made a great contribution to the reseach and development of KL1.

2) Design of KL1

Research on KL1 was begun with the studies of such languages as Concurrent Prolog and PARLOG. We intended primarily to design the core language from which we could design the machine language and also the system description language. From the viewpoint of hardware, this core language is required to be as simple as possible. From the viewpoint of software, it must be clean and powerful to be able to introduce new programmig concepts and paradigms for describing operating systems and application programs.

Through discussions with researchers from abroad and experimental construction of language interpreters and sample programs, we designed a new language, GHC (Gurded Horn Clauses). It is a stream-base AND parallel language and fullfils most of the software and hardware requirements. Main features of GHC are summarized as follows:

For description of parallel processing;
1) Dynamic inter-process communications via logical variables
2) Flexibility in the size of processing granularity
3) Simplicity of description

As a logic programming language;
4) Pattern driven clause selection
5) Single assignment via logical variables

In the intermediate stage, we started to consider the detailed structure of KL1. Currently KL1 is divided into three layers, namely a machine language (KL1-b), a core language (KL1-c) a pragma (KL1-p), and a user language (KL1-u).

KL1-b is the machine language of PIM. Its design is almost the same as the design of PIM machine architecture, especially, the design of the PE. The execution mechanism for GHC is now being studied for an experimental interpreter in C. Optimization by compiler is also being considered.

KL1-c is the core language of KL1, and its language features determine the principles of KL1 itself. KL1-c is now being designed based on GHC and extended so that we can describe important functions of the operating system, PIMOS, such as interrupt handling and resource management.

KL1-p is a set of declarations to specify the way of dividing a job into parallel subjobs, and to specify the estimated amount of load for each subjob.

KL1-u is a user language used to describe the operaing system and users programs. KL1-u must have modularization functions and we are working on introducing the object-oriented modular structure.

The evaluation of these language specifications must be done by actually writing many sample programs. This work is currently done using PSIs and VAXs. Parallel exection environments are also desired and the multi-PSI system will be used for this purpose.

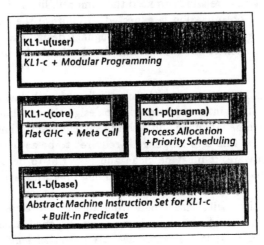

KL1 Language System

3.4 Development of SIM

In the initial stage, we developed the sequential inference machine (SIM) as a software development tool. In the development of SIM, we built two types of machines. One is named PSI and the other is named CHI. The programming and operating system, SIMPOS, was also developed on PSI. It is written in ESP and its current size is about 200K lines in ESP.

1) Personal sequential inference machine (PSI)

PSI is a personal workstation run under SIMPOS and provides researchers with an execution speed of about 30KLIPS with 80MB of main memory plus a multi-window based efficient programming environment. To run logic programming languages efficiently, PSI uses a tag architecture and a hardware supported stack mechanism. KL0 is interpreted by microprogram using specialized hardware mechanism. As we intended to distribute PSIs to many researchers, we used TTL devices and made a reliable and maintainable implementation. Its cycle time is 200 ns.

The high execution speed of PSI is attained by microprogramming techniques and specialized hardware supports. The key features of the hardware supports are for dynamic data type checking, shortening memory access time, especially stack access time, and dynamic memory allocation.

2) Cooperative high-speed sequential inference machine (CHI)

CHI was developed as a high speed prolog engine connected as a back-end processor to PSI, intended as the fastest possible machine for logic programming. It introduced the low level machine instruction set proposed by David H.D. Warren, called *abstract prolog machine instruction set*. and fully utilized the static optimizing technique by its compiler. CHI was implemented using CML (Current Mode Logic) device technology and attained 100 ns in machine cycle time. It attained about 280KLIPS in *append* operation and about 200 KLIPS for usual programs.

3) Improved version of PSI and CHI

In the intermediate stage, these machines are being improved using LSIs to make smaller-size models. They are called PSI-II and CHI-II.

PSI-II has the low-level machine instruction set similar to Warren's set, but, it has more optimized instructions. The design of PSI-II employs the following.

1) The low-level machine instruction set
2) Equipment of argument registers
3) Using 3 stacks, local, global, and trail stack
4) Structure copying for the structured data

Specifically, the new PSI's CPU will be used as element processors of the multi-PSI system. The execution speeed of PSI-II is expected to be improved to 150 KLIPS. We expect that this improvement will be effective to implement the interpreter of a parallel logic programming language such as GHC.

In the design of CHI-II, we intended to make it much smaller than the previous model because the implementation using CML device made the size of the previous model too large to use it as a practical programming tool. CHI-II uses CMOS VLSIs and 1 Mbit memory chips to obtain the size like a desk-side locker keeping almost the same performance as the previous model.

Through the development of SIM, we learned a lot of things about the hardware and software implementations for logic programming. They are effectively being applied for the research and development of PIM.

a) Effective implementation methods of the tag architecture for logic programming.
b) The static optimization techniques and design methods of the efficient machine instruction set.
c) Dynamic behavior of many logic programs through the evaluation of PSI's micro interpreter.
d) System programming techniques using logic programming through the development of SIMPOS.
e) Great merits of using logic programming for writing complex programs like operating systems.

f) Great contribution of the object-oriented modularization to software productivity and reliability through the use of ESP for SIMPOS and other various applications.

3.5 PIM research in the intermediate stage

Considering about the research results in the initial stage research and development, we made the more detailed plan for PIM research in the intermediate stage.

1) The intermediate stage goal for PIM

The research goal of PIM is redefined as follows:
1) The experimental hardware contains about 100 PEs.
2) Machine language is KL1-b based on GHC.
3) Target processign speed is 2 to 5 MLIPS.
4) The hardware systm must be stable and maintainable enough to support PIMOS.
5) The experimental PIM operating system is developed in parallel with the hardware development.

This new goal puts more weight on the effective combination of the hardware and software. The hardware system is required to be simple, fast and stable. The PE is based on a sequential execution mechanism and optimized for the execution of KL1-b. This experimental hardware system is informaly called PIM-I.

For the PIMOS development, we need a stable parallel hardware environment as its development tool. To encourage software researchers, this hardware environment is desired to be fast, flexible and stable as much as possible and also must be provided as soon as possible. The multi-PSI system is almost the best solution in this project to fullfil these requirements.

2) Design of the intermediate stage PIM, PIM-I

The research of PIM-I was begun with the design of the machine language, KL1-b. The execution mechanism of KL1-b is also being designed writing experimental interpreters in ESP and C. In this functional design phase, we are studying following items:
1) For synchronization and schduling: internal structure of goals, priority scheduling queues and goal trees to manage logical goal relationship; suspend-hook mechanism; and efficient context switching mechansim.
2) For communication: shared buffer communication and packet communication; and efficient context switching mechanisms for remote data access.
3) For stream: CDR-coding and special primitives.
4) For fine grained activities: optimizing compilers; improved bounded depth-first scheduling; and a low level instruction set based on sequential execution.
5) For large grained activities: load distribution primitives.

The design of the machine language and its execution mechanism has to be proceed with the functional design of the PE and the connection mechanism. We are now intending to introduce a cluster concept and a shared memory to reduce inter-PE communication delay. Concerning to the hardware of PIM-I, we are studying following items:
1) Functions of the cluster: logical cluster and address transformation; physical cluster and its implementation; and inter-cluster network and cluster controler.

2) For memory system design: parallel cache mechanisms; proper usage of local and shared (global) memories; and specialized memory mechanisms dediacted to KL1-b.

3) For the design of PE: implementaions of tag architectures for KL1-b; efficient context switching mechanisms; and communication hardware and interrupt handling mechanisms.

To attain the target processing speed for PIM-I, we are trying to make the PE at least faster than PSI-II for KL1-b and also introduce fast inter-PE comunication mechanisms such as a global shared memory so that the overhead in the communication can be reduced by a variety of optimization techniques to be developed by software researchers.

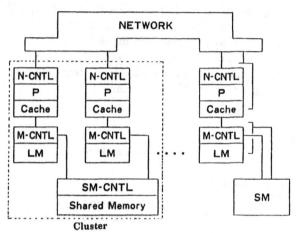

Organization of PIM-I

3.6 PIMOS research and the multi-PSI system

1) PIMOS research

The ultimate goal of the parallel software research may be to develop various useful software technology on parallel computational models and actually construct various software systems on prallel machines. As a small step toward this goal, we aims to build an experimental operating system, PIMOS which will be operational on PIM-I. The primary goal of PIMOS research is to build the experimental software system for hardware resource management of PIM-I. This software system may correspond to the kernel and supervisor layers of usual operating systems.

The research is begin with the studies on such items:

1) Control methods for job allocation and locality of communication between PEs.
2) Memory management and GC for distributed environments.
3) Program code management and distribution methods.
4) Methods to handle input/output and interrupt.
5) Debugging and monitoring of parallel programs.

These research items have long been realized as important but difficult research themes in parllel processing. We start this research with the implementation of KL1 interpreter on the multi-PSI system.

For the job allocation problem, we have decided to have a policy of persuading programmers to explicitly specify the way of dividing their jobs and the amount of load for each divided jobs. We are now trying to introduce a two-dimensional processing power plene (PPP) model where a programmer assumes that processing power is uniformely distributed on a two-dimensional plane. The size of the plane area corresponds to the amount of processing power. The distance between two points on the plane corresponds to the cost of the communication. By specifying the way of dividing this plane and the correspondence between the divided area and the divided job, the programmer can represent his or her suggestion about the job allocation. The specification is written using KL1-p (pragma). It is unlikely that this suggestion is completly correct. Then dynamic reallocation of divided jobs must be made by PIMOS and PIM-I to attain better performance. This idea of job allocation has not been examined deeply, however, it may be a suitable start point of this research. Many ideas of this kind will be studied actually writing programs on the multi-PSI system.

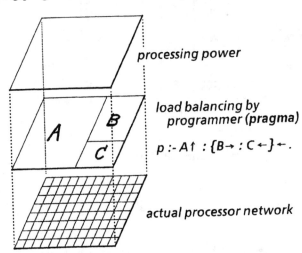

processing power

load balancing by programmer (pragma)

$p :- A\uparrow : \{B \rightarrow : C \leftarrow \} \leftarrow .$

actual processor network

Process Allocation Strategy (Load Balancing)

2) Development of the multi-PSI system

The multi-PSI system is developed for parallel software experiments. It is desirable to be provided as soon as possible to promote PIMOS research. We plan to build two versions of the multi-PSI system, namely, MPSI-V1 and MPSI-V2.

MPSI-V1 uses 6 to 8 current PSIs (PSI-I) as its PEs. They are connected with a two-dimensional mesh type network. Each node of this network has five input/output channels and a simple routing mechanism. One of these channels is connected to the PSI's internal bus. Its basic data transfer is controlled by PSI's microprogram. Its data transfer rate is about 500 KByte/sec for each channel. The routing mechanism of each node passes each packet one channel to another without interrpting the PSI connected to that node if the destination of the packet is not that PSI. On MPSI-V1, the interpreter of KL1, actually GHC, is written in ESP using SIMPOS. Then, the execution speed of GHC will be slow, however, the parallel interpreter using communication facility can be build and evaluated. MPSI-V1 will be avilable in August, 1986.

MPSI-V2 will use 16 to 64 CPUs of PSI-II as its PEs. The connection network is almost similar to that of MPSI-V1, however, its size will be smaller using LSIs (Gate arrays) and its transfer rate will be improved. On MPSI-V2, the interpreter of KL1 will be written in microprogram so that faster execution speed can be attained. We are expecting that it can attain around 100 KLIPS if given programs do not cause suspentions often. Thus, larger scale software experiments will be possible on MPSI-V2 including the building of PIMOS. MPSI-V2 is planed to be available around the end of 1987.

4. Concluding remarks

In this paper, the effective combination of software and hardware systems on PIM is emphasized. To promote the research and development of parallel software technolgy, the intimate cooperation of software and hardware people is essential. The primary role of the hardware people is to povide parallel hardware environments which can be attractive tools for the software people. In the FGCS project, we are building the multi-PSI system for providing this tool. We also intend that PIM-I will be a next version of the tools. Prallel software research has so many unknown problems that these tools have to be improved repeatedly in many years. Our current effort may be regarded as starting the first step of this repetition toward the realization of fully parallel inference machines.

Reference

[1] H. Ishibasi, et al: SIMPOS: Sequential Inference Machine Programming and Op-erationg System,— Its User Interface—, to apper in FJCC'86, Nov. 1986.

[2] A. Goto and S. Uchida: Current research status of PIM: Parallel Inference Machine, ICOT TM-140, Nov. 1985.

[3] K. Ueda: Gurded Horn Clauses, Lecture Notes in Computer Science 221, Spring-Verlag, 1986.

[4] T. Chikayama: Load Balancing in Very Large Scaled Multi-Processor Systems, Proc. of fourth Japanese and Swedish Workshop on Fifth Generation Computer Systems, Jul. 1986., also to appear ICOT TR.

[5] E. Shapiro: A Subset of Concurrent Prolog and Its interpreter, ICOT TR-003, 1983.

[6] K. Clark and S. Gregory: PARLOG: Parallel Programming in Logic, Research report DOC 84/4. Dept. of Computing, Imperial College, London.

[7] D.H.D. Warren: An Abstract Prolog Instruction Set, Tech. Note 309, AI Center, SRI International, 1983.

[8] S. Uchida: Sequential Infernce Machine: SIM - Progress Report, Proc. of FGCS'84, Nov. 1984.

[9] T. Chikayama: Unique features of ESP, Proc. of FGCS, Nov. 1084.

[10] R. Nakazaki, et al: Design of A High-speed Prolog Machine (HPM), Proc. of the 12th ISCA, pp.191-197, Jun. 1985.

[11] K. Nakajima, et al: Evaluation of PSI micro-interpreter, Proc. of COMPCON'86, Mar. 1986.